Fluid Mechanics
and
Hydraulics

(Revised & Updated)

Fluid Mechanics and Hydraulics

(Revised & Updated)

Dr. Suresh Ukarande
B.E. (Civil), M. Tech., Ph.D. (IIT, Bombay)

Dean
Faculty of Technology,
Chairman Board of Studies in Civil Engineering
Member of Management Council, Senate, Academic Council
University of Mumbai, Mumbai

Principal
SES YTCEM,
Affiliated to University of Mumbai, Mumbai

Ane Books Pvt. Ltd.
New Delhi ♦ Chennai

Fluid Mechanics and Hydraulics

Dr. Suresh Ukarande

First Edition : 2003
Revised & Updated : 2014
Reprint : 2017, 2018, **2020, 2023**

Published by

Ane Books Pvt. Ltd.

4821, Parwana Bhawan, 1st Floor, 24 Ansari Road, Darya Ganj,
New Delhi - 110 002, Tel.: +91(011) 23276843-44, Fax: +91(011) 23276863
e-mail: kapoor@anebooks.com, Website: www.anebooks.com

Branch Office :

- Avantika Niwas, 1st Floor, 19 Doraiswamy Road, T. Nagar,
Chennai - 600 017, Tel.: +91(044) 28141554, 28141209
e-mail: anebookschennai@gmail.com, rathinam@anebooks.com

ISBN : 978-93-8116-253-8

Printed at : Repro Knowledgecast Limited, Thane

Dedicated to

My Parents, Wife Asmita

&

Daughter Prajakta

Preface

I am happy to revise this book entitled "Fluid Mechanics and Hydraulics" to the students pursuing their Engineering in Civil, Mechanical and Chemical disciplines at any college across India. This book will be useful to diploma, degree and A. M.I.E. examinations. Since I have taught the subject for more than decade, I thought it is worthwhile to give it in the most palatable from the subject matter to the engineering students. Besides giving detailed fundamental coverage to the subject matter, I have tried to illustrate the matter by giving number of solved problems topic wise as well as in the form of exercise problems with their answers. This will help the student to understand the basic fundamentals through problems. This book is written in a simple language, so that average student will understand the subject with self-study.

I do not claim any originality of the basic concepts in this book. The manuscript is checked thoroughly to make this book, near to perfect. I will be grateful to the users / readers of this book to point out mistakes, if any, so that they can be rectified in the next edition of this book.

It is difficult to mention names of all the persons who have helped in making this project successful. However, I would like to place on record my gratitude towards Dr. P.R. Mehta, retired principal of SVRCE, Surat and Prof. U.W. Mate and Ane Books Pvt. Ltd. for publishing this book.

Dr. Suresh Ukarande

Contents

1

Fluid Properties

1.1 INTRODUCTION TO FLUID MECHANICS

Matter has three states *i.e.*, solid, liquid and gas. A substance which is either in liquid or gaseous state is called fluid. Therefore fluid is defined as a substance which is capable of flowing, and fluid mechanics is defined as a science concerned with the behaviour of fluid at rest and in motion.

While dealing with fluid we come across three aspects of fluids—statics, kinematics and dynamics.

The study of fluid at rest is called fluid statics.

The study of fluids in motion without considering the forces causing flow is called fluid kinematics.

The study of fluids in motion considering the forces causing flow is called fluid dynamics.

1.2 FLUID PROPERTIES

1.2.1 Density or Mass Density

The density or mass density of a substance is defined as a mass per unit volume and is denoted by 'ρ'. Its SI unit is kg/m^3. The mass density of water is taken as 1000 kg/m^3.

Mathematically it can be expressed as $\rho = \dfrac{\text{Mass}}{\text{Volume}}$.

1.2.2 Specific Weight or Weight Density

Specific weight or weight density of a substance is defined as a weight per unit volume and is denoted by 'γ'. Its SI unit is N/m^3. Mathematically it can be expressed as

$$\gamma = \frac{\text{Weight}}{\text{Volume}}.$$

Relation between 'γ' and 'ρ':

$$\gamma = \rho g$$

(units are $\gamma \rightarrow N/m^3$, $\rho \rightarrow kg/m^3$, $g \rightarrow m/sec^2$)

Note: Specific weight of water is generally denoted by 'γ' and its value is 1000×9.81 N/m³ in SI units.

1.2.3 Specific Volume

Specific volume of a substance is defined as a volume per unit mass and is denoted by '$\forall$'. Its SI unit is m³/kg.

Bulk modulus of elasticity 'K' is defined as the ratio of compressive stress to volumetric strain.

Mathematically it can be expressed as

$$\text{Bulk modulus} = K = \frac{dp}{-\left(\frac{dv}{v}\right)}$$

where dp = change in pressure and unit is N/m²
dv = change in volume and unit is m³
v = initial volume and unit is m³ and

$$\text{Compressibility} = \frac{1}{K}.$$

1.2.4 Specific Gravity

Specific gravity of substance is defined as a ratio of the specific weight of a substance to the specific weight of standard substance. For liquids standard fluid is water and for gases standard fluid is air. It is represented by symbol 'S'.

Mathematically it can be expressed as:

$$\text{Specific gravity of liquid} = \frac{\text{Specific weight of liquid}}{\text{Specific weight of water}}$$

$$S = \frac{\gamma_2}{\gamma_w} = \frac{\rho_L \times g}{\rho_w \times g} = \frac{\rho_L}{\rho_L}$$

Note: For water, $\rho_w = 1000$ kg/m³ and specific gravity of water = 1.0.

1.2.5 Compressibility

Compressibility is defined as a reciprocal of bulk modulus of elasticity 'K'

Bulk modulus of elasticity 'K' is defined as the ratio of compressive stress to volumetric strain.

Mathematically it can be expressed as

$$\text{Bulk modulus} = K = \frac{dp}{-\left(\frac{dv}{v}\right)}$$

where dp = change in pressure and its unit is N/m^2

dv = change in volume and unit is m^3

v = initial volume and its unit is m^3.

■ **Problem 1.1:** *A 12 cm diameter cylinder is closed at the bottom and is filled with water upto a height of 60 cms. A force of 2.5×10^6 N is applied on it. Calculate the height of water after the application of the force if K for water = 2×10^9 N/m^2.*

Solution:

$$d = 12 \text{ cm} = 0.12 \text{ m}$$

$$h = 60 \text{ cms} = 0.6 \text{ m}$$

$$F = 2.5 \times 10^6 \text{ N}$$

$$K = 2 \times 10^9 \text{ N/m}^2$$

Now

$$dp = \frac{F}{A} = \frac{2.5\times10^6}{\left(\frac{\pi\times0.12^2}{4}\right)}$$

$$= 221.0485 \times 10^6 \text{ N/m}^2$$

$$= 0.221 \times 10^9 \text{ N/m}^2$$

$$\text{Volume of water} = V = \frac{\pi\times0.12^2}{4}\times0.6 \text{ m}^3$$

$$= 6.7858 \times 10^{-3} \text{ m}^3$$

Using the relation,

$$K = \frac{dp}{\left(-\frac{dV}{V}\right)}$$

$$2 \times 10^9 = \frac{0.221\times10^9}{-\left(\frac{dV}{6.7858\times10^{-3}}\right)}$$

$$\text{Change in volume} = dV = -\frac{0.221\times10^9\times6.7858\times10^{-3}}{2\times10^9}$$

$$= -0.7498 \times 10^{-3} \text{ m}^3$$

$$\text{Change in height} = -\frac{dV}{A} = -\frac{0.7498\times10^{-3}}{\left(\frac{\pi\times0.12^2}{4}\right)}$$

$$= -66.2996 \times 10^{-3} \text{ m}$$
$$= -6.629 \text{ cm}$$

∴ The height of water after application of the force = 60 – 6.629 = 53.371 cm.

1.3 VISCOSITY

The viscosity is the property of fluid by virtue of which a fluid offers resistance to deformation under the effect of shear force.

In case of viscous fluid flow it is assumed that one layer of fluid glides over the adjacent layer.

Shear stress 'τ' offered by a layer '1' to layer '2' or vice versa is proportional to $\frac{du}{dy}$ and hence can be expressed as

$$\tau \propto \frac{du}{dy}$$

or
$$\tau = \mu \frac{du}{dy} \qquad \text{...(1.1)}$$

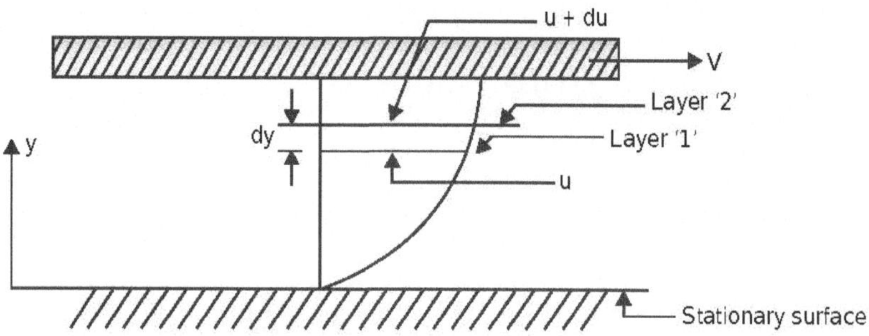

Fig. 1.1 Fluid flow between two parallel plates one is at rest and second is moving with velocity 'V'

Equation (1.1) is known as the Newton's law of viscosity or Newton's law of fluid friction.

where τ = Shear stress and its unit is N/m^2.

μ = dynamic viscosity and its unit is Ns/m^2 in SI system.

$\frac{du}{dy}$ = Velocity gradient or rate of shear deformation or rate of shear strain and its unit is 'per second'.

Shear stress is defined as the ratio of force to transverse area.

∴
$$\tau = \frac{F}{A} \qquad \text{...(1.2)}$$

where, F is the force applied on plate and A is the area (transverse) of the plate.

1.3.1 Dynamic Viscosity

Dynamic viscosity is denoted by 'μ' (mu).

Newton's law of viscosity may be expressed as

$$\tau = \mu \frac{du}{dy} \quad \text{or} \quad \mu = \frac{\tau}{\left(\frac{du}{dy}\right)}$$

Thus dynamic viscosity may be defined as the shear stress required to produce unit velocity gradient.

Units of dynamic viscosity in SI unit is $\frac{\text{N.S}}{\text{m}^2}$ and in CGS unit is $\frac{\text{dyne .sec}}{\text{cm}^2}$ which is called as poise.

Thus $\quad 10 \text{ poise} = \frac{1\text{N.S}}{\text{m}^2}$

and $\quad 1 \text{ poise} = 100 \text{ centipoise.}$

1.3.2 Kinematic Viscosity

Kinematic viscosity is denoted by 'υ' (nu) and its relation with dynamic viscosity is expressed as

$$\upsilon = \frac{\mu}{\rho}$$

where υ = Kinematic viscosity and its unit is m^2/sec.

μ = Dynamic viscosity and its units is $\frac{\text{N} - \text{S}}{\text{m}^2}$.

ρ = Mass density and its unit is kg/m^3.

Units of kinematic viscosity in SI unit is m^2/sec. and in CGS unit is cm^2/sec. and is called as stoke.

Thus $\quad 1 \text{ stoke} = 10^{-4} \text{ m}^2/\text{sec.}$

and $\quad 1 \text{ stoke} = 100 \text{ centistoke.}$

1.3.3 Effect of Temperature on Viscosity

The viscosity of a fluid depends upon its intermolecular structure.

The viscosity of a fluid is due to intermolecular cohesion and transfer of molecular momentum in direction normal to the flow.

In liquids cohesive forces predominate the molecular momentum transfer in a direction normal to the flow and hence viscosity of liquids decreases with the increase of temperature.

In gases the transfer of molecular momentum in a direction normal to the flow predominates the cohesive forces and hence viscosity of gases increases with the increase of temperature.

The effect of temperature on viscosity may be given by

(*a*) For liquids

$$\upsilon = \frac{0.0179}{1+0.0337T+0.000211T^2} \text{ – Poiseuille equation}$$

(*b*) For gases

$$\mu = 1.715 \times 10^{-5}\,(1 + 0.00275\,T - 3.4 \times 10^{-7}\,T^2) \text{ – Holman equation}$$

where υ = kinematic viscosity and its unit is cm^2/sec.

T = temperature and its unit is degree centigrade

μ = dynamic viscosity and its unit is Ns/m^2.

1.4 CLASSIFICATION OF FLUIDS

Fluids

- Newtonian (Time-independent)
- Non-Newtonian
  - (Time-independent)
    - (*a*) Dilatent (Examples-butter, printing ink)
    - (*b*) Bingham plastic (Examples-sewage sludge, mud)
    - (*c*) Pseudoplastic (Examples-paper pulp, paint)
  - (Time-dependent)
    - (*a*) Thixotropic
    - (*b*) Rheopectic

1.4.1 Graphical Classification of Fluids

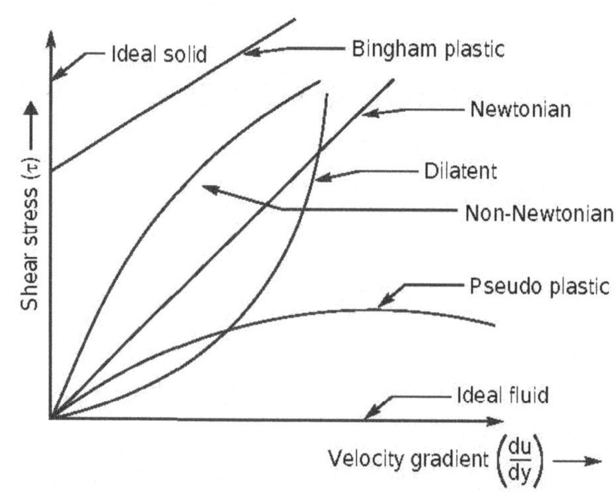

Fig. 1.2 Graphical classification of fluids

1.4.2 Types of Fluids

1. **Ideal fluids:** Ideal fluid is an imaginary, non-realistic fluid which does not possess the properties like -compressibility, surface tension, viscosity etc.
2. **Real fluids:** All fluids which exist in nature are real fluids and possess the properties like compressibility, surface tension, viscosity etc.
3. **Newtonian fluid:** Newtonian fluids are those fluids which obey Newton's law of viscosity given by the expression $\tau = \mu \frac{du}{dy}$.
4. **Non-Newtonian fluid:** Non-Newtonian fluids are those fluids which do not obey Newton's law of viscosity.

A relationship between shear stress and velocity gradient for non-newtonian fluid is given as

$$\tau = A\left(\frac{du}{dy}\right)^n + B \qquad \text{...(1.3)}$$

where A and B are constants which depend on the type of fluid and conditions imposed on the flow:

For dilatent fluid	$n < 1$
Bingham plastic fluid	$n = 1$
Pseudoplastic fluid	$n > 1$.

5. **Time dependent fluid:** In time dependent fluids the velocity gradient depends on shear stress and time of application of force.
6. **Time independent fluid:** In time independent fluids the velocity gradient depends on shear stress only and not on the time for which the force is applied.

■ **Problem 1.2:** *There are two parallel plates at a distance of 0.6 mm and the gap is filled with a oil of viscosity 1.5 Ns/m². The upper plate is moving at 3m/s to the right and the lower plate is at rest. Find the force and power required to maintain the speed of upper plate. Take area of plate = 0.5 m².*

Solution:

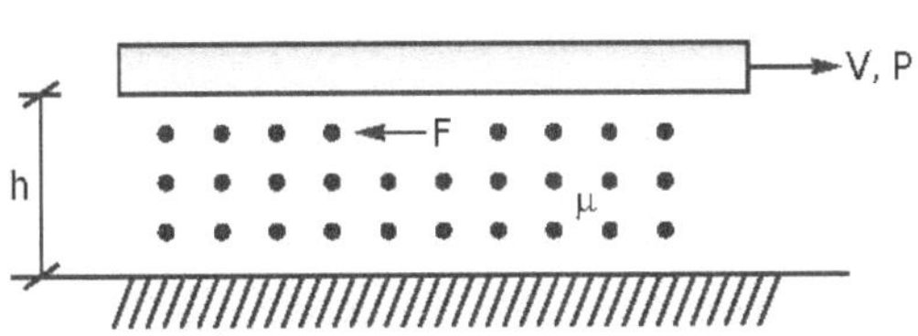

Fig. 1.3

Given:

$h = 0.6 \text{ mm} = 0.6 \times 10^{-3}$ m

$\mu = 1.5$ Ns/m²

$V = 3$ m/s

$A = 0.5$ m²

$$\text{Velocity gradient} = \frac{du}{dy} = \frac{V}{h} = \frac{3}{0.6 \times 10^{-3}}$$

$$= 5 \times 10^3 \text{ per sec.}$$

Using Newton's law of viscosity

$$\tau = \mu \frac{du}{dy} = 1.5 \times 5 \times 10^3 \text{ N/m}^2$$

$$= 7.5 \times 10^3 \text{ N/m}^2$$

(*a*) $F = \tau \times A$

$$= 7.5 \times 10^3 \times 0.5 \text{ N}$$

$$= 3750 \text{ N}$$ ...(**Ans.**)

(*b*) Power required $= F \times V$

$$= 3750 \times 3 = 11250 \text{ Nm/sec. or watts}$$ ...(**Ans.**)

■ **Problem 1.3:** *Two large horizontal plates of infinite extent are 2.5 cm apart and have liquid viscosity of 0.8 Ns/m² filled between them.*

What force is required to pull a thin plate of negligible thickness and area 0.5 m² between the two large plates at a speed of 0.5 m/sec. if

(a) The thin plate is in the middle of the two large plates?

(b) The thin plate is at a distance of 1.0 cm from one of the large plates?

Solution: Given:

$$h = 2.5 \text{ cm} = 2.5 \times 10^{-2} \text{ m}$$
$$\mu = 0.8 \text{ Ns/m}^2$$
$$A = 0.5 \text{ m}^2$$
$$V = 0.5 \text{ m/sec.}$$

(*a*) When the plate is in the middle of two large plates

$$\left(\frac{du}{dy}\right)_1 = \frac{V}{y_1} = \frac{V}{(h/2)}$$

$$= \frac{0.5}{\left(\frac{2.5}{2} \times 10^{-2}\right)} = 40 \text{ per sec.}$$

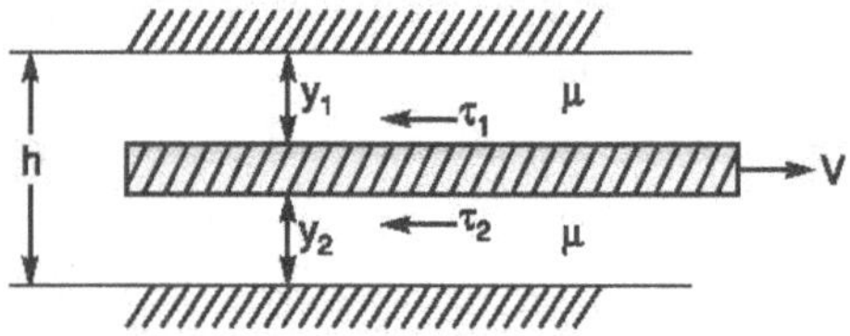

Fig. 1.4

Shear stress on the top portion

$$\tau_1 = \mu \left(\frac{du}{dy}\right)_1$$

$$= 0.8 \times 40 = 32 \text{ N/m}^2$$

$$F_1 = \tau_1 \times A = 32 \times 0.5 = 16 \text{ N}$$

Since the moving plate is equidistant from the stationary plates

$$F_1 = F_2$$

∴ Hence pull required to pull the plate

$$F = 2F_1 = 32 \text{ N}$$ ...(Ans.)

(*b*) Let the moving plate is at a distance of $y_1 = 1$ cm from the top stationary plate.

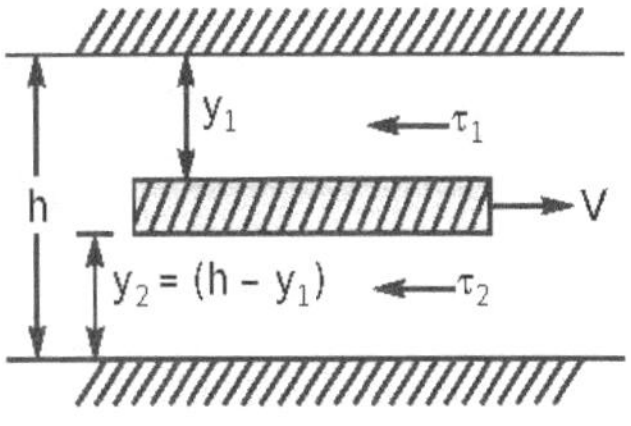

Fig. 1.5

$$\left(\frac{du}{dy}\right)_1 = \frac{V}{y_1} = \frac{0.5}{1 \times 10^{-2}}$$

$$= 50 \text{ per sec.}$$

Shear stress on the top portion

$$\tau_1 = \mu\left(\frac{du}{dy}\right)_1 = 0.8 \times 50 = 40 \text{ N/m}^2$$

$$F_1 = \tau_1 \times A = 40 \times 0.5 = 20 \text{ N}$$

Similarly

$$\left(\frac{du}{dy}\right)_1 = \frac{V}{y_2} = \frac{V}{(h - y_1)} = \frac{0.5}{(2.5 - 1.0) \times 10^{-2}}$$

$$= \frac{0.5}{1.5 \times 10^{-2}} = 33.33 \text{ per sec.}$$

Shear stress on the bottom portion

$$\tau_2 = \mu\left(\frac{du}{dy}\right)_1 = 0.8 \times 33.33 = 26.67 \text{ N/m}^2$$

$$F_2 = \tau_2 \times A = 26.67 \times 0.5 = 13.33 \text{ N}$$

Hence pull required to pull the plate

$$F = F_1 + F_2 = 20 + 13.33 = 33.33 \text{ N.}$$

■ **Problem 1.4:** *A piston 9.95 cm in diameter works in a cylinder 10 cm diameter and 12 cm long. The space between the two is filled with an oil of viscosity 0.5 poise. Calculate the speed of the piston through the cylinder under the action of an axial force of 5 N.*

Solution: Given:

$$d = 9.95 \text{ cm} = 9.95 \times 10^{-2} \text{ m}$$

$$D = 10 \text{ cm} = 10 \times 10^{-2} \text{ m}$$

$$L = 12 \text{ cm} = 12 \times 10^{-2} \text{ m}$$

$$\mu = 0.5 \text{ poise} = 0.05 \text{ Ns/m}^2$$

$$F = 5 \text{ N}$$

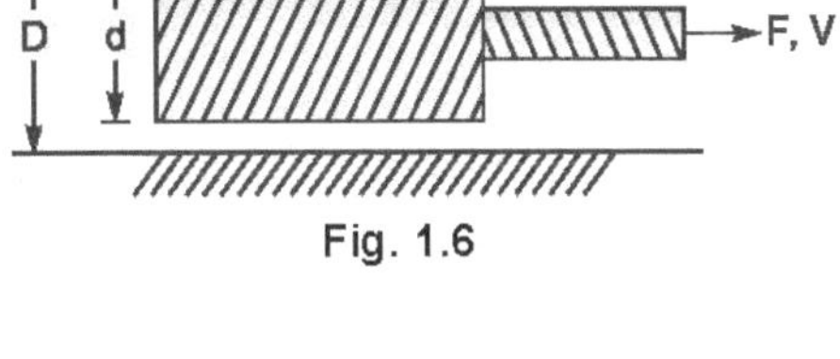

Fig. 1.6

$$\frac{du}{dy} = \frac{V}{y} = \frac{V}{\left(\frac{D-d}{2}\right)}$$

$$= \frac{V}{\left(\frac{10\times10^{-2} - 9.95\times10^{-2}}{2}\right)}$$

$$= \frac{V}{0.025\times10^{-2}}$$

Shear stress on the piston

$$\tau = \mu\frac{du}{dy}$$

$$= 0.05 \times \frac{V}{0.025\times10^{-2}} = 200\text{ V}$$

$$F = \tau \times A = \tau \times \pi dL = 200\text{ V} \times \pi \times 9.95 \times 10^{-2} \times 12 \times 10^{-2}$$

$\therefore$ $5 = 7.50\text{ V}$

$\therefore$ $V = 0.66$ m/sec.

■ **Problem 1.5:** *A piston 9.95 cm in diameter works in a cylinder 10 cm diameter and 12 cm long. The space between the two is filled with an oil of viscosity 0.5 poise. Calculate a force required to push the piston in downward direction with a velocity of 0.5 m/sec. Weight of piston is 2.5 Newtons.*

Solution: Given:

$d = 9.95\text{ cm} = 9.95 \times 10^{-2}\text{ m}$

$D = 10\text{ cm} = 10 \times 10^{-2}\text{ m}$

$L = 12\text{ cm} = 12 \times 10^{-2}\text{ m}$

$\mu = 0.5\text{ poise} = 0.05\text{ Ns/m}^2$

$V = 0.5$ m/sec., $W = 2.5$ N

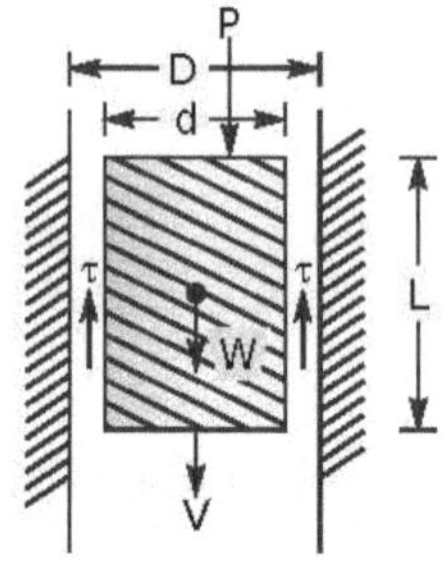

Fig. 1.7

$$\frac{du}{dy} = \frac{V}{y} = \frac{0.5}{\left(\frac{10\times10^{-2} - 9.95\times10^{-2}}{2}\right)}$$

$$= \frac{0.5}{0.025\times10^{-2}} = 2000\text{ per sec.}$$

$$\tau = \mu\frac{du}{dy} = 0.05 \times 2000 = 100\text{ N/m}^2$$

Shear resistance on the side of piston = $F = \tau \times A$

$$= \tau \times \pi dL = 100 \times \pi \times 9.95 \times 10^{-2} \times 12 \times 10^{-2}$$

$$= 3.75 \text{ N}$$

From Fig. 1.7, $W + P = F$

∴ Push required to maintain the velocity of piston as 0.5 m/sec.

$$= F - W = 3.75 - 2.5 = 1.25 \text{ N.}$$

■ **Problem 1.6:** *A vertical gap 12 mm wide of infinite extent contains fluid of viscosity 1.2 Ns/m² and sp. gravity 0.8. A metallic plate 1.2 m × 2.4 m and 2 mm thick is to be lifted up with a constant velocity of 0.2 m/sec. through the gap. Find the force required if the plate is in the middle of the gap and weights 60 N.*

Solution: Given:

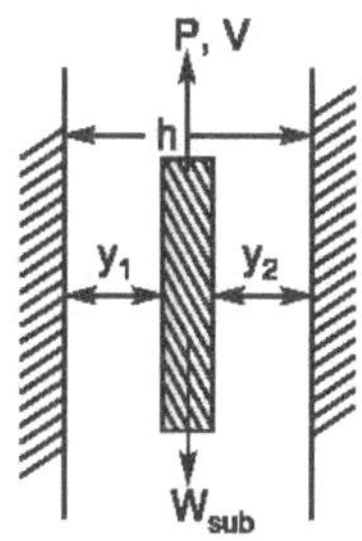

Fig. 1.8

$$h = 12 \text{ mm} = 12 \times 10^{-3} \text{ m}$$

$$\mu = 1.2 \text{ Ns/m}^2$$

$$S = 0.8$$

$$\text{Size of plate} = 1.2 \text{ m} \times 2.4 \text{ m} \times 2 \text{ mm}$$

$$V = 0.2 \text{ m/sec.}$$

$$W = 60 \text{ N}$$

$$\left(\frac{du}{dy}\right)_1 = \frac{V}{y_1} = \frac{V}{\left(\dfrac{h - \text{thickness of plate}}{2}\right)}$$

$$= \frac{0.2}{\left(\dfrac{12\times10^{-3} - 2\times10^{-3}}{2}\right)} = 40 \text{ per sec.}$$

$$\text{Shear stress on one face} = \tau_1 = \mu\left(\frac{du}{dy}\right)_1$$

$$= 1.2 \times 40 = 48 \text{ N/m}^2$$

$$F_1 = \tau_1 \times A = 48 \times 1.2 \times 2.4 = 138.24 \text{ N}$$

∴ Total resistance = $F = F_1 + F_2$

Since the plate is equidistant from stationary plates

$$F_1 = F_2$$

∴ $$F = 2F_1$$

$$= 2 \times 138.24 = 276.48 \text{ N}$$

Also $W_{\text{sub merged}} = W -$ weight of fluid displaced by the plate

$$= W - (\text{sp. Weight of fluid} \times \text{volume of plate})$$

$$= 60 - (0.8 \times 9810 \times 1.2 \times 2.4 \times 2 \times 10^{-3})$$

$$= 60 - 45.20 = 14.8 \text{ N}$$

From Fig. 1.8,

Force required to lift the plate = $P = F + W_{sub} = 276.48 + 14.8 = 291.28$ N.

■ **Problem 1.7:** *A block of base area 20 cm², weight 120 N slides down plane over an oil film of thickness 1 mm. Coefficient of viscosity of oil 500 poise. Estimate the steady state velocity of the block if the inclination of plane is 30°.*

Solution: Given:

$$A = 20 \text{ cm}^2 = 20 \times 10^{-4} \text{ m}^2$$
$$W = 120 \text{ N}$$
$$y = 1 \text{ mm} = 1 \times 10^{-3} \text{ m}$$
$$\mu = 500 \text{ poise} = 50 \text{ Ns/m}^2$$
$$\theta = 30°$$

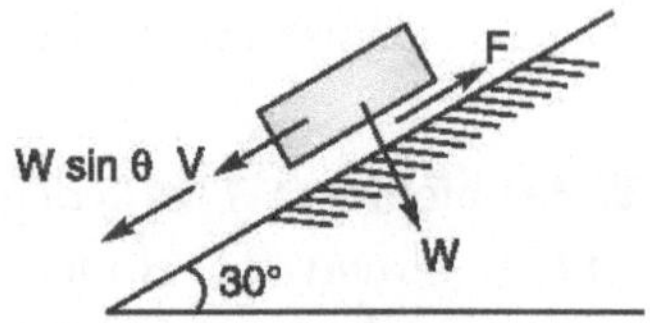

Fig. 1.9

$$\frac{du}{dy} = \frac{V}{y} = \frac{V}{1\times10^{-3}}$$

$$\tau = \mu\frac{du}{dy} = 50\times\frac{V}{1\times10^{-3}}$$
$$= 50000\ V \text{ N/m}^2$$
$$F = \tau \times A$$
$$= 50000\ V \times 20 \times 10^{-4}$$
$$= 100\ V \text{ N}$$

But from Fig. 1.9

$$F = W \sin\theta$$
$$100\ V = 120 \times \sin 30°$$

∴ $$V = 0.6 \text{ m/sec.}$$

■ **Problem 1.8:** *A thin plate is pulled through a gap 'h' present between two plates such that the viscosity of liquid on two sides of moving plate are* μ_1 *and* μ_2*. Determine the position of the moving plate such that minimum drag force will be required to maintain a constant velocity 'V'.*

Solution:

Ref. Fig. 1.10.

Shear stress $$\tau_1 = \mu_1\left(\frac{du}{dy}\right)_1 = \mu_1\frac{V}{y}$$

$$F_1 = \tau_1 A = \mu_1\frac{V}{y}A$$

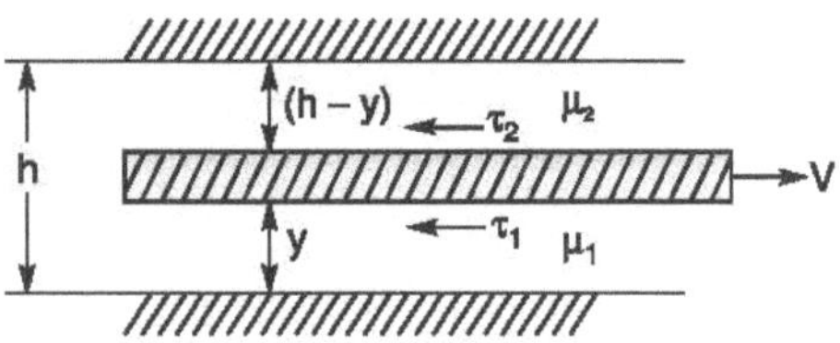

Fig. 1.10

Shear stress $$\tau_2 = \mu_2\left(\frac{du}{dy}\right)_2 = \mu_2\frac{V}{(h-y)}$$

and $$F_2 = \tau_2 A = \mu_2\frac{V}{(h-y)}A$$

Total shear force $= F = F_1 + F_2$

$$= \mu_1 \frac{V}{y} A + \mu_2 \frac{V}{(h-y)} A$$

For drag force to be minimum

$$\frac{dF}{dy} = 0$$

$$\frac{\mu_1 A}{y^2} + \frac{\mu_2}{(h-y)^2} A = 0$$

$$\frac{\mu_1}{y^2} = \frac{\mu_2}{(h-y)^2}$$

$$\frac{(h-y)^2}{y^2} = \frac{\mu_2}{\mu_1}$$

$$\frac{h^2 - 2hy + y^2}{y^2} = \frac{\mu_2}{\mu_1}$$

$$\left(\frac{h}{y}\right)^2 - 2\left(\frac{h}{y}\right) + 1 = \frac{\mu_2}{\mu_1}$$

$$\left(\frac{h}{y}\right)^2 - 2\left(\frac{h}{y}\right) + \left(1 - \frac{\mu_2}{\mu_1}\right) = 0$$

$$\frac{h}{y} = \frac{2 \pm \sqrt{4 - 4\left(1 - \frac{\mu_2}{\mu_1}\right)}}{2}$$

$$\therefore \quad \frac{h}{y} = 1 + \sqrt{\frac{\mu_2}{\mu_1}}$$

$$\therefore \quad y = \frac{h}{1 + \sqrt{\frac{\mu_2}{\mu_1}}}.$$

■ **Problem 1.9:** *A cylinder of 0.12 m radius rotates concentrically inside a fixed cylinder of 0.13 m radius. Both cylinders are 3 m long. Determine the viscosity of the liquid which fills the space between the cylinders if a torque of 0.08 kgm is required to maintain an angular velocity of 211 radian/sec. Assume a linear velocity profile.*

Solution: Given:

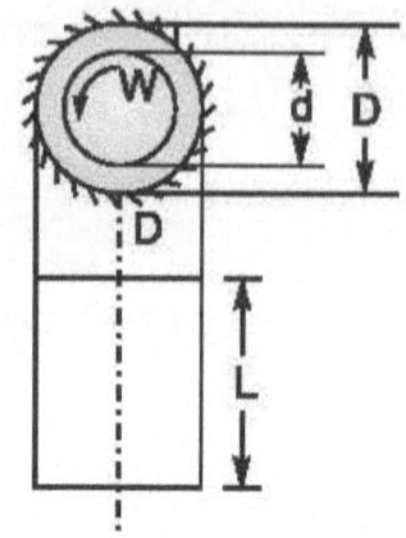

Fig. 1.11

$$r = 0.12 \text{ m}$$
$$R = 0.13 \text{ m}$$
$$L = 3 \text{ m}$$
$$T = 0.08 \text{ kg m}$$
$$= 0.08 \times 9.81 = 0.7848 \text{ N.m}$$
$$\omega = 211 \text{ rad/sec.}$$

Now
$$d = 2r = 0.12 \times 2 = 0.24 \text{ m}$$
$$D = 2R = 0.13 \times 2 = 0.26 \text{ m}$$

$$\text{Linear velocity} = V = r\omega$$
$$= 0.12 \times 211 = 25.32 \text{ m/sec.}$$

Gap between two cylinders

$$= y = R - r = 0.13 - 0.12 = 0.01 \text{ m}$$

$$\text{Shear stress} = \tau = \mu\frac{du}{dy} = \mu\frac{V}{y} = \mu \times \frac{25.32}{0.01} = 2532\,\mu$$

$$\text{Shear force} = F = \tau \times A = \tau \times \pi dL$$
$$= 2532\,\mu \times \pi \times 0.24 \times 3$$
$$= 5727.2491\,\mu$$

$$\text{Shear torque} = T = F \times r$$
$$0.7848 = 5727.2491\,\mu \times 0.12 = 687.2699\,\mu$$

$$\therefore \quad \mu = \frac{0.7848}{687.2699} = 1.1419 \times 10^{-3} \text{ Nm/sec.}$$

Note: Power required to rotate the cylinder is calculated by using the relation

$$\text{Power} = P = \omega T$$

where P is in Nm/sec. or watts, ω = angular velocity in rad/sec., T = torque in Nm]

■ **Problem 1.10:** *In a 5 cm long journal bearing arrangement, the clearance between the shaft and bearing is 0.1 mm. The shaft is 2 cm in diameter and rotates at 3000 rpm. The dynamic viscosity of the liquid used is 0.01 Ns/m². Considering the liquid is Newtonian estimate the frictional torque journal has to overcome and corresponding power loss.*

Solution: Given:

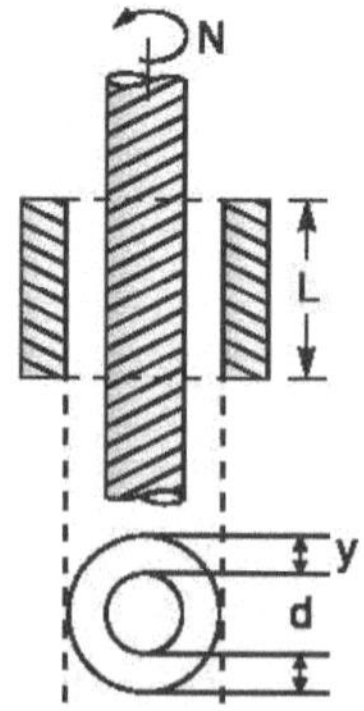

Fig. 1.12

$$L = 5 \text{ cm} = 5 \times 10^{-2} \text{ m}$$
$$y = 0.1 \text{ mm} = 0.1 \times 10^{-3} \text{ m}$$
$$d = 2 \text{ cm} = 2 \times 10^{-2} \text{ m}$$
$$N = 3000 \text{ rpm}$$
$$\mu = 0.01 \text{ Ns/m}^2$$
$$\omega = \frac{2\pi N}{60}$$

$$= \frac{2\times\pi\times 3000}{60} = 314.16 \text{ rad/sec.}$$

and $$V = r\omega = \frac{d}{2}\times\omega = \frac{2}{2}\times 10^{-2}\times 314.16$$

$$= 3.14 \text{ m/sec.}$$

$$\text{Velocity gradient} = \frac{du}{dy} = \frac{V}{y} = \frac{3.14}{0.1\times 10^{-3}} = 31.4\times 10^3 \text{ per sec.}$$

$$\text{Shear stress} = \tau = \mu\frac{du}{dy} = 0.01\times 31.4\times 10^3 = 0.314\times 10^3 \text{ N/m}^2$$

$$\text{Shear force} = F = \tau\times A = \tau\times \pi dL$$

$$= 0.314\times 10^3\times\pi\times 2\times 10^{-2}\times 5\times 10^{-2}$$

$$= 0.986 \text{ N}$$

$$\text{Shear torque} = T = F\times r$$

$$= 0.986\times 1\times 10^{-2}$$

$$= 0.986\times 10^{-2} \text{ Nm}$$

$$\text{Power required} = P = \omega T$$

$$= 314.16\times 0.986\times 10^{-2}$$

$$= 3.0986 \text{ Nm/sec. or watts.}$$

■ **Problem 1.11:** *A uniform film of oil 0.13 mm thick separates two discs each of 200 mm diameter mounted co-axially. Ignoring edge effects calculate the torque necessary to rotate one disc relative to the other at a speed of 7 rad./sec. If foil has a viscosity 0.4 poise.*

Solution: Consider a strip of width dr at a distance of 'r' from the axis of rotation.

Shear stress at a distance of r from centre

$$= \tau = \mu\frac{du}{dy} = \mu\frac{V}{y} = \mu\frac{r\omega}{y}$$

Shear force on elemental ring $= dF = \tau\times dA$

$$= \mu\frac{r\omega}{y}\times 2\pi r\,dr$$

Shear torque on elemental ring $= dT = dF\times r$

$$= \frac{\mu r\omega}{y} = 2\pi r dr\times r = \frac{2\pi\mu\omega}{y} r^3\,dr$$

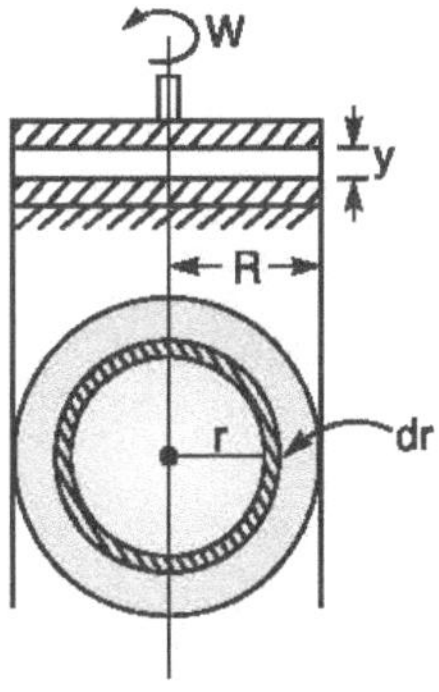

Fig. 1.13

$$\text{Total torque} = T = \int_0^T dT = \int_0^R \frac{2\pi\mu\omega}{y} r^3\,dr$$

$$T = \frac{2\pi\mu\omega}{y}\left[\frac{r^4}{4}\right]_0^R = \frac{\pi\mu\omega R^4}{2y} \text{ Nm}$$

Now given: $y = 0.13 \text{ mm} = 0.13 \times 10^{-3}$ m

$D = 200 \text{ mm} = 200 \times 10^{-3}$ m

∴ $R = 100 \times 10^{-3} = 0.1$ m

$N = 7$ rev./sec. $= 7 \times 60 = 420$ rev./min.

$\mu = 0.4$ poise $= 0.04$ Nm/sec.

Using the derived relation

$$T = \frac{\pi\mu\omega R^4}{2y} = \frac{\pi \times \mu \times \left(\frac{2\pi N}{60}\right) R^4}{2y}$$

$$= \frac{\pi \times 0.04 \times \frac{2\pi \times 420}{60} \times (0.1)^4}{2 \times 0.13 \times 10^{-3}}$$

$= 2.125$ Nm.

■ **Problem 1.12:** *Derive the expression for its power required to rotate 9 shaft at an angular velocity 'ω' in a conical bearing as shown in Fig. 1.14.*

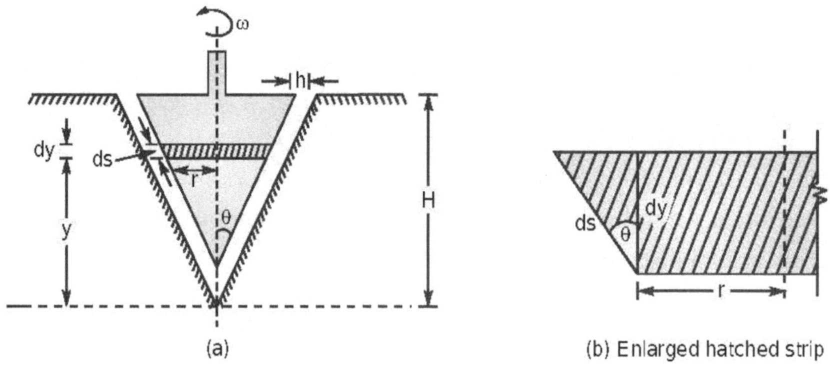

Fig. 1.14

Solution:

Using Newton's law of viscosity

$$\tau = \mu \frac{du}{dy}$$

and
$$\frac{du}{dy} = \frac{v}{y} = \frac{r\omega}{h}$$

put in the above expression

$$\tau = \frac{\mu r\omega}{h}$$

shear resistance offered by the hatched surface

$$dF = \tau \times A$$

$$= \frac{\mu r \omega}{h} \times 2\pi r ds$$

$$= \frac{2\pi\mu r^2 \omega}{h} \frac{dy}{\cos\theta} \qquad \because \quad ds = \frac{dy}{\cos\theta}$$

Torque

$$dT = dF \times r = \frac{2\pi\mu r^2 \omega}{h} \frac{dy}{\cos\theta} \times r$$

$$= \frac{2\pi\mu r^2 \omega}{h} \frac{dy}{\cos\theta}$$

Power

$$dP = dT \times \omega$$

$$= \frac{2\pi\mu r^3 \omega^2}{h \cos\theta} dy$$

But

$$r = y \tan\theta$$

$$dP = \frac{2\pi\mu y^3 \tan^3\theta\, \omega^2}{h\cos\theta} dy$$

therefore total power required to maintain the speed of shaft.

$$\int_0^P dP = \int_0^H \frac{2\pi\mu y^3 \tan^3\theta \omega^2}{h\cos\theta} dy$$

$$\therefore \qquad P = \frac{2\pi\mu\omega^2 \tan^3\theta}{h\cos\theta} \left[\frac{y^4}{4}\right]_0^H$$

$$= \frac{\pi\mu\omega^2 \tan^3\theta\, H^4}{2h\cos\theta}.$$

1.5 CAPILLARITY

1.5.1 Capillary Rise in a Glass Tube

When a glass tube is dipped in water, the water rises in the tube. If a glass tube is dipped in mercury, the mercury level inside the tube will be lower than the outside. The rise of water and fall of mercury in the tube is termed as capillary rise and capillary depression respectively. This phenomenon of rise and fall of liquid in a capillary tube is called capillarity and is due to surface tension.

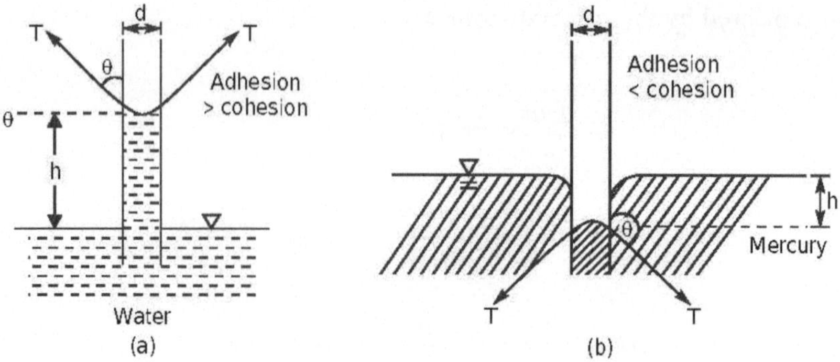

Fig. 1.15 Capillary

Ref. Fig. 1.15 (*a*)

Resolving the forces in vertical direction

$$T \cos \theta = \text{Weight of liquid in the tube}$$

$$T \cos \theta = \frac{\pi d^2}{4} \times h \times \gamma$$

$$\sigma \pi d \cos \theta = \frac{\pi d^2}{4} \times h \times \gamma \qquad (\because \quad T = \sigma \pi d)$$

$$h = \frac{4\sigma \cos \theta}{\gamma d} \qquad \text{...(1.4)}$$

where h = capillary rise in m

σ = surface tension in N/m

θ = angle of contact

γ = specific weight in N/m^3

d = diameter of capillary tube in '*m*'

1.5.2 Capillary Rise in a Gap between Concentric Tube

Resolving the forces in vertical direction,

$$T_0 \cos \theta + T_i \cos \theta = \frac{\pi(d_0^2 - d_i^2)}{4} \times h \times \gamma$$

$$\sigma \pi d_0 \cos \theta + \sigma \pi d_i \cos \theta = \pi \frac{(d_0^2 - d_i^2)}{4} \times h \times \gamma$$

$$\sigma \pi (d_0 + d_i) \cos \theta = \pi \frac{(d_0 + d_i)(d_0 - d_i) \times h \times \gamma}{4}$$

$$h = \frac{4\sigma \cos \theta}{\gamma (d_0 - d_i)} \qquad \text{...(1.5)}$$

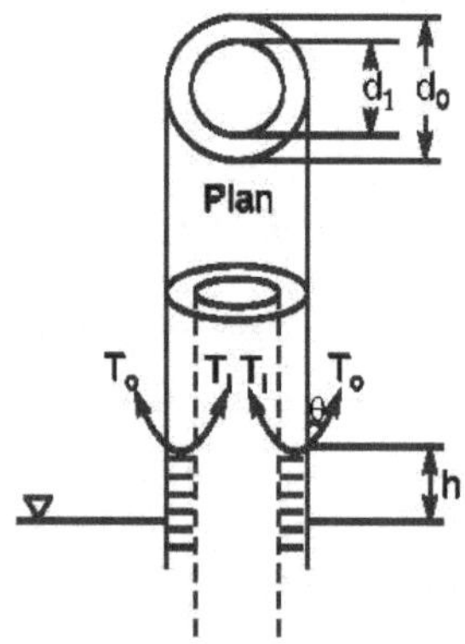

Fig. 1.16

where d_0 = diameter of outer tube in m

d_i = diameter of inner tube in m

1.5.3 Capillary Rise in a Gap between Two Parallel Plates

Consider two parallel plates of length 'L' and separated by distance 't' and 'h' is the capillary rise, then,

$$2T\cos\theta = L \times t \times h \times \gamma$$

$$2\sigma L\cos\theta = L \times t \times h \times \gamma$$

$$h = \frac{2\sigma\cos\theta}{\gamma t} \quad \text{...(1.6)}$$

where t gap between plates in m.

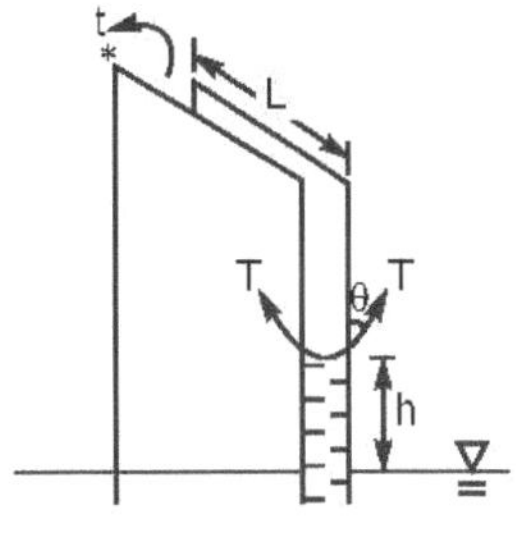

Fig. 1.17

■ Problem 1.13: *Determine the minimum diameter of the glass tube required if water level is not to rise more than 0.5 mm. Surface tension of water = 0.074 N/m. Angle of contact 0°.*

Solution: Given:

$$h = 0.5 \text{ mm} = 0.5 \times 10^{-3} \text{ m}$$

$$\sigma = 0.074 \text{ N/m}$$

$$\theta = 0°$$

Using
$$h = \frac{4\sigma\cos\theta}{\gamma d}$$

$$0.5 \times 10^{-3} = \frac{4 \times 0.074 \times \cos 0°}{9810 \times d}$$

$$\therefore \quad d = \frac{4 \times 0.074 \times 1}{9810 \times 0.5 \times 10^{-3}}$$

$$= 6.0346 \times 10^{-2} \text{ m}$$

$$= 6.03 \text{ cm.}$$

■ Problem 1.14: *For having a blood sample a fine glass capillary of dia 2 mm was held touching a freshly punctured finger tip. Estimate in 'ml' the volume of blood sample so drawn. Take density of blood as 1060 kg/m³, surface tension as 5 × 10⁻² N/m and its contact angle with glass as zero degrees.*

Solution: Given:

$$d = 2 \text{ mm} = 2 \times 10^{-3} \text{ m}$$

$$\rho = 1060 \text{ kg/m}^3$$

$$\gamma = \rho g = 1060 \times 9.81 \text{ N/m}^3$$

$$= 10398.6 \text{ N/m}^3$$

$$\sigma = 5 \times 10^{-2} \text{ N/m}$$

$$\theta = 0°$$

Using
$$h = \frac{4\sigma\cos\theta}{\gamma d} = \frac{4 \times 5 \times 10^{-2} \times \cos 0°}{10398.6 \times 2 \times 10^{-3}}$$

$$= 9.6167 \times 10^{-3} \text{ m}$$

Volume of blood sample drawn

$$= \frac{\pi d^2}{4} \times h$$

$$= \frac{\pi (2 \times 10^{-3})^2}{4} \times 9.6167 \times 10^{-3} \text{ m}^3$$

$$= 30.2118 \times 10^{-9} \text{ m}^3$$

$$= 30.2118 \times 10^{-9} \times 10^{6} \text{ ml}$$

$$= 30.2118 \times 10^{-3} \text{ ml.}$$

1.6 SURFACE TENSION

Consider a mass of liquid. A molecule '*O*' of liquid which is inside the liquid get attracted in all directions by the surrounding molecules. But a molecule at the surface of the liquid will get attracted in downward direction only. Hence the surface of the liquid acts as it is an elastic membrane under tension. Due to surface tension if a needle is gently placed on the liquid it floats.

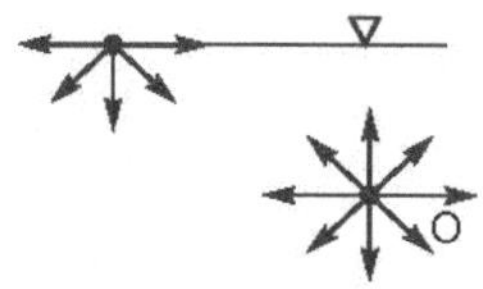

Fig. 1.18

Surface tension of a liquid is same on the liquid surface. It is affected by temperature. Surface tension is expressed in Newton per metre (N/m), and denoted by Greak letter **σ**(sigma). The pressure difference between inside and outside of a curved surface Δp is related to the diameter d and surface tension σ is:

(*a*) For a bubble

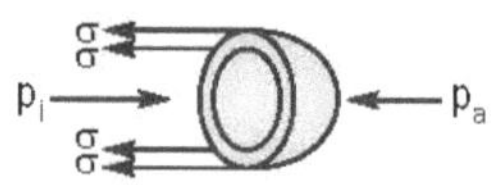

Fig. 1.19

$$p_i \times \frac{\pi d^2}{4} = \sigma \times 2\pi d + p_a \times \frac{\pi d^2}{4}$$

$$(p_i - p_a)\frac{\pi d^2}{4} = 2\pi\sigma d$$

$$p_i - p_a = \frac{8\sigma}{d}$$

$$\Delta p = \frac{8\sigma}{d} \qquad \text{...(1.7)}$$

where p_i = pressure inside the bubble

p_a = pressure outside the bubble *i.e.*, atmospheric pressure.

(*b*) For a droplet

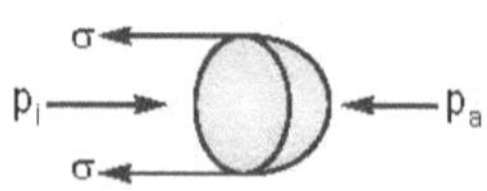

Fig. 1.20

$$p_i \times \frac{\pi d^2}{4} = \sigma \times \pi d + p_a \times \frac{\pi d^2}{4}$$

$$p_i - p_a = \frac{4\sigma}{d}$$

$$\Delta p = \frac{4\sigma}{d} \qquad \text{...(1.8)}$$

(c) For a liquid cylinder

$$p_i \times d \times L = \sigma \times 2L + p_a \times d \times L$$

$$(p_i - p_a) = \Delta p = \frac{2\sigma}{d} \qquad \text{...(1.9)}$$

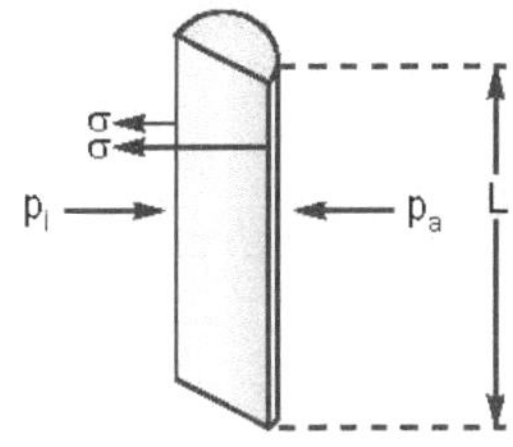

Fig. 1.21

■ **Problem 1.15:** *Calculate the gauge pressure and the absolute pressure within:*

(a) a jet of water 0.4 cm dia.

(b) a droplet of water 0.4 cm dia.

(c) a bubble of water 0.4 cm dia.

Assume surface tension of water as 0.073 N/m and atmospheric pressure as 101300 N/m².

Solution: Given:

$$d = 0.4 \text{ cm} = 0.4 \times 10^{-2} \text{ m}$$

$$\sigma = 0.073 \text{ N/m}$$

$$p_a = 101300 \text{ N/m}^2$$

(*a*) Using a relation for a jet of water

$$\Delta p = p_i - p_a = \frac{2\sigma}{d}$$

$$p_i \text{ (absolute)} = \frac{2\sigma}{d} + p_a$$

$$= \frac{2 \times 0.073}{0.4 \times 10^{-2}} + 101300$$

$$= 101336.5 \text{ N/m}^2 \text{ (absolute)}$$

$$p_i \text{ (gauge)} = \frac{2\sigma}{d} = \frac{2 \times 0.073}{0.4 \times 10^{-2}} = 36.5 \text{ N/m}^2$$

(*b*) Using a relation for a droplet of water

$$\Delta p = p_i - p_a = \frac{4\sigma}{d}$$

$$p_i \text{ (absolute)} = \frac{4\sigma}{d} + p_a$$

$$= \frac{4 \times 0.073}{0.4 \times 10^{-2}} + 101300$$

$$= 73 + 101300$$

$$= 101373 \text{ N/m}^2$$

$$p_i \text{ (gauge)} = \frac{4\sigma}{d} = \frac{4 \times 0.073}{0.4 \times 10^{-2}} = 73 \text{ N/m}^2$$

(*c*) Using a relation for a bubble of water

$$\Delta p = p_i - p_a = \frac{8\sigma}{d}$$

$$p_i \text{ (absolute)} = \frac{8\sigma}{d} + p_a = \frac{8 \times 0.073}{0.4 \times 10^{-2}} + 101300$$

$$= 146 + 101300 = 101446 \text{ N/m}^2$$

$$p_i \text{ (gauge)} = \frac{8\sigma}{d} = \frac{8 \times 0.073}{0.4 \times 10^{-2}} = 146 \text{ N/m}^2.$$

Note: Gauge atmospheric pressure = zero N/m^2, Refer Chapter 2

■ **Problem 1.16:** *What is the pressure with which you will need to blow to get soap bubble of 3 cm diameter if the ambient pressure is 1.03 kg/cm^2 and the surface tension coefficient for the soap is 0.25 N/m.*

Solution: Given:

$$d = 3 \text{ cm} = 3 \times 10^{-2} \text{ m}$$

$$p_a = 1.03 \text{ kg/cm}^2$$

$$= 1.03 \times 9.81 \times 10^4 \text{ N/m}^2$$

$$\sigma = 0.25 \text{ N/m}$$

Using a relation for bubble

$$\Delta p = p_i - p_a = \frac{8\sigma}{d}$$

$$p_i = \frac{8\sigma}{d} + p_a$$

$$= \frac{8 \times 0.25}{3 \times 10^{-2}} + 1.03 \times 9.81 \times 10^4$$

$$= 101109.67 \text{ N/m}^2$$

The pressure to blow to get soap bubble is 101109.67 N/m^2.

■ **Problem 1.17:** *What force is needed to lift a thin wire ring 3 cm in diameter from a water surface? Assume surface tension for water as 0.07 N/m and angle of contact as zero.*

Solution: Given:

$$d = 3 \text{ cm} = 3 \times 10^{-2} \text{ m}$$

$$\sigma = 0.07 \text{ N/m}$$

$$\theta = 0°$$

$$\text{Force needed to lift} = 2\pi d\, \sigma \cos\theta$$

$$= 2\pi \times 3 \times 10^{-2} \times 0.07 \times \cos 0°$$

$$= 0.0132 \text{ N.}$$

1.7 VAPOUR PRESSURE

All liquids have a tendency to vaporise when they come in contact with gaseous atmosphere. The vaporization takes place due to liquid molecules escaping from the free surface.

Rage of vaporization depends on:

(*a*) Molecular energy of the liquid

(*b*) Condition of the atmosphere adjoining it.

Consider a liquid enclosed in a closed vessel, the ejected vapour molecules get accumulated in the space between the free liquid surface and top of the vessel. This accumulated vapour of the liquid exerts their own pressure on the liquid surface, called vapour pressure.

The vapour pressure will have a constant value when the molecules leave and enter the liquid at the same rate. The constant vapour pressure is called the saturated vapour pressure.

If the external absolute pressure imposed on the liquid is reduced by some means to such an extent that it becomes equal to or less than the vapour pressure of the liquid, the boiling of the liquid starts whatever be the temperature.

■ **Problem 1.18:** *Find the power required to rotate a vertical shaft rests in a foot-step bearing. The diameter of the shaft is 15 cm and rotating with 1000 rpm. The gap between the rotating part and bearing is 5 mm and filled with a fluid of viscosity 0.2 Ns/m². Derive an expression for the power for foot step bearing.*

Solution: Using Newton's law of viscosity

$$\tau = \mu \frac{du}{dy}$$

$$= \mu \frac{V}{h}$$

shear stress on the ring

$$\tau = \mu \frac{r\omega}{h} \quad \because \quad V = r\omega$$

shear force = $dF = \tau \times A$

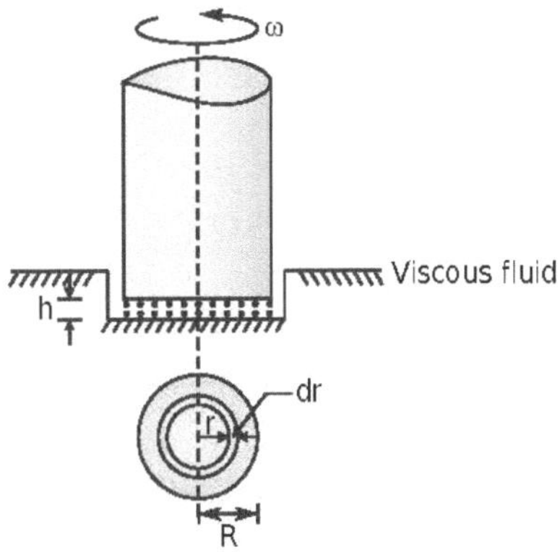

Fig. 1.22 Foot-step bearing

$$dF = \frac{\mu r\omega}{h} \times 2\pi r\, dr$$

Torque required $= d\tau = dF \times r$

$$= \frac{\mu r\omega}{h} \times 2\pi r\, dr \times r$$

$\therefore$ Total torque required

$$T = \int_0^T dT = \int_0^R \frac{2\pi\mu\omega}{h} r^3\, dr$$

$$= \frac{2\pi\mu\omega}{h}\left[\frac{r^4}{4}\right]_0^R = \frac{2\pi\mu\omega R^4}{4h}$$

$$= \frac{\pi\mu\omega R^4}{2h} \qquad \text{...(1.10)}$$

and power required to rotate the shaft

$$P = \omega T$$

$$= \frac{\pi\mu\omega^2 R^4}{2h} \qquad \text{...(1.11)}$$

Given: $D = 15$ cm

$R = 7.5 \text{ cm} = 0.075 \text{ m}$

$N = 1000$ rpm

$h = 5 \text{ mm} = 5 \times 10^{-3} \text{ m}$

$\mu = 0.2 \text{ Ns/m}^2$

Now $$P = \frac{\pi\mu\omega^2 R^4}{2h}$$

But $$\omega = \frac{2\pi N}{60}$$

$\therefore$ $$P = \frac{\pi\mu R^4}{2h}\left(\frac{2\pi N}{60}\right)^2 = \frac{\mu\pi^2 R^4 N^2}{1800\, h}$$

$$= \frac{0.2 \times \pi^2 \times (0.075)^4 \times 1000^2}{1800 \times 5 \times 10^{-3}}$$

$= 6.9396$ Nm/sec.

Problem 1.19: *Derive an expression for power absorbed in overcoming viscous resistance for collar bearing. Also find it for the given data: Internal and external radius of collar in 5 cm and 15 cm respectively. Speed is 1000 rpm. The gap between the rotating part and bearing is 5 mm and filled with a fluid of viscosity 0.2 Ns/m².*

Solution:

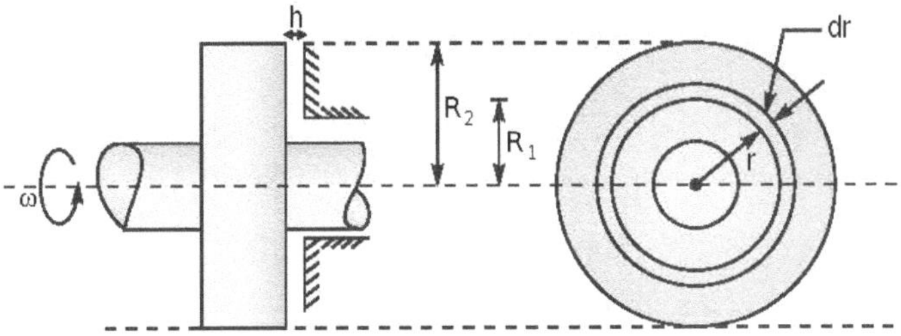

Fig. 1.23 Collar bearing

Using Newton's law of viscosity

$$\tau = \mu \frac{du}{dy} = \mu \frac{v}{h}$$

for the elementary ring at a distance of r from the axis of shaft and thickness dr

$$\text{Shear stress} = \tau = \mu \frac{r\omega}{h}$$

$$\text{Shear force} = dF = \tau \times dA$$

$$dF = \frac{\mu r\omega}{h} \times 2\pi r\, dr$$

$$\text{Torque required} = dT = dF \times r$$

$$= \mu \frac{r\omega}{h} \times 2\pi r\, dr \times r$$

∴ Total torque required

$$T = \int_0^T dT = \int_{R_1}^{R_2} \frac{\mu r\omega}{h} \times 2\pi r\, dr \times r$$

∴ $$T = \frac{2\pi\mu\omega}{h}\left[\frac{r^4}{4}\right]_{R_1}^{R_2} = \frac{2\pi\mu\omega(R_2^4 - R_1^2)}{4h}$$

$$T = \frac{\pi\mu\omega}{2h}(R_2^4 - R_1^4) \quad \text{...(1.12)}$$

and the power required to rotate the shaft

$$P = \omega T$$

$$= \frac{\pi\mu\omega}{2h}(R_2^4 - R_1^4) \quad \text{...(1.13)}$$

Given: $R_1 = 5 \text{ cm} = 0.05 \text{ m}$

∴ $R_2 = 15 \text{ cm} = 0.15 \text{ m}$

$N = 1000$ rpm

$h = 5 \text{ mm} = 5 \times 10^{-3} \text{ m}$

$\mu = 0.2 \text{ Ns/m}^2$

Now $$P = \frac{\pi\mu\omega^2}{2h}(R_2^4 - R_1^4)$$

But $$\omega = \frac{2\pi N}{60}$$

∴ $$P = \frac{\mu\pi^2 N^2}{1800\,h}(R_2^4 - R_1^4)$$

$$= \frac{0.2 \times \pi^2 \times 1000^2}{1800 \times 5 \times 10^{-3}}(0.15^4 - 0.05^4)$$

$$= 109.66 \text{ Nm/sec.}$$

■ **Problem 1.20:** *A flywheel weighing 600 N has a radius of gyration of 30 cm. When it is rotating at 600 rpm, its speed reduces by 1 rpm per sec. due to viscous friction. If the length of sleeve bearing is 5 cm, the shaft diameter 20 mm and the radial clearance between the shaft and sleeve 0.05 mm, determine the fluid viscosity.*

Given:

$W = 600\ N$

$K = 30\ cm = 30 \times 10^{-2}\ m = 0.3\ m$

$N = 600\ rpm$

$L = 5 \times 10^{-2}\ m$

$d = 20 \times 10^{-3}\ m$

Radial clearance $= h = 0.05\ mm$

$= 0.05 \times 10^{-3}\ m.$

Solution:

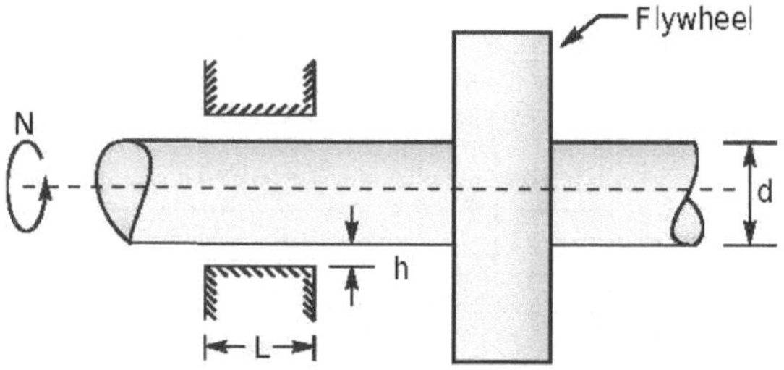

Fig. 1.24 Symbolic diagram of flywheel

Torque $= T =$ Moment of Inertia × Angular acceleration

$$= I \times \alpha$$

But $$I = mK^2$$

$$= \frac{600}{9.81} \times 0.3^2 = 5.5045 \text{ m}^4$$

and $$\omega = \frac{2\pi N}{60} = \frac{2\pi \times 600}{60}$$

$$= 2\pi = 62.83 \text{ rad/sec}$$

and $$\alpha = \frac{\text{Change in angular speed}}{\text{Time}}$$

$$= \frac{\frac{1}{60} \times 2\pi}{1} = 0.1047 \text{ rad/sec}^2$$

$\therefore$ $$\text{Torque} = T = I \times \alpha$$
$$= 5.5045 \times 0.1047$$
$$= 0.5764 \text{ Nm} \quad ...(1)$$

Similarly from Newton's law of viscosity

Using Newton's law of viscosity

$$\tau = \mu \frac{du}{dy} = \mu \frac{v}{h}$$

$$\tau = \mu \times \frac{r\omega}{h}$$

$$\tau = \mu \times \frac{10 \times 10^{-3} \times 62.83}{0.05 \times 10^{-3}}$$
$$= 12566 \text{ mN/m}^2$$

$\therefore$ $$F = \tau \times A = \tau \times \pi dL$$
$$= 12566\,\mu \times \pi \times 20 \times 10^{-3} \times 5 \times 10^{-2}$$
$$= 39.48\,\mu\text{N}$$

$\therefore$ $$T = F \times r$$
$$= 39.48\mu \times 10 \times 10^{-3}$$
$$= 0.3948\,\mu \text{ Nm} \quad ...(2)$$

Equating equations (1) and (2)

$$0.3948\,\mu = 0.5764$$

$\therefore$ $$\mu = 1.46 \text{ Ns/m}^2 = 14.6 \text{ poise.}$$

Exercises

1. Find (*i*) mass density (*ii*) specific weight and specific volume of a fluid of specific gravity 0.8. (**Ans.** $\rho = 800$ kg/m^3, $\gamma = 7848$ N/m^3, $\forall = 1.25 \times 10^{-3}$ m^3/kg)
2. The pressure on the fluid filled in a cylinder is increased from 8×10^5 N/m^2 to 15×10^5 N/m^2. Find the percentage reduction in a volume of fluid if bulk modules of elasticity is 6×10^8 N/m^2. (**Ans.** 0.1167%)
3. Determine the diameter of (*i*) Droplet (*ii*) Bubble and (*iv*) Liquid jet, inside pressure is 102500 N/m^2 (absolute). Assume surface tension of water as 0.073 N/m and atmospheric pressure as 101300 N/m^2. (**Ans.** (*i*) 0.24 mm (*ii*) 0.48 mm (*iii*) 0.12 mm)

4. Find a capillary rise through the gap between two concentric tubes of diameter 6 cm and 7 cm. If the assembly of concentric tubes are dipped in water having surface tension 0.075 N/m and angle of contact 0°. (**Ans.** 3.0581 mm)

5. A plate is moving over the another stationary plate with a velocity of 3.5 m/sec the gap between the plate is of 0.5 mm and is filled with a oil of viscosity 1.75 Ns/m^3. Find a shear stress on the top plate. (**Ans.** 12250 N/m^2)

6. Two large horizontal plates of infinite extent are 2.5 cm apart. Find a position of a thin plate of negligible thickness having area 0.6 m^2 and being pulled with a velocity of 0.65 m/sec for minimum resistance condition. Let the two gaps are filled with liquid of viscosities 0.8 Ns/m^2 and 1.75 Ns/m^2 respectively.

   (**Ans.** 1 cm from the fixed plate in contact with liquid of viscosity 0.8 Ns/m^2)

   $$\left(\textbf{Hint. } y = \frac{h}{1+\sqrt{\mu_2/\mu_1}}\right)$$

7. A pipe of diameter 10 cm and length 30 cm slides along a shaft of diameter 9.5 cm in a downward direction. The shaft is properly lubricated with an oil of viscosity 0.5 poise. Calculate the constant speed of the pipe if its weight is 5 N. (**Ans.** 2.65 m/sec)

8. A shaft 6.0 cm in diameter is being pushed axially through a bearing sleeve 6.02 cm in diameter and 40 cm long. The clearance assumed uniform is filled with oil whose properties are v = 0.003 m^2/s and specific gravity 0.88. Estimate the force required to pull the shaft at steady velocity of 0.4 m/sec. (**Ans.** 796.20 N)

9. A vertical gap 25 mm wide of infinite extent contains oil of specific gravity 0.9 and viscosity 2.5 Ns/m^2. A metal plate 1.0 m × 1.5 m × 3 mm weighing 140 N moves down under its own weight. Find the velocity of the plate. (**Ans.** 0.2/ sec)

10. A block of base area 30 cm^2 and mass 8 kg moves over a horizontal plane lubricated with oil film of 0.1 cm thick. If the initial velocity of the block is 2.5 m/sec. Find the distance covered by the block before coming to rest. How much time it would take to reduce its velocity to 0.5 m/sec? Take μ = 0.05 Ns/m^2. (**Ans.** 66.67 m , 64 sec)

11. A cylinder of 0.15 m radius rotates concentrically inside a fixed cylinder of 0.17 m radius. Both cylinders are having 3.5 m length. Assuming linear velocity profile find the viscosity of the liquid filled in a gap between the two cylinders if a torque of 120 Nm is required to maintain a rotational velocity of 250 rad/sec.

    (**Ans.** 0.0647 Ns/m^2)

12. In a 5 cm long journal bearing arrangement the clearance between the shaft and bearing is 0.1 mm. The shaft is 2 cm in diameter and the torque need to be applied to maintain a rotational speed 'N'rpm is 0.986 × 10^{-2} Nm. Find 'N' rpm. Take dynamic viscosity of liquid used in 0.001 Ns/m^2. (**Ans.** 3000 rpm)

13. Derive the expression for frictional torque in a conical bearing when the shaft is rotating at angular velocity 'ω' as shown in Fig. 1.25.

Take viscosity of fluid = μ.

$$\left(\textbf{Ans}: T = \frac{\pi\omega\mu}{2h\sin\theta}(R_2^4 - R_1^4)\right)$$

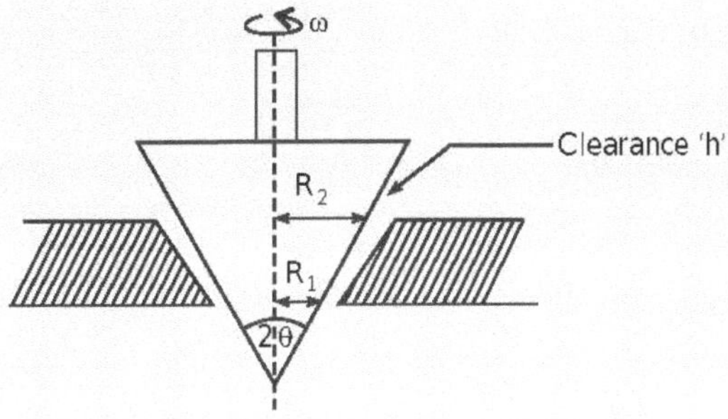

Fig. 1.25

14. A circular disc of diameter 'D' is rotating at a speed of 'N' ram above a fixed plate and the gap 'h' between the plates is filled with a fluid of viscosity 'μ' obtain an expression for viscous torque 'T' to maintain the speed of the disc. (Refer Fig. 1.26)

$$\left(\textbf{Ans}: T = \frac{\pi^2 \mu N D^4}{960\, h}\right)$$

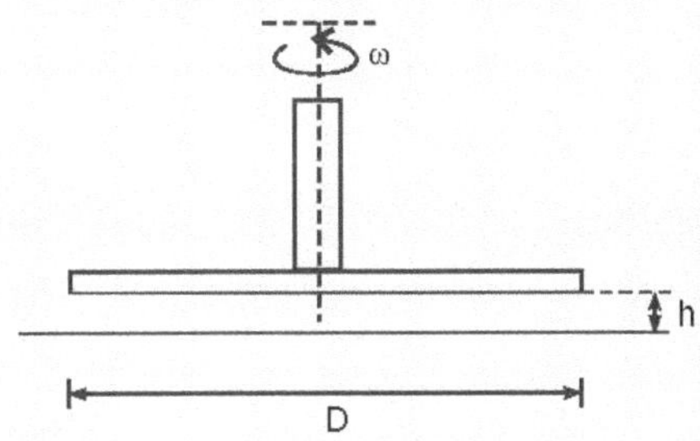

Fig. 1.26

❑❑❑

2

Fluid Pressure Measurement

2.1 INTRODUCTION

Pressure or intensity of pressure at a point in a fluid is defined as the force exerted pre unit area. It always acts in a normal direction to the surface in contact and is compressive in nature. If F is the total force distributed over area A, then the intensity of pressure is represented as,

$$P = \frac{F}{A} \quad \text{...(2.1)}$$

If the force is not uniformly distributed, then

$$P = \frac{dF}{dA} \quad \text{...(2.2)}$$

where dF is the force exerted on small area dA.

The unit of pressure is SI system is given on N/m^2 and in MKS as kgf/m^2.

2.2 PRESSURE VARIATION IN STATIC FLUID

Consider a small element of fluid for the analysis of the pressure variation. Let the size of element is $\delta x \times \delta y \times \delta z$ as shown in Fig. 2.1 in the fluid at rest. The element is in equilibrium under the action of compressive pressure forces acting on all its faces and the self weight.

Let P is the intensity of pressure at centroid of the element through which its own weight ($\gamma\delta \times \delta y \times \delta z$) acts vertically downwards, where 'γ' is the weight density of fluid.

The intensity of pressure on face $AEFB$ is $\left(p - \frac{\partial p}{\partial x}\frac{\partial x}{2}\right)$.

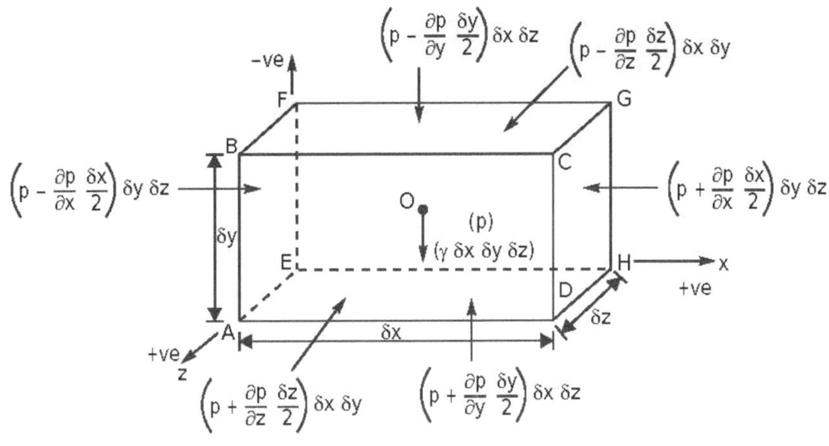

Fig. 2.1 Fluid element in fluid at rest

This acts on area $\delta y\,\delta z$. Hence the pressure force acting on face *AEFB* is

$$\left(p - \frac{\partial p}{\partial x}\frac{\delta x}{2}\right)\delta y\,\delta z.$$

Similarly the pressure force acting on the face *DHGC* is $\left(p + \frac{\partial p}{\partial x}\frac{\delta x}{2}\right)\delta y\,\delta z$. Other intensity of pressures and pressure forces acting normal to the faces are shown in Fig. 2.1.

As the element is in equilibrium under the action of the said forces, the algebraic sum of forces acting in any direction is zero.

$\therefore$ $\Sigma F_x = 0$, gives

$$\left(P - \frac{\partial p}{\partial x}\frac{\partial x}{2}\right)\partial y\,\partial z - \left(P + \frac{\partial p}{\partial x}\frac{\partial x}{2}\right)\partial y\,\partial z = 0$$

i.e.
$$\frac{\partial p}{\partial x} = 0 \qquad (\because \text{ since } \delta x\,\delta y\,\delta z \neq 0) \qquad ...(2.3)$$

$\Sigma F_y = 0$, gives

$$\left(p + \frac{\partial p}{\partial y}\frac{\delta y}{2}\right)\delta x\,\delta z - \left(p - \frac{\partial p}{\partial y}\frac{\delta y}{2}\right)\delta x\,\delta z - \gamma\,\delta y\,\delta y\,\delta z = 0$$

$$\frac{\partial p}{\partial y} = \gamma \qquad ...(2.4)$$

and $\Sigma F_z = 0$, gives

$$\left(p - \frac{\partial p}{\partial}\frac{\delta z}{2}\right)\delta x\,\delta y - \left(p + \frac{\partial p}{\partial z}\frac{\delta z}{2}\right)\delta x\,\delta y = 0$$

$$\frac{\partial p}{\partial z} = 0 \qquad ...(2.5)$$

The equations (2.3) and (2.5) shown that the intensity of pressure does not vary along x and z directions. The equation (2.4) shows that intensity of pressure varies in y-direction only and hence can be written as:

$$\frac{dp}{dy} = \gamma \qquad ...(2.6)$$

The above expression shows that the pressure increases in the downward direction and varies directly with weight density, γ of fluid. This is law of hydrostatics. This law holds good for both compressible and incompressible fluids. For incompressible fluids its weight density is constant. By integrating the equation (2.6)

$$\int dp = \int \gamma dy$$

$$p_2 - p_1 = \gamma (y_2 - y_1) \qquad ...(2.7)$$

where p_1 and p_2 are intensity of pressures at depth y_1 and y_2 from free surface of liquid, as shown in Fig. 2.2. At a point in fluid, the expression is written as,

$$p = \gamma y \qquad ...(2.8)$$

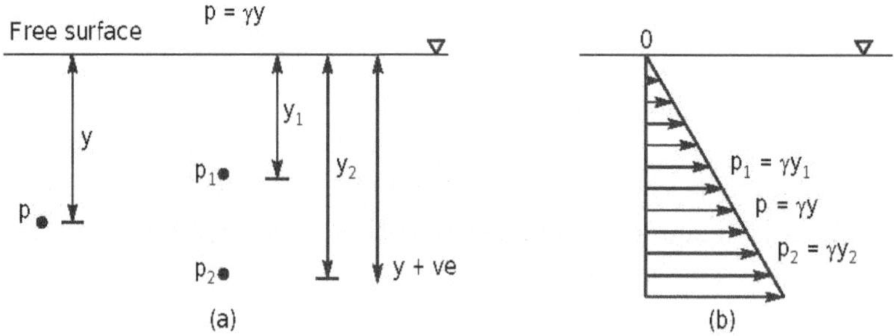

Fig. 2.2 Pressure variation and pressure diagram

From the expression (2.8) it is clear that the pressure variation is linear and is shown in Fig. 2.2 (*b*). Here p is the pressure above atmospheric pressure.

2.3 PRESSURE HEAD

The expression (2.8) can be written as

$$y = \frac{p}{\gamma} \qquad ...(2.9)$$

Here, y is the pressure head and is the vertical distance from the point to the free surface of liquid. It is expressed in 'm' or 'cm'.

2.4 PASCAL'S LAW

The pressure or intensity of pressure at any point in a fluid at rest is equal in all directions. This is known as Pascal's Law.

Proof of Pascal's Law:

Consider a small wedge shaped element in a static mass of fluid as a free body as shown in Fig. 2.3.

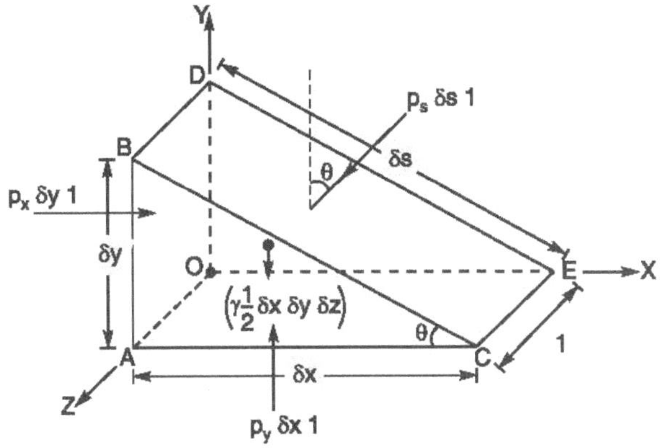

Fig. 2.3 Wedge shaped element in static mass

The size of the element is $\delta x \times \delta y \times 1$. The forces acting normal to the faces are p_x, p_y and p_s. The pressure force acting on face *OABD* is $(p_x \cdot \delta_y \cdot 1)$ and is along +ve x-axis. Similarly the other forces are as shown in Fig. 2.3. The fluid element is in equilibrium under action of pressure forces and self weight and hence algebraic sum of forces acting in any direction is zero.

$\Sigma F_x = 0$, gives

$$p_x \cdot \delta_y .1 - p_s \cdot \delta_s \cdot 1 \cdot \sin\theta = 0$$

But, $\delta_s \cdot \sin\theta = \delta_y$

$\therefore \quad p_x \cdot \delta_y \cdot 1 - p_s \cdot \delta_y \cdot 1 = 0$

$$p_x = p_s \qquad \text{...(2.10)}$$

$\Sigma F_y = 0$, gives

$$p_y \cdot \delta_x \cdot 1 - p_s \delta_s \cos\theta - \gamma \delta_x \cdot \delta_y \cdot 1 = 0$$

But $\delta_s \cdot \cos\theta = \delta_x$ and the term $\delta_x \cdot \delta_y$ is very small and can be neglected.

$$p_y \cdot \delta_x \cdot 1 - p_s \cdot \delta_x \cdot 1 = 0$$

$$p_y = p_s \qquad \text{...(2.11)}$$

Hence from equations (2.10) and (2.11) it is understood that

$$p_x = p_y = p_s \qquad \text{...(2.12)}$$

Hence for any fluid, pressure at point in the fluid mass is same in all directions.

2.5 ATMOSPHERIC, GAUGE, ABSOLUTE AND VACUUM PRESSURES

An air in the atmosphere exerts pressure in normal direction to the surface in contact and it is called atmospheric pressure. The two systems to measure pressure acting on fluid are (*i*) atmospheric pressure and (*ii*) absolute zero pressure or complete vacuum.

The relationship between gauge, absolute and vacuum pressure is illustrated in Fig. 2.4.

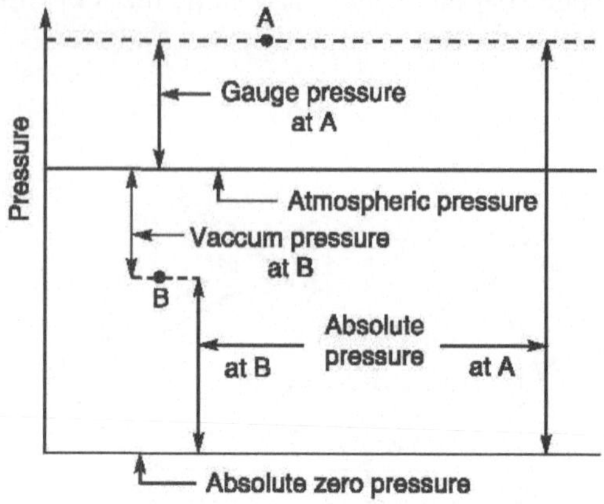

Fig. 2.4 Relationship between gauge absolute and vacuum pressures

When pressure is measured w.r.t. atmospheric pressure as datum it is called gauge pressure. It is measured with the help of pressure measuring device called gauges or pressure gauges. It shows zero reading on scale for normal atmospheric pressure. If the pressure is above atmospheric pressure it is called gauge pressure (positive) and below as negative gauge pressure or vacuum pressure.

The pressure measured w.r.t. absolute zero pressure is called as absolute pressure. This will have all positive values:

These pressure can be written in the following relation form:

(*a*) Absolute pressure = Atmospheric pressure + Gauge pressure

(*b*) Absolute pressure = Atmospheric pressure – Vacuum pressure

The atmospheric pressure at sea level is 10.13 N/cm^2 in SI units and 1.013 kgf/cm^2 in MKS system OR in terms of pressure head it is 10.3 m of water or 76 cm of mercury.

2.6 SOLVED PROBLEMS

■ **Problem 2.1:** *A hydraulic press has a ram of 25 cm diameter and a plunger of 4 cm diameter. Find the force required to lift load of 40 kN.*

Solution. Pascal's law states that intensity of pressure is transmitted equally in all directions.

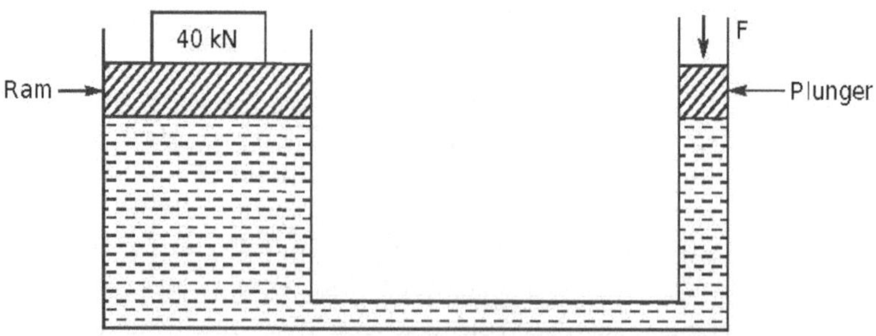

Fig. 2.5 Hydraulic press

Intensity of pressure at plunger = intensity of pressure at ram

$$\frac{F}{a} = \frac{W}{A}$$

$$F = W \times \left(\frac{a}{A}\right)$$

$$F = 40 \times 1000 \times \frac{\frac{\pi}{4} \times (0.04)^2}{\frac{\pi}{4} \times (0.25)^2}$$

$$= 40000 \times \frac{0.0016}{0.0625}$$

$$F = 1024 \text{ N.}$$ ...(Ans.)

■ **Problem 2.2:** *In a hydraulic jack the area of small piston is 8 cm² and that of large piston is 80 cm². A force of 200 kg is applied on small piston. What load can be fitted on large piston:*

(*a*) *if the pistons are at the same level?*

(*b*) *if the small piston is 50 cm above the large piston?*

specific weight of liquid in jack = 1000 kg/m³.

Solution. Pascal's low states that intensity of pressure transmits equally in all directions.

∴ Pressure intensity at ram and piston must be same.

(*a*) **Piston at same level:**

Let W is the load fitted on large piston.

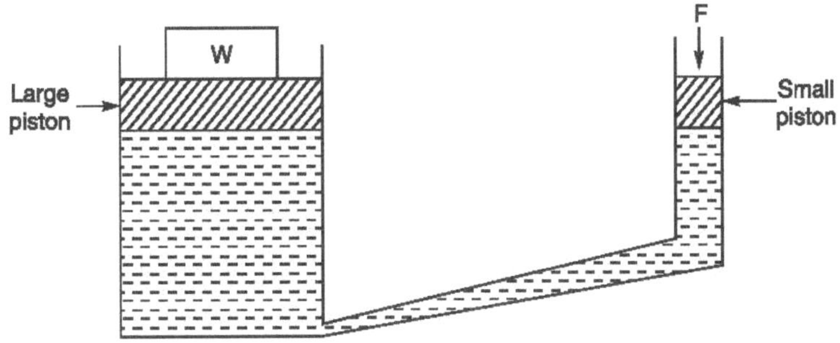

Fig. 2.6 Hydraulic press

∴ Pressure intensity on large piston = Pressure intensity on small piston

$$\frac{W}{80} = \frac{F}{8}$$

$$W = \frac{200}{8} \times 80$$

$$W = 2000 \text{ kg}$$ ...(Ans.)

(*b*) **Piston at different levels:**

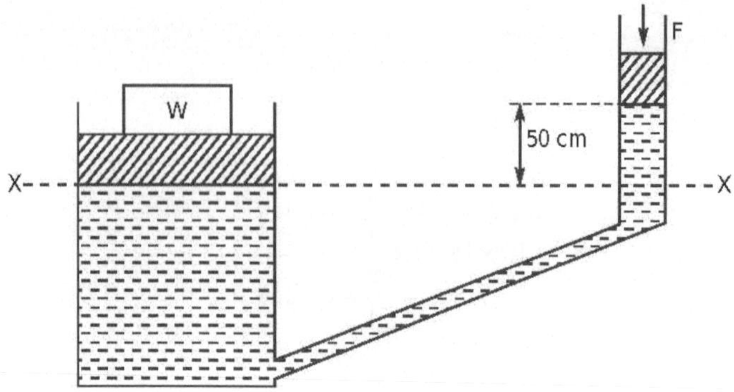

Fig. 2.7

$$\text{Pressure intensity on large piston at level } X\text{–}X = \left(\text{Pressure intensity on small piston}\right) + \left(\text{Pressure intensity due to 50 cm fiuid at } X\text{–}X \text{ level}\right)$$

$$\frac{W}{80} = \frac{200}{8} + \frac{0.50 \times 1000}{10^4}$$

$$W = \left(\frac{200}{8} + 0.05\right)80$$

$$W = 2000 + 40$$

$$W = 2004 \text{ kg}$$ ...(Ans.)

2.7 PRESSURE MEASUREMENT

Fluid pressure is measured by using either of the following two devices:

(1) Manometers

(2) Mechanical gauges.

2.7.1 Manometers

Manometers are the device used for measuring pressure at a point in a fluid by balancing the column of fluid by the same or another column of fluid. These manometers are classified as:

(*i*) Simple manometers

(*ii*) Differential manometers.

2.7.2 Mechanical Gauges

Mechanical gauges are the devices used for measuring pressure at a point by balancing the column of fluid by the spring or weight.

Most commonly used gauges are as follows:

(1) Bourdon tube pressure gauge

(2) Diaphragm pressure gauge

(3) Dead weight pressure gauge

(4) Bellows pressure gauge.

2.8 SIMPLE MANOMETERS

A simple manometer consists of glass tube of specific diameter, with one end connected to a point where pressure is to be measured and other end open to the atmosphere.

Most commonly used manometers are as follows:

(1) Piezometer

(2) *U*-tube manometer

(3) Single column manometer.

2.8.1 Piezometer

It is the simple glass tube used for measuring moderate pressures. One end of the tube is connected to the point where pressure is to be measured and other end open to atmosphere, as shown in Fig. 2.7. The fluid where the pressure is to be measured may be at rest or in motion.

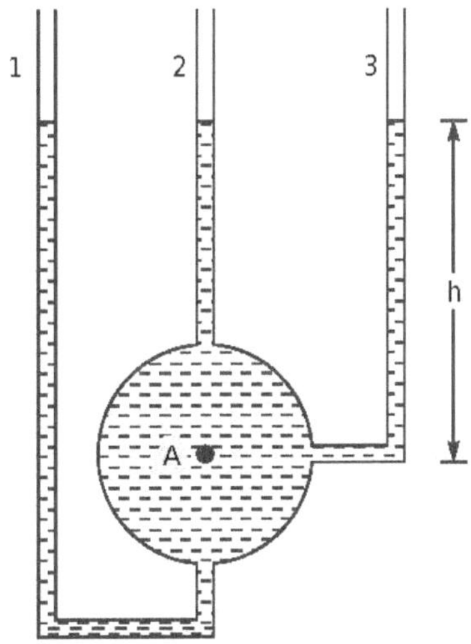

Fig. 2.7 Piezometers

The height of liquid in the glass tube gives the pressure head at that point. If 'h' is the height of liquid column above point A and γ is the weight density of that liquid, then pressure at point A, is $p = \gamma h$. Piezometers measure gauge pressures only as the other end is (surface at liquid in tube) open to the atmosphere (*i.e.*, subjected to atmospheric pressure). It should be observed strictly that, liquid should not overflow the Piezometer. Piezometers are not used for measuring small pressures as it will not give accurate results. Also it is not used for measuring high pressure since the height of tube required will be more and will not be easy to handle.

The internal diameter of the tube should not be less than 12 mm, otherwise capillary rise will affect the height of liquid column and in turn the result. Also the diameter of tube should not be more than 25 mm.

2.8.2 Solved Problems

■ **Problems 2.3:** *A closed tank contains 0.6 m of mercury, 1.5 m of water, 2.5 m of oil of relative density 0.75 and the empty space above it is filled with air at a pressure of 15 N/cm². What would be readings of the gauges installed at the bottom and in the top of the tank? Take atmospheric pressure as 10.2 N/cm².*

Solution:

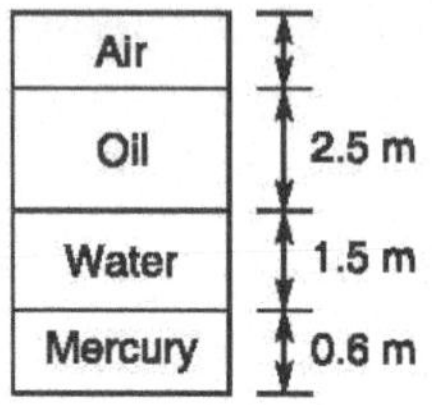

Fig. 2.8

Reading of the gauge installed at the top of the gauge = 15 – 10.2 = 4.8 N/cm² ...**(Ans.)**

Reading of gauge at the bottom of the gauge

$$= (15 - 10.2) + \frac{0.75 + 1000 \times 9.81}{10^6} \times 250 + \frac{1.0 \times 1000 \times 9.81}{10^6} \times 150 + \frac{13.6 \times 1000 \times 9.81}{10^6} \times 60$$

$$= 16.116 \text{ N/cm}^2. \qquad \text{...(Ans.)}$$

■ **Problem 2.4:** *A Piezometer tube is fitted to a tank containing water at a point 50 cm above the bottom of tank. The liquid in manometer is carbon di-sulphide having a specific gravity 1.9. Find the height of the free water surface above the bottom of the tank if the piezometer reading is 40 cm. Find the pressure intensity at the bottom of the tank.*

Solution: Consider level *BC* as datum and equate pressure on both sides.

Pressure head at B = Pressure head at C

$= 1.9 \times 0.4$

Pressure heat at $B = 0.76$ m

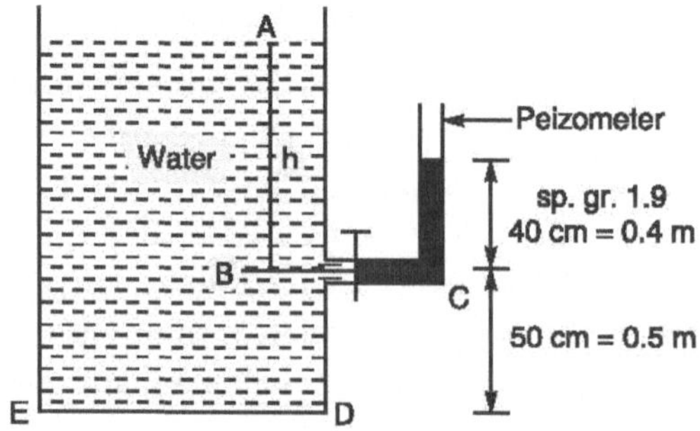

Fig. 2.9

Height of free surface above the base of the tank = 0.5 + 0.76 = 1.26 m of water

Pressure intensity at the bottom of the tank = $\frac{1.26 \times 1000}{10^4}$ = 0.126 kg/cm^2.

2.8.3 U-Tube Manometer

U-tube manometers are used to measure small, moderate and high pressures at point in a fluid at rest or in motion. It consists of a glass tube of *U*-shape, with one of its end connected to the point where pressure is to be measured and other open to the atmosphere as shown in Fig. 2.10. It is used for measuring gauge as well as vacuum pressures. The tube contains liquid having higher specific gravity, (generally mercury) than the specific gravity of the liquid whose pressure is to be measured. Such liquid is called manometric liquid and it should not get mixed with the liquid of which pressure is to be measured.

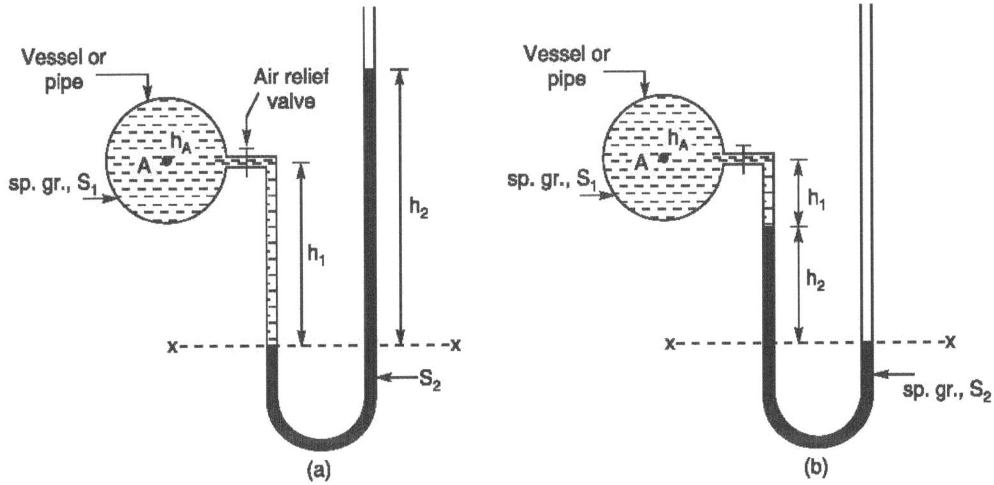

Fig. 2.10 *U*-tube manometer

(I) Measurement of Gauge Pressure

One end of *U*-tube manometer, having heavy liquid of specific gravity, S_2 is connected to the vessel or pipe. The liquid having sp. gravity S_1 from vessel or pipe enters the manometer and reduces the heavy liquid level in left limb and rise in heavy liquid level in right limb as shown in Fig. 2.10 (*a*). An air relief valve is provided at the top of connecting tube, which removes air from left limb and helps to give fairly accurate results.

Let, h_1 = height of liquid column in left limb above datum *X–X*

and h_2 = height of heavy liquid column in right limb above datum *X–X*.

We know that, the intensity of pressure or pressure head is same for the horizontal level. Hence pressure head above the horizontal datum *X–X* in the left and right limb of *U*-tube must be same.

$\therefore$ Pressure head in left limb above datum *X–X*

= Pressure head in right limb above datum *X–X*

$$h_1S_1 + h_A = h_2S_2$$

$$\therefore \qquad h_A = h_2S_2 - h_1S_1 \qquad \text{...(2.13)}$$

where, h_A is pressure head of point A.

(II) Measurement of Vacuum Pressure

Let there is vacuum pressure at A in the vessel or pipe. When the one end of U-tube is connected to vessel or pipe, the heavy liquid will rise in left limb and fall in right limb as shown in Fig. 2.10 (*b*).

Now, pressure head above datum X–X in left limb

= Pressure head above datum X–X in right limb

$$h_2S_2 + h_1S_1 + h_A = 0$$

$$\therefore \qquad h_A = -(h_2S_2 + h_1S_1) \qquad \text{...(2.14)}$$

2.8.4 Solved Problems

■ **Problem 2.5:** *Find the pressure of fluid in a pipe A for manometer readings as shown in Figs. 2.11 (a) and (b).*

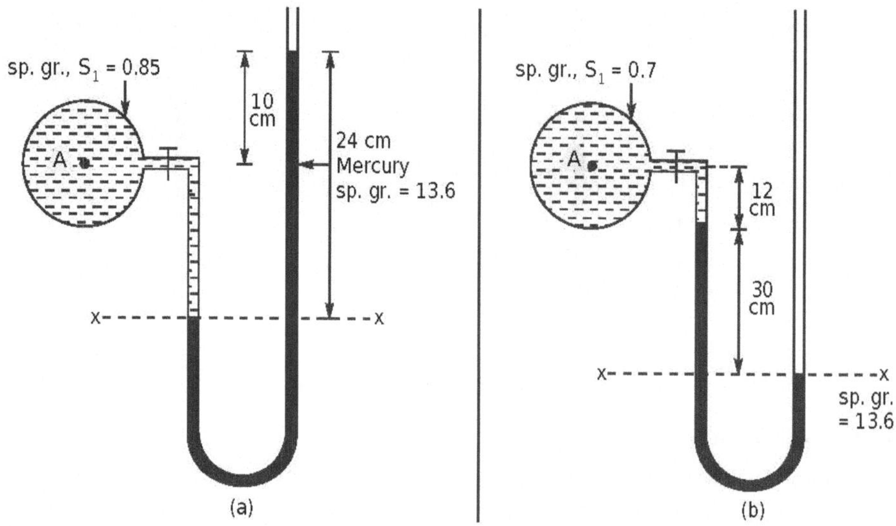

Fig. 2.11

(*a*) For gauge pressure: Equating pressures on both sides above the datum X–X.

Pressure head in left limb above X–X = Pressure head in right limb above X–X

$$h_A + (24 - 10) \times 0.85 = 24 \times 13.6$$

$\therefore$ Pressure head, $h_A = 314.5$ cm of water

$$P_A = \text{Pressure intensity} = \frac{314.5 \times 1000 \times 9.81}{10^6}$$

$$P_A = 3.085 \text{ N/cm}^2 \qquad \text{...(Ans.)}$$

(b) For vacuum pressure:

Pressure head in left limb above datum X–X

= Pressure head in right limb above datum X–X

$$30 \times 13.6 + 12 \times 0.7 + h_A = 0$$

$$\therefore \quad h_A = -416.4 \text{ cm of water}$$

$$P_A = \text{Pressure at } A$$

$$= \frac{-416.4 \times 1000 \times 9.81}{10^6}$$

$$= -4.084 \text{ N/cm}^2. \qquad \text{...(Ans.)}$$

■ **Problem 2.6:** *To find the pressure at a point in a pipe line a U-tube mercury manometer is connected to the point. Calculate the pressure when the free surface of mercury coincides with the centre line of the pipe and deflection is 6 cm.*

Solution. Equating pressure heads above datum X–X on both sides.

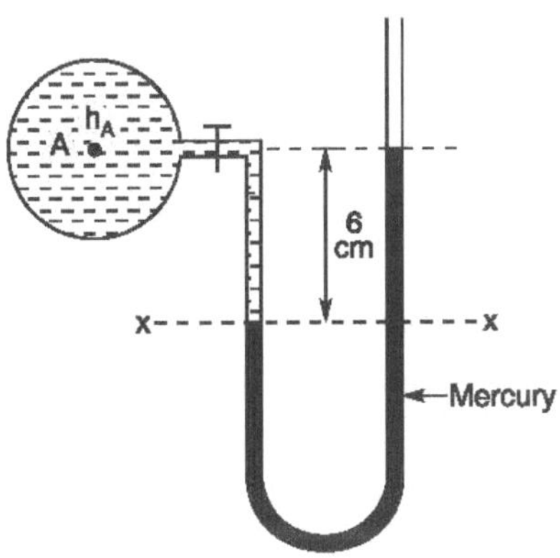

Fig. 2.12

Pressure head in left limb above datum X–X

= Pressure head in right limb above datum X–X

$$h_A + 6 \times 1.0 = 6 \times 13.6$$

$$h_A = 75.6 \text{ cm of water}$$

The pressure at point A is $P_A = \gamma h_A$

$$\therefore \quad P_A = \frac{1000 \times 9.81}{10^6} \times 75.6$$

$$P_A = 0.742 \text{ N/cm}^2 \qquad \text{...(Ans.)}$$

where, weight density, $\gamma = 100 \times 9.81 \text{ N/m}^2 \text{ ... } \left(\frac{\text{kg}}{\text{m}^3} \times \frac{\text{m}}{\text{s}^2} = \frac{\text{N}}{\text{m}^3}\right)$

$$= \frac{1000 \times 9.81}{10^6} \frac{\text{N}}{\text{cm}^3}$$

2.8.5 Single Column Manometer

In the U-tube manometer, it is required to take readings at two points if single U-tube is used and of course more readings if number of U-tubes are used. This can be avoided by using single column manometer. A single column manometer is a modified form of U-tube manometer, in which a reservoir having large cross-sectional area (about 100 times) as compared to the area of tube is introduced to the left limb as shown in Fig. 2.13.

For any variation in pressure in vessel or pipe the drop in heavy liquid level in the reservoir is very small and rise in heavy liquid level will be more. This small drop can be neglected and height of liquid in right limb gives pressure head. The right limb may be vertical or inclined. Based on this the single column manometers are classified as:

(I) Vertical single column manometer

(II) Inclined single column manometer.

(I) Vertical Single Column Manometer

A vertical single column manometer is shown in Fig. 2.13. Let, the liquid in vessel or pipe has specific gravity S_1 and heavy liquid in reservoir and right limb has specific gravity S_2. Initially when the manometer was not connected to pipe, the datum level is X–X in the reservoir and the right limb. When the manometer is connected to vessel or pipe, which is under high pressure, the liquid level in reservoir will drop down to Z–Z level by amount of Δh and rise to h_2 in the right limb above datum X–X.

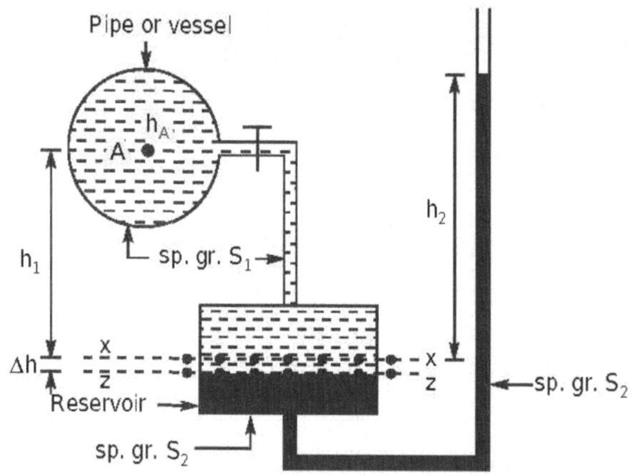

Fig. 2.13 Vertical single column manometer

Hence we can write,

$$A \times \Delta h = a \times h_2$$

where 'A' is cross-sectional area of reservoir and 'a' is cross-sectional area of right limb.

$$\therefore \quad \Delta h = \frac{a}{A} \times h_2$$

Now, consider pressure heads above datum Z–Z.

$$\therefore \quad \begin{pmatrix}\text{Pressure head in the left limb} \\ \text{above datum } Z\text{–}Z\end{pmatrix} = \begin{pmatrix}\text{Pressure head in the right limb} \\ \text{above datum } Z\text{–}Z\end{pmatrix}$$

$$(\Delta h + h_1) S_1 + h_A = (\Delta h + h_2) S_2$$

$$\therefore \quad h_A = (\Delta h + h_2) S_2 - (\Delta h + h_1) S_1$$

$$= \Delta h (S_2 - S_1) + h_2 S_2 - h_1 S_1$$

$$h_A = \frac{a}{A} h_2 (S_2 - S_1) + h_2 S_2 - h_1 S_1 \quad ...(2.15)$$

Knowing h_2, the pressure head (h_A) at A can be calculated using above equation.

The above equation reduces to,

$$h_A = h_2 S_2 - h_1 S_1 \quad ...(2.16)$$

if the term $\left(\frac{a}{A}\right)$ is neglected, as its value is very small.

(II) Inclined single column manometer

For measuring small gauge pressure at a point it is better to use inclined single column manometer than vertical. The reading L recorded on the inclined single column manometer is higher than that over a vertical single column manometer by a factor of cosec θ, where θ is the angle made by inclined limb with the horizontal.

From the Fig. 2.14 it is clear that for the same vertical h_2 the length of liquid in the inclined limb is h_2 cosec θ.

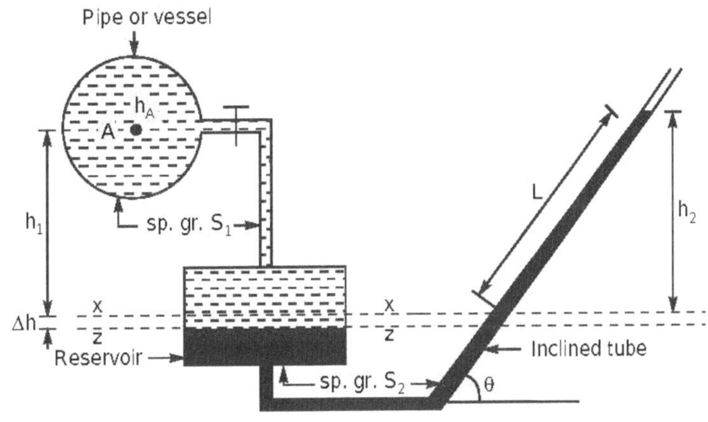

Fig. 2.14 Inclined single column manometer

Smaller the angle θ, provides larger length L and in turn accurate results. The angle θ, in any case should not be less than 20°.

The pressure head at A can be calculated by equating pressure heads above datum X–X on both sides or simply by putting $L \sin\theta$ for h_2 in equation (2.16).

$$\therefore \quad h_A = L \sin\theta \times S_2 - h_1 S_1 \quad ...(2.17)$$

2.8.6 Solved Problem

■ **Problem 2.7**: Find the pressure head in the pipe A, if the area of the reservoir is 90 times the area of the tube for the readings as shown in Fig. 2.15 for a single column vertical manometer.

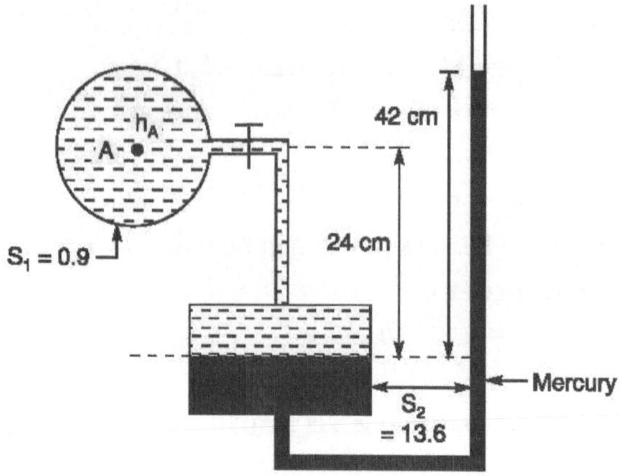

Fig. 2.15

Pressure head,

$$h_A = \frac{a}{A}h_2\,(S_2 - S_1) + h_2S_2 - h_1S_1$$

$$= \frac{1}{90} \times 42\,(13.6 - 0.9) + 42 \times 13.6 - 24 \times 0.9$$

$$= 5.93 + 549.6$$

$$h_A = 555.53 \text{ cm of water}$$

Here, h_A = 549.6 cm of water if the term $\left[\frac{a}{A} \times h_2\,(S_2 - S_1)\right]$ is neglected.

2.9 DIFFERENTIAL MANOMETERS

Differential manometers are used to measure the difference of pressure between the two points. The two points may either be connected to same vessel (pipe) or different vessels (pipe) containing the same or different fluids. These two points may be at the same level or different.

Most commonly used differential manometers are of two types:

(1) U-tube differential manometer.

(2) Inverted U-tube differential manometer.

2.9.1 U-tube Differential Manometer

Figure 2.16 shows the U-tube differential manometers at different and same levels.

Let the two points A and B, where differential manometer is connected, are at different levels as shown in Fig. 2.16 (a) and have liquids of different specific gravity. The specific gravity of liquid is pipe A is S_1 and in pipe B is S_2 and manometric (heavy) liquid have specific gravity S_m. Here, h is the difference in mercury levels and h_1 and h_2 are as shown in Fig. 2.16. h_A and h_B are pressure heads at points A and B.

Take the datum at X–X and equate the pressure heads on both sides.

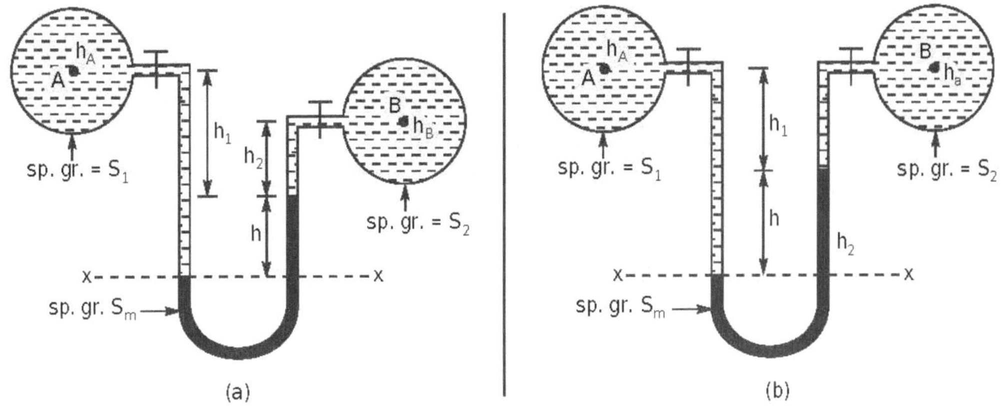

Fig. 2.16 *U*-tube differential manometer

Pressure head in left limb above datum *X-X* = Pressure head in right limb above datum *X–X*

$$(h + h_1) S_1 + h_A = hS_m + h_2S_2 + h_B$$

$$h_A - hB = hS_B - hS_1 + h_2S_2 - h_1S_1$$

$$h_A - h_B = h (S_m - S_1) + h_2S_2 - h_1S_1 \quad ...(2.18)$$

The equation (2.18) is general expression for calculating pressure difference between points *A* and *B* when they are connected to same or different pipes and at same and different levels.

Special Cases:

Case 1: Points *A* and *B* connected to same pipe but at different levels. In this case

$$S_1 = S_2 = S.$$

$$\therefore \quad h_A - h_B = h (S_m - S) + (h_2 - h_1) S \quad ...(2.19)$$

Case 2: Points *A* and *B* connects to same pipe and at same level. In this case

$$S_1 = S_2 = S \text{ and } h_1 = h_2.$$

$$\therefore \quad h_A - h_B = h (S_m - S) \quad ...(2.20)$$

Case 3: Points *A* and *B* are connected to different pipes but at same level: In this case $h_1 = h_2$.

$$\therefore \quad h_A - h_B = h(S_m - S_1) + h_1 (S_2 - S_1) \quad ...(2.21)$$

2.9.2 Solved Problems

■ **Problem 2.8:** *A U-tube differential manometer connects two pressure pipes A and B. Pipe A contains carbon tetrachloride having a specific gravity 1.594 under a pressure of 1.2 kgf/cm² and pipe B contains oil of sp. gravity 0.8 under a pressure of 2 kgf/cm². Pipe A lies 2.5 m above pipe B. Find the difference of pressure measured by mercury as fluid filling U-tube. Mercury level in left limb is 3.75 m below pipe A.*

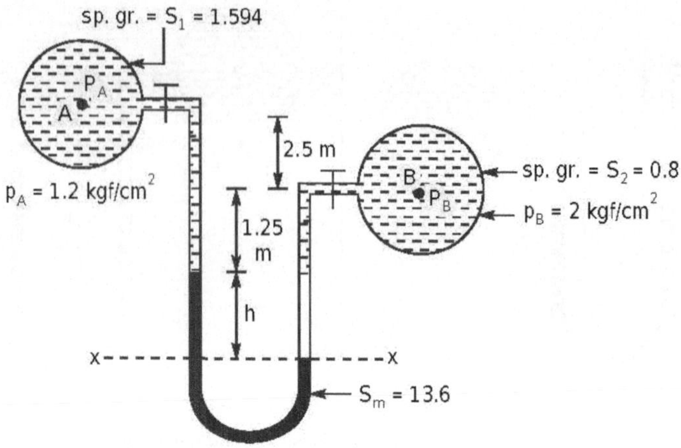

Fig. 2.17

Solution. Pressure head at A, $h_A = \dfrac{P_A}{\gamma}$

$$\therefore \qquad h_A = \frac{1.2}{1000} \times 10^4 = 12 \text{ m}$$

Pressure head at B, $h_B = \dfrac{P_B}{\gamma} = \dfrac{2.0}{1000} \times 10^4 = 20$ m

Equate pressure above datum X–X on both sides.

$$\begin{pmatrix}\text{Pressure head in left limb} \\ \text{above datum } X\text{–}X\end{pmatrix} = \begin{pmatrix}\text{Pressure head in right limb} \\ \text{above datum } X\text{–}X\end{pmatrix}$$

$$13.6 \times h + 3.75 \times 1.544 + 12 = 0.8 \times h + 0.8 \times 1.25 + 20$$

$$h = 0.251 \text{ m}$$

$$h = 25.1 \text{ cm}$$

Difference of pressure head = 25.1 cm.

■ **Problem 2.9:** *Petrol of specific gravity 0.80 flows upwards through a vertical pipe. A and B are two points in the pipe, B being 30 cm higher than A. Connections are led from A and B to a U-tube containing mercury. If the difference of pressure between A and B is 0.18 kg/cm². Find the reading shown by the differential mercury gauge.*

Solution:

Given the pressure difference:

$$(P_A - P_B) = 0.18 \text{ kg/cm}^2$$

$\therefore$ Difference of pressure head

$$h_A - h_B = \frac{0.18 \times 10^4}{1000}$$

$$= 1.8 \text{ m}$$

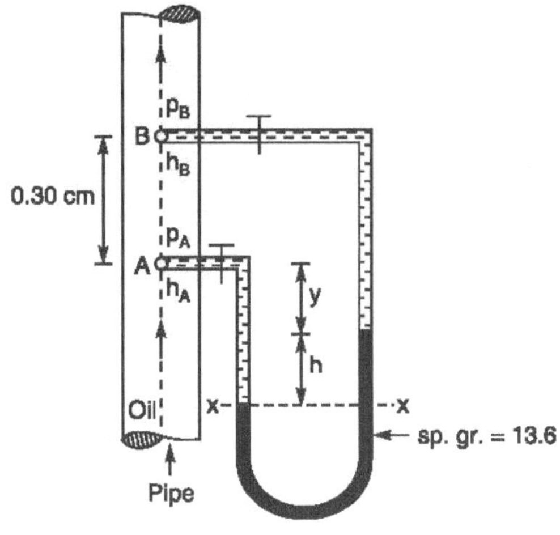

Fig. 2.18

Let, the difference in mercury levels = h

Equating pressures on both sides,

$$\begin{pmatrix}\text{Pressure head above datum}\\ X\text{–}X \text{ in left limb}\end{pmatrix} = \begin{pmatrix}\text{Pressure head above datum}\\ X\text{–}X \text{ in right limb}\end{pmatrix}$$

$$(h + y) \times 0.8 + h_A = 13.6 \times h + 0.8 \times y + 0.3 \times 0.8 + h_B$$

$$\therefore \quad h_A - h_B = (13.6 - 0.8)\, h + 0.24$$

$$1.8 = 12.8\, h + 0.24$$

$$h = 0.122 \text{ m} = 12.2 \text{ cm}$$

$\therefore$ Difference in mercury level = 12.2 cm.

2.9.3 Inverted U-Tube Manometer

This type of manometer is used for measuring small pressure difference between the two points. These two points may be connected to the same vessel (pipe) or different vessel containing same or different fluid at same or different levels as shown in Fig. 2.19.

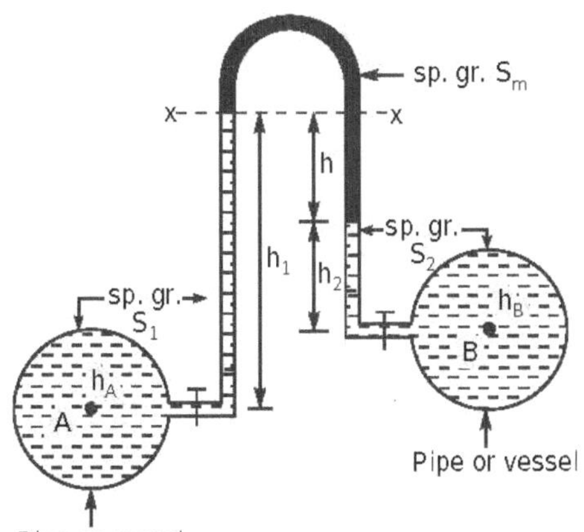

Fig. 2.19 Inverted *U*-tube different of manometer

Let the two points A and B, where the inverted U-tube manometer is connected are at different levels as shown in Fig. 2.17 and have fluids of different specific gravities. The specific gravity of manometric liquid (light) in U-tube is S_m and that in pipe A and B is S_1 and S_2 respectively. The difference in manometric liquid levels is 'h' and; h_1 and h_2 are as shown in Fig. 2.10. The pressure heads at A and B are h_A and h_B respectively.

Take the datum level at X–X and equate the pressure heads on both sides.

$$\begin{pmatrix}\text{Pressure head in left limb}\\ \text{below datum } X\text{–}X\end{pmatrix} = \begin{pmatrix}\text{Pressure head in right limb}\\ \text{below datum } X\text{–}X\end{pmatrix}$$

$$h_A - h_1 \times S_1 = h_B - S_2 h_2 - S_m h$$

$$h_A - h_B = h_1 S_1 - S_2 h_2 - S_m h \qquad ...(2.22)$$

The equation (2.22) is general expression and is used to calculate pressure difference between two points A and B, when they are connected to same or different pipes and at same or different levels.

Special Case: Ends of manometer connected to same pipe but at different levels:

In this case $\quad S_1 = S_2 = S$

$$\therefore \quad h_A - h_B = S(h_1 - h_2) - S_m h \qquad ...(2.23)$$

2.9.4 Solved Problem

■ **Problem 2.10:** *An inverted U-tube manometer is connected to the two pipes A and B in which water flows. The manometric fluid has specific gravity 0.75. Find the pressure difference between the points A and B for the manometer readings as shown in Fig. 2.20.*

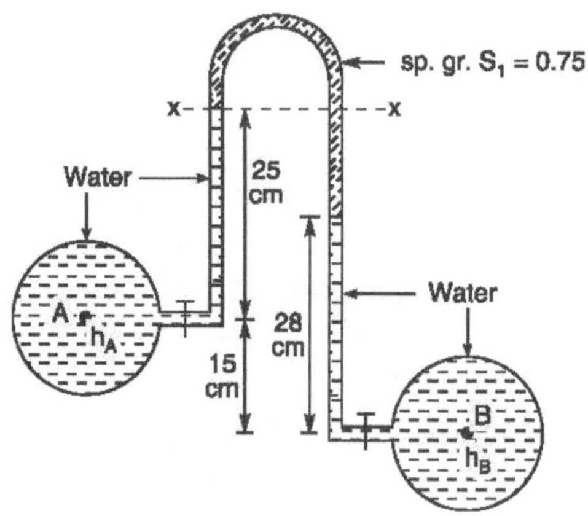

Fig. 2.20

Solution: Equate pressure heads on both sides below X–X datum

$$h_A - 0.25 \times 1.0 = h_B - 0.28 \times 1.0 - (15 + 25 - 28) \times 0.75$$

$$h_A - h_B = -9.03 \text{ cm}$$

$$h_A - h_B = -0.09 \text{ m of water}$$

$$\text{Pressure difference} = h_A - h_B = -0.9 \text{ m of water.}$$

Exercises

1. Find the intensity of pressure at a depth of 18 m below the free surface of water in the reservoir. (**Ans.** $p = 176.58$ kN/m^2)
2. The pressure intensity at a point is 48 kN/m^2. Find the corresponding height of water column. (**Ans.** $h = 4.893$ m)
3. A hydraulic press has a ram of 30 cm diameter and a plunger of 5 cm diameter. Find the force required to lift the load of 50 kN. (**Ans.** $F = 1388.89$ N)
4. In a hydraulic jack the area of small piston is 10 cm^2 and that of large piston is 100 cm^2. A force of 1000 N is applied on small piston. What load can be lifted on large piston if the small piston is 40 cm above the large piston? Assume specific weight of liquid in jack = 9810 N/m^2. (**Ans.** $W = 10{,}004$ N)
5. A U-tube manometer is used to measure pressure at a point in a pipe. The left limb contains water is connected to pipe full of water at a pressure and right limb contains mercury and is open to the atmosphere. The free surface of mercury is 15 cm above the centre of the pipe and difference between mercury levels is 27 cm. Find the pressure intensity of water in the pipe. (**Ans.** $p = 3.4845$ N/cm^2)
6. A tank stores water under pressure. A U-tube mercury manometer is connected to the tank through a rubber tubing. The outlet point of tank is 2.4 m above the free surface of mercury in the U-tube. For a deflection of 24 cm in the manometer, calculate the pressure of water in the tank. Atmospheric pressure = 10.3 m of water. (**Ans.** $p = 8436$ N)
7. A simple manometer containing mercury is connected to a pipe in which oil of specific gravity = 0.8 is flowing. The pressure in the pipe is vacuum. The other end of the manometer is open atmosphere. Find the vacuum pressure in the pipe, if the difference in mercury level in the two limbs is 15 cm, and the height of oil in the left limb from the centre of the pipe is 20 cm below. Draw a neat sketch of the arrangement. (**Ans.** $h_A = -2.2$ m)
8. A U-tube manometer as shown in figure given below is used to measure pressure at a point A in a pipe. The pipe contains oil of specific gravity 0.85. Find the pressure at point A. (**Ans.** $h_A = 3.625$ m of oil)

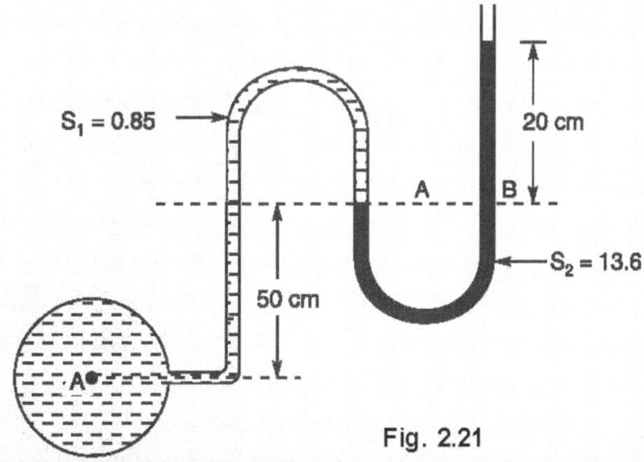

Fig. 2.21

9. A U-tube differential manometer connects two pressure pipes A and B. Pipe A contains liquid of specific gravity 1.4 under pressure of 1.5 kgf/cm^2 and pipe B contains liquid of specific gravity 0.72 under a presure of 2.4 kgf/cm^2. Pipe A lies 3.0 m above pipe B. Mercury level in the left limb is 4 m below pipe A. **(Ans.** h = 39.75 cm)

10. A pipe containing water at 172 kN/m^2 pressure is connected by a differential mercury manometer to another pipe 1.5 m lower than the first pipe and containing water at high pressure. If the difference in height of the mercury columns of the manometer is equal to 7.5 cm, what is the pressure in the lower pipe? Draw a neat sketch of the arrangement. **(Ans.** h_B = 177.44 kN/m^2)

11. Two points M and N in a pipe system are connected to a mercury differential manometer. The connecting tube is filled with an oil of relative density 0.85. The high pressure point M is 0.8 m above point N. If the mercury column reading is 8 cm, what is the pressure difference between M and N in (*i*) KPa and (*ii*) Meters of water. **(Ans.** (*i*) 3.335 KPa (*ii*) $h_M - h_N$ = 0.34 m)

12. A differential manometer is used to measure the pressue difference due to flow of oil of specific gravity 0.85 in a vertical conical pipe with oil flowing upwards from broader end to smaller end. Distance between the two point between which the manometer is connected is 95 cm and the mercury column difference in the manometer reads 12 cms. The manometer limbs above mercury are filled with oil. Taking specific gravity of mercury as 13.6. Find the pressure difference measured. **(Ans.** $h_A - h_B$ = 233.75 cm)

13. A U-tube differential manometer is connected to a pipe containing water and inclined at 45° at two points X and Y 10 m apart. Find the deflection of mercury in the manometer. (*MU Dec. 1997*) **(Ans.** h = 56.12 cm)

14. Find the pressure head in a pipe A, if the area of the reservoir is 100 times the area of the tube for the readings as shown in figure given below for a single column vertical manometer. **(Ans.** h_A = 399 cm)

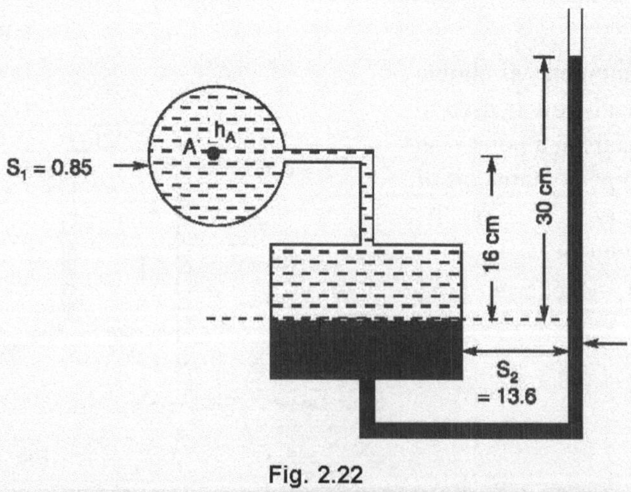

Fig. 2.22

15. A pressure gauge consists of two cylindrical bulbs *A* and *B* each of 12 cm^2 cross-sectional area. These two bulbs are connected by a *U*-tube with vertical limbs each of 0.30 cm^2 cross-sectional area. Water is filled into *A* and liquid of specific gravity 0.85 is filled into *B*. The surface of separation is in the limb *B*. Find the displacement of the surface of separation when the pressure on the surface in bulb *B* is greater than bulb *A* by an amount equal to 1.2 cm head of water. (**Ans.** δ = 5.0.95 cm)

16. Find pressure difference between two points *A* and *B* when inverted *U*-tube manometer is connected to pipes *A* and *B* as shown in figure given below.

(**Ans.** $h_A - h_B = -39.52$ cm of liquid in pipe)

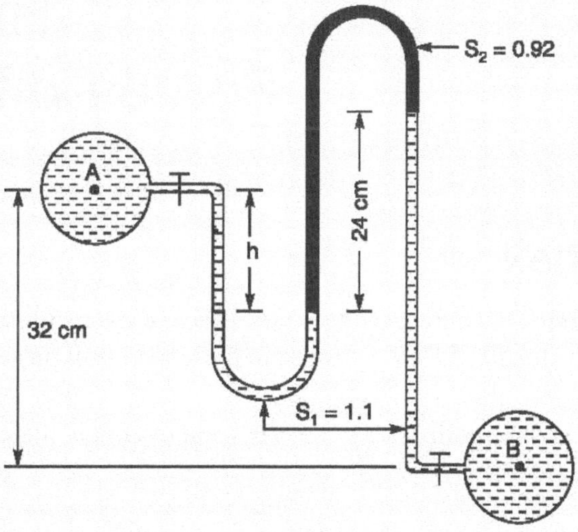

Fig. 2.23

❑❑❑

3

Hydrostatic Forces on Surfaces

3.1 INTRODUCTION

When a liquid at rest comes in contact with plane surface, it exerts pressure force normal to the surface in contact. The velocity of fluid particles in each layer will be zero, if the fluid is at rest. Then in this case the velocity gradient $\left(\frac{du}{dy}\right)$ is zero and of course the shear stress $\left(\mu\frac{du}{dy}\right)$ will also be zero.

The pressure force exerted by a fluid at rest on a plane lamina (surface) is known as total pressure. This always acts normal to the surface in contact. The point at which the total pressure acts is known as centre of pressure.

3.2 TOTAL PRESSURE AND CENTRE OF PRESSURE

The plane lamina submerged in fluid may be in horizontal, vertical or inclined position or it may be a curved surface.

3.2.1 Horizontal Plane Lamina Submerged in Liquid

Consider a plane lamina submerged in a liquid of specific weight γ at a depth y from the free surface in a horizontal position as shown in Fig. 3.1. As every point of the plane lamina is at same depth from free surface of liquid, the intensity of pressure is same on the entire lamina, equal to $p = \gamma y$. This is well known Pascal's Law. The total pressure on the horizontal surface will be equal to the product of pressure intensity and total surface area (A) on which it act.

$$\therefore \quad F = p \times A$$

$$= \gamma y A$$

$$F = \gamma A y \qquad ...(3.1)$$

In this case the depth of centre of gravity $\bar{y}$ and depth of centre of pressure y^* will coincide with each other and is equal to y.

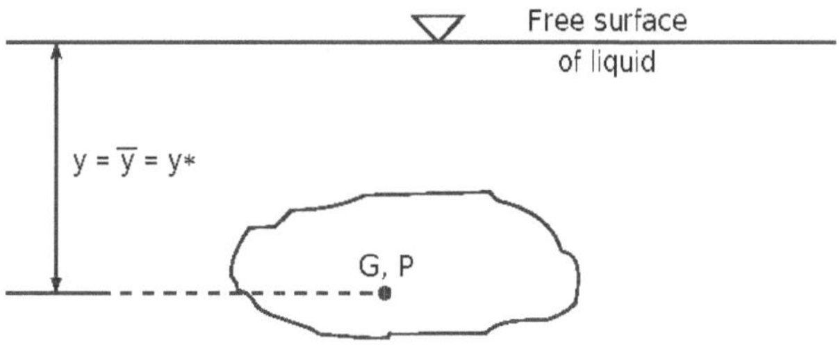

Fig. 3.1 Horizontal plane lamina

3.2.2 Solved Problem

■ **Problem 3.1:** *There are four vessels of same base area. The top area of each vessel is A, 1.6 A, 0.7 A and 0.2 A respectively. The vessels are filled with water to the same height. What will be force exerted on the base of each vessel? (Refer Fig. 3.2)* [MU Dec. 1993]

Solution:

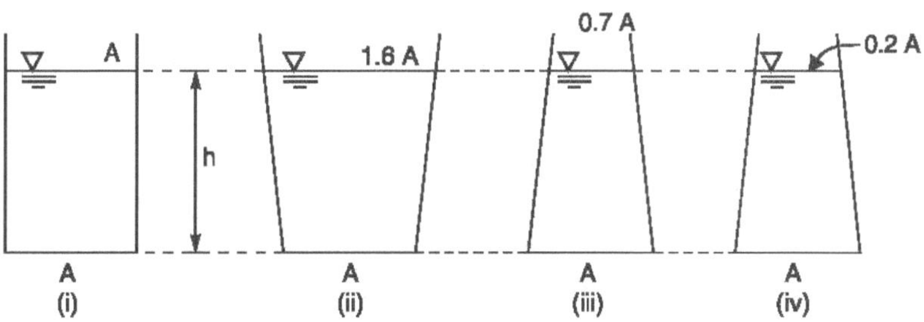

Fig. 3.2

The four vessel have same base Area 'A' and are filled with water to the same height 'h'. The force exerted on each case will be same and equal to:

$$F = \gamma A\bar{y}$$

$$F = 100 \times A \times h \text{ kg} \qquad \text{(since } \bar{y} = h)$$

Note: The force exerted on the base of each vessel is same. It does not depend upon the shape, volume or weight of fluid contained in it. It depends only on base area and height of liquid. This is known as " Hydrostatic Paradox".

3.2.3 Vertical Plane Lamina Submerged in Liquid

Consider a plane lamina of arbitrary shape is submerged in a static liquid of specific weight γ in a vertical position as shown in Fig. 3.3. The centre of gravity (G) and centre of pressure (P) are at a depth of $\bar{y}$ and y^* respectively from free surface of liquid.

(*a*) **Total Pressure (F):** The intensity of pressure varies directly with the depth and hence it will not be constant on entire surface. In such case, the total pressure is determined by dividing the figure in number of small strips and calculating total pressure on each of the strip. The total pressure on entire lamina will be obtained by summing up the total pressure on each small elemental strips.

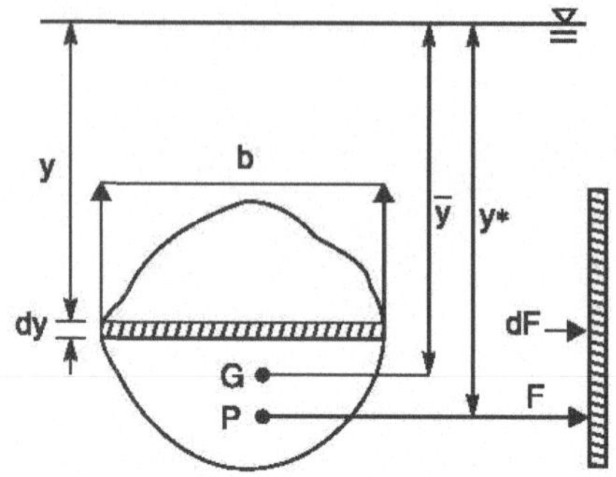

Fig. 3.3 Vertical plane surface

Consider a small elemental strip of width b and thickness dy at a depth of y from free surface of liquid. The intensity of pressure on strip will be $p = \gamma y$. The area of small strip will be $dA = b \times dy$.

∴ Total pressure force $= dF = p \times dA$

∴ $$dF = \gamma y \times bdy$$

∴ Total pressure force on entire plane lamina is

$$F = \int \gamma y \times bdy$$

$$= \gamma \int y \times bdy$$

Here, $\int y \times bdy$ represents sum of first moment of area of strips about free surface, which is equal to the product of total area A and distance $\bar{y}$ from the same free surface.

∴ $$\int yb \times by = \int y\,dA = A\bar{y}$$

∴ $$F = \gamma A\bar{y} \qquad ...(3.2)$$

(*b*) **Centre of pressure:** In case of vertical submerged plane lamina, centre of pressure will lie below centre of gravity of the plane lamina as intensity of pressure increases with the increase in depth. Centre of pressure is calculated by using the "Principle of Moments", which states that the sum of moment of all the component forces about an axis is equal to the moment of the resultant force about the same axis.

Hence moment of total force F about free surface of the liquid $= F \times y^*$ ...(3.2)

The moment of force dF acting on small elemental strip about free surface is;

$$= dF \times y$$

$$= \gamma y \times bdy \times y$$

Summing up the moments of all forces about free surface,

$$= \int \gamma y \times b \times dy \times y$$

$$= \gamma \int y^2 b dy$$

$$= \gamma \int y^2 dA \quad \text{...(3.3)}$$

$$= \gamma I_0$$

where, $I_0 = \int y^2 dA$ is the moment of inertia of the plane lamina about free surface of liquid.

Equating (3.2) and (3.3)

$$F \times y^* = \gamma I_0$$

$$\gamma A \bar{y} \times y^* = \gamma I_0$$

$$\therefore \quad y^* = \frac{I_0}{A\bar{y}} \quad \text{...(3.4)}$$

By parallel axis theorem, we can write

$$I_0 = I_G + A\bar{y}^2 \quad \text{...(3.5)}$$

where, I_G is equal to the moment of inertia of a plane lamina about its own centriodal axis, parallel to the free surface of liquid.

$$\therefore \quad y^* = \frac{I_G + A\bar{y}^2}{A\bar{y}}$$

$$y^* = \bar{y} + \frac{I_G}{A\bar{y}} \quad \text{...(3.6)}$$

From the equation (3.6), it is clear that centre of pressure well lie below the centre of gravity, as $\left(\frac{I_G}{A\bar{y}}\right)$ is always positive term.

3.2.4 Solved Problems

■ **Problem 3.2:** *A rectangular plane lamina is of size 3 m ×4 m. Determine the total pressure and centre of pressure on the plane lamina when it is in vertical position 2 m below free surface when (a) 3 m edge is in horizontal position (b) 4 m edge is in horizontal position.*

Solution:

(*a*) 3 m edge in horizontal position

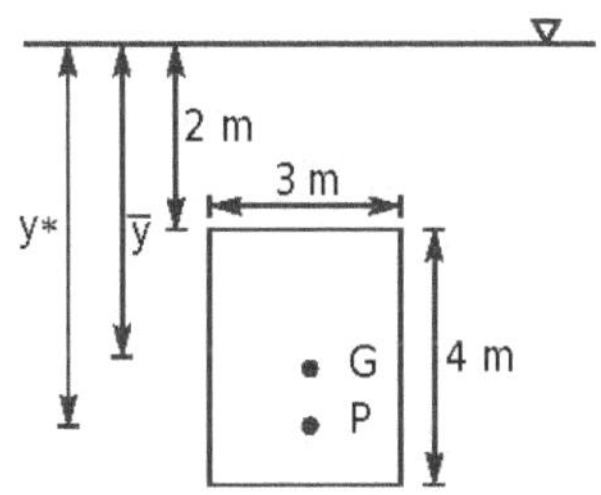

Fig. 3.3

$$\bar{y} = 2 + \frac{4}{2} = 4\,\text{m}$$

$$F = \gamma A\bar{y}$$

$$= (9.81 \times 1000) \times (3 \times 4) \times 4$$

$$F = 470880\ \text{N} \quad \text{...(Ans.)}$$

$$y^* = \bar{y} + \frac{I_G}{A\bar{y}}$$

$$I_G = \frac{bd^3}{12} = \frac{3 \times 4^3}{12} = 16 \text{ m}^4$$

$\therefore$ $$y^* = 4 + \frac{16}{(3 \times 4) \times 4}$$

$$y^* = 4.333 \text{ m}$$ ...(Ans.)

(*b*) 4 m edge in horizontal position:

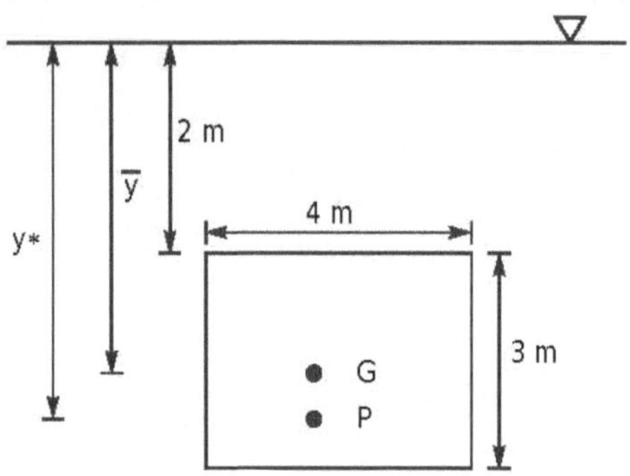

Fig. 3.4

$$\bar{y} = 2 + \frac{3}{2} = 3.5 \text{ m}$$

$$F = \gamma A\bar{y}$$

$$= (9.81 \times 1000) \times (4 \times 3)(3.5)$$

$$F = 412020 \text{ N}$$ ...(Ans.)

$$y^* = \bar{y} + \frac{I_G}{A\bar{y}}$$

$$I_G = \frac{4 \times 3^3}{12} = 9 \text{ m}^4$$

$$y^* = 3.5 + \frac{9}{(4 \times 3) \times 3} = 3.75 \text{ m}$$ ...(Ans.)

■ **Problem 3.3:** *A triangular lamina of base and altitude equal to 3.2 m is submerged in water, vertically. Determine the total pressure and centre of pressure, when (a) Base of lamina coincides with free surface and (b) Apex of triangular lamina coincides with free surface.*

Solution: (*a*) Base of lamina coincides with free surface

$$F = \gamma A\bar{y}$$

$$= (9.81\times1000)\left(\frac{1}{2}\times3.2\times3.2\right)\times\frac{1}{3}\times3.2$$

$$= 53575.68 \text{ N}$$

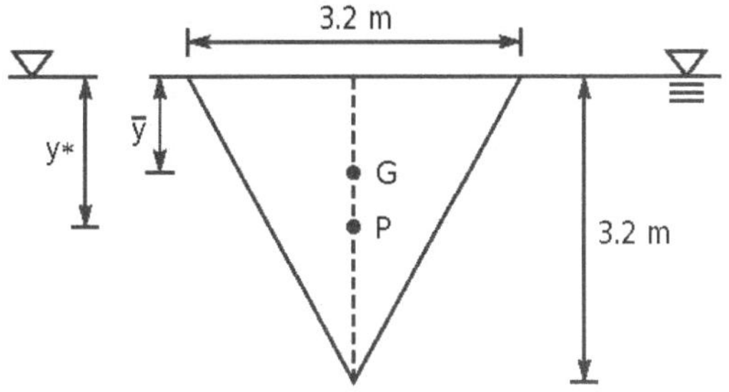

Fig. 3.5

Now,
$$y^* = \bar{y} + \frac{I_G}{A\bar{y}}$$

$$I_G = \frac{bh^3}{36} = \frac{3.2\times3.2^3}{36}$$

$$= 2.91 \text{ m}^4$$

$$y^* = \frac{3.2}{3} + \frac{2.91}{\frac{1}{2}\times3.2\times3.2\times\frac{3.2}{3}}$$

$$= 1.067 + 0.533$$

$$= 1.6 \text{ m}$$

(*b*) Apex of the triangular lamina coincides with the free surface:

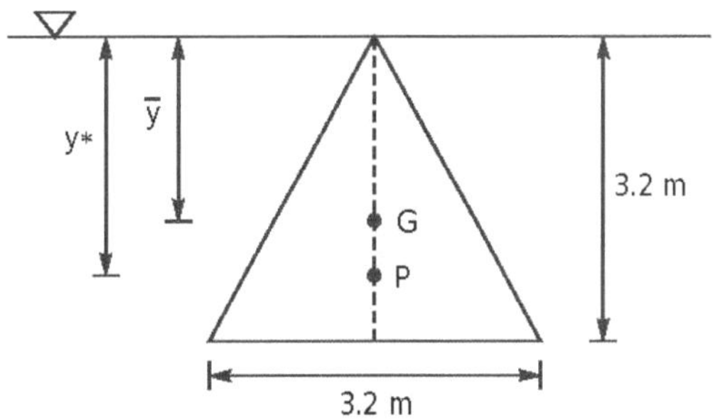

Fig. 3.6

$$A = \frac{1}{2}\times3.2\times3.2 = 5.12\,\text{m}^2$$

$$\bar{y} = \frac{2}{3}\times3.2 = 2.133\,\text{m}$$

$$F = \gamma A\bar{y}$$
$$= 9810 \times 5.12 \times 2.133$$
$$F = 107151.36 \text{ N}$$

Now,
$$y^* = \bar{y} + \frac{I_G}{A\bar{y}}$$
$$= 2.133 + \frac{2.91}{5.12 \times 2.133}$$
$$= 2.133 + 0.266$$
$$= 2.399$$
$$y^* \approx 2.4 \text{ m}$$

■ **Problem 3.4:** *A vertical sided 1.5 m height tank is square in plan whose side is 1 m long. The tank contains oil of specific gravity 0.8 to a depth of 50 cm floating on 1m depth of water. Determine:*

(*a*) *Total pressure on one side of the tank.*

(*b*) *Height of centre of pressure above the base.*

Solution:

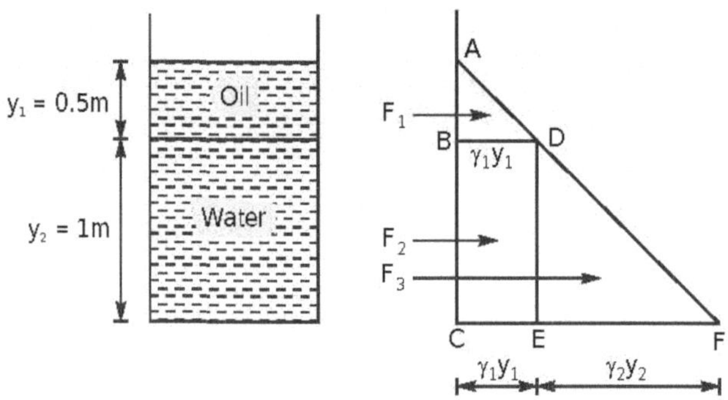

Fig. 3.7

(*a*) **Total pressure on one side of a tank:**

Total pressure is calculated by drawing pressure diagram as shown in Fig. 3.7.

Intensity of pressure on top, (*i.e.*, at *A*), $P_A = 0$.

Intensity of pressure at the interface of oil and water (*i.e.*, at BD) = $P_B = \gamma_1 y_1$

$$= 0.8 \times 1000 \times 0.5$$
$$= 400 \text{ kgf/m}^2$$

Intensity of pressure of Base *CF*, P_C is,

$$P_C = \gamma_1 y_1 + \gamma_2 y_2$$
$$= 400 + 1000 \times 1.0$$
$$= 1400 \text{ kg/m}^2$$

Now pressure force F_1 = Area of ΔABD × width of tank

$$= \frac{1}{2} \times BD \times AB \times \text{width of tank}$$

$$= \frac{1}{2} \times 400 \times 0.5 \times 1$$

$$= 100 \text{ kgf}$$

Pressure force F_2 = Area of rectangle × width of tank

$$= BD \times BC \times \text{width of tank}$$

$$= 400 \times 1 \times 1$$

$$= 400 \text{ kgf}$$

Pressure force F_3 = Area of ΔDEF × width of tank

$$= \frac{1}{2} \times EF \times DE \times \text{width of tank}$$

$$= \frac{1}{2} \times 1000 \times 1 \times 1$$

$$= 500 \text{ kgf}$$

Total pressure force = $F_1 + F_2 + F_3$

$F = 100 + 400 + 500 = 1000$ kgf ...(Ans.)

(*b*) **Centre of Pressure:**

Take moments of all force about top, point A,

$$F \times y^* = F_1 \times \frac{2}{3}(AB) + F_2\left(AB + \frac{1}{2}BC\right) + F_3 \times \left(AB + \frac{2}{3}DE\right)$$

$$1000 \times y^* = 100 \times \frac{2}{3} \times 0.5 + 400 \times \left(0.5 + \frac{1}{2} \times 1\right) + 500 \times \left(0.5 + \frac{2}{3} \times 1\right)$$

$$y^* = 1.0168 \text{ m}$$

∴ Height of centre of pressure above base

$$= 1.5 - 1.0168$$

$$= 0.483 \text{ m.}$$

■ **Problem 3.5:** *An opening 1 m wide and 2 m high in the wall of a tank is closed by the gate of same size hinged at its centre. Water level in the tank is 3 m above the hinge and the gate is held in position by the force F applied at its bottom edge. Find F.*

Solution: Pressure force on gate,

$$p = \gamma A\bar{y}$$

$$= (9.81 \times 1000) \times (1 \times 2) \times 3$$

$$= 58860 \text{ N}$$

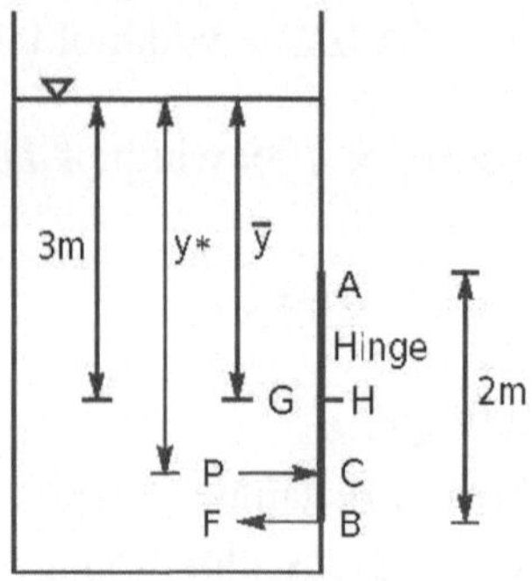

Fig. 3.8

Centre of pressure, of force P,

$$y^* = \bar{y} + \frac{I_G}{A\bar{y}}$$

$$= \bar{y} + \frac{\frac{bd^3}{12}}{b \times d \times \bar{y}}$$

$$= 3 + \frac{\frac{1 \times 2^3}{12}}{1 \times 2 \times 3}$$

$$= 3 + 0.111 \text{ m}$$

$$y^* = 3.111 \text{ m}$$

Point of application of pressure force P, from hinge,

$$= 3.111 - 3.0$$

$$= 0.111 \text{ m}$$

Now taking moments about hinge to calculate force required at bottom to held gate in position.

$$F \times 1 = P \times 0.111$$

$$= 58860 \times 0.111$$

$$F = 6540 \text{ N} \qquad \text{...(Ans.)}$$

■ **Problem 3.6:** *A tank with top area 2 m × 3 m contains water of density 998.23 kg/m² upto a height of 4m above the base. An immiscible liquid of specific gravity 0.8 is filled on top of that over 1.5 m depth. Calculate pressure at a point (i) 1m below the free surface, (ii) at the interface and (iii) at 2.5 m below the free surface. Calculate also the force on a vertical wall 5 m wide.*

Solution:

(*i*) Pressure at point 1 m below

$$\text{Free surface} = P_K = 0.8 \times 998.23 \times 1$$

$$P_K = 798.58 \text{ kg/m}^2 \qquad \text{...(Ans.)}$$

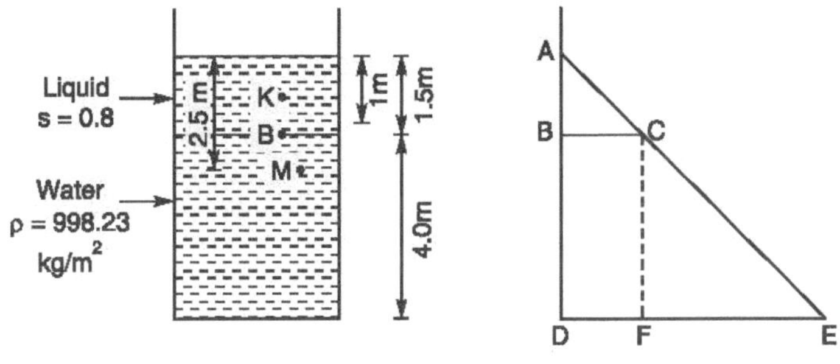

Fig. 3.9

(*ii*) Pressure at the interface = P_B = 0.8 × 998.23 × 1.5

$$P_B = 1197.876 \text{ kg/m}^2 \quad \text{...(Ans.)}$$

(*iii*) Pressure at a point 2.5 m below the free surface:

$$P_M = \gamma_1 y_1 + \gamma_2 y_2$$

$$P_M = 0.8 \times 998.23 \times 1.5 + 998.23 \times (2.5 - 1.5)$$

$$= 1197.876 + 998.23$$

$$P_M = 2196.106 \text{ kg/m}^2 \quad \text{..(Ans.)}$$

(*iv*) Force on vertical wall 5 m wide

$$F = \text{Area of pressure diagram} \times \text{Width of wall}$$

$$= (\text{Area of } \Delta ABC + \text{Area of rectangle } BCDF + \text{Area of } \Delta CFE) \times \text{Width}$$

$$= \left[\left(\frac{1}{2} \times 1{,}197.876 \times 1.5\right) + (1{,}197.876 \times 4) + \left(\frac{1}{2} \times 998.23 \times 4\right)\right] \times 5$$

$$F = 38431.855 \text{ kg.} \quad \text{...(Ans.)}$$

■ **Problem 3.7:** *A vertical gate closes a horizontal tunnel 5 m high and 3m wide running full with water. The pressure at the bottom of the gate is 2 × 10⁴ kg/m². Determine the total pressure on the gate and position of the centre of pressure.*

Solution:

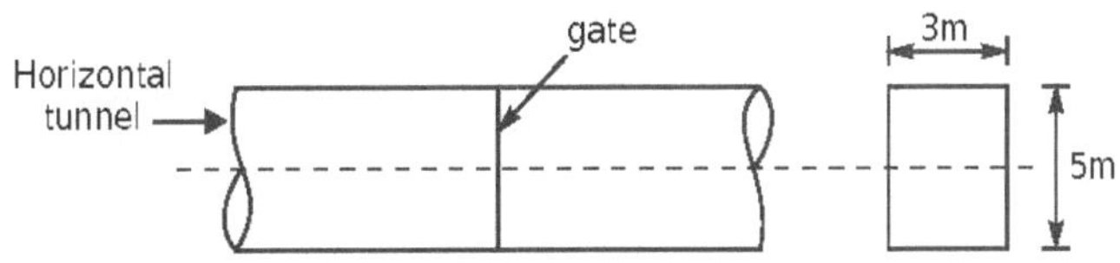

Fig. 3.10

The pressure at the bottom of the gate = 2×10^4 kg/m²

∴ The pressure head at the bottom of gate

$$h = \frac{2 \times 10^4}{1000} = 20 \text{ m}$$

∴ The height of equivalent water surface from the bottom of gate = 20 m

∴ The height of equivalent water surface from the centre of the gate

$$= 20 - \frac{5}{2} = 17.5 \text{ m}$$

∴ The depth of centre of gate from free surface = $\bar{y}$ = 17.5 m

(*i*) ∴ Force exerted by the water on the gate,

$$F = \gamma A\bar{y}$$

$$= 1{,}000 \times 5 \times 3 \times 17.5$$

$$F = 2{,}62{,}500 \text{ kg.}$$ ...(Ans.)

(*ii*) Position of centre of pressure, y^*

$$y^* = \bar{y} + \frac{I_G}{A\bar{y}}$$

$$= 17.5 + \frac{\frac{3\times5^3}{12}}{(5\times3)\times17.5}$$

$$= 17.5 + 0.119$$

$$y^* = 17.619 \text{ m.}$$ ...(Ans.)

■ **Problem 3.8**: *The gate 3 m wide and 2 m high separates a liquid of specific gravity 1.5 and height 2 m on one side and water upto a height of 1.5 m on other side of gate. Find the resultant force acting on the gate and position of centre of pressure.*

Solution:

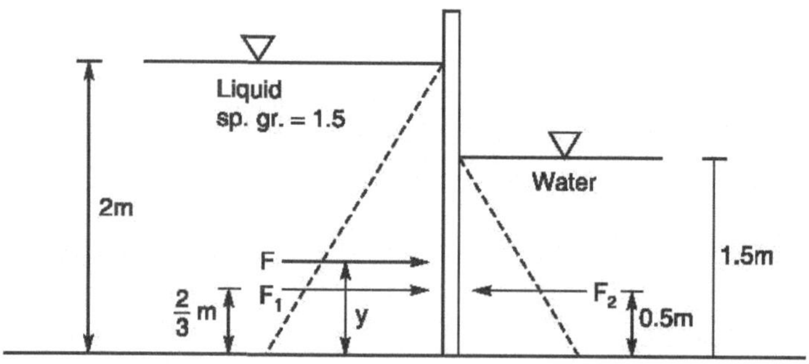

Fig. 3.11

Force exerted by liquid of specific gravity, 1.5 on gate on one side

$$F_1 = \gamma_1 A_1 \bar{y}_1$$

$$= 1.5 \times 1{,}000 \times (2 \times 3) \times \frac{2}{2}$$

$$F_1 = 9{,}000 \text{ kg}$$

This act at $\left(\frac{1}{3}\times2\right)$ distance from base

Force exerted by water on other side,

$$F_2 = \gamma_2 A_2 \bar{y}_2$$

$$= 1.0 \times 1{,}000 \times (1.5 \times 3) \times \frac{1.5}{2}$$

$$F_2 = 3{,}375 \text{ kg}$$

This act at $\left(\frac{1}{3} \times 1.5\right)$ distance from base

∴ Resultant force acting on gate, is

$$F = F_1 - F_2$$

$$= 9{,}000 - 3{,}375$$

$$F = 5{,}625 \text{ kg}$$

To calculate point of application of this total force take moment at the base

$$F \times y = F_1 \times \left(\frac{1}{3} \times 2\right) - F_2 \times \left(\frac{1}{3} \times 1.5\right)$$

$$5625 \times y = 9{,}000 \times \frac{2}{3} - 3{,}375 \times 0.5$$

$$y = 0.767 \text{ m, from Base.} \qquad \text{...(Ans.)}$$

■ **Problem 3.9**: *ABCD is a square plate of side '2a' and is immersed in a liquid such that its diagonal BD is horizontal. A is the upper most point and is at a depth 'a' below the surface. Two points 'E' and 'F' are middle points of AD and AB respectively. Find the centre of pressure of figure EFBCD.*

Solution: Here, from geometry

$$AH = 0.707\,a$$

$$EF = 1.414\,a$$

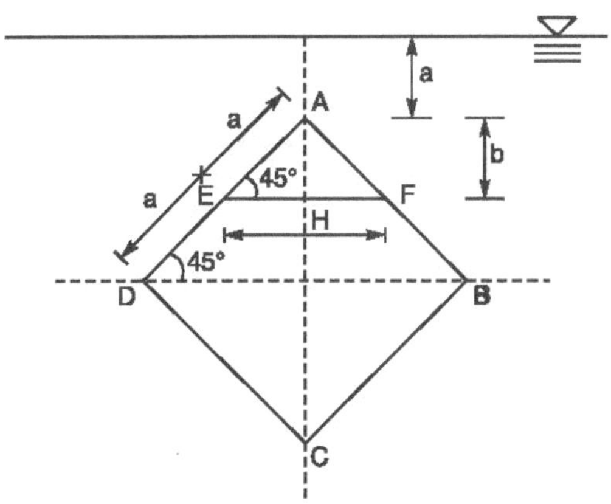

Fig. 3.12

Consider, F_1, F_2 and F_3 be the pressure forces on *AEF*, *EFBCD* and *ABCD* respectively and y_1^*, y_2^* and y_3^* their corresponding centre of pressures.

(*a*) Consider triangle *AEF*

$$A_1 = \frac{1}{2} \times 1.414a \times 0.707a = \frac{a^2}{2}$$

$$\bar{y}_1 = a + \frac{2}{3} \times 0.707\,a = 1.4713a$$

$$I_{G1} = \frac{1.414a \times (0.707a)^3}{36} = \frac{a^4}{72}$$

$$\therefore \quad F_1 = \gamma A_1 \bar{y}_1 = \gamma \times \frac{a^2}{2} \times 1.4713a = 0.7356 \times \gamma a^3$$

and

$$y_1^* = \bar{y}_1 + \frac{I_{G1}}{A_1 \bar{y}_1} = 1.4713a + \frac{\frac{a^4}{72}}{\frac{a^2}{2} \times 1.4713a}$$

$$y_1^* = 1.49a$$

(*b*) Consider square ABCD

$$A_3 = 2a \times 2a = 4a^2$$

$$\bar{y}_3 = a + 1.414a = 2.414a$$

$$I_{G3} = \frac{(2a)^4}{12} = 1.333\,a^4$$

$$F_3 = \gamma A_3 \bar{y}_3 = \gamma \times 4a^2 \times 2.414a = 9.656\gamma a^3$$

$$y_3^* = \bar{y}_3 + \frac{I_{G3}}{A\bar{y}_3} = 2.414a + \frac{1.333a^4}{4a^2 \times 2.414a}$$

$$y_3^* = 2.552\,a$$

Now, $F_2 = F_3 - F_1 = 9.656\,\gamma a^3 - 0.7356\,\gamma a^3 = 8.9204\,\gamma a^3$

But, we know,

$$F_1 y_1^* + F_2 y_2^* = F_3 y_3^*$$

$$\therefore \quad y_2^* = \frac{F_3 y_3^* - F_1 y_1^*}{F_2} = \frac{9.657\gamma a^3 \times 2.552a - 0.7356\gamma a^3 \times 1.49a}{8.9204\gamma a^3}$$

$$\therefore \quad y_2^* = 2.64a$$ ...(Ans.)

■ **Problem 3.10:** *The water face of the dam is in the form of trapezium. The bottom width is 'a' metre and top width at the water level is (a + b) metre. The face of the dam is vertical and at a depth 'h' metre of water.*

Show that:

(a) Resultant pressure at dam is $\frac{\gamma h^2\,(3a+b)}{b}$ *kg and*

(b) The depth of centre of pressure is: $\left(\frac{4a+b}{6a+2b}\right)$ *h metre,* γ *= specific weight of water.*

Solution:

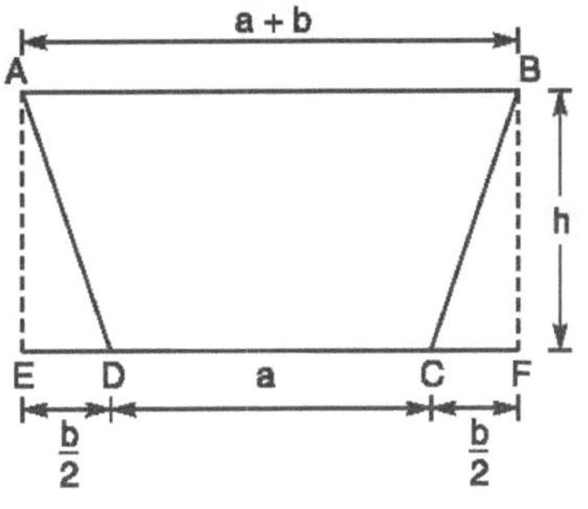

Fig. 3.13

Consider $ABCD$ as the face of dam

$$A = \text{Area of face } ABCD = \left(\frac{(a+b)+a}{2}\right)\times h$$

$$A = \left(\frac{2a+b}{2}\right)h$$

Depth of centroid from top edge AB

$$\bar{y} = \left(\frac{AB+2CD}{AB+CD}\right)\times\frac{h}{3}$$

$$= \frac{(a+b)+2a}{(a+b)+a}\times\frac{h}{3} = \left(\frac{3a+b}{2a+b}\right)\frac{h}{3}$$

(*a*) Resultant pressure on dam face:

$$F = \gamma A\,\bar{y}$$

$$= \gamma\left(\frac{2a+b}{2}\right)h\times\left(\frac{3a+b}{2a+b}\right)\frac{h}{3}$$

$$F = \frac{\gamma h^2\,(3a+b)}{6} \qquad \text{...(Ans.)}$$

(*b*) Depth of centre of pressure:

$$y^* = \frac{I_0}{A\bar{y}} \qquad \text{...(from equation, 3.4)}$$

I_0 = M.I. of trapezium about AB.

= M.I. of rectangle $ABFE$ – M.I. of triangle AED and BFC about B.

$$= \frac{(a+b)\,h^3}{3} - 2\times\frac{\frac{b}{2}\times h^3}{4} = \frac{h^3}{12}(4a+b)$$

$$y^* = \frac{\frac{h^3}{12}(4a+b)}{\left(\frac{2a+b}{2}\right)h \times \left(\frac{3a+b}{2a+b}\right)\frac{h}{3}}$$

$$y = \left(\frac{4a+b}{6a+2b}\right)h. \qquad \text{...(Ans.)}$$

3.2.5 Inclined Plane Lamina Submerged in a Liquid

Consider a plane lamina of arbitrary shape of area A is submerged in a liquid of specific weight γ, such that the plane of the lamina makes an angle θ with the free surface of a liquid as shown in Fig. 3.14. The centre of gravity and centre of pressure are at a depth of $\bar{y}$ and y^* from free surface of a liquid.

The inclined plane when extended, it intersects free surface of liquid with line 0–0.

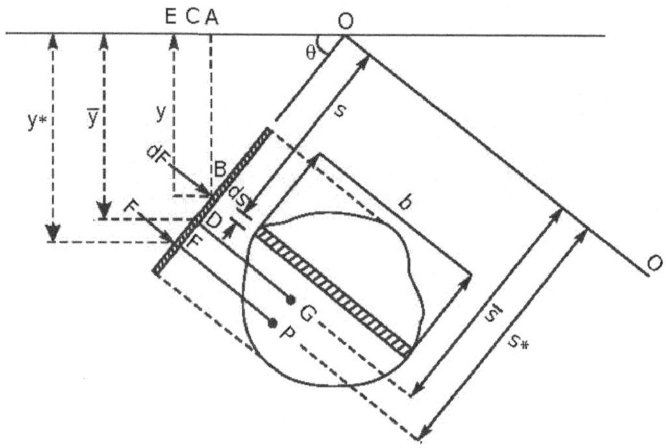

Fig. 3.14 Inclined plane surface

The distance of centre of gravity and centre of pressure from axis 0–0 are $\bar{S}$ and S^* respectively.

The total pressure on entire lamina will be obtained by summing up the total pressure on each small elemental strips.

Consider a small elemental strip of width b and thickness dS at a distance of S from axis 0–0. The intensity of pressure on strip will be $p = \gamma y$ and area of each strip will be $dA = b \times dS$.

Total pressure force acting on each strip,

$$dF = p \times dA$$

Total pressure force on entire lamina $= F = \int dF$

$$= \int p dA$$

$$= \int \gamma y \, dA$$

Now from geometry of Fig. 3.14 we have

$$y = S \sin \theta$$

$$\bar{y} = \bar{S} \sin \theta$$

and $$y^* = S^* \sin \theta$$

$\therefore$ $$F = \int \gamma \times S \times \sin \theta \times dA$$

$$= \gamma \sin \theta \int S \, dA$$

$$F = \gamma \sin \theta \, . \, A\bar{S} \qquad \text{...(As } \int S \, dA = A\bar{S}\text{)}$$

$$= \gamma \bar{y} A \qquad \text{(as } \bar{S} \sin \theta = \bar{y}\text{)}$$

$$F = \gamma A \bar{y} \qquad \text{...(3.7)}$$

Centre of pressure: Similar to vertical plane lamina the centre of pressure will lie below the centre of gravity for inclined plane lamina.

Moment of total force F about axis 0–0 $= F \times S^*$ ...(3.8)

The pressure force on elemental strip is,

$$dF = \gamma y \, dA$$

$$dF = \gamma S \sin \theta \, dA \qquad \text{(as } y = S \sin \theta\text{)}$$

Moment of force, dF, acting on small elemental strip about axis 0–0 is,

$$= dF \times S$$

$$= \gamma S \sin \theta \, dA \times S$$

$$= \gamma \sin \theta \, S^2 \, dA$$

Summing up the moment of all forces about 0–0 axis,

$$= \int \gamma \sin \theta \, S^2 \, dA$$

$$= \gamma \sin \theta \int S^2 \, dA = \gamma \sin \theta \, I_0 \qquad \text{...(3.9)}$$

where, $I_0 = \int S^2 \, dA$ is the moment of inertia of inclined plane lamina about 0–0 axis

Equating (3.8) and (3.9)

$$F \times S^* = \gamma \sin \theta \, I_0 \qquad \text{...(3.10)}$$

we know, $$F = \gamma A \bar{y};$$

$$S^* = \frac{y^*}{\sin \theta}$$

and I_0 = Moment of inertia about axis 0–0,

$$= I_G + A\bar{S}^2$$

where I_G = Moment of inertia about its own centroidal axis.

Substitute for F, S^* and I_0 in equation (3.10), we get

$$\gamma A\bar{y} \times \frac{y^*}{\sin\theta} = \gamma \sin\theta\,(I_G + A\bar{S}^2)$$

$$y^* = \frac{\sin^2\theta}{A\bar{y}}\left[I_G + A\left(\frac{\bar{y}}{\sin\theta}\right)^2\right]$$

$$= \frac{I_G \sin^2\theta}{A\bar{y}} + \bar{y}$$

$$\therefore \quad y^* = \bar{y} + \frac{I_G \sin^2\theta}{A\bar{y}} \qquad ...(3.11)$$

For $\theta = 90°$ the above equation will be same as equation (3.6), which is applicable to vertical plane lamina submerged totally in liquid.

3.2.6 Solved Problems

■ **Problem 3.11:** *A circular plate 2.5 m diameter is immersed in water with its greatest and least depth below the free surface being 3 m and 1 m respectively. Find (i) the total pressure on one face of the plate and (ii) the position of centre of pressure.*

Solution:

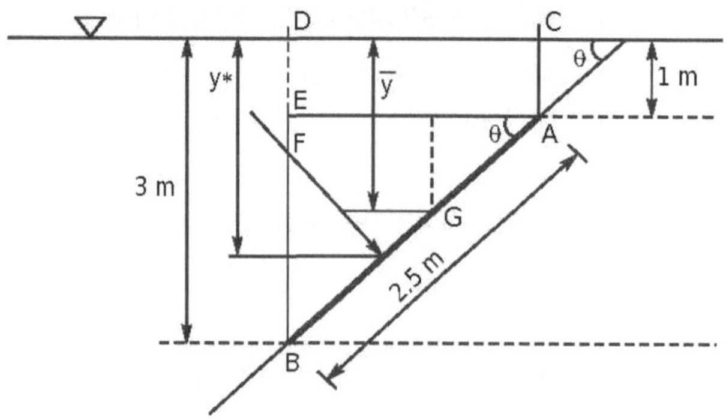

Fig. 3.15

From ΔABE, $\quad \sin\theta = \frac{BE}{AB} = \frac{3.0 - 1.0}{2.5} = \frac{2}{2.5}$

$\therefore \quad \theta = 53.13°$

Now, $\quad \bar{y} = CA + AG\sin\theta$

$$= 1.0 + \frac{2.5}{2} \times \sin 53.13°$$

$$\bar{y} = 2.0 \text{ m}$$

(*i*) Total pressure $= F = \gamma A \bar{y}$

$$= (1{,}000 \times 9.81) \times \frac{\pi}{4} \times (2.5)^2 \times 2.0$$

$F = 96{,}309.45$ N ...(Ans.)

(*ii*) Centre of pressure (y^*):

$$y^* = \bar{y} + \frac{I_G \sin^2 \theta}{A\bar{y}}$$

$$= 2.0 + \frac{\frac{\pi}{64} \times (2.5)^4 \times \sin^2 53.13}{\frac{\pi}{4} \times (2.5)^2 \times 2.0}$$

$$= 2.0 + 0.125$$

$y^* = 2.125$ m. ...(Ans.)

■ **Problem 3.12:** *An inclined rectangular gate 1.22 m × 5 m size is shown in Fig. 3.16 is installed against a sluice opening to control discharge of water. What force normal to the gate will be required at its end B to open it, if A is hinged?*

Solution:

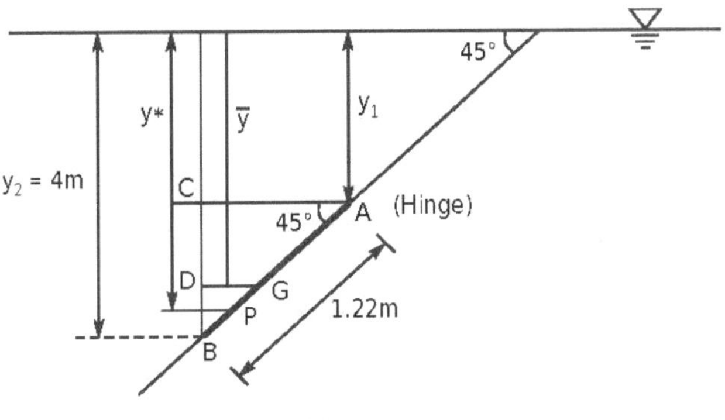

Fig. 3.16

A = Area of gate = 5 × 1.22 = 6.1 m²

$$\bar{y} = y_2 - BD$$

$$= 4.0 - BG \sin 45$$

$$= 4.0 - \frac{1.22}{2} \times \sin 45$$

$$= 4.0 - 0.432$$

$$\bar{y} = 3.568 \text{ m}$$

(*i*) Total pressure force $= F = \gamma A\bar{y}$

$F = (1{,}000 \times 9.81) \times 6.1 \times 3.568$

$F = 2{,}13{,}512.7$ N

(*ii*) Centre of pressure, y^*

$$y^* = \bar{y} + \frac{I_G \sin^2 \theta}{A\bar{y}}$$

$$= 3.568 + \frac{\frac{5 \times (1.22)^3}{12} \times \sin^2 45}{6.1 \times 3.568}$$

$$y^* = 3.568 + 0.0174$$

$$y^* = 3.585 \text{ m}$$

(*iii*) Normal force P at end B to open the gate:

From Fig. 3.17

$$GM = y^* - \bar{y} = 3.585 - 3.568$$

$$GM = 0.0174 \text{ m}$$

$$GP = \frac{GM}{\sin 45} = \frac{0.0174}{0.707} = 0.0246 \text{ m}$$

Now, $AP = AG + GP$

$$= \frac{1.22}{2} + 0.0246 \text{ m}$$

$$AP = 0.6346 \text{ m}$$

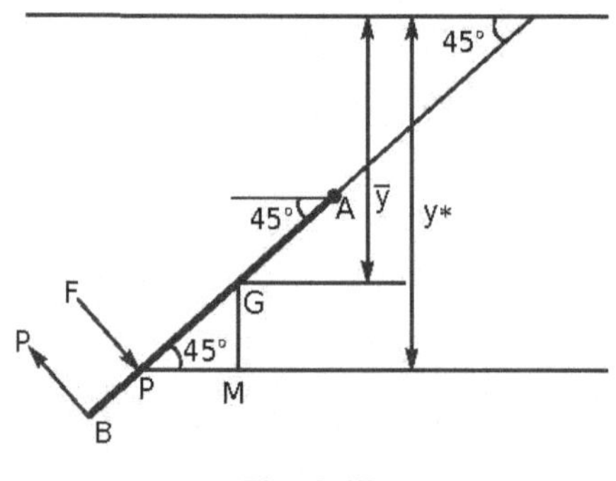

Fig. 3.17

Take moment about A.

$$P \times GB = F \times AP$$

$$P \times 1.22 = 2{,}13{,}552.47 \times 0.6346$$

$\therefore$ $P = 1{,}11{,}082.3$ N ...(Ans.)

3.2.7 Curved Surface Submerged in a Liquid

Consider a curved surface AB submerged totally, in a liquid of specific weight γ as shown in Fig. 3.18.

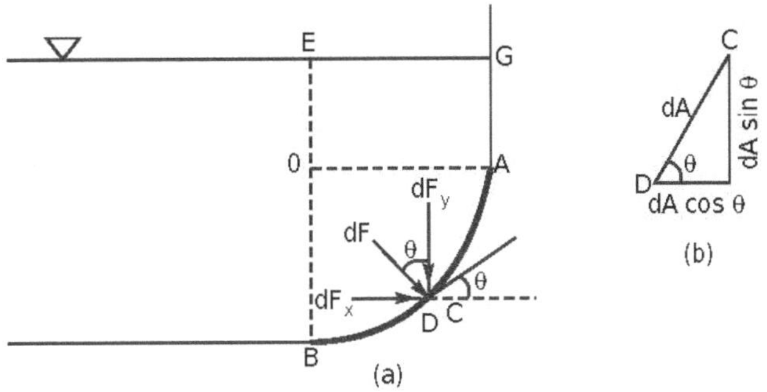

Fig. 3.18 Curved surface

Pressure force always acts normal to the surface and so is true for curved surface also. If 'dA' is the area of small element CD of the curved surface AB at a depth y below the free surface of liquid, then intensity of pressure is

$$dF = p \times dA$$

$$= \gamma y \times dA \quad \text{...(3.12)}$$

$\therefore$ Total pressure force on the curved surface AB is

$$F = \int dF = \int \gamma y \, dA \quad \text{...(3.13)}$$

But the direction of pressure force in case of curved surface on elementary small strip varies from point to point. Hence determination of pressure force by integration of equation (3.13) is not at all possible.

This problem can be solved by resolving the force dF in two components along x and y directions viz. dF_x and dF_y. The total pressure force along x and y direction can be calculated by integrating dF_x and dF_y and total force as

$$F = \sqrt{F_x^2 + F_y^2} \quad \text{...(3.14)}$$

and angle θ, the inclination of resultant with the horizontal as

$$\theta = \tan^{-1}\left(\frac{F_y}{F_x}\right) \quad \text{...(3.15)}$$

Now resolving dF along horizontal and vertical (*i.e.*, along x and y) directions.

$$dF_x = dF \sin\theta = \gamma y \, dA \sin\theta$$

and $$dF_y = dF \cos\theta = \gamma y \, dA \cos\theta$$

Integrating dF_x and dF_y we will get total forces along x and y directions.

$\therefore$ $$F_x = \int dF_x = \int \gamma y \, dA \sin\theta \quad \text{...(3.16)}$$

and $$F_y = \int dF_y = \int \gamma y \, dA \cos\theta \quad \text{...(3.17)}$$

In the expression (3.16), ($dA \sin\theta$) is the vertical projection of the small elemental area dA and term ($dA \cos\theta$) in equation is the horizontal projection of the elemental area dA. Hence ($\int \gamma y \, dA \sin\theta$) represents the total pressure force on the vertical projection of the curved surface on the vertical plane and ($\int \gamma y \, dA \cos\theta$) represents the weight of liquid lying above the curved surface upto free surface, (*i.e.*, portion AB OF GA) as shown in Fig. 3.18 (*a*).

Hence,

$\therefore$ F_x = Total pressure on the projected area of the curved surface on vertical plane.

This will act through centre of pressure of plane surface

and F_y = Total weight of liquid supported by the curved surface upto free surface.

This will act through centre of gravity of the volume of liquid supported by curved surface upto free surface.

In some cases, the lower side of curved surface is subjected to hydrostatic pressure force. In such cases F_y is calculated by assuming imaginary liquid supported by the curves surface upto the free surface liquid and it is considered to act upwards.

3.2.8 Solved Problem

■ **Problem 3.13:** *A cylindrical gate of 3m diameter 2m long has water upto its top on one side and upto a height of 1.5 m on the other. Determine the magnitude, location and direction of the resultant force exerted by the water on the gate. Find also the least weight of the cylinder so that it may not be lifted away from the floor.*

Solution:

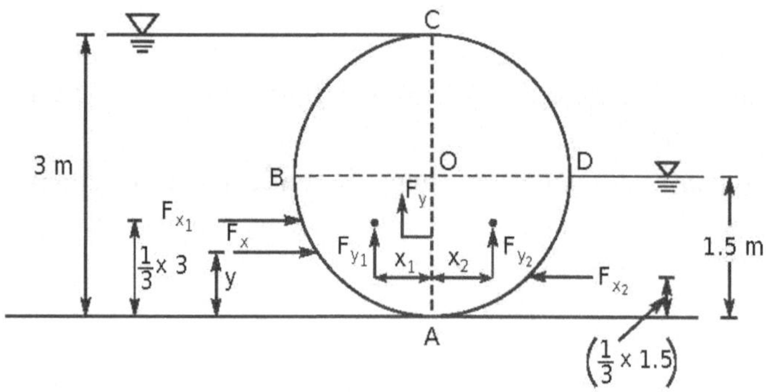

Fig. 3.19

(I) Horizontal Forces:

$$F_{x_1} = \text{Force exerted by water on projected vertical plane}$$

$$= \text{Force on plane } AOC$$

$$= \gamma A_1 \bar{y}_1$$

$$= (1{,}000 \times 9.81) \times (3 \times 2) \times \frac{3}{2}$$

$$F_{x_1} = 88{,}290 \text{ N}$$

$$= 88.29 \text{ kN}$$

$$F_{x_2} = \text{Force exerted by water on projected vertical plane}$$

$$= \text{Force on } AO$$

$$= \gamma A_2 \bar{y}_2$$

$$= (1{,}000 \times 9.81) \times (1.5 \times 2) \times \frac{1.5}{2}$$

$$= 22{,}072.5 \text{ N}$$

$$= 22.73 \text{ kN}$$

Resultant force in X-direction $= F_x = F_{x_1} - F_{x_2} = 88.29 - 22.73 = 65.56$ kN

Vertical Forces:

$$F_{y_1} = \text{Weight of water enclosed by portion } AOCBA$$

$$= \gamma \times A \times \text{width of gate}$$

$$= (1{,}000 \times 9.81) \times \left(\frac{\pi \times 1.5^2}{2}\right) \times 2.0$$

$$= 69{,}342.8 \text{ N}$$

$$F_{y_1} = 69.343 \text{ kN}$$

$$F_{x_2} = \text{Weight of water enclosed by portion } AODA$$

$$= (1{,}000 \times 9.81) \times \frac{\pi \times (1.5^2)}{4} \times 2.0$$

$$= 34{,}671.4 \text{ N}$$

$$F_{x_2} = 34.671 \text{ kN}$$

Resultant force in y-direction $= F_y = F_{y_1} + F_{y_2}$

$$= 69.343 + 34.671$$

$$F_y = 104.014 \text{ kN}$$

Resultant Force

(*i*) Magnitude,

$$F = \sqrt{F_x^2 + F_y^2}$$

$$= \sqrt{65.56^2 + 104.014^2}$$

$$F = 122.95 \text{ kN} \qquad \text{...(Ans.)}$$

(*ii*) Direction

Let the resultant force act at angle θ with the horizontal.

$$\therefore \qquad \theta = \tan^{-1}\frac{F_y}{F_x} = \tan^{-1}\frac{104.014}{65.56}$$

$$\theta = 57.78° \qquad \text{...(Ans.)}$$

(*iii*) Location

Taking moments about base

$$F_x \times y = F_{x_1} \times y_1 - F_{x_2} \times y_2$$

$$65.56 \times y = 88.29 \times \left(\frac{1}{3} \times 3\right) - 22.73 \times \left(\frac{1}{3} \times 1.5\right)$$

$$y = 1.173 \text{ m from base} \qquad \text{...(Ans.)}$$

Horizontal component of force, ($F_x = 65.56$) act at a distance of 1.173 m from base. The vertical component act through the centre of gravity of respective portion.

$$x_1 = \frac{4\gamma}{3\pi} = \frac{4 \times 1.5}{3\pi} = 0.637 \text{ m from point } A \text{ towards left.}$$

and
$$x_2 = \frac{4\gamma}{3\pi} = \frac{4 \times 1.5}{3\pi} = 0.637 \text{ m from point } A \text{ towards right}$$

∴ Taking moment about A, we get

$$F_y \times x = F_{y_1} \times x_1 - F_{y_2} \times x_2$$

$$104.014 \times x = 69.34 \times 0.637 - 34.671 \times 0.637$$

$$x = 0.212 \qquad \text{...(Ans.)}$$

∴ The vertical component of force, ($F_y = 104.014$ kN) act at distance of 0.212 m towards left from point A.

(II) Last Weight of Cylinder:

The least weight of cylinder must be equal to the upward force so that cylinder may not get lifted from floor.

∴
$$W = F_y$$

$$W = 104.014 \text{ kN} \qquad \text{...(Ans.)}$$

3.3 PRACTICAL APPLICATION OF TOTAL PRESSURE AND CENTRE OF PRESSURE

In actual practice, there are various hydraulic structures subjected to hydrostatic pressure forces. While designing these structures it is necessary to know the total pressure force and point through which it acts. Some of common structures are:

(*a*) Dams

(*b*) Gates-sluice gates, and lock gates

(*c*) Tanks

Computation of total pressure and centre of pressure acting on dams, sluice gates and tanks is explained later in the solved problems.

3.3.1 Total Pressure and Centre of Pressure on Lock Gates

Lock gates are used for changing water level in a canal or a river for navigation. Fig. 3.5 shows the plan and elevation on the single pair of lock gates. Let *AB* and *BC* are two lock gates placed such as to meet at *B* in the closed position. Each gate is fixed by two hinges at the top and bottom at the ends *A* and *C*.

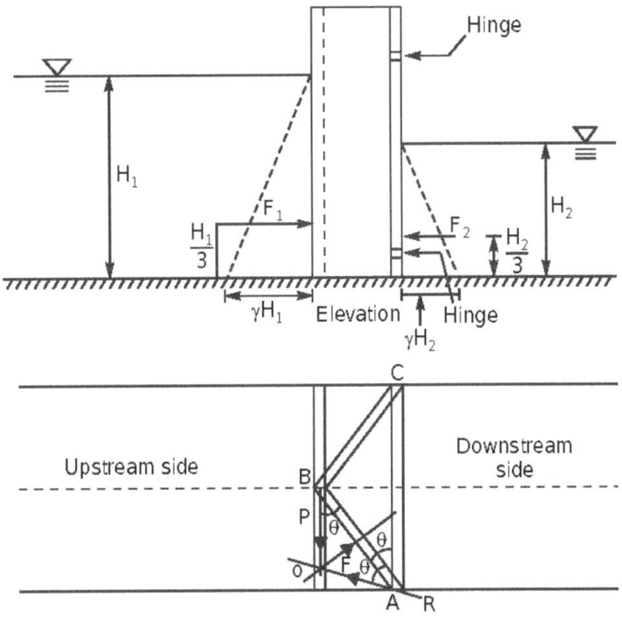

Fig. 3.20 Pair of lock gates

Let H_1 and H_2 be the depths of water on upstream and downstream sides of gates respectively. Consider gates *AB* of width *l*.

The resultant pressure force acting on gate *AB* is

$$F = F_1 - F_2 \qquad \text{...(3.18)}$$

where, F_1, total pressure force on *u/s* face of gate *AB* is

$$F_1 = \gamma A_1 \bar{y}_1$$

$$= \gamma (l \times H_1) \times \frac{H_1}{2}$$

$$F_1 = \frac{\gamma l H_1^2}{2} \qquad \text{...(3.19)}$$

It acts at $\left(\frac{H_1}{3}\right)$ from base and F_2 the total pressure force on *d/s* face of gate *AB* is

$$F_2 = \gamma A_2 \bar{y}_2$$

$$= \gamma (l + H_2) + \frac{H_2}{2}$$

$$F_2 = \frac{\gamma l H_2^2}{2} \quad \text{...(3.20)}$$

which acts at $\left(\frac{H_2}{3}\right)$ from the base.

The point of application of resultant force F can be calculated by taking moments of F, F_1 and F_2 about the bottom edge.

Under the action of pressure force the gates remains closed at B. Hence the other force acts on gate is reaction at common contact surface of the two gates, which acts normal to the contact surface. In addition to F and P forces, the third force act on gate is resultant reaction 'R' of the hinges.

Since the gate is in equilibrium under the action of these forces, then they must intersect at the same point. If we assume that the forces F and P meet at O, then R will also pass through O. Let θ is the inclination of the gate with the perpendicular to the side of the lock.

From ΔABO

$$\angle OAB = \angle OBA = \theta$$

Here, it is assumed, for the purpose of analysis that all the three forces are coplanar.

As the gate is in equilibrium the unknowns P and R can be calculated by applying the condition of equilibrium.

Resolving the forces along the gate, we get

$$P \cos \theta = R \cos \theta$$

$$P = R \quad \text{...(3.21)}$$

and resolving the forces perpendicular to the gate, we have

$$F = P \sin \theta + R \sin \theta$$

$$F = (P + R) \sin \theta$$

$$F = 2R \sin \theta \quad \text{...(since } P = R\text{)}$$

$$\therefore \quad R = \frac{F}{2 \sin \theta} \quad \text{...(3.22)}$$

and

$$P = \frac{F}{2 \sin \theta} \quad \text{...(3.23)}$$

The force F is known from equation (3.18) and angle θ from geometry of figure. Substituting for F and θ in equation (3.22) and (3.23) the unknowns R and P can be calculated.

The reactions at top and bottom hinges R_T and R_B respectively, can be calculated by writing two equations.

(*a*) $R_T + R_B = R$ and (*b*) By principle of moments *i.e.*, taking moment about bottom hinge.

3.3.2 Solved Problem

■ **Problem 3.14:** *Each gate of lock is 5 m high and is supported by two hinges placed on the top and bottom of the gate. When the gates are closed, they make an angle of 120°. The width of lock chamber is 4 m. The depth of water on two sides of the gate are 4 m and 3 m respectively. Determine the resultant pressure on each gate and value of hinge reactions.*

Solution:

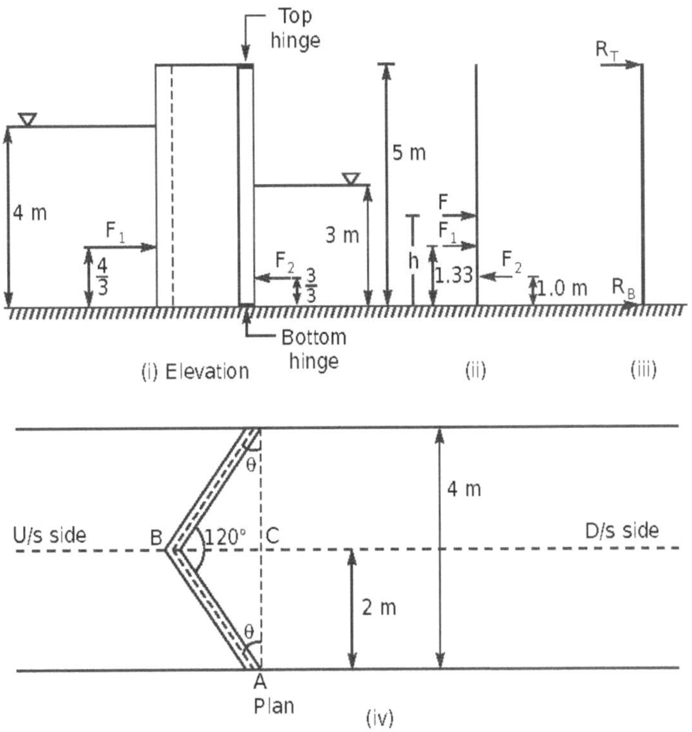

Fig. 3.21

From ΔABD,

$$\angle ABD = 120°$$

$$\therefore \quad 2\theta = 180° - 120°$$

$$\theta = 30°$$

$$\text{Width of each lock gate} = AB = l = \frac{AC}{\cos 30}$$

$$l = \frac{2.0}{\cos 30} = 2.31 \text{ m}$$

Now,

$$F_1 = \gamma A_1 \bar{y}_1 = \gamma \times (H_1 \times l) \times \frac{H_1}{2}$$

$$= (1{,}000 \times 9.81) \times (4 \times 2.31) \times \frac{4}{2}$$

$$= 1{,}81{,}288.8 \text{ N}$$

$$F_1 = 181.289 \text{ kN}$$

$$F_2 = \gamma A_2 \bar{y}_2 = \gamma \times (H_2 \times l) \times \frac{H_2}{2}$$

$$= (1{,}000 \times 9.81) \times (3 \times 2.31) \times \frac{3}{2}$$

$$= 1{,}01{,}974.95 \text{ N}$$

$$F_2 = 101.975 \text{ kN}$$

$\therefore$ Resultant water pressure $= F = F_1 - F_2$

$$= 181.289 - 101.975$$

$$F = 79.314 \text{ kN}$$

Let this resultant pressure act at a distance h from bottom.

$\therefore$ Taking moment about the bottom (Fig. (*ii*))

$$F \times h = F_1 \times \frac{4}{3} - F_2 \times \frac{3}{3}$$

$$79.314 \times h = 181.289 \times 1.33 - 101.975 \times 1$$

$$h = 1.754 \text{ m}$$

Now, from equations (3.22) and (3.22), we have

$$R = \frac{F}{2\sin\theta} = \frac{79.314}{2 \times \sin 30} = 79.314 \text{ kN}$$

$$P = \frac{F}{2\sin\theta} \times \frac{79.314}{2 \times \sin 30} = 79.314 \text{ kN}$$

To calculate reactions at the hinges:

Let R_T and R_B be reactions at top and bottom hinges:

$\therefore$ $$R_T + R_B = R$$

Now, taking moments about bottom hinge (Fig. (*iii*))

$$R \times h = R_T \times 5.0 + R_B \times 0$$

$$79.314 \times 1.754 = R_T \times 5$$

$$R_T = 27.83 \text{ kN}$$ **...(Ans.)**

$\therefore$ $$R_B = R - R_T = 79.314 - 27.83$$

$$R_B = 51.486 \text{ kN.}$$ **...(Ans.)**

Exercises

1. A tank 10 m × 10 m base contains water upto the height of 5 m. Find the intensity of pressure and total pressure on the bottom of tank.
(**Ans.** p = 49.05 kN/m^2, F = 4905 kN)

2. Find the total pressure and cenre of pressure on the rectangular plane lamina of size 3 m × 2 m, when its 3 m edge is 1 m below the free surface of water.
(**Ans.** F = 117.72 kN, y^* = 2.167 m)

3. A triangular lamina of base and altitude equal to 3 m is submerged in water vertically. Determine total pressure and centre of pressure on one of its face when apex of it is 1.5 m below the free surface of water. (**Ans.** F = 154.51 kN, y^* = 3.643 m)

4. A right angled triangular plate having a base width of 4 m and height 6 m is immersed vertically in water such that the base is parallel to the water surface and at a depth of 1 m below the free surface of water level and apex is below the base. Determine total pressure and position of centre of pressure. (**Ans.** F = 360 kN, y^* = 3.66 m)

5. Find the position and magnitude of resultant water pressure acting on the plane lamina as shown in Fig. 3.22. (**Ans.** F = 177084.6 N, y^* = 2.44 from free surface)

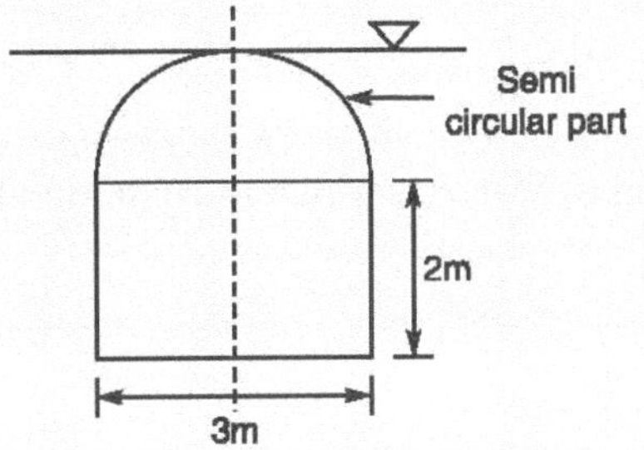

Fig. 3.22

6. An opening 1.5 m wide and 3 m high in the wall of tank is closed by the gate of the same size hinged at its centre. Water level in the tank is 4 m above the hinge and the gate is held in position by a force F applied at its bottom edge. Find force F.
(**Ans.** F = 88.29 kN)

7. A vertical gate closes a horizontal tunnel 6 m high and 4 m wide running full with water. The pressure at the bottom of the gate is 2.4 × 10^4 kg/m^2. Find out the total pressure on the gate and position centre of pressure.
(**Ans.** F = 504 kN, y^* = 21.143 m)

8. A gate 4 m wide and 3 m high separates a liquid of specific gravity 1.2 and height 2.4 m on one side and water upto a height of 1.6 m on other side of the gate. Compute the resultant force acting on the gate and position of centre of pressure.
(**Ans.** F = 8704 N, Y = 0.9567 from base)

9. A sluice gate 2.4 m wide and 1.5 m high is hinged at the bottom. On upstream side the water is 3 m above the bottom of gate and downstream side upto top of gate. Find the resultant force acting on gate and position of centre of pressure. Also find minimum force required at the top of gate to open it. Take density of sea water = 1025 kg/m^3.

(**Ans.** (*i*) F = 5602.5 N; (*ii*) y^* = 0.667 m above hinge and minimum force = 2791.85 N)

10. A triangular aperture in the vertical side of tank is closed by a plate of same dimension. The base width and height of triangular plate are 40 cm and 32 cm respectively. The base of the plate is 30 cm below the free surface of water is placed with apex downwards. The plate is held in position by three stops, one at each corners. Determine the reactions at the stop. (**Ans.** Reaction at base stops = 80.5 N, Reaction at apex stop = 96.3 N)

11. A circular plate 3 m diameter is immersed in water with its greatest and least depth below the free surface being 3.5 m and 1.5 m respectively. Find the total pressure on one face of the plate and the position of centre of pressure.

(**Ans.** F = 143.64 kN, y^* = 2.358 m)

12. A tank 2 m deep is 4 m square at the top and 2.5 m square at the bottom. The four sides are plane and each has the same trapezoidal shape. The tank is full of water. Obtain from first principles the resultant pressure on each side and the position of centre of pressure.

(**Ans.** (*i*) Pressure on sloping side = 58860 N; (*ii*) Pressure on bottom = 122625 N)

13. The gate AB as shown in Fig. 3.23 supports water on its upstream side and is hinged at point C. Find the height of water at which the gate tip about the hinge.

(**Ans.** h = 5.091 m)

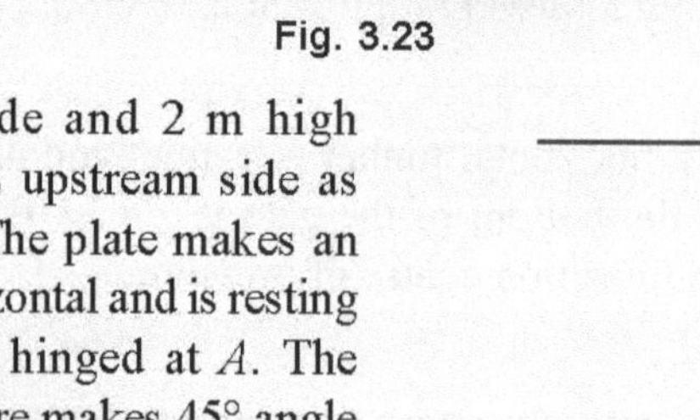

Fig. 3.23

14. A plate AB 5 m wide and 2 m high supports water on its upstream side as shown in Fig. 3.24. The plate makes an angle of 60° with horizontal and is resting on support at C and hinged at A. The support shown in figure makes 45° angle with the plate AB. Calculate the thrust in the support. (**Ans.** Thrust, F = 80098)

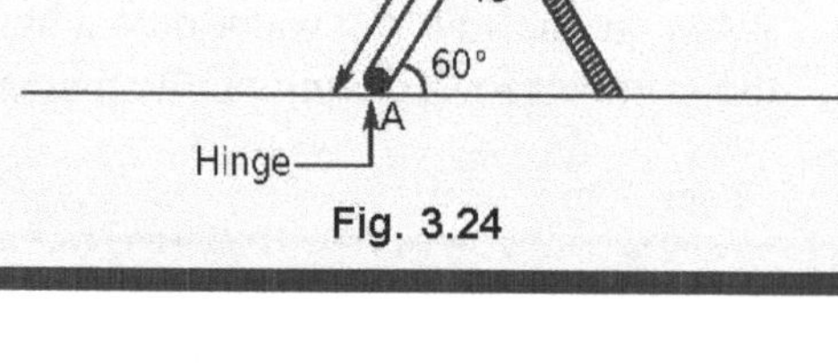

Fig. 3.24

15. Show that for a quarter-circular gate as shown in Fig. 3.25 the resultant reaction passes through the Hinge A.

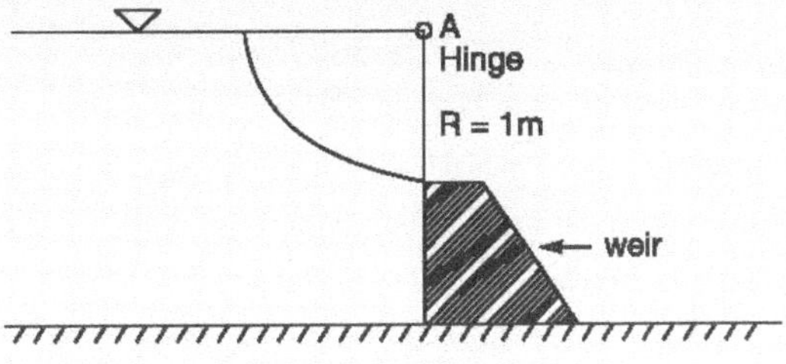

Fig. 3.25

16. Calculate the horizontal and vertical components of forces exerted on the Tainter gate, which retains water as shown in Fig. 3.26. Assume unit width of gate.

(**Ans.** F_x = 78480 N, F_y = 14218.6 N)

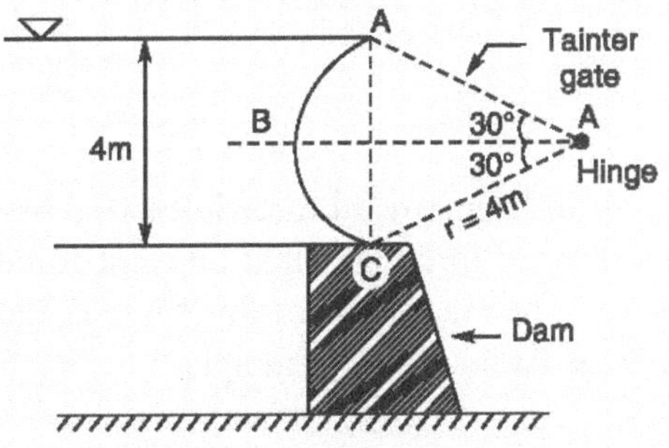

Fig. 3.26

17. Each gate of lock is 6 m high and is supported by two hinges placed on the top and bottom of the gate. When the gates are closed, they make an angle of 120°. The width of the lock chamber is 5 m. The depth of water on two sides of the gate are 4.2 m and 3.2 m respectively. Determine the resultant pressure on each gate and value of hinge reactions. (**Ans.** F = 104.8 kN, R_T = 32.51 kN and R_B = 72.29 kN)

❑❑❑

4

Buoyancy and Floatation

4.1 BUOYANCY

When a body is immersed in a fluid, an upward force is exerted by the fluid on the body, which tends to lift it upwards. This upward force is called buoyant force or buoyancy. This force is opposite to the action of gravity. The magnitude of this force is equal to the weight of the fluid displaced and it is well known as Archimedes' principle.

4.2 CENTRE OF BUOYANCY

It is defined as the point of application of buoyant force on the body. The buoyant force is vertical force and is equal to the weight of fluid displaced. The centre of buoyancy is therefore equal to the centre of gravity of the fluid displaced.

$$F_B = \gamma V$$

where, F_B = buoyant force

γ = specific weight of fluid

V = volume of submerged body.

4.3 PRINCIPLE OF FLOATATION

The weight of a body floating in any fluid is equal to the force of buoyancy and which is also equal to the weight of fluid displaced by the same body.

$$F_B = W$$

where, W = weight of body.

If $W > F_B$: the body tends to sink down till $W = F_B$

If $W < F_B$: the body tends to lift up till $W = F_B$.

4.4 SOLVED PROBLEMS

■ **Problem 4.1:** *A wooden block 2 m wide, 1.2 m deep and 5 m long floats in water. Find the volume of water displaced and position of centre of buoyancy. The density of wooden block is 600 kg/m³.*

Solution:

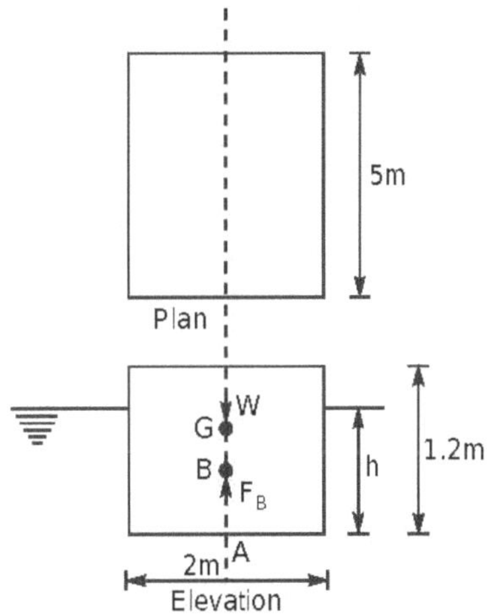

Fig. 4.1

G = Centre of gravity

B = Centre of buoyancy

and A is the bottom-most point on the vertical axis.

Let, h = Depth of immersion

Now,

Weight of wooden block

$$= \rho \times g \times \text{Volume of block}$$
$$= 600 \times 9.81 \times 2 \times 1.2 \times 5$$
$$= 70632 \text{ N}$$

From Archimedes principle, or for equilibrium

Weight of block = Weight of water displaced by the block

70632 = Weight density of water × Volume of water displaced

$$\therefore \quad \text{Volume of water displaced} = \frac{70632}{9.81 \times 1000} = 7.2$$

Now,

Volume of block in water = Volume of water displaced

$$2 \times 5 \times h = 7.2$$
$$h = 0.72 \text{ m}$$
$$\therefore \quad AB = \frac{h}{2} = 0.36 \text{ m}$$

∴ Centre of buoyancy from base = 0.36 m.

■ **Problem 4.2:** *Calculate specific gravity of a concrete block when it weight 50 kg in air and 32 kg in water.*

Solution: For the equilibrium

$$\begin{pmatrix}\text{Weight of block}\\ \text{in air}\end{pmatrix} - \begin{pmatrix}\text{Weight of block}\\ \text{in water}\end{pmatrix} = \begin{pmatrix}\text{Weight of water}\\ \text{displaced}\end{pmatrix}$$
$$50 - 32 = 18$$

$$\text{Now, Volume of water displaced} = \frac{\text{Weight of water displaced}}{\text{Density of water}}$$
$$= \frac{18}{1000} = 0.018 \text{ m}^2$$

$$\text{Volume of concrete block} = \text{Volume of water displaced} = 0.018 \text{ m}^3$$

$$\text{Weight density of concrete block} = \frac{\text{Weight of block in air}}{\text{Volume of block}}$$

$$= \frac{50}{0.018}$$

$$= 2777.78 \text{ kg/m}^3$$

$$\therefore \quad \text{Specific gravity of concrete block} = \frac{\text{Weight density of block}}{\text{Weight density of water}}$$

$$= \frac{2777.78}{1000}$$

$$\text{Specific gravity} = 2.778. \qquad \text{...(Ans.)}$$

4.5 METACENTRE AND METACENTRIC HEIGHT

Metacentre is defined as the point about which a body oscillates when it is given a small angular displacement.

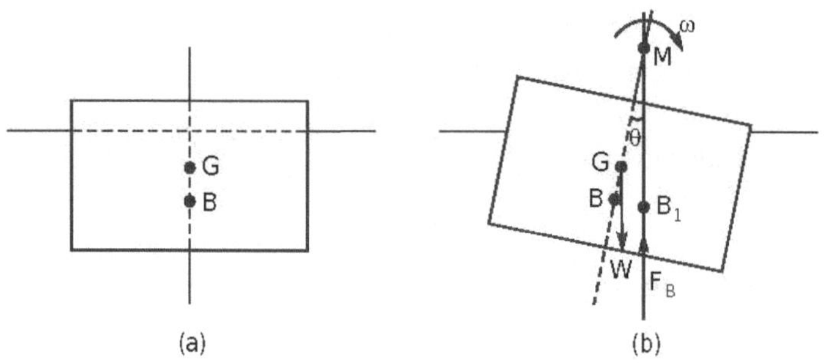

Fig. 4.2 Metacentre and Metacentric Height

Consider a body floating in a liquid as shown in Fig. 4.2 (*a*), which is in equilibrium. The weight, *W* of the body acts through point *G*, and buoyant force F_B through point *B*. Both the points lie on the same vertical line called normal axis of the body.

Let us consider that body is given small angular displacement θ, (Fig. 4.2 (*b*)). The centre of gravity of body remains at point *G* itself but centre of buoyancy *B* shifts towards right of normal axis at B_1 as the right side of body sinks down and left part emerges out of the liquid. Now the line of action of buoyant force which is vertical, intersects the normal axis at some point *M*, which is known as metacentre. Hence metacentre is defined as the point of intersection between vertical line passing through B_1 and normal axis. The distance (*GM*) between the metacentre, *M* and centre of gravity, *G* of a floating body is called metacentric height.

4.6 STABILITY OF FLOATING AND SUBMERGED BODIES

A body whether it is floating or submerged is said to be stable, when it will come back to its original position even after it has been displaced slightly.

When a small angular displacement is given to submerged or floating body, either of the three conditions of equilibrium will be developed,

(*i*) Stable equilibrium.

(*ii*) Unstable equilibrium.

(*iii*) Neutral equilibrium.

4.6.1 Stability of Submerged Body

The positions of centre of gravity and centre of buoyancy are fixed for wholly submerged bodies.

The relative positions of G and B defines the stability conditions of a submerged bodies.

(*i*) **Stable Equilibrium**

Consider a body such as balloon floating in air, *i.e.*, submerged totally in air. Let us assume that the centre of gravity is below the centre of buoyancy as shown in Fig. 4.3. The weight of balloon, W acts through G vertically downwards and the buoyant force, F_B acts vertically upwards through B, and for equilibrium, $W = F_B$. If the balloon is given an angular displacement in anticlockwise direction then the weight W and buoyant force F_B constitute a couple in clockwise direction and brings the balloon to its original position.

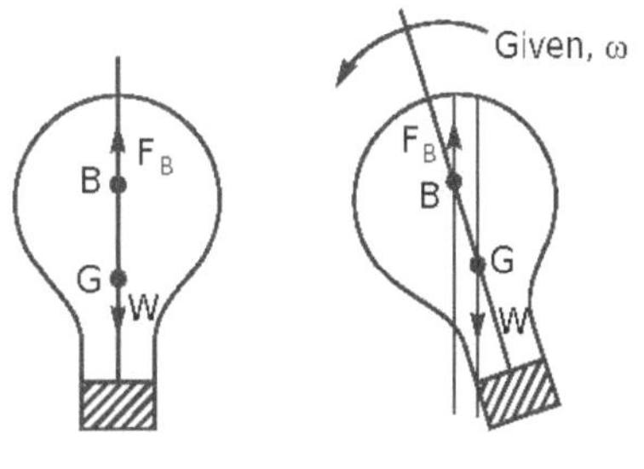

Fig. 4.3 Stable Equilibrium

$\therefore$ Condition for stable equilibrium $\Rightarrow$ Point B should be above point G.

(*ii*) **Unstable Equilibrium**

For the balloon submerged in air, let us consider centre of buoyancy B, below the centre of gravity G, when $W = F_B$. If the balloon is given a slight angular displacement in anticlockwise direction as shown in Fig. 4.4, then the W and F_{B}, constitutes couple in anticlockwise direction and does not bring the body to its original position, and hence it is in unstable equilibrium.

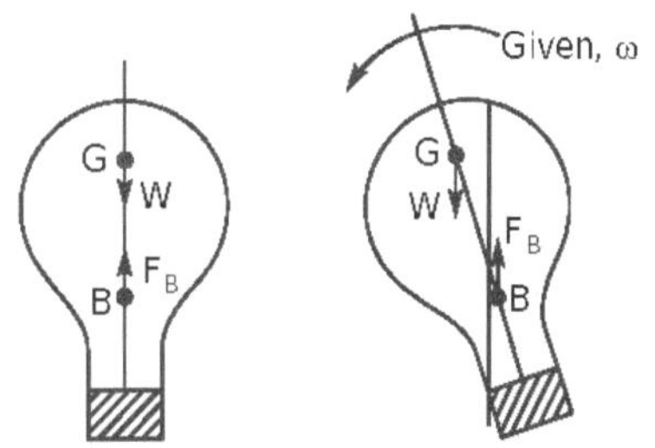

Fig. 4.4 Unstable Equilibrium

$\therefore$ Condition for unstable equilibrium

$\Rightarrow$ Point B should be below point G.

(*iii*) **Neutral Equilibrium**

When point B and G are at the same point and if $W = F_B$ as shown in Fig. 4.5, the body is said to be in neutral equilibrium.

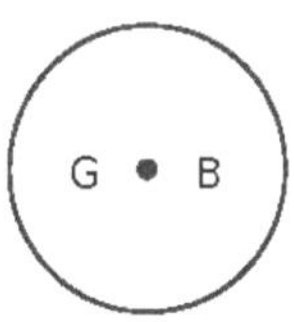

Fig. 4.5 Neutral Equilibrium

4.6.2 Stability of Floating Body

The position of metacentre M relative to the position of centre of gravity G of floating (partially submerged) bodies determine the stability conditions of a body.

(*i*) **Stable Equilibrium.** Consider a body floating (partially submerged) in liquid as shown in Fig. 4.6 (*e.g.*, ship floating in seawater). If the body is displaced by giving a slight angular displacement in clockwise direction, the centre of buoyancy shifts from B to its new position B_1. If the vertical line is drawn through B_1, it intersects normal axis at M, where the position of M is above G. In this case buoyant force F_B passing through B_1 and weight passing through G forms a restoring couple acting in anticlockwise direction and bring the body to its original position.

∴ Condition for stable equilibrium ⇒ Point M should be above G *i.e.*, $BM > BG$.

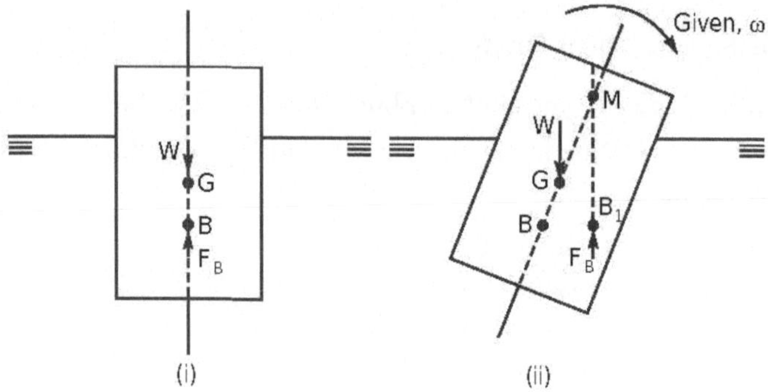

Fig. 4.6 Stable Equilibrium

(*ii*) **Unstable Equilibrium.** If a body is displaced by giving small angular displacement in clockwise direction, the point B shifts to B_1 as shown in Fig. 4.7. The vertical line drawn through B_1 cuts normal axis at M, where M is below G. In this case F_B and W from a couple in clockwise direction, thus disturbing the equilibrium more, and does not bring the body to its original position.

∴ Condition for unstable equilibrium ⇒ Point M should be below G.

i.e., $BM < BG$.

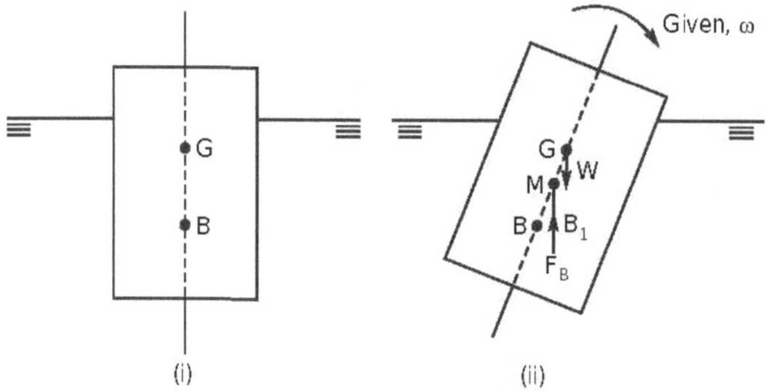

Fig. 4.7 Unstable Equilibrium

(*iii*) **Neutral Equilibrium.** For a floating body if metacentre, M coincides with the centre of gravity, G *i.e.*, $BM = BG$, the body is said to be in neutral equilibrium.

4.7 DETERMINATION OF METACENTRIC HEIGHT

Metacentric height of a floating body can be calculated by either analytical or experimental method.

4.7.1 Analytical Method for the Determination of Metacentric Height

Consider floating body as shown in Fig. 4.8 is in equilibrium. The position of centre of gravity and centre of buoyancy are fixed as shown in Fig. 4.8 (*a*) at G and B. Fig. 4.8 (*b*) shows the position of body in tilted position when it is given a small angular displacement in clockwise sense. The centre of gravity remains at the same point but centre of buoyancy shifts to the new position B_1. This is due to the more portion of body on right side of vertical axis sinks in the liquid. Due to the angular displacement, the body tilts and the wedge shaped portion AOA_1 on left side of axis emerges out from liquid and portion DOD_1 on right side of axis sinks down in the liquid. The total weight of body is same as the volume immersed remains same and hence the volumes of wedge shaped portions AOA_1 and DOD_1 on either sides are equal. The portion DOD_1 represents positive buoyant force, dF_B acting vertically upwards through centre of gravity of DOD_1. Similarly the portion AOA_1 represents the negative buoyant force, dF_B acting vertically downwards through the centre of gravity of AOA_1. These two equal and opposite forces form a couple and tends to rotate the body in anticlockwise direction.

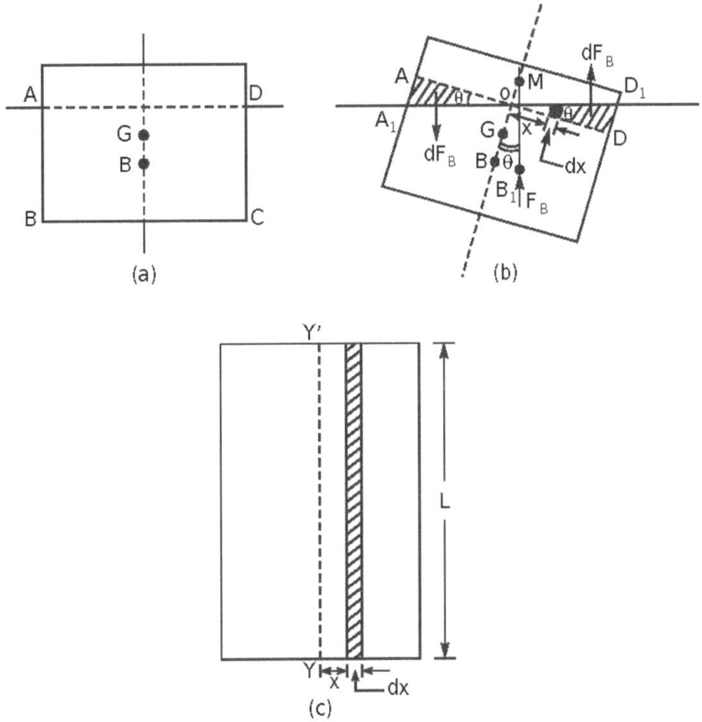

Fig. 4.8 Metacentric Height

The centre of buoyancy has been shifted from B to B_1 and due to this moment developed is in anticlockwise direction. The effect of these two couples must be same.

∴ Moment of couple due to the shift of centre of buoyancy from B to B_1 is

$$= F_B \times BB_1$$
$$= F_B \times BM \times \theta$$
$$= W \times BM \times \theta \qquad ...(4.1)$$

As, $\tan\theta = \sin\theta = \theta$, when θ is very small.

Couple formed due to positive and negative buoyancy forces

Consider a small strip of thickness 'dx' at a distance x from 0, for the wedge shaped portion DOD_1.

$$\text{The height of strip} = x \cdot \theta$$

$$\text{The area of small strip} = \text{thickness} \times \text{height}$$

$$= dx \cdot x \cdot \theta$$

$$\text{Area} = x \cdot \theta \cdot dx$$

$$\text{Volume of strip} = \text{Area} \times \text{length of floating body}$$

$$= x \cdot \theta \cdot dx \cdot L$$

$$\text{Weight of strip} = w \cdot x\theta L dx$$

Similarly, if small strip of thickness 'dx' at a distance x from 0 is considered, then the weight will be equal to $(wx\theta Ldx)$. These two weights constitutes couple as they are acting in opposite directions.

$$\text{Moment of couple} = \text{Weight of strip} \times \text{distance between the two strip weights.}$$

$$= (wx\theta Ldx) \times (2x)$$

$$= 2wx^2\theta Ldx$$

$$\text{Moment of couple for entire wedge} = \int 2wx^2\theta Ldx \qquad \text{...(4.2)}$$

Equating equations (4.1) and (4.2), we get

$$W \times BM \times \theta = \int 2wx^2\theta Ldx$$

$$W \times BM = 2w \int x^2 Ldx$$

Now the Ldx represents the area of small strip at the water surface.

$$\therefore \quad Ldx = dA$$

$$\therefore \quad W \times BM = 2w \int x^2 dA$$

The term $2\int x^2 dA$ represents the moment of inertia of a body at the water surface (in plan) about Y–Y axis

$$\therefore \quad 2\int x^2 dA = I$$

$$\therefore \quad W \times BM = wI$$

$$\therefore \quad BM = \frac{wI}{W}$$

$$= \frac{wI}{wV}$$

$$BM = \frac{I}{V} \qquad \text{...(4.3)}$$

where V = Volume of fluid displaced by a body.

Now, $GM = BM - BG$

$$GM = \frac{I}{V} - BG$$

$\therefore$ Metacentric height $= GM = \frac{I}{V} - BG$ ...(4.4)

Conditions of Equilibrium:

(*i*) $GM \rightarrow$ +ve, ... Stable equilibrium

(*ii*) $GM \rightarrow$ –ve, ... Unstable equilibrium

(*iii*) $GM \rightarrow 0$, ... Neutral equilibrium.

4.7.2 Solved Problems

■ **Problem 4.3:** *A uniform body of size 3 m × 3 m and 1 m deep floats in water. What is the weight of the body if depth of immersion is 0.8 m? Calculate the density of the body material and its metacentric height.*

Solution:

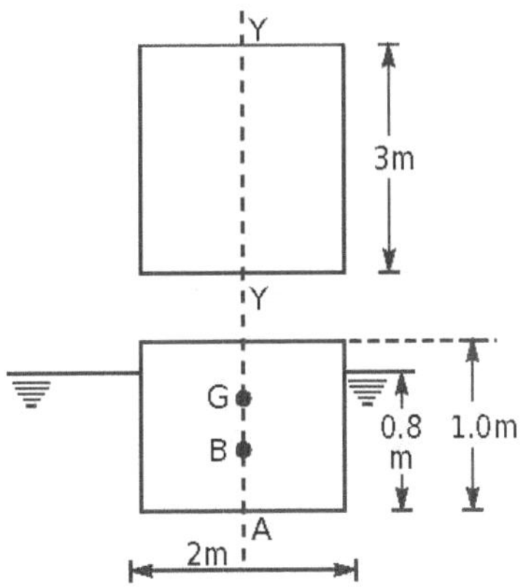

Fig. 4.9

(*i*) Weight of body, W

Weight of body, W = Weight of water displaced

$W = \rho \times g \times$ Volume of water displaced

$= 1000 \times 9.81 \times 3 \times 2 \times 0.8$

$W = 47088$ N ...(Ans.)

(*ii*) Density of body, material, ρ_m

Weight of body = Density of body material × g × Volume of body

$47088 = S \times 1000 \times 9.81 \times 3 \times 2 \times 1$

$\therefore$ $S = 0.8$

Density of body material $= S \times 1000$

$= 0.8 \times 1000$

$\rho_m = 800 \text{ kg/m}^3$

(*iii*) Metacentric height, GM

$$GM = \frac{I}{V} - BG$$

From the figure,

$$BG = AG - AB$$

$$= \frac{1.0}{2} - \frac{0.8}{2}$$

$$BG = 0.1 \text{ m}$$

$$I = \frac{bd^3}{12} = \frac{3 \times 2^3}{12} = 2.0 \text{ m}^3$$

$$V = 3 \times 2 \times 0.8 = 4.8 \text{ m}^3$$

$$\therefore \quad GM = \frac{2}{4.8} - 0.1$$

$$= 0.4167 - 0.1$$

$\therefore$ Metacentric height, $GM = 0.3167$ m. ...(**Ans.**)

■ **Problem 4.4:** *A metallic body floats at the interface of mercury (specific gravity 13.6) and water in such a way that 30% of its volume is submerged in mercury and 70% in water. Find the density of the metallic body.*

Solution:

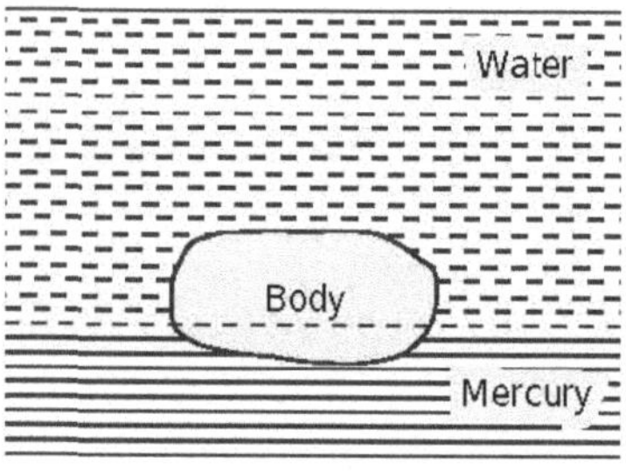

Fig. 4.10

Let volume of body $= V \text{ m}^3$

Volume of body submerged in water $= 0.7V \text{ m}^3$

and volume of body submerged in mercury $= 0.3V \text{ m}^3$

For the equilibrium of body,

Weight of body $W =$ Buoyant force, F_B

Now, Force of buoyant $F_B =$ Force of buoyancy of water + Force of buoyancy of mercury

$=$ Weight of water displaced by body + Weight of mercury displaced by body

$$= (\text{Density of water} \times g \times \text{Volume of water displaced})$$
$$+ (\text{Density of mercury} \times g \times \text{Volume of mercury displaced})$$

$$\rho \times g \times V = 1000 \times g \times 0.7\,V + 13.6 \times 1000 \times g \times 0.3\,V$$
$$\rho = 700 + 4080$$
$$\rho = 4780 \text{ kg/m}^3$$

$\therefore$ Density of metallic body = 4780 kg/m^3.

■ **Problem 4.5:** *A wooden cylinder of diameter 'd' and length '2d' floats in water with its axis vertical. Is the equilibrium stable? Locate the meta-centre with reference to water surface. Specific gravity of wood is 0.60.*

Solution:

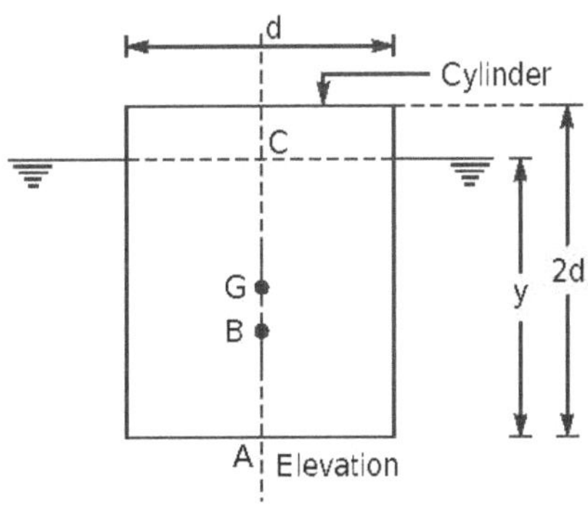

Fig. 4.11

Weight of water displaced by the cylinder = Weight of cylinder

$$\text{Volume of water displaced} \times 9.81 \times 1000 = \frac{\pi}{4}d^2 \times 2d \times 0.6 \times 9.81 \times 1000$$

$\therefore$ Volume of water displaced = $0.942\,d^3$

$$\therefore \quad \text{Depth of immersion, } y = \frac{\text{Volume of water displaced}}{c/s \text{ Area of cylinder}}$$

$$y = \frac{0.942\,d^3}{\frac{\pi}{4}d^2}$$

$$y = 1.2d$$

$$\therefore \quad AB = \frac{y}{2} = 0.6d$$

$$\therefore \quad BG = AG - AB = d - 0.6d = 0.4d$$

$$GM = \frac{I}{V} - BG$$

$$= \frac{\frac{\pi}{64} d^4}{0.942 d^3} - 0.4 d$$

$$= 0.0521d - 0.4d$$

$$GM = -0.348d$$

Metacentric height, GM is –ve, *i.e.*, M lies below G and hence the cylinder is in unstable equilibrium.

The location of metacentre below water surface $= 0.6d - 0.0521d$

$$= 0.548d.$$

■ **Problem 4.6:** *A block of wood has a cross-section 50 cm × 50 cm in plan and the height 'h'. It floats vertically in water. If the specific gravity of wood is 0.7. Find the maximum height of the block so that it can remain in stable equilibrium.*

Solution:

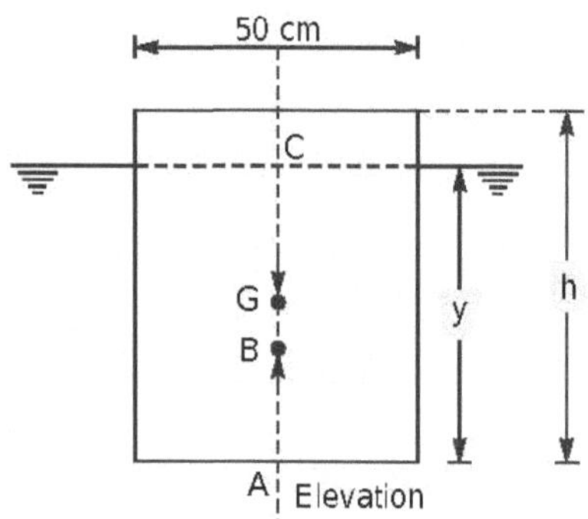

Fig. 4.12

Weight of wooden block = Weight of water displaced

$$0.5 \times 0.5 \times h \times 0.7 \times 1000 \times 9.81 = 0.5 \times 0.5 \times y \times 1000 \times 9.81$$

$$h \times 0.7 = y$$

$$\therefore \quad y = 0.7\, h \qquad \text{...}(i)$$

Here,

$$AG = 0.5\, h$$

and

$$AB = \frac{y}{2} = \frac{0.7h}{2} = 0.35\, h$$

$$\therefore \quad BG = AG - AB$$

$$= 0.5\, h - 0.35\, h$$

$$BG = 0.15h$$

Metacentric height, $GM = \dfrac{I}{V} - BG$

$$GM = \frac{\frac{0.5 \times 0.5^3}{12}}{0.5 \times 0.5 \times 0.7h} = 0.15h$$

$$GM = \frac{0.03}{h} - 0.15h$$

The stable equilibrium will attain when $GM > 0$.

The block will remain in equilibrium with the condition of maximum possible height h, when neutral equilibrium exists.

$\therefore \quad GM = 0$

$\therefore \quad \frac{0.03}{h} - 0.15h = 0$

$\therefore \quad 0.15h^2 = 0.03$

$$h^2 = \frac{0.03}{0.15}$$

$$h = 0.447 \text{ m.}$$

■ **Problem 4.7:** *A body has the cylindrical upper portion of 4 m diameter and 2 m deep. The lower portion is a curved on which displaces a volume of 0.9 m³ of water. The centre of buoyancy of the curved portion is at a distance of 2.10 m below the top of the cylinder. The centre of gravity of the whole body is 1.5 m below the top of the cylinder. The total displacement of water is 4.5 tonnes. Find the metacentric height of the body.*

Solution:

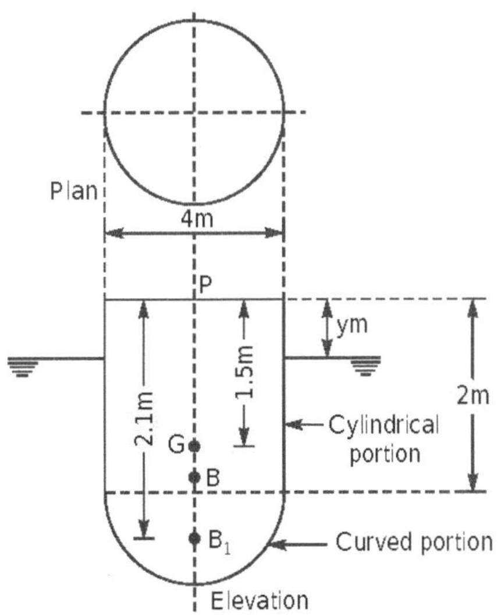

Fig. 4.13

Let $\quad B_1$ = Centre of buoyancy of curved portion

$PG = 1.5$ m

$$PB_1 = 2.1 \text{ m}$$

Now, Let $\quad y$ = height of body above water surface.

$$\begin{pmatrix}\text{Total weight of water} \\ \text{displaced by body}\end{pmatrix} = (\text{Weight density of water}) \times (\text{Volume of water displaced})$$

$$4.5 \times 1000 = 1000 \times \text{Volume of body in water}$$

$$= 1000 \times \begin{bmatrix}\text{Volume of} \\ \text{cylindrical portion} + \text{Volume of} \\ \text{curved portion}\end{bmatrix}$$

$$4.5 \times 1000 = 1000\left[\frac{\pi}{4}D^2 \times (2-y) + 0.9\right]$$

$$4.5 = \frac{\pi}{4} \times 4^2\ (2-y) + 0.9$$

$$12.566(2-y) = 3.6$$

$$y = 1.71 \text{ m}$$

Let B_2 is centre of buoyancy of cylindrical portion.

$$\therefore \quad PB_2 = y + \frac{2-y}{2}$$

$$= 1.71 + \frac{2-1.71}{2}$$

$$PB_2 = 1.85 \text{ m}$$

Now, to calculate distance PB:

$$PB = \frac{\begin{pmatrix}\text{Volume of} \\ \text{curved portion} \times PB_1\end{pmatrix} + \begin{pmatrix}\text{Volume of cylindrical} \\ \text{portion in water} \times PB_2\end{pmatrix}}{\text{Volume of water displaced}}$$

$$= \frac{0.9 \times 2.1 + \frac{\pi}{4} \times (4)^2 \times (2-1.71) \times 1.85}{0.9 + \frac{\pi}{4} \times 4^2\ (2-1.71)}$$

$$PB = \frac{8.63}{4.544} = 1.8995$$

$$\therefore \quad BG = PB - PG = 1.8995 - 1.5 = 0.3995 \text{ m}$$

$$\therefore \quad \text{Metacentric height, } GM = \frac{I}{V} - BG$$

$$= \frac{\frac{\pi}{64} \times 4^4}{4.5} - 0.3995$$

$$GM = 2.393 \text{ m.} \qquad \text{...(Ans.)}$$

■ **Problem 4.8:** *A solid cylinder 10 cm diameter and 40 cm long is made of two materials. The bottom 1 cm is of material of sp. gr. 6.5 and the portion above of sp. gr. 0.6. Does the cylinder float vertically in water of sp. wt. 1000 kg/m³?*

Solution:

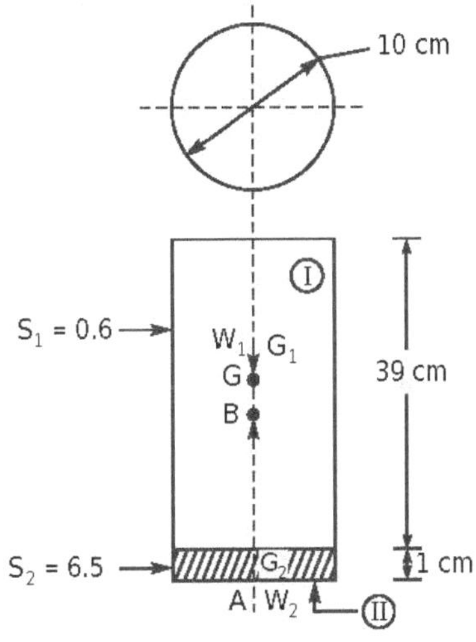

Fig. 4.14

To float the body vertically in water, the metacentric height, *GM* should be positive. To know the *GM*, the location of *G* and *B* are to be determined for whole body.

Now,

$$AG = \frac{W_1 \times AG_1 + W_2 \times AG_2}{W_1 + W_2}$$

$$= \frac{\left[\frac{\pi}{4} \times D^2 \times 39 \times 0.6 \times \left(1.0 + \frac{39}{2}\right)\right] + \left[\frac{\pi}{4} \times D^2 \times 1.0 \times 6.5 \times \frac{1.0}{2}\right]}{\left(\frac{\pi}{4} \times D^2 \times 39 \times 0.6\right) + \left(\frac{\pi}{4} \times D^2 \times 1 \times 6.5\right)}$$

$$= \frac{(39 \times 0.6 \times 20.5) + (1 \times 6.5 \times 0.5)}{(39 \times 0.6) + (1 \times 6.5)}$$

$$AG = \frac{479.7 + 3.25}{23.4 + 6.5}$$

$$AG = \frac{482.95}{29.9} = 16.15 \text{ cm}$$

To find the distance of centre of buoyancy, *AB*.

Now, Let us assume depth of immersion of cylinder as '*h*' cm.

∴ Weight of cylinder = Weight of water displaced

$$\left(\frac{\pi}{4}\times D^2\times\frac{39}{100}\times1000\times0.6\right)+\left(\frac{\pi}{4}\times D^2\times\frac{1.0}{100}\times1000\times6.5\right)=\frac{\pi}{4}\times D^2\times\frac{h}{100}\times1000$$

$\therefore\ 39\times0.6+1.0\times6.5=h$

$$\therefore\qquad h=29.9\text{ cm}$$

$$\therefore\qquad AB=\frac{h}{2}=\frac{29.9}{2}=14.95\text{ cm}$$

$$\therefore\qquad BG=AG-AB=16.15-14.95=1.2\text{ cm}$$

Now,
$$GM=\frac{I}{V}-BG$$

$$\therefore\qquad I=\frac{\pi}{64}\times D^4=\frac{\pi}{64}\times(10)^4=490.87\text{ cm}^4$$

$$V=\frac{\pi}{4}\times D^2\times h=\frac{\pi}{4}\times(10)^2\times29.9=2348.34\text{ cm}^3$$

$$\therefore\qquad GM=\frac{490.87}{2348.34}-1.2$$

$$=0.209-1.2$$

$$GM=-0.991\text{ cm}$$

Here –ve sign, indicates that metacentre, M is below centre of gravity, G. Hence the cylinder is in unstable equilibrium and will not float vertically in water.

■ **Problem 4.9:** *A solid cone of diameter 'D' and height 'h' is floating vertically in water with its apex below the base. The semicone is* α *and the specific gravity of material of cone is 'S' prove that the depth of centre of gravity of cone below the free surface of water is given by the expression* $\dfrac{D}{2\tan\alpha}\left(S^{1/3}-\dfrac{3}{4}\right)$.

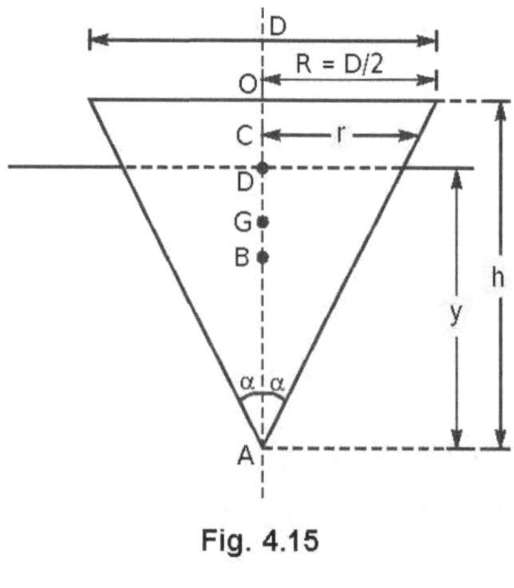

Fig. 4.15

Solution:

$$\tan\alpha = \frac{R}{h}$$

$$\therefore \quad h = \frac{R}{\tan\alpha}$$

$$h = \frac{D}{2\tan\alpha}$$

For equilibrium condition

Weight of body = Weight of liquid displaced

$$\frac{1}{3}\pi R^2 h \times S \times w = \frac{1}{3}\pi r^2 \times y \times w$$

$$R^2 hS = r^2 y$$

$$y = \frac{R^2}{r^2} hS$$

From geometry, $\dfrac{R}{r} = \dfrac{h}{y}$

$$y = \frac{h^2}{y^2} hS$$

$$y^3 = Sh^3$$

$$y = S^{1/3} h$$

Now depth of centre of gravity from free surface

$$DG = \frac{h}{4} - (h - y)$$

$$= y - \frac{3}{4}h$$

$$= S^{1/3}h - \frac{3}{4}h$$

$$= h\left(S^{1/3} - \frac{3}{4}\right)$$

$$= \frac{R}{\tan\alpha}\left(S^{1/3} - \frac{3}{4}\right)$$

$$DG = \frac{D}{2\tan\alpha}\left(S^{1/3} - \frac{3}{4}\right). \qquad \text{...(Ans.)}$$

■ **Problem 4.10:** *A right solid cone with apex angle 60° is having density "K" times the density of liquid in which it floats with its apex downwards. Determine what range of "K" is consistent with stable equilibrium.*

Solution:

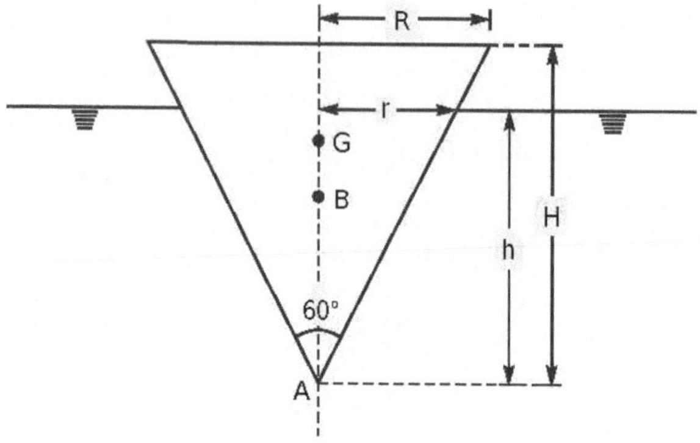

Fig. 4.16

Point A is the apex of the right circular cone of height H and base radius R. Let 'h' is the depth of immersion and 'r' radius at water surface.

$$w = \text{weight density of liquid}$$

$\therefore$ $$Kw = \text{weight density of cone}$$

From geometry,

$$\frac{H}{h} = \frac{R}{r}$$

and $$\tan 30 = \frac{r}{h} = \frac{R}{H}$$

$$r = \frac{h}{\sqrt{3}} \text{ and } R = \frac{H}{\sqrt{3}}$$

Also, we know $AG = \frac{3}{4}H$ and $AB = \frac{3}{4}h$ for right circular cone.

For equilibrium condition

Weight of body = Weight of liquid displaced

$$\frac{1}{3}\pi R^2 H.Kw = \frac{1}{3}\pi r^2 h.w$$

$$R^2HK = r^2h$$

$$h = \frac{R^2}{r^2}HK$$

$$h = \frac{R^2}{h^2}HK$$

$$\therefore \qquad h^3 = KH^3$$

$$\therefore \qquad h = K^{1/3}H$$

$$AB = \frac{3}{4}h = \frac{3}{4}K^{1/3}H$$

Now, $$AG = \frac{3}{4}H \text{ and } AB = \frac{3}{4}h$$

$$\therefore \qquad BG = AG - AB$$

$$= \frac{3}{4}H - \frac{3}{4}h$$

$$= \frac{3}{4}(H - h)$$

Metacentric height, $GM = \dfrac{I}{V} - BG$

$$GM = \frac{\frac{\pi r^4}{4}}{\frac{1}{3}\pi r^2 h} - \frac{3}{4}(H - h)$$

$$= \frac{3}{4}\frac{r^2}{h} - \frac{3}{4}(H - h)$$

$$= \frac{3}{4}\frac{h^2}{3h} - \frac{3}{4}(H - h) \qquad \left(\text{Since } r = \frac{h}{\sqrt{3}}\right)$$

$$= \frac{3}{4}\frac{h}{3} - \frac{3}{4}(H - h)$$

$$= \frac{3}{4}\frac{K^{1/3}H}{3} - \frac{3}{4}(H - K^{1/3}H)$$

$$= \frac{3}{4}H\left(\frac{K^{1/3}}{3} - 1 + K^{1/3}\right)$$

$$= \frac{3}{4}H\left(\frac{4K^{1/3} - 3}{3}\right)$$

$$GM = \frac{H}{4}(4K^{1/3} - 3)$$

For stable equilibrium, $GM > 0$

$$\therefore \qquad \frac{H}{4}(4K^{1/3} - 3) > 0$$

$$\therefore \quad 4K^{1/3} - 3 > 0$$

$$K^{1/3} > \frac{3}{4} \quad \therefore \quad K > \left(\frac{3}{4}\right)^{4/3}$$

$$K > 0.422$$

For the body to float $K < 1$ $\therefore$ Range of values of K is from 0.422 to 1.0.

4.7.3 Experimental Method for Determination of Metacentric Height

Consider a body (ship or boat) floating in water as shown in Fig. 4.17 (*a*). Let w be a moveable weight placed on the top surface of the body (deck) at the centre and W be the total weight of body including w. Let centre of gravity and centre of buoyancy be at G and B respectively in equilibrium position of the body. Now the weight w be moved towards right through a distance x on the top surface of the body so that it gets tilted through small angle θ. The angle θ, called as angle of heel may be measured by using plumb line or pendulum and the horizontal scale, both attached to the body. As the weight w moves through distance x, the centre of gravity of the body shifts from G to G_1 and also centre of buoyancy from B to B_1. The moment caused by the shift of load w must be equal to the moment caused due to shift of centre of gravity.

$$\therefore \quad w \,.\, x = W \times GG_1$$

$$= W \times GM \tan \theta$$

$$\therefore \quad GM = \frac{wx}{W \tan \theta}$$

Fig. 4.17 Metacentric height

The metacentric height for a body which is constructed is determined by using this method.

4.7.4 Solved Problems

■ **Problem 4.11:** *A body has a displacement of 28,00,000 kg of fresh water when it floats with its axis vertical. A mass of 20,000 kg placed centrally moved through a distance of 12 m across the deck, causing lower end of pendulum 3.2 long to more 25 cm horizontally. Find the metacentric height.*

Solution:

$$\text{Weight of body} = W = 28{,}00{,}000 \text{ kg}$$

and $$w = 20{,}000 \text{ kg}$$

$$\tan\theta = \frac{0.25}{3.2} = 0.078$$

$$GM = \frac{wx}{W\tan\theta}$$

$$= \frac{20{,}000 \times 12}{28{,}00{,}000 \times 0.078}$$

$$= 1.0989$$

$$GM \cong 1.1 \text{ m.}$$

Exercises

1. A wooden block 2.4 m wide, 1.5 m deep and 6 m long floats in water. Find the volume of water displaced and position of centre of buoyancy. Assume density of wood as 650 kg/m^3. (**Ans.** V = 14.04 m^3, Centre of buoyancy from base = 0.4875 m)
2. Calculate specific gravity of concrete block when it weights 48 kg in air and 30 kg in water. (**Ans.** Specific gravity of concrete = 2.667)
3. A uniform body of size 4 m × 3 m and 1.4 m deep floats in water. What is the weight of the body if depth of immersion is 1.0 m? Compute the density of the body material and its metacentric height. (**Ans.** W = 117.72 kN, ρ_m = 714 kg/m^3, GM = 0.707 m)
4. A block of wood has a cross-section 60 cm × 60 cm in plan and the height 'h'. It floats vertically in water. If the specific gravity of wood is 0.8. Find the maximum height of the block so as to remain in stable equilibrium. (**Ans.** h = 61.2 cm)
5. A cylinder of diameter 'D' length L and having specific gravity 's' floats in water. Show that for stable equilibrium with its axis vertical.
$$L < \frac{D}{\sqrt{8s(1-s)}}.$$
6. A cone of semivertex angle 'θ' and made up of material having specific gravity 's' floats in water with its apex downwards. Show that for stable equilibrium.
$$\theta = \cos^{-1}(s^{1/6}).$$
7. A cone of base diameter 'D' and height 'H' floats in water with its axis vertical and vertex downwards. The cone is made up of material having specific gravity 's'. Show that for stable equilibrium.
$$H < \frac{D}{2}\left(\frac{s^{1/3}}{1-s^{1/3}}\right)^{1/2}.$$

8. A wooden cone weighing 30 kg floats in liquid of specific gravity 0.9 with its apex below the free surface of liquid. Taking specific gravities of wood and steel 0.8 and 8 respectively, calculate weight of steel which must be suspended from the apex of the cone by a thread to just submerge the cone. (**Ans.** $W_{steel} = 33.3$ kg)
9. A cylindrical buoy 3 m long and weighing 40 kg floats vertically in water so that it is immersed upto 2 m height. When the same buoy was placed in a liquid having specific gravity 's', the depth of immersion was 1.6 m. Find the specific gravities 's' and that of buoy. (**Ans.** $s = 1.25$, Specific Gravity of buoy = 0.666)
10. A solid cylinder of diameter 4 m has a height of 3 m. Determine its stability when floating in water with its axis vertical. Specific gravity of cylinder material is 0.6. (**Ans.** Unsuitable equilibrium)
11. Show that a cylindrical buoy 1.2 meter diameter and 2 meter high weighing 1200 kg will not float vertically in water. Find the tension necessary in a vertical anchor chain attached to the centre of the base so that to keep the cylinder vertical, water weighs 1025 kg/m^3. (**Ans.** $T = 393$ kg)
12. A cube of side 2 m floats with half its volume immersed and its bottom face horizontal. The centre of gravity of the cube is 60 cm below the geometric centre in a vertical line passing through it. A weight equal to $\frac{1}{20}$ of the weight of the cube in placed of the middle point of one of the top edges of the cube. Find the angle through which cube will tilt due to additional weight. (**Ans.** $\theta = 7.78°$)
13. A wooden cylinder of mass density 600 kg/m^3 is required to float in a liquid of mass density 800 kg/m^3. Find the ratio of diameter 'd' and length 'l' of the cylinder in order that the cylinder can just float with its longitudinal axis vertical. (**Ans.** $\frac{d}{l} = 1.225$)
14. A pontoon of 1600 tonnes displacement is floating in water. A weight of 16 tonnes is moved through a distance of 8 m across the deck of pontoon, which tilts the pontoon through an angle of 6°. Find metacentric height of the pontoon. (**Ans.** $GM = 0.761$ m)
15. A ship weights 12,000 tonnes. The ships boats are filed on one side with 60 tonnes of water. The boats are at a mean distance of 10 m from centre of ship. If the angle of displacement is 2°16′. Calculate the metacentric height. (**Ans.** $GM = 1.267$ m)
16. A body has a displacement of 30,00,000 kg of fresh water when it floats with its axis vertical a mass of 21,000 kg placed at its centre moves through a distance of 14 m across the deck, which causes the lower end of pendulum 3.5 m long to more 28 cm horizontally. Find the metacentric height. (**Ans.** $GM = 1.125$ m)

❑❑❑

5

Fluids in Relative Equilibrium

5.1 INTRODUCTION

Consider a vessel partially filled with a fluid and subjected to a constant acceleration. In such a case there is no relative motion between fluid and vessel and hence law of hydrostatics can be used to find the fluid pressure. When this fluid with vessal is subjected to uniform horizontal, vertical and rotational motion then pressure is exerted by fluid due to different new position occupied by the fluid. This pressure can be determined as follows:

5.2 VESSEL CONTAINING LIQUID SUBJECTED TO UNIFORM HORIZONTAL ACCELERATION

Fig. 5.1 shows a vessel containing liquid moving in horizontal direction with acceleration a_x. Since the vessel is not accelerated in vertical direction, vertical force on the vessel is zero.

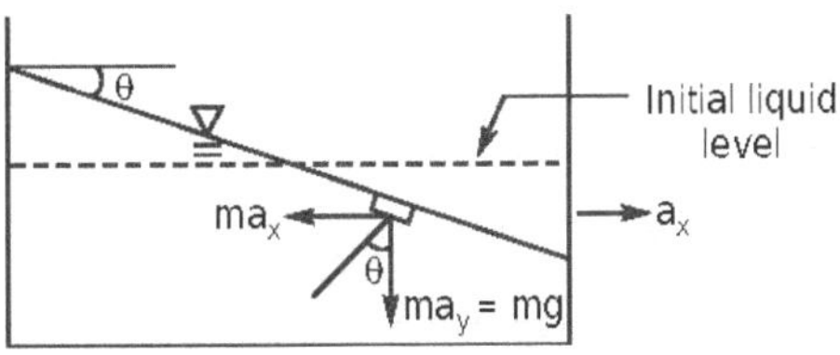

Fig. 5.1

Consider a small fluid element on the liquid surface of mass 'm' and let pressure on this element be 'F' then resolving the forces in horizontal and vertical direction.

$$F \sin \theta = ma_x \text{ and } F \cos \theta = mg \text{ respectively.}$$

Therefore $$\tan \theta = \frac{a_x}{g} \quad ...(5.1)$$

It should be noted that in the above case the pressure intensity varies vertically in the same way as fluid at rest and given by the expression

$$p = \gamma h \qquad ...(5.2)$$

where p = gauge pressure intensity in N/m^2

γ = specific weight in N/m^3

h = depth below the liquid surface where pressure is p.

Equation (5.2) can be written as

$$p_{\text{absolute}} = p_{\text{atmospheric}} + \gamma h \qquad ...(5.3)$$

5.2.1 Solved Problems

■ **Problem 5.1:** *A container having dimensions 7 m × 2 m and 2.5 m deep contains water 1.25 m deep. The container accelerated at 3 m/sec^2 in the horizontal direction. Find*

(a) Inclination of free surface with horizontal.

(b) Pressure intensities at A, B, C.

(c) Total force due to water on faces AD and CE of the container.

Solution:

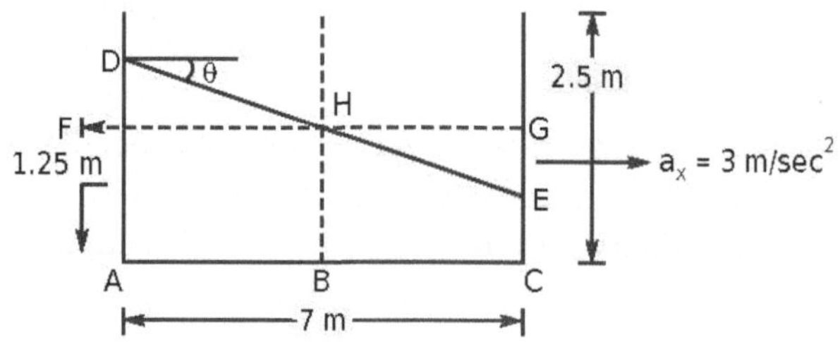

Fig. 5.2

(*a*) By using equation (5.1)

$$\tan\theta = \frac{a_x}{g}$$

$$\tan\theta = \frac{3}{9.81} = 0.3058$$

$\therefore \qquad \theta = 17°0'13''$

(*b*) From Fig. 5.2, $\overline{DF} = \overline{GE} = \dfrac{7\tan\theta}{2} = \dfrac{7\tan(17°0'13'')}{2}$

$= 1.07$ m

Also $\qquad \overline{AD} = \overline{AF} + \overline{FD} = 1.25 + 1.07 = 2.32$ m

and $\qquad \overline{CE} = \overline{CG} - \overline{EG} = 1.25 - 1.07 = 0.18$ m

Pressure intensity at point A

$$p_A = \gamma h$$

$$= \gamma \times \overline{AD}$$
$$= 9810 \times 2.32 = 22759.2 \text{ N/m}^2$$

Pressure intensity at point C

$$p_C = \gamma h$$
$$= \gamma \times \overline{CE}$$
$$= 9810 \times 0.18 = 1765.8 \text{ N/m}^2$$

Pressure intensity at point B

$$p_B = \gamma h$$
$$= \gamma \times \overline{BH}$$
$$= 9810 \times \left(\frac{2.32 + 0.18}{2}\right) = 12262.5 \text{ N/m}^2$$

(*c*) Total force on $\overline{AD}$ (Fig. 5.2) (*a*))

$$P_{AD} = \frac{1}{2} \times \gamma \times \overline{AD} \times \overline{AD} \times \text{width of container}$$
$$= \frac{1}{2} \times 9810 \times 2.32^2 \times 2$$
$$= 52801.344 \text{ N}$$

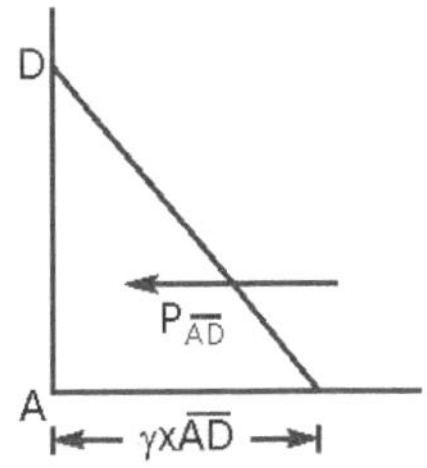

Fig. 5.2 (*a*)

Total force on $\overline{CE}$ (Fig. 5.2 (*b*))

$$P_{\overline{CE}} = \frac{1}{2} \times \gamma \times \overline{CE} \times \overline{CE} \times \text{width of container}$$
$$= \frac{1}{2} \times 9810 \times 0.18 \times 0.18 \times 2$$
$$= 317.844 \text{ N.}$$

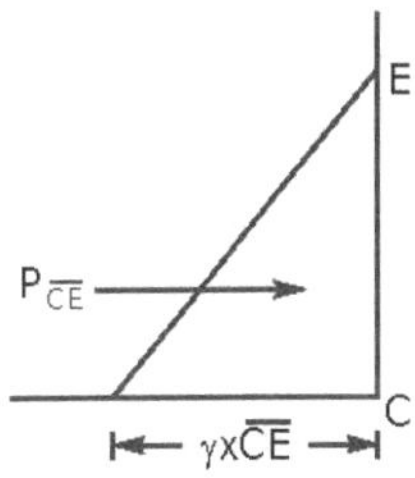

Fig. 5.2 (*b*)

5.3 VESSEL CONTAINING LIQUID SUBJECTED TO UNIFORM VERTICAL ACCELERATION

Fig. 5.3 shows vessel containing liquid and moving upwards with uniform acceleration a_y.

Consider an elementary prism of liquid of cross sectional dA and of height 'h' as shown in Fig. 5.3 and subjected to pressure intensity p. Let w is the weight of prism. The liquid in the tank will have a free horizontal surface but the pressure intensity at any point is different than static pressure.

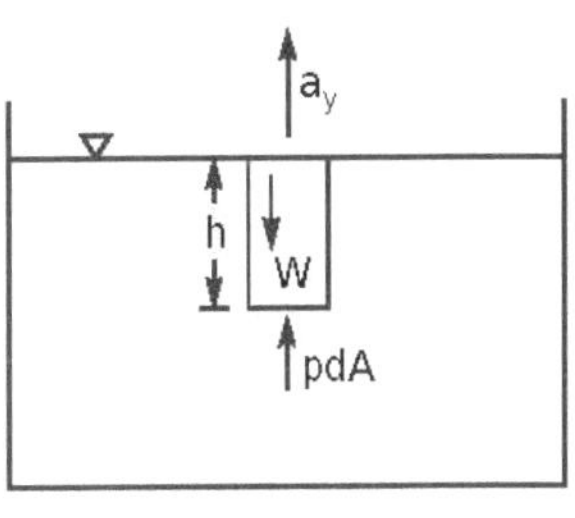

Fig. 5.3

Using Newton's second law of motion

$$\Sigma F_y = \text{Mass} \times \text{acceleration in } y \text{ direction}$$
$$= m \times a_y$$
$$pdA - W = \rho \times \text{volume of elementary prism} \times a_y$$

$$\therefore \quad pdA - \gamma hdA = \frac{\gamma}{g} \times hdA \times a_y$$

$$p = \gamma h\left(1+\frac{a_y}{g}\right) \quad \text{...(5.4)}$$

Similarly for a vessel moving in downward direction

$$p = \gamma h\left(1-\frac{a_y}{y}\right) \quad \text{...(5.5)}$$

■ **Problem 5.2:** *A container having dimensions 7 m × 2 m and 2.5 m deep contains water 1.25 m deep. The container is accelerated at 3 m/sec² in the vertically upward direction. Find the total force due to water on the side and bottom of the container.*

Solution:

Pressure intensity at the top = zero

Pressure intensity at the bottom

$$= p = \gamma h\left(1+\frac{a_y}{g}\right)$$

$$= 9810 \times 1.25\left(1+\frac{3}{9.81}\right)$$

$$= 16012.5 \text{ N/m}^2$$

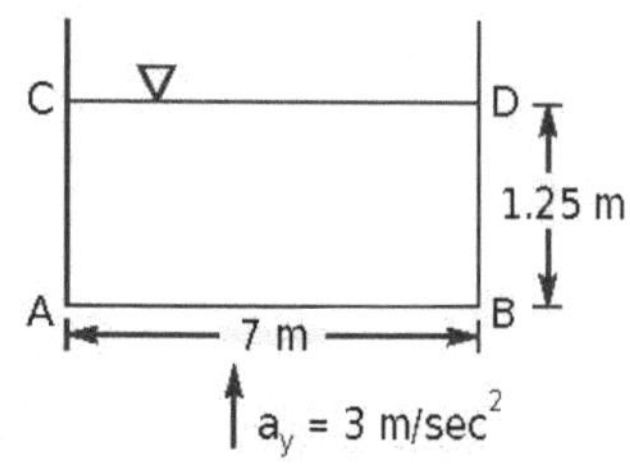

Fig. 5.4

$\therefore$ Average pressure intensity on the sides

$$= \frac{0+16012.5}{2} = 8006.25 \text{ N/m}^2$$

Total force on each side = average pressure intensity × area

$$= 8006.25 \times 1.25 \times 2$$

$$= 20015.625 \text{ N}$$

Total force on bottom $= 16012.5 \times 7 \times 2 = 224175$ N.

5.4 VESSEL CONTAINING LIQUID SUBJECT TO UNIFORM ACCELERATION ALONG INCLINED PLANE (MOVING UP THE SLOPE)

Let the vessel is moving along the inclined plane with an acceleration '*a*'.

If '*a*' is resolved in *x* and *y* direction then we will get

$$a_x = a\cos\beta$$

and $$a_y = a\sin\beta$$

Now consider a small fluid element on the water surface of weight *mg* and let *F* is the force acting on this fluid element.

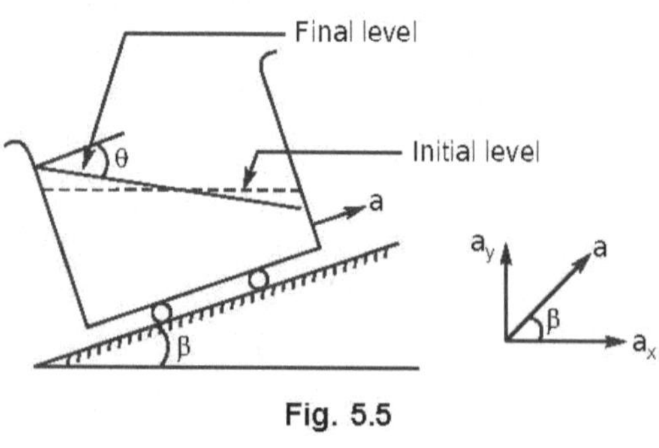

Fig. 5.5

Resolving the forces in x and y direction

$$F \sin \theta = ma_x$$

And $$F \cos \theta = ma_y + mg$$

Therefore $$\tan \theta = \frac{a_x}{a_y + g} \quad ...(5.6)$$

Similarly, when the vessel is moving down the slope

$$\tan \theta = \frac{a_x}{g - a_y} \quad ...(5.7)$$

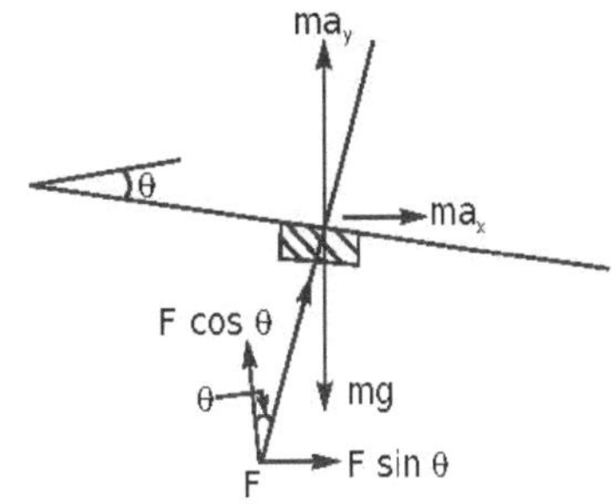

Fig. 5.6

■ **Problem 5.3:** *A container having dimensions 7 m × 2 m and 2.5 m deep contains water 1.25 m deep. The container moves with an acceleration 3 m/sec² up a 20° inclined plane. Find the inclination of water surface with a horizontal.*

Solution: Now using the relation

$$a_x = a \cos \beta = 3 \times \cos 20 = 2.819 \text{ m/sec}^2$$

and

$$a_y = a \sin \beta = 3 \times \sin 20 = 1.026 \text{ m/sec}^2$$

when the tank moves up the inclined plane using equation (5.6)

$$\tan \theta = \frac{a_x}{a_y + g} = \frac{2.819}{1.026 + 9.81} = 0.28$$

$$\theta = \tan^{-1} 0.28 = 15.64 = 15° \, 38' \, 32''$$

The inclination of water surface with horizontal is 15° 38′ 32″.

5.5 VESSEL CONTAINING LIQUID SUBJECTED TO CONSTANT ROTATION

5.5.1 Vessel Open to Atmosphere

Consider a open cylindrical tank partly filled with liquid and rotated about its vertical axis with a constant angular velocity 'ω' as shown in Fig. 5.7.

For any two points A and B on the free surface

$$Z_B - Z_A = \frac{\omega^2}{2g}(r_B^2 - r_A^2) \quad ...(5.8)$$

If the point A lies on the axis of rotation then $z_A = 0$, $r_A = 0$. The above equation becomes

$$z_B = \frac{\omega^2 r_B^2}{2g} \quad \text{...(5.9)}$$

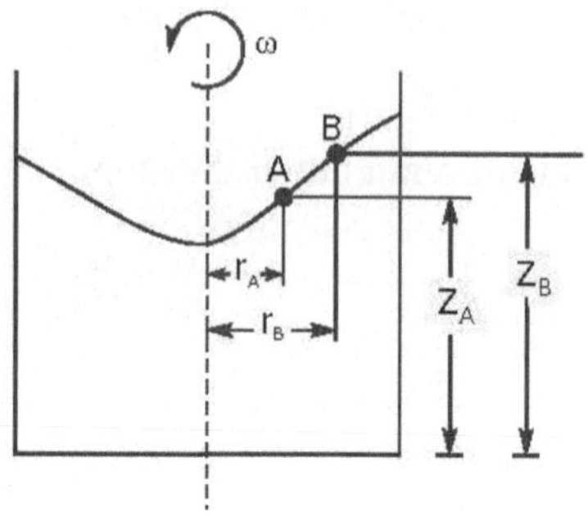

Fig. 5.7

This shows the free surface of the liquid is a parabolic.

In general equation (5.9) can be written as

$$z = \frac{\omega^2 r^2}{2g} \quad \text{...(5.10)}$$

(refer Fig. 5.8)

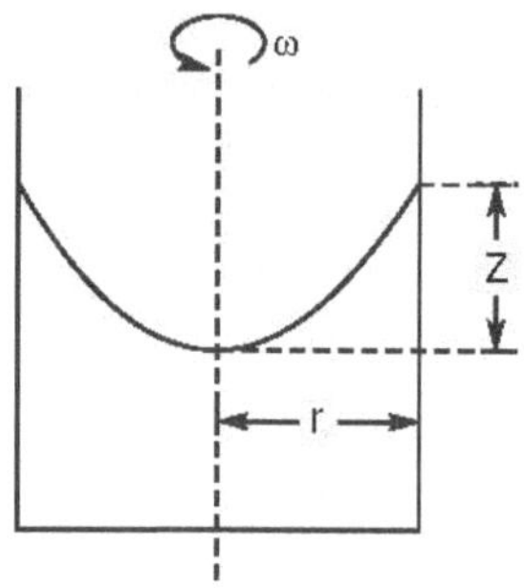

Fig. 5.8

Similarly if the axis of rotation is eccentric (refer Fig. 5.9).

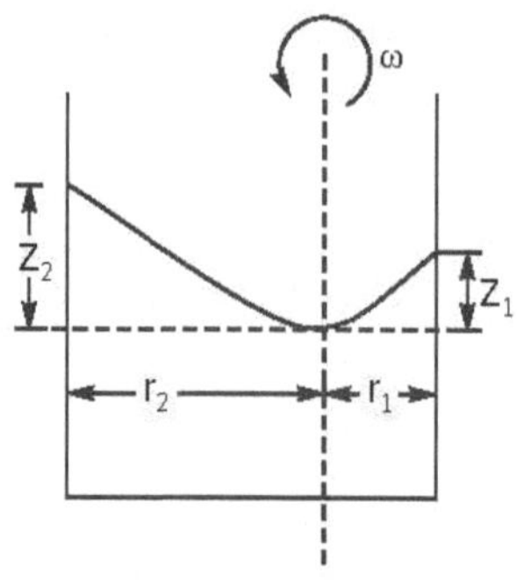

Fig. 5.9

$$z_1 = \frac{\omega^2 r_1^2}{2g} \text{ and } z_2 = \frac{\omega^2 r_2^2}{2g} \qquad ...(5.11)$$

■ **Problem 5.4:** *Show that for a vessel containing liquid subjected to constant rotation, the rise of liquid level at the wall is equal to the fall of liquid level at the axis of rotation.*

Solution:

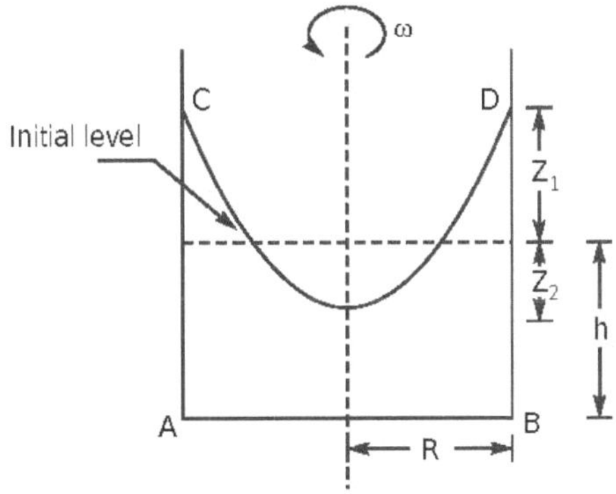

Fig. 5.10

Refer Fig. 5.10.

Volume of liquid before rotation

$$= \pi R^2 \times (h) = \pi R^2 h \qquad ...(1)$$

Volume of liquid after rotation

$$= \text{Volume } ABDC - \text{Volume of paraboloid}$$

$$= \pi R^2 (h + z_1) - \frac{\pi R^2}{2}(z_1 + z_2) \qquad ...(2)$$

Equating (1) and (2)

$$\pi R^2 h = \pi R^2 (h + z_1) - \frac{\pi R^2}{2}(z_1 + z_2)$$

$$\pi R^2 h = \pi R^2 h + \pi R^2 z_1 - \frac{\pi R^2}{2} z_1 - \frac{\pi R^2}{2} z_2$$

$$\frac{\pi R^2}{2} z_1 = \frac{\pi R^2}{2} z_2$$

$$\therefore \qquad z_1 = z_2$$

Hence it is proved that fall of liquid level at axis of rotation is equal to the rise of liquid level near the wall.

■ **Problem 5.5:** *An open circular tank of 30 cm diameter and 80 cm long and is filled with a water to a depth of 50 cm. What is maximum speed at which it can be rotated so that water just touches centre of bottom of the tank?*

Solution:

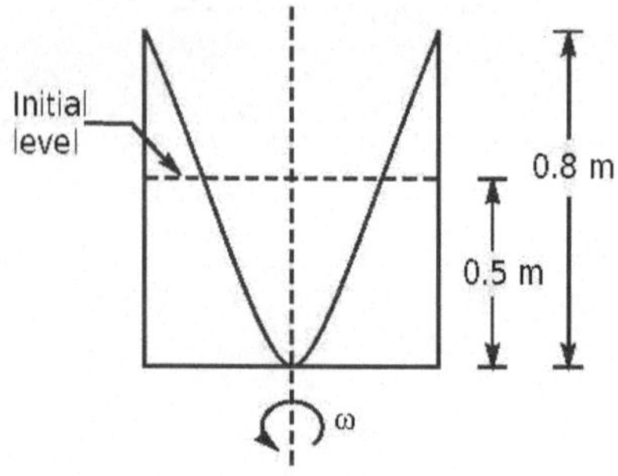

Fig. 5.11

Using a equation $z = \dfrac{\omega^2 R^2}{2g}$

$$0.8 = \frac{\omega^2 \times 0.15^2}{2 \times 9.81}$$

$$\omega = \sqrt{\frac{0.8 \times 2 \times 9.81}{0.15^2}}$$

$$= 26.41 \text{ rad/sec.}$$

Now $\omega = \dfrac{2\pi N}{60}$

$\therefore$ $N = \dfrac{60\omega}{2\pi} = \dfrac{60 \times 26.41}{2 \times \pi} = 252.197$ rpm.

■ **Problem 5.6:** *For the problem 5.5 find the height of paraboloid formed on free surface when the tank is rotated at a speed of 200 rpm.*

Solution:

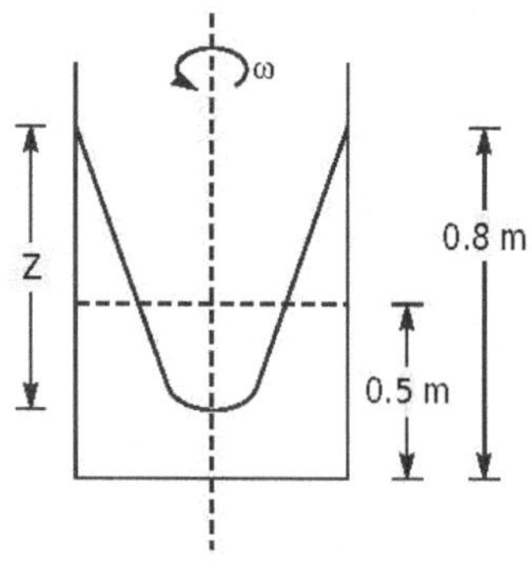

Fig. 5.12

$$\omega = \frac{2\pi N}{60} = \frac{2\pi \times 200}{60}$$

$$= 20.94 \text{ rad/sec.}$$

and $$z = \frac{\omega^2 R^2}{2g}$$

$$= \frac{20.94^2 \times 0.15^2}{2 \times 9.81} = 0.50 \text{ m.}$$

■ **Problem 5.7:** *For the problem 5.5 find the water spilled out when the tank is rotated at a speed of 300 rpm.*

Solution.

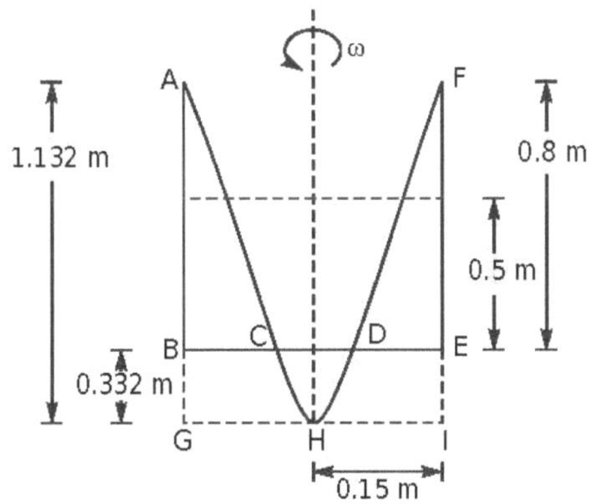

Fig. 5.13

$$\omega = \frac{2\pi N}{60}$$

$$= \frac{2\pi \times 300}{60}$$

$$= 31.42 \text{ rad/sec.}$$

$$z = \frac{\omega^2 R^2}{2g}$$

$$= \frac{31.42^2 \times 0.15^2}{2 \times 9.81}$$

$$= 1.132 \text{ m}$$

In this case height of paraboloid formed is greater than the height of cylinder and hence water will spill out.

Hence height of imaginary parabola

$$z_1 = 1.132 - 0.8 = 0.332$$

and radius of imaginary parabola

$$z_1 = \frac{\omega^2 R_1^2}{2g}. \quad \therefore \quad 0.332 = \frac{31.42^2 \times R_1^2}{2 \times 9.81}$$

$\therefore \quad R_1 = 0.08$ m

Volume of water before rotation $= \pi \times 0.15^2 \times 0.5 = 0.035$ m^3

Volume of water left in tank after rotation = Volume of ABC + Volume of FDE

= Volume $ABEF$ – Volume $ACDF$

= Volume $ABEF$ – [Volume of paraboloid AHF – Volume of paraboloid CHD]

$$= \pi \times R^2 \times \text{height tank} - \left[\frac{1}{2}\pi R^2 z - \frac{1}{2}\pi R_1^2 z_1\right]$$

$$= \pi \times 0.15^2 \times 0.8 - \left[\frac{1}{2} \times \pi \times 0.15^2 \times 1.132 - \frac{1}{2} \times \pi \times 0.08^2 \times 0.332\right]$$

$= 0.0565 - [0.040 - 3.3376 \times 10^{-3}]$

$= 0.0198$ m^3

Therefore water spilled out = Volume of water before rotation – Volume of water left in tank after rotation

$= 0.035 - 0.0198 = 0.0152$ m^3

Area of bottom exposed to atmosphere

$= \pi R_1^2 = \pi \times 0.08^2 = 0.02$ m^2.

5.5.2 Closed Vessels

If closed cylindrical vessel is rotated about its vertical axis following type of paraboloid may from. Refer Fig. 5.14.

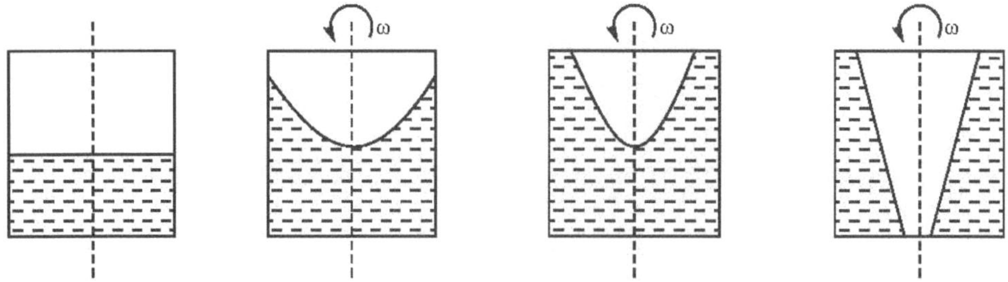

Fig. 5.14

For a closed vessel following relation should be noted.

Volume of air before rotation = Volume of air after rotation = Volume of paraboloid formed.

■ **Problem 5.8:** *A cylindrical tank closed at both the ends of size 30 cm radius and 100 cm high contains water to a height of 70 cm. If this is rotated at a speed of 80 rpm find the height of paraboloid formed on free surface of water.*

Solution.

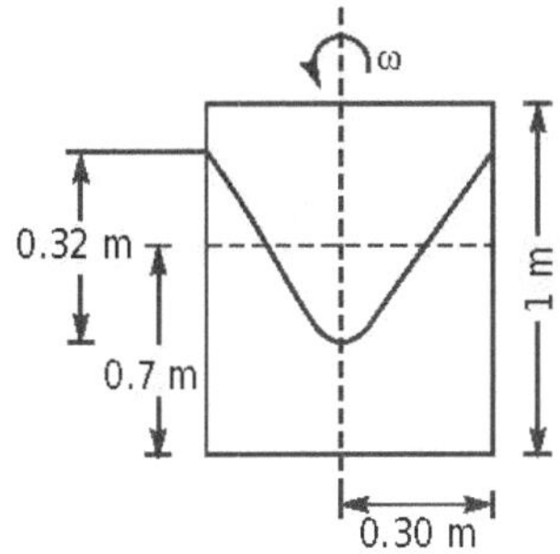

Fig. 5.15

$$\omega = \frac{2\pi N}{60}$$

$$= \frac{2\pi \times 80}{60} = 8.378 \text{ rad/sec.}$$

$$z = \frac{\omega^2 R^2}{2g}$$

$$= \frac{8.378 \times 0.3^2}{2 \times 9.81} = 0.32 \text{ m.}$$

■ **Problem 5.9**: *For the problem 5.8 find the speed of rotation of tank when axial depth of water is zero.*

Solution.

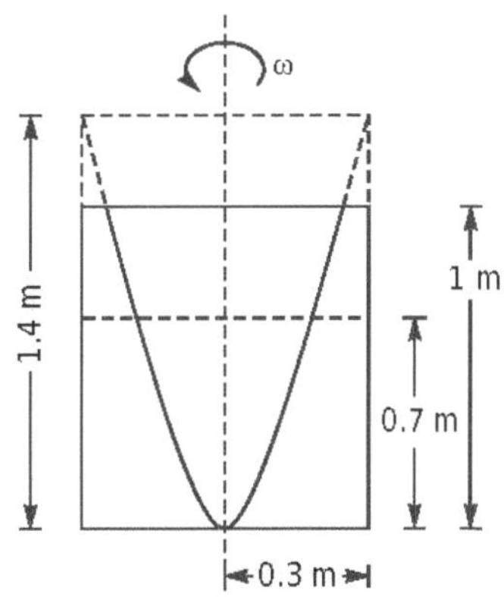

Fig. 5.16

Let the vessel would not have been closed at the top then height of paraboloid formed so that it will touch the bottom at axis of rotation.

$$Z = 2 \times 0.7 = 1.4 \text{ m}$$

(Refer the result of problem No. 5.4)

$$Z = \frac{\omega^2 R^2}{2g}$$

$$1.4 = \frac{\omega^2 \times 0.3^2}{2 \times 9.81}$$

$\therefore$
$$\omega = \sqrt{\frac{1.4 \times 2 \times 9.81}{0.3^2}} = 17.46 \text{ rad/sec.}$$

and
$$\omega = \frac{2\pi N}{60}$$

$\therefore$
$$\omega = \frac{60\omega}{2\pi} = \frac{60 \times 17.46}{2 \times \pi}$$
$$= 166.73 \text{ rpm.}$$

■ **Problem 5.10**: *For the problem 5.8 find the area of bottom exposed for a rotational speed of 200 rpm.*

Solution:

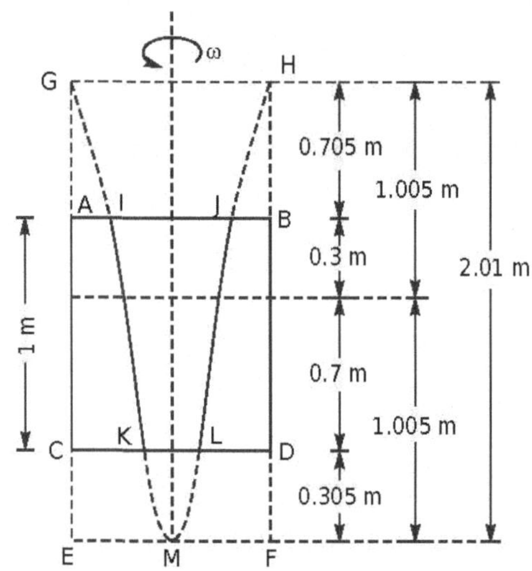

Fig. 5.17

Let the vessel would not have been closed at the top. Then height of paraboloid formed

$$Z = \frac{\omega^2 R^2}{2g}$$

here
$$\omega = \frac{2\pi N}{60} = \frac{2\pi \times 200}{60}$$
$$= 20.94 \text{ rad/sec.}$$

Put in (1) $$Z = \frac{20.94^2 \times 0.3^2}{2 \times 9.81} = 2.01 \text{ m}$$

Now near the ends the paraboloid will rise by $\frac{2.01}{2} = 1.005$ m and at axis of rotation it will move down by 1.005 m with relative to initial water level (Refer the result of problem 5.4)

Refer Fig. 5.17.

Consider paraboloid *KLM*

$$Z = \frac{\omega^2 r^2}{2g} \quad \text{here } r = \frac{KL}{2}$$

$$0.305 = \frac{20.94^2 \times r^2}{2 \times 9.81}$$

$$r = \sqrt{\frac{0.305 \times 2 \times 9.81}{20.94^2}} = 0.1168 \text{ m} = 11.69$$

Therefore the area of bottom exposed $= \pi r^2 = \pi \times 0.1168^2 = 0.0429 \text{ m}^2$.

Exercises

1. A tank having dimensions 10 m × 3 m × 2 m deep contains water 1.25 m deep. The container accelerated at 4 m/sec^2 in the horizontal direction. Find the inclination of free surface with horizontal. **(Ans.** 22°, 10′, 59″**)**
2. A container 7 m × 3 m × 2.5 m deep is filled with water to a depth of 1 m. Find the horizontal acceleration of a container so that the bottom front end of the tank is just exposed. **(Ans.** 2.8 m/sec^2**)**
3. A container 7 m × 3 m × 1.5 m deep is filled with water to a depth of 1 m. Find the horizontal acceleration of the container so that water just starts spilling out the container. **(Ans.** 1.4 m/sec^2**)**
4. For a problem no. 3, find the horizontal acceleration of a container so that the bottom front end of the tank is just exposed. **(Ans.** 2.102 m/sec^2**)**
5. A tank 7 m × 3 m × 2.5 m deep is completely filled with water. It is accelerated in the horizontal direction at the rate of 3 m/sec^2 how many litres of water is spilled out? **(Ans.** 22.477 m^3**)**
6. A container having dimensions 5 m × 2 m × 1.5 m deep contains water 1 m deep. The container is accelerated at 2.5 m/sec in the vertically downward direction. Find the total force due to water on the side and bottom of the container. **(Ans.** *F* on sides = 7310 N, *F* on bottom = 73100 N**)**

7. A container having dimensions 7 m × 2 m × 2.5 m deep contains water 1.25 m deep. The container moves with an acceleration 3 m/sec^2 down a 20° inclined plane. Find the inclination of water surface with a horizontal. **(Ans.** 17°, 47′, 34″)
8. An open circular tank of 50 cm diameter and 1.2 m long is completely filled with a water to a depth of 75 cm. What is maximum speed at which it can be rotated so that water depth at the centre of the bottom of tank reaches to zero. **(Ans.** 185.34 rpm)
9. For the problem no. 8, find the water retained in the tank when it is rotated at a speed of 200 rpm. **(Ans.** 0.1011 m^3)
10. A cylindrical tank closed at both the ends of size 30 cm radius and 100 cm high contains water to a height of 70 cm. If the height of the paraboloid formed on free surface of water is 0.32 m find the rotational speed of the tank. **(Ans.** 80 rpm)
11. For the problem no. 10, if the speed of rotation of tank is 166.73 rpm. Find the depth of water at the axis of rotation. **(Ans.** zero)

❑❑❑

6

Kinematics of Fluid Flow

6.1 INTRODUCTION

The kinematics of fluid flow is the branch of science which deals with velocity and acceleration neglecting the forces causing the flow.

6.2 CLASSIFICATION OF FLUID FLOW

6.2.1 Steady and Unsteady Flow

Steady flow is defined as a flow in which fluid and flow characteristics such as velocity, pressure, density, acceleration, etc. at a point do not change with time, thus for steady flow,

$$\left(\frac{\partial V}{\partial t}\right)_{x_0, y_0, z_0} = 0$$

$$\left(\frac{\partial p}{\partial t}\right)_{x_0, y_0, z_0} = 0$$

$$\left(\frac{\partial \rho}{\partial t}\right)_{x_0, y_0, z_0} = 0 \quad ...(6.1)$$

Here x_0, y_0 and z_0 refers to a fixed point in the fluid flow.

Ex: Flow through a pipe of uniform diameter with varying flow rate.

Unsteady flow is define as the flow in which one or more fluid and flow characteristics at a point changes with respect to time.

Thus for unsteady flow,

$$\left(\frac{\partial V}{\partial t}\right)_{x_0, y_0, z_0} \neq 0, \left(\frac{\partial p}{\partial t}\right)_{x_0, y_0, z_0} \neq 0,$$

$$\left(\frac{\partial \rho}{\partial t}\right)_{x_0,\, y_0,\, z_0} \neq 0, \text{ etc.} \qquad ...(6.2)$$

Ex: Flow through a pipe of uniform diameter with varying flow rate.

6.2.2 Uniform and Non-Uniform Flow

Uniform flow is defined as a flow in which the velocity vector at all point does not change with respect to space, thus, for uniform flow,

$$\left(\frac{\partial V}{\partial s}\right)_{t_0} = 0 \qquad ...(6.3)$$

Ex: Flow through a straight pipe of uniform diameter.

Now-uniform flow is that type of flow in which the velocity vector changes with respect to space, thus,

$$\left(\frac{\partial V}{\partial s}\right)_{t_0} \neq 0 \qquad ...(6.4)$$

Ex: Flow through a straight pipe of varying diameter.

In uniform flow streamlines are straight and parallel.

6.2.3 Rotational and Irrotational Flow

Rotational flow is defined as a flow in which a fluid particle while moving along a streamline also rotate about its mass centre. *Ex*: Tank filled with liquid and rotated about its vertical axis.

Irrotational flow is defined as a flow in which a fluid particle while moving along a streamline, do not rotate about its mass centre. *Ex*: Flow above drain hole of stationary tank.

6.2.4 Laminar and Turbulent Flow

Laminar flow is a flow in which it is assumed that fluid flow takes place in laminar *i.e.*, one layer moves over another layer and fluid particles moves along well defined paths. Laminar flow is also called as viscous flow. *Ex*: Ground water flow.

In a turbulent flow fluid particles are not moving along a well defined paths but in a random way. Also in turbulent flow eddies are formed which results into loss of energy. *Ex*: High velocity flow in large pipes.

Reynold's number is given by

$$R = \frac{\rho V D}{\mu} \qquad ...(6.5)$$

where D = Diameter of pipe in m

V = Velocity of flow in m/sec

ρ = Mass density in kN/m^3

μ = Dynamic viscosity in N sec./m^2

R = Reynold's number, no unit since it is a dimensionless number.

Fluid flow in conduit can be classified as:

(*a*) $R < 2000 \rightarrow$ Flow is laminar

(*b*) $R > 4000 \rightarrow$ Flow is turbulent

(*c*) $2000 < R < 4000 \rightarrow$ Flow is in transition stage or may be laminar or turbulent.

6.2.5 Compressible and Incompressible Flow

Compressible fluid flow is defined as a flow in which the density of a fluid changes with space.

i.e. $$\rho \neq \text{constant} \quad ...(6.6)$$

In incompressible fluid flow density is constant. *i.e.* ρ = constant.

6.3 ONE, TWO AND THREE DIMENSIONAL FLUID FLOW

6.3.1 One Dimensional Flow

In this type of flow, characteristics such as velocity, acceleration etc. are functions of time and one co-ordinate only.

Thus for one dimensional unsteady flow

$$u = f(x, t),\ v = 0,\ w = 0 \quad ...(6.7)$$

where u, v, w are the velocity components in x, y, z directions respectively.

If $$u = f(x) \text{ i.e. } u \text{ is not a function of time} \quad ...(6.8)$$

then it represents one dimensional steady flow.

6.3.2 Two Dimensional Flow

In this type of flow, the flow characteristics are functions of time and two co-ordinates only.

Thus, flow two dimensional unsteady flow

$$u = f_1(x, y, t)$$
$$v = f_2(x, y, t)$$
$$w = 0 \quad ...(6.9)$$

and for two dimensional steady flow

$$u = f_1(x, y)$$
$$v = f_2(x, y)$$
$$w = 0 \quad ...(6.10)$$

6.3.3 Three Dimensional Flow

In this type of flow, the flow characteristics are functions of time and three co-ordinates.

Thus for three dimensional unsteady flow

$$u = f_1(x, y, z, t)$$
$$v = f_2(x, y, z, t)$$
$$w = f_3(x, y, z, t) \quad ...(6.11)$$

and for three dimensional steady flow

$$u = f_1(x, y, z)$$
$$v = f_2(x, y, z)$$
$$w = f_3(x, y, z) \quad ...(6.12)$$

6.4 STREAMLINE, PATHLINE, STREAKLINE

6.4.1 Streamline

Streamline is an imaginary line drawn in flow field such that velocity of particle at any point moving along the streamline is represented by a tangent drawn at that point.

Differential equation for a streamline is given by

$$\frac{dx}{u} = \frac{dy}{v} = \frac{dz}{w} \quad ...(6.13)$$

6.4.2 Pathline

Pathline is a path traced by a individual fluid particle while moving along a flow:

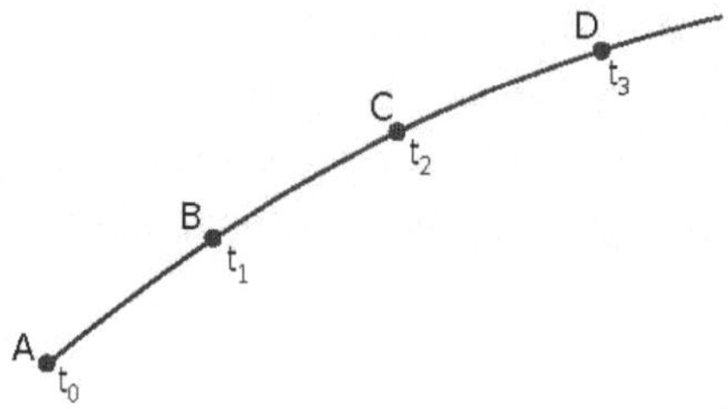

Fig. 6.1

Fig. 6.1 shows path traced by and A, B, C, D are the position of particle corresponding to time t_0, t_1, t_2, t_3 respectively.

6.4.3 Streakline

When the position of particles passing through a fixed point for a given instant of time are connected by a line, the resulting line is called streakline. *Ex*: path traced by smoke coming out form chimney.

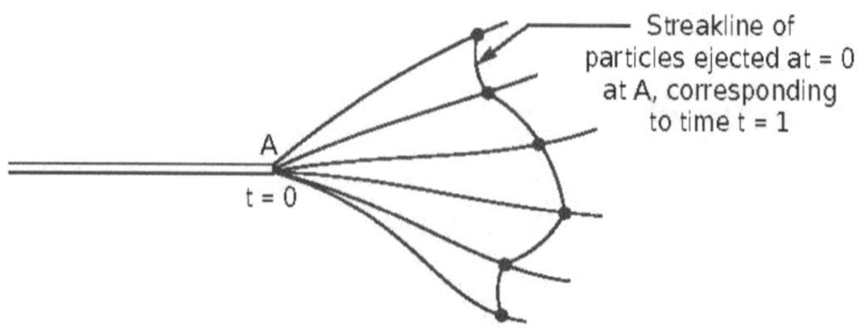

Fig. 6.2

6.5 CONTINUITY EQUATION

6.5.1 Continuity Equation for One Dimensional Flow

The continuity equation for compressible fluids will be written as (principle of conservation of mass)

$$\rho_1 A_1 V_1 = \rho_2 A_2 V_2 \quad ...(6.14)$$

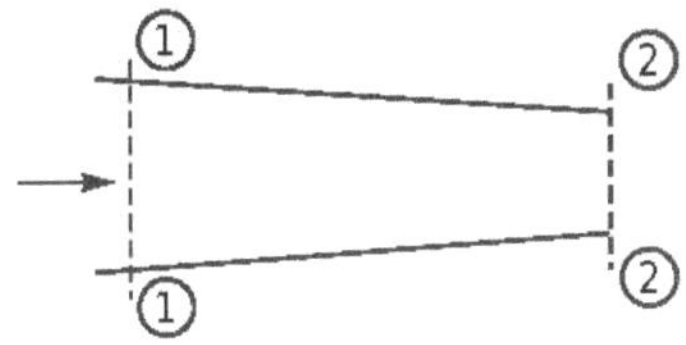

Fig. 6.3

where ρ_1, A_1, V_1 are the density, cross sectional area of flow and velocity at section (1) –(1) and similarly, ρ_2, A_2, V_2 for section (2)–(2).

For incompressible fluids equation (6.14) can be writtern as (as density of constant)

$$A_1 V_1 = A_2 V_2 \quad ...(6.15)$$

since $\rho_1 = \rho_2$

6.5.2 Continuity Equation for Three Dimensional Flow

Consider a fluid element of dimensions *dx*, *dy*, *dz* and velocity components *u*, *u*, *w* being along *x*, *y*, *z* direction respectively. Refer Fig. 6.4.

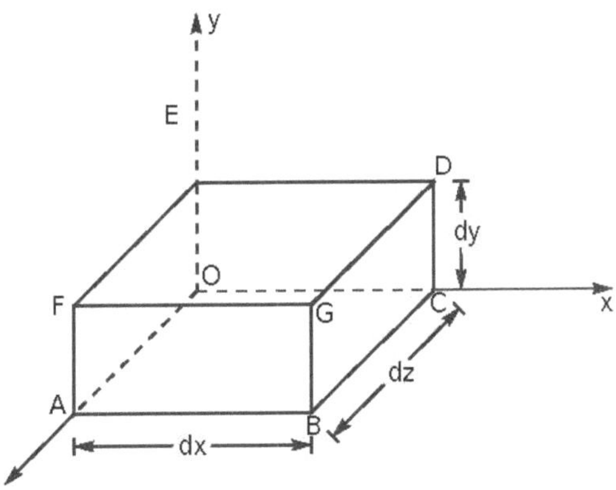

Fig. 6.4

The rate of mass flow entering the face *AOEF* = ρ × velocity in *x*-direction × area *AOEF*

$$= \rho \times u \times dy \times dz \quad ...(6.16)$$

The rate of mass flows leaving the face *BCDG*

$$= \rho u \, dy \, dz + \frac{\partial}{\partial x}(\rho u \, dy \, dz) \, dx \quad ...(6.17)$$

The net mass rate of flow gained in x-direction

$$= \text{mass rate entering} - \text{mass rate leaving}$$

$$= \rho u \, dy \, dz - \rho u \, dy \, dz - \frac{\partial}{\partial x}(\rho y \, dy \, dz) \, dx$$

$$= -\frac{\partial}{\partial x}(\rho u) \, dx \, dy \, dz \qquad \text{...(6.18)}$$

∴ The net mass rate of flow gained in y-direction

$$= -\frac{\partial}{\partial y}(\rho v) \, dx \, dy \, dz \qquad \text{...(6.19)}$$

and the net mass rate of flow gained in z-direction

$$= -\frac{\partial}{\partial z}(\rho w) \, dx \, dy \, dz \qquad \text{...(6.20)}$$

Therefore the total net gain of mass for the given fluid element

$$= -\frac{\partial(\rho u)}{\partial x} dx \, dy \, dz - \frac{\partial(\rho v)}{\partial y} dx \, dy \, dz - \frac{\partial(\rho w)}{\partial z} dx \, dy \, dz$$

$$= -\left[\frac{\partial(\rho u)}{\partial x} + \frac{\partial(\rho v)}{\partial y} + \frac{\partial(\rho w)}{\partial z}\right] dx \, dy \, dz \qquad \text{...(6.21)}$$

Now if fluid flow is assumed to be steady and compressible.

ρ = constant and there will be no accumulation of mass rate of flow in a given fluid element and hence equation (6.21) can be equated to zero to get

$$\frac{\partial u}{\partial x} + \frac{\partial v}{\partial y} + \frac{\partial w}{\partial z} = 0 \qquad \text{...(6.22)}$$

This is a continuity equation for three dimensional flow.

For two dimensional continuity equation (6.22) can be reduced to

$$\frac{\partial u}{\partial x} + \frac{\partial v}{\partial y} = 0 \text{ since } w = 0 \qquad \text{...(6.23)}$$

6.5.3 Equation of Continuity in Polar Co-ordinates

The equation of continuity in polar co-ordinates for compressible fluids is

$$\frac{1}{r}(\rho V_r) + \frac{\partial}{\partial r}(\rho V_r) + \frac{1}{r}\frac{\partial}{\partial \theta}(\rho V_\theta) = 0 \qquad \text{...(6.24)}$$

For incompressible fluid it reduces to

$$\frac{V_r}{r} + \frac{\partial V_r}{\partial_r} + \frac{1}{r} \cdot \frac{\partial V_\theta}{\partial \theta} = 0 \qquad \text{...(6.25)}$$

6.5.4 Solved Problems

■ **Problem 6.1:** *The velocity components in a two dimensional flow fluid for an incompressible fluid are expressed as*

$$u = \frac{y^3}{3} + 2x - x^2 y$$

$$v = xy^2 - 2y - \frac{x^3}{3}$$

Show whether the given velocity distribution is possible field of flow.

Solution: We have a two dimensional continuity equation

$$\frac{\partial u}{\partial x} + \frac{\partial v}{\partial y} = 0$$

$$u = \frac{y^3}{3} + 2x - x^2 y \qquad \text{...(1)}$$

$$v = xy^2 - 2y - \frac{x^3}{3}$$

$$\therefore \qquad \frac{\partial u}{\partial x} = 2 - 2xy,$$

$$\frac{\partial v}{\partial y} = 2xy - 2$$

Substituting in eqn. (1)

$$\frac{\partial u}{\partial x} + \frac{\partial v}{\partial y} = 2 - 2xy + 2xy - 2$$

$$= 0$$

Since the continuity equation is satisfied, the given velocity distribution is a possible field of flow.

■ **Problem 6.2:** *The two velocity components for a flow field are given. Find the third velocity component so as to satisfy the continuity equation.*

$$u = x^2 y, \qquad v = y^2 z.$$

Solution:

$$u = x^2 y, \qquad v = y^2 z.$$

$$\frac{\partial u}{\partial x} = 2xy, \qquad \frac{\partial v}{\partial y} = 2yz$$

Substituting in continuity equation

$$\frac{\partial u}{\partial x} + \frac{\partial v}{\partial y} + \frac{\partial w}{\partial z} = 0$$

$$2xy + 2yz + \frac{\partial w}{\partial z} = 0$$

$$\frac{\partial w}{\partial z} = -2xy - 2yz$$

Integrating
$$w = -2xyz - \frac{2yz^2}{2} + C$$
$$= -2xyz - yz^2 + C.$$

6.6 VELOCITY AND ACCELERATION

Let u, v, w are the velocity component in x, y, z direction respectively.

Thus, resultant velocity $V = ui + vj + wk$

$$= \sqrt{u^2 + v^2 + w^2} \quad \text{...(6.26)}$$

The total acceleration in x-direction can be expressed as

$$a_x = \frac{du}{dt} = \frac{\partial u}{\partial x}\frac{dx}{dt} + \frac{\partial u}{\partial y}.\frac{dy}{dt} + \frac{\partial u}{\partial z}.\frac{dz}{dt} + \frac{\partial u}{\partial t}$$

$$= u\frac{\partial u}{\partial x} + v\frac{\partial u}{\partial y} + w\frac{\partial u}{\partial z} + \frac{\partial u}{\partial t} \quad \text{...(6.27)}$$

Similarly total acceleration in y and z direction can be expressed as

$$a_y = u\frac{\partial v}{\partial x} + v\frac{\partial v}{\partial y} + w\frac{\partial v}{\partial z} + \frac{\partial v}{\partial t} \quad \text{...(6.28)}$$

and
$$a_z = u\frac{\partial w}{\partial x} + v\frac{\partial w}{\partial y} + w\frac{\partial w}{\partial z} + \frac{\partial w}{\partial t} \quad \text{...(6.29)}$$

Thus resultant acceleration

$$a = a_x i + a_y j - a_z k$$
$$= \sqrt{a_x^2 + a_y^2 + a_z^2} \quad \text{...(6.30)}$$

The term which shows a change is velocity with respect to time are called a local acceleration.

The term which shows change in velocity with respect to space is called convective acceleration.

Thus for steady flow local acceleration is zero.

i.e.
$$\frac{\partial u}{\partial t} = 0, \frac{\partial v}{\partial t} = 0, \frac{\partial w}{\partial t} = 0$$

and for uniform flow convective acceleration is zero, *i.e.*

$$\frac{\partial u}{\partial x} = \frac{\partial u}{\partial y} = \frac{\partial u}{\partial z} = \frac{\partial v}{\partial x} = \frac{\partial v}{\partial y} = \frac{\partial v}{\partial z} = \frac{\partial w}{\partial x} = \frac{\partial w}{\partial y} = \frac{\partial w}{\partial z} = 0$$

Therefore, if $a_x = 0$, $a_y = 0$ and $a_z = 0$

i.e. $a = 0$, the fluid flow is steady and uniform.

In such cases the streamlines are straight and parallel.

6.6.1 Solved Problems

■ **Problem 6.3:** *If* $V = x^2 y\,\hat{i} + y^2 z\,\hat{j} - (2xyz + yz^2)\,\hat{k}$

Calculate the velocity and acceleration at the point (2, 1, 3).

Solution:
$$V = x^2 y\,\hat{i} + y^2 z\,\hat{j} - (2xyz + yz^2)\,\hat{k}$$
$$u = x^2y,\ v = y^2z,\ w = 2xyz - yz^2$$

Substituting

$u = 2^2 \times 1 = 4, \quad v = 1^2 \times 3 = 3, \quad w = -2 \times 2 \times 1 \times 3 - 1 \times 3^2 = -12 - 9 = -21$

Substituting in equation

$$V = \sqrt{u^2 + v^2 + w^2}$$
$$= \sqrt{16 + 9 + 441} = \sqrt{466}$$
$$= 21.58 \text{ units}$$

Now,

$$\frac{\partial u}{\partial x} = 2xy = 2 \times 2 \times 1 = 4, \quad \frac{\partial u}{\partial y} = x^2 = 2^2 = 4, \quad \frac{\partial u}{\partial z} = 0$$

$$\frac{\partial v}{\partial x} = 0, \quad \frac{\partial v}{\partial y} = 2yz = 2 \times 1 \times 3 = 6, \quad \frac{\partial v}{\partial z} = y^2 = 1^2 = 1$$

$$\frac{\partial w}{\partial x} = -2yz - 0, \quad \frac{\partial w}{\partial y} = -2xz - z^2, \quad \frac{\partial w}{\partial z} = -2xy - 2yz$$

$$= -2 \times 1 \times 3 \qquad = -2 \times 2 \times 3 \times 3^2 \qquad = -2 \times 2 \times 1 - 2 \times 1 \times 3$$

$$= -6 \qquad = -12 - 9 \qquad = -4 - 6$$

$$= -21 \qquad = -10$$

Substituting in the following equations:

$$a_x = u\frac{\partial u}{\partial x} + v\frac{\partial v}{\partial y} + w\frac{\partial w}{\partial z}$$
$$= 4 \times 4 + 3 \times 4 \times 21 \times 0$$
$$= 16 + 12 + 0 = 28 \text{ units}$$

$$a_y = u\frac{\partial v}{\partial x} + v\frac{\partial v}{\partial y} + w\frac{\partial v}{\partial z}$$
$$= 4 \times 0 + 3 \times 6 + 21 \times 1$$
$$= 0 + 18 + 21 = 38 \text{ units}$$

$$a_z = u\frac{\partial w}{\partial x} + v\frac{\partial w}{\partial y} + w\frac{\partial w}{\partial z}$$
$$= 4(-6) + 3(-21) + 21(-10)$$

$$= -24 - 63 - 210 = -297 \text{ units}$$

and
$$a = \sqrt{a_x^2 + a_y^2 + a_z^2}$$

$$= \sqrt{28^2 + 39^2 + (-297)^2}$$

$$= 300.8554 \text{ units.}$$

■ **Problem 6.4:** *A pipe converges uniformly from 0.6 m diameter to 0.3 m diameter over 3 length. (i) water flows through the pipe at a rate of 30 lit/sec. Find the convective acceleration at the middle of the pipe.*

(ii) If the rate of flow changes from 30 lit/sec. to 50 lit/sec. uniformly in 20 seconds, find the total acceleration at the middle of the pipe at 10th second.

Solution: (*i*)

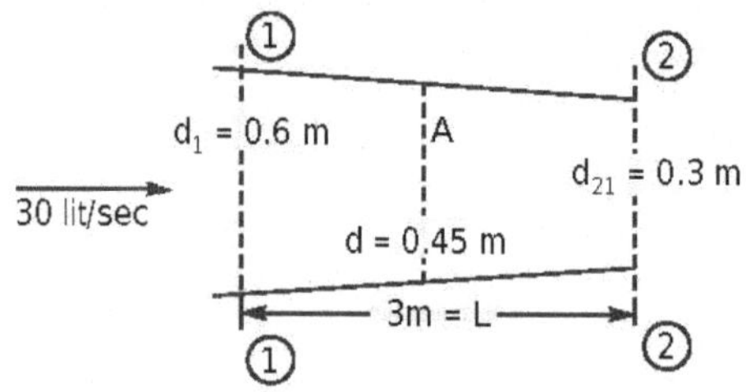

Fig. 6.5

Diameter at a distance of 1.5 m from section (1) – (1) $= \dfrac{0.6 + 0.3}{2} = 0.45$ m

Velocity at this section $= u = \dfrac{Q}{\dfrac{\pi d^2}{4}}$

$$= \frac{30 \times 10^{-3}}{\left(\dfrac{\pi \times 0.45^2}{4}\right)} = 0.1886 \text{ m/sec.}$$

Velocity at section (1) – (1)

$$u_1 = \frac{Q}{\dfrac{\pi d_1^2}{4}} = \frac{30 \times 10^{-3}}{\left(\dfrac{\pi \times 0.6^2}{4}\right)} = 0.1061$$

Velocity at section (2) – (2)

$$u_2 = \frac{Q}{\left(\dfrac{\pi d_2^2}{4}\right)} = \frac{30 \times 10^{-3}}{\left(\dfrac{\pi \times 0.3^2}{4}\right)}$$

$$= 0.4244 \text{ m/sec.}$$

Now, $$\frac{\partial u}{\partial x} = \frac{u_2 - u_1}{L} = \frac{0.4244 - 0.1061}{3}$$

$$= 0.1061 \text{ per sec.}$$

Thus convective acceleration at a midpoint

$$= u\frac{\partial u}{\partial x} = 0.1886 \times 0.1061$$

$$= 0.02 \text{ m/sec}^2.$$

(*ii*) Now the flow changes from 30 lit./sec to 50 lit/sec. in 20 seconds so the rate of flow will be 40 lit./sec. at 10th second.

Velocity at midpoint at 10th second

$$u = \frac{40 \times 10^{-3}}{\left(\frac{\pi \times 0.45^2}{4}\right)} = 0.2515 \text{ m/sec.}$$

Velocity at (1)–(1) at 10th second

$$u_1 = \frac{40 \times 10^{-3}}{\left(\frac{\pi \times 0.6^2}{4}\right)} = 0.1415 \text{ m/sec.}$$

Velocity at (2)–(2) at 10th second

$$u_2 = \frac{40 \times 10^{-3}}{\left(\frac{\pi \times 0.3^2}{4}\right)} = 0.5658 \text{ m/sec.}$$

Convective acceleration at midpoint

$$= u\frac{\partial u}{\partial x}$$

$$= u \times \frac{u_2 - u_1}{L}$$

$$= 0.2515 \times \frac{0.5658 - 0.1415}{3}$$

$$= 0.0356 \text{ m/sec}^2.$$

Now at $t = 0$ velocity at midpoint

$$= \frac{30 \times 10^{-3}}{\left(\frac{\pi \times 0.45^2}{4}\right)} = 0.1886 \text{ m/sec.}$$

At $t = 20$ seconds velocity at midpoint

$$= \frac{50 \times 10^{-3}}{\left(\frac{\pi \times 0.45^2}{4}\right)} = 0.3143 \text{ m/sec.}$$

Local acceleration at midpoint

$$= \frac{\partial u}{\partial t} = \frac{0.3143 - 0.1886}{20}$$

$$= 0.006285 \text{ m/sec}^2$$

Therefore total acceleration at the midpoint at 10th sec.

= Convective acceleration + local acceleration

= 0.0356 + 0.006285

= 0.0419 m/sec^2.

6.7 VELOCITY POTENTIAL FUNCTION AND STREAM FUNCTION

6.7.1 Velocity Potential Function

The velocity potential (ϕ) is defined as a scalar function of space and time such that its negative derivative with respect to any direction gives the fluid velocity in that direction.

Mathematically, $$-\frac{\partial \phi}{\partial x} = u \quad \text{...(6.31 (a))}$$

$$-\frac{\partial \phi}{\partial y} = v \quad \text{...(6.31 (b))}$$

$$-\frac{\partial \phi}{\partial z} = w \quad \text{...(6.31 (c))}$$

The negative sign indicates that ϕ decreases with increase in the values of x, y, z, *i.e.*, flow is always in the direction of decreasing ϕ.

For steady incompressible fluid continuity equation is given as

$$\frac{\partial u}{\partial x} + \frac{\partial v}{\partial y} + \frac{\partial w}{\partial z} = 0$$

Substituting from equation (6.31)

$$\frac{\partial}{\partial x}\left(-\frac{\partial \phi}{\partial x}\right) + \frac{\partial}{\partial y}\left(-\frac{\partial \phi}{\partial y}\right) + \frac{\partial}{\partial z}\left(-\frac{\partial \phi}{\partial z}\right) = 0$$

$$\frac{\partial^2 \phi}{\partial x^2} + \frac{\partial^2 \phi}{\partial y^2} + \frac{\partial^2 \phi}{\partial z^2} = 0 \quad \text{...(6.32)}$$

This equation is known as Laplace equation.

For a rotational flow the rotation components are given by

$$\omega_x = \frac{1}{2}\left(\frac{\partial w}{\partial y} - \frac{\partial v}{\partial z}\right) \quad ...(6.33\ (a))$$

$$\omega_y = \frac{1}{2}\left(\frac{\partial u}{\partial z} - \frac{\partial w}{\partial x}\right) \quad ...(6.33\ (b))$$

$$\omega_z = \frac{1}{2}\left(\frac{\partial v}{\partial x} - \frac{\partial u}{\partial y}\right) \quad ...(6.33\ (c))$$

Substituting from equation (6.31)

$$\omega_x = \frac{1}{2}\left(-\frac{\partial^2 \phi}{\partial y \partial z} + \frac{\partial^2 \phi}{\partial z \partial y}\right) \quad ...(6.34\ (a))$$

$$\omega_y = \frac{1}{2}\left(-\frac{\partial^2 \phi}{\partial z \partial x} + \frac{\partial^2 \phi}{\partial x \partial z}\right) \quad ...(6.34\ (b))$$

$$\omega_z = \frac{1}{2}\left(-\frac{\partial^2 \phi}{\partial x \partial y} + \frac{\partial^2 \phi}{\partial y \partial x}\right) \quad ...(6.34\ (c))$$

Following points to be noted for potential function:

(1) If $\omega_x = \omega_y = \omega_z = 0$, the flow is irrotational.

(2) Velocity potential exists only for irrotational flow.

(3) Any function ϕ that satisfies Laplace equation is a possible steady, incompressible irrotational flow.

6.7.2 Stream Function

The stream function ψ is defined as a scalar function of space and time such that its partial derivative with respect to any direction gives the velocity component at right angles to this direction.

Mathematically,

$$\frac{\partial \psi}{\partial x} = v \quad ...(6.35(a))$$

$$\frac{\partial \psi}{\partial y} = -u \quad ...(6.35\ (b))$$

Substituting in continuity equation

$$\frac{\partial}{\partial x}\left(-\frac{\partial \psi}{\partial y}\right) + \frac{\partial}{\partial y}\left(\frac{\partial \psi}{\partial x}\right) = 0$$

$$-\frac{\partial^2 \psi}{\partial x \partial y} + \frac{\partial^2 \psi}{\partial x \partial y} = 0 \quad ...(6.36)$$

Putting the values of u, v in terms of ψ in the rotation component ω_z.

$$\omega_z = \frac{1}{2}\left[\frac{\partial}{\partial x}\left(\frac{\partial \psi}{\partial x}\right) - \frac{\partial}{\partial y}\left(-\frac{\partial \psi}{\partial y}\right)\right]$$

$$= \frac{1}{2}\left[\frac{\partial^2 \psi}{\partial x^2} + \frac{\partial^2 \psi}{\partial y^2}\right] \quad ...(6.37)$$

The equation is called as Poisson's equation.

For an irrotational flow $\omega_z = 0$. Equation (6.37) will reduce to

$$\frac{\partial^2 \psi}{\partial x^2} + \frac{\partial^2 \psi}{\partial y^2} = 0 \quad ...(6.38)$$

This equation is called as Laplace equation.

Following points to be noted for stream function:

1. Any function ψ which is continuous is a possible case of rotational or irrotational fluid flow.
2. If function ψ satisfies Laplace equation then it is a possible case of an irrotational flow.

6.8 FLOW NET

A family of equipotential lines and constant streamlines is called flow net or in other words it can be defined as a grid obtained by a drawing a series of streamlines and equipotential lines.

A flow net may be drawn for a two dimensional irrotational flow and is used to analyse flow.

6.9 STREAMLINES AND POTENTIAL LINES

6.9.1 Relation between Stream Function and Potential Function

From section (6.7) following relation can be derived.

$$\frac{\partial \psi}{\partial x} = \frac{\partial \psi}{\partial y} \quad ...(6.39)$$

and

$$\frac{\partial \phi}{\partial y} = -\frac{\partial \psi}{\partial x} \quad ...(6.40)$$

6.9.2 Slope of Equipotential Line and Constant Streamline

Equipotential line is defined as a line for which the velocity potential is same at every point.

Fot equipotential line ϕ = constant

i.e. $d\phi = 0$

Mathematically, $d\phi = \frac{\partial \phi}{\partial x} dx + \frac{\partial \phi}{\partial y} dy$

$$= -u\,dx - vdy$$

For equipotential line $d\phi = 0$

Hence $0 = -udx - vdy$

or $$\frac{dy}{dx} = -\frac{u}{v} \quad \text{...(6.41)}$$

Similarly for constant streamline

$$\psi = \text{constant}$$

or $d\psi = 0$

Mathematically, $d\psi = \frac{\partial \psi}{\partial x} dx + \frac{\partial \psi}{\partial y} \cdot dy$

For constant streamline $d\psi = 0$

Hence $0 = vdx - udy$

or $$\frac{dy}{dx} = \frac{v}{u} \quad \text{...(6.42)}$$

From equation (6.41) and (6.42), by multiplying the slopes of equipotential line and constant streamline is equal to –1. Thus it shows that equipotential lines and constant streamlines are orthogonal to each other.

6.9.3 Solved Problems

■ **Problem 6.5**: *A two dimensional flow is described by the velocity components.*

$$u = 5x^3 \text{ and } v = -15x^2y$$

Calculate the stream function.

Solution:

$$u = 5x^3 \text{ and } v = -15x^2y$$

$$\frac{\partial \psi}{\partial x} = v = -15x^2y \quad \text{...(1)}$$

$$\frac{\partial \psi}{\partial y} = -u = -5x^3 \quad \text{...(2)}$$

Integrating equation (1) w.r.t. x, we get

$$\int \partial\psi = \int -15x^2 y\, \partial x$$

$$\psi = -15\frac{x^3}{3} y + c$$

Constant of integration 'c' may be a function of y, then

$$\psi = -5x^3y + f(y) \quad ...(3)$$

Differentiating w.r.t. y

$$\frac{\partial \psi}{\partial y} = -5x^3 + f'(y)$$

From equation (2), $\frac{\partial \psi}{\partial y} = -5x^3$

$\therefore$
$$-5x^3 = -5x^3 + f'(y)$$
$$f'(y) = 0$$

Integrating w.r.t. y

$$f(y) = 0$$

Substituting in equation (3)

$$\psi = -5x^3y$$

■ **Problem 6.6:** *The velocity for potential flow is given by $\phi = 4(x^2 - y^2)$. Determine stream function ψ for the field.*

Solution:
$$\phi = 4(x^2 - y^2) = 4x^2 - 4y^2$$

By definition
$$-\frac{\partial \phi}{\partial x} = -\frac{\partial}{\partial x}(4x^2 - 4y^2) = -(8x) = u \quad ...(1)$$

$$-\frac{\partial \phi}{\partial y} = -\frac{\partial}{\partial y}(4x^2 - 4y^2) = -(-8y) = 8y = v \quad ...(2)$$

Also,
$$\frac{\partial \psi}{\partial x} = v = 8y \quad ...(3)$$

$$\frac{\partial \psi}{\partial y} = -u = -(-8x) = 8x \quad ...(4)$$

Integrating equation (3)

$$\int \frac{\partial \psi}{\partial x} = \int 8y$$

$$\psi = \frac{8y^2}{2} + C$$

'C' may be a function of y

$\therefore$
$$\psi = 4y^2 + f(y) \quad ...(5)$$

Differentiating this equation w.r.t. y

$$\frac{\partial \psi}{\partial y} = 8y + f'(y)$$

But from equation (4)

$$\frac{\partial \psi}{\partial y} = 8x$$

$$\therefore \quad 8x = 8y + f'(y)$$

$$\therefore \quad f'(y) = 8x - 8y$$

Integrating w.r.t. y

$$f(y) = 8xy - 4y^2$$

Putting in equation (5)

$$\psi = 4y^2 + 8xy - 4y^2 = 8xy \qquad \text{...(Ans.)}$$

■ **Problem 6.7:** *The velocity potential function ϕ is given by an expression*

$$\phi = \frac{xy^3}{3} - x^2 + \frac{x^3 y}{3} + y^2$$

1. *Find volocity component in x and y direction.*
2. *Show that ϕ represents a possible case of flow.*

Solution:

$$\phi = \frac{xy^3}{3} - x^2 + \frac{x^3 y}{3} + y^2$$

1. By definition

$$u = -\frac{\partial \phi}{\partial x}$$

$$= -\frac{\partial}{\partial x}\left(\frac{xy^3}{3} - x^2 + \frac{x^3 y}{3} + y^2\right)$$

$$= -\left(\frac{y^3}{3} - 2x + \frac{3x^2 y}{3} + 0\right)$$

$$\therefore \quad u = -\frac{y^3}{3} + 2x - x^2 y \qquad \text{...(1)}$$

$$v = -\frac{\partial \phi}{\partial y}$$

$$v = -\frac{\partial}{\partial y}\left(\frac{xy^3}{3} - x^2 + \frac{x^3y}{3} + y^2\right)$$

$$= -\left(\frac{3xy^2}{3} - 0 + \frac{x^3}{3} + 2y\right)$$

$$= -xy^2 - \frac{x^3}{3} - 2y \quad ...(2)$$

2. If ϕ represents a possible case of flow it should satisfy Laplace equation

$$\frac{\partial^2\phi}{\partial x^2} + \frac{\partial^2\phi}{\partial y^2} = 0 \quad ...(3)$$

Now,
$$\frac{\partial\phi}{\partial x} = \frac{y^3}{3} - 2x + x^2y$$

$$\frac{\partial^2\phi}{\partial x^2} = -2 + 2xy \quad ...(4)$$

and
$$\frac{\partial\phi}{\partial y} = xy^2 + \frac{x^3}{3} + 2y$$

$$\frac{\partial^2\phi}{\partial y^2} = 2xy + 2 \quad ...(5)$$

Substituting in equation (3)

$-2 + 2xy + 2xy + 2 = 4xy \neq 0$

Hence ϕ does not represent a possible case of flow.

■ **Problem 6.8**: *In a two dimensional fluid motion the stream function is given by*

$$\psi = 4xy$$

1. *Sketch the streamlines*
2. *Determine the potential function.*

Solution:

1. $\psi = 4xy$

For $\psi = 10 = 4xy$

x	–3	–2	–1	0	1	2	3
y	–0.8	–1.25	–2.5	0	2.5	1.25	0.8

Similarly streamline.

For $\psi = 20$ can be sketched.

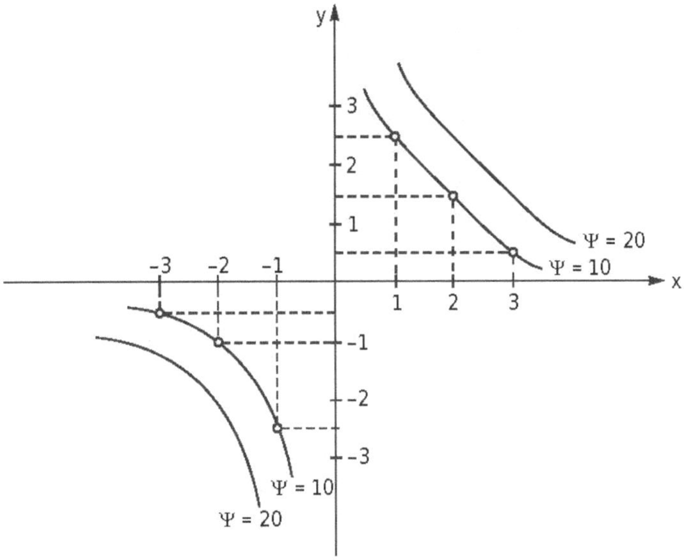

Fig. 6.6

2. By definition

$$\frac{\partial \psi}{\partial x} = v = 4y \quad ...(1)$$

$$\frac{\partial \psi}{\partial y} = -u = 4x \quad ...(2)$$

Also

$$-\frac{\partial \phi}{\partial y} = u = -4x \quad ...(3)$$

$$-\frac{\partial \phi}{\partial y} = v = 4y \quad ...(4)$$

Integrating equation (3) w.r.t. x

$$\phi = \frac{4x^2}{2} + C$$

'C' may be a function of y

$$\therefore \qquad \phi = 2x^2 + f(y) \quad ...(5)$$

Differentiating w.r.t. y

$$\frac{\partial \phi}{\partial y} = f'(y)$$

From equation (4)

$$\frac{\partial \phi}{\partial y} = f'(y) = -4y$$

Integrating w.r.t. y

$$f(y) = -\frac{4y^2}{2} = -2y^2$$

Put in equation (5)

$$\phi = 2x^2 - 2y^2.$$

Exercises

1. The velocity component in x-direction for a two dimensional flow is given by

$$u = \frac{y^3}{3} + 2x - x^2y$$

Find the velocity component in y-direction such that it satisfies the continuity equation.

(**Ans.** $v = xy^2 - 2y + c$)

2. If $V = 2x^2 y\hat{i} + 3y^2 z\hat{j} + (xyz + xyz^2)\hat{k}$.

Calculate the velocity and the acceleration at the point (1, 2, 3).

(**Ans.** $V = 43.45$ units, $a = 1855.12$ units)

3. Find whether $\phi = \frac{x^2y}{2} - 2x + \frac{y^2x}{2} + y^2$ represents a possible case of flow or not.

(**Ans.** No. **Hint:** *Use Laplace equation*)

4. Show that $u = 2x^2y$ and $v = -2y^2x$ represents a case of possible steady incompressible fluid flow.

(**Ans.** $\frac{\partial u}{\partial x} + \frac{\partial v}{\partial y} = 0$, hence proved)

5. The velocity potential function is given by

$$\phi = x^2 - y^2.$$

Calculate the velocity component at the point (3, 4).

(**Ans.** $u = -6$, $v = 8$)

6. The stream function is given by

$$\psi = x^2 - y^2 + y.$$

Calculate the velocity component at the point (1, 2). (**Ans.** $u = 3$, $v = 2$)

7. The velocity components in a two dimensional flow are

$$u = 2x^2y + \frac{2}{3}y^3 \text{ and } v = -2y^2x - \frac{2}{3}x^3.$$

Show that these functions represent a possible case of an irrotational flow.

(**Ans. Hint:** *Show* $\frac{\partial u}{\partial x} + \frac{\partial v}{\partial y} = 0$ *and* $\omega_z = 0$)

8. For a two dimensional flow the velocity components are given by

$$u = x^2 - x^2y \text{ and } v = xy^2 - 2xy.$$

Show velocity potential exist and find ϕ and ψ.

(**Ans. Hint:** $\frac{\partial u}{\partial x} + \frac{\partial v}{\partial y} = 0 \therefore \phi$ *exist*, $\phi = -\frac{x^3}{3} + \frac{xy^3}{3} - xy^2, \psi = \frac{x^2y^2}{2} - x^2y + y$)

9. The velocity potential is given by

$$\phi = x^2 + y^2.$$

Find the stream function ψ. (**Ans.** $\psi = 6xy$)

10. The stream function is given by

$$\psi = x^2 - y^2.$$

Find the velocity potential function ϕ. (**Ans.** $\phi = -2xy$)

❑❑❑

7

Dynamics of Fluid Flow

7.1 INTRODUCTION

The study of fluids in motion considering the forces causing flow is called fluid dynamics.

The laws of nature which are used to analyse a fluid flow are:

(1) The principle of conservation of mass
(2) Newton's first law of motion
(3) Newton's second law of motion
(4) Newton's third law of motion
(5) First law of thermodynamics
(6) Second law of thermodynamics.

7.2 EQUATIONS OF MOTION

Using Newton's second law of motion the general equation of motion in the x-direction can be written as

$$ma_x = (F_g)_x + (F_p)_x + (F_v)_x + (F_t)_x + (F_c)_x \quad ...(7.1)$$

where $ma_x = F_x$

F_x = Force acting in the x-direction on a fluid mass 'm' producing acceleration 'ax.'

F_g = Gravity force

F_p = Pressure force

F_v = Viscous force

F_t = Force due to turbulence

F_c = Force due to compressibility.

If a fluid is assumed to be incompressible, equation (7.1) can be written as

$$ma_x = (F_g)_x + (F_p)_x + (F_v)_x + (F_t)_x \quad ...(7.2)$$

Equation (7.2) is called as Reynolds equation.

If the force due to turbulence is neglected equation (7.2) can be written as

$$ma_x = (F_g)_x + (F_p)_x + (F_v)_x \qquad ...(7.3)$$

Equation (7.3) is called as Navier Stokes equation.

If the force due to viscosity is neglected equation (7.3) can be written as

$$ma_x = (F_g)_x + (F_p)_x \qquad ...(7.4)$$

Equation (7.4) is called as Euler's equation.

It should be noted that equations (7.1), (7.2), (7.3) and (7.4) can be written for y and z directions by replacing x by y and z respectively.

7.3 EULER'S EQUATION OF MOTION

In Euler's equation of motion only forces due to gravity and pressure are taken into account.

Let us consider a fluid element of cross-sectional area dA and length dS moving along a streamline, as shown in Fig. 7.1.

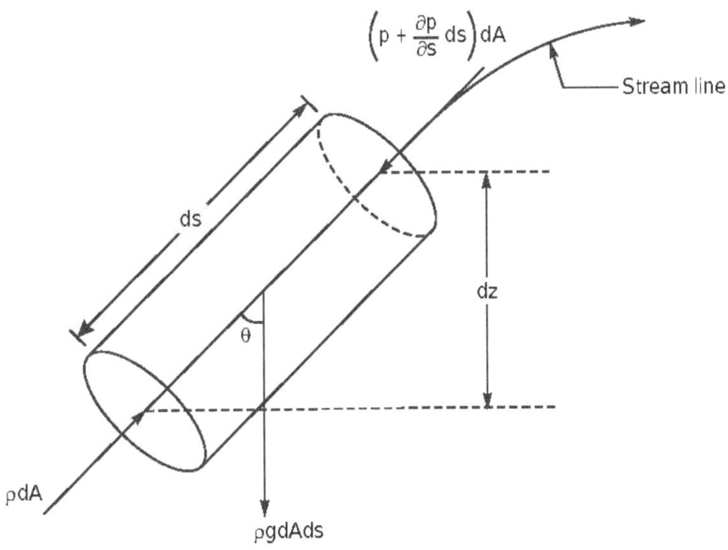

Fig. 7.1 Forces on a cylindrical fluid element

As per Newton's law of motion the equation in the S-direction can be written as

$$(\rho dA dS)\, a_s = pdA - \left(p + \frac{\partial p}{\partial s} ds\right) dA + \rho g dA\, ds \cos\theta \qquad ...(7.5)$$

where
$$a_s = \frac{dv}{dt} = \frac{\partial v}{\partial s} \times \frac{ds}{dt} + \frac{\partial v}{\partial t}$$
$$= \frac{v\partial v}{\partial s} + \frac{\partial v}{\partial t}$$

For steady flow $$\frac{\partial v}{\partial t} = 0$$

$$\therefore \quad a_s = \frac{v\partial v}{\partial s}$$

Put in equation (7.5)

$$(\rho dAds)\frac{v\partial v}{\partial s} = pdA - \left(p + \frac{\partial p}{\partial s}ds\right)dA + \rho gdAds\cos\theta$$

Dividing each term by $\rho dsdA$

$$\frac{v\partial v}{\partial s} = \frac{-\partial p}{\rho\partial s} - g\cos\theta$$

$$\therefore \quad \frac{\partial p}{\rho\partial s} + \frac{v\partial v}{\partial s} + g\cos\theta = 0$$

From Fig. 7.1 $$\cos\theta = \frac{dz}{ds}$$

$$\therefore \quad \frac{\partial p}{\rho\partial s} + \frac{v\partial v}{\partial s} + \frac{gdz}{ds} = 0$$

$$\therefore \quad \frac{\partial p}{\rho} + v\partial v + gdz = 0 \qquad ...(7.6)$$

Equation (7.6) is called as Euler's Equation in S-direction.

7.4 BERNOULLI'S EQUATION DERIVED FROM EULER'S EQUATION

Integrating equation (7.6) with respect to s taking limit $dA \to 0$, $ds \to 0$

$$\int\frac{dp}{\rho} + \int vdv + \int gdz = \text{constant}$$

For compressible fluid ρ = constant

$$\therefore \quad \frac{p}{\rho} + \frac{V^2}{2} + gz = \text{constant}$$

Dividing all terms by g

$$\frac{p}{\rho g} + \frac{V^2}{2g} + z = \text{constant}$$

or $$\frac{p}{\gamma} + \frac{V^2}{2g} + z = \text{constant} \quad (\text{as, } \rho g = \gamma) \qquad ...(7.7)$$

Equation (7.7) is called as Bernoulli's equation.

where, $\frac{p}{\gamma}$ = work done by the pressure force per unit weight of fluid or popularly called as pressure head.

$\frac{V^2}{2g}$ = kinetic energy of flow per unit weight of fluid or popularly called as velocity head.

z = potential energy per unit weight of fluid or popularly called as datum head or potential head.

Therefore Bernoulli's Theorem can be stated as for steady, irrotational flow of incompressible, non-viscous (ideal) fluid the total energy at any point along the flow is constant.

Mathematically, Bernoulli's theorem is written as

$$\frac{p}{\gamma}+\frac{V^2}{2g}+z = \text{constant}$$

Following assumptions are made while deriving Bernoulli's equation

1. The fluid is non viscous (ideal fluid)
2. The fluid is incompressible (ρ = constant)
3. The flow is steady. $\left(\frac{\partial p}{\partial t}=0, \frac{\partial v}{\partial t}=0, \frac{\partial p}{\partial t}=0\right)$
4. The flow is irrotational. (No eddy losses)

7.5 LIMITATIONS OF BERNOULLI'S THEOREM

1. The theorem is not valid for unsteady flow.
2. In irrotational flow eddies and vortices are formed and due to this energy loss is there which is not considered in Bernoulli's theorem.
3. Loss due to friction or viscosity is not taken into account.
4. Theorem has considered only a flow of incompressible fluids.
5. This theorem is not applicable to fluid flowing along curved path (pipe bend etc.) since energy due to centrifugal force is not taken into account.
6. No provision for separation of flow or the flow where cavitation takes place, hence in such cases if Bernoulli's theorem is used it does not give good results.

7.6 BERNOULLI'S EQUATION FOR A REAL FLUID

Real fluids are viscous and hence when it flows losses occurs. So to use Bernoulli's equation for real fluids, Bernoulli's equation should be modified to accommodate head losses.

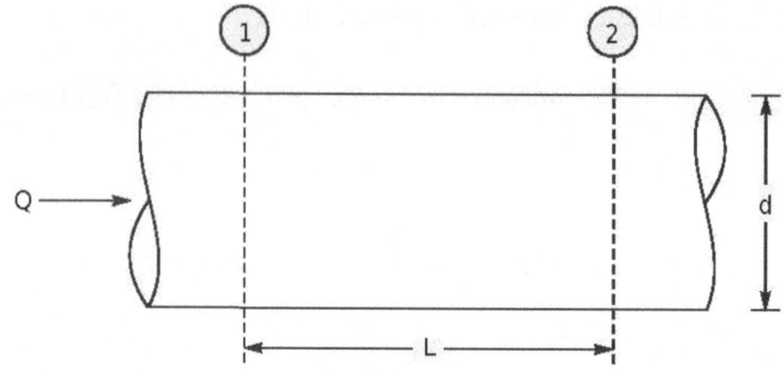

Fig. 7.2

Thus when a Bernoulli's equation is used for a fluid flow through pipe for section (1) and (2) as shown in Fig. 7.2. It can be written as

$$\frac{p_1}{\gamma}+\frac{V_1^2}{2g}+z_1 = \frac{p_2}{\gamma}+\frac{V_2^2}{2g}+z_2+h_L$$

where, h_L = Head loss between section (1) and (2) *i.e.*, for length '*L*'. It may include friction loss and also other minor losses like entry loss, loss due to change in cross-section of pipe, fittings loss, exit loss etc.

7.6.1 Solved Problems

■ **Problem 7.1:** *Water flows through a horizontal pipe of diameter 20 cm with a velocity of 20 m/sec. The pressure at A and B is given as 25 N/cm² and 20 N/cm² respectively. Find a head loss between A and B.*

Given:

$$d = 20 \text{ cm} = 0.2 \text{ m}$$
$$V = 20 \text{ m/sec}$$
$$p_A = 25 \text{ N/cm}^2 = 25 \times 10^4 \text{ N/m}^2$$
$$p_B = 20 \text{ N/cm}^2 = 20 \times 10^4 \text{ N/m}^2.$$

Solution: Using Bernoulli's equation for *A* and *B*

$$\frac{p_A}{\gamma}+\frac{V_A^2}{2g}+Z_A = \frac{p_B}{\gamma}+\frac{V_B^2}{2g}+Z_B+h_L$$

Pipe is horizontal hence $Z_A = Z_B$

Pipe is of uniform diameter hence = $V_A = V_B$

$$\therefore \quad \frac{p_A}{\gamma} = \frac{p_B}{\gamma}+h_L$$

$$\therefore \quad \frac{p_A - p_B}{\gamma} = h_L$$

$$\therefore \quad h_L = \frac{25\times10^4 - 20\times10^4}{9810} = 5.09 \text{ m}.$$

■ **Problem 7.2:** *For the same data given in problem 1.1. If the pipe is inclined and B is 1 m above the datum line passing through A, find a head loss between A and B.*

Solution:

Now $Z_A = 0$ and $Z_B = 1$ m

Using Bernoulli's equation for A and B

$$\frac{p_A}{\gamma}+\frac{V_A^2}{2g}+Z_A = \frac{p_B}{\gamma}+\frac{V_B^2}{2g}+Z_B+h_L$$

Pipe is of uniform diameter hence $V_A = V_B$

$$\therefore \quad \frac{p_A}{\gamma}+Z_A = \frac{p_B}{\gamma}+Z_B+h_L$$

$$\frac{25\times10^4}{9810}+0 = \frac{20\times10^4}{9810}+1+h_L$$

$$\therefore \quad h_L = 4.09 \text{ m.}$$

■ **Problem 7.3:** *A pipe is converging from 20 cm diameter at A to 15 cm diameter at B in a direction of flow. The discharge through the pipe is 0.5 m³/ sec. The pipe is inclined, A is on a datum line and B is 1.5 m above the datum line. Find a pressure difference between A and B for a head loss of 5 m between A and B.*

Given: $d_A = 20\ cm = 0.2\ m$

$d_B = 15\ cm = 0.15\ m$

$Q = 0.5\ m^3/sec$

$Z_A = 0$

$Z_B = 1.5\ m$

$h_L = 5\ m.$

Solution:

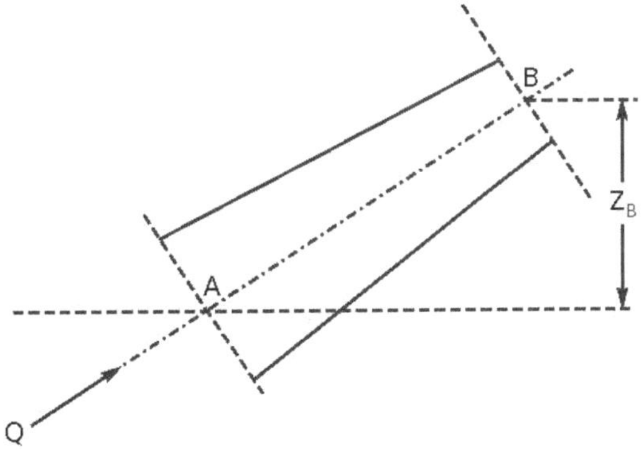

Fig. 7.3

$$V_A = \frac{Q}{\left(\frac{\pi d_A^2}{4}\right)} = \frac{0.5}{\left(\frac{\pi\times0.2^2}{4}\right)} = 15.92\text{ m/sec}$$

$$V_B = \frac{Q}{\left(\frac{\pi d_B^2}{4}\right)} = \frac{0.5}{\left(\frac{\pi \times 0.15^2}{4}\right)} = 28.29 \text{ m/sec}$$

Using Bernoulli's equation for A and B

$$\frac{p_A}{\gamma} + \frac{V_A^2}{2g} + Z_A = \frac{p_B}{\gamma} + \frac{V_B^2}{2g} + Z_B + h_L$$

$$\frac{p_A}{\gamma} - \frac{p_B}{\gamma} = \left(\frac{V_B^2}{2g} - \frac{V_A^2}{2g}\right) + (Z_B - Z_A) + h_L$$

$$= \left(\frac{28.29^2}{2\times 9.81} - \frac{15.92^2}{2\times 9.81}\right) + (1.5 - 0) + 5$$

$$= 40.80 - 12.92 + 6.5 = 34.38 \text{ m}$$

Also $$p_A - p_B = 34.38 \times 9810 = 337267.8 \text{ N/m}^2.$$

7.7 PRACTICAL APPLICATIONS OF BERNOULLI'S EQUATION

Some of the flow measuring devices designed based on Bernoulli's equation are listed below:

(1) Venturimeter
(2) Orificemeter
(3) Nozzlemeter
(4) Pitot tube.

7.7.1 Venturimeter

Venturimeter is a device used to measure a rate of flow through a pipe.

Venturimeter consists of three parts:

(1) Convergent cone
(2) Cylindrical throat
(3) Divergent cone

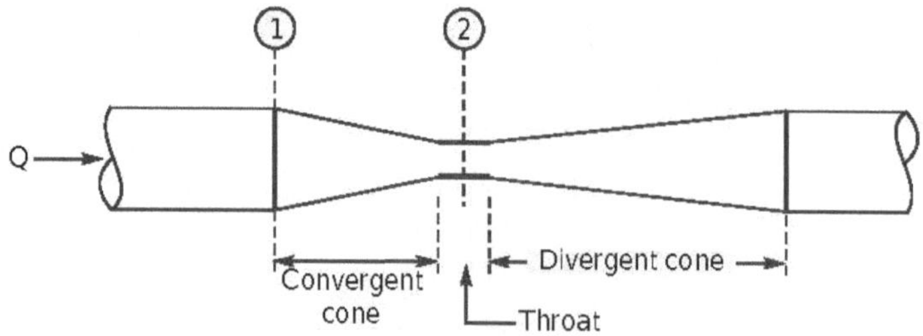

Fig. 7.4

(1) Convergent cone: Convergent cone tapers from the diameter of a pipe to the diameter of throat. The convergent cone has a included angle of 20° to 22° and its length is approximately 2.7 $(d_1 - d_2)$ where d_1 is a diameter of a pipe to which venturimeter is connected and d_2 is a diameter of a throat.

(2) Throat: The throat of the venturimeter is a short pipe of uniform diameter. Generally, the ratio of the diameter of throat to the diameter of pipe is $\frac{1}{3}$ to $\frac{3}{4}$ and preferably it is $\frac{1}{2}$. The length of throat is equal to its diameter.

When a fluid moves from pipe to throat through convergent cone the velocity of flow increases resulting decrease in pressure. The ratio of diameter of throat to diameter of pipe should be such that pressure in the throat should not drop below vapour pressure to avoid cavitation.

(3) Divergent cone: Divergent cone diverges from throat diameter to the diameter of pipe. The divergent cone has a included angle of 5° to 15°, generally it is 6°. Length of a divergent cone is more than the convergent cone. Length of a divergent cone should be sufficient since in divergent cone flow retards which may lead to separation of flow resulting energy loss.

Though the coefficient of discharge (C_d) depends on discharge, surface roughness, viscosity of flowing fluid etc., for general cases $C_d = 0.98$, can be used for venturimeter but coefficient of discharge varies from 0.95 to 0.99.

By applying Bernoulli's equation at sections (1) and (2) (Refer Fig. 7.4)

$$\frac{p_1}{\gamma} + \frac{V_1^2}{2g} + Z_1 = \frac{p_2}{\gamma} + \frac{V_2^2}{2g} + Z_2 \qquad \text{...(7.8)}$$

where all these terms carries general meaning.

Since the pipe is horizontal $Z_1 = Z_2$

$$\therefore \quad \frac{p_1}{\gamma} - \frac{p_2}{\gamma} = \frac{V_2^2}{2g} - \frac{V_1^2}{2g}$$

$$\frac{p_1 - p_2}{\gamma} = \frac{V_2^2}{2g} - \frac{V_1^2}{2g}$$

But $$\frac{p_1 - p_2}{\gamma} = h$$

$$\therefore \quad h = \frac{V_2^2}{2g} - \frac{V_1^2}{2g} \qquad \text{...(7.9)}$$

Using continuity principle for section (1) and (2)

$$a_1 V_1 = a_2 V_2$$

$$\therefore \quad V_1 = \frac{a_2}{a_1} V_2$$

put in equation (7.9)

$$\therefore \qquad h = \frac{V_2^2}{2g} - \frac{\left(\frac{a_2}{a_1}V_2\right)^2}{2g}$$

$$= \frac{V_2^2}{2g} - \frac{a_2^2 V_2^2}{a_1^2\, 2g}$$

$$= \frac{V_2^2}{2g}\left(1 - \frac{a_2^2}{a_1^2}\right)$$

$$= \frac{V_2^2}{2g}\left(\frac{a_1^2 - a_2^2}{a_1^2}\right)$$

$$\therefore \qquad V_2^2 = \frac{2gh\, a_1^2}{(a_1^2 - a_2^2)}$$

$$\therefore \qquad V_2 = \frac{a_1\sqrt{2gh}}{\sqrt{a_1^2 - a_2^2}}$$

Now discharge $= Q = a_2 V_2$

$$\therefore \qquad Q = \frac{a_1 a_2\sqrt{2gh}}{\sqrt{a_1^2 - a_2^2}} \qquad ...(7.10)$$

and actual discharge $= Q_{\text{act.}} = C_d \dfrac{a_1 a_2\sqrt{2gh}}{\sqrt{a_1^2 - a_2^2}}$ ...(7.11)

where C_d = coefficient of discharge for venturimeter.

7.7.2 Orificemeter

Orificemeter is a flow measuring device. It works on Bernoulli's principle. Orificemeter is cheaper than venturimeter and requires less length for its installation.

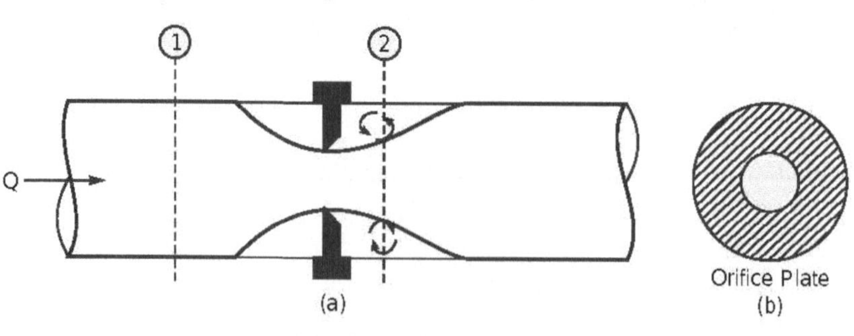

Fig. 7.5 Orificemeter

An orifice meter consists of a flat circular plate with a circular hole through which water can flow is called orifice (Fig.7.5 (*b*))

The ratio of orifice diameter to pipe diameter may vary from 0.2 to 0.8 but the orifice diameter is kept generally 0.5 times the diameter of the pipe.

Pressure measuring devices are connected to section (1) which is 0.9 to 1.1 times the pipe diameter upstream from the orifice plate and to section (2) where the cross-sectional area of flow is minimum called vena-contracta.

In case of orificemeter change in the cross-sectional areas is sudden and hence as compared to venturimeter energy losses are more.

An expression for discharge can be derived in the same way as that of venturimeter *i.e.*, by applying Bernoulli's and continuity equation as section (1) and (2) and is given by

$$Q_{act} = C_d \frac{a_1 a_2 \sqrt{2gh}}{\sqrt{a_1^2 - a_2^2}} \quad ...(7.12)$$

where C_d = coefficient of discharge and for turbulent flow it ranges from 0.59 to 0.88.

7.7.3 Nozzlemeter

Nozzlemeter is a flow measuring device and consists of a streamlined convergent nozzle through which water flows.

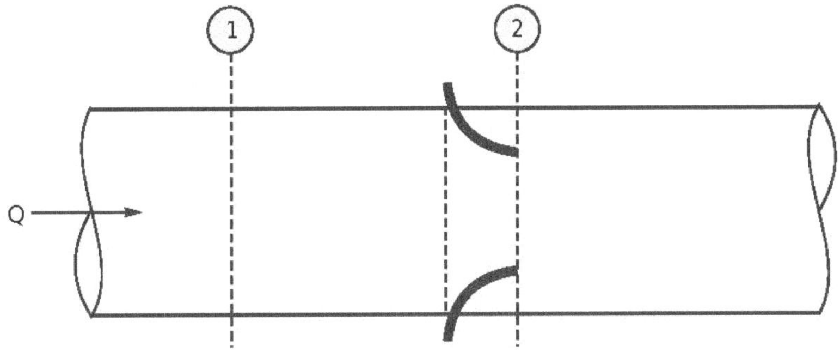

Fig. 7.6 Nozzlemeter

Since divergent cone is not provided on downstream side of nozzle energy loss will be more as compared to venturimeter.

An expression for discharge can be derived in the same way as that of venturimeter *i.e.*, by applying Bernoulli's and continuity equation at section (1) and (2) and is given by

$$Q_{act} = \frac{C_d a_1 a_2 \sqrt{2gh}}{\sqrt{a_1^2 - a_2^2}} \quad ...(7.13)$$

where, C_d = coefficient of discharge and for nozzlemeter its range is same as that of venturimeter.

7.7.4 Hints for Solving Problems Based on Venturimeter, Orificemeter, Nozzlemeter

Case I: Pressure gauges are used at section (1) and (2)

$$\frac{p_1}{\gamma}+\frac{V_1^2}{2g}+Z_1 = \frac{p_2}{\gamma}+\frac{V_2^2}{2g}+Z_2$$

here put the values of p_1 and p_2 (unit $\rightarrow$ N/m^2).

Case II: Simple manometers are used are section (1) and (2)

$$\frac{p_1}{\gamma}+\frac{V_1^2}{2g}+Z_1 = \frac{p_2}{\gamma}+\frac{V_2^2}{2g}+Z_2$$

Here put the values of $\frac{p_1}{\gamma}=h_1$ and $\frac{p_2}{\gamma}=h_2$ (unit $\rightarrow m$) where h_1 and h_2 are the manometric readings if manometric fluid and flowing fluid is same. If it is different then

$$\frac{p_1}{\gamma} = h_1 = x_1\left(\frac{S_m}{S_o}-1\right)$$

and,
$$\frac{p_2}{\gamma} = h_2 = x_2\left(\frac{S_m}{S_o}-1\right)$$

where x_1 and x_2 are the manometric readings at 1 and 2 respectively.

S_m = Specific gravity of manometric fluid

S_o = Specific gravity of flowing fluid.

Case III: Simple manometer and pressure gauge both are used

Let at section (1) simple manometer and at section (2) pressure gauge is used

then,
$$\frac{p_1}{\gamma} = h_1 \rightarrow \text{if same fluid}$$

$$h_1 = x_1\left(\frac{S_m}{S_o}-1\right) \rightarrow \text{is manometric fluid different that the flowing}$$

fluid and $p_2 \rightarrow$ pressure gauge reading in N/m^2.

Case IV: Differential manometer is used

$$\frac{p_1}{\gamma}+\frac{V_1^2}{2g}+Z_1 = \frac{p_2}{\gamma}+\frac{V_2^2}{2g}+Z_2$$

$$h = \left(\frac{p_1}{\gamma}+Z_1\right)-\left(\frac{p_2}{\gamma}+Z_2\right)=\frac{V_2^2}{2g}-\frac{V_1^2}{2g}$$

where
$$h = x\left(\frac{S_m}{S_o}-1\right) \text{ for } S_m > S_o$$

and $$h = x\left(1 - \frac{S_m}{S_o}\right) \text{ for } S_m < S_o$$

General Note: In Bernoulli's equation all terms shall be expressed in terms of flowing fluid column and hence

$$\gamma = 9810 \text{ N/m}^3 \text{ for water}$$

and $$\gamma = 9810 \times S_o \text{ N/m}^3 \text{ for other fluids.}$$

■ **Problem 7.4:** *A 10 cm × 5 cm horizontal venturimeter carries 50 lit/sec of water and has $C_d = 0.97$. Find the deflection in a mercury manometer connected between entrance and throat.*

Given: $d_1 = 10 \text{ cm} = 0.1 \text{ m}$

$d_2 = 5 \text{ cm} = 0.05 \text{ m}$

$Z_1 = Z_2$ ∵ *Venturimeter is horizontal*

$Q = 50 \text{ lit/sec} = 50 \times 10^{-3} \text{ m}^3\text{/sec}$

$C_d = 0.97$

$S_o = 1.0$ *(Flowing fluid is water)*

$S_m = 13.6$ *(Manometric fluid is mercury).*

Solution:

Using Bernoulli's equation at entrance and throat

$$\frac{p_1}{\gamma} + \frac{V_1^2}{2g} + Z_1 = \frac{p_2}{\gamma} + \frac{V_2^2}{2g} + Z_2$$

$$\therefore \quad h = \left(\frac{p_1}{\gamma} + Z_1\right) - \left(\frac{p_2}{\gamma} + Z_2\right) = \frac{V_2^2}{2g} - \frac{V_1^2}{2g}$$

Also $$h = x\left(\frac{S_m}{S_o} - 1\right) = \frac{V_2^2}{2g} - \frac{V_1^2}{2g} \quad ...(7.14)$$

using continuity equation

$$Q = C_d a_1 V_1 = C_d a_2 V_2$$

$$\therefore \quad 50 \times 10^{-3} = 0.97 \times \frac{\pi \times 0.1^2}{4} \times V_1$$

$$\therefore \quad V_1 = 6.56 \text{ m/sec}$$

Similarly $$50 \times 10^{-3} = \frac{0.97 \times \pi \times 0.05^2}{4} V_2$$

$$\therefore \quad V_2 = 26.25 \text{ m/sec}$$

put in equation (7.14)

$$\therefore \quad x\left(\frac{13.6}{1.0} - 1\right) = \frac{26.25^2}{2 \times 9.81} - \frac{6.56^2}{2 \times 9.81}$$

$$\therefore \qquad x = \frac{35.12 - 2.19}{12.6} = 2.61\,\text{m}$$

∴ Deflection in a mercury manometer is 2.61 m.

■ **Problem 7.5:** *A 15 cm ×5 cm venturimeter is provided in a vertical pipe carrying crude oil (sp. gr = 0.8). The flow is in upward direction. The difference of elevation between the entrance and throat section of the venturimeter is 25 cm. The difference in level between the two limbs of U-tube mercury manometer recorded is 20 cm. Calculate (i) Flow rate of oil (ii) Pressure difference between the entrance and the throat section. Take coefficient discharge as 0.95.*

Given:

$$d_1 = 15\ cm = 0.15\ m$$
$$d_2 = 5\ cm = 0.05\ m$$
$$S_o = 0.8,\ S_m = 13.6$$
$$Z_2 - Z_1 = 25\ m = 0.25\ m$$
$$x = 20\ cm = 0.2\ m$$
$$C_d = 0.95.$$

Solution:

$$a_1 = \frac{\pi d_1^2}{4} = \frac{\pi \times 0.15^2}{4} = 0.0177\ \text{m}^2$$

$$a_2 = \frac{\pi d_2^2}{4} = \frac{\pi \times 0.05^2}{4} = 1.963 \times 10^{-3}\ \text{m}^2$$

Using
$$h = x\left(\frac{S_m}{S_o} - 1\right)$$
$$= 0.2\left(\frac{13.6}{0.8} - 1\right) = 3.2\ \text{m}$$

Applying Bernoulli's equation at entrance and throat of venturimeter

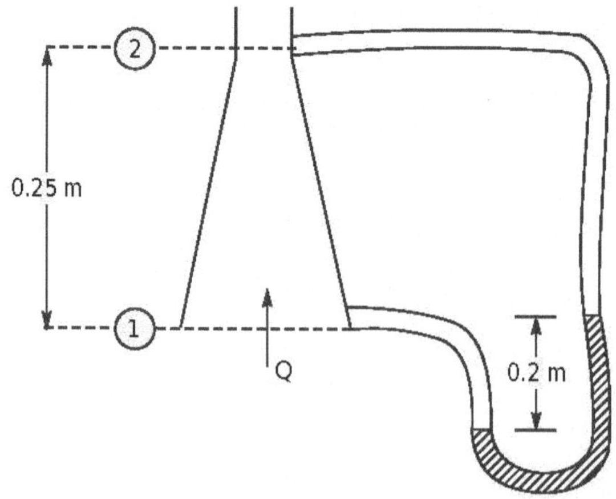

Fig. 7.7

$$\frac{p_1}{\gamma}+\frac{V_1^2}{2g}+Z_1 = \frac{p_2}{\gamma}+\frac{V_2^2}{2g}+Z_2$$

Now, $$h = \left(\frac{p_1}{g}+Z_1\right)-\left(\frac{p_2}{\gamma}+Z_2\right)=\frac{V_2^2}{2g}-\frac{V_1^2}{2g}$$

$\therefore$ $$h = \frac{V_2^2}{2g}-\frac{V_1^2}{2g} \qquad ...(7.15)$$

Also applying continuity principle at section (1) and (2)

$$a_1V_1 = a_2V_2$$

$$0.0177\ V_1 = 1.963 \times 10^{-3}\ V_2$$

$\therefore$ $$V_1 = \frac{1.963\times10^{-3}}{0.0177}V_2$$

$$= 0.11\ V_2$$

Put in equation (7.15)

$\therefore$ $$h = \frac{V_2^2}{2g}-\frac{(0.11V_2)^2}{2g}$$

$\therefore$ $$3.2 = V_2^2\left(\frac{1-0.11^2}{2\times9.81}\right)$$

$\therefore$ $$V_2 = 7.97 \text{ m/sec}$$

$\therefore$ $$Q_{act} = C_d\,a_2\,V_2$$

$$= 0.95 \times 1.963 \times 10^{-3} \times 7.97 = 0.0149 \text{ m}^2\text{/sec}$$

Now $$h = \left(\frac{p_1}{\gamma}+Z_1\right)-\left(\frac{p_2}{\gamma}+Z_2\right)$$

$\therefore$ $$\frac{p_1}{\gamma}-\frac{p_2}{\gamma} = h - Z_1 + Z_2$$

$$= 3.2 - 0 + 0.25$$

$$= 3.45 \text{ m of oil.}$$

■ **Problem 7.6:** *A venturimeter with a throat diameter of 10 cm is connected to a 20 cm diameter main carrying water. The head loss between the inlet and the throat is known to be 0.1* $\frac{V_2^2}{2g}$ *where* V_2 *is the velocity at the throat. Estimate the discharge when the inverted differential U-tube manometer connected to the inlet and throat records a reading of 30 cm. The manometric fluid has a relative density of 0.75. What is the coefficient of discharge of the meter?*

Given:

$$d_1 = 20\ cm = 0.2\ m$$
$$d_2 = 10\ cm = 0.1\ m$$
$$h_L = 0.1\frac{V_2^2}{2g}$$
$$x = 30\ cm = 0.3\ m$$
$$S_m = 0.75$$
$$S_o = 1.0.$$

Solution:

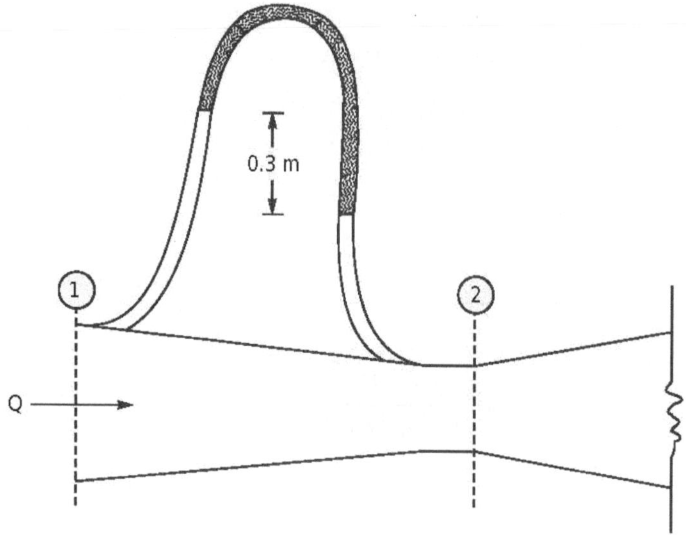

Fig. 7.8

Applying continuity equation at section (1) and (2)

$$a_1V_1 = a_1V_2$$

$$\frac{\pi \times 0.2^2}{4} \times V_1 = \frac{\pi \times 0.1^2}{4} \times V_2$$

$\therefore$ $$V_1 = 0.25\ V_2 \qquad ...(7.16)$$

Applying Bernoulli's equation at entrance and throat of venturimeter

$$\frac{p_1}{\gamma} + \frac{V_1^2}{2g} + Z_1 = \frac{p_2}{\gamma} + \frac{V_2^2}{2g} + Z_2 + h_L$$

$\therefore$ $$h_L = \left(\frac{p_1}{g} + Z_1\right) - \left(\frac{p_2}{g} + Z_2\right) = \frac{V_2^2}{2g} - \frac{V_1^2}{2g} + h_L \qquad ...(7.17)$$

In this case $S_m < S_o$

$\therefore$ $$h = x\left(1 - \frac{S_m}{S_o}\right) \qquad ...(7.18)$$

From equations (7.17) and (7.18)

$$x\left(1-\frac{S_m}{S_o}\right) = \frac{V_2^2}{2g}-\frac{V_1^2}{2g}+0.1\frac{V_2^2}{2g}$$

$$0.3\left(1-\frac{0.75}{1.0}\right) = \frac{V_2^2}{2g}-\frac{V_1^2}{2g}(1-0.1)$$

$$0.3\left(1-\frac{0.75}{1.0}\right) = \frac{V_2^2}{2g}-\frac{(0.25\,V_2)^2}{2g}(0.9)$$

$$0.075 = V_2^2\left(\frac{1-0.05625}{2\times 9.81}\right)$$

$$V_2 = 1.19 \text{ m/sec}$$

and $$Q = a_2V_2$$

$$= \frac{\pi\times 0.1^2}{4}\times 1.19$$

$$= 9.81\times 10^{-3} \text{ m}^3\text{/sec}$$

Now $$h_L = \frac{0.1\,V_2^2}{2g}$$

$$= \frac{0.1\times 1.19^2}{2\times 9.81}$$

$$= 7.9638\times 10^{-3} \text{ m}$$

and $$h = x\left(1-\frac{S_m}{S_o}\right)$$

$$= 0.3\left(1-\frac{0.75}{1.0}\right)$$

$$= 0.075 \text{ m}$$

∴ $$C_d = \sqrt{\frac{h_L-h_a}{h}}$$

$$= 0.94.$$

■ **Problem 7.7:** *A horizontal venturimeter with inlet diameter 20 cm and throat diameter 10 cm is used to measure the flow of oil of sp. gr. 0.8. The discharge of oil through venturimeter is 60 lit/sec. Find the reading of oil-mercury differential manometer. Take C_d = 0.98.*

Given: d_1 = 20 cm = 0.2 m

d_2 = 10 cm = 0.1 m

$S_o = 0.8, S_m = 13.6$

$Q = 60\ lit/sec = 60 \times 10^{-3}\ m^3/sec$

$C_d = 0.98.$

Solution:

$$a_1 = \frac{\pi d_1^2}{4} = \frac{\pi \times 0.2^2}{4} = 0.0314\ \text{m}^2$$

$$a_2 = \frac{\pi d_2^2}{4} = \frac{\pi \times 0.1^2}{4} = 7.85 \times 10^{-3}\ \text{m}^2$$

Using continuity equation

$$Q = C_d a_1 V_1 = C_d a_2 V_2$$

$\therefore$ $60 \times 20^{-3} = 0.98 \times 0.0314 \times V_1$

$\therefore$ $V_1 = 1.95$ m/sec

Similarly $60 \times 10^{-3} = 0.98 \times 7.85 \times 10^{-3} \times V_2$

$\therefore$ $V_2 = 7.8$ m/sec

Using Bernoulli's equation

$$\frac{p_1}{\gamma} + \frac{V_1^2}{2g} + Z_1 = \frac{p_1}{\gamma} + \frac{V_2^2}{2g} + Z_2$$

Also

$$h = x\left(\frac{S_m}{S_o} - 1\right) = \left(\frac{p_1}{\gamma} + Z_1\right) - \left(\frac{p_2}{\gamma} + Z_2\right) = \frac{V_2^2}{2g} - \frac{V_1^2}{2g}$$

$\therefore$

$$x\left(\frac{S_m}{S_o} - 1\right) = \frac{V_2^2}{2g} - \frac{V_1^2}{2g}$$

$$x\left(\frac{13.6}{0.8} - 1\right) = \frac{7.8^2}{2 \times 9.81} - \frac{1.95^2}{2 \times 9.81}$$

$\therefore$

$$x = \frac{2.9071}{16} = 0.1817\ \text{m} = 18.17\ \text{cm}$$

$\therefore$ Reading of oil mercury manometer is 18.17 cm.

■ **Problem 7.8:** *A venturimeter measures the flow of water in a 75 mm diameter pipe. The difference of head between the throat and the entrance of the meter is measured by a U-tube containing mercury, the mercury being in contact with the water. What should be the diameter of the throat of the meter in order that the difference in level of the mercury be 25 cm. When the quantity of water flowing in the pipe is 650 lpm. Assume 'C_d' of the meter as 0.97.*

Given: $d_1 = 75\ mm = 0.075\ m$

$S_o = 1.0$

$S_m = 13.6$

$x = 25\ cm = 0.25\ m$

$$Q = 650\ lpm = \frac{650}{60}\ lps = \frac{650}{60}\ 10^{-3}\ m^3/sec = 0.01083\ m^3/sec$$

$$C_d = 0.97.$$

Solution:

$$a_1 = \frac{\pi d_1^2}{4} = \frac{\pi \times 0.075^2}{4} = 4.4179 \times 10^{-3}\ \text{m}^2$$

$$a_1 = \frac{\pi d_2^2}{4} = 0.7854\, d_2^2\ \text{m}^2$$

Using continuity equation

$$Q = C_d\, a_1\, V_1 = C_d\, a_2 V_2$$

$\therefore$ $0.01083 = 0.97 \times 4.4179 \times 10^{-3} \times V_1$

$\therefore$ $V_1 = 2.53$ m/sec

Similarly $0.01083 = 0.97 \times 0.7854\ d_2^2 \times V_2$

$\therefore$ $V_2 = \dfrac{0.0142}{d_2^2}$ m/sec

Using Bernoulli's equation

$$\frac{p_1}{\gamma} + \frac{V_1^2}{2g} + Z_1 = \frac{p_2}{\gamma} + \frac{V_2^2}{2g} + Z_2$$

$$\therefore \quad h = x\left(\frac{S_m}{S_o} - 1\right) = \left(\frac{p_1}{\gamma} + Z_1\right) - \left(\frac{p_2}{\gamma} + Z_2\right) = \frac{V_2^2}{2g} - \frac{V_1^2}{2g}$$

$$\therefore \quad x\left(\frac{S_m}{S_o} - 1\right) = \frac{V_2^2}{2g} - \frac{V_1^2}{2g}$$

$$0.25\left(\frac{13.6}{1.0} - 1\right) = \left(\frac{0.0142}{d_2^2}\right)^2 \frac{1}{2 \times 9.81} - \frac{2.53^2}{2 \times 9.81}$$

$$3.15 = \frac{1.0277 \times 10^{-5}}{d_2^4} - 0.3562$$

$$\therefore \quad d_2 = \left(\frac{1.0277 \times 10^{-5}}{3.15 + 0.3262}\right)^{1/4}$$

$= (0.2956 \times 10^{-5})^{1/4}$

$= 0.041$ m

$= 4.1$ cm

$= 41$ mm.

■ **Problem 7.9:** *A 30 cm × 15 cm venturimeter is fitted in a horizontal pipeline carrying oil of specific gravity 0.8. The pressure at the inlet of the meter is 14 N/cm² and at the throat the vacuum pressure is 37 cm of mercury. Assuming 5% of the differential head is lost between the inlet and throat, determine the rate of flow of oil through the pipeline.*

Given:

$$d_1 = 30\ cm = 0.3\ m$$

$$d_2 = 15\ cm = 0.15\ m$$

$$S_o = 0.8$$

$$p_1 = 14\ N/cm^2 = 14 \times 10^4\ N/m^2$$

$$\frac{p_2}{\gamma} = -37\ cm\ of\ mercury$$

$$h_L = 0.05\left(\frac{p_1}{\gamma} - \frac{p_2}{\gamma}\right).$$

Solution:

$$\frac{p_2}{\gamma} = -37 \text{ cm of mercury}$$

$$= -0.37 \text{ m of mercury}$$

$$= -0.37 \times 13.6 = -5.032 \text{ m of water}$$

$$= \frac{-5.032}{0.8} = -6.29 \text{ m of oil}$$

$$h_L = 0.05\left(\frac{p_1}{\gamma} - \frac{p_2}{\gamma}\right)$$

$$= 0.05\left(\frac{14 \times 10^4}{9810 \times 0.8} - (-6.29)\right)$$

$$= 0.05\ (17.83 + 6.29)$$

$$= 1.206 \text{ m}$$

Horizontal venturimeter ∴ $Z_1 = Z_2$

Using continuity equation

$$a_1 V_1 = a_2 V_2$$

$$\frac{\pi d_1^2}{4} \times V_1 = \frac{\pi d_2^2}{4} \times V_2$$

$$0.0707\ V_1 = 0.01767\ V_2$$

$$\therefore \quad V_1 = 0.25\ V_2$$

Using Bernoulli's equation

$$\frac{p_1}{\gamma} + \frac{V_1^2}{2g} + Z_1 = \frac{p_2}{\gamma} + \frac{V_2^2}{2g} + Z_2 + h_L$$

$$\frac{14\times10^4}{0.8\times9810}+\frac{(0.25V_2)^2}{2\times9.81}=-6.29+\frac{V_2^2}{2\times9.81}+1.206$$

$$17.83 + 3.18 \times 10^{-3} V_1^2 = -6.29 + 0.05 V_2^2 + 1.206$$

$$V_2 = 20.79 \text{ m/sec}$$

∴ Rate of flow of oil through the pipeline

$$= Q = a_2V_2 = 0.1767 \times 20.79$$

$$= 3.67 \text{ m}^3\text{/sec.}$$

■ **Problem 7.10:** *An orifice meter of orifice diameter 10 cm is inserted in pipe of 20 cm diameter. The pressure gauge fitted on upstream and downstream give readings of 20 N/cm² and 10 N/cm² respectively. C_d = 0.6. Find the discharge.*

Given:

$$d_1 = 20 \text{ cm} = 0.2 \text{ m}$$

$$d_2 = 10 \text{ cm} = 0.1 \text{ m}$$

$$p_1 = 20 \text{ N/cm}^2 = 20 \times 10^4 \text{ N/m}^2$$

$$p_2 = 10 \text{ N/cm}^2 = 10 \times 10^4 \text{ N/m}^2$$

$$C_d = 0.6.$$

Solution:

$$a_1 = \frac{\pi d_1^2}{4} = \frac{\pi\times0.2^2}{4} = 0.0314 \text{ m}^2$$

$$a_2 = \frac{\pi d_2^2}{4} = \frac{\pi\times0.1^2}{4} = 0.00785 \text{ m}^2$$

Using continuity equation

$$a_1V_1 = a_2V_2$$

∴ $$0.0314\ V_1 = 0.00785\ V_2$$

∴ $$V_1 = 0.25\ V_2$$

Using Bernoulli's equation

$$\frac{p_1}{\gamma}+\frac{V_1^2}{2g}+Z_1 = \frac{p_2}{\gamma}+\frac{V_2^2}{2g}+Z_2$$

Let $$Z_1 = Z_2$$

$$\therefore \frac{20\times10^4}{9810}+\frac{(0.25V_2)^2}{2\times9.81} = \frac{10\times10^4}{9810}+\frac{V_2^2}{2\times9.81}$$

$$20.387 + 3.185 \times 10^{-3} V_2^2 = 10.194 + 0.051 V_2^2$$

∴ $$V_2^2 = \frac{10.194}{0.0478} = 213.26$$

$$V_2 = 14.60 \text{ m/s}$$

∴ $$Q = C_d a_2 V_2 = 0.6 \times 0.00785 \times 14.60$$

$$Q = 0.06878 \text{ m}^3\text{/sec.}$$

7.8 SOME IMPORTANT FLOW MEASURING DEVICES

7.8.1 Rotameter

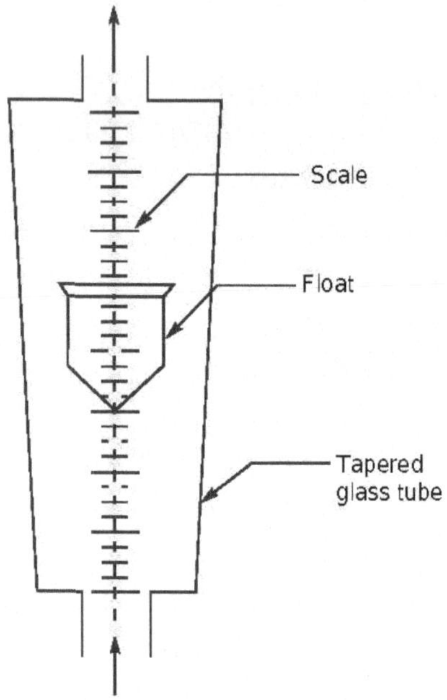

Fig. 7.9 Rotameter

Rotameter consists of a transparent tube of variable area in which a sharp circular upper edged float is inserted. The tube is graduated properly. The float has grooves on its head because of which float rotates when fluid flows through the tube. When there is no flow float rests on the bottom of the tube. As liquid flows through the tube, the float get lifted to a level which directly shows a discharge.

7.8.2 Elbow Meter

It consists of a 90° pipe bend. Pressure measuring devices are provided on the inner and outer side of the bend.

If a differential pressure head is 'h' then the discharge is given by

$$Q = C_d A \sqrt{2gh}$$

where Q = Discharge (m^3/sec)

C_d = Coefficient of discharge depends on $\frac{R}{r}$ ratio and its general range is in between 0.56 to 0.83

A = Cross-sectional area (m^2)

h = Differential pressure head.

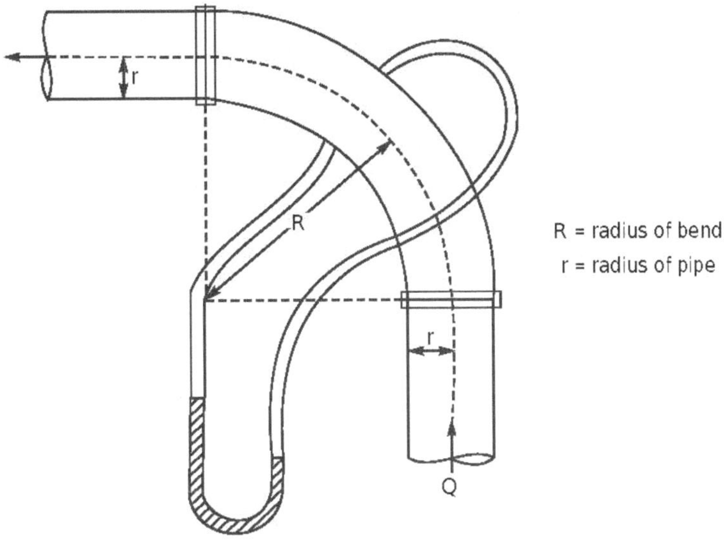

Fig. 7.10 Elbow-meter

7.9 VELOCITY MEASURING DEVICES

7.9.1 Hot Wire Anemometer

Hot wire anemometer is generally used to measure a rapidly fluctuating flow. In this a very fine wire heated between two small probes. The probe is introduced into the flowing fluid. The rate of cooling of wire depends on velocity keeping other factors constant.

Hot wires can be arranged in groups to measure multidimensional flows.

7.9.2 Simple Pitot Tube

Pitot tube is used to measure a velocity of flowing fluid. It consists of a glass tube bent in a '*L*' shape. Its one end is immersed in a fluid facing the flow. From the rise of fluid in the tube a velocity can be calculated.

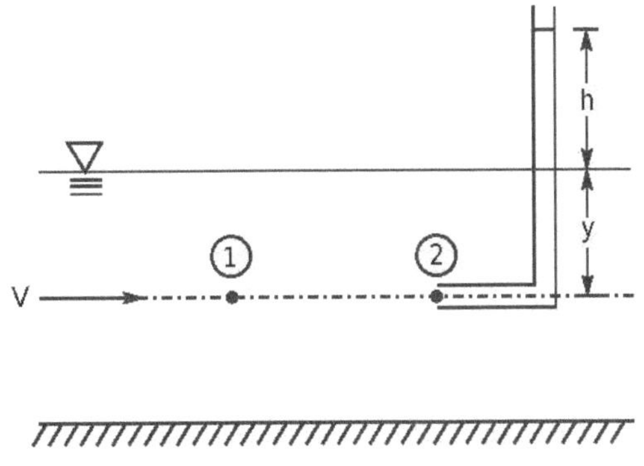

Fig. 7.11 Simple Pitot Tube

Applying Bernoulli's equation at (1) and (2) where (1) and (2) are on the same level, (1) inside the flow and (2) at the entrance of pilot tube.

$$\therefore \qquad \frac{p_1}{\gamma} + \frac{V_1^2}{2g} + Z_1 = \frac{p_2}{\gamma} + \frac{V_2^2}{2g} + Z_2$$

Now $\qquad Z_1 = Z_2,$

$$\frac{p_1}{\gamma} = y,$$

$$\frac{p_2}{\gamma} = y + h$$

Let $\qquad V_1 = V =$ velocity of flow

$V_2 = 0 =$ since (2) is a stagnation point

$$\therefore \qquad y + \frac{V^2}{2g} = y + h + 0$$

$$\therefore \qquad \frac{V^2}{2g} = h$$

$$\therefore \qquad V = \sqrt{2gh}$$

if $\qquad C_V =$ Coefficient of velocity

then $\qquad V \text{ actual} = C_V \sqrt{2gh} \qquad \text{...(7.19)}$

7.9.3 Static Pitot Tube

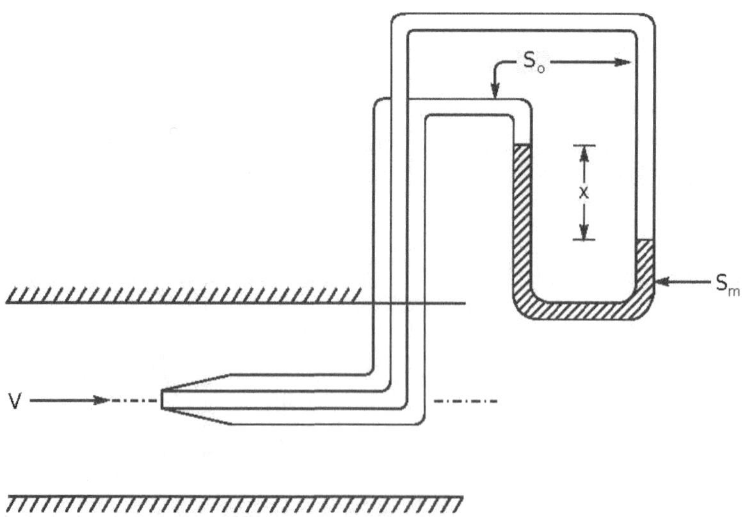

Fig. 7.12 Static Pitot Tube

It consists to two concentric tubes. The outer one is perforated one. The two ends of the concentric tubes are connected to differential manometer. From the differential pressure velocity of flow can be calculated by using equation (7.19).

$$V_{act} = C_V\sqrt{2gh}$$

where $$h = x\left(\frac{S_m}{S_o} - 1\right) \text{ for } S_m > S_o$$

or $$h = x\left(1 - \frac{S_m}{S_o}\right) \text{ for } S_m < S_o.$$

■ **Problem 7.11:** *Sketch and explain the principles behind a pitot static tube and hence find the speed of a submarine moving in sea water for a deflection of 4 cm in a mercury differential manometer which is connected to pitot static tube. Take coefficient as unity and specific gravity of sea water as 1.03.*

Given: $x = 4\ cm = 0.04\ m$

$C_v = 1.0$

$S_m = 13.6$

$S_o = 1.03.$

Solution: For theory part see subtopic number 7.9.3

Now $S_m > S_o$

∴ Using $$h = x\left(\frac{S_m}{S_o} - 1\right)$$

$$= 0.04\left(\frac{13.6}{1.03} - 1\right) = 0.488 \text{ m}$$

Using equation (7.19)

$$V_{act} = C_v\sqrt{2gh}$$

$$= 1.0\sqrt{2 \times 9.81 \times 0.488} = 3.09 \text{ m/sec}$$

∴ Speed of the submarine is 3.09 m/sec.

7.10 MOMENTUM EQUATION

Momentum equation can be derived from Newton's second law of motion which states that the rate of change of momentum is proportional to the applied force and takes place in the direction of that force.

Mathematically $$F = m \times a$$

$$= m \times \frac{dv}{dt}$$

$$\therefore \quad F \times dt = d(m \times v) \qquad \text{...(7.20)}$$

Equation (7.20) is called impulse momentum equation and is used for the dynamic analysis of fluid flow.

7.11 APPLICATIONS OF MOMENTUM EQUATION

7.11.1 Flow Through Pipe Bend

Consider a pipe bend with angle of deflection of water flow is θ as shown in Figure 7.13.

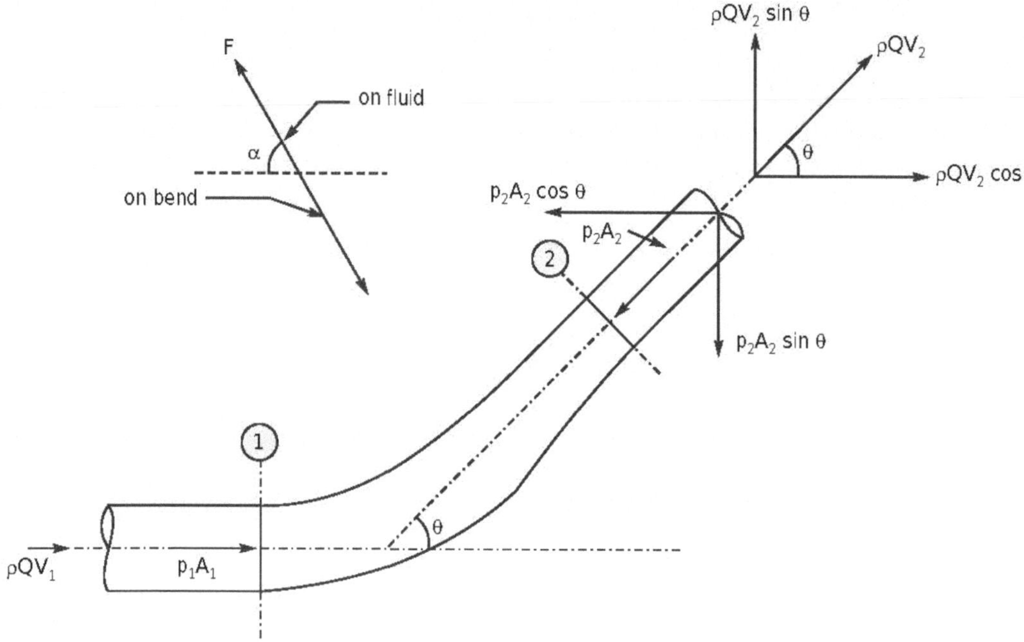

Fig. 7.13

Let p_1, V_1, A_1 are the pressure, velocity, area of cross-section of flow at section (1) and similarly p_2, V_2, A_2 at section (2).

The momentum equation in the x-direction can be stated as

$$p_1A_1 - p_2A_2 \cos \theta + F_x = \rho Q (V_2 \cos \theta - V_1) \quad ...(7.21)$$

Similarly for y-direction

$$-p_2A_2 \cos \theta + F_y = \rho Q (V_2 \sin \theta - 0) \quad ...(7.22)$$

$\therefore$ The force exerted by the pipe bend on the fluid $= F = \sqrt{F_x^2 + F_y^2}$ ...(7.23)

and as per the Newton's third law of motion the force exerted by the fluid on the bend will have the same magnitude but opposite direction to F.

The inclination of F with the horizontal is calculated as $\alpha = \tan^{-1}\left(\dfrac{F_y}{F_x}\right)$ ...(7.24)

7.11.2 Flow Through Nozzle

Refer Figure 7.14

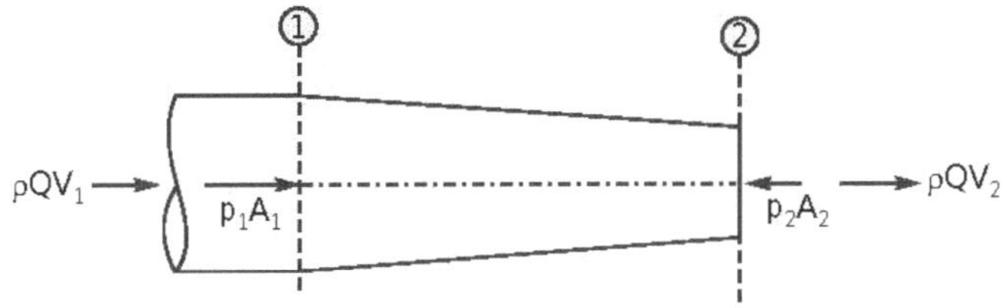

Fig. 7.14

The momentum equation in x-direction

$$p_1A_1 - p_2A_2 + F_x = \rho Q(V_2 - V_1) \quad ...(7.25)$$

Since nozzle discharges water to atmosphere at section (2) pressure will be atmospheric

$$\therefore \quad p_2 = 0$$

∴ Equation (7.25) can be written as

$$p_1A_1 + F_x = \rho Q(V_2 - V_1) \quad ...(7.26)$$

where F_x = Force exerted by nozzle on fluid.

The force acting on fluid in the y-direction *i.e.*, F_y will be zero since there is no change in momentum in y-direction.

$$\therefore \quad F = F_x$$

The force exerted by the fluid on the nozzle will have the same magnitude but opposite direction to F.

Solved Problems

■ **Problem 7.12:** *A reducing bend is placed in A pipeline such that the direction of flow of water is turned through 60° in the horizontal plane and the pipe diameter is reduced from 0.25 m to 0.15 m. The velocity and pressure at the entry to the bend are 1.5 m/s and 300 kN/m² gauge respectively. At the exit the pressure is 287.2 kN/m² gauge. Determine the force exerted by the bend on the water.*

Given: *Angle of bend* = θ = 60°

Bend is in horizontal plane i.e., $Z_1 = Z_2$

$d_1 = 0.25$ m

$d_2 = 0.15$ m

$V_1 = 1.5$ m/sec

$p_1 = 300$ kN/m² $= 300 \times 10^3$ N/m²

$p_2 = 287.2$ kN/m² $= 287.2 \times 10^3$ N/m².

Solution: Using continuity equation

$$A_1V_1 = A_2V_2$$

$$\frac{\pi d_1^2}{4} \times V_1 = \frac{\pi d_2^2}{4} \times V_2$$

$$\frac{\pi \times 0.25^2}{4} V_1 = \frac{\pi \times 0.15^2}{4} V_2$$

$$0.0491\, V_1 = 0.0177\, V_2$$

$\therefore$ $V_1 = 0.3599\, V_2$ ...(7.27)

But $V_1 = 1.5$ m/sec $\therefore$ $V_2 = 4.17$ m/sec

$\therefore$ $Q = A_1V_1 = 0.0491 \times 1.5$

$= 0.07365$ m³/sec

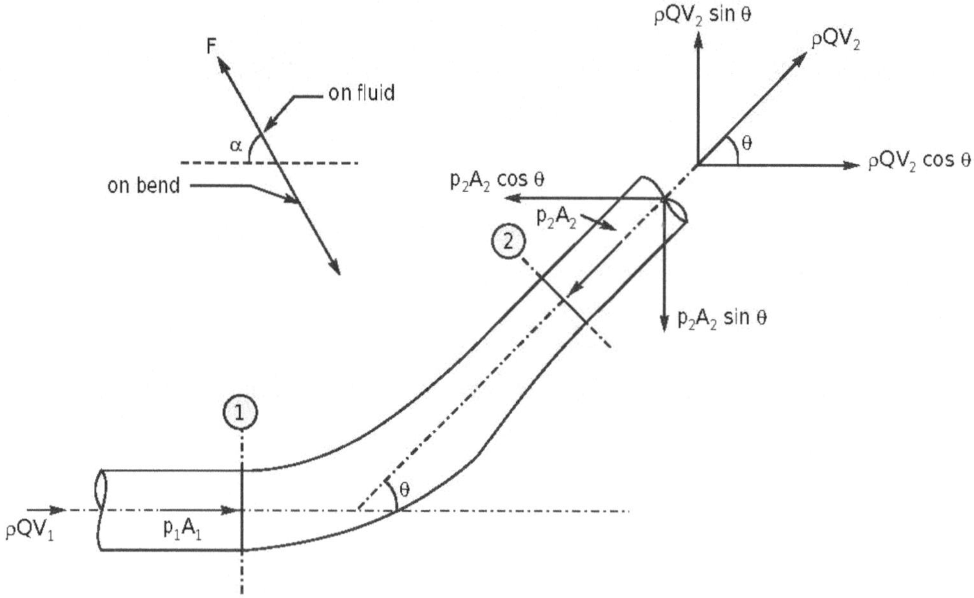

Fig. 7.15

The momentum equation in x-direction is given by equation (7.21) as

$$p_1A_1 - p_2A_2 \cos \theta + F_x = \rho Q\,(V_2 \cos \theta - V_1)$$

$$300 \times 10^3 \times 0.0491 - 287.2 \times 10^3 \times 0.0177 \cos 60° + F_x$$

$$= 1000 \times 0.07365\,(4.17 \cos 60° - 1.5)$$

$\therefore$ $F_x = -\,12145.19$ N

Similarly the momentum equation in y-direction is given by equation (7.22)

$$-\,p_2A_2 \cos \theta + F_y = \rho Q\,(V_2 \sin \theta - 0)$$

$$287.2 \times 10^3 \times 0.0177 \cos 60° + F_y$$

$$= 1000 \times 0.07365\,(4.17 \sin 60° - 0)$$

$\therefore$ $2541.72 + F_y = 265.974$

$\therefore$ $F_y = -\,2275.745$

∴ Force exerted by bend on fluid

$$= F = \sqrt{F_x^2 + F_y^2}$$

$$= \sqrt{(-12145.19)^2 + (-2275.745)^2}$$

$$= 12356.56 \text{ N.}$$

■ **Problem 7.13:** *A 90° degree bend in a 15 cm diameter pipe carries oil of specific gravity 0.8 at 110 lit/sec under a pressure of 0.8 m of oil at the entrance. Find the force on the bend.*

Given: Angle of bend = angle through which water get deflected = $\theta = 90°$

$$d_1 = d_2 = 15 \text{ cm} = 0.15 \text{ m}$$

$$S_0 = 0.8$$

$$Q = 110 \text{ lit/sec} = 110 \times 10^{-3} \text{ m}^3\text{/sec}$$

$$= 0.110 \text{ m}^3\text{/sec}$$

$$p_1 = 0.8 \text{ m of oil.}$$

Solution: Assuming the bend is in a horizontal plane *i.e.*, $Z_1 = Z_2$

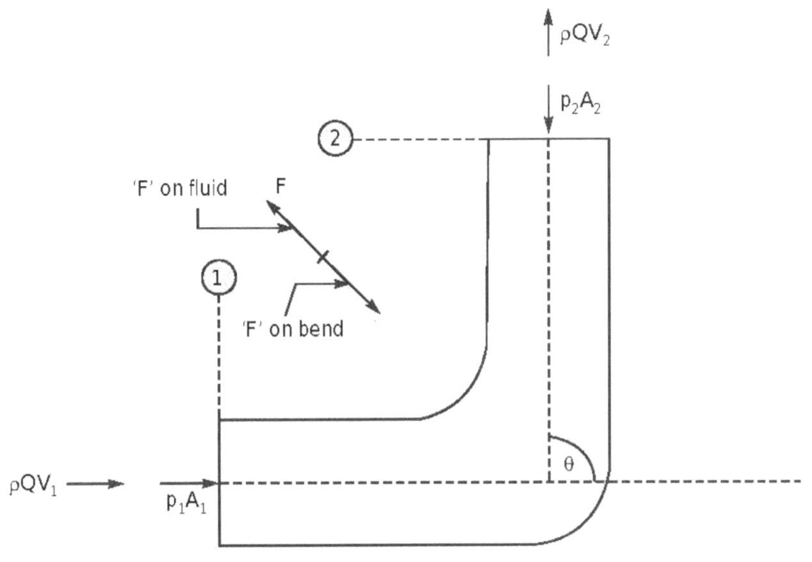

Fig. 7.16

Using continuity equation

$$Q = A_1 V_1 = A_2 V_2$$

Since $A_1 = A_2 \rightarrow V_1 = V_2$

∴ $$Q = \frac{\pi d_1^2}{4} \times V_1$$

$$0.110 = \frac{\pi \times 0.15^2}{4} \times V_1$$

∴ $$0.110 = 0.0177\, V_1$$

$\therefore \quad V_1 = 6.22$ m/sec

Applying Bernoulli's equation at (1) and (2)

$$\frac{p_1}{\gamma} + \frac{V_1^2}{2g} + Z_1 = \frac{p_2}{\gamma} + \frac{V_2^2}{2g} + Z_2$$

$$\because \quad V_1 = V_2,\ Z_1 = Z_2$$

$$p_1 = p_2$$

The momentum equation in x-direction

$$p_1 A_1 + F_x = \rho Q\,(0 - V_1)$$

$$0.8 \times 0.0177 + F_x = -1000 \times 0.110 \times 6.22$$

$$= -\,684.2142 \text{ N}$$

The momentum equation in y-direction

$$-p_2 A_2 + F_y = \rho Q\,(V_2 - 0)$$

$$-\,0.8 \times 0.0177 + F_y = +\,1000 \times 0.110 \times 6.22$$

$$\therefore \quad F_y = 684.2142 \text{ N}$$

$$\therefore \quad \text{Force on fluid} = \sqrt{F_x^2 + F_y^2}$$

$$= \sqrt{(684.2142)^2 + (+\,684.2142)^2}$$

$$= 967.62 \text{ N}$$

$\therefore$ Force exerted on the bend will have the same magnitude but opposite direction to F.

■ **Problem 7.14:** *A 120° bend cum reducer has 300 mm diameter at inlet and 200 mm diameter at the outer end. When it carries a flow 0.3 m³/s of water, the pressure at the inlet section is 210 kN/m². Assuming no energy loss in the bend determine the force exerted by the water on the bend. The bend is in a horizontal plane.*

Given: Angle of bend $= \theta = 120°$

$$d_1 = 300 \text{ mm} = 0.3 \text{ m}$$

$$d_2 = 200 \text{ mm} = 0.2 \text{ m}$$

$$Q = 0.3 \text{ m}^3/\text{sec}$$

$$p_1 = 210 \text{ kN/m}^2 = 210 \times 10^3 \text{ N/m}^2$$

Bend is in a horizontal plane i.e., $Z_1 = Z_2$.

Solution: Using continuity equation

$$Q = A_1 V_1 = A_2 V_2$$

$$\therefore \quad V_1 = \frac{Q}{A_1} = \frac{Q}{\frac{\pi d_1^2}{4}} = \frac{0.3}{\left(\frac{\pi \times 0.3^2}{4}\right)} = \frac{0.3}{0.07} = 4.29 \text{ m/sec}$$

and

$$V_2 = \frac{Q}{A_2} = \frac{Q}{\frac{\pi d_2^2}{4}} = \frac{0.3}{\left(\frac{\pi \times 0.2^2}{4}\right)} = \frac{0.3}{0.03} = 10 \text{ m/sec}$$

Applying Bernoulli's equation at (1) and (2)

$$\frac{p_1}{\gamma}+\frac{V_1^2}{2g}+Z_1 = \frac{p_2}{\gamma}+\frac{V_2^2}{2g}+Z_2$$

$$\frac{210\times10^3}{9810}+\frac{4.29^2}{2\times9.81} = \frac{p_2}{9810}+\frac{10^2}{2\times9.81} \qquad \because Z_1 = Z_2$$

$$21.4067 + 0.9380 = \frac{p_2}{9810} + 5.0968$$

$$\therefore \qquad p_2 = 169201.899 \text{ N/m}^2$$

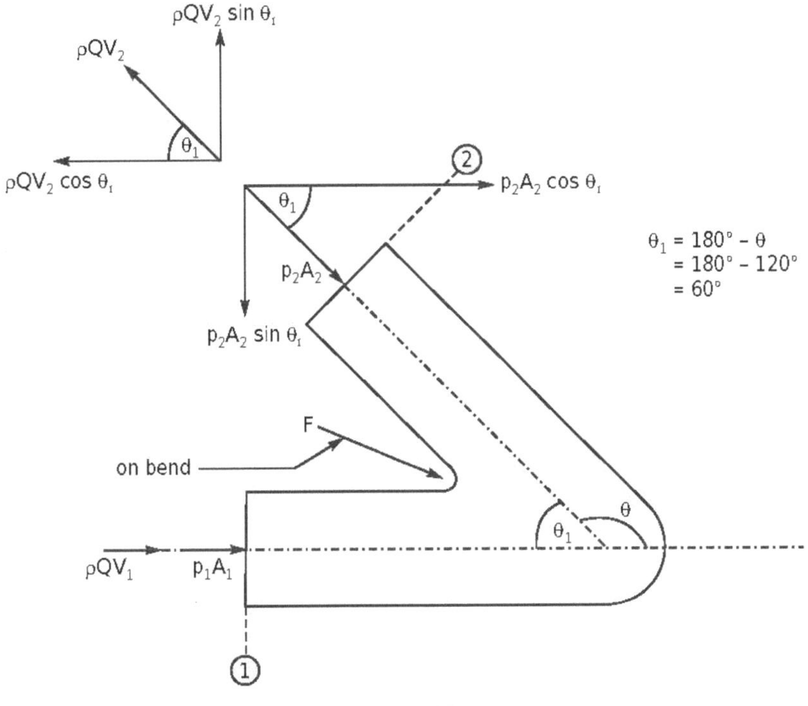

Fig. 7.17

The momentum equation in x-direction

$$p_1A_1 + p_2A_2 \cos \theta_1 + F_x = \rho Q\,(-V_2 \cos \theta_1 - V_1)$$

$$210 \times 10^3 \times 0.07 + 169201.899 \times 0.03 \cos 60° + F_x$$
$$= 1000 \times 0.3\,(-10 \cos 60° - 4.29)$$

$$\therefore \qquad 14700 + 2538.03 + F_x = -2787$$

$$\therefore \qquad F_x = -20025.03 \text{ N}$$

The momentum equation in y-direction

$$-p_2A_2 \sin \theta_1 + F_y = \rho Q\,(V_2 \sin \theta_1 - 0)$$

$$-169201.899 \times 0.03 \times \sin 60° + F_y = 1000 \times 0.3\,(10 \sin 60°)$$

$$-4395.99 + F_y = 2598.08$$

$\therefore \quad F_y = 6994.07$ N

$\therefore$ Force acting on the fluid $= F = \sqrt{F_x^2 + F_y^2}$

$$= \sqrt{(-20025.03)^2 + (6994.07)^2}$$

$$= 21211.29 \text{ N}$$

The force exerted by the water on the bend will have same magnitude but opposite direction to 'F'.

■ **Problem 7.15:** *A U-bend is placed in a horizontal plane. Its diameter at inlet is 100 mm. At outlet a nozzle having an exit diameter of 50 mm is connected. C_v for the nozzle is 0.97. If the head lost in the bend due to friction is 5% of its velocity head, determine the force on the bend given that the flow rate is 2000 lpm and pressure at inlet of bend is 200 kN/m².*

Given:

$$d_1 = 100 \text{ mm} = 0.1 \text{ m}$$

$$d_3 = 50 \text{ mm} = 0.05 \text{ m}$$

$$C_v = 0.97$$

$$h_L = 0.05 \frac{V_1^2}{2g}$$

$$Q = 2000 \text{ lpm} = \frac{2000}{60} = 33.33 \text{ lps}$$

$$= 33.33 \times 10^{-3} = 0.0333 \text{ m}^3/\text{sec}$$

$$p_1 = 200 \text{ kN/m}^2$$

$$= 200 \times 10^3 \text{ m}^2.$$

Solution:

Now $\quad d_1 = d_2$

$\therefore \quad a_1 = a_2$

$\therefore$ By continuity equation $V_1 = V_2$

applying Bernoulli's equation at (1) and (2)

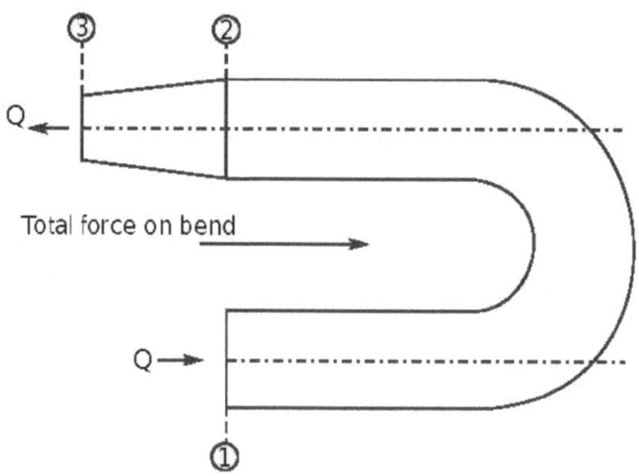

Fig. 7.18 (*a*)

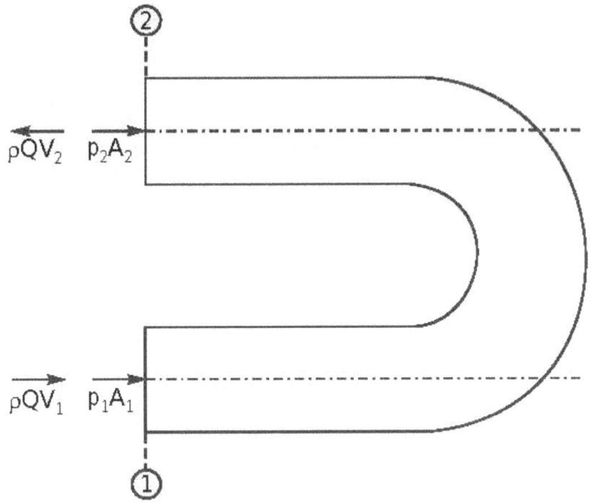

Fig. 7.18 (*b*)

$$\frac{p_1}{\gamma}+\frac{V_1^2}{2g}+Z_1 = \frac{p_2}{\gamma}+\frac{V_2^2}{2g}+Z_2+0.05\frac{V_1^2}{2g}$$

Now bend is horizontal $\therefore$ $Z_1 = Z_2$

Also $V_1 = V_2$ and $V_1 = \dfrac{Q}{A_1}$

$$= \frac{0.03333}{\left(\dfrac{\pi\times 0.12}{4}\right)}$$

$$= \frac{0.03333}{0.0078} = 4.27 \text{ m/sec}$$

Put in Bernoulli's equation

$$\frac{200\times 10^3}{9810} = \frac{p_2}{9810}+0.05\times\frac{4.27^2}{2\times 9.81}$$

$$20.39 = \frac{p_2}{9810}+0.046$$

$\therefore$ $p_2 = 199574.64 \text{ N/m}^2$

Using momentum equation in x-direction

$$p_1A_1 + p_2A_2 + F_x = \rho Q\,(-V_2 - V_1)$$

$$200\times 10^3 \times 0.0078 + 199574.64\times 0.0078 + F_x = 1000\times 0.03333\,(-4.27-4.27)$$

$$1560 + 1556.68 + F_x = -284.64$$

$\therefore$ $F_x = -3401.32 \text{ N}$ ...(7.28)

Equation (7.28) gives a force on the water in the absence of nozzle.

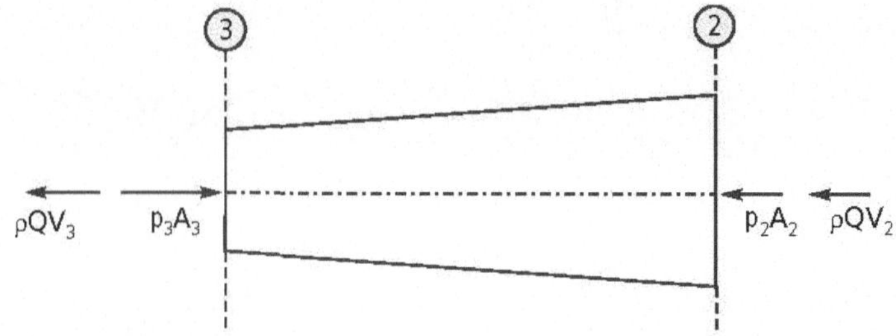

Fig. 7.18 (*c*)

Now $C_v = 0.97$, at the outlet of the nozzle cross-sectional area of nozzle is equal to cross-section of flow *i.e.*, $C_c = 1.0$

$$\therefore \quad C_d = C_v \times C_c = 0.97 \times 1.0 = 0.97$$

Now $$Q = C_d A_3 V_3$$

$$0.03333 = 0.97 \times \frac{\pi \times 0.05^2}{4} \times V_3$$

$$\therefore \quad 0.03333 = 0.97 \times 1.96 \times 10^{-3} \times V_3$$

$$V_3 = 17.53 \text{ m/sec}$$

Using momentum equation in *x*-direction

$$-p_2A_2 + p_3A_3 - F_{x1} = \rho Q\,(-V_3 - (-V_2))$$

Now $p_3 = 0$ (Nozzle discharges water to atmosphere)

$$\therefore \quad -p_2A_2 - F_{x1} = \rho Q\,(-V_3 + V_2)$$

$$-199574.64 \times 0.0078 - F_x = 1000 \times 0.03333\,(-17.53 + 4.27)$$

$$F_{x1} = -1114.73 \text{ N} \qquad \text{...(7.29)}$$

Equation (7.29) gives force exerted on water by nozzle

∴ The total force on the water

$$F = F_x + F_{x1}$$

$$= -3401.32 - 1114.73$$

$$= -4516.05 \text{ N}$$

Hence the total force on the bend will be equal to 4516.05 but direction opposite to '*F*'.

7.11.3 Hint to Solve Problems Based on Bend Placed in Vertical Plane

After applying the Bernoulli's equation to section (1) and (2), put $Z_1 = 0$ and the value of Z_2 from given data (as shown in Fig. 7.19) in the equation

$$\frac{p_1}{\gamma} + \frac{V_1^2}{2g} + Z_1 = \frac{p_2}{\gamma} + \frac{V_2^2}{2g} + Z_2.$$

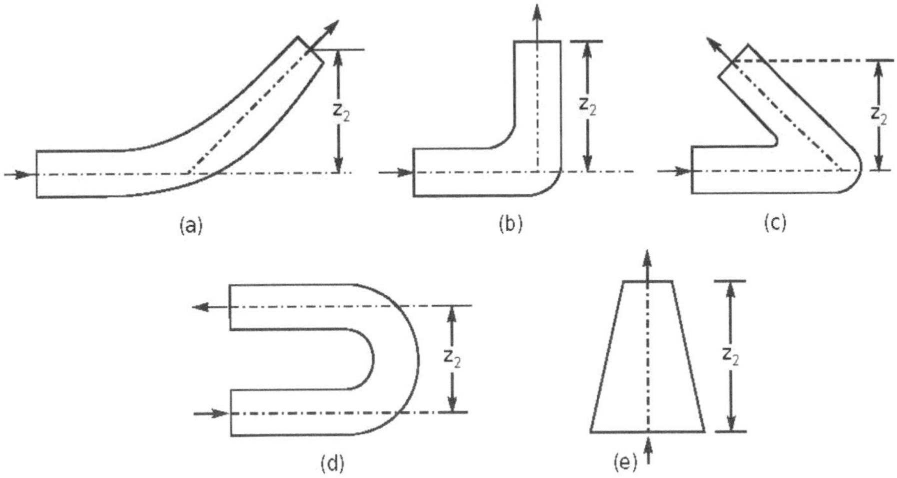

Fig. 7.19

7.12 MOMENT OF MOMENTUM EQUATION

As per the moment of momentum principle, the resulting torque is equal to the rate of change in moment of momentum.

Thus,

Resulting Torque = Rate of change in moment of momentum

$$\therefore \quad T = \rho Q\, V_2 r_2 - \rho Q V_1 r_1$$

$$= \rho Q\, (V_2 r_2 - V_1 r_1)$$

where ρ = mass density of flowing fluid (kg/m^3)

Q = rate of flow (m^3/sec)

V_1 = velocity of flow (m/sec) at section (1)

r_1 = radius of curvature at section (1) (m)

V_2 = velocity of flow (m/sec) at section (2)

r_2 = radius of curvature at section (2) (m)

and T = resulting torque (Nm)

Moment of momentum equation find its application in analysing the problem based on turbomachinery and sprinklers.

7.12.1 Solved Problems

■ **Problem 7.16:** *The 1 cm diameter jets of a lawn sprinkler face opposite directions. A flow of 3 lit/sec enters the rotating arm in a normal direction. The jets are equidistant from the centre. The centre to centre distance between the jets is 64 cm. Find the speed of rotation and the torque required to hold the sprinkler stationary.*

Given: $d = 1 \text{ cm} = 0.01 \text{ m}$

$Q = 3 \text{ lit/sec} = 3 \times 10^{-3} \text{ m}^3\text{/sec}$

$$r_1 = r_2 = \frac{64}{2}\ cm = 32\ cm = 0.32\ m.$$

Solution: Area of nozzle $= A_1 = A_2 = \dfrac{\pi d^2}{4}$

$$= \frac{\pi \times 0.01^2}{4} = 7.8539 \times 10^{-5}$$

Discharge through each nozzle $= \dfrac{Q}{2} = \dfrac{3\times10^{-3}}{2} = 1.5 \times 10^{-3}\ m^3/sec$

Velocity of water at the outlet of nozzle

$$= V_1 = V_2 = \frac{Q_1}{A_1} = \frac{1.5\times10^{-3}}{7.8539\times10^{-5}} = 19.10\ m/sec$$

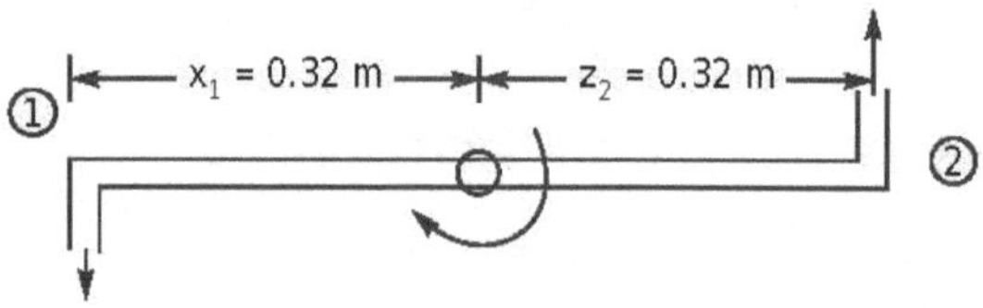

Fig. 7.20

(*i*) Speed of rotation of sprinkler

The absolute velocity of flow at (1) and (2)

$$(V_{ab})_1 = V_1 - \omega r_1$$
$$= 19.10 - \omega \times 0.32$$

and
$$(V_{ab})_2 = V_2 - \omega \times r_2$$
$$= 19.10 - \omega \times 0.32$$

Total torque exerted by water on sprinkler

$$= T = \rho Q_1 (V_{ab})_1 r_1 + \rho Q_2 (V_{ab})_2 r_2$$
$$= 1000 \times 1.5 \times 10^{-3} (19.10 - 0.32\omega)\ 0.32$$
$$+ 1000 \times 1.5 \times 10^{-3} (19.10 - 0.32\omega)\ 0.32$$

Since the sprinkler is free to rotate

$$T = 0$$

$\therefore$ $0 = 1000 \times 1.5 \times 10^{-3} \times 0.32 \times 2\ (19.10 - 0.32\omega)$

$\therefore$ $19.10 - 0.32\omega = 0$

$\therefore$ $\omega = \dfrac{19.10}{0.32} = 59.6875\ rad/sec$

Now $\omega = \dfrac{2\pi N}{60}$

$$\therefore \qquad N = \frac{60\omega}{2\pi} = \frac{60 \times 59.6875}{2 \times \pi}$$

$$= 569.97 \text{ rpm}$$

(*ii*) Torque required to hold the sprinkler stationary

Now

$$T = \rho Q_1 V_1 r_1 + \rho Q_2 V_2 r_2$$

$$\because \qquad Q_1 = Q_2,\ V_1 = V_2 \text{ and } r_1 = r_2$$

$$T = 2\rho Q_1 V_1 r_1$$

$$= 2 \times 1000 \times 1.5 \times 10^{-3} \times 19.10 \times 0.32$$

$$= 18.336 \text{ Nm.}$$

■ **Problem 7.17:** *A twin jet unequal arm lawn sprinkler delivers a total discharge of 1.5 lps. Taking jet diameter as 0.9 cm, inclination of jets with axis of pipe 45° in opposite directions, and distance from axis of rotation to jets 15 cm and 30 cm and neglecting friction, find speed of sprinkler and torque to keep the sprinkler stationary.*

Given: $Q = 1.5 \text{ lps} = 1.5 \times 10^{-3} \text{ m}^3/\text{sec}$

$d_1 = d_2 = 0.9 \text{ cm} = 0.009 \text{ m}$

$\theta = 45°$

$r_1 = 15 \text{ cm} = 0.15 \text{ m}$

$r_2 = 30 \text{ cm} = 0.3 \text{ m}$

Solution:

$$A_1 = A_2 = \frac{\pi \times d_1^2}{4} = \frac{\pi \times 0.009^2}{4} = 6.36 \times 10^{-5} \text{ m}^2$$

$$Q_1 = Q_2 = \frac{Q}{2} = \frac{1.5 \times 10^{-3}}{2} = 0.75 \times 10^{-3} \text{ m}^3/\text{sec}$$

$$\therefore \qquad V_1 = V_2 = \frac{Q_1}{A_1} = \frac{0.75 \times 10^{-3}}{6.36 \times 10^{-5}} = 11.79 \text{ m/sec}$$

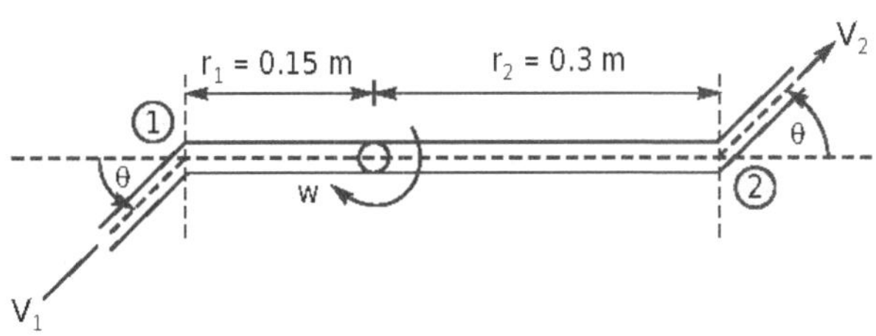

Fig. 7.21

(*i*) Speed of rotation of sprinkler

The absolute velocity of flow at (1) and (2) is *y*-direction

$$(V_{ab})_1 = V_1 \sin\theta - \omega r_1$$

$$= 11.79 \times \sin 45° - \omega \times 0.15$$

$$= 8.3368 - 0.15\,\omega$$

$$(V_{ab})_2 = V_2 \sin\theta - \omega r_2$$
$$= 11.79 \times \sin 45° - \omega \times 0.30$$
$$= 8.3368 - 0.3\,\omega$$

Total torque exerted by water on sprinkler

$$T = \rho Q_1 (V_{ab})_1 r_1 + \rho Q_2 (V_{ab})_2 r_2$$
$$= 1000 \times 0.75 \times 10^{-3} \times (8.3368 - 0.15\omega) \times 0.15$$
$$+ 1000 \times 0.75 \times 10^{-3} \times (8.3368 - 0.3\omega) \times 0.30$$

Since the sprinkler is free to rotate

$$T = 0$$

$\therefore \quad (8.3368 - 0.15\omega) \times 0.15 + (8.3368 - 0.3\omega) \times 0.3 = 0$

$\therefore \quad 1.25 - 0.0225\omega + 2.50 - 0.09\omega = 0$

$\therefore \quad \omega = 33.33$ rad/sec

But,

$$\omega = \frac{2\pi N}{60}$$

$\therefore \quad N = \dfrac{60\omega}{2\pi} = \dfrac{60 \times 33.33}{2 \times \pi} = 318.28$ rpm

(*ii*) Torque required to keep the sprinkler stationary

$$T = \rho Q_1 V_1 \sin\theta\, r_1 = \rho Q_2 V_2 \sin\theta\, r_2$$
$$= 1000 \times 0.75 \times 10^{-3} \times 11.79 \sin 45° \times 0.15$$
$$+ 1000 \times 0.75 \times 10^{-3} \times 11.79 \sin 45° \times 0.30$$
$$= 1000 \times 0.75 \times 10^{-3} \times 11.79 \sin 45° \,(0.15 + 0.30)$$
$$= 2.81 \text{ Nm.}$$

■ **Problem 7.18:** *A twin jet unequal arm lawn sprinkler delivers a total discharge of 1.5 lps. Taking jet diameter as 0.9 cm and distance from axis of rotation to jets 15 cm and 30 cm and neglecting friction, find speed of sprinkler and torque to keep the sprinkler stationary if both jets are in same direction.*

Given:

$Q_1 = 1.5$ lps $= 1.5 \times 10^{-3}$ m³/sec

$d_1 = d_2 = 0.9$ cm $= 0.009$ m

$r_1 = 15$ cm $= 0.15$ m

$r_2 = 30$ cm $= 0.3$ m.

Solution:

$$A_1 = A_2 = \frac{\pi d_1^2}{4} = \frac{\pi \times 0.009^2}{4} = 6.36 \times 10^{-5} \text{ m}^2$$

$$Q_1 = Q_2 = \frac{Q}{2} = \frac{1.5 \times 10^{-3}}{2} = 0.75 \times 10^{-3} \text{ m}^3/\text{sec}$$

$$V_1 = V_2 = \frac{Q_1}{A_1} = \frac{0.75 \times 10^{-3}}{6.36 \times 10^{-5}} = 11.79 \text{ m/sec}$$

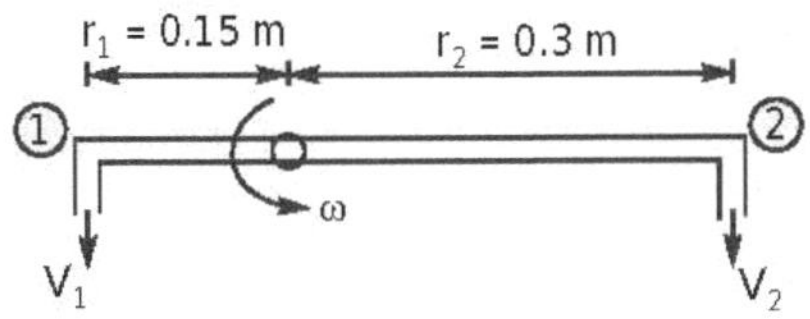

Fig. 7.22

(*i*) Speed of rotation of sprinkler

The absolute velocity of flow at (1) and (2) is *y*-direction

$$(V_{ab})_1 = V_1 + \omega r_1$$
$$= 11.79 + 0.15\,\omega$$
$$(V_{ab})_2 = V_2 - \omega r_2$$
$$= 11.79 - 0.3\,\omega$$

Total torque exerted by water on sprinkler

$$T = \rho Q_2 (V_{ab})_2 r_2 + \rho Q_1 (V_{ab})_1 r_1$$
$$= 1000 \times 0.75 \times 10^{-3} \times (11.79 + 0.15\omega) \times 0.15$$
$$- 1000 \times 0.75 \times 10^{-3} \times (11.79 - 0.3\omega) \times 0.3$$

Since the sprinkler is free to rotate

$$T = 0$$

$\therefore \quad (11.79 + 0.15\omega)\, 0.15 - (11.79 - 0.3\omega) \times 0.3 = 0$

$\therefore \quad 1.7685 + 0.0225\omega - 3.537 + 0.09\omega = 0$

$\therefore \quad \omega = 15.72$ rad/sec

Now $\quad \omega = \dfrac{2\pi N}{60}$

$\therefore \quad N = \dfrac{60\omega}{2\pi} = \dfrac{60 \times 15.72}{2 \times \pi} = 150.11$ rpm

(*ii*) Torque required to keep the sprinkler stationary

Now

$$T = \rho Q_2 V_2 r_2 + \rho Q_1 V_1 r_1$$
$$= 1000 \times 0.75 \times 10^{-3} \times 11.79 \times 0.3$$
$$- 1000 \times 0.75 \times 10^{-3} \times 11.79 \times 0.15$$
$$= 1000 \times 0.75 \times 10^{-3} \times 11.79 \times (0.3 - 0.15)$$
$$= 1.326 \text{ Nm.}$$

■ **Problem 7.19:** *Water is admitted at the axis of rotation of a four arm lawn sprinkler. The nozzle has a diameter of 6 mm sprinkler arms have a radius of 28 cm. For a flow of 1.2 lit/sec. Find speed of rotation, neglecting friction.*

(*b*) *For problem 7.19 find the torque to keep the sprinkler stationary.*

Given: $\quad d_1 = d_2 = d_3 = d_4 = 6\ mm = 6 \times 10^{-3}\ m$

$r_1 = r_2 = r_3 = r_4 = 28\ cm = 0.28\ m$

$Q = 1.2\ lit/sec = 1.2 \times 10^{-3}\ m^3/sec.$

Solution: Discharge through each nozzle

$$= Q_1 = Q_2 = Q_3 = Q_4 = \frac{Q}{4} = \frac{1.2\times10^{-3}}{4} = 0.3 \times 10^{-3}\ \text{m}^3/\text{sec}$$

Also $$V_1 = V_2 = V_3 = V_4 = \frac{Q_1}{A_1} = \frac{0.3\times10^{-3}}{\left(\dfrac{\pi\times(6\times10^{-3})^2}{4}\right)} = 10.6\ \text{m/sec}$$

Absolute velocity of flow at (1), (2), (3), (4) is same

and $$= (V_{ab})_1 = (V_1 - r_1\omega) = 10.6 - 0.28\ \omega$$

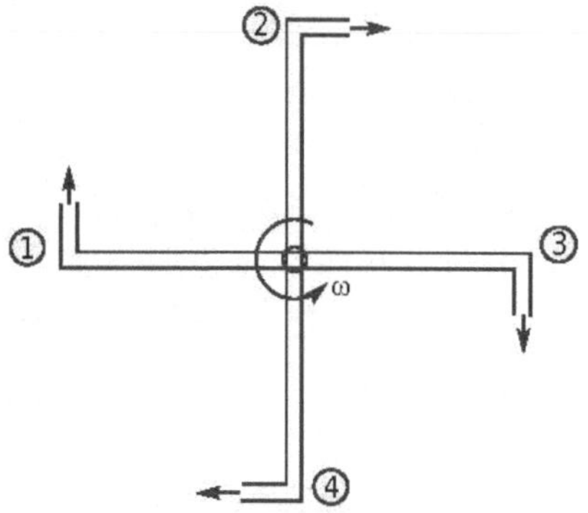

Fig. 7.23

(*i*) Speed of rotation of sprinkler

Torque exerted by each nozzle

$$T_1 = \rho Q_1 (V_{ab})_1 \times r_1$$
$$= 1000 \times 0.3 \times 10^{-3} \times (10.6 - 0.28\omega) \times 0.28$$
$$= 0.89 - 0.023\omega$$

Total torque exerted by water on sprinkler

$$T = T_1 + T_2 + T_3 + T_4$$
$$= 4T_1$$
$$= 4\ (0.89 - 0.023\omega)$$

Since the sprinkler is free to rotate

$$T = 0$$

$\therefore$ $$0.89 - 0.023\omega = 0$$

$\therefore$ $$\omega = 38.69\ \text{rad/sec}$$

Now

$$\omega = \frac{2\pi N}{60}$$

$\therefore$ $$N = \frac{60\omega}{2\pi} = \frac{60\times38.69}{2\times\pi} = 369.46\ \text{rpm}$$

(*ii*) Torque required to keep the sprinkler stationary

Now

$$T = 4T_1$$
$$= 4\,(\rho Q_1 V_1 r_1)$$
$$= 4\,(1000 \times 0.3 \times 10^{-3} \times 10.6 \times 0.28)$$
$$= 3.5616 \text{ Nm.}$$

7.13 FREE JETS

A jet of water discharging to atmosphere is called free jet. Consider a free jet which makes an angle of $\theta°$ with the horizontal when it is issued from the nozzle.

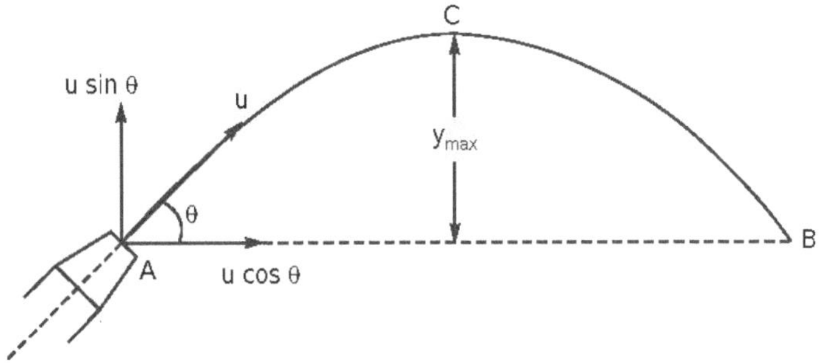

Fig. 7.24

Let in time t the particle of liquid is displaced in horizontal and vertical direction by x and y respectively.

$$\therefore \quad x = u \cos \theta \times t \quad ...(7.30)$$

and

$$y = u \sin \theta \times t - \frac{1}{2} g t^2 \quad ...(7.31)$$

From equation (7.30)

$$t = \frac{x}{u \cos \theta}$$

Put in equation (7.31)

$$y = u \sin \theta \frac{x}{u \cos \theta} - \frac{1}{2} g \left(\frac{x}{u \cos \theta} \right)^2$$

$$= x \tan \theta - \frac{g x^2}{2u^2 \cos^2 \theta}$$

$$= x \tan \theta - \frac{g x^2}{2u^2} \sec^2 \theta \quad ...(7.32)$$

This is an equation of a parabola. Hence it is proved that a path traced by a free jet is parabolic.

7.13.1 Maximum Displacement of Free Jet in y-Direction

Using a basic equation

$$V^2 = u^2 + 2as$$

here V = final velocity at the highest point $= 0$

u = initial velocity in y-direction $= u \sin \theta$

$$a = -g$$

$$s = y_{max}$$

$$\therefore \quad 0 = u^2 \sin^2 \theta - 2g\, y_{max}$$

$$\therefore \quad y_{max} = \frac{u^2 \sin^2 \theta}{2g} \qquad \text{...(7.33)}$$

7.13.2 Time to Reach the Highest Point

Using the basic equation

$$V = u + at$$

here

$$V = 0$$

$$u = u \sin \theta$$

$$a = -g$$

$$t = T_1$$

$$\therefore \quad 0 = u \sin \theta - gT_1$$

$$\therefore \quad T_1 = \frac{u \sin \theta}{g} \qquad \text{...(7.34)}$$

7.13.3 Time of Flight

Using the basic equation

$$S = ut + \frac{1}{2}at^2$$

here

$$S = y = 0$$

$$u = u \sin \theta$$

$$t = T$$

$$a = -g$$

$$\therefore \quad 0 = u \sin \theta \times T - \frac{1}{2} gT^2$$

$$\therefore \quad T = \frac{2u \sin \theta}{g} \quad \text{...(7.35)}$$

7.13.4 Horizontal Range of the Free Jet

Let x_R is the horizontal range of the free jet

then
$$x_R = u \cos \theta \times T$$
$$= u \cos \theta \times \frac{2u \sin \theta}{g}$$
$$= \frac{u^2}{g} \sin 2\theta \quad \text{...(7.36)}$$

7.13.5 Condition for Maximum Range

We have equation (7.36)

i.e.
$$x_R = \frac{u^2}{g} \sin 2\theta$$

It is clear from this equation that x_R is maximum when sin 2θ is maximum

or
$$\sin 2\theta = 1$$
or
$$2\theta = 90°$$
or
$$\theta = 45°$$
put in equation (7.36)

$$\therefore \quad x_{R(\max)} = \frac{u^2}{g} \sin 90°$$
$$= \frac{u^2}{g} \quad \text{...(7.37)}$$

7.13.6 Solved Problems

■ **Problem 7.20:** *A jet of water issued from a nozzle with a velocity of 18 m/sec. If the nozzle makes an angle of 40° with the horizontal find*

(1) the maximum height attained by the free jet and time required to reach the maximum height

(2) time of flight

(3) horizontal range of the free jet

Given: $u = 18$ *m/sec*

$\theta = 40°$.

Solution:

(1) For y_{max}

Using equation (7.33)

$$y_{max} = \frac{u^2 \sin^2 \theta}{2g} = \frac{18^2 \sin^2 40°}{2 \times 9.81}$$

$$= 6.82 \text{ m}$$

Time to reach the maximum height

$$= T_1 = \frac{u \sin \theta}{g} = \frac{18 \times \sin 40°}{9.81}$$

$$= 1.18 \text{ sec}$$

(2) Time of flight

$$T = \frac{2u \sin \theta}{g} = \frac{2 \times 18 \times \sin 40°}{9.81}$$

$$= 2.36 \text{ sec}$$

(3) Horizontal range of free jet

$$x_R = \frac{u^2}{g} \sin 2\theta°$$

$$= \frac{18^2}{9.81} \sin 80°$$

$$= 32.53 \text{ m}$$

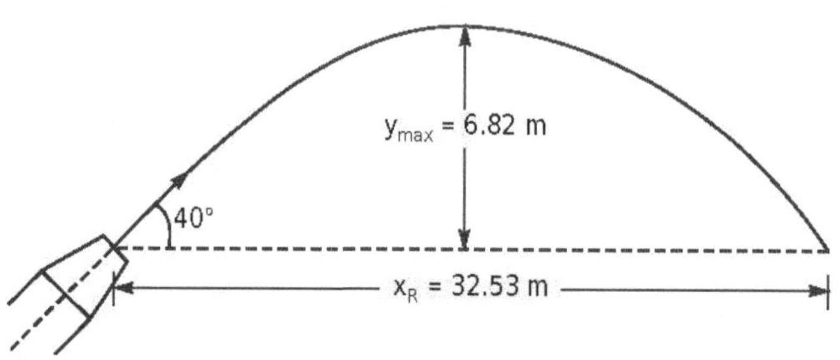

Fig. 7.25

■ **Problem 7.21:** *Find the inclination angle of a fire hose nozzle, held at a height of 1.9 m above the ground to direct the jet, having a velocity of 33 m/sec to reach a point which is at a height of 24 m and 30 m away horizontally.*

Given: $h = 1.9\,m$

$u = 33\,m/sec$

$H = 24\,m \quad \therefore \quad y = H - h = 24 - 1.9 = 22.1\,m$

$x = 30\,m.$

Solution:

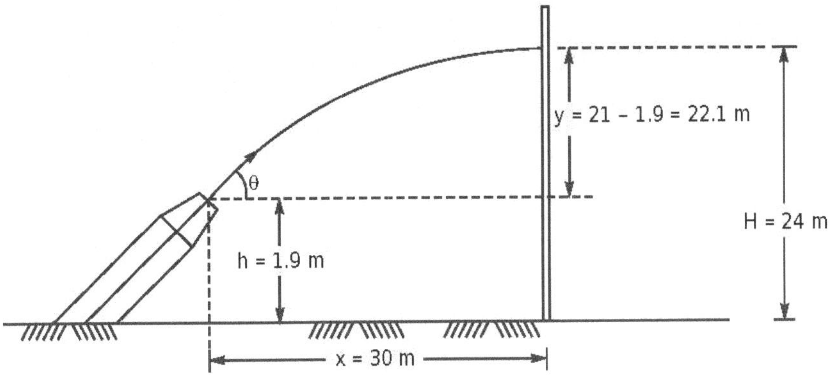

Fig. 7.26

Using equation (7.32)

$$y = x\tan\theta - \frac{gx^2}{24^2}\sec^2\theta$$

$$(24 - 1.9) = 30\tan\theta - \frac{9.81 \times 30^2}{2 \times 33^2}\sec^2\theta$$

$\therefore$ $22.1 = 30\tan\theta - 4.05\,(1 + \tan^2\theta)$

$\therefore$ $4.05\tan^2\theta - 30\tan\theta + 26.15 = 0$

$\therefore$ $\tan^2\theta - 7.41\tan\theta + 6.46 = 0$

Solving this quadratic equation

$$\tan\theta = \frac{7.41 \pm \sqrt{7.41^2 - 4 \times 1 \times 6.46}}{2 \times 1}$$

$$= \frac{7.41 \pm \sqrt{54.91 - 25.84}}{2}$$

$$= \frac{7.41 \pm 5.39}{2}$$

$\therefore$ $\theta = \tan^{-1} 1.01$ or $\tan^{-1} 6.4$

$= 45.28°$ or $81.12°$.

Exercises

1. Water flows through a pipe of diameter 10 cm with a velocity of 12 m/sec. The pressure at A is 2.25 kg/cm^2 and pressure at B which is on downstream to A is 15 m. Find a head loss between A and B. **(Ans. 7.5 m)**

2. A pipe is diverging from 10 cm diameter at A to 20 cm diameter at B in the direction of flow of fluid of specific gravity 0.8. The discharge through the pipe is 0.25 m^3/sec. If a pressure difference between A and B is 33.75 N/cm^2. Find the head loss between A and B. (**Ans.** 5.4 m of oil)
3. Find a direction of flow and head loss for a pipe having diameter 10 cm and 15 cm, pressure 1.5 kg/cm^2 and 1.25 kg/cm^2 and elevation 1 m and 2.5 m at A and B respectively. Let discharge through pipe is 0.25 m^3/sec.
(**Ans.** Water flows from A to B, head loss = 42.44 m)
4. A 10 cm × 5 cm horizontal venturimeter carries 10 lit/sec of water and reading of differential mercury manometer is 104.53 mm. Find coefficient of discharge of venturimeter. (**Ans.** C_d = 0.97)
5. The difference of elevation between the entrance and throat section of the venturimeter of size 15 cm and 5 cm is 25 cm. Find the manometric reading of mercury-oil differential manometer. The venturimeter is fitted to a vertical pipe carrying crude oil of specific gravity 0.81 at a rate of 15 lit/sec. The difference of elevation and pressure difference between the throat and entrance section is 25 cm and 3.45 m of oil respectively. Take coefficient of discharge as 0.95. (**Ans.** 20 cm)
6. A venturimeter is connected to a pipe of diameter 20 cm and carrying water at a rate of 9.81 lit/sec. The head loss between the inlet and the throat is known to be 0.1 $\frac{V_2^2}{2g}$.
Where v^2 is the velocity at the throat. The manometric fluid has a relative density of 0.75. The U-tube manometer connected to the inlet and the throat records a reading of 30 cm. Find the diameter of the throat. Take C_d = 0.94. (**Ans.** 10 cm)
7. A horizontal venturimeter with inlet diameter 20 cm and the throat diameter 10 cm is used to measure the flow of oil of specific gravity 0.8. The reading of oil-mercury differential manometer is 18.17 cm. Find the discharge of oil through venturimeter. Take C_d = 0.98. (**Ans.** 60 lit/sec)
8. A venturimeter measures the flow of water in a 75 mm diameter pipe. The difference of head between the throat and the entrance of the meter is measured by a U-tube containing mercury, the mercury being in contact with the water. The discharge through the meter is 650 lpm and throat diameter is 41 mm. Find the difference in level of the mercury. Assume 'C_d' of the meter as 0.97. (**Ans.** 25 cm)
9. A 30 cm × 15 cm venturimeter is fitted in a horizontal pipeline carrying oil of specific gravity 0.8. At the throat the vacuum pressure is 37 cm of mercury. Assuming 5% of the differential head is lost between the inlet and throat and discharge of oil through the pipeline as 3.67 m^3/sec. Find the pressure at the inlet of the meter.
(**Ans.** 14 N/cm^2)

10. An orifice meter is inserted in a pipe of 20 cm diameter carrying 68.78 lit/sec. The pressure gauge fitted on upstream and downstream give readings of 20 N/cm^2 and 10 N/cm^2 respectively. $C_d = 0.6$. Find the diameter of orifice. (**Ans.** 10 cm)

11. A submarine is moving in a sea water with a velocity of 3.09 m/sec. Find the deflection in a mercury differential manometer which is connected to pitot static tube. Take coefficient as unity and specific gravity of sea water as 1.03. (**Ans.** 4 cm)

12. A reducing bend is placed in a pipeline carrying discharge 73.65 lit/sec. The water is turned through 60° in the horizontal plane. The pipe diameter is reduced from 0.25 m to 0.15 m. The pressure of the entry to the blend is 300 kN/m^2 gauge and the exist the pressure is 287.2 kN/m^2 gauge. Determine the force exerted on the bend. (**Ans.** 123.56 kN)

13. Find a pressure at the entrance of 90° bend in a 15 cm diameter pipe carrying oil of specific gravity 0.8 at 110 lit/sec. Force on the bend in x-direction is 684.214 N. Find the total force on the bend. (**Ans.** 0.8 m of oil, 967.62 N)

14. The 1 cm diameter jets of a lawn sprinkler face opposite direction. The jets are equidistant from the centre. The centre to centre distance between the jets is 64 cm. Find the flow which enters the rotating arm in a normal direction. The torque required to hold the sprinkler stationary is 18.336 km. (**Ans.** 3 lit/sec)

15. A twin jet unequal arm lawn sprinkler delivers a total discharge of 2 lps. Taking jet diameter as 0.9 cm and distance from axis of rotation to jets 20 cm and 35 cm and neglecting friction. Find the speed of sprinkler and torque to keep the sprinkler stationary if both jets are in same direction. (**Ans.** $N = 184.2$ rpm, $T = 2.35$ Nm)

16. The jet of water issued from a nozzle with a velocity of 18 m/sec. If the maximum height attained by the free jet is 6.82 m. Find

    (*i*) Angle made by the nozzle with the horizontal.

    (*ii*) Time of flight.

    (*iii*) Horizontal range of the free jet. (**Ans.** 40°, 2.36 sec, 32.53 m)

❑❑❑

8

Orifices and Mouthpieces

8.1 INTRODUCTION

An orifice is a small opening provided in a side or at the bottom of the tank through which fluid flows. As compared to the size of tank the size of orifice is very small and it may be of any shape such as circular, square, rectangular or triangular. A mouthpiece is a pipe of very small length, about two to three times the diameter fitted to a circular opening or orifice on the side of the tank, through which water flows. The orifices and mouthpieces are generally provided on the side or bottom of tank and used for measuring the rate of flow of liquid.

8.2 CLASSIFICATION OF ORIFICES

The orifices are classified as follows:

(1) The orifices are classified based upon their shape (*i*) Circular orifices (*ii*) Rectangular orifice (*iii*) Square orifice and (*iv*) Triangular orifice.

(2) The orifices are classified based upon their size and head above the centre of it as (*i*) Small orifice and (*ii*) Large orifice.

(3) Based on the shape of upstream edge of the orifice, they are classified as (*i*) Sharp edged orifice and (*ii*) Bell mouthed orifice.

(4) Based on the discharge conditions, orifices are classified as (*i*) Free discharging orifices and (*ii*) Submerged or drowned orifice. The submerged orifice is further classified as (*a*) Fully submerged orifice and (*b*) Partially submerged orifice.

In general, rectangular or circular shaped orifices are used and they may be small or large depending upon the head above the centre and may be sharp edged or bell mouthed with free or partial discharging jet of liquid.

8.3 FLOW THROUGH SHARP EDGED FREE DISCHARGING ORIFICE

Consider a tank provided with a small sharp edged orifice in one side as shown in Fig. 8.1. The tank contains liquid equal to height H above the centre of the orifice. The liquid will emerge from the orifice as a free jet. The jet of water discharges in the atmosphere and it deflects downwards due to action of gravity force acting on it. The jet of liquid has a less cross-sectional area at a certain distance from orifice as compared to the area of orifice. The section C-C at which it has minimum cross-sectional area, have all streamlines straight and parallel and are perpendicular to the plane of orifice. This section is known as Vena-contracta.

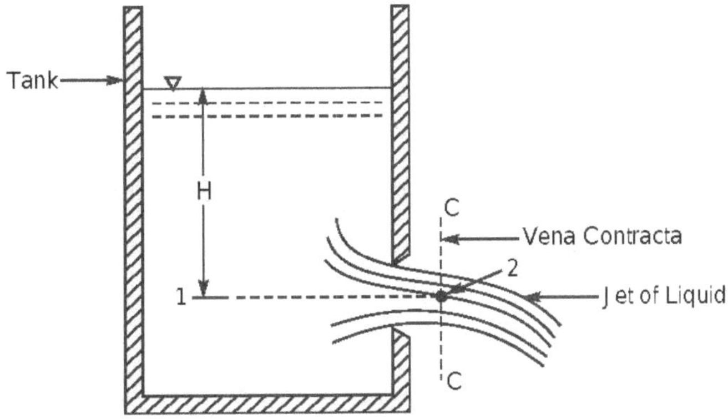

Fig. 8.1 Tank with Sharp Edged Orifice

As the cross-sectional area of jet is minimum at vena-cotracta, the velocity of flow of liquid will be maximum (continuity equation). The jet of liquid deflects downwards due to the action of gravity and diverges after this section.

Let the depth of liquid in the tank be maintain constant equal to H by adjusting outflow through orifice equal to inflow in the tank. Hence in this case flow will be steady under constant head H. Now, apply the Bernoulli's equation between two points 1 and 2, which are as shown in Fig. 8.1. The point 1 is in the tank on the centre line of orifice on upstream of it and point 2 at the centre of jet at vena-contracta.

Where P_1, V_1 are intensity of pressure and velocity of flow at point 1 and P_2, V_2 are intensity of pressure and velocity of flow at point 2 respectively.

$$\frac{P_1}{\gamma} + \frac{V_1^2}{2g} + Z_1 = \frac{P_2}{\gamma} + \frac{V_2^2}{2g} + Z_2$$

Here, $Z_1 = Z_2$, as centre line passing through point 1 and 2 is considered as a datum.

$$\therefore \qquad \frac{P_1}{\gamma} + \frac{V_1^2}{2g} = \frac{P_2}{\gamma} + \frac{V_2^2}{2g}$$

Now, $$\frac{P_1}{\gamma} = H$$

and as point 2 is under atmospheric pressure,

$$\frac{P_2}{\gamma} = 0$$

In the case, V_1 the velocity of flow is very small as compared to V_2 as the area of tank is very large compared to the area of jet of liquid. Here, V_1 is known as velocity of approach as it approaches the orifice.

$$\therefore \qquad H + 0 = 0 + \frac{V_2^2}{2g}$$

$$\therefore \qquad V_2 = \sqrt{2g\,H} \qquad ...(8.1)$$

This velocity V_2 is known as theoretical velocity and it will always be more than actual velocity.

8.4 HYDRAULIC COEFFICIENTS AND THEIR EXPERIMENTAL METHODS OF DETERMINATION

8.4.1 Coefficient of Velocity (C_v)

In the derivation of equation (8.1), we have neglected the loss of energy due to friction and surface tension. Hence the actual velocity of flow will be slightly less than the theoretical velocity given by equation (8.1). In such case the actual velocity of jet at vena-contracta can be determined by multiplying the theoretical velocity by some coefficient, known as coefficient of velocity.

The coefficient of velocity, C_v is defined as the ratio of the actual velocity of jet at vena-contracta to the theoretical velocity of jet.

$$\therefore \qquad C_v = \frac{V}{V_{th}} = \frac{V}{\sqrt{2g\,H}} \qquad ...(8.2)$$

where, V = Actual velocity of jet at vena-contracta

and V_{th} = Theoretical velocity of jet.

The value of C_v = 0.98 is adopted in general, whereas it varies from 0.95 to 0.99 for different orifices depending on the shape and size of orifice. It also depends on the head of liquid under which flow takes place.

Experimental Method

Consider a tank fitted with an orifice on one of its sides flowing under constant head of water as shown in Fig. 8.2.

Let section *C-C* represents the vena-contracta of jet of water and V is the velocity at that point. Consider a liquid particle at any instant of time at vena-contracta and it takes the new position at B in the jet in time t. Let x and y represents the horizontal and vertical distances of point B from vena-contracta. The horizontal distance travelled by particle in time t is

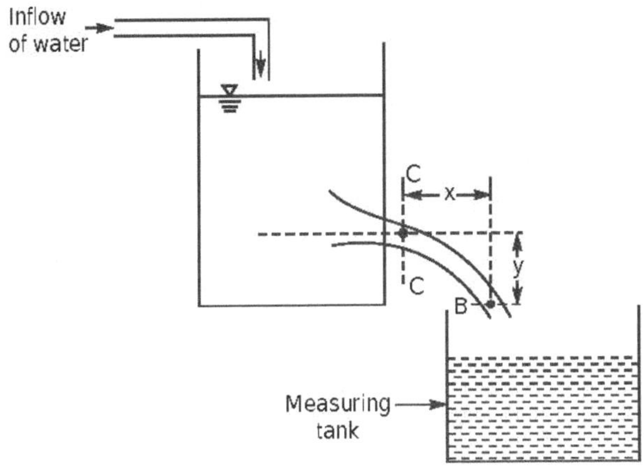

Fig. 8.2 Experimental set for Determination of C_v and C_d

$$x = Vt \quad \text{...}(i)$$

and vertical distance in the same time 't' is

$$y = \frac{1}{2} gt^2 \quad \text{...}(ii)$$

Substituting for $t = \frac{x}{V}$ from equation (i) in (ii), we get

$$y = \frac{1}{2} g \left(\frac{x}{V}\right)^2$$

$$\therefore \quad V^2 = \frac{gx^2}{2y}$$

$$\therefore \quad V = \sqrt{\frac{gx^2}{2y}} \quad \text{...}(8.3)$$

But, the theoretical velocity, from equation (8.1) is,

$$V_{\text{th}} = \sqrt{2g\,H}$$

$\therefore$ Coefficient of velocity,

$$C_v = \frac{\sqrt{\frac{gx^2}{2y}}}{\sqrt{2g\,H}}$$

$$\therefore \quad C_v = \sqrt{\frac{x^2}{4Hy}}$$

$$\therefore \quad C_v = \frac{x}{\sqrt{4Hy}} \quad \text{...}(8.4)$$

8.4.2 Coefficient of Contraction (C_c)

As discussed in the earlier section, the cross-sectional area of jet at vena-contracta is less than the area of orifice. Hence the actual area of jet at vena-contracta can be calculated by multiplying the area of orifice by a coefficient, known as coefficient of contraction.

The coefficient of contraction, C_c is defined as the ratio of the area of jet at vena-contracta to the area of the orifice.

$$\therefore \quad C_c = \frac{a_c}{a} \qquad ...(8.5)$$

where, a_c = area of jet at vena-contracta

and a = area of the orifice.

The value of $C_c = 0.64$ is adopted in general, where as it varies from 0.61 to 0.65 depending on the shape and size of the orifice. It also depends on the head under which flow takes place.

Experimental Method

The radius of jet at vena-contracta is measured with the help of micrometer contraction gauge and from which the actual area of jet at vena-contracta (a_c) is calculated. The area of orifice (a) is already known. Thus knowing a_c and a the coefficient of contraction C_c can be calculated from equation (8.5).

It is quite difficult to measure the area of jet emerging from circular orifice at vena-contracta accurately with the help of micrometer contraction gauge. Hence it is advisable to use following expression to obtain C_c.

$$C_c = \frac{C_d}{C_v} \qquad ...(8.6)$$

where, C_d is coefficient of discharge and is explained as follows.

8.4.3 Coefficient of Discharge (C_d)

In case of real fluids, the actual velocity of jet is sightly less than the theoretical (ideal) velocity due to the loss of energy due to friction, and due to contraction of jet of liquid, the actual discharge through an orifice is always less than the theoretical discharge. Hence the actual discharge through an orifice can be calculated by multiplying the theoretical discharge by a coefficient called coefficient of discharge.

The coefficient of discharge C_d is defined as the ratio of the actual discharge from an orifice to the theoretical discharge.

$$\therefore \quad C_d = \frac{Q}{Q_{th}} \qquad ...(8.7)$$

where, Q = Actual discharge from an orifice

and Q_{th} = Theoretical discharge.

But, $Q = a_C \times V$

$$Q = C_c \times a \times C_v \sqrt{2gH}$$

and $Q_{th} = a \times V_{th}$

$$= a \times \sqrt{2gH}$$

Substituting for Q and Q_{th} in equation (8.7), we get.

$$C_d = \frac{Q}{Q_{th}} = \frac{(C_c \times a) \times (C_v \sqrt{2gH}}{a \times \sqrt{2gH}}$$

$$\therefore \quad C_d = C_c \times C_v \qquad ...(8.8)$$

Thus coefficient of discharge is defined as the product of coefficient of contraction C_c and coefficient of velocity C_v.

The value of $C_d = 0.62$ is adopted in general, whereas it varies from 0.61 to 0.65.

Experimental Method

The water is allowed to flow through an orifice provided in a side of tank into a measuring tank (refer Fig. 8.2). The constant head h is maintained in the tank by adjusting the inflow of water to the tank equal to the outflow from the tank. The rise of water level (h) in the measuring tank is noted in time t. Knowing the area of measuring tank (A) the actual discharge through an orifice can be calculated as

$$Q = \frac{A \times h}{t}$$

The theoretical discharge, Q_{th} is given as

$$Q_{th} = a \times \sqrt{2gH}$$

where, a = area of orifice

$$\therefore \quad C_d = \frac{Q}{Q_{th}} = \frac{Q}{a\sqrt{2gH}} \qquad ...(8.9)$$

8.4.4 Solved Problems

■ **Problem 8.1:** *The head of water over the centre of an orifice is 2 m. The diameter of orifice is 24 mm. The actual discharge through an orifice is 1.756 lps. Find the coefficient of discharge.*

Solution:

Diameter of orifice = d = 24 mm = 0.024 m

$$\text{Area, } a = \frac{\pi}{4} \times (0.024)^2 = 4.5239 \times 10^{-4}\ \text{m}^2$$

Head of water, H = 2 m

$$\text{Theoretical velocity, } V_{th} = \sqrt{2gH}$$

$$= \sqrt{2 \times 9.81 \times 2}$$

$\therefore \qquad V_{th} = 6.261$ m/s

Theoretical discharge, $Q_{th} = a \times V_{th}$

$= 4.5239 \times 10^{-4} \times 6.261$

$Q_{th} = 2.8324 \times 10^{-3}$

Actual discharge = 1.756 lps

$Q = 1.756 \times 10^{-3}$ m³/s

$$\therefore \qquad C_d = \frac{Q}{Q_{th}} = \frac{1.756 \times 10^{-3}}{2.8324 \times 10^{-3}} = 0.62.$$

■ **Problem 8.2:** *Oil of relative density 0.85 issues out of an orifice under a pressure of 0.2 kg/cm² at the rate of 4.5 lps. The diameter at vena-contracta is 3 cm. Find coefficient of velocity.*

Solution:

P = Pressure intensity = 0.2 kg/cm²

= 2000 kg/m²

$$H = \text{Pressure head} = \frac{P}{\rho g} = \frac{2000}{0.85 \times 1000}$$

$\therefore \qquad H = 2.353$ m

Q = Discharge through orifice

= 4.5 lps

$= 4.5 \times 10^{-3}$ m³/s

Diameter of jet at vena-contracta = 3 cm = 0.03 m

$$\therefore \quad \text{Area of jet at vena-contracta} = a_c = \frac{\pi}{4} \times (0.03)^2$$

$= 7.068 \times 10^{-4}$ m²

$$\therefore \quad \text{Velocity of jet at vena-contracta} = \frac{Q}{a_c}$$

$$V = \frac{4.5 \times 10^{-3}}{7.068 \times 10^{-4}} = 6.366 \text{ m/s}$$

$$\therefore \qquad C_v = \frac{V}{\sqrt{2gH}}$$

$$= \frac{6.366}{\sqrt{2 \times 9.81 \times 2.353}}$$

$$= \frac{6.366}{6.7945} = 0.937$$

■ **Problem 8.3**: *The head of water over the centre of orifice is 9.0 m. The diameter of orifice is 8.0 cm. The jet of water discharges into a circular tank of diameter 1.17 m. The water level rises 0.8 m in 20 seconds. The x and y co-ordinates are 5 m and 0.75 m respectively. Find the coefficients, C_d, C_v and C_c.*

Solution:

Area of orifice; $a = \frac{\pi}{4} d^2 = \frac{\pi}{4} \times (0.08)^2$

$= 5.026 \times 10^{-3}\ \text{m}^2$

Theoretical velocity, $V_{th} = \sqrt{2gH} = \sqrt{2 \times 9.81 \times 9.0}$

$V_{th} = 13.29$ m/s

Theoretical discharge $= Q_{th} = V_{th} \times a$

$= 13.29 \times 5.026 \times 10^{-3}$

$Q_{th} = 0.0668\ \text{m}^3/\text{s}$

Actual discharge $= Q = \frac{A \times h}{t}$

$$= \frac{\frac{\pi}{4} \times (1.17)^2 \times 0.8}{20}$$

$Q = 0.0430\ \text{m}^3/\text{s}$

Coefficient of discharge $= C_d = \frac{Q}{Q_{th}}$

$$= \frac{0.043}{0.0608}$$

$C_d = 0.644$

$$C_v = \sqrt{\frac{x^2}{4\,Hy}}$$

$$C_v = \sqrt{\frac{5^2}{4 \times 9 \times 0.75}}$$

$C_v = 0.962$ ...(**Ans.**)

$$C_c = \frac{C_d}{C_v}$$

$$= \frac{0.644}{0.962}$$

$C_c = 0.669.$ ...(**Ans.**)

■ **Problem 8.4:** *An orifice is located in the side of a tank with its centre 10 cm above the base of tank. The constant water level is 1 m above the centre of the orifice. The coefficient of velocity is 0.98. Find the distance travelled by a point which is 10 cm below vena-contracta.*

Solution:
$$C_v = \sqrt{\frac{x^2}{4\,Hy}}$$

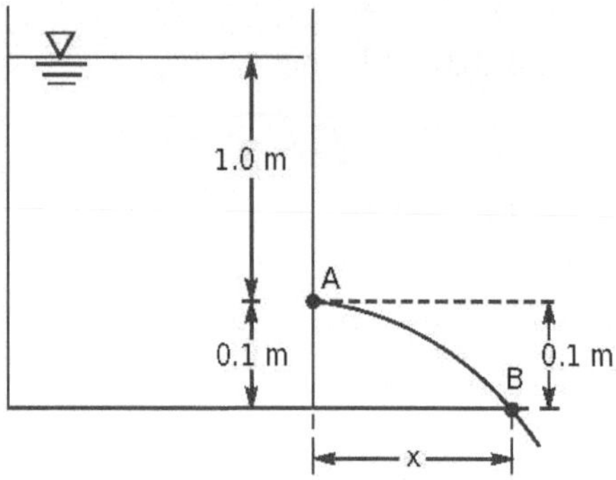

Fig. 8.3

$$x^2 = (C_v)^2 \times 4\,Hy$$
$$= (0.98)^2 \times 4 \times 1.0 \times 0.1$$
$$x^2 = 0.3842$$
$$x = 0.62. \qquad \text{...(Ans.)}$$

The horizontal distance travelled by a point = 62 cm.

■ **Problem 8.5:** *A tank has two identical orifices in one of its vertical sides, the upper orifices is 3.2 m below the water surface and lower one is 5.5 m below the water surface. If the value of C_v for each orifice is 0.96, find the point of intersection of two jets.*

Solution:

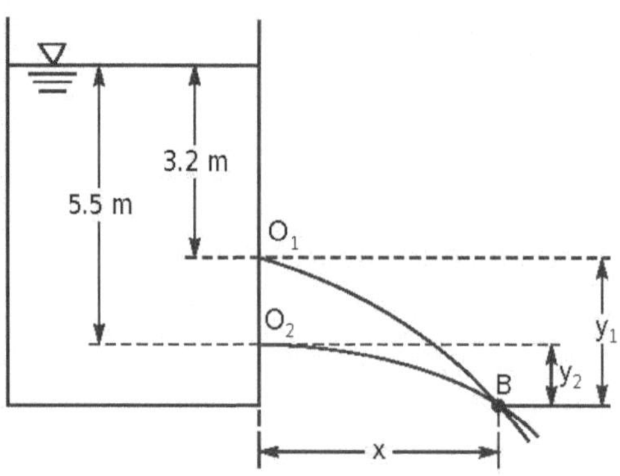

Fig. 8.4

Let two orifices intersect at point B.

$\therefore$ From Fig. 8.4, $H_1 = 5.5$ m and $H_2 = 3.2$ m

$$y_1 = y_2 + (5.5 - 3.2) = y_2 + 2.3$$

As both orifices are identical, C_v for both must be same

$$\therefore \quad C_{v1} = C_{v2}$$

$$\sqrt{\frac{x^2}{4\,H_1 y_1}} = \sqrt{\frac{x^2}{4\,H_2 y_2}}$$

$$\frac{x^2}{4 \times 3.2 \times y_1} = \frac{x^2}{4 \times 5.5 \times y_2}$$

$$\therefore \quad 3.2\,y_1 = 5.5\,y_2$$

But $\quad y_1 = y_2 + 2.3$

$$\therefore \quad 3.2\,(y_2 + 2.3) = 5.3\,y_2$$

$$\therefore \quad 2.3\,y_2 = 7.36$$

$$y_2 = 3.2$$

$$\therefore \quad C_{v2} = \sqrt{\frac{x^2}{4\,H_2 y_2}}$$

$$(0.96)^2 = \frac{x^2}{4 \times 5.5 \times 3.2}$$

$$\therefore \quad x = 8.055 \text{ m.} \qquad \text{...(Ans.)}$$

■ **Problem 8.6:** *Compensation water is to be discharged by two circular orifice of the same diameter, situated at the bottom of a vessel having a constant head of 2m. If the demand is 18, 000,000 list/day. What diameter will be required for each orifice ? Take coefficient of contraction and velocity as 0.62 and 0.98 respectively.*

Solution:

$$C_d = C_v \times C_c$$

$$= 0.98 \times 0.62$$

$$C_d = 0.6076$$

$$Q = 18{,}000{,}000 \text{ lit/day}$$

$$= 18{,}000 \text{ m}^3\text{/day}$$

$$= \frac{18000}{24 \times 60 \times 60} \text{ m}^3\text{/s}$$

$\therefore$ Actual discharge $Q = 0.2083 \text{ m}^3\text{/s}$

$$C_d = \frac{Q}{Q_{th}}$$

$$\therefore \qquad Q_{th} = \frac{Q}{C_d}$$

$$= \frac{0.2083}{0.6076} = 0.3428 \text{ m}^2/\text{s}$$

$$\text{Theoretical velocity} = \sqrt{2g\,H} = \sqrt{2\times 9.81\times 2}$$

$$V_{th} = 6.264 \text{ m/s}$$

Q_{th} is the discharge from two orifices of the same area under same head. Hence discharge from one orifice is

$$Q_{th} = \frac{Q_{th}}{2} = \frac{0.3428}{2} = 0.1714 \text{ m}^3/\text{s}$$

$$\text{Now, Area of orifice, } a = \frac{Q_{th}}{V_{th}}$$

$$= \frac{0.1714}{6.264}$$

$$a = 0.02736 \text{ m}^2$$

i.e.,

$$\frac{\pi}{4}\times d^2 = 0.02736$$

$$d = 0.1866 \text{ m}$$

$$d = 18.66 \text{ cm}$$

Diameter of each orifice = 18.66 cm.

8.5 FLOW THROUGH LARGE ORIFICES

Based on the size of orifices and head of liquid above the centre of it the orifices are classified as small orifices and large orifices. In the earlier study we have dealt with the small orifices, in which vertical dimension of orifice is small as compared to the head and the velocity in the entire cross-section of jet is considered to be constant and the discharge can be calculated by equation, $Q = C_d\, a\, \sqrt{2g\,H}$. In case of large orifices the size of orifice (vertical dimension) is large enough as compared with head and velocity varies over the entire cross-section of orifice. Hence discharge cannot be calculated by the above equation, but it has to be calculated by integrating discharges through small horizontal strips.

8.5.1 Flow Through Large Rectangular Orifice

Consider a large rectangular orifice of size ($b \times d$) fitted in the side of tank and discharging freely into the atmosphere as shown in Fig. 8.5. The head H above centre of orifice is maintained constant by adjusting inflow into the tank and outflow from orifice.

Let H_1 and H_2 be the head of liquid above the top and bottom edge of the orifice respectively and C_d is coefficient of discharge.

Consider an elementary horizontal strip of depth '*dh*' at a depth '*h*' below the free surface of liquid in the tank.

∴ Area of horizontal strip $= b \times dh$

The theoretical velocity of water through strip $= \sqrt{2gh}$

∴ Discharge through an elementary horizontal strip is given as:

$$dQ = C_d \times \text{Area of strip} \times \text{theoretical velocity}$$

$$dQ = C_d \times b \times dh \times \sqrt{2gh}$$

Now, integrate the above expression to get the total discharge through the orifice.

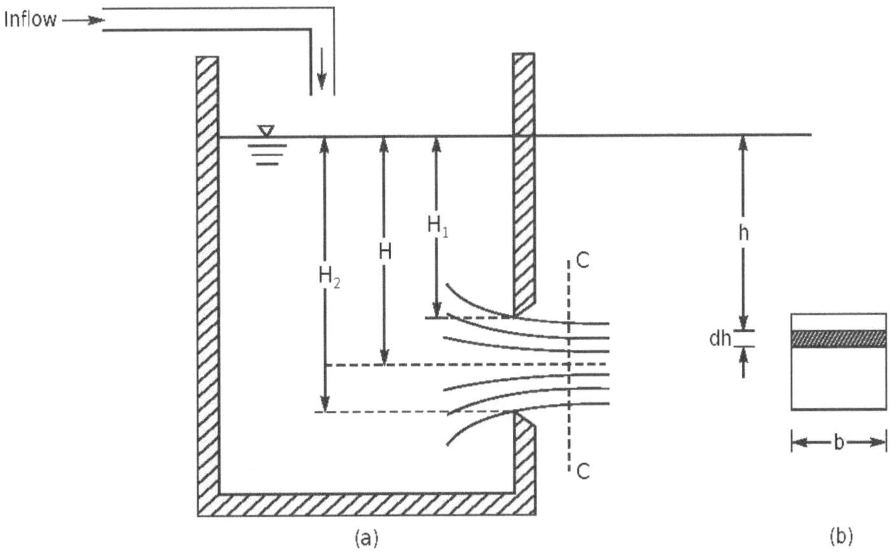

Fig. 8.5 Large Rectangular Orifice

$$Q = \int_{H_1}^{H_2} C_d \times b \times dh \times \sqrt{2gh}$$

$$= C_d \times b \times \sqrt{2g} \int_{H_1}^{H_2} h^{\frac{1}{2}}\, dh$$

$$= C_d \times b \times \sqrt{2g} \left[\frac{h^{\frac{3}{2}}}{\frac{3}{2}} \right]_{H_1}^{H_2}$$

$$Q = \frac{2}{3} C_d \times b \times \sqrt{2g}\, [H_2^{\frac{3}{2}} - H_1^{\frac{3}{2}}] \qquad ...(8.10)$$

where, $H_1 = H - \dfrac{d}{2}$ and $H_2 = H + \dfrac{d}{2}$

In deriving the above expression the velocity of approach was neglected. If the velocity of approach is not negligible, then the above expression with velocity of approach, V_1 can be written as:

$$Q = \frac{2}{3} C_d \times b \times \sqrt{2g} \left[\left(H_2 + \frac{V_1^2}{2g} \right)^{\frac{3}{2}} - \left(H_1 + \frac{V_1^2}{2g} \right)^{\frac{3}{2}} \right] \quad ...(8.11)$$

8.6 FLOW THROUGH FULLY SUBMERGED ORIFICE

If an orifice has its total outlet side submerged under liquid so that it discharges a jet of liquid into a liquid of the same kind, is known as fully submerged orifice. It is also known as fully drowned orifice.

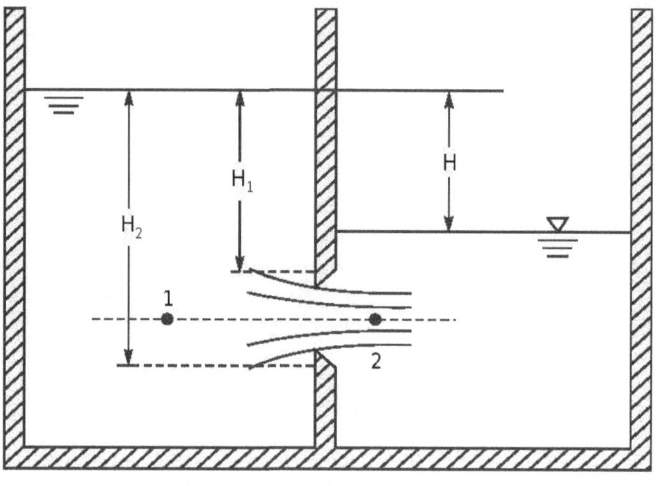

Fig. 8.6 Fully Submerged orifice

Fig. 8.6 shows the fully submerged orifice.

Let H_1 and H_2 be the head of liquid above the top and bottom edge of the orifice respectively and H is the difference of water levels.

Applying Bernoulli's equation between the points 1 and 2, we get

$$\frac{P_1}{\gamma} + \frac{V_1^2}{2g} + Z_1 = \frac{P_2}{\gamma} + \frac{V_2^2}{2g} + Z_2 \quad ...(i)$$

Consider datum level as centre line of orifice

$$Z_1 = Z_2$$

$$\frac{P_1}{\gamma} = \text{Head of water above the center of orifice in the up-stream tank}$$

$$= \frac{H_1 + H_2}{2}$$

$$\frac{P_2}{\gamma} = \text{Head of water above the centre of orifice in the down-stream side}$$

$$= \frac{H_1 + H_2}{2} - H$$

V_1 = Velocity of approach, which is negligible.

Substituting these values in the equation (*i*)

$$\frac{H_1 + H_2}{2} + 0 = \frac{H_1 + H_2}{2} - H + \frac{V_2^2}{2g}$$

$$\frac{V_2^2}{2g} = H$$

$$\therefore \quad V_2 = \sqrt{2g\,H}$$

The area of orifice $= b \times (H_2 - H_1)$ ...(b = width of orifice)

$\therefore$ Discharge through the orifice

$$= C_d \times \text{Area} \times \text{Velocity}$$

$$= C_d \times b\,(H_2 - H_1) \times \sqrt{2g\,H}$$

$$\therefore \quad Q = C_d \times b\,(H_2 - H_1) \times \sqrt{2g\,H} \qquad \text{...(8.12)}$$

8.7 FLOW THROUGH PARTIALLY SUBMERGED ORIFICE

If an orifice has its outlet side partially submerged under liquid, then it is known as partially submerged orifice. It is also known as partially drowned orifice. The discharging of liquid in partially submerged orifice is considered to be in two parts. The upper portion behaves as an orifice discharging freely in the atmosphere and the lower portion behaves as a submerged orifice as shown in Fig. 8.7. It must be remembered here that only a large orifice can behave as partially submerged orifice. The discharge through partially submerged orifice can be calculated by adding the discharge through the free and submerged portions.

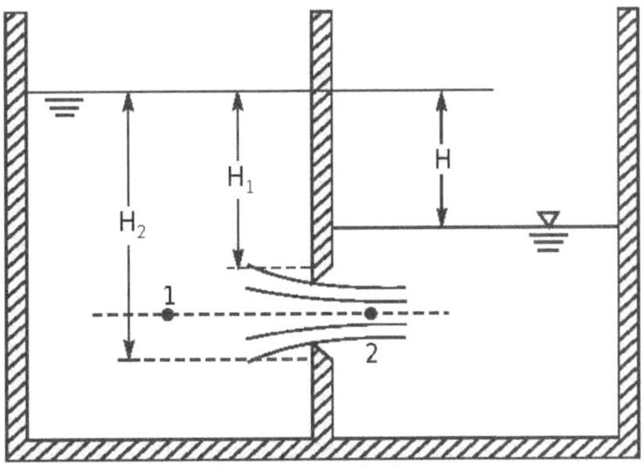

Fig. 8.7 Parially Submerged Orifice

The discharge through the free portion is calculated earlier and is given by equation (8.10) as:

$$Q_1 = \frac{2}{3} C_d \times b \times \sqrt{2g}\,[H_2^{\frac{3}{2}} - H_1^{\frac{3}{2}}]$$

The discharge through the partially submerged orifice is calculated and is given by equation (8.12)

$$Q_2 = C_d \times b\,(H_2 - H_1) \times \sqrt{2g\,H}$$

Hence the total discharge $Q = Q_1 + Q_2$

$$Q = \frac{2}{3} C_d \times b \times \sqrt{2g}\,[H_2^{\frac{3}{2}} - H_1^{\frac{3}{2}}] + C_d \times b\,(H_2 - H_1) \times \sqrt{2g\,H} \quad ...(8.13)$$

8.8 SOLVED PROBLEMS

■ **Problem 8.7:** *A rectangular orifice of size 1.8 m wide and 1.2 m deep is discharging water from a tank. The water level in the tank is 3.5 m higher from the centre of orifice. Find the discharge through the orifice. Take* $C_d = 0.62$.

Solution:

The discharge through orifice is given by equation (8.10) for large rectangular orifice.

$$Q = \frac{2}{3} C_d \times b \times \sqrt{2g}\,[H_2^{\frac{3}{2}} - H_1^{\frac{3}{2}}]$$

Given, $C_d = 0.62$

$$H_1 = 3.5 - \frac{1.2}{2} = 2.9 \text{ m}$$

$$H_2 = 3.5 + \frac{1.2}{2} = 4.1 \text{ m}$$

Substitute these values in above equation

$$Q = \frac{2}{3} \times 0.62 \times 1.8 \times \sqrt{2 \times 9.81}\,[(4.1)^{\frac{3}{2}} - (2.9)^{\frac{3}{2}}]$$

$$= 3.296\,(8.302 - 4.939)$$

$$Q = 11.084 \text{ m}^3\text{/s.} \quad ...(\textbf{Ans.})$$

■ **Problem 8.8:** *A rectangular orifice of size 1.2 m wide and 1.5 m deep is discharging water from a tank. The water level in the tank is 1.0 m above the top edge of the orifice. Calculate the discharge through the orifice and percentage error if the orifice if treated as small orifice. Take* $C_d = 0.61$.

Solution: Discharge through large rectangular orifice is given by equation (8.10)

$$Q = \frac{2}{3} C_d \times b \times \sqrt{2g}\,[H_2^{\frac{3}{2}} - H_1^{\frac{3}{2}}]$$

Given,
$$C_d = 0.61$$
$$b = 1.2 \text{ m}$$
$$H_1 = 1.0 \text{ m}$$
$$H_2 = 1.5 + 1.0 = 2.5 \text{ m}$$

Substitute these values in above equation

$$Q = \frac{2}{3} \times 0.61 \times 1.2 \times \sqrt{2 \times 9.81}\,[(2.5)^{\frac{3}{2}} - (1.0)^{\frac{3}{2}}]$$
$$= 2.162\,(3.953 - 1)$$
$$Q = 6.384 \text{ m}^3\text{/s.} \qquad \text{...(Ans.)}$$

If the given orifice is treated as a small orifice, then

$$Q_s = C_d \times a \times \sqrt{2g\,H}$$
$$= 0.61 \times (1.2 \times 1.5) \times \sqrt{2 \times 9.81 \times 1.75}$$
$$Q_s = 6.434 \text{ m}^3\text{/s} \qquad \left(\text{where, } H = H_1 + \frac{d}{2} = 1.0 + \frac{1.5}{2} = 1.75\right)$$

$$\% \text{ error} = \frac{Q_s - Q}{Q}$$
$$= \frac{6.434 - 6.384}{6.384}$$
$$= 0.00783$$
$$\text{Error} = 0.783\%. \qquad \text{...(Ans.)}$$

■ **Problem 8.9**: *Find the discharge through fully submerged orifice of width 1.8 m. The difference of water levels on both the sides of the orifice is 48 cm. The head of water above top and bottom edges of the orifice are 2.4 m and 2.8 m respectively. Take $C_d = 0.62$.*

Solution: Discharge through the fully submerged orifice is given by the following equation:

$$Q = C_d \times b \times (H_2 - H_1)\sqrt{2g\,H}$$

Given,
$$b = 1.8 \text{ m}$$
$$H = 48 \text{ cm} = 0.48 \text{ m}$$
$$H_1 = 2.4 \text{ m}$$
$$H_2 = 2.8 \text{ m}$$

and
$$C_d = 0.62$$

Substitute these values in the above equation

$$Q = 0.62 \times 1.8 \times (2.8 - 2.4)\,\sqrt{2 \times 9.81 \times 0.48}$$
$$Q = 1.37 \text{ m}^3\text{/s.} \qquad \text{...(Ans.)}$$

■ **Problem 8.10**: *Find the discharge through the rectangular orifice of 2.0 m wide and 1.0 m deep provided in the side of tank. The head of water on one side of orifice is 3.2 m above the top edge of the orifice while on other side the head of water is 0.4 m below the top edge. Take $C_d = 0.62$.*

Solution: The discharge through partially submerged orifice can be calculated by using the equation (8.13)

$$Q = C_d \times b \times (H_2 - H_1)\sqrt{2g\,H} + \frac{2}{3} \times C_d \times b \times \sqrt{2g}\,[H^{\frac{3}{2}} - H_1^{\frac{3}{2}}]$$

Given,

$$b = 2.0 \text{ m}$$
$$d = 1.0 \text{ m}$$
$$H_1 = 3.2 \text{ m}$$
$$H_2 = 3.2 + 1.0 = 4.2 \text{ m}$$
$$H = H_1 + 0.4 = 3.2 + 0.4 = 3.6 \text{ m}$$

Substitute these values in the above equation to get Q.

$$Q = 0.62 \times 2.0 \times (4.2 - 3.2) \times \sqrt{2 \times 9.81 \times 3.6}$$
$$+ \frac{2}{3} \times 0.62 \times 2.0 \times \sqrt{2 \times 9.81} \times [(3.6)^{\frac{3}{2}} - (3.2)^{\frac{3}{2}}]$$
$$= 10.42 + 4.05$$
$$Q = 14.47 \text{ m}^3/\text{s}. \qquad \text{...(Ans.)}$$

8.9 TIME OF EMPTYING A TANK

In the earlier study, we have assumed the flow as steady *i.e.*, the head of liquid above centre of orifice is constant. This may be achieved by adjusting the inflow into the tank and outflow from the orifice. But this may not be true all the time. The liquid head in the tank may vary depending upon the inflow into the tank and outflow from orifice. If there is no inflow of liquid into the tank, then liquid level will decrease with the discharge of liquid from the orifice or tank may become empty in certain amount of time. The aim of further study is to determine time required for free surface of liquid to change from initial level to some another level or to determine time of emptying the tank with no inflow.

8.9.1 Cylindrical Tank (Vertical)

Consider a tank containing liquid upto height H_1. Let an orifice is provided on the bottom of the tank. The aim of study is to find the time required for the free liquid surface to fall from height H_1 to H_2 or total emptying of tank. The discharge through orifice depends upon the head above the centre of orifice, which is varying with time and hence the time can be determined by integration.

Let, H_1 and H_2 be initial and final heads of water above the centre of orifice respectively (Fig. 8.8) and T is the time required to fall the liquid surface from H_1 to H_2 in seconds.

Let any instant, the head of liquid above the orifice is h and let the head of liquid fall by a small amount dh in time dT. The volume of liquid leaving the tank in time dT is $A \times dh$, where A is area of tank. If the discharge through orifice in time dT is dQ, then volume of liquid flowing through orifice is $dQ\ dT$.

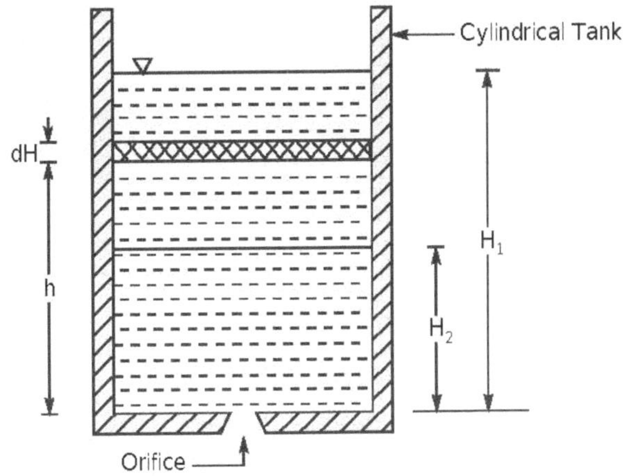

Fig. 8.8 Cylindrical Tank with Orifice at Bottom

Discharge through orifice is given by equation (8.9)

$$dQ = C_d \, a\sqrt{2gh}$$

∴ Volume of liquid flowing through orifice is

$$dQdT = C_d \, a\sqrt{2gh} \cdot dT$$

But the volume of liquid leaving the tank is equal to the volume of liquid flowing through the orifice.

∴ $$-A \times dh = C_d \, a\sqrt{2gh} \, dT$$

Negative sign is introduced because, the liquid head on orifice decreases with increase in time.

∴ $$dT = \frac{-A \times dh}{C_d \, a\sqrt{2gh}}$$

∴ $$dT = \frac{-A \, h^{\frac{-1}{2}}}{C_d \cdot a \cdot \sqrt{2g}} dh \qquad \text{...(8.14)}$$

Integrate the equation (8.14) between the limits H_1 to H_2 to get the total time, T.

∴ $$T = \int_0^T dT = \int_{H_1}^{H_2} \frac{-A \, h^{\frac{-1}{2}}}{C_d \cdot a \cdot \sqrt{2g}} dh$$

$$= \frac{-A}{C_d \cdot a \cdot \sqrt{2g}} \left[\frac{h^{\frac{1}{2}}}{\frac{1}{2}} \right]_{H_1}^{H_2}$$

$$= \frac{-2A}{C_d \cdot a \cdot \sqrt{2g}} [H_2^{\frac{1}{2}} - H_1^{\frac{1}{2}}]$$

$$T = \frac{-2A}{C_d \cdot a \cdot \sqrt{2g}} [H_1^{\frac{1}{2}} - H_2^{\frac{1}{2}}] \quad ...(8.15)$$

For emptying the tank totally, $H_2 = 0$,

$$\therefore \quad T = \frac{-2A\, H_1^{\frac{1}{2}}}{C_d \cdot a \cdot \sqrt{2g}} \quad ...(8.16)$$

The above equations (8.15) and (8.16) are also applicable to rectangular or square tank with their axis vertical and having constant horizontal cross-sectional area.

8.9.2 Conical Tank

In general conical tank has a shape of frustum of cone, where in the horizontal cross-sectional area A varies. (Refer Fig. 8.9)

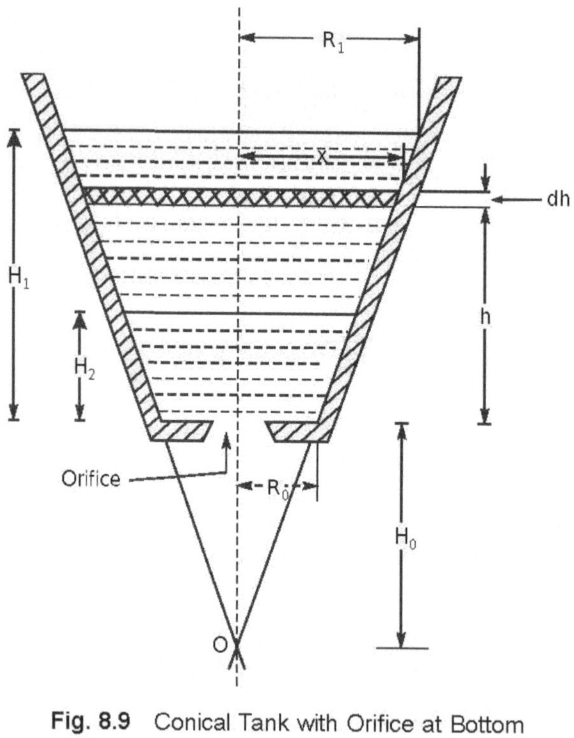

Fig. 8.9 Conical Tank with Orifice at Bottom

The aim of this is to find time required for the free liquid surface to fall from height H_1 to H_2 or for total emptying the tank. The equation (8.14) can be used to find the time T.

$$dT = \frac{-A\, h^{\frac{-1}{2}}}{C_d \cdot a \cdot \sqrt{2g}} dh \quad ...(8.17)$$

In this case the cross-sectional area A varies with time as the head of liquid in the container reduces. Let x is the radius of cone at height h above the bottom.

$$\therefore \quad A = \pi x^2$$

The value of x can be calculated using similar triangles

$$\frac{x}{H_0 + h} = \frac{R_1}{H_0 + H_1}$$

$$\therefore \quad x = \frac{R_1(H_0 + h)}{H_0 + H_1}$$

$$\therefore \quad A = \pi x^2 = \frac{\pi R_1^2 (H_0 + h)^2}{(H_0 + H_1)^2}$$

Substituting for A in equation (8.17)

$$T = \int_0^T dT = \frac{-\pi R_1^2}{C_d \times a \times \sqrt{2g}\,(H_0 + H_1)^2} \int_{H_1}^{H_2} (H_0 + h)^2 h^{\frac{-1}{2}} dh$$

$$= \frac{-\pi R_1^2}{C_d a \sqrt{2g}\,(H_0 + H_1)^2} \int_{H_1}^{H_2} (H_0^2 h^{\frac{-1}{2}} + 2H_0 h^{\frac{1}{2}} + h^{\frac{3}{2}})\, dh$$

$$= \frac{-\pi R_1^2}{C_d a \sqrt{2g}\,(H_0 + H_1)^2} \left[2H_0^2\, h^{\frac{1}{2}} + \frac{4}{3} H_0 h^{\frac{3}{2}} + \frac{2}{5} h^{\frac{2}{5}} \right]_{H_1}^{H_2}$$

$$= \frac{+\pi R_1^2}{C_d a \sqrt{2g}\,(H_0 + H_1)^2}$$

$$\left[2H_0^2 (H_1^{\frac{1}{2}} - H_2^{\frac{1}{2}}) + \frac{4}{3} H_0 (H_1^{\frac{3}{2}} - H_2^{\frac{3}{2}}) + \frac{2}{5} (H_1^{\frac{5}{2}} - H_2^{\frac{5}{2}}) \right] \quad \text{...(8.18)}$$

Hence the equation (8.18) gives the time 'T' required to fall water level from H_1 and H_2. For emptying the tank completely, $H_2 = 0$.

$$\therefore \quad T = \frac{\pi R_1^2}{C_d a \sqrt{2g}\,(H_0 + H_1)^2} \left[2H_0^2 H_1^{\frac{1}{2}} + \frac{4}{3} H_0 H_1^{\frac{3}{2}} + \frac{2}{5} H_1^{\frac{5}{2}} \right] \quad \text{...(8.19)}$$

In the above expression, the value of H_0, can be calculated by similar triangles

$$\frac{R_0}{H_0} = \frac{R_1}{H_0 + H_1} \quad \text{...(8.20)}$$

8.9.3 Hemispherical Tank

Fig. 8.10 shows the hemispherical tank of radius R provided with an orifice of area at the bottom. The aim of this study is to find the time T required to fall liquid level from H_1 to H_2 or for total emptying the tank.

The equation (8.19) can be used for determining the time T.

$$dT = \frac{-A \times h^{\frac{-1}{2}}}{C_d a \sqrt{2g}} dh \qquad ...(8.21)$$

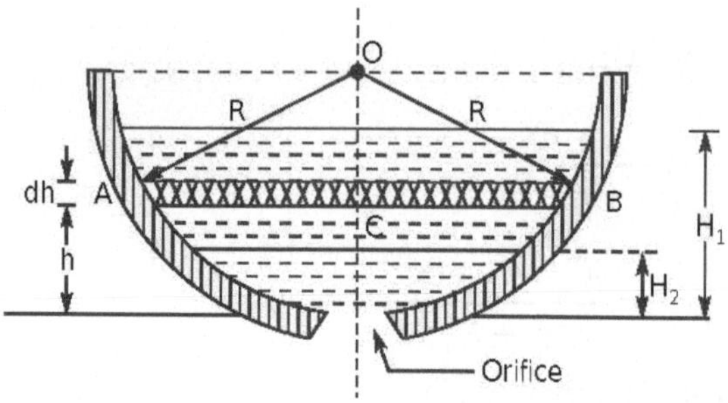

Fig. 8.10 Hemispherical Tank with Orifice at the Bottom

Let the area of liquid surface at any instant of time is

$$A = \pi x^2$$

where, x = Radius of liquid surface at height 'h' above the orifice at bottom

$$x = AC$$

$$= \sqrt{AO^2 - CO^2}$$

$$x = \sqrt{R^2 - (R-h)^2}$$

$$x^2 = R^2 - (R^2 - 2RH + h^2)$$

$$x^2 = 2Rh - h^2$$

∴ Area, $A = \pi x^2 = \pi(2Rh - h^2)$

Substitute for A in equation (8.21)

$$T = \int_0^T dT = \frac{-\pi}{C_d a\sqrt{2g}} \int_{H_1}^{H_2} (2Rh - h^2) \times h^{\frac{-1}{2}} dh$$

$$= \frac{-\pi}{C_d a\sqrt{2g}} \int_{H_1}^{H_2} (2Rh^{\frac{1}{2}} - h^{\frac{3}{2}}) dh$$

$$= \frac{-\pi}{C_d a\sqrt{2g}} \left[\frac{4}{3} Rh^{\frac{3}{2}} - \frac{2}{5} h^{\frac{5}{2}}\right]_{H_1}^{H_2}$$

$$\therefore \quad T = \frac{-\pi}{C_d a\sqrt{2g}} \left[\frac{4}{3} R(H_2^{\frac{3}{2}} - H_1^{\frac{3}{2}}) - \frac{2}{5}(H_2^{\frac{5}{2}} - H_1^{\frac{5}{2}})\right]$$

$$T = \frac{-\pi}{C_d a\sqrt{2g}} \left[\frac{4}{3} R(H_1^{\frac{3}{2}} - H_2^{\frac{3}{2}}) - \frac{2}{3}(H_1^{\frac{5}{2}} - H_2^{\frac{5}{2}})\right] \qquad ...(8.22)$$

For completely emptying the tank, $H_2 = 0$

$$\therefore \quad T = \frac{-\pi}{C_d \cdot a\sqrt{2g}}\left[\frac{4}{3}RH_1^{\frac{3}{2}} - \frac{2}{5}H_1^{\frac{3}{2}}\right] \quad ...(8.23)$$

8.9.4 Cylindrical Horizontal Tank

Consider a cylindrical horizontal tank of length L and radius R provided with an orifice of area a at the bottom of the tank as shown in Fig. 8.11. The initial level of liquid is H_1, which reduced the H_2 in time T. Aim of this study is to find the time T.

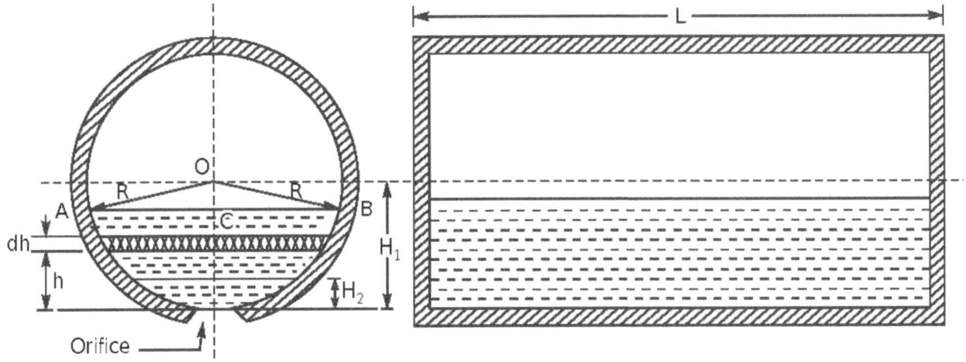

Fig. 8.11 Cylindrical Horizontal Tank

The equation (8.14) can be used for determining T

$$dT = \frac{-A\,h^{\frac{-1}{2}}}{C_d\,a\sqrt{2g}}\,dh \quad ...(8.24)$$

Let the area of liquid surface at any instant of time is:

$$A = L \times AB$$

where,

$$AB = 2 \times AC = 2\sqrt{AO^2 - CO^2}$$

$$= 2\sqrt{R^2 - (R-h)^2}$$

$$= 2\sqrt{R^2 - (R^2 - 2Rh + h^2)}$$

$$= 2\sqrt{2Rh - h^2}$$

$$\therefore \quad A = L \times 2\sqrt{2Rh - h^2}$$

$$A = 2L\sqrt{2Rh - h^2}$$

Substitute for A in equation (8.24),

$$T = \int_0^T dT = \int_{H_1}^{H_2} \frac{-2L(2Rh - h^2)^{\frac{1}{2}}\,h^{\frac{-1}{2}}}{C_d\,a\sqrt{2g}}\,dh$$

$$\therefore \quad = \frac{-2L}{C_d\, a\sqrt{2g}} \int_{H_1}^{H_2} (2R-h)^{\frac{1}{2}} \times h^{\frac{1}{2}} \times h^{\frac{-1}{2}}\, dh$$

$$= \frac{-2L}{C_d\, a\sqrt{2g}} \int_{H_1}^{H_2} (2R-h)^{\frac{1}{2}}\, dh$$

$$= \frac{-2L}{C_d\, a\sqrt{2g}} \left[\frac{(2R-h)^{\frac{3}{2}}}{\frac{3}{2}} \right]_{H_1}^{H_2}$$

$$T = \frac{4L}{3C_d\, a\sqrt{2g}} [(2R-H_2)^{\frac{3}{2}} - (2R-H_1)^{\frac{3}{2}}] \quad ...(8.25)$$

For emptying the tank completely, $H_2 = 0$

$$\therefore \quad T = \frac{4L}{3C_d\, a\sqrt{2g}} [(2R)^{\frac{3}{2}} - (2R-H_1)^{\frac{3}{2}}] \quad ...(8.26)$$

8.9.5 Solved Problems

■ **Problem 8.11:** *It takes 200 sec to empty the top $\frac{1}{6}$th of a rectangular tank. Find how long will it take to empty the bottom $\frac{1}{4}$th.*

Solution: Let H is the head of water in the tank. It requires 200 sec. to fall the water level to $0.4\,H$.

$$\therefore \quad 200 = \frac{2A}{C_d\, a\sqrt{2g}} [H^{\frac{1}{2}} - (0.833\,H)^{\frac{1}{2}}] \quad ...(i)$$

Let T is the time required to fall the water level from $0.4\,H$ to 0.

$$\therefore \quad T = \frac{2A}{C_d\, a\sqrt{2g}} [(0.25\,H)^{\frac{1}{2}} - 0] \quad ...(ii)$$

Dividing equation (*i*) by (*ii*)

$$\frac{200}{T} = \frac{\frac{2A}{C_d\, a\sqrt{2g}} [H^{\frac{1}{2}} - (0.833\,H)^{\frac{1}{2}}}{\frac{2A}{C_d\, a\sqrt{2g}} [(0.25\,H)^{\frac{1}{2}} - 0]}$$

$$\frac{200}{T} = \frac{H^{\frac{1}{2}}(1-0.833)}{H^{\frac{1}{2}}(0.25)}$$

$$\frac{200}{T} = \frac{0.833}{0.25}$$

$$T = 300 \text{ sec.}$$

Time required to empty the bottom $\frac{1}{4}$th of tank = T = 300 seconds. ...(**Ans.**)

■ **Problem 8.12:** *A tank has the form of a frustum of a cone, with the 2.44 m diameter uppermost and 1.22 m diameter at the bottom and 3.05 m deep. The bottom contains an orifice whose average coefficient of discharge may be taken as 0.60. What size orifice will empty the tank in 6 minute if the depth fall is 3.05?*

Solution: Time of emptying the conical tank is given on:

$$T = \frac{\pi R_1^2}{C_d\, a\sqrt{2g}(H_0 + H_1)^2}\left[2H_0^2 H_1^{\frac{1}{2}} + \frac{4}{3}H_0 H_1^{\frac{3}{2}} + \frac{2}{5}H_1^{\frac{5}{2}}\right]$$

Given,

$$R_1 = \frac{2.44}{2} = 1.22 \text{ m}$$

$$R_0 = \frac{1.22}{2} = 0.61 \text{ m}$$

$$H_1 = 3.05 \text{ m}$$

$$C_d = 0.6$$

$$T = 6 \text{ min} = 360 \text{ sec.}$$

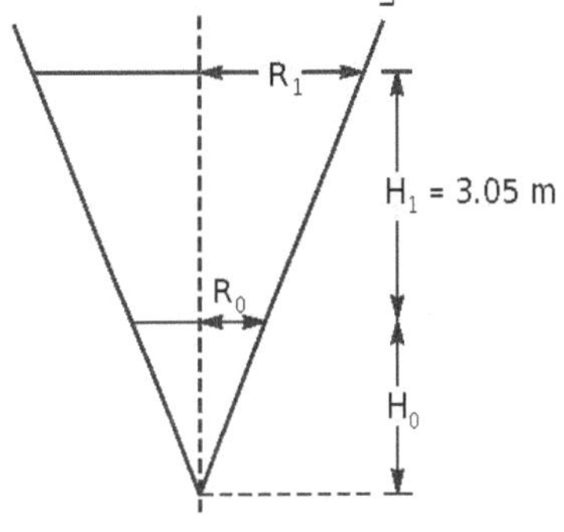

Fig. 8.12

From similar triangles;

$$\frac{R_0}{H_0} = \frac{R_1}{H_0 + H_1}$$

$$H_0 R_1 = H_0 R_0 + H_1 R_0$$

$$1.22\, H_0 = 0.61\, H_0 + 3.05 \times 0.61$$

$$H_0 = 3.05 \text{ m}$$

Substitute all the values in the above equation to get '*a*'

$$360 = \frac{\pi(1.22)^2}{0.6 \times a \times \sqrt{2 \times 9.81}(3.05 + 3.05)^2}$$

$$\left[2 \times (3.05)^2 (3.05)^{\frac{1}{2}} + \frac{4}{3}(3.05)(3.05)^{\frac{3}{2}} + \frac{2}{5}(3.05)^{\frac{5}{2}}\right]$$

$$\therefore \qquad a = \frac{4.676}{35601.1}\left[\left(2+\frac{4}{2}+\frac{2}{5}\right)\times 3.05^{\frac{5}{2}}\right]$$

$$= \frac{4.676}{35601.1}\times 60.60$$

$$a = 7.959 \times 10^{-3}\ \text{m}^2$$

$$\frac{\pi}{4}d^2 = 7.959 \times 10^{-3}$$

$$d = 0.1007\ \text{m}$$

$$d = 10.07\ \text{cm.} \qquad \text{...(Ans.)}$$

■ **Problem 8.13:** *A cylindrical boiler, diameter 2 m and length 10 m is lying horizontally and is half full of water. It is to be emptied by an external cylindrical mouthpiece of diameter 7.5 cm fixed at the bottom of the boiler. How long will the mouthpiece take to empty the boiler? Take* $C_d = 0.82$.

Solution: Diameter of cylindrical boiler = 2 m

$\therefore$ Radius = 1.0 m

$\therefore$ Head, H_1 = 1.0 m

Length, L = 10 m

Diameter of mouthpiece = 7.5 cm = 0.075 m

$$a = \frac{\pi}{4}(0.0075)^2 = 4.418\times 10^{-3}\ \text{m}^2$$

$$C_d = 0.82$$

$$\text{Time of emptying, } T = \frac{4L}{3C_d\, a\sqrt{2g}}\left[(2R)^{\frac{3}{2}} - (2R-H_1)^{\frac{3}{2}}\right]$$

$$T = \frac{4\times 10}{3\times 0.82\times 4.418\times 10^{-3}\times\sqrt{2\times 9.81}}\left[(2\times 1.0)^{\frac{3}{2}} - (2\times 1 - 1.0)^{\frac{3}{2}}\right]$$

$$= \frac{40}{0.0481}[2.828 - 1.0]$$

$$T = 1525\ \text{sec.} = 25\ \text{min}\ 25\ \text{sec.} \qquad \text{...(Ans.)}$$

■ **Problem 8.14:** *A hemispherical tank of diameter 4 m contains water upto height 2.0 m. An orifice of diameter 5 cm is provided at the bottom. Find the time required by water (i) to fall from 2.0 m to 1.0 m (ii) for completely emptying the tank. Take* $C_d = 0.6$.

Solution:

(*i*) Time required to fall water level from H_1 to H_2 in case of hemispherical tank is given by equation (8.22)

$$T = \frac{\pi}{C_d\, a\sqrt{2g}}\left[\frac{4}{3}R(H_1^{\frac{3}{2}} - H_2^{\frac{3}{2}}) - \frac{2}{5}(H_1^{\frac{5}{2}} - H_2^{\frac{5}{2}})\right]$$

Given, Dia. of tank = 4 m

$\therefore$ Radius, $R = \frac{4}{2} = 2$ m

$H_1 = 2.0$ m

$H_2 = 1.0$ m

Dia. of orifice = 5 cm = 0.05 m

$$a = \frac{\pi}{4}\times(0.05)^2 = 1.9635\times 10^{-3}\ \text{m}^2$$

$C_d = 0.6$

Substitute these values in above equation to get time required to fall water level from 2.0 m to 1.0 m.

$$T = \frac{\pi}{0.6\times1.9635\times10^{-3}\times\sqrt{2\times9.81}}\left[\frac{4}{3}\times2.0(2^{\frac{3}{2}} - 1^{\frac{3}{2}}) - \frac{2}{5}(2^{\frac{5}{2}} - 1^{\frac{5}{2}})\right]$$

$T = 602.03\ [4.876 - 1.863]$

$T = 1814.07$ sec. ...(**Ans.**)

(*ii*) Time required for completely emptying the tank

$$T = \frac{\pi}{C_d\, a\sqrt{2g}}\left[\frac{4}{3}RH_1^{\frac{3}{2}} - \frac{2}{5}H_1^{\frac{5}{2}}\right]$$

$$T = 602.03\left[\frac{4}{3}\times 2(2.0)^{\frac{3}{2}} - \frac{2}{5}(2.0)^{\frac{5}{2}}\right]$$

$= 602.03\ (7.542 - 2.263)$

$T = 3178.27$ sec. ...(**Ans.**)

■ **Problem 8.15:** *A swimming pool 140 m long and 15 m wide with vertical sides and bottom at a slope of so that the depth of water at shallow side and deep side are respectively 1 m and 1.75 m. The pool is provided with an orifice of area 0.1 m². Find the time taken to discharge total water from swimming pool. Take C_d of orifice 0.61.*

Solution: The swimming pool as shown in Fig. 8.13 can be considered in two parts, viz.

(I) Constant cross-sectional area for a depth of 1.0 m and

(II) The shallow portion where cross-sectional area varies.

Thus total time T required to empty the pool can be divided into two parts T_1 and T_2 required to empty (I) and (II) portions.

(*i*) Time of emptying top portion (T_1):

Let Q is the discharge through an orifice and h is the height above the centre of orifice at any instant and in time dT the level of water decrease by dh.

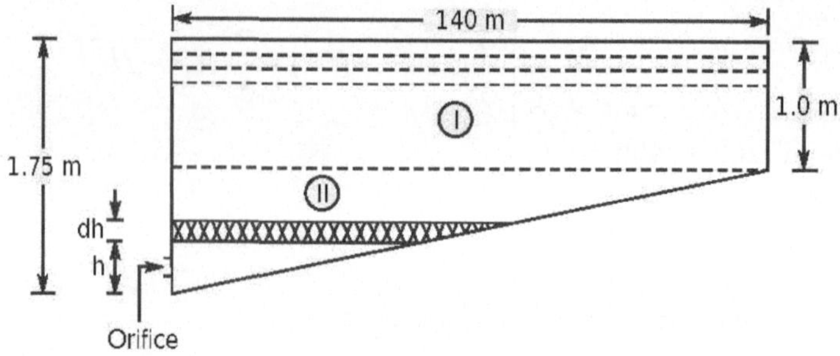

Fig. 8.13

$$\therefore \quad Q\,dT = -A\,dh$$

$$\therefore \quad dT = \frac{-A\,dh}{Q} \qquad \ldots(i)$$

where,
$$Q = C_d \times a \times \sqrt{2gh}$$
$$Q = 0.61 \times 0.1 \times \sqrt{2gh}$$
$$Q = 0.27\sqrt{h}$$
$$A = 140 \times 15 = 2100 \text{ m}^2$$
$$H_1 = 1.75 \text{ m and } H_2 = 0.75 \text{ m}$$

Integrating Equation (*i*) above

$$T_1 = \int_0^{T_1} dT = -\int_{1.75}^{0.75} \frac{2100}{0.27\sqrt{h}}\,dh$$

$$= \frac{-7777.78}{\frac{1}{2}}\left[h^{\frac{1}{2}}\right]_{1.75}^{0.75}$$

$$T_1 = 2 \times 7777.78\left[(1.75)^{\frac{1}{2}} - (0.75)^{\frac{1}{2}}\right]$$
$$T_1 = 15555.50\,(1.323 - 0.866)$$
$$T_1 = 7108.5 \text{ seconds.}$$

(*i*) Time of emptying shallow portion (T_2):

If the water in the pool is h at any instant of time then cross-sectional area at this level is as follows.

$$A = 140 \times 15 \times \left(\frac{h}{0.75}\right)$$

$$A = 2800\,h$$

If in time dT, water decreases by dh, then

$$Q\,dT = -A\,dh$$

$$dT = \frac{-A}{Q}\,dh$$

$$T_2 = \int_0^{T_2} dT = \int_{0.75}^{0} \frac{-2800\,h}{0.27\sqrt{h}}\,dh$$

$$T_2 = 10370.4 \int_{0.75}^{0} h^{\frac{1}{2}}\,dh$$

$$= -10370.4 \times \frac{2}{3} \times [h^{\frac{3}{2}}]_{0.75}^{0}$$

$$= -10370 \times \frac{2}{3} \times (0.75)^{\frac{3}{2}}$$

$$T_2 = 4490.5 \text{ seconds.}$$

Total time required for emptying the pool is:

$$T = T_1 + T_2$$

$$= 7108.5 + 4490.5$$

$$= 11499.0 \text{ seconds.}$$

T = 3 hrs 11 mm 39 sec. ...(Ans.)

8.10 CLASSIFICATION OF MOUTHPIECES

The mouthpieces are classified as follows:

(1) The mouthpieces are classified on the basis of shape as (*i*) Cylindrical (*ii*) Convergent (*iii*) Divergent (*iv*) Convergent-Divergent Mouthpieces.

(2) The mouthpieces are classified as (*i*) External (*ii*) Internal depending upon their position. External mouthpiece is one which is fitted to the tank and projecting outside the tank. An internal mouthpiece is also known as Borda's or re-entrant mouthpiece and is fitted to the tank projecting inside.

(3) The mouthpieces are classified on the basis of discharge conditions as (*i*) Mouthpiece running full and (*ii*) Mouthpiece running free. This classification is only for internal mouthpiece.

8.11 FLOW THROUGH EXTERNAL CYLINDRICAL MOUTHPIECE

A mouthpiece is a short length pipe (2 to 3 times its diameter) fitted to circular orifice in the tank. If the mouthpiece is fitted externally it is called external cylindrical mouthpiece and it is observed that the discharge increases if the mouthpiece runs full. This is explained as under. If the length of mouthpiece is two to three times its diameter and head above mouthpiece does not exceed certain value, then it runs full. If length is small equal to its diameter and for low heads the mouthpiece runs free *i.e.*, the jet of liquid emerge out without touching the sides of mouthpiece and it can be considered as the orifice. Hence following study aims to determine the discharge through an external cylindrical mouthpiece running full.

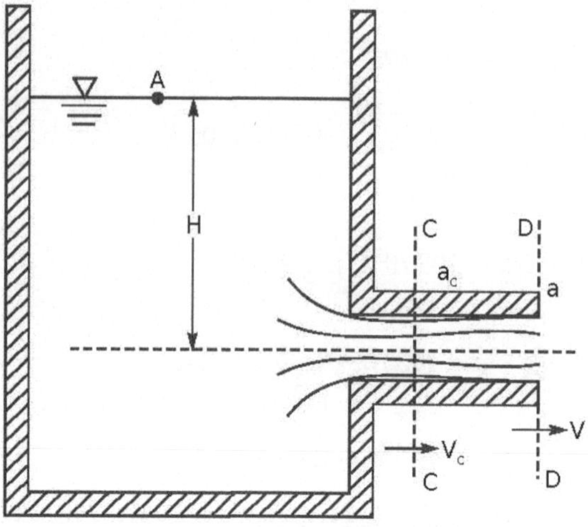

Fig. 8.14 External Cylindrical Mouthpiece

Consider a tank having cylindrical mouthpiece of cross-sectional area 'a' provided externally on one of its sides as shown in Fig. 8.14. The head of liquid above the centre of mouthpiece is H. The jet of liquid emerges out from mouthpiece and contracts to form vena-contracta at a Section C-C. The cross-sectional area of jet at Section C-C is a_c and velocity of flow equal to V_c. The jet again expands and occupies the mouthpiece completely. The velocity of jet at outlet *i.e.*, at Section D-D is V. Apply the continuity equation between Section C-C and D-D, as flow through mouthpiece is same.

$$a_c V_c = aV$$

$$V_c = \frac{a}{a_c} V$$

But $$C_c = \frac{a_c}{a} = 0.62 \qquad \text{(Assume, } C_c = 0.62\text{)}$$

∴ $$V_c = \frac{V}{0.62}$$

Now, there will be some loss of head, h_L when the jet of liquid enlarges from Section C-C to Section D-D. The flow pattern between these two sections is similar, that due to sudden enlargement in pipe, which can be calculated by using following equation. (Please refer Chapter 12 for the derivation of loss of head due to sudden enlargement)

$$h_L = \frac{(V_c - V)^2}{2g}$$

$$= \frac{\left(\dfrac{V}{0.62} - V\right)^2}{2g}$$

$$= \frac{V^2}{2g}\left(\frac{1}{0.62}-1\right)^2$$

$$h_L = 0.375\frac{V^2}{2g}$$

Applying Bernoulli's equation between free surface of liquid at A and section D-D.

$$H_a + H = H_a + \frac{V^2}{2g} + h_L$$

where, H_a = atmospheric pressure head

$$\therefore \quad H = \frac{V^2}{2g} + 0.375\frac{V^2}{2g}$$

$$H = 1.375\frac{V^2}{2g}$$

$$\therefore \quad V = \sqrt{\frac{2g\,H}{1.375}}$$

$$V = 0.855\sqrt{2g\,H}$$

The theoretical velocity of flow of liquid through mouthpiece is,

$$V_{th} = \sqrt{2g\,H}$$

∴ Coefficient of velocity for mouthpiece = $C_v = \dfrac{V}{V_{th}}$

$$= \frac{0.855\sqrt{2g\,H}}{\sqrt{2g\,H}}$$

$$\therefore \quad C_v = 0.855$$

The coefficient of contraction C_v for the mouthpiece be equal 1, as the area of liquid jet emerging out from mouthpiece is equal to area of mouthpiece at outlet.

∴ The coefficient of discharge for mouthpiece is

$$C_d = C_c \times C_v = 1.0 \times 0.855$$

$$C_d = 0.855$$

Since the coefficient of discharge C_d for mouthpiece is more than the value to C_d for orifice, the discharge through mouthpiece will be more.

∴ Discharge through the mouthpiece is given as follows:

$$Q = C_d\,a\sqrt{2g\,H}$$

$$Q = 0.855 \times a \times \sqrt{2g\,H} \qquad \text{...(8.27)}$$

8.12 FLOW THROUGH CONVERGENT-DIVERGENT MOUTHPIECE

In the case of external cylindrical mouthpiece, there is some loss of energy due to formation of vena-contracta and the enlargement of jet thereafter, which reduces the coefficient of discharge of the mouthpiece. This can be avoided by making the shape of mouthpiece to match the shape of jet of liquid upto vena-contaracta to eliminate loss of energy. Such a mouthpiece is known as convergent mouthpiece (refer Fig. 8.15). Theoretical value of C_d for such mouthpiece is unity but in actual practice due to loss of energy it is less than one. The acceptable value for $C_d = 0.975$.

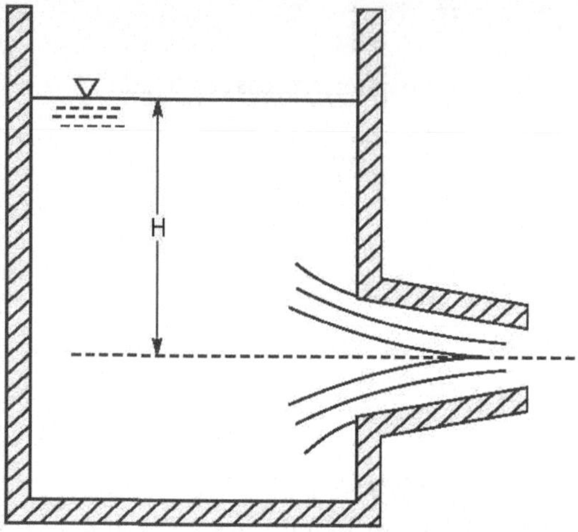

Fig. 8.15 Convergent Mouthpiece

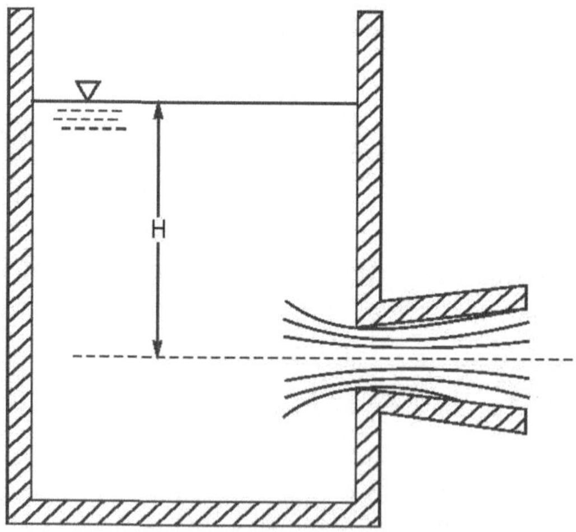

Fig. 8.16 Divergent Mothpiece

The loss of energy due to sudden enlargement of liquid jet in mouthpiece can be eliminated by making the shape of mouthpiece as gradually diverging as shown in Fig. 8.16. Such mouthpiece is called as divergent mouthpiece.

When the shape of mouthpiece is made convergent upto vena-contracta and thereafter diverges, then such type of mouthpiece is known as convergent-divergent mouthpiece. In such mouthpiece the velocity at vena-contracta increases with the increase in divergence. The increase in velocity leads to increase in vacuum pressure at vena-contracta. But this vacuum pressure should not reduce to absolute zero. Thus there is a limit for the maximum divergence to be provided to the mouthpiece and is explained as under:

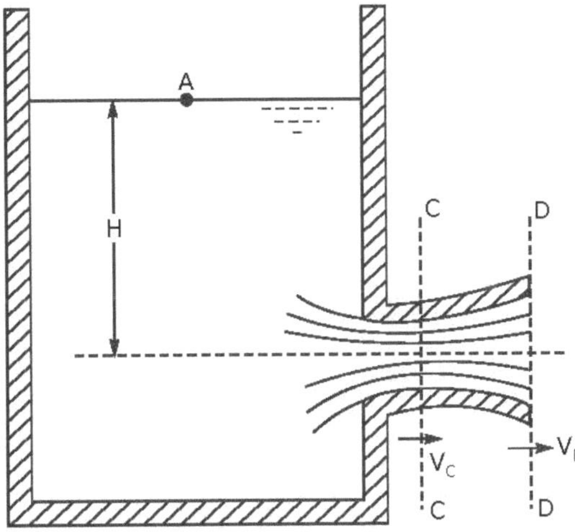

Fig. 8.17 Convergent-Divergent Mouthpiece

Apply Bernoulli's equation between the free liquid surface in the tank and Section *C-C*.

$$\frac{P_A}{\gamma} + \frac{V_A^2}{2g} + Z_A = \frac{P_C}{\gamma} + \frac{V_C^2}{2g} + Z_C$$

But, $\frac{P_A}{\gamma} = H_a,\ V_A = 0,\ \frac{P_C}{\gamma} = H_C$ and

$Z_A = H$ and $Z_C = 0$ if centre of orifice is considered as datum.

$$\therefore \quad H_a + 0 + H = H_c + \frac{V_c^2}{2g} + 0$$

$$\frac{V_c^2}{2g} = H_a + H - H_c \quad ...(i)$$

$$\therefore \quad V_c = \sqrt{2g\,(H_a + H - H_c)} \quad ...(ii)$$

Now apply Bernoulli's equation between Section *C-C* and Section *D-D*.

$$\frac{P_C}{\gamma} + \frac{V_C^2}{2g} + Z_C = \frac{P_D}{\gamma} + \frac{V_D^2}{2g} + Z_D$$

But, $Z_C = Z_D$ and $\frac{P_D}{\gamma} = H_a$

$$\therefore \qquad H_c + \frac{V_C^2}{2g} = H_a + \frac{V_D^2}{2g} \qquad \text{...(iii)}$$

Substitute for $\frac{V_C^2}{2g}$ from equation (*i*) in (*iii*)

$$H_a + H = H_a + \frac{V_D^2}{2g}$$

$$\therefore \qquad V_D = \sqrt{2g\,H} \qquad \text{...(iv)}$$

By using the continuity equation, we can write

$$a_D V_D = a_C V_C$$

$$\frac{a_D}{a_D} = \frac{V_C}{V_D}$$

$$= \frac{\sqrt{2g\,(H_a + H - H_c)}}{\sqrt{2g\,H}}$$

$$\therefore \qquad \frac{a_D}{a_C} = \sqrt{\frac{H_a + H - H_c}{H}}$$

$$\frac{a_D}{a_C} = \sqrt{1 + \frac{H_a - H_c}{H}} \qquad \text{...(8.28)}$$

Thus the equation (8.28) gives the maximum value of ratio of $\left(\frac{a_D}{a_C}\right)$.

8.13 FLOW THROUGH INTERNAL OR RE-ENTRANT OR BORDA'S MOUTHPIECE

An internal mouthpiece is short cylindrical tube fitted to the circular orifice in the side of tank projecting inside as shown in Fig. 8.18. The internal mouthpiece is also known as re-entrant or Borda's mouthpiece. Based on discharge conditions the internal mouthpieces are classified as mouthpiece running free and mouthpiece running full. Both the conditions do exits in practice and hence studied as under.

8.13.1 Borda's Mouthpiece Running Free

If the length of tube is small and is approximately equal to its diameter, the jet of liquid emerges out from mouthpiece without touching the sides of tube as shown in Fig. 8.18 (*a*) such type of mouthpiece is known as Borda's mouthpiece running free.

Let a_c is cross-sectional area of jet and V_c be its velocity. The area of mouthpiece is a and head of liquid above centre of mouthpiece is H.

The liquid flows through the mouthpiece because of the pressure force exerted by the fluid on the entrance section of mouthpiece.

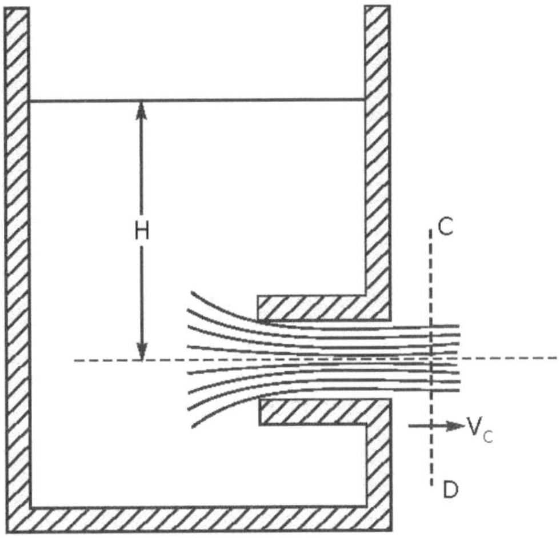

Fig. 8.18 (*a*) Borda's Mouthpiece Running Free

∴ Total pressure force exerted on entrance = $\gamma.a.H$ ...(*i*)

Now mass of liquid flowing per second = $\rho a_C V_C$

$$\begin{pmatrix}\text{Rate of change}\\ \text{of momentum}\end{pmatrix} = \begin{pmatrix}\text{Mass of liquid flow}\\ \text{per second}\end{pmatrix} \times \begin{pmatrix}\text{Final velocity}\\ -\text{Initial velocity}\end{pmatrix}$$

Rate of change of momentum = $\rho\, a_C V_C (V_C - 0)$ ...(*ii*)

But according to Newton's second law of motion, the net force is equal to the rate of change of momentum.

∴ Equating (*i*) and (*ii*),

$$\gamma.a.H = \rho a_C V_C^2 \quad ...(iii)$$

Now applying the Bernoulli's equation between the free surface of liquid and Section *D-D*. Considering centre line of mouthpiece as datum.

$$\frac{P}{\gamma} + \frac{V_2}{2g} + H = \frac{P_D}{\gamma} + \frac{V_D^2}{2g} + 0$$

$$\frac{P}{\gamma} = \frac{P_D}{\gamma} = 0,\ V = 0 \text{ and } V_D = V_C$$

$$\therefore \quad 0 + 0 + H = 0 + \frac{V_C^2}{2g} + 0$$

$$V_C = \sqrt{2g\,H}$$

Substitute V_C in equation (*iii*),

$$\gamma.a.H = \frac{\gamma}{g} \cdot a_c \cdot 2g\,H$$

$$a = 2\,a_C$$

$$\frac{a_c}{a} = \frac{1}{2} = 0.5$$

Hence coefficient of contraction = 0.5

As the jet of liquid flows free, there is no loss of energy.

∴ Coefficient of velocity = C_v = 1.0

∴ Coefficient of discharge = $C_d = C_c . C_v$

$$= 0.5 \times 1.0$$

$$C_d = 0.5$$

∴ Flow through the Borda's mouthpiece running free is,

$$Q = C_d \times a \times \sqrt{2g\,H}$$

$$Q = 0.5 \times a \times \sqrt{2g\,H} \qquad \text{...(8.29)}$$

8.13.2 Borda's Mouthpiece Running Full

If the length of tube is 2 to 3 times its diameter, the jet of liquid emerges out and contracts at vena-contracta and thereafter enlarges to occupy it completely and runs full as shown in Fig. 8.18. (*b*).

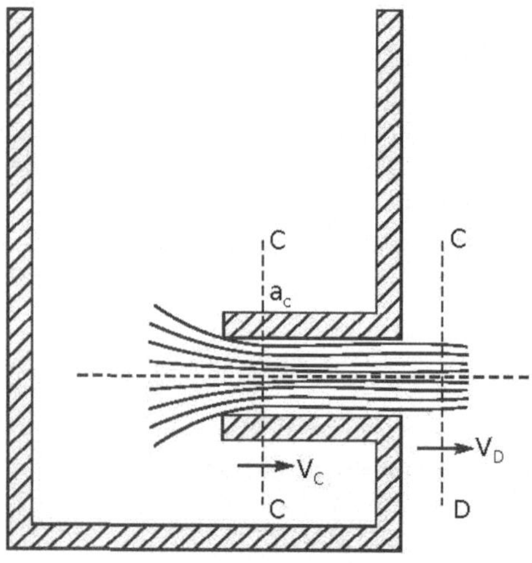

Fig. 8.18 (*b*) Borda's Mouthpiece Running Full

Let, H is the head of liquid above the mouthpiece and a_D and a_C are areas at outlet (Section D-D) and at vena-contracta (Section C-C) respectively. Also V_D and V_C are the velocities at outlet and vena-contracta respectively.

When jet of liquid moves from Section C-C it enlarges suddenly. Hence there will be loss of head between Section C-C and Section D-D due to sudden enlargement and is given as

$$h_L = \frac{(V_C - V_D)^2}{2g} \qquad \text{...}(i)$$

Now from continuity equation, we can write,

$$a_C V_C = a_D V_D$$

$$V_C = \frac{a_D}{a_C} V_D$$

$$V_C = \frac{V_D}{\frac{a_C}{a_D}} = \frac{V_D}{C_C} = \frac{V_D}{0.5}$$

$\therefore$ $$V_C = 2\,V_D$$

Substitute for V_C in equation (*i*),

$$h_L = \frac{(2V_D - V_D)^2}{2g} = \frac{V_D^2}{2g}$$

Apply Bernoulli's equation between free surface of water and the Section *D-D*, considering centre of mouthpiece as datum.

$$\frac{P}{\gamma} + \frac{V^2}{2g} + Z = \frac{P_D}{\gamma} + \frac{V_D^2}{2g} + Z_D + h_L$$

$$0 + 0 + H = 0 + \frac{V_D^2}{2g} + 0 + \frac{V_D^2}{2g}$$

$\therefore$ $$H = \frac{V_D^2}{2g} + \frac{V_D^2}{2g}$$

$$H = \frac{V_D^2}{g}$$

$\therefore$ $$V_D = \sqrt{gH}$$

The theoretical velocity is given as

$$V_{th} = \sqrt{2g\,H}$$

$\therefore$ Coefficient of velocity,

$$C_v = \frac{V_D}{V_{th}} = \frac{\sqrt{gH}}{\sqrt{2g\,H}} = \frac{1}{\sqrt{2}}$$

$\therefore$ $$C_v = 0.707$$

In this case $C_c = 1$ as the area of jet at outlet and mouthpiece are same.

$\therefore$ $$C_d = C_c \times C_v$$

$$= 1.0 \times 0.707$$

$$C_d = 0.707$$

$\therefore$ Discharge through Borda's mouthpiece running full is given as

$$Q = C_d \times a \times \sqrt{2g\,H}$$

$$Q = 0.707 \times a \times \sqrt{2g\,H} \qquad ...(8.30)$$

8.14 SOLVED PROBLEMS

■ **Problem 8.16:** *An external cylindrical mouthpiece of diameter 20 cm is discharging water under a constant head of 8 m. Determine the discharge and absolute pressure head of water at vena-contracta. Take $C_d = 0.855$ and C_c for vena-contracta = 0.62. Atmospheric pressure head = 10.3 m of water.* (MU May 1994, Const.)

Solution: Discharge,

$$Q = C_d \times a \times \sqrt{2gH}$$

$$= 0.855 \times \frac{\pi}{4}(0.2)^2 \times \sqrt{2 \times 9.81 \times 8}$$

$$Q = 0.3365 \text{ m}^3/\text{s} \qquad \text{...(Ans.)}$$

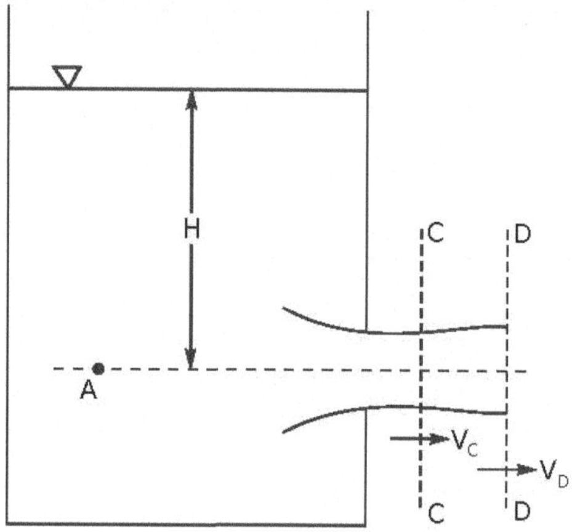

Fig. 8.19

Apply Bernoulli's equation between point *A* on the centre of mouthpiece and Section *C-C*. Consider centre of mouthpiece as datum.

$$\therefore \quad \frac{P_A}{\gamma} + \frac{V_A^2}{2g} + 0 = \frac{P_C}{\gamma} + \frac{V_C^2}{2g} + 0$$

$$H_A + H + 0 + 0 = H_C + \frac{V_C^2}{2g}$$

$$\therefore \quad H_C = H_A + H - \frac{V_C^2}{2g}$$

But $$V_C = \frac{V_D}{0.62}$$

$$\therefore \quad H_C = H_A + H - \left(\frac{V_D}{0.62}\right)^2 \times \frac{1}{2g}$$

$$H_C = H_A + H - \frac{1}{(0.62)^2} \times \frac{V_D^2}{2g}$$

But $$H = 1.375 \frac{V_D^2}{2g}$$

$\therefore$ $$\frac{V_D^2}{2g} = \frac{H}{1.375}$$

$\therefore$ $$H_C = H_A + H - \frac{1}{(0.62)^2} \times \frac{H}{1.375}$$

$$= H_A + H - 1.892\,H$$

$$= H_A - 0.892\,H$$

$$= 10.3 - 0.892 \times 8.0$$

$$H_C = 3.164 \text{ m (Absolute)}$$ ...(Ans.)

■ **Problem 8.17:** *An external convergent-divergent mouthpiece has 5 cm diameter at the section where the convergent and divergent portions meet. Water is discharged through the mouthpiece under a head of 3 m above its centre line. Determine the maximum discharge and the corresponding diameter at outlet. The maximum vacuum head allowed is 8 m of water.*

Solution: The discharge through convergent-divergent mouthpiece is:

$$Q_{max} = a_c \times \sqrt{2gH}$$

$$= \frac{\pi}{4}(0.05)^2 \times \sqrt{2 \times 9.81 \times 3}$$

$$Q_{max} = 0.0151 \text{ m}^3\text{/s}$$ ...(Ans.)

The ratio of areas at outlet and throat is:

$$\frac{a}{a_c} = \sqrt{1 + \frac{H_a - H_c}{H}}$$

Pressure head at throat = 8 m (vacuum)

or $$H_c = H_a - 8.0 \text{ (absolute)}$$

$$H_c = 10.3 - 8.0$$

$$H_c = 2.3$$

Substitute these values in equation above

$$\frac{\frac{\pi}{4}d^2}{\frac{\pi}{4}dc^2} = \sqrt{1 + \frac{10.3 - 2.3}{3.0}}$$

$$\frac{d^2}{dc^2} = 1.915$$

$$\frac{d}{dc} = \sqrt{1.915}$$
$$d = 1.384 \times dc$$
$$d = 1.384 \times 5$$
$$d = 6.92 \text{ cm}$$

Diameter corresponding to maximum discharge = 6.92 cm. ...**(Ans.)**

■ **Problem 8.18:** *A Borda's mouthpiece 2.5 cm in diameter is provided to the side of a tank full of water upto the height of 5 m above the centre line of the mouthpiece. If the mouthpiece runs free and if its coefficient of velocity is 0.99, calculate the discharge through it.*

Solution: For the Borda's mouthpiece running free

$$Q = D_d \times a \times \sqrt{2gH}$$

and
$$C_d = C_c \times C_v$$
$$= 0.5 \times 0.99$$
$$C_d = 0.495$$
$$a = \frac{\pi}{4} \times (0.025)^2 = 4.91 \times 10^{-4} \text{ m}^2$$
$$H = 5 \text{ m}$$

Substitute these values in above equation:

∴
$$Q = 0.495 \times 4.91 \times 10^{-4} \times \sqrt{2 \times 9.81 \times 5}$$
$$Q = 2.407 \times 10^{-3} \text{ m}^3/\text{s}.$$ ...**(Ans.)**

Exercises

1. The head of water over the centre of an orifice is 2.4 m. The diameter of orifice is 20 mm. The actual discharge through an orifice is 1.337 lps. Find the coefficient of discharge. **(Ans.** $C_d = 0.62$**)**
2. Oil of relative density 0.8 issues out of an orifice under a pressure of 1.8 kg/cm^2 at the rate of 5 lps. The diameter of vena-contracta is 3.2 cm. Find coefficient of velocity. **(Ans.** $C_v = 0.936$**)**
3. The head of water over the centre of orifice is 10.0 m. The diameter of orifice is 10.0 cm. The jet of water discharges into a rectangular tank of size 1.3 m × 1.3 m. The water level rises 1.0 m in 25 seconds. The *x* and *y* co-ordinates are 5.6 and 0.8 m respectively. Find the coefficient C_d, C_v and C_c. **(Ans.** $C_d = 0.615$, $C_v = 0.98$, $C_c = 0.627$**)**
4. In an experiment of determination of coefficient of 2.5 cm diameter sharp edged circular orifice it was found that jet issuing horizontally under head of 1 m, travel a horizontal distance of 1.92 m from vena-contracta in the course of a vertical drop of 1 m from same point. Further if a flat plate were held normal to the jet at vena-contracta, the jet

exerted a force of 5.7 N on jet. Determine coefficients of contraction, velocity and discharge. Assume coefficient of impact to be unity.

(**Ans.** $C_v = 0.96$, $C_d = 0.644$, $C_c = 0.618$)

5. A short tube is connected to a water tank so as to produce a vertical jet. If the head of water in the tank above the outlet of the short tube is 4 m. Find the height to which the jet will rise. Take $C_v = 0.94$. (**Ans.** Height = 3.534 m)
6. From a circular orifice a jet of water is issued vertically upwards under a pressure of 9 N/cm^2. Calculate height above the plane of orifice, where diameter of jet is equal to diameter of orifice. Take $C_v = 0.64$ and $C_v = 0.97$. (**Ans.** $h = 5.026$ m)
7. An orifice plate with an orifice of 5 cm diameter is attached to the end of 10 cm diameter pipeline. If the pressure head just upstream of the plate is 5 m of water and coefficient of discharge of orifice is 0.62. Assuming that orifice discharges water into atmosphere, evaluate discharge through pipe taking into account the effect of velocity of approach. (**Ans.** $Q = 0.0122$ m^3/s)
8. An orifice is located in the side of a tank with its centre 12 cm above the base of tank. The constant water level is 1.2 above the centre of the orifice. The coefficient of velocity is 0.98. Find the distance travelled by a point which is 12 cm below vena-contracta.

   (**Ans.** $x = 74.37$ cm)
9. A tank has two identical orifices in one of its vertical sides. The upper orifices is 3.0 m below the water surface and lower one is 5.0 m below the water surface. If the value of C_v for each orifice is 0.96, find the point of intersection of two jets.

   (**Ans.** $x = 7.436$ m)
10. An orifice is to be located in the side of a tank of depth H, resting on ground, such that the jet shall strike the ground at maximum distance. Find the height of orifice above the base in terms of H. $\left(\textbf{Ans. } h = \dfrac{H}{2}\right)$
11. A vessel has two identical orifices provided in one of its sides at depth H_1 and H_2 below the free surface of water in the tank. Determine the position of the point of intersection of the two jets.

    If $H_1 = 2$ m, $H_2 = 5$ m and $C_v = 0.98$ for each orifice. Locate the point of intersection of two jets.

    (**Ans.** $y_2 = H_1$, $y_1 = H_2$, $x = 2C_v\sqrt{H_1H_2}$, $y_2 = 2$ m, $y_1 = 5$ m, $x = 6.198$ m)
12. Oil of specific gravity 0.75 discharges into atmosphere through the 8 cm diameter orifice, whose coefficient of velocity and contraction are 0.95 and 0.65 respectively. At what pressure should air be pumped in the space above the oil surface so that the power in the jet may be 10 kW. Take height of oil above centre of orifice as 24 m.

    (**Ans.** Air pressure = 8.84 N/cm^2)

13. A closed vessel contains water upto a height of 2 m and over the water surface there is an air having pressures 8.829 N/cm^2 above the atmospheric pressure. At the bottom of the vessel there is an orifice of diameter 15 cm. Find the rate of flow of water from the orifice. Take $C_d = 0.6$. *(MU May 2002)*

(Ans. $Q = 0.1539$ m^3/s)

14. Compensation water is to be discharged by two circular orifices of the same diameter, situated at the bottom of a vessel having a constant head of 2.2 m. If the demand is 20,000,000 lits/day. What diameter will be required for each orifice? Take coefficient of contraction and velocity as 0.62 and 0.98 respectively. **(Ans.** $d = 14.98$ cm)

15. A rectangular orifice of size 1.6 m wide and 1.0 m deep is discharging water from a tank. The water level in the tank is 3.2 m higher from the centre of orifice. Find the discharge through the orifice. Take $C_d = 0.62$. **(Ans.** $Q = 7.852$ m^3/s)

16. A rectangular orifice of size 1.0 m wide and 1.2 m deep is discharging water from a tank. The water level in the tank is 1.0 m above the top edge of the orifice. Calculate the discharge through the orifice and percentage error if the orifice is treated as small orifice. Take $C_d = 0.62$. **(Ans.** $Q = 4.143$, Error = 0.616%)

17. Find the discharge through fully submerged orifice of width 1.6 m. The difference of water levels on both the sides of the orifice is 60 cm. The head of water above top and bottom edge of the orifice are 2.5 m and 3.0 m respectively. Take $C_d = 0.62$.

(Ans. $Q = 1.702$ m^3/s)

18. Find the discharge through the rectangular orifice of 1.8 m wide and 0.8 m deep provided in the side of tank. The head of water on one side of orifice is 3.0 m above the top edge of the orifice while on other side the head of water is 0.3 m below the top edge. Take $C_d = 0.62$. **(Ans.** $Q = 9.815$ m^3/s)

19. Two tanks circular in cross-section are connected by a small orifice. The tank is closed and contains compressed air at a pressure of 7 kN/cm^2. Both the tanks contain water. The level in the tank B is 1 m above that in A. A load of 2 kN is placed on a piston in B, whose area is 1 m^2. Find discharge through orifice at this instant if its diameter is 5 cms. Find also the rate and direction of movement of load. Take $C_d = 0.62$.

(Ans. $Q = 0.01314$ m^3/s, $V = 0.01314$ m/s upwards)

20. It takes 150 seconds to empty the top $\frac{1}{4}$th of the cylindrical tank. Find how long it will take to empty bottom $\frac{1}{6}$th portion. **(Ans.** $T = 515.47$ sec.)

21. Show that for a vertical cylindrical tank, the time required to lower the liquid level by a given amount is equal to the volume of liquid discharged divided by the average of initial and final rate of discharge.

22. A tank has uniform cross-section area of 2 m^2 and has two orifices. Each 4 cm diameter in one of the vertical sides provided at 2.9 m and 6.5 m above the bottom of the tank. Find the time required to lower the depth of water from 9.5 m to 5 m. Take $C_d = 0.62$. (**Ans.** $T = 1142.2$ sec)

23. A tank with vertical sides is being emptied through an orifice situated in one of the vertical sides. As the head reduces the point of impact of the jet on the horizontal flow starts moving towards the orifice. The point of impact of the jet was observed to move from 7 m to 5 m in 40 seconds measured from the orifice. How long will it take to move from 5 m to 2 m. Prove that formula used? (**Ans.** $T = 60$ sec.)

24. A tank 20 m diameter at top converges to 4 m diameter at the bottom in its 10 m vertical height. An orifice of 15 cm^2 area is situated at its bottom. If the tank is full initially, find the time required to empty it. (**Ans.** $T = 38$ hr 1 min 5 sec.)

25. A hemispherical tank 2.5 m diameter is full of water. What will be the time required for the water level to fall by 1 m through an orifice of 50 cm^2 in area fitted at the bottom? Take $C_d = 0.62$. (**Ans.** $T = 3$ min 40 sec.)

26. A closed hemispherical tank 2 m diameter and having vertical sides is emptied through sharp edged circular orifice of 10 cm diameter. Initially the tank contains an oil of specific gravity of 0.75 to a height of 1.5 m above the centre of the orifice. The space above the oil contains compressed air at an equivalent pressure of 10 cms of mercury. Assuming that the air pressure will remain constant throughout, calculate the time required to empty the tank. Assume $C_d = 0.6$. (**Ans.** Time = 2 min 29.5 sec.)

27. A cylindrical boiler of diameter 2.4 m and length 12 m is lying horizontally and is half full of water. It is to be emptied by an external cylindrical mouthpiece of diameter 10 cm fixed at the bottom of the boiler. How long will the mouthpiece take to empty the boiler? Take $C_d = 0.82$. (**Ans.** $T = 1782.92$ sec.)

28. Find the time required to empty the swimming pool through the orifice of 0.5 m^2 area provided at the bottom of the dipper end of the pool. The depths at dipper end = 4 m and that at shallow end = 1 m. The width and length of pool are 10 m and 24 m respectively. The bottom of the pool is uniformly sloping. Take $C_d = 0.62$. (**Ans.** $T = 295.44$ sec.)

29. A parabolloid shaped tank 3 m height has 2 m diameter at the top and orifice with $C_d = 0.62$ is fitted at the bottom. It is observed that, the water level fall from 2.5 m to 1.5 m above the orifice in 10 minutes. What must be the area of the orifice? (**Ans.** $a = 8960$ mm^2)

30. Two tanks A and B whose constant cross-sectional areas are 9 m^2 and 2.25 m^2 respectively are connected by 5 cm diameter orifice with $C_d = 0.62$. If the initial water level difference is 2 m. Find the time required for 3 m^2 of water to flow from tank A to tank B. (**Ans.** $T = 9$ min 17.5 sec.)

31. An external cylindrical mouthpiece of diameter 24 cm is discharging water under a constant head of 10 m. Determine the discharge and absolute pressure head of water at

vena-contracta. Take $C_d = 0.85$, $C_c = 0.62$ for vena-contracta and atmospheric pressure head = 10.3 m of water. (**Ans.** $Q = 0.5418$ m^3/s, $H_c = 1.38$ m, Abs.)

32. Water under constant head discharges through an external cylinder mouthpiece of 20 cm^2 area. If the $C_c = 0.62$, find the discharge, maximum head and coefficient of discharge for the mouthpiece. Assume separation occurs at 2 m absolute and atmospheric pressure is 10 m. (**Ans.** $Q = 0.0227$ m^3/s, $H = 9.0$ m, $C_d = 0.854$)

33. An external convergent-divergent mouthpiece has 6 cm diameter at the section where the convergent and divergent portions meet. Water is discharged through the mouthpiece under a head of 4 m above its centre line. Determine the maximum discharge and its corresponding diameter at outlet. The maximum vacuum head allowed is 8 m of water. (**Ans.** $Q_{max} = 0.025$ m^3/s, $d = 7.896$ cm)

34. Convergent-divergent mouthpiece is fitted from outside in the vertical side of a tank containing water, if discharges into atmosphere under a constant head of 4 m. Calculate the ratio of the throat diameter to the exit diameter of the mouthpiece for the maximum discharge for the data given below.
    (*i*) Atmospheric pressure head = 10.3 m of water.
    (*ii*) Separation will take place at an absolute pressure head of 2 m of water.
    (*iii*) Loss of head occurs only in the divergent part of the mouthpiece and is equal to 20% of the energy head lost a sudden expansion. $\left(\textbf{Ans.}\ \dfrac{dc}{d} = 0.729\right)$

35. A convergent-divergent mouthpiece is fitted into the vertical side of a tank containing water. Assuming that there are no losses in the convergent part of the mouthpiece and that the losses in the divergent part are equivalent to 0.2 times the velocity head at exit and that the minimum absolute pressure head at the throat is 2.44 m of water for a barometric pressures of 760 mm of mercury. Determine the throat and exit diameters of the mouthpieces when the discharge is 4.25 litres/sec. for a head of 1.52 meter. (**Ans.** $d_c = 2$ cm, $d_e = 3.1$ cm)

36. A borda's mouthpiece 3 cm in diameter is provided to the side of a tank full of water upto the height of 6 m above the centre line of the mouthpiece. If the mouthpiece runs free and if its coefficient of velocity is 0.98, calculate the discharge through it. (**Ans.** $Q = 3.43 \times 10^{-3}$ m^3/s)

❑❑❑

9

Notches and Weirs

9.1 INTRODUCTION

A notch is sharp-edged device used for the measurement of rate of flow of liquid from a tank or channel. It can be defined as the opening provided in the side of a tank in such a way that the liquid surface in the tank or channel is below the top edge of the opening. Notches are generally made of metallic plates.

A weir is an obstruction provided in open channel over which flow occurs. The obstruction may be in the form of small dam constructed across a river which allows storage of water on its upstream side and allow excess water to flow over its entire length to downstream side. It is a concrete or masonry structure used for measurement of rate of flow or water in rivers.

A sheet or water flowing over a notch or weir is known as the nappe or vein. The bottom edge of the notch or top edge of the wear is known as crest or sill.

9.2 CLASSIFICATION OF NOTCHES AND WEIRS

The notches are classified as:

(1) Based on the shape of opening:

(*a*) Rectangular (*b*) Triangular (*c*) Trapezoidal (*d*) Stepped (*e*) Circular and (*f*) Parabolic.

(2) Based on the effect of the sides on the nappe:

(*a*) Notch with end contraction and

(*b*) Notch without end contraction or suppressed notch.

In the channel if crest length of notch is less than the width of channel it is known as notch with end contraction and if both are equal it is known as notch without end contraction.

Weirs are classified based on their shape of the opening, the shape of crest, the effect of sides on the nappe and the discharge conditions:

(1) Based on the shape of opening:
   (*a*) Rectangular weir
   (*b*) Triangular weir
   (*c*) Trapezoidal weir (Cippolletti weir)
(2) Based on the shape of crest:
   (*a*) Sharp crested weir
   (*b*) Broad crested weir
   (*c*) Narrow crested weir
   (*d*) Ogee shaped weir
(3) Based on effect of sides on issuing nappe:
   (*a*) Weir with end construction
   (*b*) Weir without end construction
(4) Based on the discharge conditions:
   (*a*) Freely discharging weir and
   (*b*) Submerged weir (Drowned weir)

The flow pattern over a sharp crested weir and notch is almost similar and therefore the same expressions can be used to calculate discharge over the sharp crest weir or notch of the same type. Moreover, notch is often termed on sharp crested weir.

9.3 FLOW OVER A RECTANGULAR SHARP CRESTED WEIR OR NOTCH

Consider a rectangular sharp crested weir or notch provided in channel carrying water as shown in Fig. 9.1. Let L is the length of crest of weir or notch and H be the head of water causing the flow. The head H should be measured at a distance of 4 to 5 times the maximum head above crest on the upstream of weir, where the curvature effect is negligible.

Consider an elementary horizontal strip of water of thickness 'dh' and length L at a depth h below the free surface of water for calculating the discharge flowing over the weir or notch (Fig. 9.1).

The area of strip = $L \times dh$

Theoretical velocity of water flowing through strip = $\sqrt{2gh}$

Thus the discharge dQ through strip is

$$dQ = C_d \times L \times dh \times \sqrt{2gh} \qquad ...(i)$$

where, C_d = Coefficient of discharge

The total discharge Q for the complete weir or notch is determined by integrating equation (*i*) between limits 0 to H

$$\therefore \quad Q = \int dQ = \int_0^H C_d \sqrt{2gh}\, dh$$

$$= C_d L \sqrt{2g} \int_0^H h^{1/2} dh$$

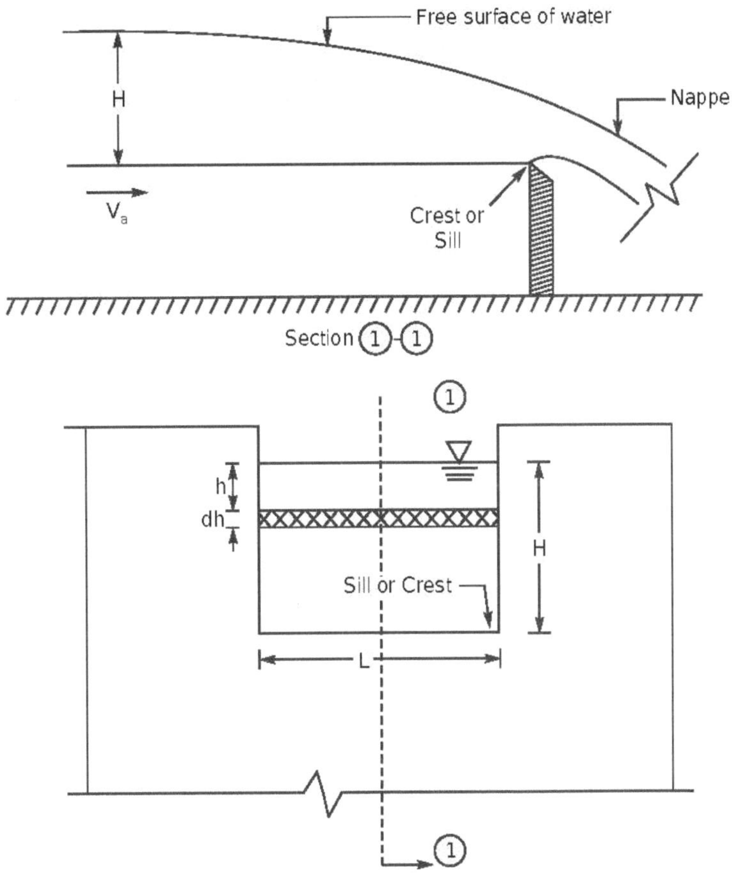

Fig. 9.1

$$= C_d L \sqrt{2g} \times \frac{2}{3} [h^{3/2}]_0^H$$

$$Q = \frac{2}{3} C_d L \sqrt{2g}\, H^{3/2} \qquad ...(9.1)$$

If the velocity of approach is to be taken into account, the above expression for Q can be written as

$$Q = \frac{2}{3} \sqrt{2g}\, L[H + h_a)^{3/2} - h_a^{2/3}] \qquad ...(9.2)$$

For the rectangular weir or notch with end contraction the effective length of crest over which flow occurs reduces and thus the discharge, which is given as below:

$$Q = \frac{2}{3} C_d \sqrt{2g}\, (L - 0.1nH)\, H^{3/2} \qquad ...(9.3)$$

where, n = Number of end contractions

If the velocity of approach is considered, the equation for Q can be written as follows:

$$Q = \frac{2}{3} C_d \sqrt{2g}\,(L - 0.1hH_1)\,(H_1^{3/2} - h_a^{3/2}) \qquad \text{...(9.4)}$$

where, $H_1 = H + h_a = H + \dfrac{V_a^2}{2g}$

and V_a = Velocity of approach.

The mean value of velocity of approach to be used in the above equation can be calculated by dividing the discharge Q by the area of flow section of the channel. If width of channel is B and height of crest above bed of channel is Z, then

$$V_a = \frac{Q}{B(H + Z)}$$

Procedure to calculate accurate value of discharge:

(1) Calculate approximate discharge Q using (9.1) or (9.3) depending on whether notch or weir is suppressed or not.

(2) Calculate area of flow section, A.

(3) Calculate velocity of approach V_a by dividing Q by A *i.e.*, $V_A = \dfrac{Q}{A}$.

(4) Calculate head, h_a by using formula, $h_a = \dfrac{V_a^2}{2g}$.

(5) The new value of Q, can be calculated using equations (9.2) or (9.4) depending on whether the weir or notch is suppressed or not.

This new value is better approximation of discharge and the same procedure is repeated until the final value of Q is within the tolerance limit. (1% of the preceding value).

9.4 EMPIRICAL FORMULA FOR DISCHARGE OVER RECTANGULAR WEIR

The empirical formulae suggested by some of the investigator's for computing discharge are as given below:

(1) Francis Formula: On the basis of experimental investigations on rectangular weir Francis proposed formulae for calculating discharge with and without end contractions [Fig. 9.2 (*a*), (*b*)]. The formula when velocity of approach is not considered is given as below:

$$Q = 1.84\,(L - 0.1\,nH)\,H^{3/2} \qquad \text{...(9.4)}$$

and when velocity of approach is considered.

$$Q = 1.84\,(L - 0.1\,nH_1)\,(H_1^{3/2} - h_a^{3/2}) \qquad \text{...(9.5)}$$

where, $H_1 = H + h_a = H + \dfrac{V_a^2}{2g}$

By comparing above formulae with equations (9.1) and (9.2), we get

$$\frac{2}{3} C_d \sqrt{2g} = 1.84$$

Thus the value of C_d for rectangular weir as per Francis' formula is 0.623. For suppressed weir *i.e.*, $n = 0$, [Fig. 9.2 (*a*)] the equations (9.4) and (9.5) reduce to

$$Q = 1.84\, LH^{3/2} \quad ...(9.6)$$

and

$$Q = 1.84\, L\,(H_1^{3/2} - h_a^{3/2}) \quad ...(9.7)$$

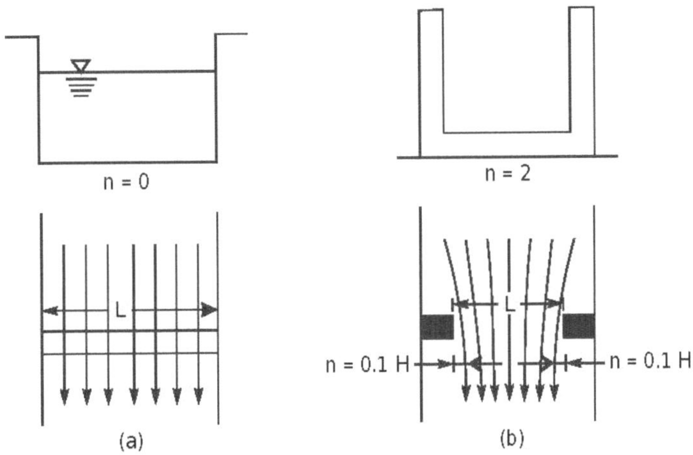

Fig. 9.2 End contractions for rectangular weir

(2) Bazin's Formula: Based on the series of experiments with rectangular weir Bazin's proposed following formula for the discharge over the rectangular weir.

$$Q = m\sqrt{2g}\, LH^{3/2} \quad ...(9.8)$$

where,

$$m = \left(0.405 + \frac{0.003}{H}\right)$$

Taking velocity of approach into account,

$$Q = m_1 \sqrt{2h}\, LH_1^{3/2} \quad ...(9.9)$$

where,

$$m_1 = \left(0.465 + \frac{0.003}{H_1}\right)$$

The head $H_1 = \left(H + \alpha \frac{V_a^2}{2g}\right)$ is called still water head.

The mean value of constant α as suggested by Bazin is 1.6.

(3) Rehbock's Formula: Rehbock suggested the following formula for C_d for the suppressed weir, based on his experiments

$$C_d = \left(0.605 + 0.08\frac{H}{Z} + \frac{0.001}{H}\right) \quad ...(9.10)$$

$$\therefore \qquad Q = \frac{2}{3}\left(0.605 + 0.08\frac{H}{Z} + \frac{0.001}{H}\right)\sqrt{2g}\,LH^{3/2} \qquad \text{...(9.11)}$$

where H is head in meters and Z is crest height in meters.

9.5 SOLVED PROBLEMS

■ **Problem 9.1:** *Find the discharge of water flowing over a rectangular notch of 2.4 m wide. The head of water over the notch is 40 cm. Take, $C_d = 0.62$.*

Solution: Data:

$$L = 2.4 \text{ m}$$

$$H = 40 \text{ cm} = 0.40 \text{ m}$$

The discharge over rectangular notch is,

$$Q = \frac{2}{3} \times C_d \times \sqrt{2g} \times L \times H^{3/2}$$

$$= \frac{2}{3} \times 0.62 \times \sqrt{2 \times 9.81} \times 2.4 \times (0.40)^{3/2}$$

$$Q = 1.112 \text{ m}^3/\text{s}.$$

■ **Problem 9.2:** *Determine the discharge over a weir 40 m long divided into 10 equal bays by vertical posts. The width of each post is 75 cm. The head of water over the crest is 1.25 m and velocity of approach is 2.1 m/sec.*

Solution: Data:

Length of weir $= L_1 = 40$ m

Number of bays $= 10$

For 10 bays, total number of post required = 9.

Width of each post = 75 cm = 0.75 m

$$\text{Effective length} = L = L_1 - 9 \times 0.75$$

$$= 40 - 9 \times 0.75$$

$$L = 33.75 \text{ m}$$

Head, $H = 1.25$ m

$$V_a = 2.1 \text{ m/s}$$

$$n = 2 \times 10 = 20$$

Discharge over rectangular weir is given as

$$Q = \frac{2}{3}\sqrt{2g}\,(L - 0.1nH_1)(H_1^{3/2} - h_a^{3/2})$$

where

$$h_a = \frac{V_a^2}{2g} = \frac{(2.1)^2}{2 \times 9.81} = 0.2248 \text{ m}$$

$$Q = \frac{2}{3} \times 0.62 \times \sqrt{2 \times 9.81}\,(33.75 - 0.1 \times 20 \times 1.4748)$$

$$\times [(1.4748)^{3/2} - (0.2248)^{3/2}]$$

$$= 1.831 \times 30.80 \times (1.791 - 0.1067)$$

$$Q = 94.98 \text{ m}^3/\text{s}. \qquad \textbf{...(Ans.)}$$

■ **Problem 9.3:** *A suppressed rectangular weir is used to measure rate of flow in a stream 2 m wide. The head of water above the weir is 25 cm. The sill of the notch is 50 cm above the stream bed. Assuming C_d = 0.62. Find the discharge. Consider velocity of approach.*

Solution: Width of channel, $b = L = 2.0$ m = width of weir

Head of water above weir, $H = 0.25$ m

Height of sill above bed of channel = 0.50 m

∴ Depth of channel = 0.50 + 0.25

= 0.75 m

Discharge over rectangular weir without velocity of approach is

$$Q = \frac{2}{3} \times C_d \times L \times \sqrt{2g} \times H^{3/2}$$

$$= \frac{2}{3} \times 0.62 \times 2 \times \sqrt{2 \times 9.81} \times (0.25)^{3/2}$$

$$Q = 0.4580 \text{ m}^3/\text{s}$$

Now, velocity of approach $= V_a = \frac{Q}{A} = \frac{0.458}{2.0 \times 0.75}$

∴ $V_a = 0.3053$ m/s

Head, due to velocity of approach,

$$h_a = \frac{V_a^2}{2g} = 0.00475 \text{ m}$$

Now the discharge with velocity of approach is

$$Q = \frac{2}{3} C_d L \sqrt{2g} \, [(H + h_a)^{3/2} - h_a^{3/2}]$$

$$= \frac{2}{3} \times 0.62 \times 2.0 \times \sqrt{19.62} \; [(0.25 + 0.00475)^{3/2} - (0.00475)^{3/2}]$$

$$= 3.661 \, [0.1286 - 0.003275]$$

$$Q = 0.4588 \text{ m}^3/\text{s}.$$ ...(Ans.)

■ **Problem 9.4:** *Water is flowing in a rectangular channel of 1.2 m width and 0.8 m deep. Find the discharge over a rectangular weir of crest length 70 cm if the head over the weir crest is 25 cm and water from the channel flows over the weir. Take C_d = 0.6. Neglect end contractions but consider velocity of approach.*

Solution:

Length of weir, $L = 0.7$ m

Width, $b = 1.2$ m

Depth, $d = 0.8$ m

$H = 25$ cm $= 0.25$ m

Discharge over rectangular channel,

$$Q = \frac{2}{3} C_d L \sqrt{2g} H^{3/2}$$

$$= \frac{2}{3} \times 0.6 \times 0.7 \times \sqrt{2 \times 9.81} \times (0.25)^{3/2}$$

$$Q = 0.155 \text{ m}^3/\text{s}$$

Now, $$V_a = \frac{Q}{A} = \frac{0.155}{1.2 \times 0.8} = 0.1615 \text{ m/s}$$

$$h_a = \frac{V_a^2}{2g} = 0.00133 \text{ m}$$

Now, discharge over channel with velocity of approach is

$$Q = \frac{2}{3} C_d L \sqrt{2g} [(H + h_a)^{3/2} - h_a^{3/2}]$$

$$= \frac{2}{3} \times 0.6 \times 0.7 \times \sqrt{2 \times 2.81} \; [(0.25 + 0.00133)^{3/2} - (0.00133)^{3/2}]$$

$$= 1.240 \times (0.12599 - 0.000048)$$

$$= 1.240 \times (0.12595)$$

$$Q = 0.1562 \text{ m}^3/\text{s}. \qquad \text{...(Ans.)}$$

■ **Problem 9.5:** *Show that a rational formula for the flow Q over a rectangular weir of width B can be expressed as $Q = A (B - CH) H^{3/2}$. Where, H is the depth of water at a point near the weir which is not affected by the curvature of the surface.*

In rectangular weir 2 m in breadth the discharge is 300 litres/sec when the head of water is 20 cm, and 830 litres/sec when the head is 40 cm. Find the values of the constants in the above expression and estimate the discharge when the head is 25 cm.

Solution:

Part I: Refer to the derivation in section 9.1 in this Chapter. The equation for flow Q over rectangular channel with end contraction is given by equation (9.3) as

$$Q = \frac{2}{3} C \sqrt{2g} (L - 0.1nH) H^{3/2}$$

which can be written as $$Q = A (B - CH) H^{3/2}$$

where, $$A = \frac{2}{3} C_d \sqrt{2g}$$

$$L = B$$

$$C = 0.1\, n$$

Part II: $$Q = A (B - CH) H^{3/2}$$

$$Q = AB H^{3/2} - A CH^{5/2}$$

Substitute the two set of values of Q, B and H in the above equation and solve the equations simultaneously.

$$0.3 = A \times 2.0 \times (0.2)^{3/2} - AC\,(0.2)^{5/2}$$

$$0.3 = 0.1789\,A - 0.01788\,AC$$

$$AC = \frac{-0.3 + 0.1789\,A}{0.01789} = 10\,A - 16.77 \qquad ...(1)$$

and

$$0.83 = A \times 2 \times (0.4)^{3/2} - AC\,(0.4)^{5/2}$$

$$0.83 = 0.506\,A - 0.1012\,AC \qquad ...(2)$$

Substitute for AC in equation (2),

$$0.83 = 0.506\,A - 0.1012 \times (10\,A - 16.77)$$

$$= 0.506\,A - 1.012\,A + 1.697$$

$$\therefore \quad 0.506\,A = 0.867$$

$$\therefore \quad A = 1.713 \qquad ...\textbf{(Ans.)}$$

Substitute in equation (1) for A

$$1.713 \times C = 1.713 \times 10 - 16.77$$

$$C = 0.210 \qquad ...\textbf{(Ans.)}$$

$$Q = 1.713\,[2.0 - 0.210 \times (0.25)]\,(0.25)^{3/2}$$

$$Q = 0.417 \text{ m}^3/\text{s}. \qquad ...\textbf{(Ans.)}$$

■ **Problem 9.6:** *Water flows over a rectangular weir of crest length with end contractions suppressed is 1.8 m. The head of water over weir is 50 cm. Find the discharge using Francis' and Bazin's formula.*

Solution: Francis's formula for calculating discharge is given as follows (for suppressed weir).

$$Q = 1.84\,LH^{3/2}$$

$$= 1.84 \times 1.8 \times (0.50)^{3/2}$$

$$Q = 1.171 \text{ m}^3/\text{s} \qquad ...\textbf{(Ans.)}$$

Bazin's formula for calculating discharge is given as

$$Q = m \times L \times \sqrt{2g} \times H^{3/2}$$

where,

$$m = 0.405 + \frac{0.003}{H} = 0.405 + \frac{0.003}{0.5}$$

$$m = 0.411$$

$$\therefore \quad Q = 0.411 \times 1.8 \times \sqrt{2 \times 9.81} \times (0.50)^{3/2}$$

$$Q = 1.158 \text{ m}^3/\text{s}. \qquad ...\textbf{(Ans.)}$$

■ **Problem 9.7:** *Show that correction factor to allow for velocity of approach to a rectangular notch be given in the form*

$$\left[\left(1 + \frac{\alpha h}{H}\right)^{3/2} - \left(\frac{\alpha h}{H}\right)^{3/2}\right]$$

where H = *Measured head*

$h = V^2/2g$

V = *Velocity of approach*

α = *Factor to allow for velocity not being uniform over section of channel.*

If rectangular channel 1.2 meter wide has at the end a rectangular sharp edged notch 90 cm wide with the sill 20 cm from the bottom. Assuming $\alpha = 1.1$*. Calculate flow when the head is 25 cm using Francis Formulae.*

Solution: The discharge over a rectangular notch considering velocity of approach is given by

$$Q = \frac{2}{3} C_d \sqrt{2g} L[(H + h_a)^{3/2} - h_a^{3/2}]$$

In the present case,

$$h_a = \alpha h$$

and

$$h = \frac{V^2}{2g}$$

$$Q = \frac{2}{3} C_d \sqrt{2g}\, L[(H + \alpha h)^{3/2} - (\alpha h)^{3/2}]$$

$$= \frac{2}{3} C_d \sqrt{2g}\, L H^{3/2} \left[\left(1 + \frac{\alpha h}{H}\right)^{3/2} - \left(\frac{\alpha h}{H}\right)^{3/2}\right]$$

Q = (Discharge without considering velocity of approach) × (Correction factor)

Francis formula considering velocity of approach with correction factor can be written as

$$Q = 1.84\,(L - 0.1\,nH)\,H^{3/2} \left[\left(1 + \frac{\alpha h}{H}\right)^{3/2} - \left(\frac{\alpha h}{H}\right)^{3/2}\right]$$

Here, $L = 90$ cm $= 0.90$ m, $n = 2$

$H = 0.25$ m, $\alpha = 1.1$

Discharge without considering velocity of approach

$$Q = 1.84\,(L - 0.1\,nH)\,H^{3/2}$$

$$Q = 1.84\,(0.90 - 0.1 \times 2 \times 0.25) \times (0.25)^{3/2}$$

$$Q = 0.195 \text{ m}^3/\text{s}$$

$$\text{Velocity of approach} = V_a = \frac{0.195}{1.2 \times 0.45} = 0.361 \text{ m/s}$$

$$h = \frac{V_a^2}{2g} = \frac{(0.361)^2}{2 \times 9.81} = 0.0066 \text{ m}$$

and

$$\left[\left(1 + \frac{1.1 \times 0.0066}{0.25}\right)^{3/2} - \left(\frac{1.1 \times 0.0066}{0.25}\right)^{3/2}\right] = 1.039$$

Discharge with velocity of approach is

$$\therefore \quad Q = 1.84\,(0.9 - 0.1 \times 2 \times 0.25) \times (0.25)^{3/2} \times 1.039$$

$$Q = 0.195 \times 1.039 = 0.203 \text{ m}^3\text{/s.} \qquad \text{...(Ans.)}$$

9.6 VENTILATION OF SUPPRESSED WEIRS

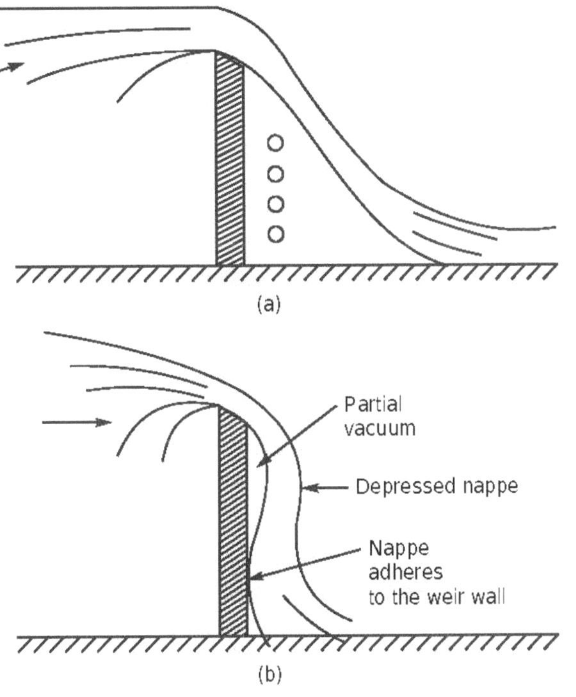

Fig. 9.3

In case of suppressed weirs, crest length is same as width of the channel or river. The nappe of over flowing water on its sides will touch the sides of the channel and due to this air is locked below the nappe of water and between the sides of channel, and gets carried away along with the flow, creating partial vacuum below the nappe. This causes the nappe to adhere to the weir wall. Such a nappe is known as depressed nappe and it draws more water and hence discharge is increased, but conditions of negative pressure below it may create cavitation and vibrations in weir wall, which is dangerous for safety of the structure. In order that free nappe is developed, ventilation to space below the nappe should be provided from the sides of the channels, such as holes shown in the Fig. 9.3 (*a*). This again makes flow of water normal and discharge is also as per predicted values.

9.7 FLOW OVER TRIANGULAR NOTCH OR WEIR

A weir which has triangular or *V*-shaped opening or notch provided in its body to discharge water is called triangular weir. Thus triangular notch and weir are same and the expression for the discharge over the triangular notch or weir is same.

Consider a triangular notch or weir with vertex angle (angle of notch) equal to θ as shown in Fig. 9.4 having head above the crest of weir equal to H. Consider a horizontal strip of water of thickness dh at a depth of h from the free surface of water.

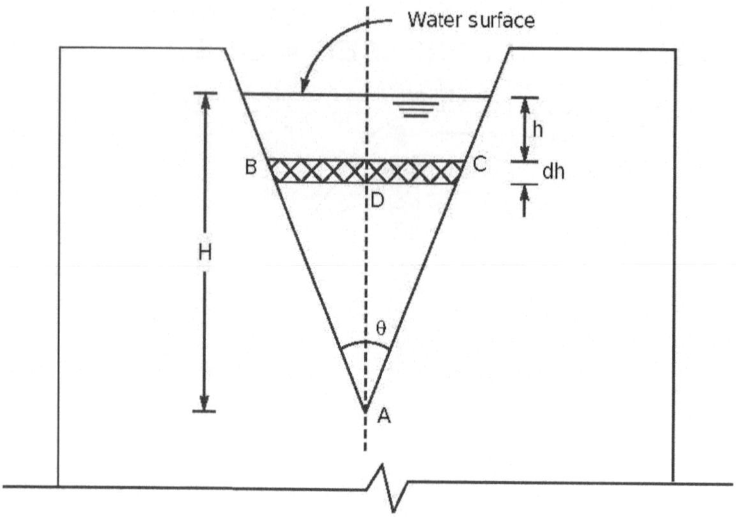

Fig. 9.4 Triangular notch of weir

Let thickness of strip is equal to BC from ΔABD

$$\tan\frac{\theta}{2} = \frac{BD}{AD} = \frac{BD}{(H-h)}$$

$$\therefore \quad BD = (H-h)\tan\frac{\theta}{2}$$

$$BC = 2BD = 2(H-h)\tan\frac{\theta}{2}$$

The area of strip $= A = BC \times dh$

$$A = 2(H-h)\tan\frac{\theta}{2}\, dh$$

The theoretical velocity of water flowing through the strip $= \sqrt{2gh}$.

If dQ is the discharge through the strip, then

$$dQ = C_d A \times \sqrt{2gh}$$

$$= C_d \times 2(H-h)\tan\frac{\theta}{2} dh \times \sqrt{2gh}$$

$$dQ = 2C_d \tan\frac{\theta}{2}\sqrt{2g}\,(H-h)h^{1/2}\, dh$$

Total discharge, Q flowing through triangular notch is determined by integrating the above expression

$$Q = \int dQ = \int_0^H 2C_d \tan\frac{\theta}{2}\sqrt{2g}\,(Hh^{1/2} - h^{3/2})\,dh$$

$$= 2C_d \tan\frac{\theta}{2}\sqrt{2g}\left[\frac{2}{3}Hh^{3/2} - \frac{2}{5}h^{5/2}\right]_0^H$$

$$Q = \frac{8}{15}C_d \tan\frac{\theta}{2}\sqrt{2g}\,H^{5/2} \qquad ...(9.12)$$

For the right angle triangular weir or notch $\theta = 90°$.

$$Q = \frac{8}{15}C_d\sqrt{2g}H^{5/2} \qquad ...(9.13)$$

and if $C_d = 0.6$, then

$$Q = 1.418\,H^{5/2} \qquad ...(9.14)$$

If the velocity of approach is considered then the equation can be modified as

$$Q = \frac{8}{15}C_d \tan\frac{\theta}{2}\sqrt{2g}\,[(H + h_a)^{5/2} - h_a^{5/2}] \qquad ...(9.15)$$

where h_a = Head due to velocity of approach

$$h_a = \frac{V_a^2}{2g}.$$

9.8 ADVANTAGES OF TRIANGULAR NOTCH OR WEIR OVER RECTANGULAR NOTCH OR WEIR

The various advantages of triangular notch or weir over rectangular notch or weir are as follows:

(1) The expression for computing discharge for right angled triangular notch is very much simplified.

(2) For measuring low discharges, the triangular weir or notch gives accurate results, as the head over triangular notch for low discharge will be more as compared with rectangular notch.

(3) The coefficient of discharge is constant for triangular notch or weir whereas it varies with for rectangular notch or weir.

(4) In case of triangular notch, velocity of approach can be neglected while calculating the discharge.

(5) Ventilation of triangular weir or notch is not necessary.

9.9 SOLVED PROBLEMS

■ **Problem 9.8:** *A rectangular notch 1 m wide having $C_d = 0.62$ and a right angled triangular notch are in series. The measured head over the rectangular notch was 10 cm. Find head over the triangular notch. If its $C_d = 0.62$.*

Solution: The discharge over rectangular weir is:

$$Q = \frac{2}{3} \times C_d \times L \times \sqrt{2g} \times H^{3/2}$$

$$Q = \frac{2}{3} \times 0.62 \times 1.0 \times \sqrt{2 \times 9.81} \times (0.1)^{3/2}$$

$$Q = 0.0579 \text{ m}^3/\text{s}$$

The discharge over the triangular notch is

$$Q = \frac{8}{15} \times C_d \times \tan\frac{\theta}{2} \times \sqrt{2g} \times H^{5/2}$$

As the same discharge passes through triangular notch, $Q = 0.0579$ m^3/s and notch is right angled, (*i.e.*, $\theta = 90°$).

$$\therefore \quad 0.0579 = \frac{8}{15} \times 0.62 \times \tan\frac{90}{2} \times \sqrt{2 \times 9.81} \times H^{5/2}$$

$$\therefore \quad H^{5/2} = 0.03953$$

$$H = 0.275 \text{ m.}$$ ...(Ans.)

■ **Problem 9.9:** *Determine the shape and design of the sharp crested notch such that the discharge will be 100 lit/sec. and 1160 lit/sec. under heads of 0.6 m and 1.6 m respectively. Take* $C_d = 0.62$.

Solution:

Case I: $Q = 100$ lps and $H = 0.6$.

When the lower discharge is to be measured then triangular notch is to be used as it gives fairly accurate results.

If rectangular notch is used then,

$$Q = \frac{2}{3} \times C_d \times L \times \sqrt{2g} \times H^{3/2}$$

$$0.1 = \frac{2}{3} \times 0.62 \times L \times \sqrt{2 \times 9.81} \times (0.6)^{3/2}$$

$$\therefore \quad L = 0.1175 \text{ m}$$

The width of crest for the discharge of 100 lps is very small and hence suggested to use triangular notch. The discharge for triangular notch is given as below:

$$Q = \frac{8}{15} \times C_d \times \tan\frac{\theta}{2} \times \sqrt{2g} \times H^{5/2}$$

$$0.1 = \frac{8}{15} \times 0.62 \times \tan\frac{\theta}{2} \times \sqrt{2 \times 9.81} \times (0.6)^{5/2}$$

$$\therefore \quad \tan\frac{\theta}{2} = 0.245$$

$$\frac{\theta}{2} = 13.76°$$

$$\theta = 27.52°$$

Thus for measuring discharge of 100 lps, the triangular notch with vertex angle equal to 27.52° may be used.

Case II: $Q = 1160$ lps and $H = 1.6$ m

For larger discharge, it is suggested to use rectangular weir or notch.

$$\therefore \quad Q = \frac{2}{3} \times C_d \times L \times \sqrt{2g} \times H^{3/2}$$

$$1.160 = \frac{2}{3} \times 0.62 \times L \sqrt{2 \times 9.81} \times (1.6)^{3/2}$$

$$\therefore \quad L = 0.313 \text{ m.}$$

9.10 FLOW OVER TRAPEZOIDAL WEIR OR NOTCH

The trapezoidal weir or notch as shown in Fig. 9.5 can be considered to be a combination of a rectangular and a triangular weir or notch. Thus the discharge can be calculated by adding discharge in two portions.

Q = Discharge through portion $BCEF$ + Discharge through ABF and DCE portions,

$$Q = \frac{2}{3} C_{d1} L \sqrt{2g}\, H^{3/2} + \frac{8}{15} C_{d2} \tan \frac{\theta}{2} \sqrt{2g}\, H^{5/2} \qquad \text{...(9.16)}$$

where C_{d1} and C_{d2} are coefficients of discharge for rectangular and triangular notch respectively.

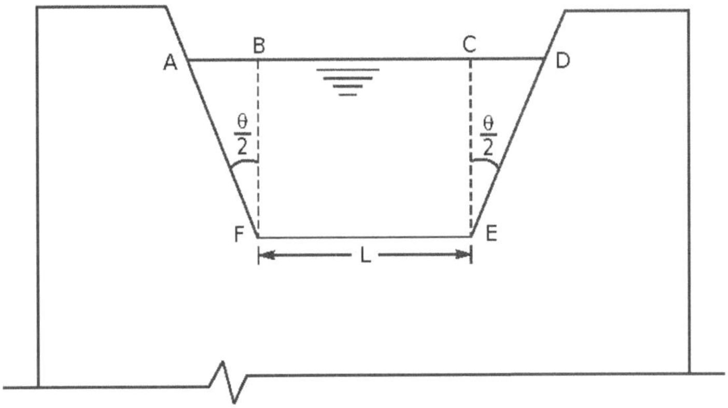

Fig. 9.5 Trapezoidal weir or notch

9.11 CIPPOLLETTI WEIR OR NOTCH

It is a trapezoidal weir which has sloping sides of inclination of 1 horizontal to 4 vertical as shown in Fig. 9.6. Due to side slopes $1\,H : 4\,V$ the decrease in discharge occurs over rectangular weir due to end contractions, which is equal to increase in discharge through the two triangular portions.

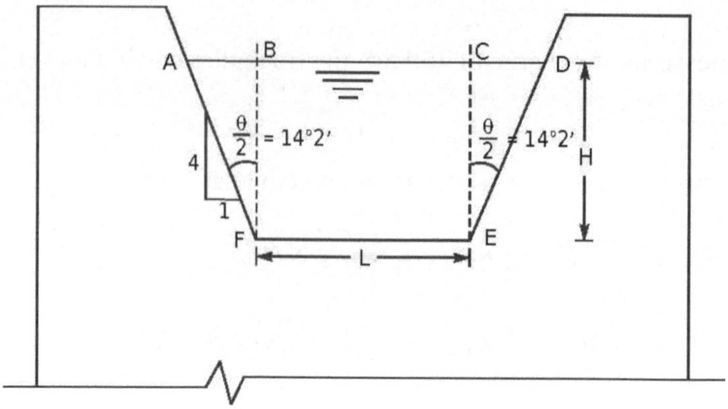

Fig. 9.6 Cippolletti weir or notch

If the discharge through rectangular portion *CEFB* is Q_1 and through two triangular portion is Q_2, then total discharge Q is given as

$$Q = Q_1 + Q_2$$

where
$$Q_1 = \frac{2}{3} C_d \sqrt{2g}\,(L - 0.2H) H^{3/2}$$

$$Q_1 = \frac{2}{3} C_d \sqrt{2g}\,(L H^{3/2} - 0.2 H^{5/2}) \qquad ...(1)$$

$$Q_2 = \frac{8}{15} C_d \tan\frac{\theta}{2} \sqrt{2g}\, H^{5/2}$$

But
$$\tan\frac{\theta}{2} = \frac{1}{4}$$

∴
$$Q = \frac{2}{15} C_d \sqrt{2g}\, H^{5/2} \qquad ...(2)$$

Adding equations (1) and (2), we get

$$Q = \frac{2}{3} C_d L H^{3/2} - \frac{2}{3} \times (0.2)\, C_d \sqrt{2g}\, H^{5/2} + \frac{2}{15} C_d \sqrt{2g}\, H^{5/2}$$

$$= \frac{2}{3} C_d \sqrt{2g}\, H^{3/2} \left(L - \frac{H}{5} + \frac{H}{5} \right)$$

$$Q = \frac{2}{3} C_d \sqrt{2g}\, L H^{3/2} \qquad ...(9.17)$$

This equation is same as the equation to calculate discharge over suppressed rectangular weir.

Cippolletti suggested value for $C_d = 0.632$, thus equation (9.17) reduce to

$$Q = 1.86\, L H^{3/2} \qquad ...(9.18)$$

If the velocity approach be considered then,

$$Q = 1.86\, L\, (H_1^{3/2} - h_a^{3/2}) \qquad ...(9.19)$$

where $$H_1 = H + h_a = H + \frac{V_a^2}{2g}.$$

9.12 DISCHARGE OVER STEPPED NOTCH

A stepped notch is combination of rectangular notches. The total discharge through stepped notch can be computed by adding the discharges through different notches.

The total discharge through the stepped notch of given crest lengths and heads as shown in Fig. 9.7 is given as

$$Q = Q_1 + Q_2 + Q_3 \quad \text{...(9.20)}$$

where,
$$Q_1 = \frac{2}{3} C_d \sqrt{2g}\, L_1 (H_1^{3/2} - H_2^{3/2})$$

$$Q_2 = \frac{2}{3} C_d \sqrt{2g}\, L_2 (H_2^{3/2} - H_3^{3/2})$$

and
$$Q_3 = \frac{2}{3} C_d \sqrt{2g}\, L_3 H_3^{3/2}$$

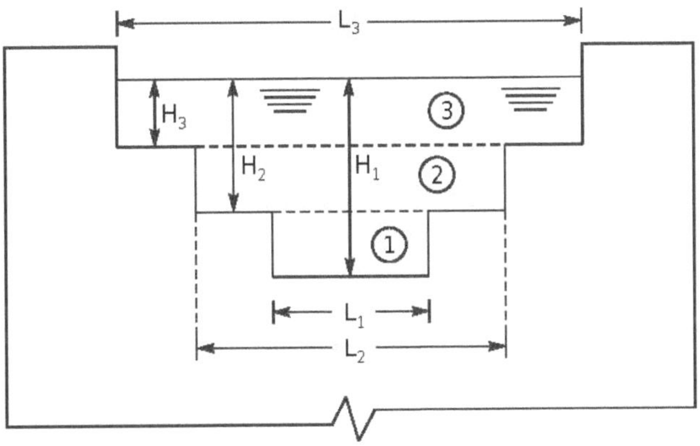

Fig. 9.7 Stepped notch

9.13 SOLVED PROBLEMS

■ **Problem 9.10:** *A trapezoidal notch 160 cm at top and 85 cm at bottom is 30 cm high. Find the discharge through the notch if head of water is 28 cm. Take $C_d = 0.62$.*

Solution: From ΔAEC, (Fig. 9.8)

$$\tan \frac{\theta}{2} = \frac{AE}{EC}$$

$$= \frac{\frac{(160-85)}{2}}{30}$$

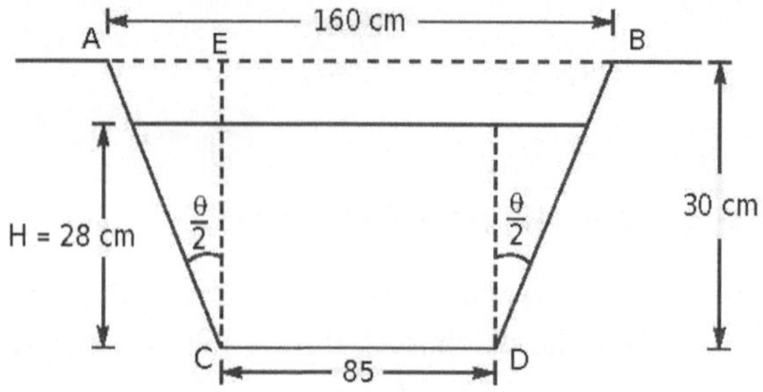

Fig. 9.8

$$\tan\frac{\theta}{2} = 1.25$$

$$\therefore \quad \frac{\theta}{2} = 51.34°$$

Discharge through the trapezoidal notch is,

$$Q = \frac{2}{3}C_d L\sqrt{2g}\,H^{3/2} + \frac{8}{15}C_d \tan\frac{\theta}{2}\sqrt{2g}\,H^{5/2}$$

$$= \frac{2}{3}\times 0.62\times 0.85\times\sqrt{2\times 9.81}\times(0.28)^{3/2}$$

$$+\frac{8}{15}\times 0.62\times\tan 51.34°\times\sqrt{2\times 9.81}\times(0.28)^{5/2}$$

$$Q = 0.2305 + 0.0759$$

$$Q = 0.3065 \text{ m}^3/\text{s}.$$ ...(Ans.)

■ **Problem 9.11:** *A Cippolletti weir of crest length 60 cm discharges water. The head of water over the weir is 360 mm. Find the discharge over the weir if the channel is 80 cm wide and 50 cm deep. $C_d = 0.62$.*

Solution: Discharge through Cippolletti weir is;

$$Q = \frac{2}{3}\times C_d\times\sqrt{2g}\times L H^{3/2}$$

$$= \frac{2}{3}\times 0.62\times\sqrt{2\times 9.81}\times 0.6\times(0.36)^{3/2}$$

$$Q = 0.2373 \text{ m}^3/\text{s}$$

Now, velocity of approach $= V_a = \dfrac{0.2373}{0.8\times 0.5}$

$$V_a = 0.5933 \text{ m/s}$$

$$h_a = \frac{V_a^2}{2g} = \frac{(0.5933)^2}{2\times 9.81} = 0.01794 \text{ m}$$

The correct discharge over Cippolletti weir (considering velocity of approach) is:

$$Q = \frac{2}{3}\times C_d \times \sqrt{2g}\times L[(H + h_a)^{3/2} - h_a^{3/2}]$$

$$= \frac{2}{3}\times 0.62\times\sqrt{2\times 9.81}\times 0.6\times[(0.36 + 0.01794)^{3/2} - (0.01794)^{3/2}]$$

$\therefore$ $$Q = 1.098\ (0.2323 - 0.0024)$$

$$Q = 0.2524\ \text{m}^3/\text{s}. \qquad \text{...(Ans.)}$$

9.14 EFFECT ON COMPUTED DISCHARGE OVER A WEIR OR NOTCH DUE TO AN ERROR IN MEASUREMENT OF HEAD

To get accurate value of discharge over a weir or notch, the head over weir or notch must be measured very accurately as the discharge is directly proportional to head. In case of triangular notch it is proportional to $H^{3/2}$. Even a small error in measurement of head of liquid over the weir or notch, will affect the computed discharge to considerable extent. Effect of error in measurement of head in triangular or rectangular notch or weir is studied as under.

9.14.1 Rectangular Weir or Notch

The discharge over a triangular weir or notch is given by equation (9.11) as

$$Q = \frac{2}{3}C_d\sqrt{2tg}\,LH^{3/2}$$

$$Q = K\,H^{3/2} \qquad \text{...(1)}$$

where $$K = \frac{2}{3}C_d\sqrt{2g}\,L$$

Differentiating equation (1) above, we get

$$dQ = K\times\frac{2}{3}H^{1/2}\,dH \qquad \text{...(2)}$$

Dividing equation (2) by (1), we get

$$\frac{dQ}{Q} = \frac{\frac{3}{2}K\,H^{1/2}dH}{K\,H^{3/2}}$$

$$\frac{dQ}{Q} = \frac{3}{2}\frac{dH}{H} \qquad \text{..(9.21)}$$

The equation (9.21) shows that an error of 1 per cent in measurement of H will produce 1.5 per cent error in the discharge over rectangular weir or notch.

9.14.2 Triangular Weir or Notch

The discharge over a triangular weir or notch is given by equation (9.12) as

$$Q = \frac{8}{15} C_d \tan\frac{\theta}{2}\sqrt{2g}\, H^{5/2}$$

$$Q = K\, H^{5/2}$$

where $$K = \frac{8}{15} C_d \tan\frac{\theta}{2}\sqrt{2g} \quad ...(3)$$

Differentiating equation (2), we get

$$dQ = K \times \frac{5}{2} H^{3/2} dH \quad ...(4)$$

Dividing equation (4) by (3), we get

$$\frac{dQ}{Q} = \frac{K \times \frac{5}{2} H^{3/2} dH}{K\, H^{5/2}}$$

$$\therefore \quad \frac{dQ}{Q} = \frac{5}{2}\frac{dH}{H} \quad ...(9.22)$$

The equation (9.22) shows that an error of 1 per cent in measurement of H will produce 2.5 per cent in the discharge over triangular weir or notch.

9.15 SOLVED PROBLEMS

■ **Problem 9.12:** *In measuring the discharge of 85 liters/sec. of water, a rectangular notch 0.3 m wide, and then a right angled triangular notch are used. If in measuring the head of water over weir and error of 0.25 cm is made each time, determine the ratio of percentage errors in finding out the discharge. Take discharge coefficient as 0.62 for notch.*

Solution:

$$Q = 85 \text{ litres/sec.} = 85 \times 10^3 \text{ cm}^3/\text{s}$$

$$L = 0.3 \text{ m} = 30 \text{ cm}$$

$$\theta = 90°$$

$$dH = 0.025 \text{ cm}$$

Part I: Discharge over rectangular notch is;

$$Q = \frac{2}{3} \times C_d \times L \times \sqrt{2g}\, H^{5/2}$$

$$8500 = \frac{2}{3} \times 0.62 \times 30 \times \sqrt{2 \times 981} \times H^{3/2}$$

$$\therefore \quad H^{3/2} = 154.76$$

$$H = 29.31 \text{ cm}$$

Now, we know $\frac{dQ}{Q} = \frac{3}{2} \times \frac{dH}{H}$

$$\frac{dQ}{Q} = \frac{3}{2} \times \frac{0.025}{29.31} = 0.00128$$

$\therefore$ $\frac{dQ}{Q} = 0.128\%$ ...(Ans.)

Part II: Discharge over right angled triangular notch is:

$$Q = \frac{8}{15} \times C_d \times \tan\frac{\theta}{2} \times \sqrt{29} \times H^{5/2}$$

$$8500 = \frac{8}{15} \times 0.62 \times \tan\frac{90}{2} \times \sqrt{2 \times 981} \times H^{5/2}$$

$$H^{5/2} = 5803.05$$

$$H = 32.02 \text{ cm}$$

We know, for triangular notch

$$\frac{dQ}{Q} = \frac{5}{2}\frac{dH}{H}$$

$$= \frac{5}{2} \times \frac{0.0125}{32.02}$$

$$\frac{dQ}{Q} = 0.001952$$

$\frac{dQ}{Q} = 0.195\%.$ ...(Ans.)

■ **Problem 9.13:** *The head of water over a triangular notch of angle 50° is 60 cm. Find the limiting value of the head if the flow measured is to be within an accuracy of 1.6%. Take $C_d = 62$.*

Solution: The discharge over triangular notch is given as

$$Q = \frac{8}{15} C_d \sqrt{2g} \tan\frac{\theta}{2} H^{5/2}$$

$$= \frac{8}{15} \times 0.62 \times \sqrt{2 \times 981} \times \tan\left(\frac{50}{2}\right) \times (60)^{5/2}$$

$$Q = 19043.5 \text{ cm}^3/\text{s}$$

We know, $\frac{dQ}{Q} = \frac{5}{2}\frac{dH}{H}$

$$\pm 0.016 = 2.5 \times \frac{dH}{H}$$

$$dH = \pm\frac{0.016\times60}{2.5}$$

$$dH = \pm\, 0.384$$

∴ Limiting values of head = 60 ± 0.384

= 60.384 cm and 59.616 cm. ...(Ans.)

9.16 TIME REQUIRED TO EMPTY A RESERVOIR OR A TANK WITH RECTANGULAR WEIR OR NOTCH

Consider a reservoir or a tank of uniform cross-sectional area A. Let it be provided with rectangular notch of crest length L and coefficient of discharge C_d. Aim of this study is to find time (T) required to lower the water level in the tank from H_1 to H_2.

Let at any instant, the height of water surface above crest of weir of notch is 'h' and in small time 'dT' the water level falls by dh. If in time dT the discharge through notch is Q, then

$$-A\,dH = Q\,dT$$

$$-A\,dh = \frac{2}{3}C_d\sqrt{2g}\,L\,h^{3/2}dT$$

(Negative sign indicates that head decrease as time increases):

$$\therefore \quad dT = \frac{-A\,dh}{\frac{2}{3}C_d\sqrt{2g}\,L\,h^{3/2}}$$

Integrating both sides,

$$T = \int_0^T dT = \int_{H_1}^{H_2} \frac{-A\,dh}{\frac{2}{3}C_d\sqrt{2g}\,L\,h^{3/2}}$$

$$T = \frac{-3A}{2C_d\sqrt{2g}\,L}\int_{H_1}^{H_2} h^{-3/2}dh$$

$$= \frac{-3A}{2C_d\sqrt{2g}\,L}(-2)\left[h^{-1/2}\right]_{H_1}^{H_2}$$

$$= \frac{3A}{C_d\sqrt{2g}\,L}[H_2^{-1/2} - H_1^{-1/2}]$$

$$\therefore \quad T = \frac{-3A}{C_d\sqrt{2g}\,L}\left[\frac{1}{\sqrt{H_2}} - \frac{1}{\sqrt{H_1}}\right] \qquad \text{...(9.23)}$$

9.17 SOLVED PROBLEM

■ **Problem 9.14:** *Water flows over a sharp edged rectangular notch. 5.4864 m wide from a reservoir in which the water surface covers an area of 8100 m². Find the time for the level to fall from 0.9144 m to 0.1524 m above the sill of the notch. Given that no water enters or leaves the reservoir by any other means. Take C_d = 0.62.*

Solution:

Data:

$$L = 5.4864 \text{ m}$$
$$A = 8100 \text{ m}^2$$
$$H_1 = 0.9144 \text{ m}$$
$$H_2 = 0.1524 \text{ m}$$

Time for level to fall from H_1 to H_2 is given as

$$T = \frac{3A}{C_d \times L \times \sqrt{2g}}\left[\frac{1}{\sqrt{H_2}} - \frac{1}{\sqrt{H_1}}\right]$$

$$= \frac{3 \times 8100}{0.62 \times 5.4864 \times \sqrt{2 \times 9.81}} \times \left[\frac{1}{\sqrt{0.1524}} - \frac{1}{\sqrt{0.9144}}\right]$$

$$T = 1613\,(2.5616 - 1.0457)$$

$$T = 2445.15 \text{ sec.} = 40 \text{ min } 45 \text{ sec.}$$ ...(Ans.)

9.18 TIME REQUIRED TO EMPTY A RESERVOIR OR A TANK WITH TRIANGULAR WEIR OR NOTCH

Consider a reservoir or a tank with uniform cross-sectional area A. Let it be provided with triangular notch or weir of angle of notch equal to θ and coefficient of discharge C_d. Aim of this study is to find the time (T) required to lower the water level in the tank or reservoir from H_1 to H_2.

Let at any instant, the height of water surface above the apex of the weir or notch is 'h' and is small time 'dT' the water level falls by 'dh'. If in time dT the discharge through weir or notch is Q, then

$$-A\,dh = Q\,dT$$

$$-A \times dh = \frac{8}{15} C_d \tan\frac{\theta}{2}\sqrt{2g}\,h^{5/2}\,dT$$

$$\therefore \quad dT = \frac{-A\,dh}{\frac{8}{15} C_d \tan\frac{\theta}{2}\sqrt{2g}\,h^{5/2}}$$

Integrating both sides $T = \int_0^T dT = \int_{H_1}^{H_2} \dfrac{-A\,dh}{\frac{8}{15} C_d \tan\frac{\theta}{2}\sqrt{2g}\,h^{5/2}}$

$$T = \frac{-15A}{8\,C_d\,\tan\frac{\theta}{2}\sqrt{2g}} \int_{H_1}^{H_2} h^{-5/2}\,dh$$

$$= \frac{-15A}{8\,C_d\,\tan\frac{\theta}{2}\sqrt{2g}} \times \left(-\frac{2}{3}\right)\left[h^{-3/2}\right]_{H_1}^{H_2}$$

$$= \frac{5A}{4\,C_d\,\tan\frac{\theta}{2}\sqrt{2g}} \left[H_2^{-3/2} - H_1^{-3/2}\right]$$

$$T = \frac{15A}{4\,C_d\,\tan\frac{\theta}{2}\sqrt{2g}} \left[\frac{1}{H_2^{3/2}} - \frac{1}{H_1^{3/2}}\right] \qquad \text{...(9.24)}$$

9.19 SOLVED PROBLEM

■ **Problem 9.15:** *Find the time required to lower the water level from 3.2 m to 2.4 m in a reservoir of uniform area equal to 7000 m² by a right angled V-notch. Take $C_d = 0.62$.*

Solution: Time required to lower water can be calculated by using following equation.

$$T = \frac{15}{4\,C_d\,\tan\frac{\theta}{2}\sqrt{2g}} \left[\frac{1}{H_2^{3/2}} - \frac{1}{H_1^{3/2}}\right]$$

$$= \frac{5 \times 7000}{4 \times 0.62 \times \tan\frac{90}{2} \times \sqrt{2 \times 9.81}} \left[\frac{1}{(2.4)^{3/2}} - \frac{1}{(3.2)^{3/2}}\right]$$

$$T = 3186.47\,(0.2679 - 0.1747)$$

$$T = 300.35 \text{ sec}$$

$$T \simeq 5 \text{ min.} \qquad \textbf{...(Ans.)}$$

9.20 FLOW OVER A BROAD CRESTED WEIR

A weir having a wide crest is known as broad crested weir. In case of broad crested weir jet of water flow over the top surface of the crest after touching the upstream edge as shown in Fig. 9.9.

Let B is the width of crest and H is the head upstream of weir, where curvature effect on water surface is negligible then if $2B > H$ the weir behaves as broad crested weir. The upstream edge of weir is made rounded shape shown in Fig. 9.9 to avoid the cavitation. If the upstream edge has sharp corner, then water level at point O will rise little and then drops down and there after it flow over the surface of weir. Thus when the air from air pocket is carried away with fluid, the pressure at the point drops and caviation process starts and weir gets damaged.

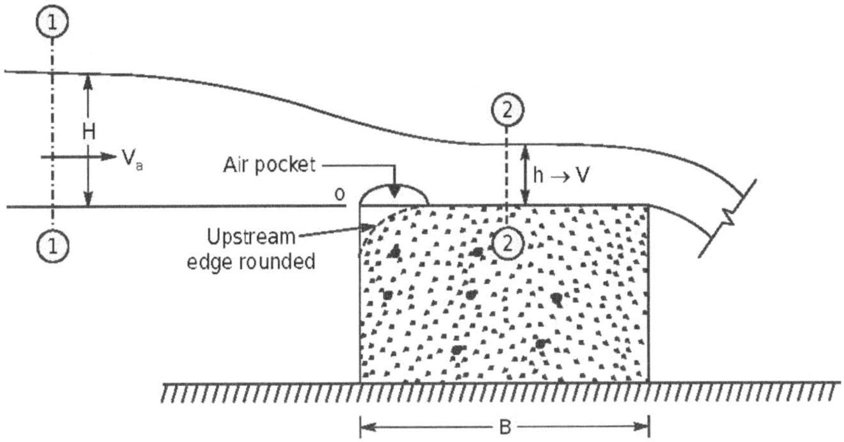

Fig. 9.9 Broad crested weir

Let V_a is the velocity of approach on upstream of weir where head is H, which subsequently reduces to 'h' on the surface of weir causing increase in velocity to V.

Consider section 1-1 and 2-2 as shown in Fig. 9.9 and apply Bernoulli's equation between them;

$$0 + 0 + H = 0 + \frac{V^2}{2g} + h \qquad \text{(As } V_a \rightarrow 0\text{)}$$

$$\therefore \qquad \frac{V^2}{2g} = H - h$$

$$\therefore \qquad V = \sqrt{2g(H-h)}$$

The discharge over weir = Area × Velocity

$$= L \times h \times \sqrt{2g(H-h)}$$

where, L = length of crest.

Theoretical discharge, $Q = C_d \times Lh\sqrt{2g(H-h)}$ ...(9.25)

Condition for maximum discharge: For constant head H, the discharge Q will be maximum if $\frac{dQ}{dh} = 0$

$$\text{i.e.} \qquad \frac{dQ}{dh} = \frac{d}{dh}(C_d\, L\, h\sqrt{2g(H+h)} = 0$$

$$\therefore \qquad C_d\, L\, h\left[\sqrt{H-h} - \frac{h}{2\sqrt{H-h}}\right] = 0$$

Solving we get, $h = \frac{2}{3}H$ ...(9.26)

Substitute for h in equation (9.25), we get

$$Q = C_d\, L\left(\frac{2}{3}H\right)\sqrt{2g\left(H - \frac{2}{3}H\right)}$$

$$= C_d\, L\left(\frac{2}{3}H\right)\sqrt{\frac{2}{3}gH}$$

$$Q = 1.70\, C_d L H^{3/2} \quad ...(9.27)$$

The equation (9.27) gives maximum discharge on broad crested weir by knowing H only. If the velocity of approach is to be taken into account, then

$$Q = 1.70\, C_d L H_1^{3/2} \quad ...(9.28)$$

where $$H_1 = H + h_a = H + \frac{V_a^2}{2g}$$

In the earlier section of the chapter, we have studied the sharp crested weir. If for any weir $2B < H$, then it is called narrow or sharp crested weir and the discharge over such weir can be calculated using the equation (9.1).

i.e. $$Q = \frac{2}{3}C_d\sqrt{2g}\, L H^{3/2} \quad ...(9.29)$$

9.21 SOLVED PROBLEM

■ **Problem 9.16:** *Find the maximum discharge over a broad crested weir of 60 m length. The head of water above crest is 54 cm and cross-sectional area on upstream side is 60 m². Take $C_d = 0.62$.*

Solution: Maximum discharge neglecting the velocity of approach is given as

$$Q = 1.70 \times C_d \times L \times H^{3/2}$$

$$= 1.70 \times 0.62 \times 60 \times (0.54)^{3/2}$$

$$\therefore \quad Q = 25.095\ \text{m}^3/\text{s}$$

Now, velocity of approach, $$V_a = \frac{Q}{A} = \frac{25.095}{60}$$

$$V_a = 0.4182\ \text{m/s}$$

$$\therefore \quad h_s = \frac{V_a^2}{2g} = \frac{(0.4128)^2}{2g} = 0.00892\ \text{m}$$

The correct value of Maximum discharge (considering the velocity of approach) is given as

$$Q = 1.70 \times C_d \times L \times H_1^{3/2}$$

where, $$H_1 = H + h_a = 0.54 + 0.00892$$

$$H_1 = 0.54892\ \text{m}$$

$$\therefore \quad Q = 1.70 \times 0.62 \times 60\ (0.54892)^{3/2}$$

$$Q = 25.719\ \text{m}^3/\text{s}. \quad ...\textbf{(Ans.)}$$

9.22 FLOW OVER SUBMERGED OR DROWNED WEIRS

The weir is said to be submerged or drowned when water level on downstream side of weir is above the crest of the weir. The discharge over a submerged weir (Fig. 9.10) can be calculated by dividing it into two parts. The portion between the upstream and downstream water level can be considered as a free weir and portion between downstream water level and crest of weir as a submerged weir. Thus, if Q_1 and Q_2 are the discharges through the free and drowned portions respectively then, total discharge Q is given as:

$$Q = Q_1 + Q_2 \quad ...(9.30)$$

where,
$$Q_1 = \frac{2}{3} C_{d1} L \sqrt{2g} (H - h)^{3/2} \quad ...(9.31)$$

and
$$Q_2 = C_{d2} L h \sqrt{2g(H - h)} \quad ...(9.32)$$

where, H and h are heads on upstream and downstream of weir and, C_{d1} and C_{d2} are coefficients of discharge for free and submerged weir respectively and L is the length of crest.

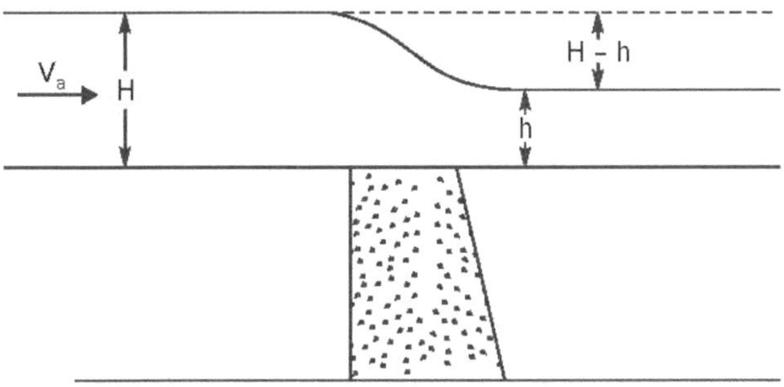

Fig. 9.10 Submerged on drowned weir

If the velocity of approach is to be taken into account, then

$$Q_1 = \frac{2}{3} C_{d1} \sqrt{2g}\, L \left[\left(H - h + \frac{V_a^2}{2g} \right)^{3/2} - \left(\frac{V_a^2}{2g} \right)^{3/2} \right] \quad ...(9.33)$$

$$Q_2 = C_{d2} \times H \times h \times \sqrt{2g (H - h) + V_a^2} \quad ...(9.34)$$

9.23 SOLVED PROBLEM

■ **Problem 9.17:** *A weir at the end of a pond is 3.5 m wide. The sill of the weir is 0.9 m below water level in the pond. The tail water level is 0.6 m above sill level. Taking coefficients of discharge as 0.6 and 0.62 for free and submerged portions and mean velocity of flow as 0.01 m sec. Calculate the discharge the weir.*

Solution:

$$L = 3.5 \text{ m}$$
$$H = 0.9$$
$$h = 0.6$$
$$C_{d1} = 0.6 \text{ and } C_{d2} = 0.62$$

The discharge over the weir considering the velocity of approach is given as

$$Q = \frac{2}{3} C_{d1} \sqrt{2g}\, L \left[\left(H - h + \frac{V_a^2}{2g} \right)^{3/2} - \left(\frac{V_a^2}{2g} \right)^{3/2} \right] + C_{d2} L\, h \sqrt{2g\,(H-h) + V_a^2}$$

$$= \frac{2}{3} \times 0.6 \times \sqrt{2 \times 9.81} \times 3.5 \times \left[\left(0.9 + \frac{(0.01)^2}{2 \times 9.81} \right)^{3/2} - \left(\frac{(0.01)^2}{2 \times 9.81} \right)^{3/2} \right]$$

$$+ 0.62 \times 3.5 \times 0.6 \times \sqrt{2 \times 9.81 \times (0.9 - 0.6) + (0.01)^2}$$

$$= 5.47068 + 3.1586$$ ...(Ans.)

$$Q = 8.629 \text{ m}^3/\text{s}.$$

Exercises

1. Find the discharge of water flowing over a rectangular notch of 2.0 m wide. The head of water over the notch is 30 cm. Tank, $C_d = 0.62$. **(Ans.** $Q = 0.602$ m^3/s**)**
2. Determine the discharge over a weir 44 m long divided into 10 equal bays by vertical posts. The width of each post is 80 cm. The head of water over the crest is 1.4 m and velocity of approach is 2.0 m/sec. **(Ans.** $Q = 111.28$ m^3/s**)**
3. The crest of the spillway consisting of 10 bays each 13 m wide is at 386 m R.L. The catchment area of reservoir is 12,800 sq. km. The average intensity of rainfall is 25.4 mm per hour and the maximum of $\frac{1}{5}$th of this quantity reaches the spillway at any time. What will be the maximum water level? Take $C_d = 0.8$. **(Ans.** R.L. of water surface = 394.55 m**)**
4. A suppressed rectangular weir is used to measure rate of flow in a stream 2.5 m wide. The head of water above the weir is 30 cm. The sill of the notch is 60 cm above the stream bed. Assuming $C_d = 0.62$. Find the discharge. Consider velocity of approach. **(Ans.** $Q = 0.7716$ m^3/s**)**
5. A sharp crested rectangular weir of 1 m height extends across a rectangular channel of 3 m width. If the head of water over the weir is 0.45 m. Calculate the discharge considering velocity of approach $C_d = 0.623$. (*MU Dec. 1994*) **(Ans.** $Q = 1.702$ m^3/s**)**
6. Water is flowing in a rectangular channel of 1.5 m width and 1.0 m deep. Find the discharge over a rectangular weir of crest length 80 cm if the head over the weir crest is 30 cm and water from the channel flow over the weir. Take $C_d = 0.6$ Neglect end contractions but consider velocity of approach. **(Ans.** $Q = 0.2342$ m^3/s**)**
7. A rectangular notch of crest width 45 cm is used to measure the flow of water in a rectangular channel 60 cm wide and 45 cm deep. If the water level in the channel is

22.50 cm above the weir crest, find the discharge in the channel. For the notch assume $C_d = 0.63$ and take velocity of approach into account. **(Ans.** $Q = 0.0824$ m³/s)

8. A stream approaching a waterfall having a fall of 20 m is gauged by a weir. The measured gauge over the weir is 32 cm and the length of the weir is 3 m. The velocity of approach, $V_a = 0.3$ m/s and the head due to this may be supposed to be increased by $\left(1.6\frac{V_a^2}{2g}\right)$. Determine the power available from the fall assuming that 60% of the energy can be used. **(Ans.** Power = 191.5 kW)

9. A tank with vertical sides and horizontal cross-sectional area of 2 m² is provided with a notch cut at the top of one of the sides. Water flowing steadily into the tank discharges over the notch with head of 18 cm over the crest with a constant rate of inflow into the tank. When the inflow is stopped, the head began to fall at the rate of 0.35 cm/sec. When the head had fallen to 9 cm, it was found that the rate of fall was 0.13 cm/sec. Estimate the rate of inflow into the tank when there is a steady head of 15 cm over the crest and what was the rate of inflow when the head was 18 cm. **(Ans.** $Q = 5.393$ lit/s)

10. Water flow over a rectangular weir of crest length with end contractions suppressed is 2.2 m. The head of water over weir is 60 cm. Find the discharge using Francis' and Bazin's formula. **(Ans.** $Q = 1.88$ m³/s –Francis's, $Q = 1.857$ m³/s–Bazin's)

11. Find the discharge over a pier by using Friancis formula and taking into account the velocity of approach and end contractions. If the total length of weir is 10 m. The number of piers carrying a bridge over the weir is 10. Width of each pier = 60 cm. Head over the weir = 1.5 m. Width of guide channel carrying water to weir = 126 m. Bed of the guide channel is 1.5 m below the crest of the pier. **(Ans.** $Q = 2999$ m³/s)

12. Show that correction factor to allow for velocity of approach to a rectangular notch be given in the form.

$$\left[\left(1+\frac{\alpha h}{H}\right)^{3/2} - \left(\frac{\alpha h}{H}\right)^{3/2}\right]$$

where H = measured head

$h = V^2/2g$

V = Velocity of approach

α = factor to allow for velocity not being uniform over section of channel.

If rectangular channel 1.2 meter wide has at the end a rectangular sharp edged notch 1m wide with the sill 25 cm from the bottom. Assuming $\alpha = 1.1$. Calculate flow when the head is 20 cm using Francis Formulae. **(Ans.** $Q = 0.163$ m³/s)

13. Find the depth and top width of a V-notch capable of discharging a maximum of 0.70 m³/sec and such that the head shall be 7.5 cm for a discharge of 5.6 litres pre second. Its C_d is the same as that of a similar (in material and sharpness of edges only) right angled V-notch for which $Q = 1.407\,H^{5/2}$. **(Ans.** $H = 0.517$ m, $B = 2.672$ m)

14. A rectangular notch 1.2 m wide having C_d = 0.62 and a right angled triangular notch are in series. The measured head over the rectangular notch was 12 cm. Find head over the triangular notch if its C_d = 0.62. (**Ans.** H = 0.3295 m)

15. Water flows over a rectangular notch 1 m wide over a depth of 15 cm and afterwards passes through a triangular right-angled notch. Find the depth of water through this triangular notch. The co-efficient of discharge for the notches are assumed to be 0.62 and 0.59 respectively. (**Ans.** H = 0.357 m)

16. Determine the shape and design of the sharp crested notch such that the discharge will be 120 lit/sec and 1400 lit/sec under heads of 0.7 m and 1.7 m respectively. Take C_d = 0.62. (**Ans.** For Q = 120 lit/s, triangular notch of θ = 15° 56 and For Q = 1400 lit/s, Rectangular notch L = 0.345 m)

17. Two notches one rectangular and other triangular are situated in the opposite side of a tank. The discharge of the notches are given by

$$Q_{\text{rect}} = 0.885\, H^{3/2} \quad \text{and} \quad Q_{\text{tri}} = 0.01415\, H^{5/2}$$

where Q and H are measured in terms of lit/sec and centimeters respectively. When the rectangular notch carries 24 lit/sec, the discharge through triangular notch was 14.5 lit/sec. If the discharge through rectangular notch was reduced by half, what would be corresponding discharge over triangular notch. (**Ans.** Q_{tri} = 8.08 lit/sec)

18. Compute the discharge over a stepped notch. The dimensions of the notch are as follows:

    Top portion: 100 cm × 40 cm

    Middle portion: 60 × 20 cm

    Bottom portion: 40 cm × 10 cm. (**Ans.** Q = 0.782 m^3/s)

19. A trapezoidal notch 2 m at top and 1.0 m at bottom is 40 cm high. Find the discharge through the notch if head of water is 32 cm. Take C_d = 0.62. (**Ans.** Q = 0.663 m^3/s)

20. A trapezoidal notch is to be designed to pass a discharge of 1 m^3/sec at a head of 0.8 m over the crest and 0.50 m^3/sec at the head of 0.51 m. Assuming C_d = 0.7 calculate the base width and side slope of the notch. (**Ans.** B = 64.2 m, θ = 2.96°)

21. A cippolletti weir of crest length 80 cm discharge water. The head of water the weir is 40 cm. Find the discharge over the weir if the channel is 1.0 m wide and 60 m deep. C_d = 0.62. (**Ans.** Q = 0.394 m^3/s)

22. Show that an error of 1% in the measurement of head will produce an error of (*i*) 0.5% in the discharge in case of an orifice. (*ii*) 1.5% in discharge in case of rectangular notch and (*iii*) 2.5% in discharge in case of triangular notch.

23. In measuring the discharge of 100 litres/sec of water, a rectangular notch 0.4 m wide, and then a right angled triangular notch are used. If in measuring the head of water over weir and error of 0.030 cm is made each time. Determine the ratio of percentage errors in finding out the discharge. Take discharge coefficient as 0.62 for notch.

    (**Ans.** (*i*) Rectangular notch, Error = 0.169% (*ii*) Triangular notch, Error = 0.219%)

24. The head of water over a triangular notch of angle 45° is 50 cm. Find the limiting value of the head if the flow measured is to be within an accuracy of 1.8% Take $C_d = 0.62$. **(Ans.** Limiting Value of Head = 50.36 cm and 49.64 cm)
25. Water flows over a sharp edged rectangular notch 6 m wide from a reservoir in which the water surface covers an area of 10,000 m^2. Find the time for the level to fall from 1.0 m to 0.2 m above the sill of the notch. Given that no water enters or leaves the reservoir by any other means. Take $C_d = 0.62$. **(Ans.** $T = 37$ min 30 sec.)
26. Find the time required to lower the water level from 4.0 m to 3.0 m in a reservoir of uniform area equal to 8,000 m^3 by a right angled V-notch. Take C_d 0.62. **(Ans.** $T = 4$ min 5 sec.)
27. Find the time required to lower the water level from 3 m to 2 m in a reservoir of dimension 80 m × 80 m by a rectangular notch of length 1.5 m. $C_d = 0.62$ **(Ans.** T = 605 sec.)
28. A sharp edged V-notch inserted in the side of a rectangular tank 4 m long and 1.5 m wide gives the calibration, $Q = 6\,H^{2.5}$ where Q is in m^3/s and H in meter. Find the time required for the head over the notch to decrease from 10 cm to 2.5 cm, assuming no inflow in the tank. **(Ans.** $T = 3$ min 7 sec)
29. Find the maximum discharge over a broad crested weir of 50 m length. The head of water above crest is 48 cm and cross-sectional area on upstream side is 55 m^2. Take $C_d = 0.62$. **(Ans.** $Q = 17.81$ m^3/s)
30. A weir 2 m long has its crest 1 m below the water level on its upstream side and 0.5 m below the water level on its downstream side. Calculate the discharge passing over the weir if C_d for the free portion is 0.6 and for submerged portion is 0.8. Water approach the weir with the velocity = 2 m/s. **(Ans.** $Q = 4.74$ m^3/s)

❑❑❑

10

Laminar Flow

10.1 INTRODUCTION

Laminar flow is also called as viscous flow. In laminar flow fluid moves in layers and since velocity changes across section it is assumed that one layer glides over another.

A dimension less number called as Reynolds number is used to ascertain the type of flow.

10.2 REYNOLDS EXPERIMENT

Using Reynolds experiment laminar flow and turbulent flow can be observed. The apparatus designed by Reynolds for his experiment is given below:

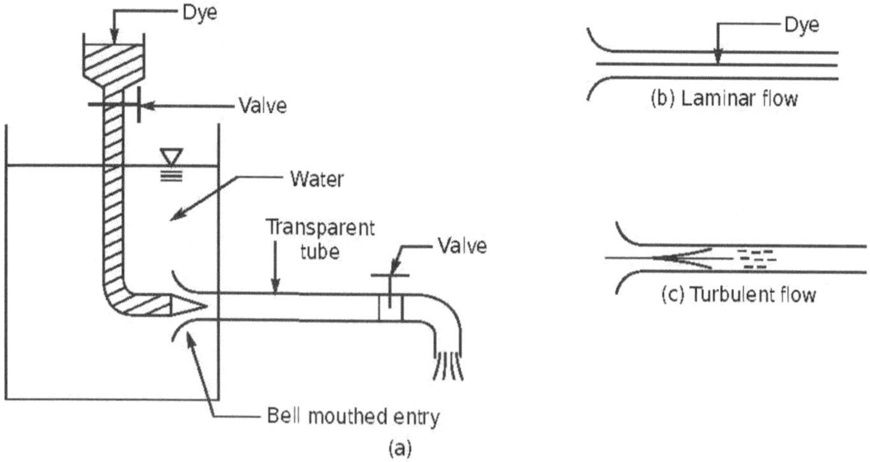

Fig. 10.1

For low discharge the flow will be laminar when the rate of flow crosses a certain limit then the dye spreads, get mixed with flowing water, showing turbulent flow.

Also by using Reynolds number.

i.e., $R = \frac{\rho VD}{\mu}$ one can identify a type of flow. Approximately, for circular pipe.

For $R < 2000 \rightarrow$ laminar flow

$R > 4000 \rightarrow$ turbulent flow

$2000 < R < 4000 \rightarrow$ transition stage.

10.3 LAMINAR FLOW THROUGH A CIRCULAR PIPE

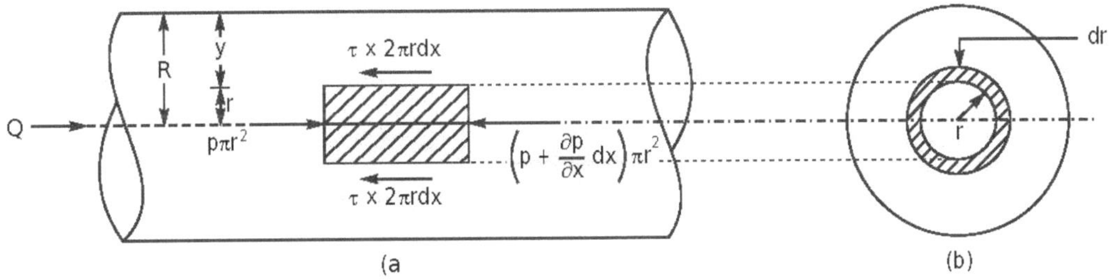

Fig. 10.2

From Fig. 10.2 (*a*).

By summing the forces in *x*-direction

$$p\pi r^2 - \left(p + \frac{\partial p}{\partial x}dx\right)\pi r^2 - \tau \times 2\pi r\, dx = 0$$

$$p\pi r^2 - p\pi r^2 - \frac{\partial p}{\partial x}dx\,\pi r^2 - \tau \times 2\pi r\, dx = 0$$

$$\frac{-\partial p}{\partial x}r = 2\tau$$

$$\tau = -\frac{\partial p}{\partial x}\frac{r}{2} \qquad \text{...(10.1)}$$

For $r = R$, τ will be maximum hence equation (10.1) can be written as

$$\tau_0 = \tau_{max} = -\frac{\partial p}{\partial x}\frac{R}{2} \qquad \text{...(10.2)}$$

Refer Fig. 10.2

$$y = R - r$$

Differentiating

$$dy = -dr$$

Now Newton's law of viscosity is given by

$$\tau = \mu\frac{du}{dy} \qquad \text{...(10.3)}$$

Doing the substitutions

$$\rho = -\mu\frac{du}{dr} \qquad ...(10.4)$$

Equating right hand sides of equations (10.1) and (10.4)

$$-\mu\frac{du}{dr} = -\frac{\partial p}{\partial x}\frac{r}{2}$$

$$\frac{du}{dr} = \frac{1}{2\mu}\frac{\partial p}{\partial x}r$$

Integrating w.r.t. '*r*'

$$u = \frac{1}{4\mu}\frac{\partial p}{\partial x}r^2 + k \qquad ...(10.5)$$

Where k is a constant of integration. To find k substituting the boundary conditions. For $r = R$, $u = 0$.

$$0 = \frac{1}{4\mu}\frac{\partial p}{\partial x}R^2 + k$$

$\therefore$

$$k = \frac{1}{4\mu}\frac{\partial p}{\partial x}R^2$$

Put in equation (10.5)

$$u = \frac{1}{4\mu}\frac{\partial p}{\partial x}r^2 - \frac{1}{4\mu}\frac{\partial p}{\partial x}R^2$$

$$= -\frac{1}{4\mu}\frac{\partial p}{\partial x}[R^2 - r^2] \qquad ...(10.6)$$

Velocity at a distance of r from the centre of the pipe can be calculated by using equation (10.6). Velocity at the centre of the pipe (*i.e.* $r = 0$) will be maximum and given by

$$u_{max} = -\frac{1}{4\mu}\frac{\partial p}{\partial x}R^2 \qquad ...(10.7)$$

Now to find out discharge 'Q' through the pipe consider a elemental ring of thickness 'dr' (Refer Fig. 10.2).

Then discharge through this elementary ring is given by

$$dQ = u \times 2\pi r\, dr$$

$$= -\frac{1}{4\mu}\frac{\partial p}{\partial x}[R^2 - r^2]\, 2\pi r\, dr$$

Integrating

$$Q = \int_0^R dQ = \int_0^R -\frac{1}{4\mu}\frac{\partial p}{\partial x}[R^2 - r^2]\, 2\pi r\, dr$$

$$= \frac{\pi}{8\mu}\left(-\frac{\partial p}{\partial x}\right)R^4 \qquad ...(10.8)$$

Now average velocity

$$= \frac{Q}{\text{Area of pipe}}$$

$$= \frac{\frac{\pi}{8\mu}\left(-\frac{\partial p}{\partial x}\right)R^4}{\pi R^2}$$

$$\bar{u} = \frac{1}{8\mu}\left(-\frac{\partial p}{\partial x}\right)R^2 \qquad \text{...(10.9)}$$

From equation (10.7) and (10.9)

$$\frac{u_{\max}}{\bar{u}} = 2.0$$

Pressure drop in terms of average velocity:

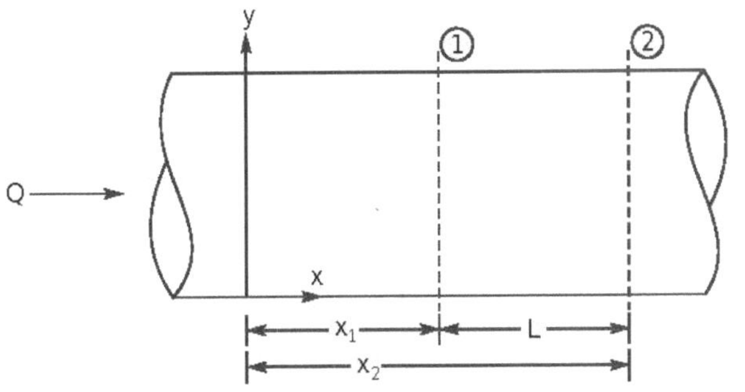

Fig. 10.3

Now

$$\bar{u} = \frac{1}{8\mu}\left(-\frac{\partial p}{\partial x}\right)R^2$$

$$-\frac{\partial p}{\partial x} = \frac{8\mu\bar{u}}{R^2}$$

Integrating

$$-\int_2^1 dp = \int_2^1 \frac{8\mu\bar{u}}{R^2}\,dx$$

$$-(p_1 - p_2) = \frac{8\mu\bar{u}}{R^2}(x_1 - x_2)$$

$$p_1 - p_2 = \frac{8\mu\bar{u}}{R^2}L$$

$$= \frac{8\mu\bar{u}\,L}{\left(\frac{D}{2}\right)^2}$$

$$= \frac{32\,\mu\bar{u}\,L}{D^2}$$

Dividing both sides by ρg

$$\therefore \quad h_f = \frac{p_1 - p_2}{\rho g} = \frac{32\mu\bar{u}\,L}{\rho g D^2} \qquad \text{...(10.11)}$$

Also,
$$Q = \frac{\pi D^2}{4} \times \bar{u}$$

$$\therefore \quad \bar{u} = \frac{4Q}{\pi D^2} \text{ put in equation (10.11)}$$

$$\frac{p_1 - p_2}{\rho g} = \frac{128\,\mu\,L}{\rho g\,\pi D^4} \qquad \text{...(10.12)}$$

Equation (10.12) is called **Hagen Poiseuille** equation.

Equation (10.12) can be written as

$$\frac{p_1 - p_2}{L} = \frac{128\,\mu}{\pi D^4} \qquad \text{...(10.13)}$$

$$= \frac{\partial p}{\partial x}$$

10.3.1 Solved Problems

■ **Problem 10.1:** *An oil of specific gravity 0.9 and viscosity 0.12 Ns/m² flow through a pipe of 2.5 cm diameter with a pressure drop of 0.35 N/cm² in a length of 30 m. Determine the discharge, shear stress intensity at the pipe wall and the power required to maintain the flow.*

Given:

$S = 0.9$

$\mu = 0.12\ Ns/m^2$

$D = 2.5\ cm = 2.5 \times 10^{-2}\ m$

$dp = p_1 - p_2 = 0.35\ N/cm^2 = 0.35 \times 10^4\ N/m^2$

$L = 30\ m.$

Solution: Using Hagen Poiseuille equation

$$\frac{p_1 - p_2}{\rho g} = \frac{128\,\mu Q L}{\rho g\,\pi D^4}$$

$$\therefore \quad Q = \frac{(p_1 - p_2)\pi D^4}{128\,\mu L}$$

$$= \frac{0.35\times 10^4 \times \pi \times (2.5\times 10^{-2})^4}{128\times 0.12\times 30}$$

$$= 0.0932 \times 10^{-4}\ m^3/sec.$$

Shear stress intensity at the pipe wall

$$\tau_0 = t_{max} = -\frac{\partial p}{\partial x}\frac{R}{2}$$

Now
$$\frac{\partial p}{\partial x} = \frac{p_1 - p_2}{L} = \frac{0.35\times10^4}{30}$$
$$= 116.67 \text{ N/m}^2 \text{ per meter}$$

Put in equation

$$t = -116.67 \times \frac{2.5\times10^{-2}}{2}$$
$$= 1.4584 \text{ N/m}^2$$

Power required to maintain the flow

$$p = \gamma Q h_f$$
$$= \gamma \times Q \times \frac{128\,\mu QL}{\rho g\,\pi D^4} \quad \text{(Refer equation 10.12)}$$
$$= \frac{0.9\times9810\times(0.0932\times10^{-4})^2\times128\times0.12\times30}{0.9\times1000\times9.81\times\pi\times(2.5\times10^{-2})^4}$$
$$= 0.0326 \text{ Nm/sec. or watts}$$

Now,
$$R = \frac{\rho\bar{u}D}{\mu}$$

where
$$\bar{u} = \frac{Q}{A} = \frac{Q}{\frac{\pi D^2}{4}}$$
$$= \frac{0.0932\times10^{-4}}{\frac{p\times(2.5\times10^{-2})^2}{4}}$$
$$= 0.019 \text{ m/sec.}$$

$\therefore$
$$R = \frac{0.019\times1000\times0.019\times2.5\times10^{-2}}{0.12}$$
$$= 3.56 < 2000 \text{ hence laminar flow.}$$

■ **Problem 10.2:** *Oil of specific gravity 0.8 flows through a pipe of 3 cm diameter and inclined at 37° to the horizontal. Pressure gauges are fitted at two points on the pipe. The gauge at A which is at the lower end records 500 kPa and at B 180 kPa. Along the pipe the distance between these is 15 m. Find the direction of flow and the flow rate in m³/hr. The viscosity of oil is 0.9 P_dS.*

Given:

$S = 0.8$

$D = 3\ cm = 3 \times 10^{-2}\ m$

$q = 37°$

$p_A = 500\ kPa = 500 \times 10^3\ N/m^3$

$p_B = 180\ kPa = 180 \times 10^3\ N/m^2$

$L = 15\ m$

$m = 0.9\ P_d S = 0.9\ Ns/m^2.$

Solution:

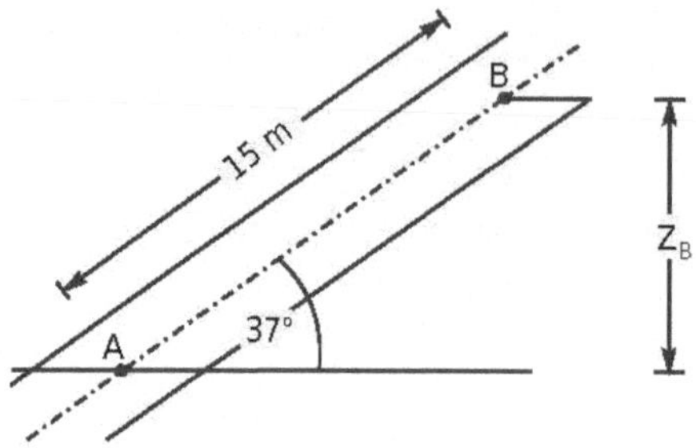

Fig. 10.4

From Fig. 10.4

$$Z_B = 15 \sin 37° = 9.027 \text{ m}$$

Total energy at
$$A = \frac{p_A}{\gamma} + \frac{V_A^2}{2g} + Z_A$$
$$= \frac{500 \times 10^3}{0.8 \times 9810} + \frac{V_A^2}{2g} + 0$$
$$= 63.71 + \frac{V_A^2}{2g}$$

Total energy at
$$B = \frac{p_B}{\gamma} + \frac{V_B^2}{2g} + Z_B$$
$$= \frac{180 \times 10^3}{0.8 \times 9810} + \frac{V_A^2}{2g} + 9.027$$
$$= 31.96 + \frac{V_A^2}{2g}$$

Now since the diameter of pipe is same

$$\frac{V_A^2}{2g} = \frac{V_B^2}{2g}$$

Therefore total energy at A > Total energy at B hence oil flows from A to B.

When oil flows from A to B, head loss h_f as given by Hagen Poiseuille equation

$$h_f = \frac{128\,\mu QL}{\rho g\, pD^4} = \text{Total energy at } A - \text{Total energy at } B$$

$$\therefore \qquad 63.71 - 31.96 = \frac{128 \times 0.9 \times Q \times 15}{0.8 \times 1000 \times 9.81 \times \pi \times (3 \times 10^{-2})^4}$$

$$\therefore \qquad Q = 3.669 \times 10^{-4} \text{ m}^3/\text{sec}$$

$$= 1.32 \text{ m}^3/\text{hr}$$

Also

$$\overline{u} = \frac{Q}{A} = \frac{3.669 \times 10^{-4}}{\dfrac{\pi \times (3 \times 10^{-2})^2}{4}}$$

$$= 0.519 \text{ m/sec.}$$

Now,

$$R = \frac{\rho \overline{u}\, D}{\mu}$$

$$= \frac{0.8 \times 1000 \times 0.519 \times 3 \times 10^{-2}}{0.9}$$

$$= 13.4 < 2000 \text{ hence laminar flow.}$$

10.4 LAMINAR FLOW THROUGH A GAP BETWEEN TWO STATIONARY PARALLEL PLATES

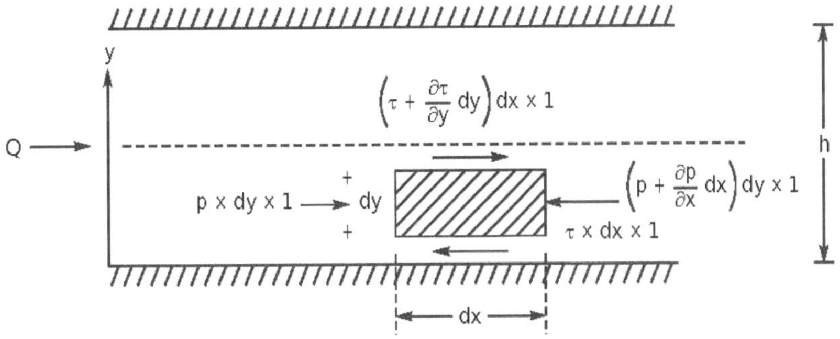

Fig. 10.5

From Fig. 10.5.

By summing the forces in x-direction

$$p \times dy \times 1 - \left(p + \frac{\partial p}{\partial x} dx\right) dy \times 1 - \tau\, dx \times 1 + \left(\tau + \frac{\partial p}{\partial x} dy\right) dx \times 1 = 0$$

$$-\frac{\partial p}{\partial x} dx\, dy + \frac{\partial \tau}{\partial x} dy\, dx = 0$$

$$\frac{\partial p}{\partial x} = \frac{\partial \tau}{\partial y} \qquad \text{...(10.14)}$$

Now $$\tau = \mu \frac{d\mu}{dy}$$ ...Newton's Law of Viscosity

Put in equation (10.14)

$$\frac{\partial p}{\partial x} = \frac{\partial}{\partial y}\left(\mu \frac{du}{dy}\right) = \mu \frac{\partial^2 u}{\partial y^2}$$

$$\therefore \quad \frac{\partial^2 u}{\partial y^2} = \frac{1}{\mu}\frac{\partial p}{\partial x}$$

Integrating w.r.t. y

$$\frac{\partial u}{\partial y} = \frac{1}{\mu}\frac{\partial p}{\partial x} y + k_1$$

Integrating again

$$u = \frac{1}{\mu}\frac{\partial p}{\partial x}\frac{y^2}{2} + k_1 y + k_2 \qquad ...(10.15)$$

where k_1 and k_2 are constant of integrations. To find k_1, k_2 putting the boundary conditions for $y = 0$, $u = 0$

$$\therefore \quad k_2 = 0$$

For $$y = h, u = 0$$

$$0 = \frac{1}{\mu}\frac{\partial p}{\partial x}\frac{h^2}{2} + k_1 h$$

$$k_1 = -\frac{1}{\mu}\frac{\partial p}{\partial x}\frac{h^2}{2h}$$

$$= -\frac{1}{2\mu}\frac{\partial p}{\partial x} h$$

Put in equation (10.15) to get

$$u = \frac{1}{2\mu}\frac{\partial p}{\partial x} y^2 + y\left(-\frac{1}{2\mu}\frac{\partial p}{\partial x} h\right)$$

$$\therefore \quad u = -\frac{1}{2\mu}\frac{\partial p}{\partial x}(hy - y^2) \qquad ...(10.16)$$

Velocity at the centre of the gap $\left(i.e.\ y = \frac{h}{2}\right)$ will be maximum and given by

$$\mu_{mix} = -\frac{1}{2\mu}\frac{\partial p}{\partial x}\left[h \times \frac{h}{2} - \left(\frac{h}{2}\right)^2\right]$$

$$= -\frac{1}{8\mu}\frac{\partial p}{\partial x}h^2 \qquad ...(10.17)$$

Now to find discharge 'Q' through the gap between the two stationary parallel plates consider a unit width of plates

$$dQ = -\frac{1}{2\mu}\frac{\partial p}{\partial x}(hy - h^2)\times dy \times 1$$

Integrating

$$Q = \int_0^h dQ$$

$$= \int_0^h -\frac{1}{2\mu}\frac{\partial p}{\partial x}(hy - h^2)\, dy$$

$$= -\frac{1}{12\mu}\frac{\partial p}{\partial x}h^3 \qquad ...(10.18)$$

$$\text{Now average velocity} = \frac{Q}{\text{Area of gap}}$$

$$= \frac{-\frac{1}{12\mu}\frac{\partial p}{\partial x}h^3}{h\times 1}$$

$$= -\frac{1}{12\mu}\frac{\partial p}{\partial x}h^2 \qquad ...(10.19)$$

From equation (10.16) and (10.19) we will get

$$\frac{u_{\max}}{\bar{u}} = \frac{3}{2} = 1.5 \qquad ...(10.20)$$

Pressure drop in terms of average velocity:

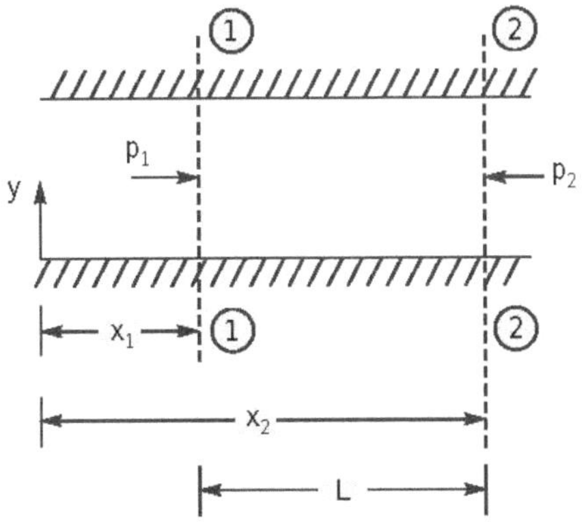

Fig. 10.6

$$\bar{u} = -\frac{1}{12\mu}\frac{\partial p}{\partial x}h^2$$

or
$$\frac{\partial p}{\partial x} = \frac{-12\mu\bar{u}}{h^2}$$

Integrating

$$\int_2^1 dp = \int_2^1 \frac{12\mu\bar{u}}{h^2}dx$$

or
$$p_1 - p_2 = \frac{-12\mu\bar{u}}{h^2}(x_2 - x_2)$$

$$= \frac{12\mu\bar{u}}{h^2}L$$

Dividing both sides by ρg

$\therefore$
$$h_f = \frac{p_1 - p_2}{\rho g} = \frac{12\mu\bar{u}L}{\rho g h^2} \quad ...(10.21)$$

Shear stress distribution:

$$\tau = \mu\frac{\partial p}{\partial y}$$

$$= \mu\frac{\partial}{\partial y}\left[-\frac{1}{2\mu}\frac{\partial p}{\partial x}(hy - h^2)\right]$$

$$= \mu\left[-\frac{1}{2\mu}\frac{\partial p}{\partial x}(hy - 2y)\right]$$

$$\tau = -\frac{1}{2\mu}\frac{\partial p}{\partial x}(hy - 2y) \quad ...(10.22)$$

Now shear stress is zero at $y = \frac{h}{2}$ *i.e.*, at centre.

Also $\tau = \tau_0 = \tau_{max}$ at $y = 0$ and $y = h$

$\therefore$
$$\tau_0 = -\frac{1}{2}\frac{\partial p}{\partial x}h \quad ...(10.23)$$

10.4.1 Solved Problems

■ **Problem 10.3**: *Two parallel plates 7.5 cm apart carrying glycerine in the space with a maximum velocity of 0.91m/sec. Find pressure difference between two section 15 m part. Find also the discharge and will shear stress.*

Take viscosity =0.8 Ns/m²

Given:

$$h = 7.5 \text{ cm} = 0.075 \text{ m}$$
$$u_{max} = 0.91 \text{ m/sec.}$$
$$L = 15 \text{ m}$$
$$\mu = 0.8 \text{ Ns/m}^2.$$

Solution:

$$u_{\max} = -\frac{1}{8\mu}\frac{\partial p}{\partial x}h^2$$

$$0.91 = -\frac{1}{8\times0.8}\times\frac{\partial p}{\partial x}\times0.075^2$$

$$\therefore \quad \frac{\partial p}{\partial x} = -1035.38$$

Now,
$$\frac{\partial p}{\partial x} = \frac{p_1 - p_2}{L}$$

$$\therefore \quad \partial p = p_2 - p_1 = -1035.38 \times 15$$
$$= -15530.7 \text{ N/m}^2$$

Using the relation

$$Q = -\frac{1}{12\mu}\frac{\partial p}{\partial x}h^3$$

$$= -\frac{1}{12\times0.8}\times(-1035.38)\times0.075^3$$

$$= 0.0455 \text{ m}^3\text{/sec.}$$

Wall shear stress
$$= \tau_0 = -\frac{1}{2}\frac{\partial p}{\partial x}h$$

$$= -\frac{1}{2}(-1035.38)\,0.075$$

$$= 38.82 \text{ N/m}^2.$$

■ **Problem 10.4:** *A oil having specific gravity 0.9 and dynamic viscosity 0.1 Ns/m² flows between parallel plates spaced 8 cm apart. Piezometers along the plate indicate that the pressure is decreasing at the rate of 90 P_a per meter length. Determine:*

(1) *Velocity of flow midway between the plates*

(2) *Average velocity of flow*

(3) *Reynolds number of flow.*

Given:

$$S = 0.9$$
$$m = 0.1 \text{ Ns/m}^2$$
$$h = 8 \text{ cm} = 0.08 \text{ m}$$

$$\frac{\partial p}{\partial x} = -\frac{90}{1} N/m^2 = -90\, N/m^2.$$

Solution:

(1) Velocity of flow midway between the plates is maximum

$$u_{max} = -\frac{1}{8\mu}\frac{\partial p}{\partial x}h^2$$

$$= -\frac{1}{8\times 0.1}\times(-90)\times 0.08^2$$

$$= 0.72 \text{ m/sec}$$

(2) Using the relation

$$\frac{u_{max}}{\bar{u}} = 1.5$$

$$\bar{u} = \frac{u_{max}}{1.5} = \frac{0.72}{1.5} = 0.48 \text{ m/sec}$$

(3)
$$R = \frac{\rho \bar{u}\, h}{\mu}$$

$$= \frac{0.9\times 1000\times 0.48\times 0.08}{0.1}$$

$= 345.6 < 2000$ hence the flow is laminar.

■ **Problem 10.5:** *There is horizontal crack 5 cm wide and 3 mm deep in a wall of thickness 15 cm. Water leaks through the crack. Find the rate of leakage of water through the creak if the difference of pressure between the two ends of the crack is 250 N/m².*

Take viscosity of water as 0.01 poise.

Given: $b = 5$ *cm* $= 0.05$ *m*

$h = 3$ *mm* $= 3\times 10^{-3}$ *m*

$L = 15$ *cm* $= 0.15$ *m*

$p_1 - p_2 = 250$ *N/m²*

$\mu = 0.01$ *poise* 0.001 *Ns/m²*.

Solution: Using the relation (10.21)

$$h_f = \frac{p_1 - p_2}{\rho g} = \frac{12\mu\bar{u}\, L}{\rho g h^2}$$

or
$$p_1 - p_2 = \frac{12\mu\bar{u}\, L}{h^2}$$

$$250 = \frac{12\times 0.001\times\bar{u}\times 0.15}{(3\times 10^{-3})^2}$$

∴ $\bar{u} = 1.25$ m/sec.

$\therefore$ The rate of leakage of water through the crack = Area × Velocity

$$= b \times h \times \bar{u} = 0.05 \times 3 \times 10^{-3} \times 1.25$$
$$= 0.1875 \times 10^{-3} \text{ m}^3/\text{sec.}$$

10.5 LAMINAR FLOW THROUGH TWO PARALLEL PLATES HAVING RELATIVE MOTION (COUNTER FLOW)

By summing the forces acting on the fluid element in x-direction

$$p \times dy \times 1 - \left(p + \frac{\partial p}{\partial x}dx\right)dy \times 1 - \tau \times dx \times 1 + \left(\tau + \frac{\partial \tau}{\partial y}dy\right)dx \times 1 = 0$$

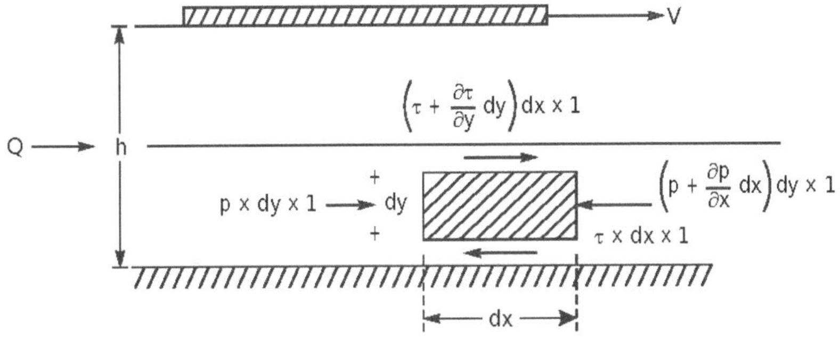

Fig. 10.6

$$-\frac{\partial p}{\partial x}dx\,dy + \frac{\partial \tau}{\partial y}dy\,dx = 0$$

$$-\frac{\partial p}{\partial x}\frac{\partial \tau}{\partial y} = 0$$

$$\frac{\partial p}{\partial x} = \frac{\partial \tau}{\partial y} \quad \text{...(10.24)}$$

Now, $\tau = \mu \dfrac{du}{dy}$ ...Newton's law of Viscosity

Put in equation (10.24)

$$\frac{\partial p}{\partial x} = \frac{\partial p}{\partial y}\left(\mu\frac{\partial u}{\partial y}\right)$$

$$= \mu\frac{\partial^2 u}{\partial y^2}$$

$$\frac{\partial^2 u}{\partial y^2} = \frac{1}{\mu}\frac{\partial p}{\partial x}$$

Integrating with respect to y

$$\frac{\partial u}{\partial y} = \frac{1}{\mu}\frac{\partial p}{\partial x} y + k_1$$

Integrating again

$$u = \frac{1}{\mu}\frac{\partial p}{\partial x}\frac{y^2}{2} + k_1 y + k_2 \quad \text{...(10.25)}$$

where k_1, k_2 are constant of integration.

To find k_1, k_2 putting the boundary conditions for $y = 0$, $u = 0$.

$$\therefore \quad k_2 = 0$$

For $y = h$, $u = V$

$$\therefore \quad V = \frac{1}{\mu}\frac{\partial p}{\partial x}\frac{y^2}{2} + k_1 h$$

$$\therefore \quad k_1 = \frac{V}{h} - \frac{1}{\mu}\frac{\partial p}{\partial x}\cdot\frac{h^2}{2h}$$

$$= \frac{V}{h} - \frac{h}{2\mu}\frac{\partial p}{\partial x}$$

Put in equation (10.25)

$$u = \frac{1}{\mu}\frac{\partial p}{\partial x}\frac{y^2}{2} + \frac{V}{h}y - \frac{hy}{2\mu}\frac{\partial p}{\partial x}$$

$$= \frac{V}{h}y - \frac{1}{2\mu}\frac{\partial p}{\partial x}(hy - y^2) \quad \text{...(10.26)}$$

Also $\quad u_{max} = V$

Now to find discharge 'Q' through the gap between the two plates consider a unit width of plates.

$$dQ = u \times dA$$

$$= \frac{V}{h}y - \frac{1}{2\mu}\frac{\partial p}{\partial x}(hy - y^2) \times dy \times 1$$

Integrating

$$Q = \int dQ = \int_0^h \left(\frac{V}{h}y - \frac{1}{2\mu}\frac{\partial p}{\partial x}(hy - y^2)\, dy\right)$$

$$= \left[\frac{V}{h}\frac{y^2}{2} - \frac{1}{2\mu}\frac{\partial p}{\partial x}\left(\frac{hy^2}{2} - \frac{y^3}{3}\right)\right]_0^h$$

$$= \frac{V}{h}\frac{h^2}{2} - \frac{1}{2\mu}\frac{\partial p}{\partial x}\left(\frac{h \times h^2}{2} - \frac{h^3}{3}\right)$$

$$= \frac{Vh}{2} - \frac{1}{2\mu}\frac{\partial p}{\partial x}\left(\frac{3h^3 - 2h^3}{6}\right)$$

$$= \frac{Vh}{2} - \frac{h^3}{12\,\mu}\frac{\partial p}{\partial x} \qquad ...(10.27)$$

Now average velocity $= \dfrac{Q}{\text{Area of gap}}$

$$\therefore \qquad \overline{u} = \frac{\dfrac{Vh}{2} - \dfrac{h^3}{12\mu}\dfrac{\partial p}{\partial x}}{h \times 1}$$

$$= \frac{V}{2} - \frac{h^2}{12\mu}\frac{\partial p}{\partial x} \qquad ...(10.28)$$

Shear stress distribution:

$$t = \mu\frac{du}{dy}$$

$$= \mu\frac{d}{dy}\left[\frac{V}{h}y - \frac{1}{2\mu}\frac{\partial p}{\partial x}(hy - y^2)\right]$$

$$= \mu\left[\frac{V}{h} - \frac{1}{2\mu}\frac{\partial p}{\partial x}(h - 2y)\right]$$

$$= \mu\frac{V}{h} - \frac{1}{2}\frac{\partial p}{\partial x}(h - 2y) \qquad ...(10.29)$$

10.5.1 Solved Problem

■ **Problem 10.6:** *Laminar flow takes place between two horizontal parallel plates 2.8 cm apart. The upper plate only moves at 0.28 m/sec. There is an adverse pressure gradient the values of pressure upstream and downstream (33 m away) in kPa are 392 and 412. Taking viscosity of fluid between the plates as 0.5 P_aS. Find rate of flow and shear stress at boundaries, also sketch variation of shear stress between the plates.*

Given:

$$h = 2.8\ cm = 0.028\ m$$

$$V = 0.28\ m/sec.$$

$$p_1 - p_2 = 392 - 412 = -20\ kPa$$

$$L = 33\ m = -20 \times 10^3\ N/m^2$$

$$\mu = 0.5\ P_a\,.\,s = Ns/m^2$$

Solution: Using the relation (10.27)

$$Q = \frac{Vh}{2} - \frac{h^3}{12\mu}\frac{\partial p}{\partial x}$$

$$= \frac{0.28 \times 0.028}{2} - \frac{0.028^3}{12 \times 0.5} \times \left(\frac{-20}{33}\right)$$

$$= 3.92 \times 10^{-3} + 2.217 \times 10^{-6}$$

$$= 3.92 \times 10^{-3} \text{ m}^3\text{/sec.}$$

Using the relation (10.29)

$$\tau = \mu\frac{V}{h} - \frac{1}{2}\frac{\partial p}{\partial x}(h - 2y)$$

For shear stress near the stationary plate *i.e.*, for $y = 0$

$$\tau = \mu\frac{V}{h} - \frac{1}{2}\frac{\partial p}{\partial x}h$$

$$= 0.5 \times \frac{0.28}{0.028} - \frac{1}{2} \times \left(\frac{-20}{33}\right)0.028$$

$$= 5 + 8.48 \times 10^{-3}$$

$$= 5.00848 \text{ N/m}^2$$

For shear stress near the moving plate *i.e.*, for $y = h$

$$\tau = \mu\frac{V}{h} - \frac{1}{2}\frac{\partial p}{\partial x}(h - 2h)$$

$$= 0.5 \times \frac{0.28}{0.028} - \frac{1}{2} \times \left(\frac{-20}{33}\right) \times (-0.028)$$

$$= 5 - 8.48 \times 10^{-3}$$

$$= -4.99 \text{ N/m}^2$$

10.6 LAMINAR FLOW THROUGH TWO PARALLEL PLATES MOVING IN OPPOSITE DIRECTION

Fig. 10.7

Velocity at a distance of y from bottom plate is given by

$$u = (V_1 + V_2)\frac{y}{h} - \frac{1}{2\mu}\frac{\partial p}{\partial x}(hy - y^2) - V_2$$

$$\text{discharge} = Q = (V_1 + V_2)\frac{y}{2} - \frac{1}{12\mu}\frac{\partial p}{\partial x}h^3$$

and $$\text{shear stress } \tau = (V_1 + V_2)\frac{\mu}{h} - \frac{\partial p}{\partial x}\left(\frac{h}{2} - y\right).$$

10.7 LAMINAR FLOW THROUGH ANNULUS

Flow through annulus is nothing but a flow through a gap between two concentric cylinders.

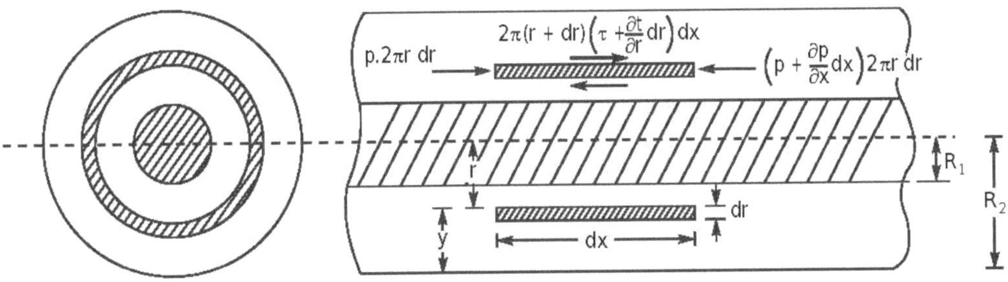

Fig. 10.8 Flow through annulus.

Let, R_1 and R_2 are the radius of inner and outer cylinders respectively. Consider a annular element of fluid of length dx and thickness dr of radius r.

Let the flow through an annulus in steady and uniform.

$$\therefore \quad p \cdot 2\pi r dr - \left(p + \frac{\partial p}{\partial x}dx\right)2\pi r dr - \tau . 2\pi r dx + 2\pi(r + dr)\left(\tau + \frac{\partial \tau}{\partial r}dr\right)dx = 0$$

$$\therefore \quad p\,.\,2\pi r\,dr - p\,.\,2\pi r dr - \frac{\partial p}{\partial x}\,dx\,.\,2\pi r dr - \tau\,.\,2\pi r\,dx$$

$$+ 2\pi r\,.\tau dx + 2\pi r\frac{\partial \tau}{\partial r}\,dr\,dx + 2\pi dr\,\tau\,dx + 2\pi\,dr\frac{\partial \tau}{\partial r}\,.\,dr\,dx = 0$$

$$-\frac{\partial p}{\partial x}dx\,2\pi r\,dr + 2\pi r\frac{\partial \tau}{\partial r}dr\,dx + 2\pi\,dr\,\tau\,dx + 2\pi\,dr\frac{\partial r}{\partial r}.\,dr\,dx$$

dividing each term by $2\pi r\,dr\,dx$ (*i.e.*, volume of the fluid element)

$$-\frac{\partial p}{\partial x} + \frac{\partial \tau}{\partial r} + \frac{\tau}{r} + \frac{dr}{r}\cdot\frac{\partial \tau}{\partial r} = 0$$

$\because \quad \dfrac{\partial r}{r}\cdot\dfrac{\partial \tau}{\partial r}$ is very small and hence neglecting this term

$$-\frac{\partial p}{2x} + \frac{\partial \tau}{\partial r} + \frac{\tau}{r} = 0 \qquad ...(10.30)$$

$$\therefore \qquad -\frac{\partial p}{2x} + \frac{1}{r}\frac{\partial(\tau r)}{\partial r} = 0$$

$$\therefore \qquad -\frac{\partial p}{2x} r + \frac{\partial(\tau r)}{\partial r} = 0$$

Integrating

$$-\int r\,dr + \int \frac{\partial}{\partial r}(\tau r)\,dr = 0$$

$$\frac{r^2}{2}\frac{\partial p}{\partial x} + \tau \cdot r = k_1 \qquad \text{...(10.31)}$$

Now, using Newton's Law of Viscosity

$$\tau = \mu \frac{du}{dy} \qquad \text{...(10.32)}$$

From Fig. 10.8

$$r + y = R$$

differentiating

$$dy = -dr \qquad \text{...(10.33)}$$

Putting in equation (10.32)

$$t = -\mu \frac{du}{dr}$$

$\therefore$ Equation (10.31) can be written as

$$-\frac{r^2}{2}\frac{\partial p}{\partial x} - \mu \frac{du}{dr} r = k_1$$

$$\therefore \qquad \frac{r}{2}\frac{\partial p}{\partial x} + \mu \frac{du}{dr} = -\frac{k_1}{r}$$

$$\frac{r}{2}\frac{\partial p}{\partial x} + \mu \frac{du}{dr} = -\frac{k_1}{r}$$

Integrating

$$\frac{\partial p}{\partial x}\frac{r^2}{4} - \mu \cdot u = -k_1 \log r + k_2 \qquad \text{...(10.34)}$$

To find the values of constant of integration k_1 and k_2 use the boundary conditions
(1) at $r = R_1$, $u = 0$ and
(2) at $r = R_2$, $u = 0$.
Put these values in equation (10.34) and simplify, we get

$$u = \frac{1}{4\mu}\frac{\partial p}{\partial x}\left[R_2^2 - r^2 + \frac{R_2^2 - R_1^2}{\log \frac{R_1}{R_2}} \log \frac{R_2}{r}\right] \qquad \text{...(10.35)}$$

The discharge through the hatched strip as shown in Fig. 10.8 is given as

$$dQ = 2\pi r\, dr \,.\, u$$

$\therefore$ Integrating
$$Q = \int_0^Q dQ = \int_{R_1}^{R_2} 2\pi r\, dr \,.\, \frac{1}{4\mu}\frac{\partial p}{\partial x}\left[R_2^2 - r^2 + \frac{R_2^2 - R_1^2}{\log \frac{R_1}{R_2}} \log \frac{R_2}{r}\right]$$

Solving
$$Q = \frac{\pi}{8\mu}\frac{\partial p}{\partial x}\left[R_2^4 - R_1^4 - \frac{\left(R_2^2 - R_1^2\right)^2}{\log \frac{R_2}{R_1}}\right] \quad \text{...(10.36)}$$

and the shear distribution

$$\tau = -\mu \frac{du}{dr}$$

$$= -\mu \frac{du}{dr}\left[\frac{1}{4\mu}\frac{\partial p}{\partial x}\left[R_2^2 - r^2 + \frac{R_2^2 - R_1^2}{\log \frac{R_1}{R_2}} \log \frac{R_2}{r}\right]\right]$$

Solving,
$$\tau = \frac{1}{4}\left(-\frac{\partial p}{\partial x}\right)\left[2r + \frac{1}{r}\frac{R_2^2 - R_1^2}{r \log \frac{R_1}{R_2}}\right] \quad \text{...(10.37)}$$

10.8 MOMENTUM CORRECTION FACTOR

It is defined as the ratio of momentum per second based on actual velocity to the momentum per second based on average velocity. Generally momentum correction factor is denoted by '**β**'.

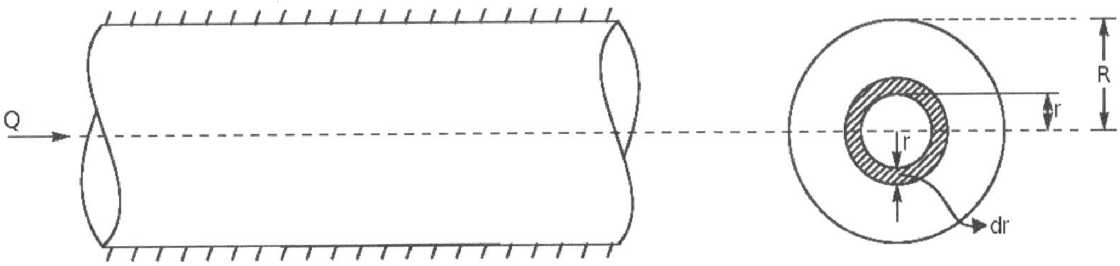

Fig. 10.9

The velocity at a distance of 'r' from the boundary of pipe for laminar flow is given by equation (10.6).

$$u = \frac{1}{4\mu}\left(-\frac{\partial p}{\partial x}\right)(R^2 - r^2)$$

Refer Fig. 10.9.

Discharge through the hatched area of ring of thickness dr is

$$dQ = u \times 2\pi r\, dr$$

∴ Momentum of the fluid passing through the hatched ring $= dm = \rho \times dQ \times u$

$$= 2\pi\rho\, u^2 r\, dr$$

Total actual momentum of the fluid

$$\int dm = \int_0^R 2\pi\rho\, u^2 r\, dr$$

$$M_{(\text{actual})} = 2\pi\rho \int_0^R \left[\frac{1}{4\mu}\left(-\frac{\partial p}{\partial x}\right)(R^2 - r^2)\right]^2 r\, dr$$

Solving

$$= \frac{\pi\rho}{48\mu^2}\left(-\frac{\partial p}{\partial x}\right)^2 R^6 \quad ...(10.38)$$

Momentum of the fluid per second based on average velocity

$$M_{(\text{average})} = \rho A \bar{u}^2$$

$$= \rho\pi R^2 \left[\frac{1}{8M}\left(-\frac{\partial p}{\partial x}\right) R^2\right]^2$$

Solving

$$= \frac{\rho\pi\left(-\frac{\partial p}{\partial x}\right)^2 R^6}{64\,\mu^2} \quad ...(10.39)$$

Therefore by definition

$$\beta = \frac{\frac{\pi\rho}{48\,\mu^2}\left(-\frac{\partial p}{\partial x}\right)^2 R^6}{\frac{\rho\pi}{64\mu^2}\left(-\frac{\partial p}{\partial x}\right)^2 R^6}$$

$$= \frac{4}{3} \quad ...(10.40)$$

10.9 KINETIC ENERGY CORRECTION FACTOR

It is defined as the ratio of kinetic energy per second based on actual velocity to the kinetic energy per second based on average velocity. Generally energy correction factor is denoted by 'α'.

Now kinetic energy of the fluid passing through the hatched ring.

$$dE = \frac{1}{2} \times \text{mass} \times \text{velocity}^2$$

$$= \frac{1}{2}\rho\, dQ\, u^2$$

$$= \frac{1}{2}\times\rho\times(u\times 2\pi r\, dr)\, u^2$$

$$= \pi\rho\, r\, u^3\, dr$$

Total kinetic energy of flow per second

$$= \int dE = \int_0^R \pi\rho r\, u^3\, dr$$

$$= \int_0^R \pi\rho r\left[\frac{1}{4\mu}\left(-\frac{\partial p}{\partial x}\right)(R^2 - r^2)\right]^3 dr$$

Solving

$$= \frac{\pi\rho}{64\mu^3}\left(-\frac{\partial p}{\partial x}\right)^3 \frac{R^8}{8} \quad \text{...(10.41)}$$

Kinetic energy of the flow based on average velocity

$$= \frac{1}{2}\times\text{Mass}\times\text{Velocity}^2_{(\text{average})}$$

$$= \frac{1}{2}\times\rho A\bar{u}\times\bar{u}^2 = \frac{1}{2}\rho A\bar{u}^3$$

$$= \frac{1}{2}\times\rho\times\pi R^2\times\left[\frac{1}{8m}\left(-\frac{\partial p}{\partial x}R^2\right)\right]^3$$

$$= \frac{\rho\pi}{128\times 8\mu^3}\left(-\frac{\partial p}{\partial x}\right)^3 R^8$$

Therefore by definition

$$a = \frac{\dfrac{\pi\rho}{64\mu^3}\left(-\dfrac{\partial p}{\partial x}\right)^3 \dfrac{R^8}{8}}{\dfrac{\rho\pi}{128\times 8\mu^3}\left(-\dfrac{\partial p}{\partial x}\right)^3 R^8}$$

$$= 2.0 \quad \text{...(10.42)}$$

10.10 DASHPOT MECHANISM

Refer Fig. 10.10.

Pressure difference across the two ends of the piston = dp

$$= \frac{W}{\dfrac{\pi D^2}{4}} \quad \text{...(10.43)}$$

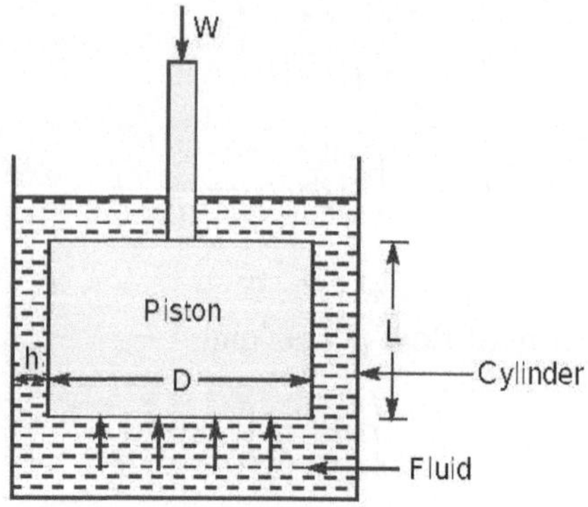

Fig. 10.10 Dashpot.

The flow through the gap between the cylinder and piston is similar as that of flow between parallel plates. Therefore using the equation (10.21).

$$\frac{p_1 - p_2}{\rho g} = \frac{12\mu \bar{u}\, L}{\rho g\, h^2}$$

or

$$dp = p_1 - p_2 = \frac{12\mu \bar{u}\, L}{h^2} \qquad \text{...(10.44)}$$

Equating equation (10.43) and (10.44)

$$\frac{12\mu \bar{u}\, L}{h^2} = \frac{W}{\frac{\pi D^2}{4}}$$

$$\therefore \qquad \bar{u} = \frac{W h^2}{3\pi \mu L\, D^2} \qquad \text{...(10.45)}$$

Rate of flow in the dashpot $= V \times \frac{\pi D^2}{4}$ ...(10.46)

Rate of flow through the gap $= \bar{u} \times \pi D \times h$ ...(10.47)

Equating equations (10.46) and (10.47)

$$\bar{u} \times \pi D \times h = V \times \frac{\pi D^2}{4}$$

$$\bar{u} = \frac{VD}{4h} \qquad \text{...(10.48)}$$

Equating equations (10.45) and (10.48)

$$\frac{VD}{4h} = \frac{W h^2}{3\pi \mu L D^2}$$

$$\therefore \qquad \mu = \frac{4WD^3}{3\pi D^3 VL} \qquad ...(10.49)$$

and piston velocity

$$= V = \frac{4Wh^3}{3\pi D^3 \mu L} \qquad ...(10.50)$$

10.10.1 Solved Problem

■ **Problem 10.7:** *A piston of 10 cm diameter is concentrically placed in a cylinder of inner diameter 10.2 cm. The piston length is 20 cm and if a pressure difference of 1 kPa exists across the two faces of the piston estimate rate of flow through the clearance, if the viscosity of liquid is 0.05 Ns/m² and specific gravity = 0.8.*

Given: $D = 10\ cm = 0.1\ m$

$$h = \frac{10.2 - 10}{2} = 0.1\ cm = 0.1 \times 10^{-2}\ m$$

$$L = 20\ cm = 0.2\ m$$

$$dp = 12\ kPa = 1 \times 10^3\ N/m^2$$

$$m = 0.05\ Ns/m^2$$

$$s = 0.8.$$

Solution: Using the relation (10.43)

$$dp = \frac{W}{\left(\frac{\pi D^2}{4}\right)}$$

$$\therefore \qquad W = dp \times \frac{\pi D^2}{4} = \frac{1 \times 10^3 \times \pi \times 0.12}{4} = 94.24\ \text{N}$$

Using the relation

$$V = \frac{4Wh^3}{3\pi D^3 \mu L}$$

$$= \frac{4 \times 94.24 \times (0.1 \times 10^{-2})^3}{3\pi \times 0.1^3 \times 0.05 \times 0.2}$$

$$= 0.003999\ \text{m/sec.}$$

∴ Rate of flow through the clearance = Rate of flow in a dash-pot

$$= \frac{\pi D^2}{4} \times V \qquad \text{using (10.38)}$$

$$= \frac{\pi \times 0.1^2}{4} \times 0.003999$$

$$= 3.14 \times 10^{-5}\ \text{m}^3/\text{sec.}$$

Exercises

1. An oil of specific gravity 0.9 and viscosity 0.12 Ns/m^2 flow through a pipe of 2.5 cm diameter with a rate of 0.00932 lit/sec. Find a pressure gradient.

   (**Ans.** $\frac{\partial p}{\partial x}$ = 116.65 N/m^2, per m)

2. An oil of specific gravity 0.9 and viscosity 0.12 Ns/m^2 flows through a pipe of 2.5 cm diameter with a pressure drop of 0.35 N/cm^2 in a length of 30 m. Determine the discharge if the power required to maintain the flow is 0.0326 Nm/sec.

   (**Ans.** 0.5592 lit/min)

3. Find the pressure difference between the two points on the pipe of 3 cm diameter and inclined at 37° to the horizontal. Along the pipe the distance between these is 15 m. An oil of specific gravity 0.8 and viscosity 0.9 P_dS moves in upward direction.

   (**Ans.** 320 kPa)

4. The pressure difference between two section 15 apart is 15530.7 N/m^2 for a two parallel plates 7.5 cm apart carrying glycerine in the space at a rate of 0.0455 m^3/sec. Find maximum velocity and wall shear stress.

   (**Ans.** U_{max} = 0.91m/sec, τ_0 = 38.82 N/m^2)

5. A oil having specific gravity 0.8 and dynamic viscosity 0.15 Ns/m^2 flows between stationary parallel plates spaced 10 cm apart. Pressure measuring devices along the plate indicate that the pressure is decreasing at the rate of 80 P_a per meter length. Determine:

   (*i*) Maximum velocity of flow.

   (*ii*) Average velocity of flow.

   (*iii*) Reynolds number. (**Ans.** U_{max} = 0.67 m/sec, $\bar{u}$ = 0.44 m/sec, R = 234.67)

6. There is a horizontal crack 5 cm wide and 3 mm deep in a wall of thickness 15 cm. Water leaks through the crack. Find the difference of pressure between the two ends of the crack if the rate of leakage of water through the crack is 0.1875 lit/sec.

   (**Ans.** $p_1 - p_1$ = 250 N/m^2)

7. Laminar flow takes place between two horizontal plates 2.8 cm apart. The upper plate only moves at 0.28 m/sec. If the rate of flow is 3.92 lit/sec of fluid having viscosity 0.5 P_dS. Find the pressure gradient and boundary shear stress.

   (**Ans.** $\frac{\partial p}{\partial x}$ = 0.606 kN/m^2 per m, τ_0 = 5.00848 N/m^2 and – 4.99 N/m^2)

8. A piston of 10 cm diameter is concentrically placed in a cylinder of inner diameter 10.2 cm. The piston length is 20 cm and its weight is 94.24 N. Find the weight of the piston and the viscosity of liquid the rate of flow through the clearance is 3.14 × 10^{-2} lit/sec. Take specify gravity of liquid as 0.8.

   (**Ans.** W = 94.24 N, m = 0.05 Ns/m^2)

❑❑❑

11

Turbulent Flow in Circular Pipes

11.1 GENERAL

Just as laminar flow is characterised by its streamlined motion, turbulent flow has also a characteristic feature of random and zigzag motion and continuous mixing of fluid particles. The limit upto which flow is laminar is decided by Reynolds number's critical value of 2000, *i.e.* at $R \leq 2000$, flow us laminar, but between 2000 to 4000 it is in transition state and generally $R \geq 4000$, the flow is turbulent. As per Reynolds experimental findings, loss of head in turbulent flow is proportional to square of average velocity of flow in a pipe line, *i.e.* $h_f \propto V^2$, more generally $h_f \propto V_n$, where n = 1.65 to 2.0 as per experimental observations for turbulent flow in pipe line.

11.1.1 Darcy-Weisbach Equation for Loss of Head in Pipe

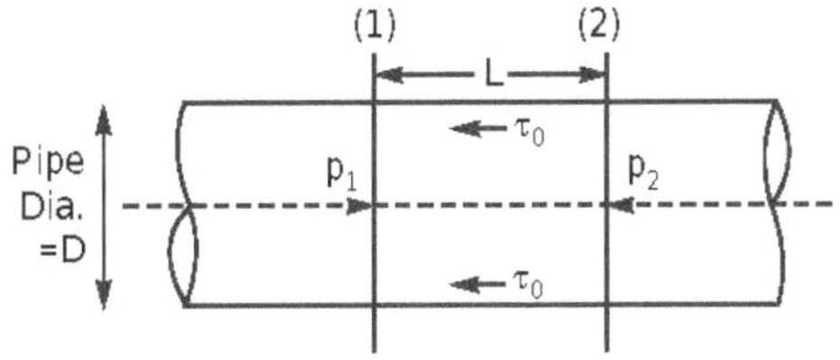

Fig. 11.1

Flow through pipe is characterized as pressure flow as the flow is taking place at the expense of pressure energy and is opposed by frictional resistance at the pipe wall. Thus if p_1 and p_2 and intensities of pressures at section (1) and (2) in Fig. 11.1, L distance apart, then

$$(p_1 - p_2)A = \tau_0 \, \pi DL$$

Putting $(p_1 - p_2) = \gamma h_f,$

we get
$$\gamma h_f = \tau_0 \left(\frac{\pi D}{A}\right) L$$

here πD = wetted perimeter P

and A = cross-sectional area of pipe.

Now, $\tau_0 = \left(\frac{\rho f}{8}\right) V^2$ as per Reynold's experimental findings for turbulent flow in pipe line. Here f is friction factor

$$\therefore \quad \gamma h_f = \left(\frac{\rho f}{8}\right) V^2 \left(\frac{\pi D}{A}\right) L$$

Putting $\gamma = \rho g$ and transferring it to RHS,

$$\therefore \quad h_f = \frac{\rho f}{\rho g 8} V^2 \frac{\pi D L}{\frac{\pi}{4} D^2}$$

$$= \frac{f L V^2}{D(2g)'} \text{ here } f = \text{friction factor}$$

If f is expressed as friction coefficient f'

then
$$f = 4f'$$

$$\therefore \quad h_f = \frac{4 f' L V^2}{D(2g)}$$

Thus Darcy – Weisbach equation can be written as

$$h_f = \frac{f L V^4}{D(2g)} \text{ where } f = \text{friction factor}$$

and also
$$h_f = \frac{(4f') L V^2}{D(2g)} \text{ where } f' = \frac{f}{4}.$$

11.2 VALUES OF FRICTION FACTOR FOR DIFFERENT RANGES OF R

(*a*) For laminar flow, friction factor $f = \frac{64}{R}$ for $R \leq 2000$. Substituting this value in Darcy–Weisbach equation, we get

$$\therefore \quad h_f = \frac{\left(\frac{64}{R}\right) L V^2}{D(2g)} = \frac{64 L V^2 \mu}{\rho V D (D(2g))}$$

$$= \frac{32\mu LV}{(\rho g)D^2} = \frac{32\mu LV}{\gamma D^2} = h_f \text{ for laminar flow as per Hegen–William equation.}$$

(*b*) For turbulent flow, as per Blasius findings,

$$f = \frac{0.316}{(R)^{1/4}} = \text{friction factor, valid for values of } R \text{ between } 10^4 \text{ and } 10^5.$$

(*c*) For all values of R for turbulent flow in **smooth** pipes.

[Pipe is **smooth** if $\frac{\varepsilon}{\delta'} \leq 0.25$

here ε = av. ht. of roughness

δ' = thickness of laminar sublayer

$= \frac{11.6\upsilon}{u^*}$

v = kinematic viscosity and

u^* = shear velocity $= \sqrt{\frac{\tau_0}{\rho}}$]

$$\frac{1}{\sqrt{f}} = 2\log(R\sqrt{f}) - 0.8$$

$$= 1.8\log(R) - 1.518$$

or

$$f = 0.0032 + \frac{0.221}{(R)^{0.237}}$$

(*d*) For all values of R for turbulent flow in **rough** pipes:

Here "rough pipe" means $\frac{e}{\delta'} \geq 6.0$ and friction factor f is given by

$$\frac{1}{\sqrt{f}} = 2\log\left(\frac{R}{e}\right) + 1.74.$$

(*e*) Colebrook equation for friction factor f for smooth, transition and rough pipes:

$$\frac{1}{\sqrt{f}} = 1.14 - 2\log\left[\frac{e}{D} + \frac{9.35}{R\sqrt{f}}\right]$$

Moody diagram for commercial pipe is a graphical plot of Cole brook equation as shown in Fig. 11.2.

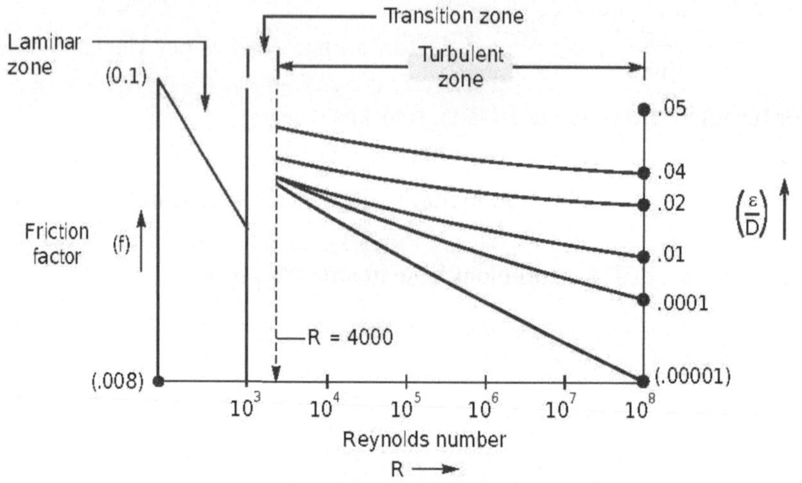

Fig. 11.2 Moody diagram (Not to scale)

11.3 CHARACTERISTICS OF TURBULENT FLOW

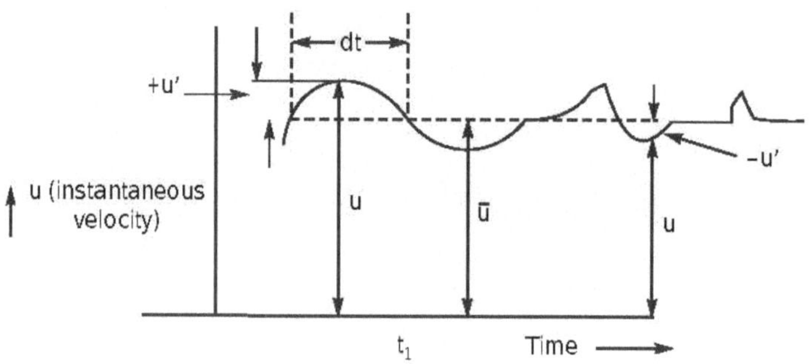

Fig. 11.3

Instantaneous velocity in x-direction, $u = \bar{u} \pm u'$

where $\bar{u} = \dfrac{1}{T}\int_0^T u\,dt$, *i.e.* it is time average of ($u\,dt$) and u' = fluctuating component in x-direction.

Similarly in y-direction, we have

$$v = \bar{v} + v'$$

where v' = fluctuating component in y-direction.

Time average of fluctuating component is always zero.

RMS, value (root mean square value) of fluctuation component $\sqrt{\overline{u'^2}}$ is

(a) known as turbulent intensity and

(b) expressed non dimensionally as $\dfrac{\sqrt{\overline{u'^2}}}{V_0}$, where V_0 is the centre line value of velocity.

Thus when we say intensity of turbulence is 10%, then $\sqrt{\overline{u'^2}} = 0.1\ (V_0)$.

Average eddy size is defined as scale of turbulence and is given by $(u\ dt)$. When $\overline{u'^2} = \overline{v'^2} = \overline{w'^2}$, *i.e.* mean of squares is fluctuating components in *x*, *y* and *z* direction are equal, the turbulence is known as **isotropic turbulence**. If these components are unequal, it is **anisotropic turbulence**.

Measurement of turbulent components u', v' etc. are possible by making use of Hot Wire Anemometer of constant temperature type or by making use of Laser Doppler techniques of flow visualizations. These are beyond the scope of the present text and hence are not described in detail here.

Shear stress in turbulent flow: As turbulent flow is characterised by its random motion and constant exchange of momentum between fluid particles, shear stresses developed are naturally quite higher than that developed in laminar flow. Reynold in 1886 gave an expression for turbulent shear stress as

$$\tau_{turb.} = \rho\overline{u'v'}.$$

As per this expression, τ_{turb} can be calculated only if u', v' are known. But measurements of u', v' are very difficult and hence Prondtl in 1925 presented his mixing length theory.

11.4 PRANDTL'S MIXING LENGTH THEORY

According to Prandtl's mixing length theory, fluid particles moving from one layer to another layer, will continue to possess its original momentum till they collide with fluid particles of another layer and assume the momentum of the fluid particles of that layer. The normal distance between these two adjacent layers of fluid particles was defined by Prandtl as mixing length l which he assumed analogous to mean free path of molecular motion of gaseous particles as per Kinetic theory of gases. Prandtl also assumed.

$$u' = l\frac{du}{dy} \text{ and } v' = l\frac{du}{dy}$$

where l = mixing length.

Substituting these in Reynolds shear stress equation,

$$\tau_{turb} = \rho\overline{u'v'} = \rho l^2\left(\frac{du}{dy}\right)^2$$

The total shear stress will then be a sum of shear stress due to viscous conditions and turbulent conditions, thus

$$\tau_{total} = \tau_{viscous} + \tau_{turb}$$

$$= \mu\frac{du}{dy} + \rho l^2\left(\frac{du}{dy}\right)^2$$

Here μ is dynamic viscosity.

Above, equation can also be written in form:

$$\tau_{total} = \mu\frac{du}{dy} + \eta\left(\frac{du}{dy}\right)$$

where η = eddy viscosity as per Boussinesq's model of turbulence and is given by

$$\eta = \rho l\left(\frac{du}{dy}\right).$$

For fully developed turbulent flow in pipe, viscous shear stress near the boundary will be negligible compared to turbulent shear and hence for turbulent flow in pipes,

$$\text{shear stress } \tau = \rho l^2\left(\frac{du}{dy}\right)^2.$$

Prandtl assumed that mixing length varies linearly as the normal distance y from the pipe wall, and accordingly,

$$l = ky$$

where k = Karman's universal constant

= 0.4 for pipe flow

$$\therefore \quad \tau = \pi k^2 y^2\left(\frac{du}{dy}\right)^2$$

$$\therefore \quad \frac{du}{dy} = \frac{1}{ky}\sqrt{\frac{\tau}{\rho}}$$

For small values or y, Prandtl assumed $\tau = \tau_0$, where τ_0 is shear stress at the boundary.

$$\therefore \quad \frac{du}{dy} = \frac{1}{ky}\sqrt{\frac{\tau_0}{\rho}} = \frac{u^*}{ky} \qquad \text{...(11.1)}$$

as $\sqrt{\frac{\tau_0}{\rho}}$ = shear velocity

$= u^*$

Integrating above equation (11.1), we get

$$u = \frac{u^*}{k}\ln(y) + C \qquad \text{...(11.2)}$$

here (ln) means natural log *i.e.* log to the base (e).

and C = integrating constant.

To find value C, we use the boundary condition that at centre line of pipe, velocity is maximum, u_m.

i.e. at $y = R, u = u_m$.

$$\therefore \quad C = u_m - \frac{u^*}{k}\ln(R) \qquad \text{...(11.3)}$$

Putting this value in equation (11.2), we get

$$u = \frac{u^*}{k}\ln(y) + u_m - (u^*/k)\ln(R)$$

$$\therefore \quad \frac{u-u_m}{u^*} = \frac{1}{k}\ln\left(\frac{y}{R}\right) \qquad ...(11.4)$$

$$= 2.5\ln\left(\frac{y}{R}\right) \text{ as } k = 0.4 \text{ for pipe flow.}$$

Equation (11.4) is Prandtl's universal velocity distribution equation for turbulent flow in pipe, and replacing natural log terms to logarithm to base 10, we get

$$\frac{u-u_m}{u^*} = 5.75\log\left(\frac{y}{R}\right) \qquad ...(11.5)$$

This can also be written in the form

$$\frac{u_m-u}{u^*} = 5.75\log\left(\frac{R}{y}\right) \qquad ...(11.6)$$

here u is value of velocity at y measured from pipe wall and u_m is maximum value of velocity at centre line of the pipe, *i.e.* at $y = R$.

11.5 VELOCITY DISTRIBUTION FOR SMOOTH AND ROUGH PIPE

This is given by Eqn. (11.2) as

$$u = \frac{u^*}{5}\ln(y) + C$$

If a given boundary is studied under a microscope, it will be seen that it consists of uneven corrugation as seen in Fig. 11.4.

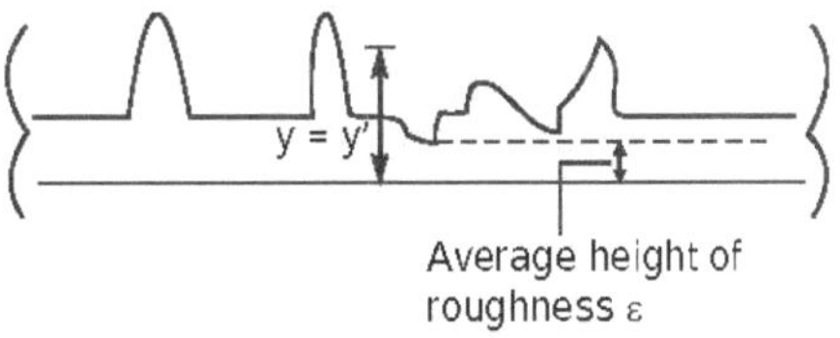

Fig. 11.4

and therefore, point at which velocity is zero, can not be well defined.

It is therefore taken that at $y = y'$, u may be zero.

As per Nikuradse Experiments for smooth pipe,

$$y' = \frac{\delta'}{107} \text{ and } \delta' = \text{laminar sublayer thickness} = \frac{11.6\,\upsilon}{u^*}$$

$$\therefore \quad y' = \frac{11.6\upsilon}{107\,u^*} \text{ for smooth pipe.}$$

∴ Integrating constant C of Eqn. (11.2) can be determined by the boundary condition that if $y = y'$, $u = 0$.

$$\therefore \quad 0 = \frac{u}{k}\ln(y') + C$$

$$\therefore \quad C = -\frac{u^*}{k}\ln(y')$$

$$\therefore \quad \frac{u}{u^*} = 2.5\ln\left(\frac{y}{y'}\right) = 5.75\log\left(\frac{y}{y'}\right)$$

and for smooth pipe,

$$y' = \frac{11.6\upsilon}{107u^*}$$

$$\therefore \quad \frac{u}{u^*} = 5.75\log\left(\frac{y(107u^*)}{11.6\upsilon}\right)$$

$$= 5.75\log\left(\frac{u^* y}{\upsilon}\right) + 5.5 \qquad \text{...(11.7)}$$

Similarly for rough pipe,

$$y' = \frac{\varepsilon}{30}$$

$$\therefore \quad \frac{u}{u^*} = 5.75\log\left(\frac{y30}{\varepsilon}\right)$$

$$\therefore \quad \frac{u}{u^*} = 5.75\log\left(\frac{y}{\varepsilon}\right) + 8.5 \text{ for rough pipe} \qquad \text{...(11.8)}$$

In terms of average velocity $V_0 = \frac{Q}{A}$, eqn. (7) for smooth pipe can be written as

$$\frac{V_0}{u^*} = 5.75\log\left(\frac{Ru^*}{\gamma}\right) + 1.75 \qquad \text{...(11.9)}$$

and for rough pipe it is

$$\frac{V_0}{u^*} = 5.75\log\left(\frac{R}{\varepsilon}\right) + 4.75 \qquad \text{...(11.10)}$$

Difference of point velocity u and average velocity V_0 for smooth and rough pipe is given by,

$$\frac{u - V_0}{u^*} = 5.75\log\left(\frac{y}{R}\right) + 3.75 \qquad \text{...(11.11)}$$

and at centre line, $y = R$, and $\log(1) = 0$,

$$\therefore \quad \frac{u_m - V_0}{u^*} = 3.75 \qquad \text{...(11.12)}$$

From above equations governing velocity distribution in a pipe line for turbulent flow, it will be seen that velocity distribution curve for laminar flow in pipe line is parabolic whereas that for turbulent flow in pipe line is logarithmic. This is shown in Fig. 11.5 (*a*).

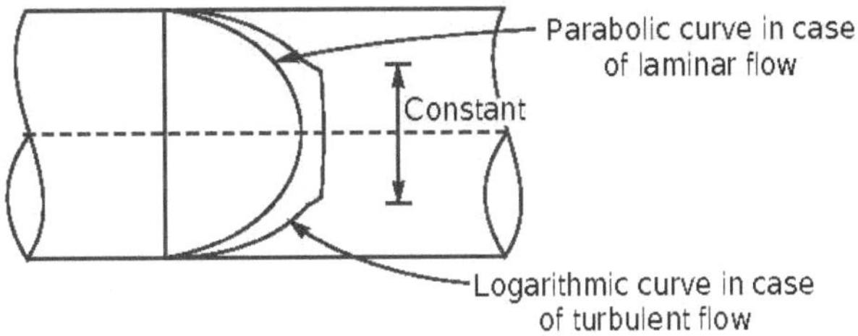

Fig. 11.5 (*a*) Velocity distribution curve for laminar and turbulent flow in pipes.

It can be seen from the curve, that velocity is almost a constant over central zone of flow and tends to have zero value at the pipe wall.

For fully developed flow in a pipe line, boundary layer thickness δ is a maximum at the centre and is equal to radius of the pipe. Shear stress is a maximum at the pipe wall and becomes zero at the centre and is given by the equation

$$\tau = \tau_0\left(1-\frac{y}{R}\right) \qquad ...(11.13)$$

here

$$\tau_0 = \rho u^{*2} = \rho V_0^2\left(\frac{f}{8}\right) \qquad ...(11.14)$$

Shear stress variation is shown in Fig. 11.5 (*b*).

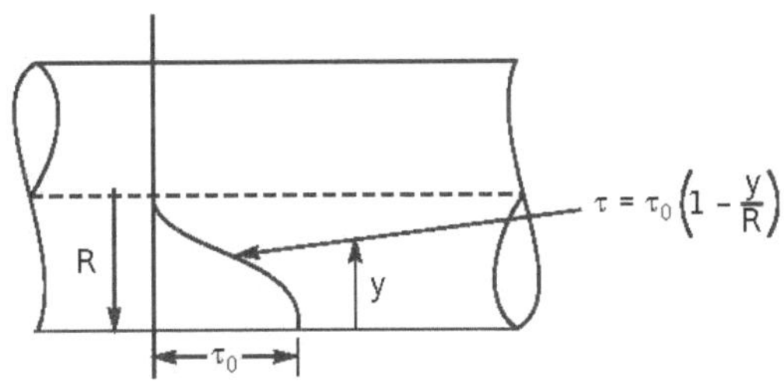

Fig. 11.5 (*b*)

11.6 KARMAN'S SIMILARITY HYPOTHESIS

Theodore Von-Karman developed important relationship for mixing length l in terms of derivation of mean velocity and based his hypothesis or similarity considerations. According to him, l is a function of distribution of $\bar{u}$ and distance y, normal to the pipe wall.

$\therefore$ As per Karman,

$$l = K\left[\frac{d\bar{u}/dy}{d^2\bar{u}/dy^2}\right]$$

and $$\tau_{turb} = \rho l^2 \left[\frac{d\bar{u}}{dy}\right]^2$$

and he assumed $K = 0.4$ pipe flow.

11.7 SOLVED PROBLEMS

■ **Problem 11.1:** *(a) Obtain velocity distribution for smooth and rough pipe in terms of average velocity for turbulent flow in pipe line.*

(b) A rough pipe of diameter 150 mm has discharge of 60 LPS. If average height of roughness $\varepsilon = 0.15$ mm, find the friction factor, μ_{max}, τ_0 and u^*.

Given: $\upsilon = 1 \times 10^{-6}\ m^2/s$ *and* $\rho = 1000\ kg/m^3$.

Solution: Reynold number

$$R = \frac{\rho V_0 D}{\mu} = \frac{V_0 D}{\upsilon}$$

$$V_0 = \frac{Q}{A} = \frac{60/1000}{\frac{\pi}{4}(0.15)^2} = 3.39 \text{ m/s}$$

$$\therefore \quad R = \frac{3.39\,(0.15)}{1\times10^{-6}} = 0.5\times10^6 > 4000$$

∴ Turbulent flow

Given pipe is rough

$$\therefore \quad \frac{u}{u^*} = 5.75\log\left(\frac{y}{\varepsilon}\right) + 8.5$$

and at $y = \text{radius} = R,\ u = u_m$

$$\therefore \quad \frac{u_m}{u^*} = 5.75\log\left(\frac{R}{\varepsilon}\right) + 8.5$$

$$= 5.75\log\left(\frac{0.15/2}{0.15\times10^{-3}}\right) + 8.5$$

$$= 15.5 + 8.5$$

$$= 24$$

Also, $$\frac{u_m - V_0}{u^*} = 5.75\log\left(\frac{R}{R}\right) + 3.75 (\text{at } y = R)$$

$$= 0 + 3.75$$

$$= 3.75$$

Putting $u_m = 24u^*$, we get

$$\frac{24u^* - V_0}{u^*} = 3.75$$

$\therefore \quad 24.u^* - 3.39 = 3.75u^*$

$\therefore \quad u^* = 0.167$ m/s ...(Ans.)

Now
$$\sqrt{\frac{\tau_0}{\rho}} = u^*$$

$$\therefore \quad \tau_0 = u^{2*}\rho = (0.167)^2\,(1000)$$
$$= 27.88 \text{ N/m}^2 \qquad \text{...(Ans.)}$$
$$u_m = 24\,u^* = 24\,(0.167)$$
$$= 4 \text{ m/s} \qquad \text{...(Ans.)}$$

For rough pipe,

$$\frac{1}{\sqrt{f}} = 2\log\left(\frac{r}{\varepsilon}\right) + 1.74$$
$$= 2\log\left(\frac{0.15/2}{0.15\times10^{-3}}\right) + 1.74$$
$$= 5.39 + 1.74$$
$$= 7.13$$
$$f = 0.0196. \qquad \text{...(Ans.)}$$

■ **Problem 11.2:** *(a) Crude oil of sp. gr. 0.9 and* $\upsilon = 0.15$ *cm²/s is flowing through a 25 cm dia. smooth pipe at the rate of 105 LPS. Calculate velocity at a distance of 6 cm from pipe axis, max. velocity and velocity at end of laminar sublayer.*

Solution:

$$V_0 = \frac{Q}{A} = \frac{105/1000}{\frac{\pi}{4}(0.25)^2} = 2.14 \text{ m/s}$$

Reynolds
$$N_0, R = \frac{V_0 D}{\upsilon} = \frac{2.14(0.25)}{0.15\times10^{-4}} = 3.56\times10^4 > 4000$$

$\therefore$ Flow is turbulent.

Given pipe is smooth.

$$\therefore \quad \frac{u}{u^*} = 5.75\log\left(\frac{u^* y}{\upsilon}\right) + 5.5$$

$$f = 0.0032 + \frac{0.221}{(R)^{0.237}}$$
$$= 0.0032 + \frac{0.221}{(3.56\times10^4)^{0.237}}$$
$$= 0.0032 + \frac{0.221}{12}$$
$$= 0.0032 + 0.018 = 0.0216$$

$$u^{*2} = V_0^2\left(\frac{f}{8}\right)$$

$$= (2.14)^2\left(\frac{0.0216}{8}\right)$$

$$= 4.57 \times 2.7 \times 10^{-3}$$

$$= 12.36 \times 10^{-3}$$

$\therefore$ $u^* = 1.11\text{m/s.}$

Now $u = ?$ at $y = 6$ cm can be obtained from

$$\frac{u}{u^*} = 5.75 \log\left(\frac{u^* y}{\upsilon}\right) + 5.5$$

$$= 5.75 \log\left(\frac{1.11 \times 0.06}{0.15 \times 10^{-4}}\right) + 5.5$$

$$= 20.97 + 5.5 = 26.47$$

$\therefore$ u at $y = 6$ cm is $26.47 \times u$

$$= 26.47 \times 1.11$$

$$= 29.38 \text{ m/s}$$ ...(Ans.)

$$\frac{u_m}{u^*} = 5.75 \log\left(\frac{1.11 \times \frac{0.15}{2}}{0.15 \times 10^{-4}}\right) + 5.5$$

$$= 21.52 + 5.5 = 27$$

$\therefore$ $u_m = 27(1.11) = 30$ m/s ...(Ans.)

$$\delta' = \frac{11.6\,\upsilon}{u^*} = \frac{11.6 \times 0.15 \times 10^{-4}}{1.11}$$

$$= 1.56 \times 10^{-4} \text{ m}$$

For u at δ', $$\frac{u}{u^*} = 5.75 \log\left(\frac{11.6 \times 1.56 \times 10^{-4}}{0.15 \times 10^{-4}}\right) + 5.5$$

$$= 6.12 + 5.5 = 11.62$$

$\therefore$ u at $\delta' = 11.62(1.11) = 12.89$ m/s. ...(Ans.)

(b) Rough turbulent flow occurs in pipe of 25 cm diameter carrying water. At $y = 3$ cm, $u = 2.1$ m/s and $\frac{du}{dy} = 10.6$/sec. Determine ε, the average height of roughness and τ_o.

Solution: $D = 25$ cm

Pipe is rough

$u = 2.1$ m/s at $y = 3$ cm

For rough pipe,

$$\frac{u}{u^*} = 5.75\log\left(\frac{y}{\varepsilon}\right) + 8.5$$

$$\frac{2.1}{u^*} = 5.75\log\left(\frac{0.03}{\varepsilon}\right) + 8.5$$

We have $$\frac{du}{dy} = \frac{1}{0.4y}\sqrt{\frac{\tau_0}{\rho}} = \frac{u^*}{0.4y}$$

$$\therefore \quad u^* = (0.4y)\frac{du}{dy}$$

$$= (0.4 \times 0.03)\ 10.6$$

$$= 0.127 \text{ m/s}$$

$$\therefore \quad \frac{21}{0.127} = 5.75\log\left(\frac{0.03}{\varepsilon}\right) + 8.5$$

$$\therefore \quad 5.75\log\left(\frac{0.03}{\varepsilon}\right) = 16.5 - 8.5 = 8.0$$

$$\therefore \quad \log\left(\frac{0.03}{\varepsilon}\right) = \frac{8}{5.75}$$

$$= 1.397$$

$$\therefore \quad \frac{0.03}{\varepsilon} = 24.97$$

$$\therefore \quad \varepsilon = \frac{0.03}{24.97} = 1.2 \times 10^{-3} \text{ m}$$

$$= 1.2 \text{ mm}$$ ...(Ans.)

$$\frac{\tau_0}{\rho} = u^{*2} = (0.127)^2$$

$$\therefore \quad \tau_0 = (0.127)^2\ 1000 = 16.12 \text{ N/m}^2.$$ ...(Ans.)

■ **Problem 11.3**: *A 15 cm diameter pipe line carries $Q = 0.25\ m^3/s$. Calculate wall shear stress and average height of roughness.*

Solution: Take, $\upsilon = 0.75 \times 10^{-6}\ \text{m}^2/\text{s}$

and $f = 0.025$

$$V_0 = \frac{Q}{A} = \frac{0.25}{\frac{\pi}{4}(0.15)^2} = 14.15 \text{ m/s}$$

Reynolds number $$R = \frac{V_0 D}{\gamma} = \frac{14.15 \times 0.15}{0.75 \times 10^{-6}}$$

$$= 2.83 \times 10^6 > 2000 \ \therefore \ \text{T.F.}$$

Assume rough pipe,

$$\frac{1}{\sqrt{f}} = 2\log\left(\frac{r}{\varepsilon}\right) + 1.74$$

$$\frac{1}{\sqrt{0.025}} = 2\log\left(\frac{0.15/2}{\varepsilon}\right) + 1.74 = 6.32$$

$$\therefore \quad 2\log\left(\frac{0.075}{\varepsilon}\right) = 6.32 - 1.74$$

$$= 4.58$$

$$\therefore \quad \log\left(\frac{0.075}{\varepsilon}\right) = \frac{4.58}{2} = 2.29$$

$$\therefore \quad \frac{0.075}{\varepsilon} = 196$$

$$\therefore \quad \varepsilon = \frac{0.075}{196} = 3.82 \times 10^{-4}\,\text{m}$$

$$= 3.82 \times 10^{-1}\,\text{mm}$$

$$= 0.382\,\text{mm}$$ ...(Ans.)

$$\tau_0 = \frac{pV_0^2 f}{8}$$

$$= \frac{1000\,(14.15)^2\,(0.025)}{8}$$

$$= 6.25\,\text{N/m}^2.$$ ...(Ans.)

■ **Problem 11.4**: *A rough pipe having* ε = *0.02 mm, is 0.2 m in dia. Q = 75 LPS, and* $\upsilon = 10^{-6}\,m^2 s$, $\rho = 1000\,kg/m^3$. *Find f,* $u_m \tau_0$ *and u*.*

Solution: $D = 0.2$ m, $r = 0.1$ m, $\varepsilon = 2$ mm, $Q = 75$ LPS

$$\therefore \quad V_0 = \frac{Q}{A} = \frac{75/1000}{\frac{\pi}{4}(0.2)^2} = 2.38\,\text{m/s}$$

$$R_N = \frac{V_0 D}{\upsilon} = \frac{2.38\,(0.2)}{10^{-6}} = 0.47 \times 10^6 > 4000 \quad \therefore \text{ T.F.}$$

Given piple is rough

$$\therefore \quad \frac{u_m}{u^*} = 5.75\log\left(\frac{r}{\varepsilon}\right) + 8.5$$

$$\therefore \quad = 5.75\log\left(\frac{0.1}{0.2 \times 10^{-3}}\right) + 8.5$$

$$= 15.5 + 8.5$$

$\therefore \quad \frac{u_m}{u^*} = 24$ ...(1)

Also $\quad \frac{u_m - V_0}{u^*} = 3.75$ at $y = r$

$\therefore \quad u_m - 2.38 = 3.75\, u^*$ ...(2)

$\therefore \quad 24u^* - 2.38 = 3.75\, u^*$

$\therefore \quad 20.26\, u^* = 2.38$

$\therefore \quad u^* = \frac{2.38}{20.26} = 0.117$ m/s ...(Ans.)

$$u_m = 24\, u^*$$
$$= 24(0.117) = 2.819 \text{ m/s}$$ ...(Ans.)

$$\tau_0 = u^2 \rho$$
$$= (0.117)^2\, 1000 = 13.6 \text{ N/m}^2$$

$$\frac{1}{\sqrt{f}} = 2\log\left(\frac{R_N}{\varepsilon}\right) + 1.74$$

$$= 2\log\left(\frac{0.47\times10^6}{0.2\times10^{-3}}\right) + 1.74$$

$$= 18.74 + 1.74 = 20.48$$

$\therefore \quad f = 2.38 \times 10^{-3} = 0.00238.$ ...(Ans.)

■ **Problem 11.5:** *Determine the maximum velocity, shear velocity, average velocity and discharge in a pipe, 150 mm, dia, 100 m long and loss of pressure over this length is 26.6 kN/m². Take pipe as smooth and $\upsilon = 10\ m^2/s$.*

Solution: Trial I, Assume friction factor = 0.02

$$h_f = \frac{fL V_0^2}{29D} = \frac{\rho}{\gamma}$$

$$\therefore \quad \frac{0.02(100)V_0^2}{29D}(\rho g) = p = 26.6 \times 10^3$$

$$\therefore \quad V_0^2 = 26.6\, D$$
$$= 26.6\,(0.15)$$
$$= 4$$

$$\therefore \quad V_0 = 2 \text{ m/s}$$

$$R = \frac{\rho V_0 D}{\mu} = \frac{V_0 D}{\upsilon} = \frac{2\times0.15}{10^{-6}}$$
$$= 3 \times 10^5$$

For smooth pipe $f = 0.0032 + \dfrac{0.221}{(R)^{0.237}}$

$$= 0.0032 + \frac{0.221}{19.86}$$

$$= 0.0032 + 0.0111$$

$$= 0.0143 < 0.02$$

$\therefore$ Trial II, assume $f = 0.015$

$$\frac{0.015(100)V_0^2}{2D} = 26.6$$

$\therefore$ $V_0^2 = 5.32$

$\therefore$ $V_0 = 2.3$ m/s

$\therefore$ $R = \dfrac{2.3 \times 0.15}{10^{-6}} = 0.345 \times 10^6$

$\therefore$ $f = 0.0032 + \dfrac{0.221}{(0.345 \times 10^6)^{0.237}} = 0.0032 + \dfrac{221}{20.5}$

$$= 0.0032 + 0.01 = 0.0132 < 0.015$$

$\therefore$ III trial, assume $f = 0.013$

$$\frac{0.013(100)V_0^2}{0.15 \times 2} = 26.6$$

$\therefore$ $V_0 = \left(\dfrac{26.6}{4.33}\right)^{1/2} = 2.47$ m/s

$$R = \frac{V_0 D}{\upsilon} = \frac{2.47 \times 0.15}{10^{-6}} = 0.37 \times 10^6$$

$$f = 0.0032 + \frac{0.221}{(0.37 \times 10^6)^{0.237}}$$

$$= 0.0032 + \frac{0.221}{20.9}$$

$$= 0.0032 + 0.0105$$

$= 0.0137 \approx 0.013$; $\therefore$ assumed value is correct.

$\therefore$ Average velocity $V_0 = 2.47$ m/s ...(Ans.)

$$Q = \frac{\pi}{4} D^2 V_0 = \frac{\pi}{4}(0.15)^2)(2.47) = 0.436 \text{ m}^3/\text{s}$$

= 43.6 LPS ...(Ans.)

$$u^* = V_0\sqrt{\frac{f}{8}} = 2.47\sqrt{\frac{0.013}{8}}$$

$$= 2.47 \times 0.04$$

$$= 0.1 \text{ m/s} \qquad \text{...(Ans.)}$$

$$\frac{u_m - V_0}{u^*} = 3.75$$

$$\therefore \quad \frac{u_m - 2.47}{0.1} = 3.75$$

$$\therefore \quad u_m - 2.47 = 0.375$$

$$\therefore \quad u_m = 2.84 \text{ m/s.} \qquad \text{...(Ans.)}$$

■ **Problem 11.6:** *Show that for Turbulent flow in pipes, ratio of maximum velocity to average velocity is given by*

$$\frac{u_m}{u_0} = 1.33\sqrt{f} + 1.$$

Solution: We have for T.F.,

$$\frac{u_m - V_0}{u^*} = 3.75$$

and

$$u^* = V\left(\sqrt{\frac{f}{8}}\right)$$

$$\therefore \quad u_m - V_0 = 3.75\, u^*$$

$$= 3.75\, V_0\left(\sqrt{\frac{f}{8}}\right)$$

$$\therefore \quad u_m = V_0[1.33\sqrt{f} + 1]$$

$$\frac{u_m}{u_0} = 1.33\sqrt{f} + 1. \qquad \text{...Proved}$$

■ **Problem 11.7:** *Water is flowing through rough pipe of D = 40 cm and length = 3 km at the rate of 0.4 m³/s. Find HP required to maintain this flow. Take* $\varepsilon = 0.3$ *mm.*

Solution: For rough pipe,

$$\frac{u}{u^*} = 5.75\log\left(\frac{y}{\varepsilon}\right) + 8.5$$

$$\therefore \text{ At } \quad y = R, \frac{u_m}{u^*} = 5.75\log\left(\frac{0.4/2}{0.3 \times 10^{-3}}\right) + 8.5$$

$$\therefore \quad \frac{u_m}{u^*} = 16.23 + 8.5 = 24.73 \qquad \text{...(1)}$$

Also $$\frac{u_m - V_0}{u^*} = 3.75, V_0 = \frac{0.4}{\frac{\pi}{4}(0.4)^2} = 3.18 \text{ m/s}$$

$$\therefore \quad \frac{u_m - 3.18}{u^*} = 3.75$$

$$\therefore \quad u_m - 3.18 = 3.75\, u^* \qquad ...(2)$$

From (1) and (2)

$$24.73u^* - 3.18 = 3.75\, u^*$$

$$\therefore \quad 21u^* = 3.18 \quad \therefore \quad u^* = 0.15 \text{ m/s}$$

$$\therefore \quad u^* = V_0\left(\sqrt{\frac{f}{8}}\right)$$

$$\therefore \quad 0.15 = 3.18\left(\sqrt{\frac{f}{8}}\right)$$

$$\therefore \quad \sqrt{\frac{f}{8}} = \frac{0.15}{3.18} = 0.047$$

$$\therefore \quad \frac{f}{8} = 2.22 \times 10^{-3}$$

$$\therefore \quad f = 0.0178$$

$$h_f = \frac{fLV_0^2}{D(2g)} = \frac{0.0178\,(3\times1000)\,(3.18)^2}{0.4\times2\times9.81}$$

$$= 68.8 \text{ m}$$

$$\text{HP} = \gamma Q h_f$$

$$= 1000\,(9.81)\,(0.4)\,(68.8)$$

$$= 270 \text{ kW.} \qquad \textbf{...(Ans.)}$$

■ **Problem 11.8:** *A 25 cm dia, pipe has a velocity of 2 m/s and 1.5 m/s at centre line and at a point 5 cm from the pipe wall. Find discharge through the pipe.*

Solution: For smooth or rough pipe, we have

$$\frac{u_m - V_0}{u^*} = 3.75$$

$$\therefore \quad \frac{2 - V_0}{u^*} = 3.75 \qquad ...(1)$$

$$\frac{u - V_0}{u^*} = 5.75 \log\left(\frac{y}{r}\right) + 3.75$$

$$u = 1.5 \text{ at } y = 5 \text{ cm}$$

$$\therefore \quad \frac{1.5 - V_0}{u^*} = 5.75 \log\left(\frac{0.05}{0.25/2}\right) + 3.75$$

$$= -2.28 + 3.75$$

$$= 1.4618$$

$$\therefore \quad 1.5 - V_0 = 1.4618\, u^* \qquad ...(2)$$

From (1) and (2), we get

$$1.5 + (3.75v^* - 2) = 1.4618\, u^*$$

$$\therefore \quad 2.29\, u^* = 0.5$$

$$\therefore \quad u^* = \frac{0.5}{2.29} = 0.218 \text{ m/s}$$

$$\therefore \quad \frac{2 - V_0}{u^*} = 3.75$$

$$\therefore \quad 2 - V_0 = 3.75\,(0.218) = 0.818$$

$$\therefore \quad V_0 = 2 - 0.818 = 1.18 \text{ m/s}$$

$$Q = \frac{\pi}{4} D^2 V_0 = \frac{\pi}{4}(0.25)^2\,(1.18)$$

$$= 0.0578 \text{ m}^3\text{/s}$$

$$= 57.8 \text{ LPS.} \qquad ...(\textbf{Ans.})$$

■ **Problem 11.9**: *A 20 cm dia. pipe has $f = 0.02$ when it was fresh. After 20 years of service f was found to be 0.025. What will be its value after another 20 years?*

Solution: Average height of Roughness **ε** is function of time.

$$\therefore \quad \varepsilon_t - \varepsilon_0 = \alpha t$$

i.e. roughness after t yrs = original roughness + αt

where t is time (age) in yrs.

Here $t = 20$ yrs. when $f_t = 0.225$

and when $t = 0$ $\quad f_0 = 0.02$

Let initial value of roughness = ε_0

$$\frac{1}{\sqrt{f_0}} = 2 \log\left(\frac{r}{\varepsilon_0}\right) + 1.74, \quad r = \frac{D}{2} = 10 \text{ cm}$$

$$\frac{1}{\sqrt{0.02}} = 2 \log\left(\frac{0.1}{\varepsilon_0}\right) + 1.74$$

$$\therefore \quad 7.07 = 2 \log\left(\frac{0.1}{\varepsilon_0}\right) + 1.74$$

$$\therefore \quad 2 \log\left(\frac{0.1}{\varepsilon_0}\right) = 7.07 - 1.74 = 5.33$$

$$\therefore \quad \log\left(\frac{0.1z}{\varepsilon_0}\right) = 2.66$$

$$\therefore \quad \frac{0.1}{\varepsilon_0} = 463$$

$$\therefore \quad \varepsilon_0 = \frac{0.1}{463} = 2.15 \times 10^{-4} \text{ m}$$

$$= 0.215 \text{ mm}$$

After 20 years, $f_t = 0.025$ and roughness $\equiv \varepsilon_t$

$$\therefore \quad \frac{1}{\sqrt{0.025}} = 2\log\left(\frac{0.1}{\varepsilon_t}\right) + 1.74 = 6.32$$

$$\therefore \quad 2\log\left(\frac{0.1}{\varepsilon_t}\right) = 4.58$$

$$\therefore \quad \log\left(\frac{0.1}{\varepsilon_t}\right) = 2.292$$

$$\therefore \quad \frac{0.1}{\varepsilon_t} = 196$$

$$\therefore \quad \varepsilon_t = \frac{0.1}{196} = 5.1 \times 10^{-4}$$

$$\therefore \quad \varepsilon_t - \varepsilon_0 = \alpha t$$

$$\therefore \quad \alpha = \frac{\varepsilon_t - \varepsilon_0}{t} = \frac{5.1 \times 10^{-4} - 2.15 \times 10^{-4}}{20} = \frac{2.95 \times 10^{-4}}{20}$$

$$= 0.147 \times 10^{-4}$$

$$= 0.0147 \text{ mm/yr}$$

In another 20 yrs, $t = 20 + 20 = 40$ yrs.

$$\varepsilon_2 = \varepsilon_0 + \alpha t$$

$$= 0.215 + (0.0147)\, 40$$

$$= 0.803 \text{ mm}$$

And corresponding value of f_2 will be

$$\therefore \quad \frac{1}{\sqrt{f_2}} = 2\log\left(\frac{0.1}{0.803 \times 10^{-3}}\right) + 1.74$$

$$= 4.19 + 1.74$$

$$= 5.93$$

$$\therefore \quad f_2 = 0.0284$$

i.e. after total of 40 yrs $f = 0.0284$. ...(Ans.)

Exercises

1. A 15 cm dia, pipe, 100 m long, had discharge of water equal to 100 LPS. If the pipe is smooth, find h_f, τ_0, u_{max} and δ'. Given $\upsilon_{water} = 1.5 \times 10^{-6}$ m²/s.
   [**Ans.** (*i*) $h_f = 13$m (*ii*) $\tau_0 = 48.5$ N/m² (*iii*) $u_{max} = 10.6$ m/s, (*iv*) $\delta' = 0.79$ mm]
2. Find discharge in a pipe of 20 cm dia. If centre line velocity is 2 m/s and u at $y = 5$ cm is 1.6 m/s. (**Ans.** $Q = 3.5$ LPS)
3. A 20 cm dia. smooth pipe has centre line velocity of 3 m/s and u and $y = 2$ cm is 2 m/s. Find discharge, friction factor, roughness height, given $\upsilon = 1 \times 10^{-6}$ m²/s.
   (**Ans.** $Q = 64.5$ LPS, $f = .0132$, $\varepsilon = .0115$ mm)
4. A 30 cm dia. rough pipe has centre line velocity of 4 m/s and u at $y = 5$ cm is 3.5 m/s. Find Q, ε, f. (**Ans.** $Q = 230$ LPS, $\varepsilon = 68$ mm and $f = 0.24$)
5. In a 20 cm dia. rough pipe velocity is found is increase by 20% if a pilot tube is moved from $y = 1$ cm to $y = 5$ cm from pipe wall. Find relative height of roughness (*i.e.* R/ε) and friction factor. (**Ans.** $R/\varepsilon = 1000$, $f = .016$)
6. A 15 cm dia rough pipe carries water. If at $y = 2.5$ cm, velocity is 1.5 m/s and velocity gradient is 7.0/sec, find relative height of roughness (R/ε), Q, and f.
   (**Ans.** $(R/\varepsilon) = 535.7$, $Q = 25$ LPS, and $f = .019$)
7. A 60 cm diameter rough pipe has mean velocity equal to 80% of centre line velocity. Find average height of roughness and friction factor. (**Ans.** $\varepsilon = 4.95$ mm, $f = .035$)
8. A rough pipe has a velocity of 75% of centre line velocity at a distance of 20% of pipe radius from the wall. Find ratio of average velocity to maximum velocity and friction factor. $\left(\textbf{Ans. } \dfrac{u_{av}}{u_{max}} = .765,\ f = .05\right)$
9. At 4 m and 8 m above a level ground wind velocity values were found to be 4 m/s and 5 m/s respectively. What will be the velocity of a height of 24 m from the same ground?

   (**Hint:** use basic eqn. $\dfrac{u}{u^*} = 5.75 \log\left(\dfrac{y}{y'}\right)$ and values of y_1, y_2 and u_1 and u_2 in the eqn., $\dfrac{u_2 - u_1}{u^*} = 5.75 \log\left(\dfrac{y_2}{y_1}\right)$, find u^* and then similarly find u_3).

   (**Ans.** $u_3 = 6.55$ m/s)
10. A 20 cm dia. smooth pipe carries water at a velocity of 3.0 m/s. If length of pipe is 100 m, find friction factor and power required to maintain the flow ($\upsilon = 1 \times 10^{-6}$ m²/s).
    (**Ans.** $P = 21$ kW, $f = 0.1$)

12

Pipe Flow System

12.1 INTRODUCTION

Principles of fluid flow discussed in earlier chapters will now be applied in the analysis is pipe flow system. Water supply in towns and cities is through pipe system. Industrial requirements of transportation of liquids and gases are also met with by pipe system. Disposal of waste water and sewage is though through pipe lines but there is free surface of flow and as such can not be considered in pipe flow system. In general pipe flow is at the expense of pressure energy and there is no free surface. Forces opposing the flow are those due to friction in pipe length, changes in pipe diameters, bends and pipe fittings. Pipes in series, pipes in parallel, two and three reservoir problem, pipe network, penstocks, water hammer problems are few special cases of pipe flow system. Pipe flow system requires careful consideration for calculations of pressure heads, friction heads and water power transmission. These are dealt with in this chapter. Problem of free surface flow in pipes are discussed in chapter on open channel flow.

12.2 MAJOR AND MINOR LOSSES

In general, pipe flow is usually turbulent type and equation used in calculation of head loss due to friction is Darcy – Weisbach equation, derived in chapter on turbulent flow,

$$h_f = \frac{fLV^2}{D2g} \qquad ...(12.1)$$

here, $f =$ friction factor

= a function of Reynolds number and relative roughness of pipe wall

$= \frac{64}{R}$ for laminar flow, R is Reynolds number

$= \frac{0.316}{R^{1/4}}$ for turbulent flow for values of R between 10^4 and 10^5.

For values of $R > 10^5$, f can be determined by logarithmic formulae given in chapter on turbulent flow.

Calculation of h_f by Darcy – Weisback equation gives major loss of head in a pipe line, whereas loss of head due to changes in pipe section, bend, fittings values, etc. constitute what are known as minor losses of head. Most useful equation in solving pipe flow problems is that due to Bernoulli's theorem, *i.e.*

$$Z + \frac{p}{\gamma} + \frac{V^2}{2g} = \text{constant} \qquad \text{...(12.2)}$$

If it is to be applied at two specific points, L distance apart, on a pipe line, then it can be written as

$$Z_1 + \frac{P_1}{\gamma} + \frac{V_1^2}{2g} = Z_2 + \frac{p_2}{\gamma} + \frac{V_2^2}{2g} + h_{f1-2}$$

where h_{f1-2} is friction loss between points 1, 2 and is given by

$$h_{f1-2} = \frac{fLV^2}{D2g} = \text{major loss of head due to friction caused by flow over pipe length } L$$

Value of f, if not specified, can be taken as in between 0.015 to 0.02, preferably 0.02. If friction coefficient f' is given then

$$h_f = \frac{4f'LV^2}{D2g}, \text{ and value of } f' = \frac{f}{4}\ i.e.\ 0.005.$$

Reynolds number is the most important ruling number for pipe flow system and is calculated by $R = \dfrac{\rho VD}{\mu}$.

Head loss on account to

(*a*) sudden expansion

(*b*) sudden contraction

(*c*) entry to pipe

(*d*) exit from pipe

(*e*) bends and fittings

(*f*) nozzle.

are known as minor losses, and are usually neglected if they are found to be less than 5% of major loss which is on account length of the pipe.

12.3 LOSS ON ACCOUNT OF SUDDEN EXPANSION

If a pipe of diameter D_1 has to get enlarged suddenly to a pipe of diameter D_2, then at entry into larger pipe, we find lot of turbulence and eddy formation coupled with loss of energy.

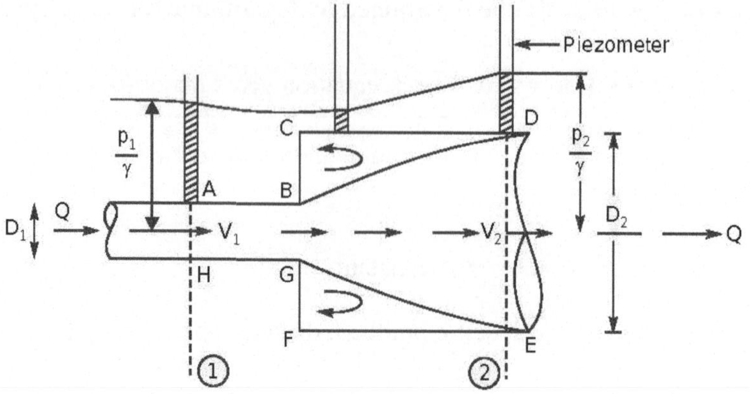

Fig. 12.1

This is mainly due to separation of streamlines from the boundary. As velocity in larger pipe for same discharge through smaller and larger pipes will be lower than that in smaller diameter pipe, pressure in larger pipe will be higher than that in the smaller diameter pipe, this will be clear from application of Bernoulli's Theorem between sections (1) and (2) as shown in Fig.12.1.

$$\therefore \quad \frac{p_1}{\gamma}+\frac{V_1^2}{2g}=\frac{p_2}{\gamma}+\frac{V_2^2}{2g}+h_L$$

datum head Z is same, as pipe line is horizontal, and

h_L = loss due to sudden enlargement

$$\therefore \quad h_L=\frac{p_1-p_2}{\gamma}+\frac{V_1^2-V_2^2}{2g} \qquad ...(12.3)$$

Applying momentum principle to the control volume *ABCDEFGH*, and assuming that on annular space *CB* and *GF*, same pressure will act as at *AH*, *i.e.* p_1, we get

$$\rho Q(V_2-V_1)=p_1A_1+p_1(A_2-A_1)-p_2A_2$$

$$=(p_1-p_2)A_2$$

$$\therefore \quad p_1-p_2=\frac{\rho Q}{A_2}(V_2-V_1)$$

$$=\rho V_2(V_2-V_1), \quad \text{as } \frac{Q}{A_2}=V_2$$

Now,

$$h_L=\frac{p_1-p_2}{\gamma}+\frac{V_1^2-V_2^2}{2g}$$

$$\therefore \quad h_L=\frac{\rho V_2(V_2-V_1)}{\rho g}+\frac{V_1^2-V_2^2}{2g}, \quad \text{as } \gamma=\rho g$$

$$=\frac{V_2(V_2-V_1)}{g}+\frac{(V_1^2-V_2^2)}{2g}$$

$$= \frac{2V_2^2 - 2V_2V_1 + V_1^2 + V_2^2}{2g}$$

$$= \frac{V_2^2 - 2V_2V_1 + V_1^2}{2g} = \frac{(V_1 - V_2)^2}{2g}$$

i.e.,

$$= \frac{(\text{higher velocity} - \text{lower velocity})^2}{2g}$$

$$\therefore \quad h_L = \frac{(V_1 - V_2)^2}{2g} \qquad \text{...(12.4)}$$

Now from continuity principles,

$$A_1V_1 = A_2V_2$$

$$\therefore \quad h_L = \frac{V_1^2}{2g}\left[1 - \frac{A_1}{A_2}\right]^2 = \frac{V_2^2}{2g}\left[\frac{A_2}{A_1} - 1\right]^2 \qquad \text{...(12.5)}$$

Head loss due to sudden enlargant as given by equations (12.4) and (12.5) was first obtained by Borda and Carnot and hence it is known as Borda–Carnot head loss equation.

12.4 LOSS DUE TO SUDDEN CONTRACTION

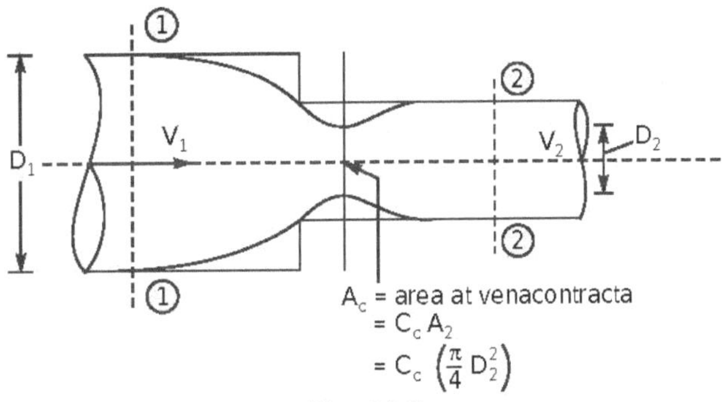

Fig. 12.2

When flow from larger diameter pipe takes place into smaller diameter pipe, the loss of head is known as loss due to sudden contraction. The fluid entering into smaller diameter pipe will have its streamlines converged upto vena contract and then expand gradually till fully established flow at section (2) takes place, thus this is actually a case of sudden expansion between section at vena contract and section (2)

$$\therefore \quad h_L = \frac{V_2^2}{2g}\left(\frac{A_2}{A_C} - 1\right)^2$$

$$= \frac{V_2^2}{2g}\left(\frac{1}{C_C} - 1\right)^2, \quad \text{as } A_C = C_C A_2$$

here C_C = coefficient of contraction
= 0.60, generally.

$$\therefore \quad \left(\frac{1}{C_C}-1\right)^2 = 0.45, \text{ usually taken as } 0.5$$

Thus
$$h_L = k\frac{V^2}{2g} \qquad \text{...(12.6)}$$

where K = minor loss coefficient.

Thus minor losses in a pipe line can be listed in the following tubular form:

Table 12.1 Minor Losses

S. No.	*Type of Loss*	h_L
1.	Sudden expansion	$\frac{(V_1-V_2)^2}{2g}$
2.	Sudden contraction	$\left(\frac{1}{C_C}-1\right)^2\frac{V^2}{2g}$
3.	Entry to pipe	$0.5\frac{V^2}{2g}$
4.	Exit from pipe	$\frac{V^2}{2g}$
5.	Bends, fittings, etc.	$K\frac{V^2}{2g}$
6.	Nozzle	$\left(\frac{1}{C_V^2}-1\right)\frac{V^2}{2g}$

Table 12.2 Value of *K* for bends and fittings

S. No.	*Type*	*Value of K*
1.	90° Elbow bend	0.9
2.	gate valve	
	(*a*) half open	5.6
	(*b*) fully open	0.2
3.	Globe valve (fully open)	10.0
4.	Foot valve	1.5
5.	45° elbow	0.4
6.	Standard Tee	0.9
7.	Sharp 90° bend	1.2

12.5 HYDRAULIC GRADIENT AND ENERGY GRADIENT

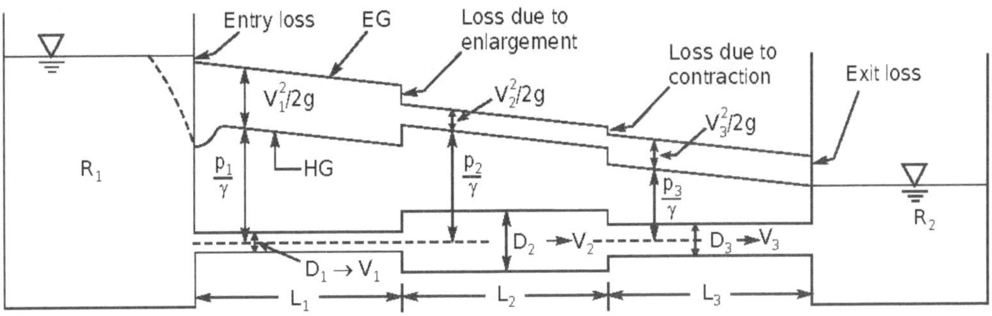

Fig. 12.3 HG and EG lines.

Hydraulic gradient (HG) is a line representing pressure energy along centre line of a given pipe system whereas Energy Gradient (EG) is a line higher by $\frac{V^2}{2g}$ compared to HG line, and represents total energy of flow.

Thus,
$$EG = Z + \frac{p}{\gamma} + \frac{V^2}{2g}$$

and
$$HG = Z + \frac{p}{\gamma} \quad (Z = \text{datum head, not shown in Fig. 12.3})$$

In Fig. 12.3, both these lines are shown. Note that pressure head in larger diameter pipe is higher than that in smaller diameter pipe. Also note that EG will always decrease in direction of flow whereas HG may increase at the point where smaller diameter pipes joins larger diameter pipe. Also note that entry, exit and sudden enlargement and sudden contraction losses should be shown on EG line as in Fig. 12.3 and 12.4.

12.5.1 Solved Problems

■ **Problem 12.1:** *Two reservoirs 1 and 2 having level difference between free surface of water equal to 5 m, are connected by pipes AB and BC of diameters 20 cm and 30 cm respectively. Length of AB is 300 m and that of BC is 200 m. If flow through the pipe line is 50 LPS, find loss due to expansion and friction factor f. Draw EG line.*

Solution: Apply Bernoulli's Theorem between water surfaces of R_1 and R_2.

$$\therefore \quad 0.5\frac{V_1^2}{2g} + \frac{fL_{AB}}{D_1}\frac{V_1^2}{2g} + \frac{(V_1 - V_2)^2}{2g} + \frac{fL_{BC}V_2^2}{D_2 2g} + \frac{V_2^2}{2g} = 5 \quad \text{...(1)}$$

$$V_1 = \frac{Q}{\frac{\pi}{4}(D_1)^2} = \frac{50 \times 10^{-3}}{\frac{\pi}{4}(0.20)^2} = 1.59 \text{ m/s}$$

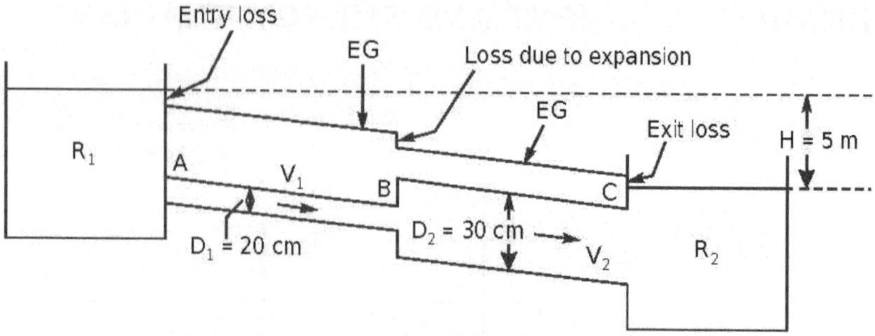

Fig. 12.4

$$V_2 = \frac{Q}{\frac{\pi}{4}(D_2)^2} = \frac{50\times10^{-3}}{\frac{\pi}{4}(0.30)^2} = 0.707 \text{ m/s}$$

$$\therefore \quad h_L = \text{loss at expansion} = \frac{(V_1 - V_2)^2}{2g} = \frac{(1.59-0.707)^2}{2g}$$

$$= \frac{0.78}{2g} = 0.0397 \text{ m} \qquad \text{...(Ans.)}$$

Putting this value in eqn. (1),
We get,

$$0.5(1.59)^2 + f\frac{(300)\times(1.59)^2}{0.2} + 0.78 + f\frac{(200)\,(0.707)^2}{0.3} + (0.707)^2 = 2g\,(5)$$

$$\therefore \quad 1.26 + f(3792) + 0.78 + f(333) + 0.49 = 98.1$$

$$2.53 + f(4125) = 98.1$$

$$\therefore \quad f(4125) = 98.1 - 2.53 = 95.51$$

$$\therefore \quad f = \frac{95.51}{4125} = 0.023. \qquad \text{...(Ans.)}$$

■ **Problem 12.2:** *Three pipes*

(*a*) *300 long, 20 cm diameter,*

(*b*) *150 m long 30 cm diameter,*

(*c*) *200 m long, 25 cm diameter,*

are connected in series between two reservoirs. Friction factor f for three pipes are 0.018, 0.02, 0.019 respectively. Find discharge in the pipe line if difference in water levels between two reservoirs is 15 m. Draw HG and EG lines. $C_C = 0.6$.

Solution: Various Losses:

$$(a) \qquad \text{entrance loss} = 0.5\frac{V_1^2}{2g} = \frac{0.5}{2g}\left(\frac{Q}{A_1}\right)^2 = 28\,Q^2$$

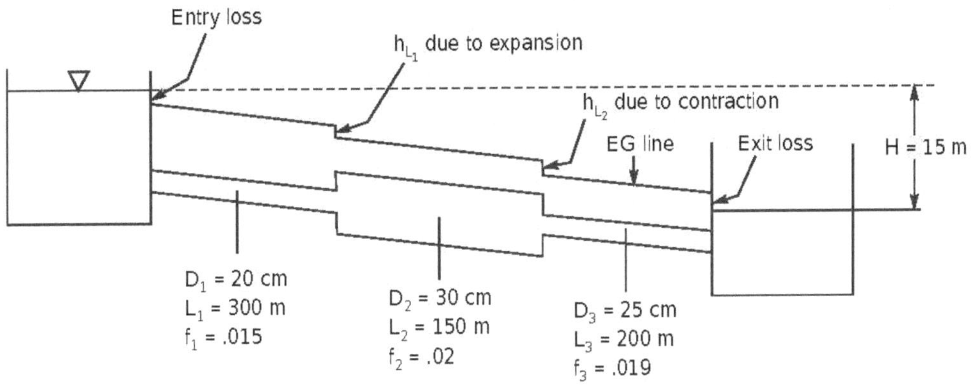

Fig. 12.5

(*b*) $$h_{f1} = \frac{f_1 L_1 V_1^2}{D_1 2g} = \frac{0.018 \times 300}{0.3(2g)}\left(\frac{Q}{A_1}\right)^2 = 1019\,Q^2$$

(*c*) $$h_{L1} = \text{loss due to expansion}$$

$$= \frac{(V_1 - V_2)^2}{2g} = \frac{Q^2\left(\frac{1}{A_1} - \frac{1}{A_2}\right)^2}{2g} = \frac{Q^2(32.2 - 14.2)^2}{2g} = 16.5\,Q^2$$

$$A_1 = \frac{\pi}{4} D_1^2 = \frac{\pi}{4}(0.2)^2 = 0.031 \text{ m}^2$$

$$A_2 = \frac{\pi}{4} D_2^2 = \frac{\pi}{4}(0.3)^2 = 0.07 \text{ m}^2$$

$$A_3 = \frac{\pi}{4} D_3^2 = \frac{\pi}{4}(0.25)^2 = 0.05 \text{ m}^2$$

(*d*) $$h_{L2} = \text{loss due to contraction} = \frac{V_3^2}{2g}\left(\frac{1}{C_C} - 1\right)^2$$

$$= 0.45\frac{V_3^2}{2g} = \frac{0.45\,Q^2}{2g\ A_3^2} = 9\,Q^2$$

(*e*) $$h_{f2} = \frac{f_2 L_2 V_2^2}{D_2 2g} = \frac{0.02(150)\,Q_2^2}{0.3\,(2g)\,A_2^2}$$

$$= \frac{0.02\,(150)\,Q^2}{0.3\,(2g)\,(0.07)^2} = 104\,Q^2$$

(*f*) $$h_{f3} = \frac{f_3 L_3 V_3^2}{D_3 2g} = \frac{(0.019)\,(200)\,Q^2}{0.25\,(2g)\,(0.05)^2} = 310\,Q^2$$

(g) exit loss $= \frac{V_3^2}{2g} = \frac{Q^2}{2g\,A_3^2} = \frac{Q^2}{2g\,(0.05)^2} = 20.38\,Q^2$

Apply Bernoulli's Theorem between water levels of two reservoirs

we get, $15 = 28\,Q^2 + 1019\,Q^2 + 16.5\,Q^2 + 104\,Q^2 + 9Q^2 + 310\,Q^2 + 20.38\,Q^2$

$= 1506.38\,Q^2$

$\therefore \quad Q^2 = \frac{15}{1506.38} = 9.96 \times 10^{-3}$

$\therefore \quad Q = 0.0998\ \text{m}^3/\text{s} = 0.1\ \text{m}^3/\text{s} = 100$ LPS ...(Ans.)

EG line is shown in the Fig.

HG line will be $\frac{V^2}{2g}$ lower than EG line in respective lengths of the pipe

(1) Entry loss $= 28\,Q^2 = 0.28$ m

(2) $h_{f1} = 1019\,Q^2 = 10.19$ m

(3) $h_{L1} = 16\,Q^2 = 0.165$ m (expansion)

(4) $h_{L2} = 9Q^2 = 0.09$ m

(5) $h_{f2} = 104\,Q^2 = 1.04$ m

(6) $h_{f3} = 310\,Q^2 = 3.1$ m

(7) Exit loss $= 20\,Q^2 = 0.2$ m

Total loss = 15 m (check).

■ **Problem 12.3:** *The difference in water levels between two tanks which are connected by three pipes in series is 15 m. Lengths and diameters of these pipes are 300 m, 150 m, 200 m and 30 cm, 20 cm, 30 cm perspectively. Find the discharge through the pipe line, and tabulate all losses, if f for the three pipes be taken as 0.02, 0.25 and 0.03.*

Solution:

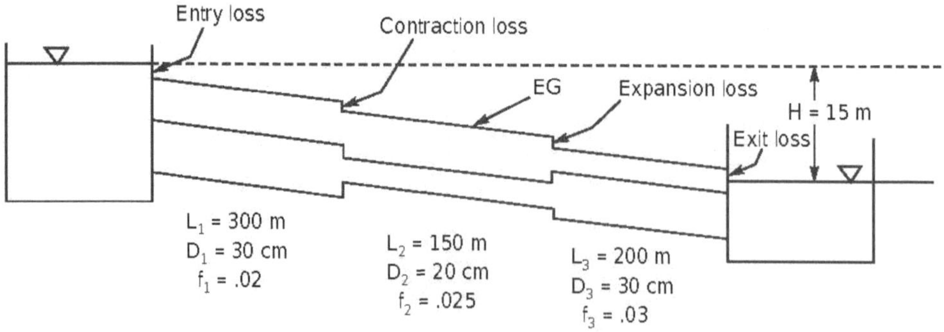

Fig. 12.6

$$V_1 = \frac{Q}{A_1} = \frac{Q}{\frac{\pi}{4}D_1^2} = \frac{Q}{\frac{\pi}{4}(0.3)^2} = \frac{Q}{0.07}\ \text{m/s}$$

$$V_2 = \frac{Q}{A_2} = \frac{Q}{\frac{\pi}{4}(D_2)^2} = \frac{Q}{\frac{\pi}{4}(0.2)^2} = \frac{Q}{0.031}\text{ m/s}$$

$$V_3 = \frac{Q}{A_3} = \frac{Q}{\frac{\pi}{4}(D_3)^2} = \frac{Q}{\frac{\pi}{4}(0.3)^2} = \frac{Q}{0.07}\text{ m/s}$$

(*a*) Entry loss $= 0.5\frac{V_1^2}{2g} = \frac{0.5}{2g}\frac{Q^2}{A_1^2} = \frac{0.5}{2g}\frac{Q^2}{(0.07)^2} = 5.2\,Q^2$

(*b*) Loss due to contraction $= 0.45\frac{V_2^2}{2g} = \frac{0.45}{2g}\frac{Q^2}{A_2^2} = \frac{0.45\,Q^2}{2g\,(0.031)^2} = 24\,Q^2$

($k = 0.45$ for $C_C = 0.6$)

(*c*) Loss due to expansion $= \frac{(V_2 - V_3)^2}{2g} = \frac{\left(\frac{1}{A_2} - \frac{1}{A_3}\right)^2 Q^2}{2g}$

$$= \frac{(32.2 - 14.2)^2}{2g}Q^2 = \frac{(18)^2 Q}{2g} = 16.5\,Q^2$$

(*d*) Loss due to exit $= \frac{V_3^2}{2g} = \frac{Q^2}{2g\,A_3^2} = 10.4\,Q^2$

(*e*) Loss due to friction in pipe 1 $= \frac{f_1 L_1 V_1^2}{D_1 2g} = \frac{f_1 L_1 Q^2}{D_1 2g\,(A_1)^2}$

$$= \frac{0.02\,(300)\,Q^2}{0.3\,(2g)\,(0.07)^2} = 208\,Q^2$$

(*f*) Loss due to friction in pipe 2 $= \frac{f_2 L_2 Q^2}{D_2\,(2g)(A_2)^2} = \frac{0.025\,(150)\,Q^2}{0.2\,(2g)\,(0.031)^2} = 994\,Q^2$

(*g*) Loss due to friction in pipe 3 $= \frac{f_3 L_3 Q^2}{D_3\,(2g)\,(A_3)^2} = \frac{0.03\,(300)\,Q^2}{0.3\,(2g)\,(0.07)^2}$

$$= 208\,Q^2$$

Apply Bernoulli's Theorem between water levels of the two tanks,

$\therefore$ $15 = 5.2\,Q^2 + 208\,Q^2 + 24\,Q^2 + 944\,Q^2 + 16.5\,Q^2 + 208\,Q^2 + 10.4\,Q^2$

$= 1466\,Q^2$

$\therefore$ $Q^2 = \frac{15}{1466} = 0.01$

$\therefore$ $Q = 0.1\text{ m}^3/\text{s} = 100$ LPS. ...**(Ans.)**

Table showing losses:

Losses	*Value*
(*a*) At entry, 5.2 $Q^2 = 0.052$ m	
(*b*) Loss due to contraction, 24	$Q^2 = 0.24$ m
(*c*) Loss due to expansion, 16.5	$Q^2 = 0.165$ m
(*d*) Friction loss in pipe 1, 208	$Q^2 = 2.08$ m
(*e*) Friction loss in pipe 2, 944	$Q^2 = 9.94$ m
(*f*) Friction loss in pipe 3, 208	$Q^2 = 2.08$ m
(*g*) Exit loss, 10.4	$Q^2 = 0.1$ m ...(**Ans.**)
	= 15.45 slightly more due to rounding of values.
	= 15 m (checked) OK.

■ **Problem 12.4**: *A pipe 0.5 m in diameter is 2 km long. To increase the discharge, another line of same diameter is introduced in parallel to the first in the second half of the length. Neglecting minor losses, find increase in discharge. Take f = 0.02 and head at inlet is 25 m.*

Solution:

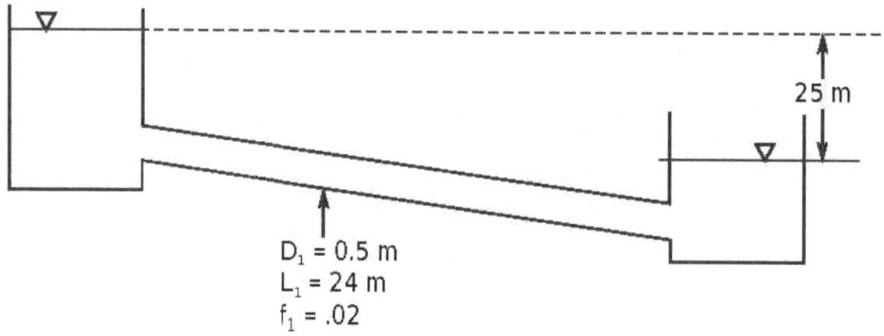

Fig. 12.7

Case (*a*):

$$25 = \frac{f_1 L_1 V_1^2}{D_1 2g} = \frac{f_1 L_1 Q^2}{D_1 2g \left(\frac{\pi}{4} D_1^2\right)^2}$$

$$= \frac{0.02\,(2000)\,(Q^2)}{0.5\,(2g)\left(\frac{\pi}{4} 0.25\right)^2} = 107.23\,Q^2$$

$$\therefore \quad Q^2 = \frac{25}{107.23} = 0.233$$

$\therefore$ $Q = 0.482$, when single line in working.

Case (*b*): Since two parallel pipe lines have same diameter and same length, head loss also same.

$\therefore$ Q passing through each most be same, *i.e.*, Q_1.

$$Q_2 = Q_1 + Q_1 = 2Q_1$$

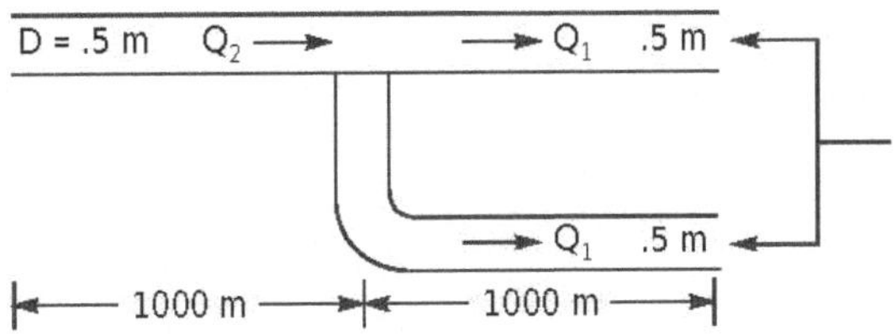

Fig. 12.7A

$$\frac{\pi}{4}(0.5)^2 V_2 = 2\left(\frac{\pi}{4}\right)(0.5)^2 V_1$$

$$\therefore \quad V_2 = 2V_1, \quad L_2 = L_1 = \frac{2000}{2} = 1000 \text{ m}$$

Now, apply B-Th:

$$25 = \frac{f_2 L_2 V_2^2}{D_2 2g} + \frac{f_1 L_1 V_1^2}{D_1 2g}$$

$$= \frac{0.02\,(1000)\,V_2^2}{0.5\,2g} + \frac{0.02\,(1000)\,V_1^2}{0.5\,(2g)}$$

$$\frac{25 \times 0.5\,(2g)}{0.02 \times 1000} = (V_2^2 + V_1^2)$$

$$= [(2V_1)^2 + V_1^2] \text{ as } V_2 = 2V_1$$

$$= 5\,V_1^2$$

$$\therefore \quad V_1^2 = \frac{25 \times 0.5 \times (2g)}{0.02 \times 1000 \times 5} = 2.45$$

$$\therefore \quad V_1 = 1.56 \text{ m/s}$$

$$\therefore \quad Q_2 = \frac{\pi}{4}(0.5)^2 \times (2 \times 1.56)$$

$$= 0.61 \text{ m}^3/\text{s}$$

Increase in discharge = 0.61 – 0.482

= 0.128 m^2/s. ...(Ans.)

12.6 PIPES IN SERIES AND PIPES IN PARALLEL

Two or more pipes can be connected in series (see Fig. 12.8) so that same discharge is passing through them but each one will have friction head as per its own length, diameter and friction factor, *i.e.*

$$Q = Q_1 = Q_2 = Q_3 \text{ etc.}$$

but $$h_f = h_{f1} + h_{f2} + h_{f3} \text{ etc.} \qquad \text{...(12.7)}$$

Similarly two or more pipes may function in parallel see Fig. 12.9 and in that case they have same head but discharge in each will be different, giving a total discharge is

$$Q = Q_1 + Q_2 + \text{etc.} \quad \text{...(12.8)}$$

but $h_f = h_{f1} = h_{f2}$ etc., see Fig. 12.9.

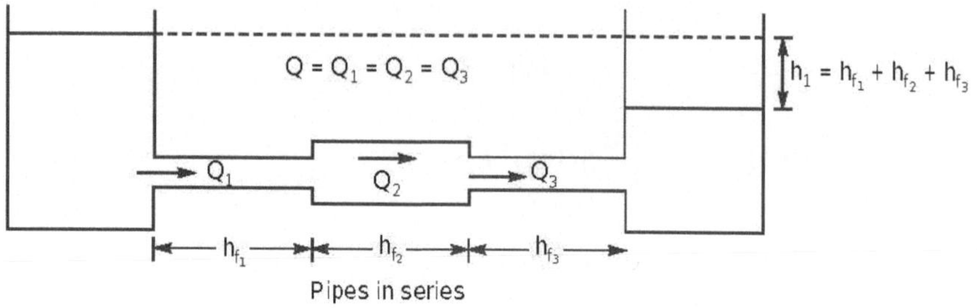

Fig. 12.8

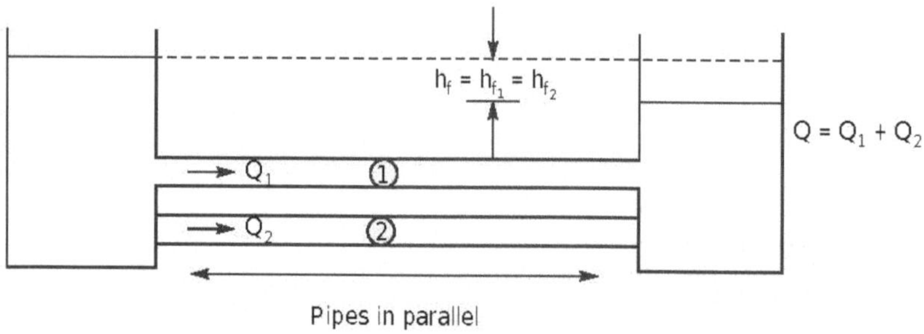

Fig. 12.9

12.6.1 Solved Problems

■ **Problem 12.5:** *Two pipes of length 2500 m each and diameters 80 cm and 60 cm respectively are connected in parallel. Coefficient of friction is 0.006. The total flow is equal to 250 LPS. Find rate of flow in each pipe.*

Solution:

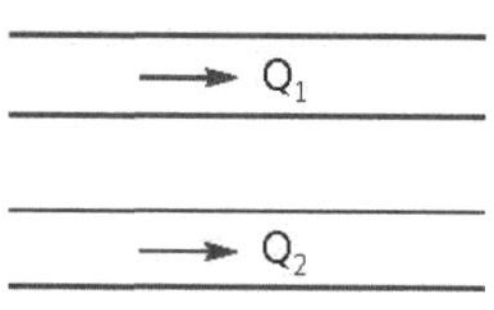

$$Q = Q_1 + Q_2 = 250 \text{ LPS}$$

$$\frac{250}{1000} = Q_1 + Q_2$$

$$h_f = h_{f1} = h_{f2}$$

$$h_f = \frac{4f'LV^2}{D2g},$$

[As data gives value of coefficient of friction, f' ∴ in place of f, put $4f'$]

For parallel pipes,

$$h_{f1} = h_{f2}$$

$$\therefore \quad \frac{4f'L_1V_1^2}{D_1 2g} = \frac{4f'L_2V_2^2}{D_2 2g} \qquad L_1 = L_2 = 2500 \text{ m}$$

$$f' = 0.006$$

$$\therefore \quad \frac{V_1^2}{D_1} = \frac{V_2^2}{D_2}$$

$$\therefore \quad V_1^2 = \frac{D_1}{D_2}V_2^2 = \frac{0.8}{0.6}V_2^2 = \frac{4}{3}V_2^2$$

$$\therefore \quad V_1 = 1.15\ V_2 \qquad \text{...(1)}$$

Now,

$$Q = Q_1 + Q_2$$

$$\therefore \quad 0.250 = \frac{\pi}{4}D_1^2\ V_1 + \frac{\pi}{4}D_2^2V_2$$

$$0.25\left(\frac{4}{\pi}\right) = (0.8)^2\ V_1 + (0.6)^2\ V_2$$

Now,

$$V_1 = 1.15\ V_2 \text{ from (1)}$$

$$\therefore \quad 0.318 = 0.64\ (1.15\ V_2) + 0.36\ V_2$$

$$= (0.736 + 0.36)\ V_2$$

$$= 1.096\ V_2$$

$$\therefore \quad V_2 = \frac{0.318}{1.096} = 0.29 \text{ m/s}. \quad \therefore \quad V_1 = 1.15\ (0.29) = 0.33 \text{ m/s}$$

$$\therefore \quad Q_2 = \frac{\pi}{4}D_2^2\ V_2 = 0.78\ (0.6)^2\ (0.29)$$

$$= 0.081 \text{ m}^3\text{/s}$$

$$= 81 \text{ LPS}$$

$$Q_1 = \frac{\pi}{4}D_1^2\ V_1 = 0.78\ (0.8)^2\ (0.33)$$

$$= 0.166 \text{ m}^3\text{/s}$$

$$= 166 \text{ LPS}$$

Check $\quad Q = Q_1 + Q_2 = 166 + 81 = 247 \simeq 250$, OK.

■ **Problem 12.6**: *Two reservoirs are connected by a pipe line of diameter 60 cm and length 4000 m and difference in water level is 20 m. At a distance of 1000 m from upper reservoir, a small pipe is connected to the 4000 m long pipe. Find discharge to lower reservoir if*

(a) No water is drawn from small pipe. (b) 100 LPS is taken from small pipe.

Take $f = 0.005$, neglect minor losses.

Solution:

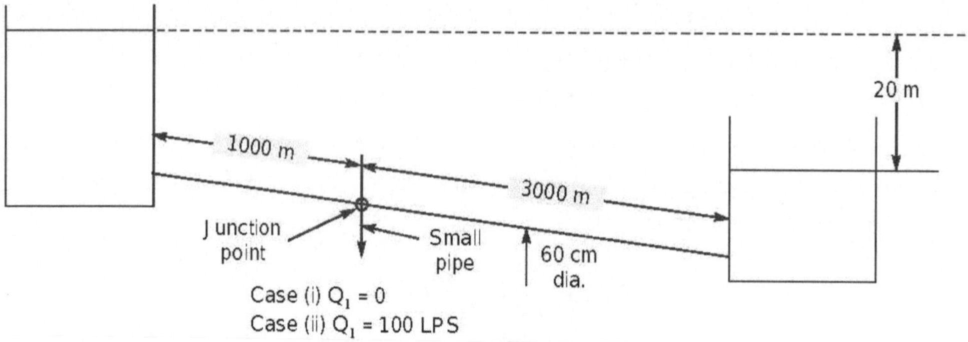

Fig. 12.10

Case 1: No water is taken from small pipe:

$$h_f = \frac{fLQ^2}{12D^5} = \frac{4f'LQ^2}{12Q^5}$$

$$\therefore \quad 20 = \frac{0.02\,(4000)\,Q^2}{12D^5} = \frac{80\,Q^2}{12\,D^5}$$

$$\therefore \quad Q^2 = \frac{20 \times 12\,(06)^5}{80} = 0.23$$

$\therefore$ $Q = 0.482$ m³/s discharge to lower reservoir in first case.

Case 2: 100 LPS is taken from small pipe.

Let small pipe and pipe of length 3000 m (*i.e.*, 4000 – 1000) be regarded as running in parallel, and let us find an equivalent pipe for them which has a length = L_e and dia = 0.6 m, then as per eqn. (12.11) given in section (12.7), we have,

$$Q_e = Q_{\text{equivalent}} = (0.1)^{1/2} + \left[\frac{12\,(0.6)^5}{0.02\,(3000)}\right]^{1/2}$$

$$\therefore \quad \left[\frac{12\,(0.6)^5}{0.02\,L_e}\right]^{1/2} = 0.316 + 0.124 = 0.44$$

$$\therefore \quad \frac{12\,(0.6)^5}{0.02\,L_e} = (.44)^2 = .1936, \quad \therefore \quad L_e = 241 \text{ m}$$

$\therefore$ New length = 1000 + 241 = 1241 m

Now,

$$h_f = \frac{f\,LQ^2}{12\,D^5} = 20$$

$$\therefore \quad Q^2 = \frac{20\,(12)(0.6)^5}{0.02\,(1241)} = 0.744$$

$\therefore \quad Q = 0.862$

$\therefore$ Discharge to lower reservoir = 0.862 – 0.1

$= 0.762 \text{ m}^3/\text{s}$

$$\% \text{ increase to lower reservoir} = \frac{(0.762 - 0.482)}{0.482}$$

$$= \frac{0.28}{0.482} = 0.58$$

$= 58\%$.

■ **Problem 12.7:** *Two reservoirs are connected by three pipes of same length laid in parallel, the diameters are 100 mm, 200 mm and 30 mm. If flow rate through 100 mm dia. pipe is 100 LPS, find flow rate through other two pipes. Assume 'f' to be same for all pipes.*

Solution:

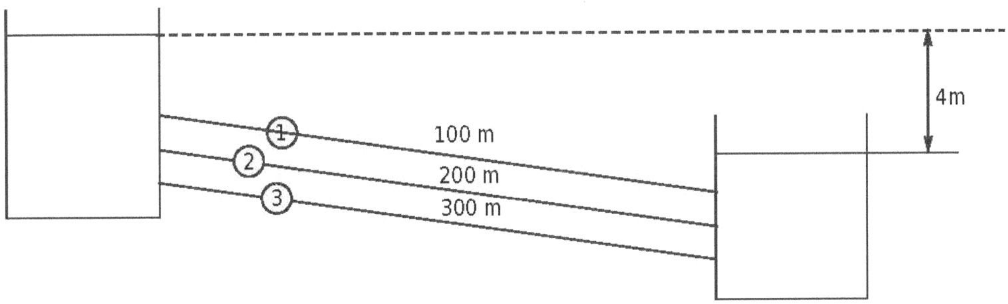

Fig. 12.11

Q_1 for pipe of dia. 100 mm = 100 LPS = 0.1 m^3/s

$$\therefore \quad h_{f1} = \frac{fLQ_1^2}{12D_1^5} = \frac{fL}{12}\left[\frac{(0.1)^2}{(0.1)^5}\right] = \frac{fL}{12}1000$$

As pipes are laid in parallel, $h_{f1} = h_{f2} = h_{f3} = \frac{fL}{12}1000$

$$\therefore \quad h_{f2} = \frac{fLQ_2^2}{12(D_2)^5}$$

$$\therefore \quad 1000 = \frac{Q_2^2}{(0.2)^5}$$

$\therefore \quad Q_2^2 = (0.2)^5 (1000) = 0.32$

$\therefore \quad Q_2 = 0.565 \text{ m}^3/\text{s}$ ...(Ans.)

Similarly, $$h_{f3} = \frac{fL\,Q_3^2}{12(D_3)^5}$$

$$\therefore \quad \frac{fL}{12}1000 = \frac{fL\,Q_3^2}{12(0.3)^5}$$

$$\therefore \qquad Q_3^2 = (0.3)^5\ 1000 = 2.43$$

$$\therefore \qquad Q_3 = 1.558 \text{ m}^3/\text{s}. \qquad \text{...(Ans.)}$$

■ **Problem 12.8:** *Two pipes have a length 'L' each, one of them is of diameter D and the other of diameter 'd'. If pipes are arranged in parallel, the loss of head when a discharge 'Q' flows through them is 'h', but if the pipes are arranged in series and same Q flows through them, the loss of head is H. If d = D/2, find ratio of H to h. Neglect minor losses. Assume same f in both cases.*

Solution:

$$h_f = \frac{fL\,Q^2}{12\,D^5}$$

Case (*a*): Two pipes in parallel.

$$\therefore \qquad h_f = h = \frac{fL\,Q_1^2}{12\,D^5} = \frac{fL\,Q_2^2}{12\,d^5}$$

$$\therefore \qquad \left(\frac{Q_1}{Q_2}\right)^2 = \left(\frac{D}{d}\right)^5$$

$$\therefore \qquad Q_1 = Q_2\left(\frac{D}{d}\right)^{5/2}$$

Also,

$$Q = Q_1 + Q_2$$

$$= Q_2\left[\left(\frac{D}{d}\right)^{5/2} + 1\right]$$

Put

$$D = 2d$$

$$\therefore \qquad Q = Q_2[(2)^{5/2} + 1] = 6.65\,Q_2$$

$$\therefore \qquad h = \frac{fL\left(\dfrac{Q}{6.65}\right)^2}{12\,d^5} = \frac{fL\,Q^2}{530\,d^5} \qquad \text{...(1)}$$

Case (*b*): Two pipes in series:

$$h_f = H = \frac{fL\,Q^2}{12\,D^5} + \frac{fL\,Q^2}{12\,d^5} = \frac{fL\,Q^2}{12}\left[\frac{1}{D^5} + \frac{1}{d^5}\right]$$

$$= \frac{fL\,Q^2}{12\,d^5}\left[\left(\frac{d}{D}\right)^5 + 1\right]$$

$$= \frac{fL\,Q^2}{12\,d^5}\left[\left(\frac{1}{2}\right)^5 + 1\right], \text{ as } D = 2d$$

$$\therefore \qquad H = (1.03)\frac{fL\,Q^2}{12\,d^5} \qquad \text{...(2)}$$

$$\therefore \quad \frac{h}{H} = \frac{fLQ^2}{530\,d^5} \times \frac{12d^5}{1.03\,fLQ^2}$$

$$= 0.0219$$

$$\therefore \quad \frac{H}{h} = 45.5. \qquad \text{...(Ans.)}$$

■ **Problem 12.9:** *Two pipes of diameters 50 cm and 25 cm are each 350 long. What will be the loss of head when they are connected in series and carry a total discharge of 0.15 mec? What will be the loss of head when same pipes are arranged in parallel and carry same total discharge? Take 'f' = 0.0075 for both pipes. Neglect minor losses.*

Solution:

Case 1: Pipe are connected in series:

$\therefore \quad h_f = h_{f1} + h_{f2}$ and $Q = Q_1 = Q_2 = 0.15$ m³/s; $f = 4f' = 4 \times 0.0076 = 0.03$

Now,
$$h_{f1} = \frac{fL_1Q_1^2}{12\,D_1^5} = \frac{0.03\,(350)\,(0.15)^2}{12\,(0.5)^5}$$

$$= \frac{0.236}{0.375} = 0.63\text{ m}$$

$$h_{f2} = \frac{fL_2Q_2^2}{12\,D_2^5} = \frac{0.03\,(350)\,(0.15)^2}{12\,(0.25)^5}$$

$$= \frac{0.236}{0.0117} = 20.13\text{ m}$$

$$\therefore \quad h_f = 0.63 + 20.13 = 20.76\text{ m} \qquad \text{...(Ans.)}$$

Case 2: Pipes are connected in parallel:

$$h_f = h_{f1} = h_{f2} \text{ and } Q = Q_1 + Q_2 = 0.15$$

$$\therefore \quad Q_1 = 0.15 - Q_2$$

$$\frac{fL_1Q_1^2}{12\,D_1^5} = \frac{fL_2Q^2}{12\,D_2^5}, \text{ here } f \text{ is same, and } L_1 = L_2$$

$$\therefore \quad \frac{Q_1^2}{D_1^5} = \frac{Q_2^2}{D_2^5}$$

$$\therefore \quad Q_1{}^2 = \left(\frac{D_1}{D_2}\right)^5 Q_2^2 = \left(\frac{0.5}{0.25}\right)^5 = Q_2^2 = 32\,Q_2^2$$

$$\therefore \quad Q_1 = 5.65\,Q_2 = 0.15 - Q_2$$

$$\therefore \quad 6.65\,Q_2 = 0.15$$

$$\therefore \quad Q_2 = \frac{0.15}{6.65} = 0.0225\text{ m}^3/\text{s}$$

$$\therefore \quad Q_1 = 0.15 - 0.225 = 0.1275\text{ m}^3/\text{s}$$

$$\therefore \qquad h_{f1} = \frac{fL_1Q_1^2}{12\,D_1^5}$$

$$= \frac{0.03\,(350)\,(0.1275)^2}{12\,(0.5)^5}$$

$$= \frac{0.17}{0.375}$$

$$= 0.453 \text{ m}$$

$$= h_{f2}. \qquad \text{...(Ans.)}$$

12.7 EQUIVALENT LENGTH OF A PIPE

Minor loss of head can be expressed in terms of equivalent length, L_e. Thus if head loss in pipe is given by

$$h_L = k\frac{V^2}{2g}$$

then equivalent length L_e of a pipe of diameter D, friction factor f and having same velocity V is given by

$$k\frac{V^2}{2g} = \frac{fL_e\,V^2}{2g\,D}$$

$$\therefore \qquad L_e = \frac{kD}{f}.$$

12.7.1 Equivalent Pipes

(*a*) A pipe of length L, diameter D, friction factor f, and having velocity V will have loss of head given by

$$h_f = \frac{fL\,V^2}{D2g}, \text{ here } V = \frac{Q}{A}$$

$$\therefore \qquad h_f = \frac{fL\,Q^2}{D2g\,A^2}$$

$$= \frac{fL\,Q^2}{D2g\left(\frac{\pi}{4}D^2\right)^2} = \frac{fL\,Q^2}{11.94\,D^5}$$

and is rounded as
$$h_f = \frac{fL\,Q^2}{12D^5} \qquad ..(12.9)$$

(*b*) If number of pipes of diameters D_1, D_2 etc. and length L_1, L_2 etc. and friction factor f_1, f_2 etc. are connected in series, then its equivalent pipe of diameter D_e, length L_e and friction factor f_e, can be obtained by using eqns. (12.7) and (12.9)

$$\frac{f_e L_e}{D_e^5} = \frac{f_1 L_1}{D_1^5} + \frac{f_2 L_2}{D_2^5} + \text{etc.} \quad ...(12.10)$$

(*c*) If number of pipes of diameter D_1, D_2 etc., length L_1, L_2 etc. and friction factor f_1, f_2 etc. are arranged in parallel then its equivalent pipe of diameter D, length L and friction factor f can be obtained by using eqns. (12.8) and (12.9) as

$$\left(\frac{D_e^5}{f_e L_e}\right)^{1/2} = \left(\frac{D_1^5}{f_1 L_1}\right)^{1/2} + \left(\frac{D_2^5}{f_2 L_2}\right)^{1/2} + \text{etc.} \quad ...(12.11)$$

12.8 SIPHON PIPE

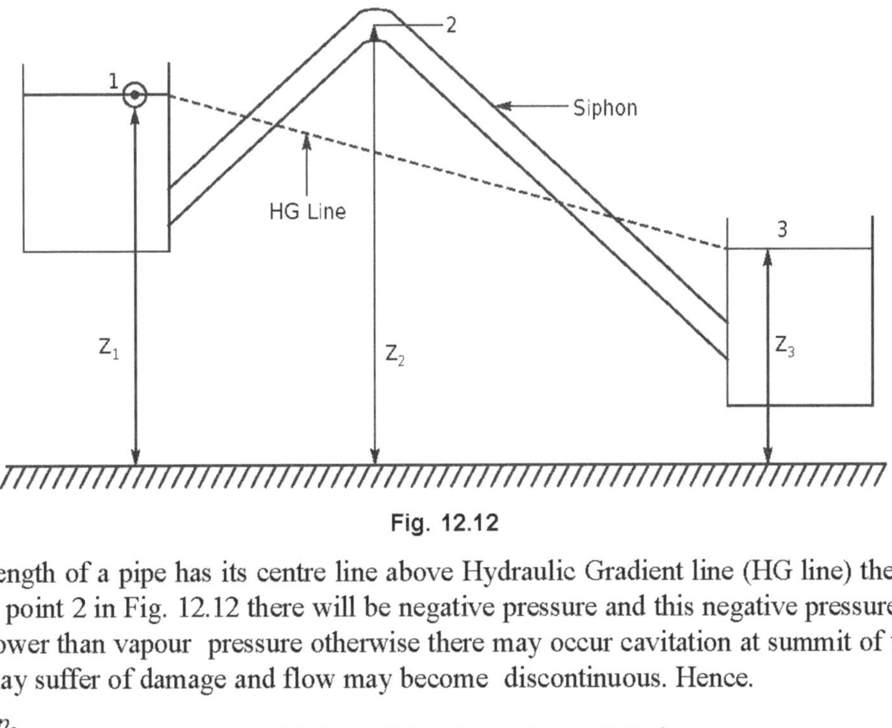

Fig. 12.12

If part length of a pipe has its centre line above Hydraulic Gradient line (HG line) then at its summit, point 2 in Fig. 12.12 there will be negative pressure and this negative pressure should not be lower than vapour pressure otherwise there may occur cavitation at summit of the pipe and it may suffer of damage and flow may become discontinuous. Hence.

$\frac{p_2}{\gamma}$ < Vapour pressure, which is –7.6 m (gauge) or (+2.7 abs)

Apply Bernoulli's Theorem between points 1 and 2,

$$Z_1 + 0 + 0 = \frac{p_2}{\gamma} + Z_2 + \frac{V_2^2}{2g} + h_{f1-2}$$

$$\therefore \quad \frac{p_2}{\gamma} = (Z_1 - Z_2) - \frac{V_2^2}{2g} - h_{f1-2} \quad ...(12.12)$$

12.9 POWER TRANSMITTED THROUGH PIPE AND NOZZLE

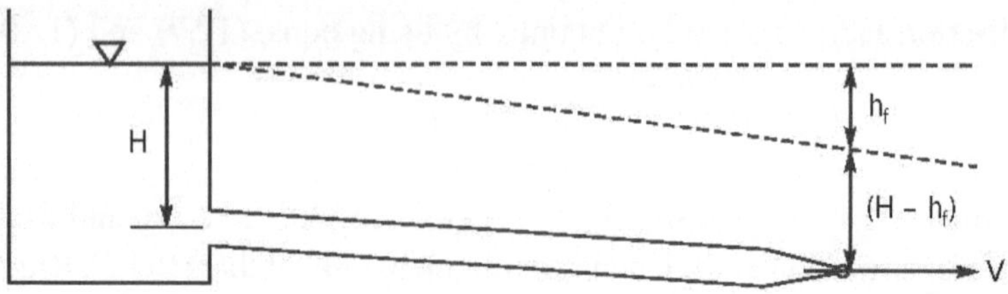

Fig. 12.13

Let v = Velocity in nozzle of diameter d and
V = Velocity in pipe of diameter D
H = Total head at inlet
h_f = Head lost in friction in the pipe.

$$\therefore \quad H - h_f = \frac{v^2}{2g} \qquad ...(12.13)$$

By law of continuity, $\frac{\pi}{4} d^2 v \frac{\pi}{4} D^2 V = Q$

$$\therefore \quad V = v\left(\frac{d^2}{D^2}\right)$$

and
$$V^2 = v^2\left(\frac{d}{D}\right)^4 \qquad ...(12.14)$$

Now power
$$P = \gamma Q\left(\frac{v^2}{2g}\right) \qquad ...(12.15)$$

From eqn. (12.13), $\frac{v^2}{2g} = H - h_f$

$$= H - \frac{fLV^2}{D2g}$$

$$\therefore \quad P = \gamma Q\left[H - \frac{fLV^2}{D2g}\right]$$

but
$$Q = \frac{\pi}{4} D^2 V$$

$$\therefore \quad P = \gamma \frac{\pi}{4} D^2 V\left[H - \frac{fLV^2}{D2g}\right]$$

$$= \gamma \frac{\pi}{4} D^2 \left[HV - \frac{fL V^2}{D 2 g} \right]$$

For P to be max, $\dfrac{dP}{dV} = 0$

$$\therefore \quad \frac{dP}{dV} = H - 3\frac{fL V^2}{D2g} = 0, \text{ but } \frac{fL V^2}{D2g} = h_f$$

$$\therefore \quad H - 3h_f = 0$$

$$\therefore \quad h_f = \frac{1}{3} H \qquad \text{...(12.16)}$$

Eqn. (12.16) gives condition for max. power transmission in the pipe.

Now we have $H - 3H_f = 0$

$$\therefore \quad 3h_f = H$$

$$3\frac{fL V^2}{D2g} = H$$

Replace V by $v\left(\dfrac{d}{D}\right)^2$

$$\therefore \quad \frac{3 fL v^2 \left(\dfrac{d}{D}\right)^4}{D2g} = H \qquad \text{...(12.17)}$$

Now from eqn. (12.13), $H - h_f = \dfrac{v^2}{2g}$

But $\quad h_f = \dfrac{1}{3} H$

$$\therefore \quad \frac{2}{3} H = \frac{v^2}{2g} \qquad \text{...(12.18)}$$

Putting value of $\dfrac{v^2}{2g}$ in eqn. (12.17)

$$\frac{3 fL \dfrac{2}{3} H \left(\dfrac{d}{D}\right)^4}{D} = H$$

$$\therefore \quad \frac{fL}{D}\left(\frac{d}{D}\right)^4 = \frac{1}{2}$$

$$\therefore \qquad fLd^4 = \frac{1}{2}D^5$$

$$\therefore \qquad d = \left(\frac{D^5}{2fL}\right)^{1/4} \qquad ...(12.19)$$

$$= \text{nozzle diameter for } P_{maz}.$$

12.9.1 Solved Problems

■ **Problem 12.10:** *Two pipes with diameters D_1, D_2, length L_1, L_2 and friction factor f_1, f_2 are connected in parallel between two points A and B in a pipe line. If an equivalent pipe of diameter D_e, length L_e, and friction factor f_e is to replace the set of parallel pipes, obtain an expression for equivalent pipe diameter, D_e.*

Solution:

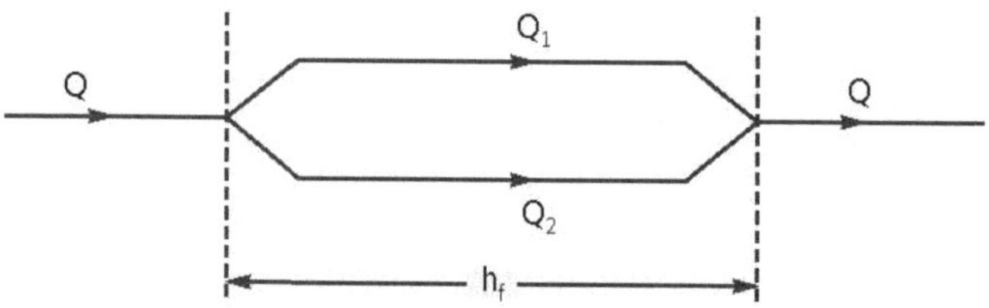

Fig. 12.14

For parallel pipes, $h_f = h_{f1} = h_{f2}$ and $Q = Q_1 + Q_2$

$$\therefore \qquad \frac{f_1L_1V_1^2}{D_1 2g} = \frac{f_2L_2V_2^2}{D_2 2g} = h_f$$

$$\therefore \qquad V_1 = \left(\frac{D_1}{f_1L_1}\right)^{\frac{1}{2}} \sqrt{2gh_f}$$

$$\therefore \qquad Q_1 = A_1V_1 = \frac{\pi}{4}D_1^2V_1$$

$$= \frac{\pi}{4}D_1^2\left(\frac{D_1}{f_1L_1}\right)^{\frac{1}{2}} \sqrt{2g\,h_f}$$

$$= \frac{\pi}{4}\left(\frac{D_1^5}{f_1L_1}\right)^{\frac{1}{2}} \sqrt{2g\,h_f}$$

Similarly,
$$Q_2 = \frac{\pi}{4}\left(\frac{D_2^5}{f_2L_2}\right)^{\frac{1}{2}} \sqrt{2g\,h_f}\,,\; Q = \frac{\pi}{4}\left(\frac{D_e^5}{fL_e}\right)^{\frac{1}{2}} \sqrt{2g\,h_f}$$

But
$$Q = Q_1 + Q_2$$

$$\therefore \quad \frac{\pi}{4}\left(\frac{D_e^5}{fL_e}\right)^{\frac{1}{2}}\sqrt{2g\,h_f} = \frac{\pi}{4}\left(\frac{D_1^5}{f_1L_1}\right)^{\frac{1}{2}}\sqrt{2g\,h_f} + \frac{\pi}{4}\left(\frac{D_2^5}{f_2L_2}\right)\sqrt{2g\,h_f}$$

$$\therefore \quad \left(\frac{D_e^5}{fL_e}\right)^{\frac{1}{2}} = \left(\frac{D_1^5}{f_1L_1}\right)^{\frac{1}{2}} + \left(\frac{D_2^5}{f_2L_2}\right)^{\frac{1}{2}}. \qquad \text{...(Ans.)}$$

■ **Problem 12.11:** *If three pipes with diameter, length and friction as D_1, L_1, f_1; D_2, L_2, f_2, D_3, L_3, f_3, respectively are connected in series, find diameter, length and friction factor of equivalent pipe.*

Solution:

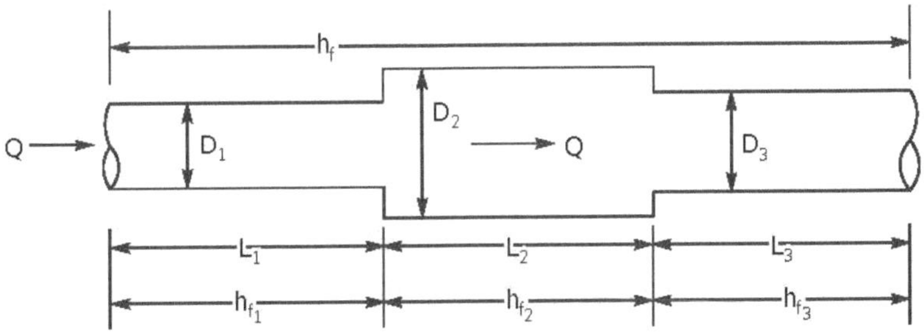

Fig. 12.15

For pipes in series as shown in Fig. 12.15,

$$Q = Q_1 = Q_2 = Q_3$$

$$h_f = h_{f1} + h_{f1} = h_{f3}$$

Now,

$$h_f = \frac{fLV^2}{D2g} = \frac{fL\,Q^2}{(D2g)\,A^2} = \frac{fL\,Q^2}{12D^5}$$

$$\therefore \quad \frac{f_eL_e\,Q^2}{12\,D_e^5} = \frac{f_1L_1\,Q^2}{12\,D_1^5} + \frac{f_2L_2\,Q^2}{12\,D_2^5} + \frac{f_3L_3\,Q^2}{12\,D_3^5}$$

$$\therefore \quad \frac{f_eL_e}{D_e^5} = \frac{f_1L_1}{D_1^5} + \frac{f_2L_2}{D_2^5} + \frac{f_3L_3}{D_3^5}.$$

■ **Problem 12.12:** *A pipe system consisting of 2000 m of 50 cm diameter and 1000 m of 40 cm diameter has same friction factor f.*

What is equivalent length of a pipe of 30 cm diameter and same f if:

(*a*) *above two pipes connected in series.*

(*b*) *above two pipes connected in parallel?*

Solution:

(*a*) Series connected of pipe 1,2:

$$\frac{f_eL_e}{D_e^5} = \frac{f_1L_1}{D_1^5} + \frac{f_2L_2}{D_2^5}$$

$$f_e = f_1 = f_2 = f, \text{ same.}$$
$$D_1 = 50 \text{ cm}, D_2 = 40 \text{ cm and } D_e = 30 \text{ cm}$$

$$\therefore \quad \frac{L_e}{(0.3)^5} = \frac{2000}{(0.5)^5} + \frac{1000}{(0.4)^5}$$

$$\frac{L_e}{0.0024} = \frac{2000}{0.0312} + \frac{1000}{0.0256}$$
$$= 64102 + 39062$$

$$\therefore \quad L_e = 0.0024\ [103164]$$
$$= 247.6 \text{ m} \qquad \text{...(Ans.)}$$

(*b*) Parallel connection of pipes 1, 2:

$$\left(\frac{D_e^5}{f_e L_e}\right)^{\frac{1}{2}} = \left(\frac{D_1^5}{f_1 L_1}\right)^{\frac{1}{2}} + \left(\frac{D_2^5}{f_2 L_2}\right)^{\frac{1}{2}}$$

f_e, f_1, f_2 can be deleted being same.

$$\therefore \quad \left[\frac{(0.3)^5}{L_e}\right]^{\frac{1}{2}} = \left[\frac{(0.5)^5}{2000}\right]^{\frac{1}{2}} + \left[\frac{(0.4)^5}{1000}\right]^{\frac{1}{2}}$$

$$\left(\frac{0.0024}{L_e}\right)^{\frac{1}{2}} = \left(\frac{0.0312}{2000}\right)^{\frac{1}{2}} + \left(\frac{0.0256}{1000}\right)^{\frac{1}{2}}$$
$$= 3.94 \times 10^{-3} + 5.06 \times 10^{-3}$$
$$= 9 \times 10^{-3}$$

$$\frac{0.0024}{L_e} = (9 \times 10^{-3})^2 = 8.1 \times 10^{-5}$$

$$L_e = \frac{0.0024}{8.1 \times 10^{-5}} = \frac{240}{8.1} = 29.6$$
$$= 29.6 \text{ m.} \qquad \text{...(Ans.)}$$

■ **Problem 12.13:** *A pipe of length 5000 m is used for power transmission. If 250 HP is to be transmitted through the pipe, in which water having a pressure of 500 N/cm² at inlet is flowing, find diameter of the pipe corresponding to maximum efficiency of transmission, take $f = 0.01$.*

Solution: Pressure in pipe at its inlet = 500 N/cm² = 500×10^4/m²

$$\therefore \quad H = \frac{p}{\gamma} = \frac{500 \times 10^4}{10^4} 500 \text{ m}$$

$$\therefore \quad h_f = \frac{1}{3} H \text{ for } P_{max} \text{ condition}$$

$$= \frac{500}{3} = 166.6 \text{ m}$$

$$166.6 = \frac{f\,LV^2}{D2g} = \frac{0.01\,(5000)\,Q^2}{12\,(D)^5}$$

Now, $$P = \gamma Q\,(H - h_f)$$

$$250 \times 750 = 9{,}810\,(Q)\,(500 - 166), \text{ here } \gamma = \rho g = 1000 \times 9.81 = 9810$$

$$Q = \frac{250 \times 750}{9810 \times 333} = \frac{563}{9810}$$

$$= 0.0573 \text{ m}^3/\text{s}$$

$\therefore$ $$166.6 = \frac{0.01\,(5000)\,(0.0573)^2}{12\,(D^5)}$$

$$D^5 = \frac{0.01\,(5000)\,(0.0573)^2}{166.6 \times 12}$$

$$= 8.27 \times 10^{-5}$$

$\therefore$ $$D = 0.157 \text{ m.}$$ **...(Ans.)**

■ **Problem 12.14:** *A pipe of 30 m length tapers uniformly from 24 cm diameter at one end to 12 cm diameter at other end and conveys a discharge of 0.08 cumec. of water. Find the loss of head due to friction in the pipe. Take f = 0.04.*

Solution:

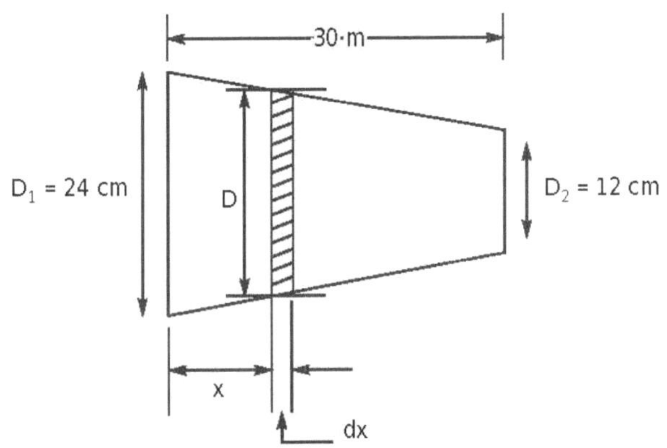

Fig. 12.16

Consider a strip of thickness dx at x from $D_1 = 24$ cm. Let dia. of strip be D.

$\therefore$ $$d(h_{fx}) = \frac{f\,(dx)\,Q^2}{12\,D^5}$$

Now, $$D = \left[24 - \frac{(24-12)}{30}x\right] \text{cm}$$

$$= (24 - 0.4x) \times 10^{-2} \text{ m}$$

$\therefore$ $$dh_f = \frac{0.04\,dx\,(0.08)^2}{12[(24 - 0.4x) \times 10^{-2}]^5}$$

$$= \frac{0.04\,(0.08)^2\,dx}{12[0.4\,(60-x)\times10^{-2}]^5}$$

$$= \frac{0.04\,(0.08)^2\,dx}{12\times1.024\times10^{-12}(60-x)^5}$$

$$= \frac{2.13\times10^{-5}\,dx}{1.024\times10^{-12}(60-x)^5}$$

$$= (2.08\times10^7)\frac{dx}{(60-x)^5}$$

$$\therefore \qquad h_f = (2.08\times10^7)\int_0^{30}\frac{dx}{(60-x)^5}$$

$$= (2.08\times10^7)\left[\frac{(60-x)^{-5+1}}{(-5+1)(-1)}\right]_0^{30}$$

$$= \frac{(2.08\times10^7)}{4}\left[(60-x)^{-4}\right]_0^{30}$$

$$= 0.52\times10^7\,[(60-30)^{-4}-(60-0)^{-4}]$$

$$= 0.52\times10^7\left[\frac{1}{(30)^4}-\frac{1}{(60)^4}\right]$$

$$= 0.52\times10^7\,[1.23\times10^{-6}-0.077+10^{-6}]$$

$$= 0.52\times10^{-7}\,(1.15\times10^{-6})$$

$$= 0.6\times10$$

$$= 6\text{ m.}$$ ...(Ans.)

■ **Problem 12.15**: *Two reservoirs R_1 and R_2 are connected through pipe system consisting of 50 cm dia. 600 m long pipe branching into two pipes of 30 cm and 40 cm diameter and each 600 m long. Pump near R_1 pumps 300 LPS of water through this pipe system to R_2 which has water surface 40 m above that of R_1. If f = 0.02, find HP required by pump taking pumping efficiency as 60 %.*

Solution: Find length of equivalent pipe of dia. 50 cm to replace 2 parallel pipes of 30 and 40 cm; by formula;

$$\left[\frac{D_e^5}{f\,L_e}\right]^{1/2} = \left[\frac{D_2^5}{f\,L_2}\right]^{1/2} + \left[\frac{D_3^5}{f\,L_3}\right]^{1/2}$$

$$\left[\frac{(0.5)^5}{L_e}\right]^{1/2} = \left[\frac{(0.3)^5}{600}\right]^{1/2} + \left[\frac{(0.4)^5}{600}\right]^{1/2}$$

$$= 2\times10^{-3}+4.13\times10^{-3}$$

$$= 6.13\times10^{-3}$$

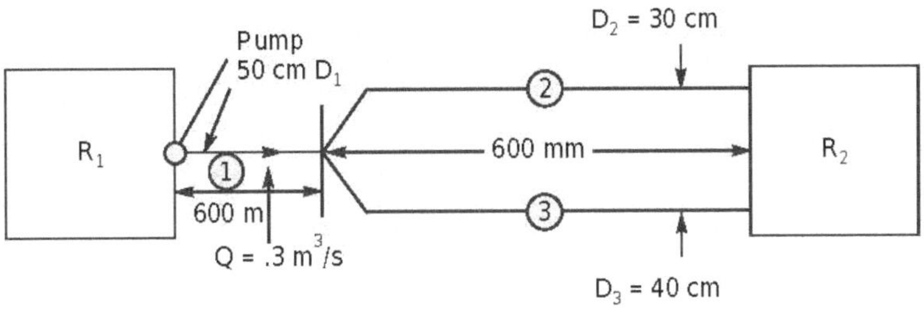

Fig. 12.17

$$\frac{(0.5)^5}{L_e} = (6.13 \times 10^{-3})^2 = 37.5 \times 10^{-6}$$

$\therefore$ $$\frac{0.031}{L_e} = 37.5 \times 10^{-6}$$

$\therefore$ $$L_e = \frac{0.031}{37.5 \times 10^{-6}} = 8.26 \times 10^{-4} \times 10^{+6} = 826 \text{ m}$$

$\therefore$ Total length of 50 cm dia. pipe = 826 + 600 = 1426 m

$$V = \frac{Q}{A} = \frac{0.3}{\frac{\pi}{4}(0.5)^2} = 1.53 \text{ m/s}$$

$\therefore$ $$h_f = \frac{f L_e V^2}{D\,2g}$$

$$= \frac{0.02\,(1426)\,(1.53)^2}{0.5\,(2 \times 9.81)}$$

$$= \frac{66.76}{9.8} = 6.8 \text{ m}$$

H = Total pumping head = 40 + 6.8 = 46.8 m

$$P = \frac{\gamma QH}{\eta}$$

$$= \frac{9810 \times (0.3)\,(46.8)}{0.6}$$

= 229 kW. ...(Ans.)

■ **Problem 12.16:** *A pipe line 60 cm in dia. and 4000 m long has water withdrawn by a series of pipes at a uniform rate of 0.1 m³/s per 200 m in its last 2000 m length. Find total head lost if f = 0.02.*

Solution: $$Q = \frac{2000}{200}(0.1) = 1 \text{ m}^3\text{/s}$$

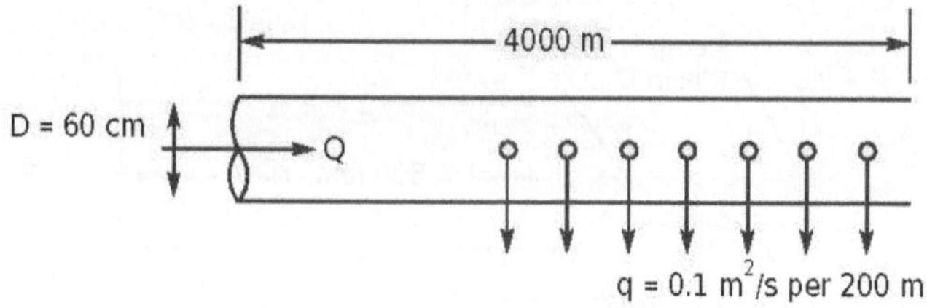

Fig. 12.18

$$q' = \frac{0.1}{200} = 5 \times 10^{-4} \text{ m}^3\text{/s/m over } L_0 = 2000 \text{ m}$$

H_f = total head loss = h_{f1} in first 2000 m + h_{f2} in last 2000 m

$$h_{f1} = \frac{0.02\,(2000)\,(1)^2}{12\,(0.6)^5} = \frac{40}{12 \times 0.077} = 42.86 \text{ m}$$

In last 2000 m, discharge = $Q_x = Q - q'x$

In a small distance dx,

$$dh_f = \frac{f\,(dx)\,(Q - q'x)^2}{12\,(D)^5}$$

$\therefore$ $$h_{f2} = \int_0^L dh_f$$ (Note that here L = 2000 m)

$$= \frac{f}{12\,(D)^5} \int_0^L (Q - q'x)^2\,dx$$

$$= \frac{f}{(12)\,(D^5)} \left[\frac{(Q - q'x)^3}{(-3q')} \right]_0^L$$

$$= \frac{-f}{(12)\,(D^5)\,3q'} \left[(Q - q'x)^3 \right]_0^L$$

$$= \frac{f}{12\,D^5\,3q'} [Q^3 - (Q - q'L)^3]$$

$$= \frac{0.02}{12\,(0.6)^5\,3(5 \times 10^{-4})} [(1)^3 - (1 - 5 \times 10^{-4} \times 2000)]$$

$$= \frac{0.02}{12\,(0.077)\,15 \times 10^{-4}} [1 - (1 - 1)]$$

$$= \frac{0.02}{13.86 \times 10^{-4}}$$

$$= \frac{1.443 \times 10^{-3}}{10^{-4}} = 14.43 \text{ m}$$

$\therefore$ Total head loss H_f = 42.86 + 14.43 = 57.29 m. ...**(Ans.)**

■ **Problem 12.17:** *A power transmillian pipe 15 cm in diameter and 500 m long is fitted with a nozzle at the exit. If inlet head is 51 m above nozzle, and f = 0.2, find maximum power transmitted and nozzle dia.*

Solution: For max. power transmillian $h_f = \frac{1}{3}H$

$$= \frac{1}{3}(51)\text{ m}$$

$$= 17\text{ m}$$

∴ H available at nozzle = 51 – 17 = 34 m

Now $$h_f = 17 = \frac{fLV^2}{D\,2g} = \frac{0.02\,(500)\,V^2}{(0.15)\,2\,(9.81)} = 3.4\,V^2$$

∴ $$V = \left(\frac{17}{3.4}\right)^{1/2} = 2.23\text{ m/s}$$

∴ $$Q = AV = \frac{\pi}{4}(0.15)^2\,(2.23)$$

$$= 0.039\text{ m}^3\text{/s}$$

$$P = \gamma QH_1$$

$$= (9810)\,(0.039)\,(34)$$

$$= 13\text{ kW}$$ ...(Ans.)

$$d_{\text{nozzle}} = \left(\frac{D^5}{2fL}\right)^{1/4} \text{ from eqn. (12.19)}$$

$$= \left[\frac{(0.15^5)}{2\,(0.02)\,500}\right]^{1/4}$$

$$= 0.044\text{ m}$$

$$= 4.4\text{ cm.}$$ ...(Ans.)

■ **Problem 12.18:** *Compare cost of pumping same fluid at same flow through 20 cm and 30 cm dia. pipes of same length. Take f = 0.02 for both pipes.*

Solution: $$h_f = \frac{fLQ^2}{12\,D^5}$$

∴ $$\frac{h_{f1}}{h_{f2}} = \frac{f_1 L_1 Q_1^2}{12\,D_1^5} \times \frac{12\,D_2^5}{f_2 L_2 Q_2^2}$$

Here $f_1 = f_2$, $Q_1 = Q_2$, and $L_1 = L_2$

∴ $$\frac{h_{f1}}{h_{f2}} = \left(\frac{D_2}{D_1}\right)^5 = \left(\frac{30}{20}\right)^5 = 7.59$$

Now cost of pumping is proportional to friction head.

∴ Cost of pumping through 20 cm dia. pipe = 7.59

(cost of pumping through 30 cm dia. pipe).

■ **Problem 12.19:** *A siphon pipe of 25 cm diameter connects two reservoirs having difference in water surface elevation equal to 20 m. Length of siphon is 600 m, and its summit is at y m above water surface of reservoir on upper level. Inlet leg is 200 m. Find discharge in siphon and value of y. Take f = 0.02.*

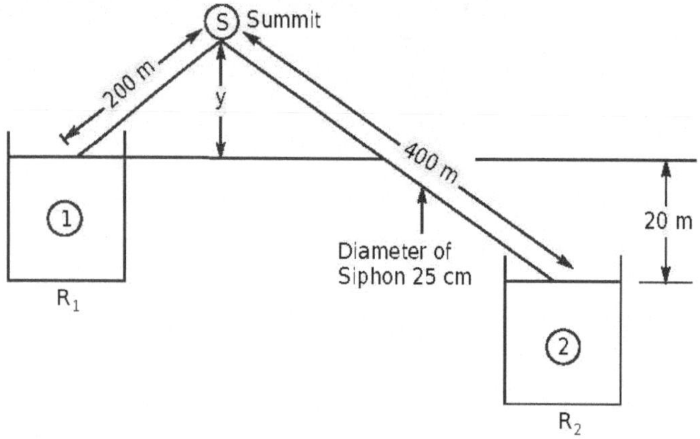

Fig. 12.19

Note: Point (*S*) in Fig. 12.19 at highest level of siphon is called summit and here pressure will be less than atmospheric. It can have theoretical value of – 10.3 but practically its limit is – 7.6 m of water or + 2.7 m absolute. If pressure at *S* falls below + 2.7 m abs, vaporization of water will start and flow will not be continuous. Hence limiting value of pressure at summit of siphon is + 2.7 m abs or – 7.6 m (gage) of water.

Solution: Apply Bernoulli's Theorem between (1) and (2)

$$\therefore \quad 20 = 0.5\frac{V^2}{2g} + f\frac{LV^2}{D\,2g} + \frac{V^2}{2g}$$

$$= \frac{V^2}{2g}\left[1.5 + \frac{0.02 \times 600}{0.25}\right] = 49.5\left(\frac{V^2}{2g}\right)$$

$$\therefore \quad V^2 = \frac{20 \times 2 \times 9.81}{49.5}$$

$$= 7.92$$

$$\therefore \quad V = 2.81 \text{ m/s}$$

$$\therefore \quad Q = \frac{\pi}{4}D^2V = 0.78\,(0.25)^2\,(2.81)$$

$$= 0.136 \text{ m}^3\text{/s}$$ ...(Ans.)

Now apply Bernoulli's Theorem between (1) and S.

$$\therefore \quad 10.3 = \frac{p_s}{\gamma} + y + \frac{V^2}{2g}\left[1.5 + \frac{fL_1}{D}\right]$$

$$= \frac{p_s}{\gamma} + y + \frac{(2.81)^2}{2g}\left[1.5 + \frac{0.02 \times 200}{0.25}\right]$$

$$= \frac{p_s}{\gamma} + y + \frac{(2.81)^2\, 17.5}{2g}$$

$$= \frac{p_s}{\gamma} + y + 7$$

Now $\frac{p_s}{\gamma}$ permissible = 2.7 abs.

$$\therefore \quad 10.3 = 2.7 + y + 7$$

$$\therefore \quad y = 10.3 - 9.7 = 0.6 \text{ m.}$$ ...(Ans.)

■ **Problem 12.20**: *A siphon of 20 cm diameter 500 m long connects two tanks having difference of level in free surface of water of 20 m. The summit is at 100 m length from upper tank and 3 m above water level of upper tank. Find Q through siphon and pressure at summit. Take f = 0.02.*

Solution:

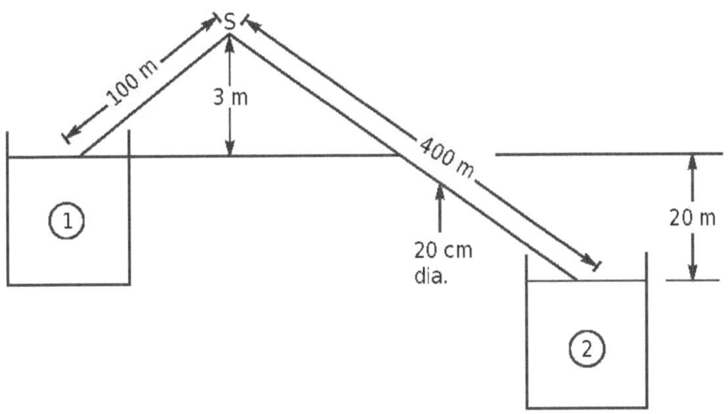

Fig. 12.20

Apply Bernoulli's Theorem between (1) and (2)

$$\therefore \quad 20 = 0.5\frac{V^2}{2g} + \frac{fL\,V^2}{D2g} + \frac{V^2}{2g}$$

$$= \frac{V^2}{2g}\left[1.5 + \frac{0.2 \times 500}{0.2}\right]$$

$$\therefore \quad 20 = 51.5\frac{V^2}{2g}$$

$$\therefore \qquad V^2 = \frac{20 \times 2 \times 9.81}{51.5} = 7.61$$

$$\therefore \qquad V = 2.76 \text{ m/s}$$

$$Q = \frac{\pi}{4} D^2 V = \frac{\pi}{4}(0.2)^2(2.76) = 0.086 \text{ m}^3/\text{s}$$

To find $\left(\frac{p_s}{\gamma}\right)$, apply Bernoulli's Theorem between (1) and S

$$\therefore \qquad 10.3 = \frac{p_s}{\gamma} + 3 + \frac{V^2}{2g}\left[1.5 + \frac{0.02 \times 100}{0.2}\right]$$

$$= \frac{p_s}{\gamma} + 3 + 4.46$$

$$\therefore \qquad \frac{p_s}{\gamma} = 10.3 - 7.46 = 2.84 \text{ m absolute} > 2.7 \text{ m abs.} \therefore \text{ OK.} \quad \text{...(Ans.)}$$

■ **Problem 12.21:** *A siphon pipe 100 mm diameter is used to transfer water from one tank to the other over an embankment. The inlet leg is 34 m and outlet leg 346 m. The pipe axis is 2.4 m above water surface of upstream tank. Take $f = 0.03$ find Q through siphon and pressure at the summit.*

Solution:

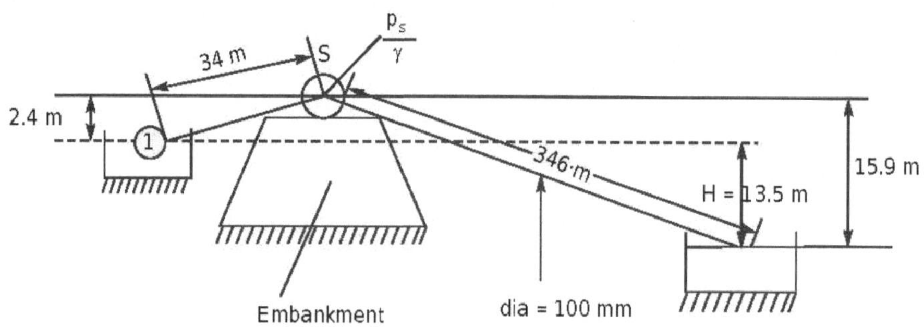

Fig. 12.21

Neglecting minor losses, $h_f = \frac{fLV^2}{D2g}$

$$\therefore \qquad (15.9 - 2.4) = \frac{0.03\,(380)\,V^2}{(0.1)\,(19.6)}$$

$$\therefore \qquad V = 1.52 \text{ m/s}$$

$$\therefore \qquad Q = \frac{\pi}{4} D^2 V = 0.78\,(0.1)^2\,(1.52)$$

$$= 0.0118 \text{ m}^3/\text{s} \qquad \text{...(Ans.)}$$

Apply Bernoulli's Theorem between (1) and (*S*),

$$\therefore \quad 10.3 = \frac{p_s}{\gamma} + 2.4 + \frac{fL_1V^2}{D2g}$$

$$= \frac{p_s}{y} + 2.4 + \frac{0.03 \times 34 \times (1.52)^2}{(0.1)\,(19.6)}$$

$$= \frac{p_s}{\gamma} + 2.4 + 1.2$$

$$\therefore \quad \frac{p_s}{\gamma} = 10.3 - 3.6 = 6.7 \text{ m absolute} > 2.7 \text{ m} \quad \therefore \text{ OK.} \qquad \text{...(Ans.)}$$

12.10 BRANCHING OF PIPES OR THREE RESERVOIR PROBLEM

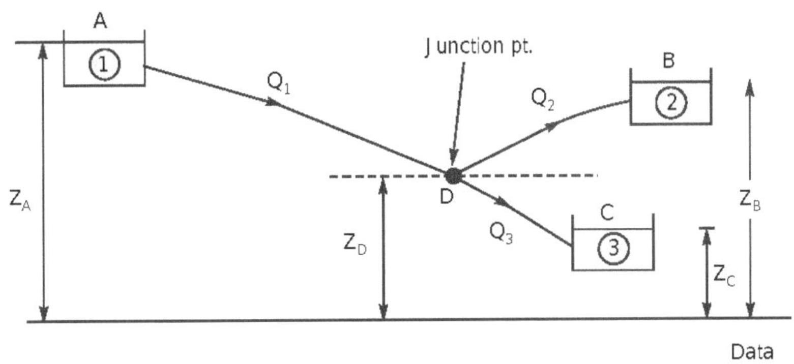

Fig. 12.22

When 3 reservoirs are connected by means of pipes, having a junction such as at *D* in Fig. 12.22, the system is called Branching Pipe System or simply a 3 reservoir problem.

Equations to be solved in this case are:

(*a*) Equation of continuity,

i.e. at the junction *D*, Inflow = Outflow

$$\therefore \quad Q_1 = Q_2 + Q_3$$

(*b*) Darcy Weisbach equation, *i.e.*

$$h_f = \frac{fLV^2}{D2g}$$

(*c*) Apply Bernoulli's Theorem between

1. *A* and *D*

$$\therefore \quad Z_A = Z_D + \frac{P_D}{\gamma} + h_{f1}$$

2. D and B

$$\therefore \quad Z_D + \frac{p_D}{\gamma} Z_C + h_{f3} = Z_B + h_{f2}$$

3. D and C

$$\therefore \quad Z_D + \frac{p_D}{\gamma} = Z_C + h_{f3}$$

There are four unknowns, V_1, V_2, V_3, $\frac{p_D}{\gamma}$ and four equations as given above, hence the problem can be solved.

12.10.1 Solved Problems

■ **Problem 12.22:** *For the branching system of pipes shown in Fig. 12.23, find Q in each pipe, given the following data:*

Pipe	*Dia.*	*Length*	*Connection*
1	*20 cm*	*400 m*	*AD*
2	*15 cm*	*200 m*	*BD*
3	*15 cm*	*200 m*	*CD*

Solution: D is junction point, $f = 0.02$ for all pipes.

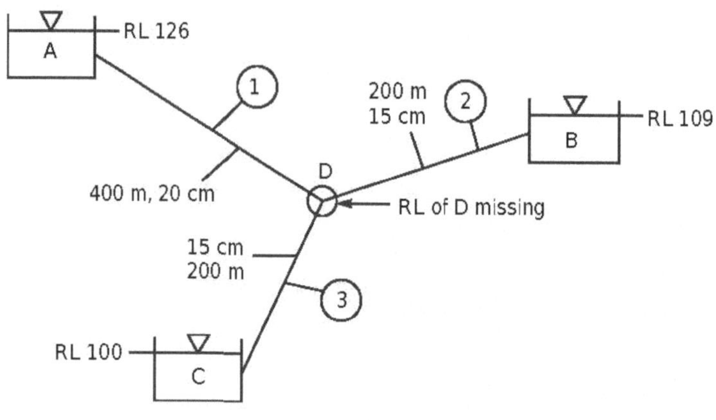

Fig. 12.23

Trial and error method is adopted as *RL* of junction point *D* is missing. Flow away from junction is – ve.

1st. Trial: Assume *RL* of $D = 114$ [nearly (1/2) of 126 *RL* and 100 *RL*]

$$h_f = \frac{fLV^2}{D2g} = \frac{(fL)Q^2}{12D^5}$$

$$= KQ^2$$

$\therefore \qquad K = \dfrac{fL}{12D^5} = \dfrac{0.02\,L}{12\,D^5} = 0.0016\left(\dfrac{L}{D^5}\right)$

$\therefore \qquad K_1 = 0.0016\dfrac{400}{(0.2)^5} = 0.0016\left(\dfrac{400}{3.2\times10^{-4}}\right) = 0.2\times10^4 = 2000$

$K_2 = 0.0016\dfrac{200}{(0.15)^5} = \dfrac{0.0016(200)}{7.59\times10^{-5}} = 0.042\times10^{-4} = 4200$

$K_3 = 0.0016\left[\dfrac{200}{(0.15)^5}\right] = 4200$

Pipe	*K*	h_f *estimated*	*Flow away from D (–ve)* $Q_{(LPS)} = \sqrt{\dfrac{h_f}{K}}$	*Mod. value i.e. (+ve only)* $\lvert Q/h_f \rvert$
1	2000	126 – 114 = 12	+ 77 LPS	6.4
2	4200	114 – 109 = 5	– 34.5 LPS	6.9
3	4200	114 – 100 = 14	– 57.7 LPS	4.12
			ΣQ = – 15.2	Σ = 17.42

$\therefore$ Correction to assumed *RL* to

$$D = \Delta H_j = \frac{2\Sigma Q}{\Sigma\left|\dfrac{Q}{h_f}\right|}$$

$$= \frac{2(-15.2)}{17.42} = -1.74$$

$\therefore$ New *RL* of *D* = 114 – 1.74 = 112.26

Pipe	*K*	h_f *estimate*	$Q = \sqrt{\dfrac{h_f}{k}}$	$\left\lvert\dfrac{Q}{h_f}\right\rvert$
1	2000	126 – 112.26 = 13.74	+ 82.3	6.0
2	4200	112.26 – 109 = 3.26	– 27.3	8.5
3	4200	112.26 – 100 = 12.26	–54	4.4
			ΔQ = + 1	$\Sigma\left\lvert\dfrac{Q}{h_f}\right\rvert$ = 19

$$\therefore \qquad \Delta H_j = \frac{2\times(1)}{\left|\dfrac{Q}{h_f}\right|} = \frac{2}{19} = +0.1$$

As $\Delta Q = 0.1$, very small, no further trial is required

$\therefore$ Assumed value of RL of $D = 112.26$ is OK.

$$\therefore \qquad Q_1 = 82.8 \text{ LPS } A \text{ to } D$$

$$Q_2 = -27.8 \text{ LPS} \qquad \text{towards } B$$

$$Q_3 = -54.0 \text{ LPS} \qquad \text{toward } C$$

...**(Ans.)**

Summary of method adopted in above problem No. 22.

1. Assume trial level of the junction, say H_j.

   This can be assumed as $\frac{1}{2}$ [level of lowest Reservoir + level of highest reservoir]

2. For the trial H_j, calculate h_f by

   $h_f = H_f -$ level of R = friction head of pipe joining R and junction.

3. For this value of h_f, find $Q = \sqrt{\dfrac{h_f}{k}}$, here $k = \dfrac{fL}{12D^5}$

   Assign + sign to Q if it is toward J and –ve if it is away from J.

4. Find $\Delta Q = \Sigma Q$, if ΔQ nearly equals to zero, assumed H_j is OK or follows steps 5, 6, 7.

5. Find $\left|\dfrac{Q}{h_f}\right|$, here Q is independent of its sign.

6. Correction to assumed value of $H_j = \dfrac{2(\Delta Q)}{\Sigma\left|\dfrac{Q}{h_f}\right|} = \Delta H_j$

7. With new value of H_j repeat above procedure.

■ **Problem 12.23:** *A 600 mm dia. pipe connects reservoir A to a junction J which branches into two pipes, 400 mm and 300 mm, connecting J to reservoir B and C. Water level in A and B are 30 m and 25 m above datum. AJ = 300 m, BJ = 200 m, CJ = 150 m. Find water level in reservoir C if from A is 100 LPS. Take f = 0.02 for all pipes.*

Solution: Here we do not know level of J and level of C.

But Q from A is known, which will give h_f for AJ pipe.

$$\therefore \qquad h_{fAj} = \frac{fL_{AJ}Q^2}{12D^5} = \frac{0.02\,(300)\,(0.1)^2}{12\,(0.6)^5} = 0.064 \text{ m}$$

$$\therefore \qquad RL \text{ of } J = 30 - 0.064$$

$$= 29.936$$

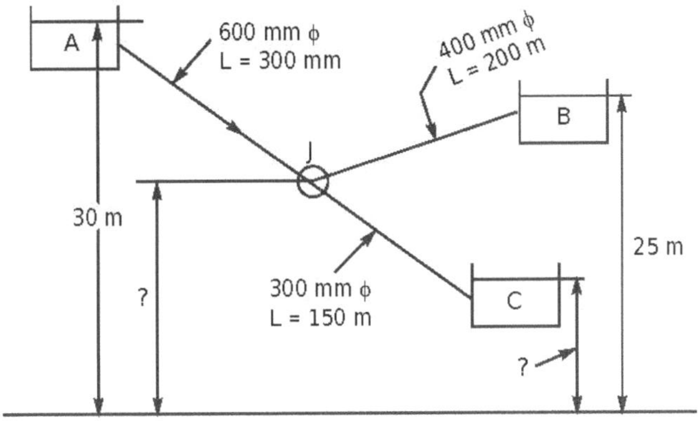

Fig. 12.24

Now RL of $B = 25$ m

$\therefore$ h_f in pipe $BJ = 29.936 - 25$

$$= 4.935 \text{ m}$$

$$= \frac{fL_{BJ}(Q_B)^2}{12(0.4)^5}$$

$$= \frac{0.02(200)(Q_B)^2}{12(0.01)}$$

$$4.935 = 33.3\,Q_B^2$$

$$\therefore \quad Q_B^2 = \frac{4.935}{33.3} = 0.148$$

$$\therefore \quad Q_B = 0.38 \text{ m}^3\text{/s from } J \text{ to } B.$$

But Q from A is only 0.1 m³/s,

$\therefore$ Q from C must come to

$$\therefore \quad J = 0.38 - 0.1 = 0.28$$

$$\therefore \quad Q = 0.28 \text{ m}^3\text{/s}$$

$$\therefore \quad h_{fJC} = \frac{0.02(150)(0.28)^2}{12(0.3)^5} = 8.11 \text{ m}$$

$$\therefore \quad RL \text{ of } C = 29.936 + 8.11 = 38.046$$

$\therefore$ RL of $C = 38.046$. ...(Ans.)

12.11 PIPE NETWORK

Water supply to a town from a water main is always by a closed system of pipe network. The main gets bifurcated by branches and the branches get bifurcated by service lines from which customers get connections. Thus a pipe system supplying water is a flow in a closed loop and several loops make pipe network, see Fig. 12.25. *ABCDE* is a network consisting of loops, I, II, III etc. *A*, *B*, *C*, *D*, *E* etc. are junction points.

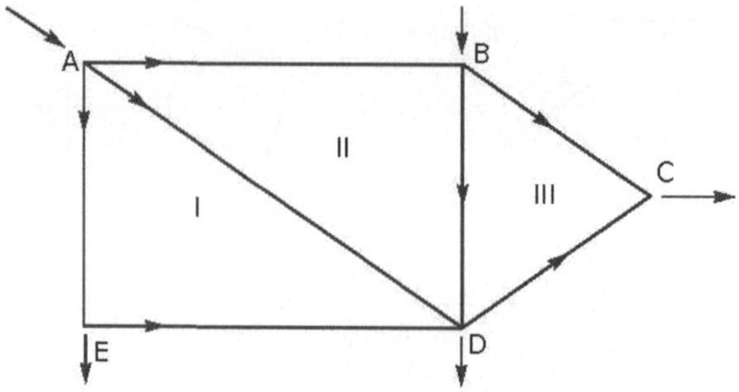

Fig. 12.25

Hardy–Cross method of trial and error is used to find discharge in each pipe of the network. The method consists of the following steps:

1. At junction, Inflow = Outflow

2. In a given loop, $h_{fc} = h_{fcc}$ *i.e.* head loss in clockwise direction is equal to head loss in counter clockwise direction. As regards direction of flow is connected, it is with respect to a junction of a loop, for example, in loop I, take junction A then flow in pipe *AD* is clockwise and in *AE* and *ED* is counter clockwise. Similarly in loop II, w.r.t. junction *B*, flow in *BD* and *AB* is clockwise and *AD* is counterclockwise. Note that pipe *AD* is common between loop I, II and flow in it in loop I is clockwise whereas for same pipe in loop II, it is counter clockwise.

Clockwise flow is considered +ve and counterclockwise flow is considered –ve.

3. $$h_f = \frac{fLV^2}{D2g}$$, as per Darcy–Weisbach equation,

here

f = function factor

L = length of pipe

D = diameter of pipe

V = velocity in pipe

$$= \frac{Q}{A}$$

$$\therefore \quad h_f = \frac{fLQ^2}{D2gA^2} = KQ^2, \text{ here}$$

$$K = \frac{fL}{D2gA^2} = \text{pipe coefficient.}$$

4. Flow in each pipe of a given loop is arbitrarily assumed with a direction and if assumed flow is correct,

$$h_{fc} = h_{fcc}$$

but if $h_{fc} \neq h_{fcc}$, then assumed flow needs correction, given by

$$\Delta Q = \frac{\Sigma KQ^n}{\Sigma |nKQ^{n-1}|} \qquad \text{...(12.20)}$$

5. Positive ΔQ means correction to be added to clockwise flow and negative ΔQ means, it should be deducted from clockwise flows.

6. For common pipe between too loops:

For loop I, ΔQ (common pipe) = $\Delta Q_I - \Delta Q_{II}$

and for loop II, ΔQ (common pipe) = $\Delta Q_{II} - \Delta Q_I$

Above procedure will be clear by going through following illustrative examples.

12.11.1 Solved Problems

■ **Problem 12.24:** *For the pipe network shown in Fig. 12.26, find discharge in each pipe and slow it in the figure with proper directional sign.*

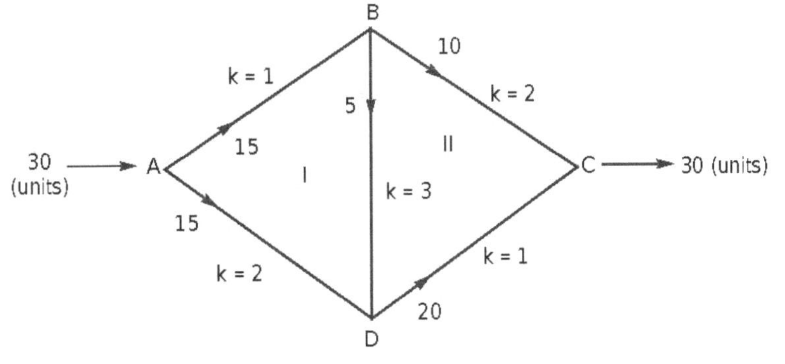

Fig. 12.26

Step I: Divide inflow at *A* into 15 for pipe *AB* and 15 for pipe *AD* as shown in Fig. 12.26. Similarly at *B*, 10 in *BC* and 5 in *BD*, so that *DC* gets 20. Now 10 of *BC* and 20 of *DC* make out flow of 30 at *C*.

Direction are shown by arrows.

Loop	*Pipe*	*K*	*Q*	*KQ²*	| *2KQ* |	$\Delta Q = \frac{\Sigma LQ^2}{\lvert 2KQ \rvert}$
I	*AB*	1	+15	+225	30	
	BD	3	+5	+75	30	$\Delta Q_I = -\frac{-150}{120} = +1.25$
BD is	*DA*	2	–15	–450	60	
common pipe				–150	120	
II	*BD*	3	–5	–75	30	
	BC	2	+10	+200	60	$\Delta Q_{II} = -\frac{-275}{130} = +2.1$
	CD	1	–20	–400	40	
				–275	130	

ΔQ for common pipe $BD = (1.25) - (2.1) = -0.85$

ΔQ for BD is loop II = (2.1) – (1.25) = + 0.85

Now apply above correction and carry out 2nd trial:

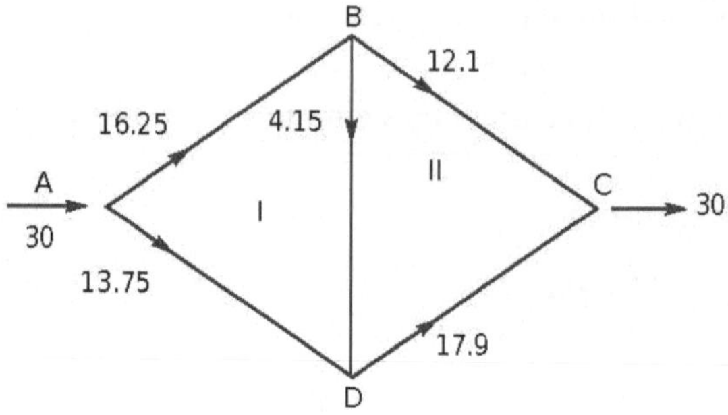

Fig. 12.26 (*a*)

Loop	*Pipe*	*K*	*Q*	KQ^2	$\|2\,KQ\|$	$\|\Delta Q\|$
I	*AB*	1	+16.25	+264	32.5	
	BD	3	+4.15	+51.6	24.9	$\Delta Q_I = -\dfrac{+126.6}{112.4}$
	DA	2	–13.75	–189	55.0	= – 1.12
				+126.6	112.4	for *BD*, ΔQ = – 1.12 – (0.72) = –1.84
II	*BD*	3	–4.15	–51.6	24.9	
	BC	2	+ 12.1	+292.8	48.4	$\Delta Q_{II} = -\dfrac{-78.8}{109.1}$
	CD	1	–17.9	–320.4	35.8	= + 0.72
				–78.8	109.1	for *BD*, ΔQ = 0.72 – (–1.12) = +1.84

Apply correction and carry out 3rd trial.

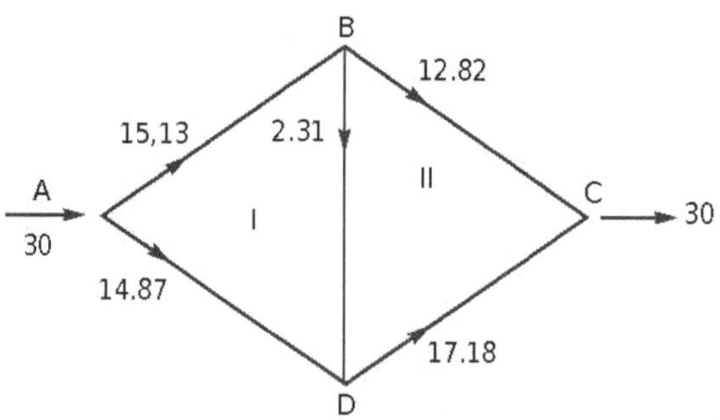

Fig. 12.26 (*b*)

Loop	*Pipe*	*K*	*Q*	*KQ²*	*2 KQ*	**ΔQ**
I	*AB*	1	+15.13	+229	30.26	
	BD	3	+2.31	+16	14.0	$\Delta Q = -\frac{-197}{103.7}$
	DA	2	–14.87	–442	59.5	= +1.89
				–197	103.7	ΔQ = 1.89 – (–0.176) = 2 for *BD*
II	*BD*	3	–2.31	–16	13.8	
	BC	2	+ 12.82	+328.7	51.28	$\Delta Q = -\frac{+78.8}{109.1}$
	CD	1	–17.18	–295.1	34.36	= – 0.176
				+17.6	99.44	ΔQ for (*BD*) = –2

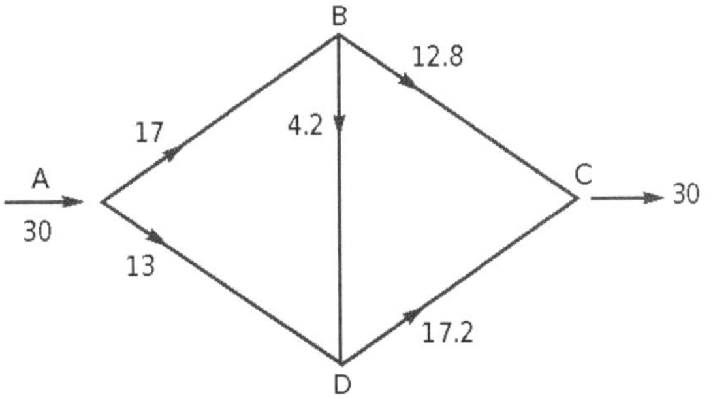

Fig. 12.26 (*c*)

4th Trial:

Loop	*Pipe*	*K*	*Q*	*KQ²*	*2 KQ*	**ΔQ**
I	*AB*	1	+17	+289	34	
	BD	3	+4.2	+53	25	$\Delta Q = -\frac{4}{111}$
	DA	2	–13	–338	52	= – 0.03 < 1
				+4	111	neglected
II	*BD*	3	–4.2	–53	25	
	BC	2	+ 12.8	+327.6	51	$\Delta Q = -\frac{-21}{100}$
	CD	1	–17.2	–295.0	34	= +0.15 < 1
				–21.2	110	∴ neglected

Hence Fig. 12.26 (*c*) is Ans.

Note: 1. Procedure needs repetition till $\Delta Q < 1$.
2. KQ^2 has same sign as Q.
3. $|2KQ|$ has no concerned with sign of Q.

■ **Problem 12.25:** *A rectangular pipe network consist of 5 pipes in which DB in diagonal pipe. The values of K in the eqn. $h_f = KQ^2$ is 1 for shorter sides, 2 longer sides and 3 for diagonal pipe.*

The input at A is 100 units and outputs at B and C are 30 and 70 units. Find Q in each pipe is not more than two trials.

Solution:

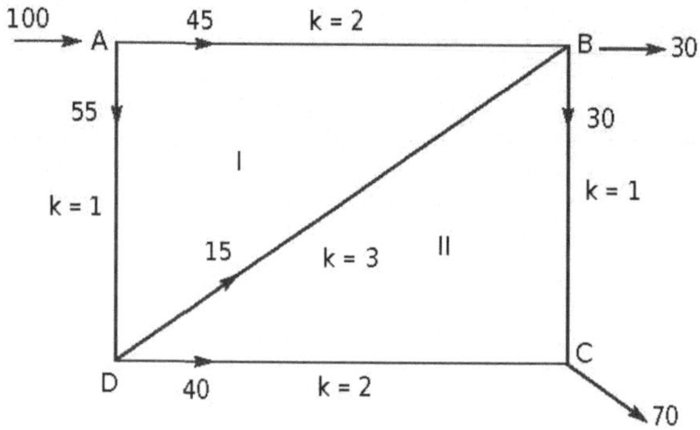

Fig. 12.27

1st Trial:

Loop	*Pipe*	*K*	*Q*	KQ^2	$\lvert 2KQ \rvert$	ΔQ
I	*AB*	2	+45	+4050	180	
	BD	3	–15	–675	90	$\Delta Q = \dfrac{\Sigma KQ^2}{\Sigma \lvert 2KQ \rvert} = -\dfrac{+350}{380} = -0.9$
	DA	1	–55	–3025	110	(rounded to – 1.0)
				+350	380	$\Delta Q(BD) = -0.9 - 5.24 = -6.14 \rightarrow -6$
II	*BC*	1	+30	+900	60	
	DC	2	–40	–3200	160	$\Delta Q = -\dfrac{-1625}{310} + 5.24$
	BD	3	+15	+675	90	(rounded to + 5)
				–1625	310	$\Delta Q(BD) = 5.25 - (-0.9) = +6.14 \rightarrow +6$

Apply correction and new values of Q are shown in Fig. 12.27 (*a*)

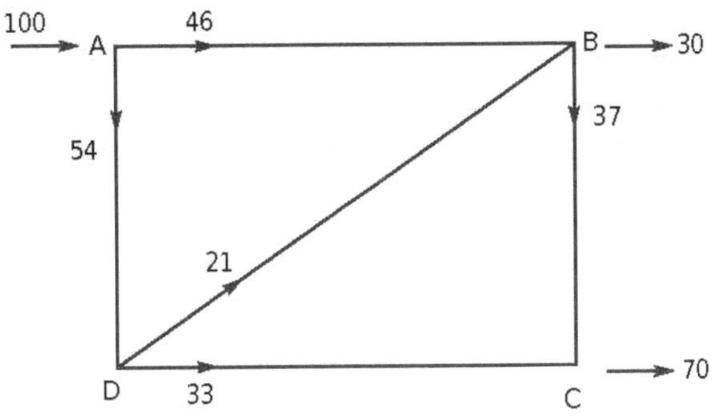

Fig. 12.27 (*a*)

2nd Trial:

Loop	*Pipe*	*K*	*Q*	KQ^2	$\|2KQ\|$	ΔQ
I	*AB*	2	+46	+4232	184	$\Delta Q = -\frac{-7}{418} = +0.016 < 1$
	BD	3	–21	–1323	126	
	DA	1	–54	–2916	108	∴ neglected
				–7	418	For *BD*, ΔQ = 1.54 = +1.5
II	*BC*	1	+37	+1369	74	
	DC	2	–33	–2178	132	$\Delta Q = -\frac{514}{332} = -1.54$
	BD	3	–21	+1323	126	= –1.5
				+514	332	

In this case ΔQ for loop I is neglected, but ΔQ for loop II is applied and new values of Q are shown in Fig. 12.27 (*b*).

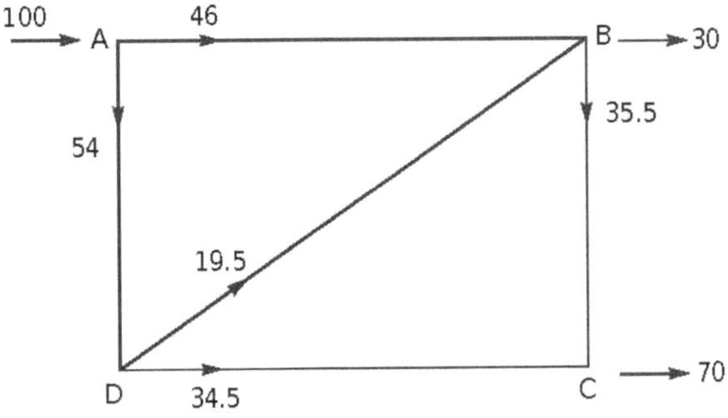

Fig. 12.27 (*b*)

Check whether $\Delta Q \rightarrow 0$ or not.

Loop	*Pipe*	*K*	*Q*	KQ^2	$\lvert 2KQ \rvert$	ΔQ
I	*AB*	2	+46	+42.32	184	$\Delta Q = -\dfrac{175}{409}$
	BD	3	–19.5	–1140	117	
	DA	1	–54	–2916	108	$= -0.42 < 1$
				+175	409	∴ neglect
II	*BC*	1	+35.5	+1260	71	
	DC	2	–34.5	–2380	138	$\Delta Q = -\dfrac{20}{326}$
	BD	3	+19.5	+1140	117	$= -0.06 < 1$
				+20	326	∴ neglect

∴ Ans. is at end of 2nd trial as shown in Fig. 12.27 (*b*).

Exercises

1. At a sudden enlargement of a pipe from 250 mm to 500 mm, the *HG* rises by 10 mm. Find discharge through the pipe. **(Ans. 35 LPS)**
2. A pipe of 80 mm diameter is suddenly expanded into a pipe of 120 mm diameter. If mercury in a differential manometer connected at abrupt expansion shows a deflection of 2 cm, find discharge in the pipe. **(Ans. 15.87 LPS)**
3. Two pipes each of 12 cm dia. and length 200 m are connected in parallel. Calculate
   (*a*) equivalent length of single pipe of dia. 12 cm.
   (*b*) diameter of equivalent single pipe of length 200 m. **(Ans. (*i*) 50 m; (*ii*) 15.8 cm)**
4. A 40 cm diameter pipe is required to be replaced by two parallel pipes of equal diameter. Assuming *f* and *L* to be same, find diameter of the parallel pipes. **(Ans. 30.3 cm)**
5. Three pipes of length 50 m each but of diameter 12, 10 and 8 cm are connected in series. Find length of the pipe of diameter 10 cm equivalent to above pipes laid in series. Take *f* same of all pipes. **(Ans. 267 m)**
6. A horizontal pipe of diameter D_1 expands abruptly to dia. D_2. What should be the value of (D_2/D_1) for differential pressure on either side of expansion to be maximum?

   What is the head loss? $\left(\textbf{Ans. } (i)\ D_2/D_1 = \sqrt{2},\ (ii)\ h_f = \dfrac{1}{4}\left(\dfrac{V_1^2}{2g}\right)\right)$

7. A pipe having flow of 20 LPS is bifurcated into two pipes laid in parallel. One pipe is 1000 m long as of 6 cm in diameter, and the other 800 m long and 8 cm in dia. If $f = 0.02$ for both pipes, find flow in each of the parallel pipes.
(**Ans.** Q_1 = 6.2 LPS, Q_2 = 13.8 LPS)
8. A 2 km long pipe carries a discharge of 380 LPS. To increase the discharge another pipe of same diameter in put in parallel to first pipe in the second half portion of its length. Find increase in discharge, if head loss in both case is 15 m. Take $f = 0.02$.
(**Ans.** 100 LPS, 26.3%)
9. A 300 mm diameter pipe, 3.2 km long, connects two reservoirs with 15 m difference in their water levels. Find discharge. If a parallel pipe, 30 cm diameter, is attached to last 1600 m length of previous pipe, find the new discharge. Take $f = 0.04$.
(**Ans.** Q_1 = 547 LPS, Q_2 = 698 LPS)
10. A fire engine supplies water to a hosepipe, 75 m long and 0.075 m in diameter, at a pressure of 3 kg/cm^2. If the discharge end of the pipe has a nozzle, find its diameter for efficient power transmission. Take $f = 0.032$. (**Ans.** d_{nozzle} = 2.65 cm)
11. Three pipes: (*a*) $L_1 = 300$ m, $D_1 = 30$ cm, $f_1 = 0.018$. (*b*) $L_2 = 150$ m, $D_2 = 20$ cm, $f_2 = 0.02$. (*c*) $L_3 = 200$ m, $D_3 = 25$ cm, $f_3 = 0.019$.
are connected in series between two reservoirs having difference in surface level = 15 m. Considering all types of losses, find discharge to lower reservoir. Draw HG and EG lines. (**Ans.** 105.7 LPS)
12. A syphon 20 cm in dia. connects two reservoirs having a 40 m surface difference. Total length of pipe is 8000 m and it crosses a ridge, summit of which is 8 m above level of water in upper reservoir. Find minimum depth of pipe below ridge summit if absolute pressure in syphon is not to fall below 3 m. Take $f = 0.024$ and atm pressure head = 10.3 m. Length of syphon from upper reservoir to summit is 50 m. Find Q.
(**Ans.** Depth = 3.24 m; Q = 28.3 LPS)
13. Obtain an expression for loss of head in a pipe of length L and diameter D fitted with laterals and discharge is drawn of uniformly along the length such that it is zero at the end. $\left(\textbf{Ans. } h_f \frac{1}{3}\left(\frac{fLV^2}{D\,2g}\right)\right)$
14. Water flows out of a reservoir through a horizontal pipe, 50 cm in diameter and 300 m long; level of water in reservoir is 10 m above the pipe. Due to some obstruction in pipe velocity of flow is 3.6 m/s at the point of obstruction. If $f = 0.025$, find pressure drop across the obstruction. Consider all losses. (*M.U. 1998*)

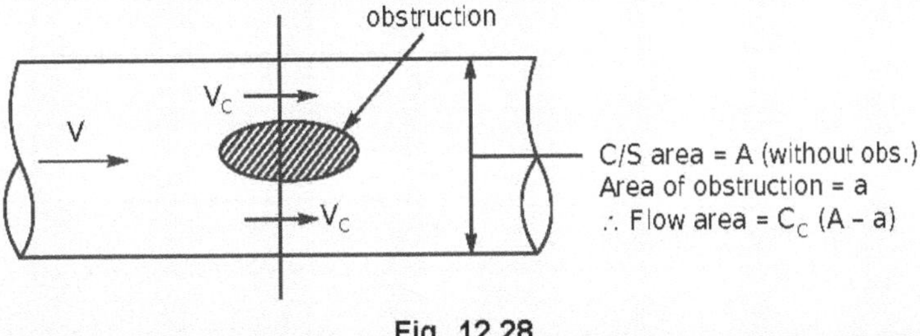

Fig. 12.28

$\therefore \quad V_C[C_C(A - a)] = A\,V$

$$\therefore \quad V_C = \frac{AV}{C_C(A-a)}, \text{ here } C_C = 0.6$$

$$h_{fC} = \text{Head loss due obstruction} = \frac{V^2}{2g}\left[\frac{A}{C_C(A-a)} - 1\right]^2.$$

(**Ans.** $h_{fC} = 1.41 \times 10^{-3}$ m)

15. Two reservoirs are connected by three parallel pipes: 280 m × 30 cm, 270 m × 25 cm, 275 m × 20 cm. Level difference between two R is 15 m. Find flow from upper to lower reservoir. Take $f = 0.02$. If it is required to increase flow by 25% by putting an additional pipe of length 300 m and $f = 0.03$, find its diameter.

(**Ans.** (*a*) $Q = Q_1 + Q_2 + Q_3 = 0.279 + 0.32 + 0.01 = 0.561$ m³/s; (*b*) $D_4 = 25$ cm)

16. Two reservoirs with a head difference of 15 m are connected by a pipe 1000 m long, $f = 0.02$ and $Q = 100$ LPS. It is desired to increase the flow by 30% by adding another pipe of same dia. from u/s R in parallel and joining previous pipe. Find length of additional pipe and head at the junction relative to d/s R. Assume length of two parallel pipes same, and $f = 0.02$ for all pipes.

(**Ans.** Length of additional pipe = 544 m; Head at junction = 11.53 m, higher than R_2)

17. Find the maximum power transmitted by a jet of water discharging freely out of a nozzle fitted to a pipe of length 300 m and 10 cm diameter. Head available at inlet is 90 m; $f = 0.01$. (**Ans.** $P = 20.64$ kW)

18. A 100 m long, 20 cm dia. pipe is bifurcated into two pipes of 60 m long, 10 cm dia. and 120 m long and 10 cm dia. These two pipes discharge into atmosphere and their outlets are at elevation of 100 m for 120 m branch and 105 m for 60 m branch. The elevation of water level in reservoir supplying water to 100 m pipe is 125 m. Take $f = 0.02$ for all pipes. Find discharge from the two outlets.

(**Ans.** Q from 120 m branch = 33 LPS; Q from 60 m branch = 40 LPS)

19. For a rectangular pipe network obtain the discharge distribution for following details:

Pipe	*K*	*n*
AB	150	2
BC	50	2
CD	100	2
DA	100	2
AC	200	2

The output at B, C and D is 5, 20 and 10 units respectively. (Solve in not more than 2 trials). (**Ans.** See Fig. 12. 29)

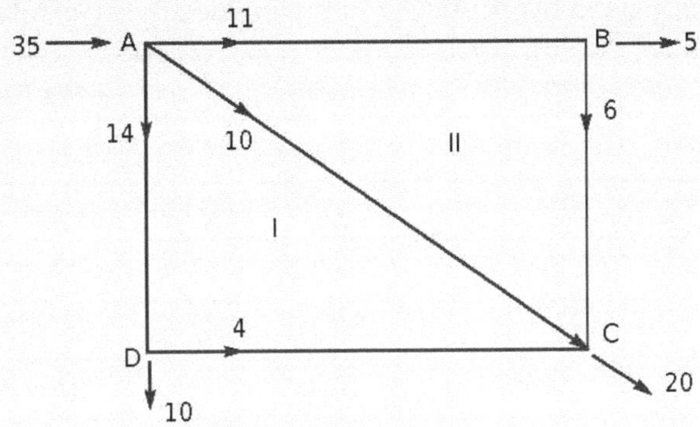

Fig. 12.29

ΔQ (loop I) = + 0.16 < 1, ΔQ (loop II) = + 0.18 < 1.

20. For the pipe network shown in Fig. 12.30 find out discharge distribution. (**Ans.** 12.31)

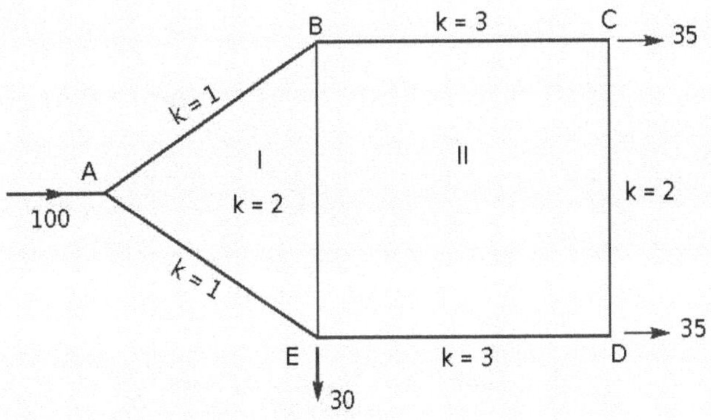

Fig. 12.30

(**Ans.** in Fig. 12.31)

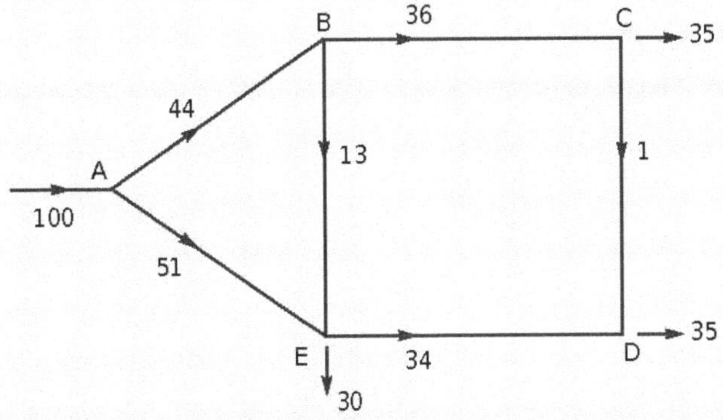

Fig. 12.31

ΔQ (I) = – 0.54 < 1

ΔQ (I) = – 0.01 < 1.

21. For a rectangular pipe network ABCD following details are available:

Pipe	*Dia.*	*Length*
AB	50 cm	200 m
BC	40 cm	100 m
CD	50 cm	200 m
DA	40 cm	100 m
BD (diagonal	50 cm	223 m

$f = 0.02$ for all pipes.

Input at *A* 100 units and outputs at *B*, *C* and *D* are 30, 50 and 20 units respectively.

Find discharge in each pipe by Hardy Cross Method. [**Hint**: Workout $k = \dfrac{fL}{12\,D^5}$ for each pipe] (**Ans.** See Fig. 12.32)

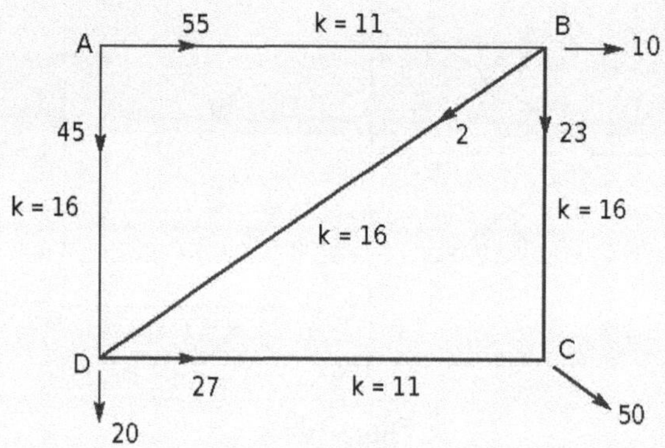

Fig. 12.32

(ΔQ I = –0.28 < 1, ΔQ II = 0.27 < 1).

❑❑❑

13

Water Hammer Theory

13.1 INTRODUCTION

General: Transportation of liquids and gases through long pipe lines may have to face the problem of sudden pressure rise in the pipe lines on account of rapid closure of a value in the pipe system. This normally happens in case of water mains or penstocks. Water mains have a long length and closure of valve may lead to pressure rise in the pipe and consequently if the pipe wall material is subject to higher stresses than permissible, then it may fail. Similarly in hydro-power stations, turnbine's speed has to be changed suddenly according to power load requirements and this will lead to sudden changes in flow of pipe line supplying water at high pressure, which are known as penstocks. Sudden rise of pressure in penstock may lead to its failure but devices such as surge tanks are provided to make penstock safe. Thus safety of penstocks, water mains, long pipes carrying gases and liquids over long distance is dependent on studies of phenomenon of water hammer which takes place on account of sudden valve closure. Kinetic energy of flowing fluid is suddenly reduced which gives rise to increase in potential energy, resulting in a hammering effect on pipe wall material and hence the phenomenon is known as water hummer. This is similar to phenomenon of hydraulic jump in open channel.

13.2 RIGID PIPE THEORY

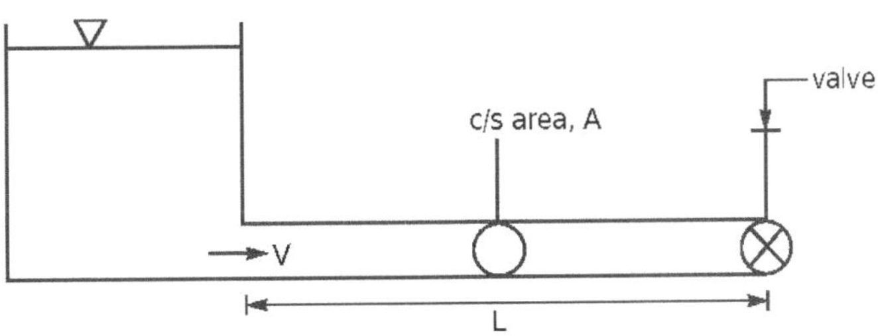

Fig.13.1

If the pipe wall material is regarded rigid, rise of pressure on account of valve closure has to be absorbed by water mass alone.

∴ Force due to pressure rise = $p_i \times A$

Here p_1 = pressure rise due to water hammer

A = cross-sectional area of pipe.

∴ Force due to pressure rise = mass × acceleration

$$p_i \times A = \left(\frac{\gamma AL}{g}\right)\frac{V}{T}$$

Here, V = velocity of fluid in pipe = Q/A

T = time of closure of valve in seconds

∴ $$p_i = \frac{\gamma LV}{gT}$$

∴ $$\frac{p_i}{\gamma} = \frac{LV}{gT} = \text{rise in pressure head}$$

Also, $$\frac{p_i}{\rho g} = \frac{LV}{gT}$$

∴ $$p_i = \frac{\rho LV}{T} = \rho cV \qquad ...(13.1)$$

here $c = \dfrac{L}{T}$ = celerity of pressure wave

∴ Rise in pressure due to rigid pipe theory is given by $p_i = \rho cV$

and $c = \sqrt{\dfrac{K}{\rho}}$ = velocity of pressure wave or velocity of sound in flowing fluid ...(13.2)

K = Bulk modulus of fluid

ρ = Mass density of fluid

Proof for $\left(c = \sqrt{\dfrac{K}{\rho}}\right)$ is given in chapter 17 on compressible flow.

Pressure wave developed due to sudden closure of valve travels upstream upto source *i.e.*, supply-tank and then gets reflected back to the valve and this cycle gets repeated till it dies down due to pipe friction. The time taken for pressure wave to reach source and come back to valve is defined as critical time and is given by

$$T = \frac{2L}{c} \qquad ...(13.3)$$

Actual closer of valve may take time = t

If $t \leq T$, it is rapid valve closure,

If $t > T$, it is a slow valve closure,

If $(p_i)_s$ = pressure rise due to slow closure,

then $$(p_i)_s = (p_i)_r \frac{T}{t}, \qquad \text{...(13.4)}$$

here, $(p_i)_r$ = pressure rise due to rapid closure

t = actual time of closure of valve

and $T = \dfrac{2L}{c}$ = critical time of closure of valve.

If flow velocity is reduced to V_2 from V_1,

then $$p_i = -\rho c(V_2 - V_1) \qquad \text{...(13.5)}$$

but if it is reduced completely,

then $p_i = \rho c V$

here V = initial value of velocity in pipe

$$= Q/A = \frac{Q}{\frac{\pi}{4}D^2}$$

After the pressure rise due to water hammer, total pressure, p_t is given by

$p_t = p_s + p_i$ where p_s = static or initial pressure in pipe

and p_i = pressure rise due to water hammer.

13.3 ELASTIC PIPE THEORY

If the pipe wall material is elastic and water compressible, then

Loss of KE due to closure of valve

= Gain in strain energy of water and that of pipe wall material.

Let D = diameter of pipe, r = radius of pipe,

t_p = thickness of pipe wall material,

v = velocity of flow in pipe,

A = c/s area of pipe,

L = length of pipe upto valve,

V_1 = volume of pipe wall material,

$= 2\pi r t_p L$

E = elasticity of pipe wall material.

f_c = hoop stress or circumferential stress in pipe wall material

$$= \frac{p_i r}{t_p} = \frac{p_i D}{2t_p}$$

f_t = longitudinal stress in pipe wall material = $\left(\dfrac{p_i r}{2t_p}\right) = \dfrac{p_i D}{4t_p}$

$\dfrac{1}{m}$ = Poison's ratio = $\dfrac{1}{4}$

K = Bulk modulus of water or fluid

$$= \frac{p_i}{\left(\dfrac{d\forall}{\forall}\right)}$$

$\forall$ = volume of flowing fluid

$\gamma = \rho g$ = wt. density of fluid

Now KE of flowing fluid = $\dfrac{1}{2}$ (mass) (velocity)^2

$$= \frac{1}{2}\left(\frac{\gamma AL}{g}\right)V^2 \qquad \text{...(13.6)}$$

Strain energy stored in fluid

$$= \frac{1}{2} \text{ stress} \times \text{strain} = \frac{1}{2}\, p_i\,(d\forall)$$

$$= \frac{1}{2} p_i \left(\frac{d\forall}{\forall}\forall\right) \qquad \text{...(13.7)}$$

Strain energy stored in pipe wall

$$= \frac{\forall_1}{2E}\left[f_c^2 + f_1^2 - \frac{2f_c f_1}{m}\right]$$

$$= \frac{2\pi r t_p L}{2E}\left[\left(\frac{p_i r}{t_p}\right)^2 + \left(\frac{p_i r}{2t_p}\right)^2 - \frac{\left(\dfrac{p_i r}{t_p}\right)\left(\dfrac{p_i r}{2t_p}\right)}{m}\right]$$

$$= \frac{2\pi r t_p L\left(\dfrac{p_i r}{t_p}\right)^2}{2E}\left[1 + \frac{1}{4} - \left(\frac{1}{4}\right)\right]$$

$$= \frac{r(\pi r^2)\,L\,p_i^2}{Et_p}$$

$$= \frac{D(AL)\,p_i^2}{2Et_p} \qquad ...(13.8)$$

Now KE of flowing fluid = strain energy stored in fluid + strain energy stored in pipe wall.

$$\therefore \qquad \frac{1}{2}\left(\frac{\rho g AL}{g}\right)V^2 = \frac{1}{2}\,p_i\left(\frac{p_i}{K}\right)AL + \frac{D(AL)p_i^2}{2Et_p}$$

Here $\frac{p_i}{K} = \frac{d\forall}{\forall}$, AL = $\forall$ and $\gamma = \rho g$

$\left(\frac{1}{2}AL\right)$ will be common on both side of eq.

$$\therefore \qquad \rho V^2 = \frac{p_i^2}{K} + \frac{Dp_i^2}{Et_p}$$

$$= p_i^2\left[\frac{1}{K} + \frac{D}{Et_p}\right]$$

$$\therefore \qquad p_i = \frac{V\sqrt{\rho}}{\left[\frac{1}{K} + \frac{D}{Et_p}\right]^{1/2}}$$

Now $p_i = \rho c V$ from eq. (13.1),

$$\therefore \qquad \rho c V = \frac{V\sqrt{\rho}}{\left[\frac{1}{K} + \frac{D}{Et_p}\right]^{1/2}} \qquad ...(13.9)$$

$$\therefore \qquad c = \frac{\sqrt{K/\rho}}{\left[1 + \frac{DK}{Et_p}\right]^{1/2}} \qquad ...(13.0)$$

Thus value of velocity of pressure wave, c, in fluid flowing in rigid pipe is reduced by $\left[1 + \frac{DK}{Et_p}\right]^{-1/2}$ when pipe wall is elastic and fluid is compressible. Always calculate first c, then $p_i = \rho c V$ will give of pressure rise due to water hammer.

13.4 VARIOUS STAGES OF PRESSURE WAVE

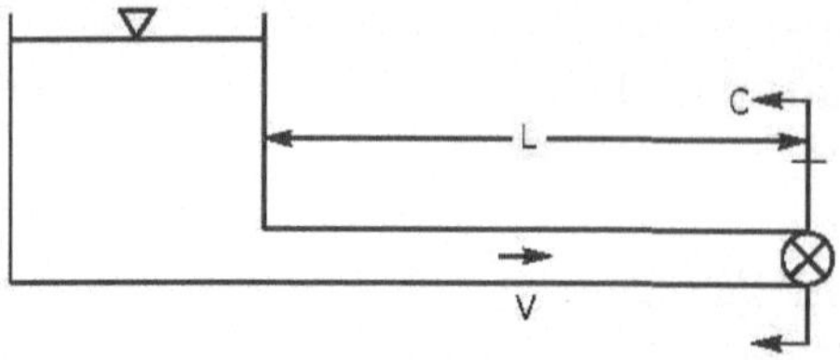

(*i*) $t = 0$, valve is closed instantaneously

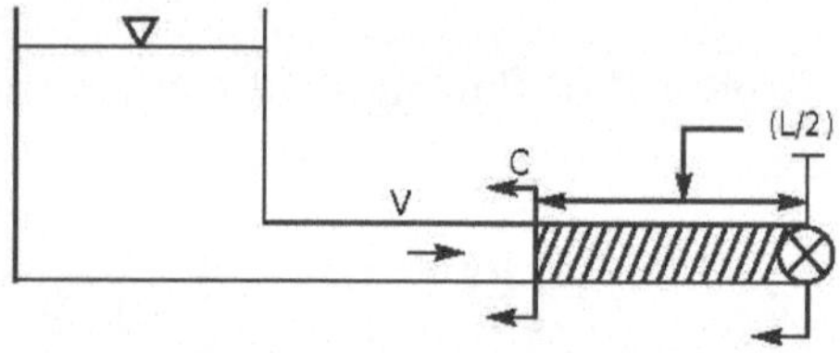

(*ii*) $t = \dfrac{L}{2c}$, pressure wave is at $\dfrac{L}{2}$ and pressure wave + ve

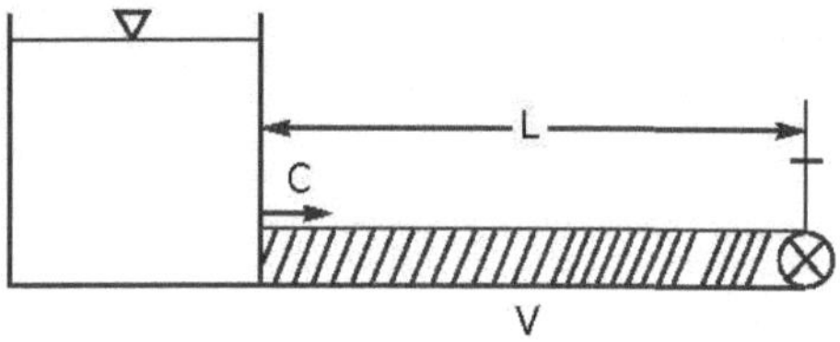

(*iii*) $t = \dfrac{L}{c}$ pressure wave reaches the source (p_i + *ve*)

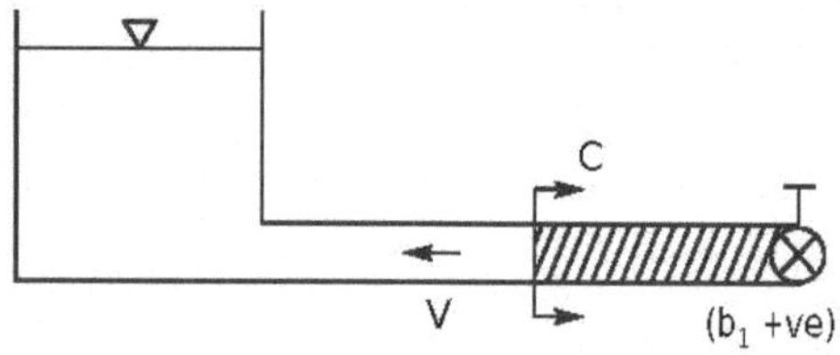

(*iv*) $t = \dfrac{3}{2}\dfrac{L}{c}$ pressure wave after getting source reflected back to valve is at $\dfrac{L}{2}$ at time $t = \dfrac{3L}{2c}$

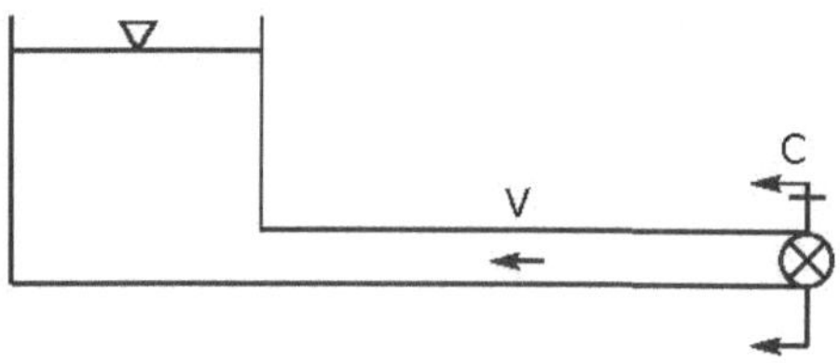

(*v*) $t = \dfrac{2L}{c}$

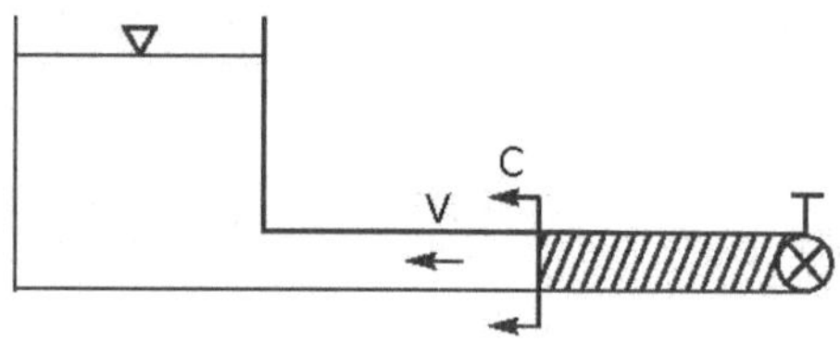

(*vi*) $t = \left(\dfrac{5L}{2}\right) c$, (pressure wave is now –ve)

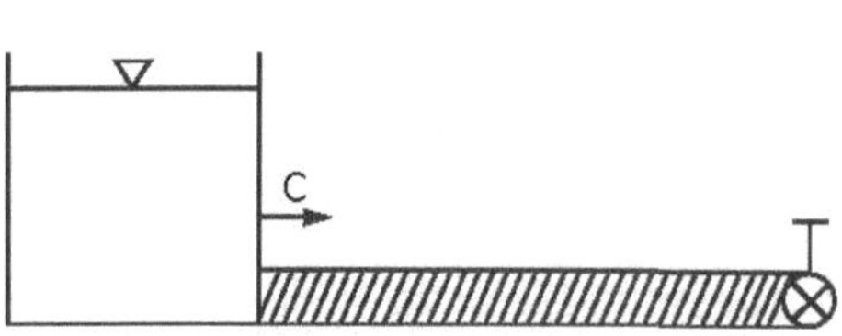

(*vii*) $t = \dfrac{3L}{c}$ (p_i – ve)

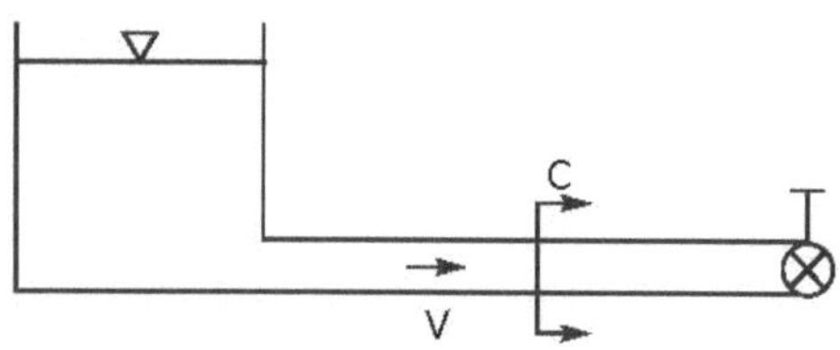

(*viii*) $t = \left(\dfrac{7L}{2}\right) c$ (p_i – ve)

Fig. 13.2 (*i*) to (*viii*)

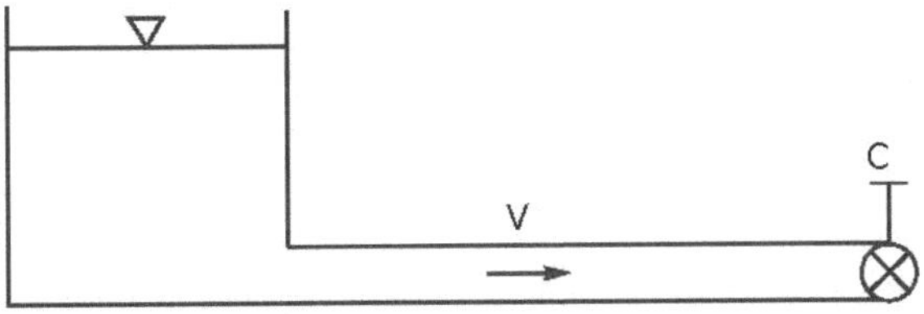

Fig. 13.2 (*ix*)

(*ix*) $t = V$ will get destroyed at valve and the cycle will get repeated till it dies down due to friction in pipe.

Fig. 13.2 (*i* to *ix*) Various Stages of Pressure Wave Travel

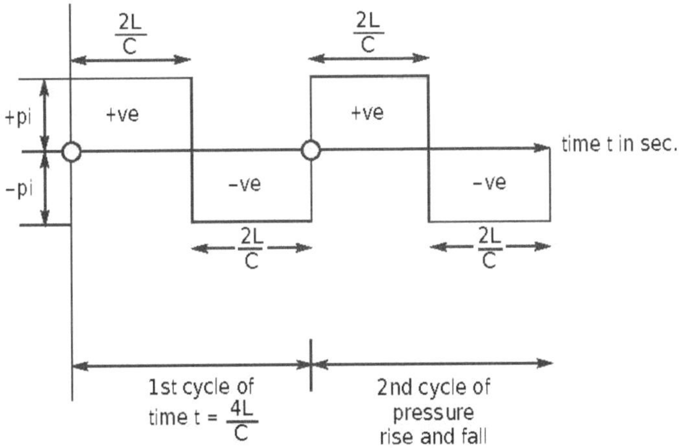

Variation of p_1 w.r.t. time t of valve closure for frictionless pipe of length L.
(x axis time, y axis p_i)

Fig. 13.3 Variation of p_i with respect to time t

Fig. 13.2 (*i*) to (*ix*) shows various stages of pressure rise p_i due to valve closure in time t seconds and Fig. 13.3 indicates graphical representation of pressure rise p_i on y axis and time t on x axis.

When the valve is closed, *i.e.*, at $t = 0$, flow with V is towards valve and pressure wave with velocity c just starts travelling towards source. At time $t = \frac{L}{c}$, pressure wave has reached the source and then gets reflected back. At time $t = \frac{2L}{c}$, p_i wave has already reached valve, but water mass with velocity V continues moving back to source, generating a cycle of –ve pressure wave from valve to source and back to valve. At time $t = \frac{4L}{c}$, first cycle of pressure wave travel is over and if there is no friction, this continues, but in actual practice, due to friction of pipe, pressure wave will die down.

If x = length of pipe from valve end, having pressure rise p_i in time $t \leq \dfrac{2L}{c}$

then $$x = L - \frac{ct}{2} \qquad ...(13.11)$$

and if $t = 0$ (*i.e.*, instantaneous closure), then

i.e., entire pipe length will be subject to instantaneous pressure rise p_i.

13.5 SURGE TANKS

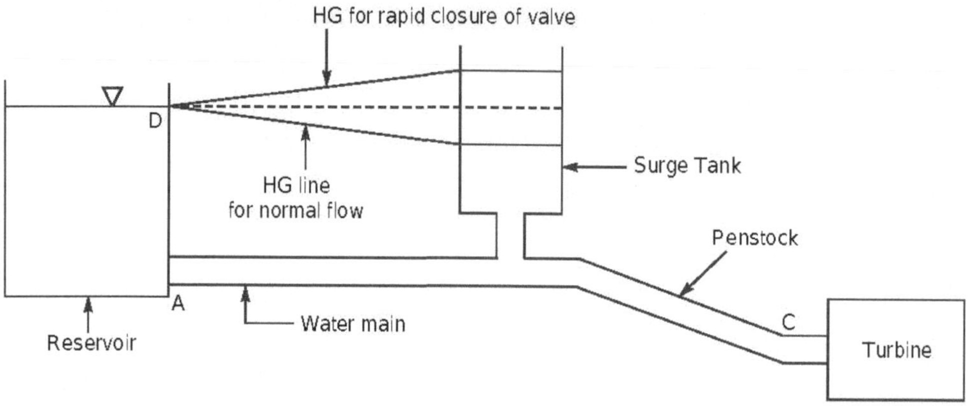

Fig. 13.4 Surge Tank

Surge tanks are safety devices for water main and penstock against water hammer. To minimise effect of sudden pressure rise in penstock and water main on account of rapid closure of valve, surge tanks are provided. Simple type of surge tank is an open cylinder provided just upstream of the valve so that when the flow is suddenly stopped part of back flow will take place into tank, and will not allow the steep rise of pressure in the penstock or the water main. When load on turbine is increased, valve is required to be opened out as large flow of water is required which is partially supplied by the water stored in the surge tank. Thus surge tank serves two purposes, (*i*) it is a safeguard against sudden rise of pressure due to closure of valve and (*ii*) it augments water supply to penstock when the demand is increased.

Surge tanks are of three types:

(*a*) simple, see Fig. 13.5 (*a*)

(*b*) orifice type, see Fig. 13.5 (*b*)

(*c*) differential type, see Fig. 13.5 (*c*)

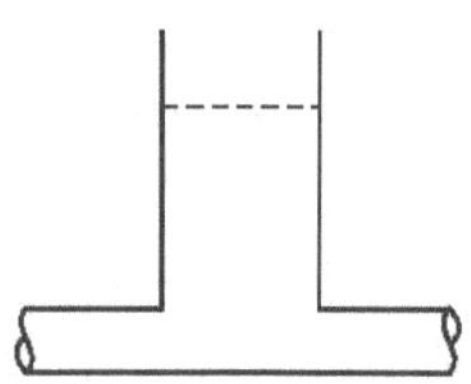

Fig. 13.5 (*a*) Simple surge tank

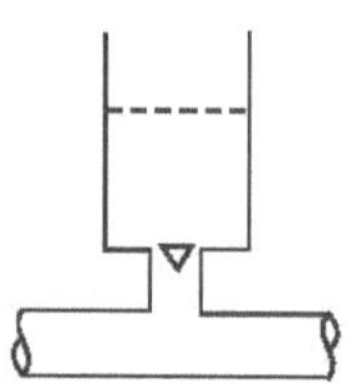

Fig. 13.5 (*b*) Orifice type surge tank

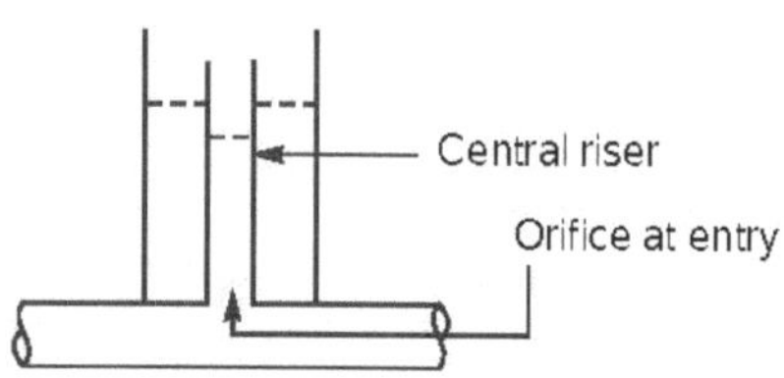

Fig. 13.5 (*c*) Differential type surge tank

In simple type, three is no restriction of entry of water in the tank, whereas orifice and differential types have restricted entry.

Orifice surge tank has orifice between the supply pipe and the tank and allows for more rapid changes in flow that the simple surge tank. The differential surge tank is a combination of an orifice surge tank and simple surge tank for sudden valve closure, the central riser overflows into the outer tank but when valve is suddenly opened, the riser supplies water to the penstock and flow from outer tank supplements this flow.

13.6 SOLVED PROBLEMS

■ **Problem 13.1:** *A 10 m tall tank is on a hill top and is drained by 7.5 mm thick steel pipe, 30 cm in diameter, into a lower tank placed 2.5 km apart. Lower tank is 100 m below hill top. If d/s valve reduces velocity from 2 m/s to 1 m/s in 4s, find total pressure on pipe wall. Is the closure rapid?*

Take $E_{steel} = 2.11 \times 10^{11}$ Pa, $K_{water} = 2.1 \times 10^{9}$ P_a

$\sigma = 0.1$ kN/mm^2

Find economical size of pipe thickness.

Solution:

$$p_i = \rho c\,(V_1 - V_2)$$

$$c = \frac{\sqrt{K/\rho}}{\sqrt{1+\dfrac{DK}{Et_p}}} = \frac{\sqrt{2.1\times10^9/10^3}}{\sqrt{1+\dfrac{0.3\,(2.1\times10^9)}{(211\times10^{11})\dfrac{7.5}{10^3}}}}$$

$$= \frac{1.45\times10^3}{\sqrt{1+0.39}} = \frac{1450}{1.179} = 1229 \text{ m/s}$$

$\therefore$ $p_i = 1000\,(1229)\,(2-1) = \mathbf{1229}$ **KPa**

Now, $p_{total} = p_s + p_i$

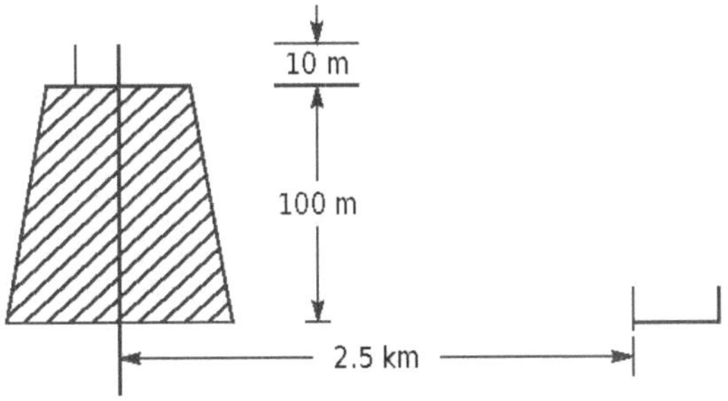

Fig. 13.4

$\therefore$ $p_s = (110)\,(1000 \times 9.81) = \mathbf{1079}$ **KPa** ...(Ans.)

$\therefore$ $p_{total} = 1079 + 1229 = 2308$ kPa

$$\text{Critical time, } T = \frac{2L}{c} = \frac{2\times2.5\times10^3}{1229} = 4.0685\text{sec.}$$

actual time $t = 4\text{s} < T$ $\therefore$ **rapid closure** ...(Ans.)

hoop stress,

$$f_c = \frac{p_{\text{total}}\, r}{t_p}$$

$$\therefore \quad t_p = \frac{2380\times10^3 \times \frac{3}{2}}{0.1\times10^3\times10^6} = 3462\times10^{-6}\,\text{m}$$

= **3.462 mm**, economic thickness of pipe. ...(Ans.)

■ **Problem 13.2:** *A 2 km long pipe, 150 mm in diameter and 8 mm thick, carries water at 100 LPS. Find pressure rise if valve at its end is closed in 2.5 s.*

Is pipe safe? Is closure rapid or slow?

hoop stress = 8 kN/cm²

$E_{steel} = 2 \times 10^7$ N/cm² $K_{water} = 2 \times 10^2$ N/cm².

Solution:

$$c = \frac{\sqrt{K/\rho}}{\sqrt{1+\frac{DK}{Et_p}}} = \frac{\sqrt{2\times10^5\times10^4/10^3}}{\sqrt{1+\frac{0.15\times2\times10^5\times10^4}{2\times10^7\times10^4\times8\times10^{-3}}}}$$

$$= \frac{1414}{\sqrt{1.1875}} = \mathbf{1298\ m/s}$$

$$p_i = \rho c V = 1000\,(1298)\,V$$

$$V = \frac{Q}{\frac{\pi}{4}D^2} = \frac{0.1}{0.78\,(.15)^2} = \mathbf{5.7\ m/s}$$

$$\therefore \quad p_i = 1000\,(1298)\,5.7 = \mathbf{7396\ KPa}$$

$$\text{hoop stress } \sigma = \frac{p_i D}{2t_p} = \frac{7396\,(.15)}{2(.008)}$$

$$= 69337.6\ \text{kN/m}^2$$

$$= \frac{69337.6}{10^4}\ \text{kN/cm}^2$$

$$= 6.93\ \text{kN/cm}^2$$

$$< 8\ \text{kN/cm}^2,\ \text{given}$$

$\therefore$ pipe is safe ...(Ans.)

actual time $t = 2.5$ s

$$T = \frac{2L}{c} = \frac{2\times2\times10^3}{1298}$$

$$= 3.08\ \text{s}$$

$$\therefore \quad t < T$$

$\therefore$ rapid closure. ...(Ans.)

■ **Problem 13.3:** *A steel pipe, 200 mm in diameter and 2 mm in thickness, has a length of 1200 m. If it carries oil of mass density 800 kg/m³ at 50 LPS, and at a static pressure of 160 m of oil. find whether the pipe is safe or not.*

If not, find minimum permissible time of closure so that pipe is safe.

$$K_{oil} = 1 \times 10^6 \ KPa, E_{steel} = 2.14 \times 10^8 \ KPa$$
$$s_{steel} = 1 \times 10^5 \ KPa.$$

Solution:

$$c = \frac{(K/\rho)^{1/2}}{\left[1+\dfrac{DK}{Et_p}\right]^{1/2}} = \frac{\left(\dfrac{1\times10^6\times10^3}{800}\right)^{1/2}}{\left[1+\dfrac{0.2\times1\times10^9}{2.14\times10^{11}\times2\times10^{-3}}\right]^{1/2}}$$

$$= \frac{1118}{(1.46)^{1/2}} = \frac{1118}{1.2} = \mathbf{930\ m/s}$$

$$T = \frac{21}{c} = \frac{2400}{930} = \mathbf{2.58\ s}$$

$$V = \frac{Q}{A} = \frac{0.05}{\frac{\pi}{4}(.2)^2} = 1.6\ \text{m/s}$$

$$p_i = \rho c V = 800 \times 930 \times 1.6$$
$$= 1190 \text{ KPa}$$

$$p_s = 160\ (800 \times 9.81)$$
$$= 1255 \text{ KPa}$$

$$p_{total} = p_i + p_s$$
$$= 1190 + 1255$$
$$= 2445 \text{ KPa}$$

$$\sigma = \frac{(p_{total})\,D}{2t_p} = 1.22\times10^5 \text{ KPa}$$

∴ pipe is not safe as $\sigma = 1.22 \times 10^5$ KPa which is greater than permissible value of **1×10^5 KPa**

In order that pipe is safe, valve closure should be slow.

$$P_{t_{new}} = \frac{\sigma_{steel} \times 2t}{D} = \frac{(1\times10^5)\times2(2\times10^{-3})}{.2}$$
$$= 2000 \text{ KPa}$$

∴ $P_{i_{slow}} = 2000 - p_s = 2000 - 1255 =$ **745 KPa for slow closure**

$$\frac{t_{slow}}{T} = \frac{P_{i_{rapid}}}{P_{i_{slow}}} = \frac{1190}{745}$$

$$\therefore \qquad t_{slow} = 2.58 \times \frac{1190}{745} = 4.12\,\text{s},$$

value of minimum permissible time of closure for pipe to be safe. ...(Ans.)

■ **Problem 13.4:** *A 30 cm diameter steel pipe, 3 km long, conveys 350 LPS of water at head of 200 m, and thickness of pipe is 8 mm. If valve is closed such that velocity of flow reduces by eighty per cent in 6 s, find pressure rise in pipe and total pressure.*

$K_{water} = 2.1 \times 10^9$ Pa, $E_{steel} = 2.1 \times 10^{11}$ Pa

If $\sigma = 0.1$ kN/mm², is pipe safe? If not find safe thickness.

Solution:

$$c = \frac{(K/\rho)^{1/2}}{\left[1+\frac{DK}{Et_p}\right]^{1/2}} = \frac{\left(\frac{2.1\times10^9}{10^3}\right)^{1/2}}{\left[1+\frac{.3\times2.1\times10^9}{2.1\times10^{11}\times8\times10^{-3}}\right]^{1/2}}$$

$$= \frac{1.45\times10^3}{(1+.375)^{1/2}} = \frac{1.45\times10^3}{1.172} = 1.273\times10^3$$

$$= \mathbf{1237\ m/s}$$

$$V_1 = \frac{Q}{A} = \frac{0.35\,D}{0.78\,(.3)^2} = 5\ \text{m/s}$$

$$V_2 = V_1 - 0.8\,V_1 = 0.2\,V_1 = \mathbf{1.0\ m/s}$$

$$P_{i_{rapid}} = -\rho c\,(V_2 - V_1) = \rho c\,(4) = 1000 \times 1237 \times 4$$

$$= 4948\ \text{KPa}$$

$$T = \frac{2L}{c} = \frac{2\times3000}{1237} = 4.85\ \text{s}$$

but actual $t = 6\ \text{s} > T, \ \therefore$ slow closure of valve

$$P_{i_{slow}} = \frac{T}{t}(4948) = \frac{4.85}{6}(4948) = 4007\ \text{KPa}$$

$\therefore$ Pressure rise due to water hammer = 4007 KPa ...(Ans.)

$$P_{total} = P_{static} + P_{i_{slow}}$$

$$= (200 \times 1000 \times 9.81) + 4007$$

$$= 1962 + 4007 = 5969\ \text{KPa}$$

$$f_c = \frac{P_{total}\,D}{2t_p} = \frac{5969\times(.3)\times10^3}{2(8\times10^{-3})} = 112\times10^6\ \text{Pa}$$

$$= 1.12 \times 10^8\ \text{Pa}$$

$$\sigma = 0.1\ \text{kN/mm}^2 = 1 \times 10^5\ \text{KPa} = 1 \times 10^8\ \text{Pa} < 1.12 \times 10^8\ \text{Pa}$$

$\therefore$ Pipe is not safe. Hence safe thickness of pipe, $t_{p_{new}}$

$$\therefore \qquad t_{p_{new}} = \frac{p_t D}{\sigma}$$

$$= \frac{5969\times10^3\times0.3}{2\times1\times10^8} = 8.95 \text{ mm}. \qquad \text{...(Ans.)}$$

■ **Problem 13.5:** *A valve at d/s end of a pipe of diameter 30 cm and 400 m long, is closed in 5 sec. If pipe is rigid and carries 100 LPS of water find pressure rise and length of pipe subject to this pressure from valve.*

Solution:

$$K_{water} = 2.1 \times 10^9 \text{ Pa}$$

For rigid pipe,
$$c = \sqrt{\frac{K}{\rho}} = \sqrt{\frac{2.1\times10^9}{10^3}} = 1450 \text{ m/s}$$

$$T = \frac{2L}{c} = \frac{2\times4000}{1450} = 5.51 \text{ s}$$

actual time $t = 5\text{s} < T$

$\therefore$ Rapid closure

$$V = \frac{Q}{A} = \frac{0.1}{.78\,(.3)^3} = 1.42 \text{ m/s}$$

$$P_i = \rho c V = 1000\,(1450)\,(1.42) = \mathbf{2065\ KPa}$$

Distance, x, from valve end over which pipe is subject to pressure rise

$$= L - \frac{ct}{2}$$

$$= 4000 - \frac{1450\,(5)}{2}$$

= **375 m** from valve end.

■ **Problem 13.6:** *A 3 km long pipe, 30 cm in diameter, supplies water at 210 LPS. If valve at its end closed instantaneously. Calculate pressure rise, considering pipe to be rigid. Sketch the variation of pressure rise w.r.t. time at (i) valve end (ii) mid point of the pipe.*

Solution:

$$K_{water} = 2 \times 10^9 \text{ Pa} \qquad Q = AV = \frac{\pi}{4}D^2V \quad \therefore \quad V = \frac{0.210}{.78\,(.3)^2} = 3 \text{ m/s}$$

$$c = \sqrt{\frac{K}{\rho}} = \sqrt{\frac{2\times10^9}{10^3}} = 1414 \text{ m/s}$$

$$\text{Critical time } T = \frac{2L}{c} = \frac{2\times3\times10^3}{1414} = \mathbf{4.24\ s}$$

period of one cycle of fluctuation = 4.24 × 2 = 8.48 s

p_i = pressure rise = $\rho cV = 10^3$ (1414) (3) = **4242 KPa.** ...(Ans.)

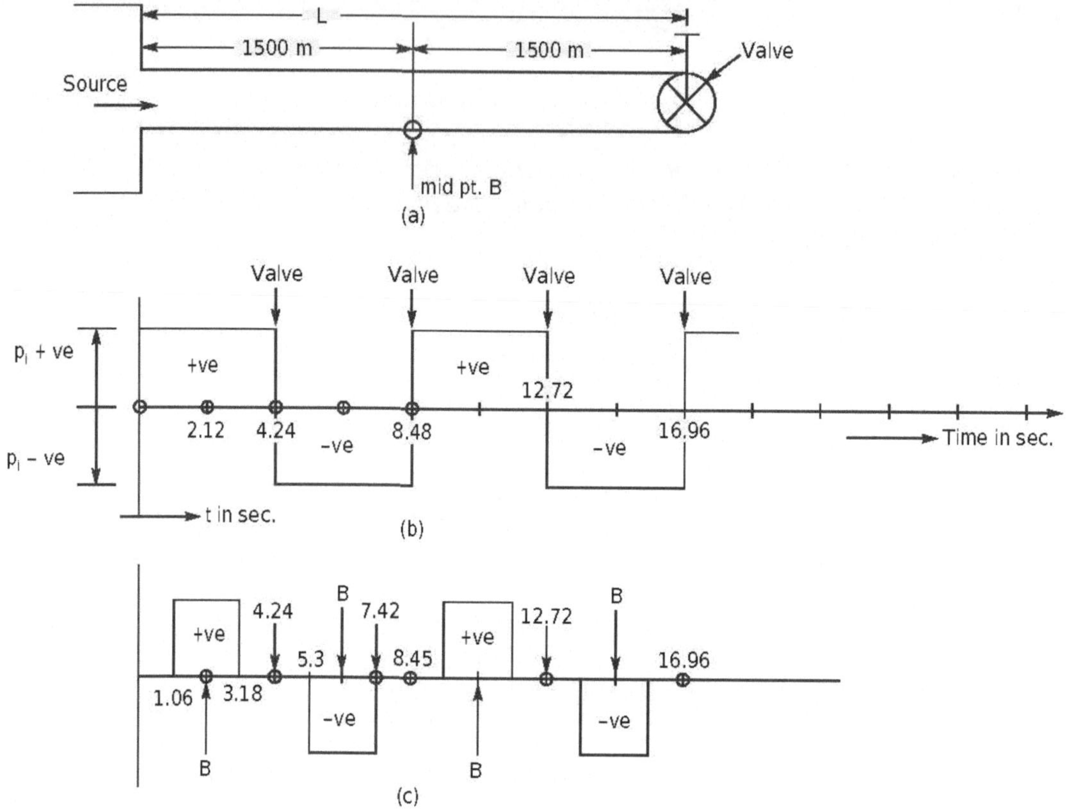

Fig. 13.5 (*a*), (*b*) and (*c*)

Fig. 13.5 (*b*) shows variation of p_i w.r.t. time t at valve end for problem (*b*).

(*i*) time taken for p_i to reach source = $\dfrac{3000}{1414} = 2.12$ s

(*ii*) time taken for p_i to get reflected back at $v = \dfrac{3000}{1414} = 2.12$ s.

Hence for time t = 0 to (2.12 + 2.12) = 4.24 s, the entire pipe length is subject to p_i +ve and from 4.24 to 8.48 it will be – p_i See Fig. 13.5 (*b*)

Again from 8.48 to 12.72, + p_i

and 12.72 to 16.96 – p_i etc.

Period of one cycle = 4.24 × 2 = 8.48 s.

Fig. 13.5 (*c*) shows variation of p_i w.r.t. time t at mid point B of pipe.

Time for p_i to reach B from valve = $\dfrac{15000}{1414} = 1.06$ s

$$\text{time for } p_i \text{ to reach source} = \frac{15000}{1414} = 1.06 \text{ s}$$

$$\text{Time for reflected wave to reach } B = \frac{15000}{1414} = 1.06 \text{ s}$$

$\therefore$ Duration of maximum pressure p_i at B is $(1.06 + 1.06) = 2.12$ s

i.e., from $t = 1.06$ s to 3.18 s

Time for reflected wave to reach valve = 3.18 + 1.06

= 4.24 s

Time for $(-p_i)$ to reach B, 4.24 + 1.06 = 5.3 s

Duration of $(-p_i)$ at B = 5.3 to (5.3 + 2.12) = 7.42 s

and time to complete 1st cycle = 8.48 s.

■ **Problem 13.7:** *A 1000 mm diameter steel pipe carries water at the rate of 1200 LPS, at a head of 200 m. Calculate pressure rise if valve at its end is closed instantaneously. Also find minimum thickness of pipe wall if permissible working stress = 1 × 10⁵ KPa.*

Solution:

$$K_{\text{water}} = 2.1 \text{ kN/mm}^2 \text{ and } E_{\text{steel}} = 210 \text{ kN/mm}^2$$

Assume pipe wall material to be rigid.

$$c = \sqrt{\frac{K}{\rho}} = \sqrt{\frac{2.1 \times 10^9}{1000}} = \mathbf{1450 \text{ m/s}}$$

$$V = \frac{Q}{A} = \frac{1.2}{.78\,(1)^2} = \mathbf{1.53 \text{ m/s}}$$

$$p_i = \rho c V = 1000\,(1450)\,1.53$$

$$= \mathbf{2230 \text{ KPa}}$$

$$p_s = \rho g(\text{head}) = 1000\,(9.81)\,(200)$$

$$= \mathbf{1962 \text{ KPa}}$$

$$\therefore \quad p_{\text{total}} = 1962 + 2230 = \mathbf{4192 \text{ KPa}}$$

$$\sigma_{\text{working}} = \frac{p_{\text{total}}\, D}{2t_p}$$

$$\therefore \quad t_p = \frac{4192\,(1)}{2\,(1 \times 10^5)} = 2096 \times 10^{-5} \text{ m}$$

$$= 20.96 \text{ mm} = 21 \text{ mm}$$

Now consider elasticity of pipe wall material, then t_p required will be less than **21 mm**

Assume t_p = **19 mm**

$$\therefore \quad c = \frac{1450}{\sqrt{1 + \dfrac{(1)\,2.1 \times 10^9}{210 \times 10^9\,(19 \times 10^{-3})}}}$$

$$= \frac{1450}{\sqrt{1.526}} = \frac{1450}{1.235} = 1174 \text{ m/s}$$

∴ $p_i = \rho c V = 1000 \times 1174 \times 1.53 = 1796$ KPa

∴ $P_t = P_{\text{total}}$ $1962 + 1796 = 3758$ KPa

$$t_p = \frac{3758(1)}{2(1\times10^5)} = 1879\times10^{-5}\times10^3$$

$= 18.79$ mm

∴ $t_p = 19$ mm ∴ assumed value of 19 mm is OK ...(Ans.)

■ **Problem 13.8:** *A cost iron pipe, 10 mm thick and 250 mm in diameter is 1000 m long, and carries discharge of 150 LPS of water. Find*

(i) rapid valve closure time

(ii) pressure rise

(iii) if T = 1.5 s, find length of pipe affected by peak water pressure.

Solution:

For water, $K = 2200$ MPa

For pipe, $E = 80 \times 10^9$ Pa

$$c = \frac{\sqrt{K/\rho}}{\sqrt{1+\dfrac{DK}{Et_p}}} = \frac{\sqrt{2200\times10^6/1000}}{\sqrt{1+\dfrac{.25\times2200\times10^6}{80\times10^9\times\dfrac{10}{1000}}}}$$

$$= \frac{1483}{\sqrt{1+.68}} = \frac{1483}{1.3}\mathbf{1140 \text{ m/s}}$$

$T = \dfrac{2L}{c} = \dfrac{2000}{1140} 1.75$ s = time for rapid closure ...(Ans.)

$p_i = \rho c V$ $1000\ (1140)\ V$

$$V = \frac{Q}{A} = \frac{0.15}{.78(.25)^2} = \mathbf{3 \text{ m/s}}$$

∴ $p_i = 1000\ (1140)\ (3) =$ **3500 KPa** ...(Ans.)

$x = L - \dfrac{Ct}{2}$, here $t = 1.5$ s

$$= 1000 - \frac{1140(1.5)}{2} = 1000 - 855$$

= 145 m from valve. ...(Ans.)

■ **Problem 13.9:** *A penstock pipe of 3 m diameter conveys 15 cumecs under a head of 190 m. Find water hammer pressure due to sudden valve closure as a percentage of static pressure.*

Solution:

$$K_{water} = 2.1 \times 10^4 \text{ kg/cm}^2 \qquad E = 2.1 \times 10^6 \text{ kg/cm}^2$$

$$c = \sqrt{\frac{K}{\rho}} = \sqrt{\frac{2.1\times10^4\times10\times10^4}{10^3}} = \mathbf{1450\ m/s}$$

$$V = \frac{Q}{A} = \frac{15}{.78(3)^2} = 2.12\ \text{m/s}$$

$$p_i = \rho c V = 1000\ (1450)\ (2.12) = \mathbf{3078\ KPa}$$

$$p_s = 190 \text{ m of water} = 1000 \times 9.81 \times 190$$

$$= \mathbf{1862\ KPa}$$

$\therefore$ $$\frac{p_i}{p_s} = \frac{3078}{1862} = 1.65 \text{ i.e., } p_i \text{ is } 165\% \text{ of } p_s.$$ ...**(Ans.)**

■ **Problem 13.10:** *A penstock line supplying water to turbines is fitted with a valve at turbine end and is vulnerable to instantaneous closure. Pipe line is 25 cm in diameter and 2.5 cm thick. If σ = 2.0 kN/cm², find maximum possible discharge it can carry.*

Solution:

$$E_{steel} = 1.2 \times 10^7 \text{ N/cm}^2 \qquad K_{water} = 2.1 \times 10^5 \text{ N/cm}^2$$

$$c = \sqrt{\frac{K/\rho}{\left(1+\frac{DK}{Et_p}\right)}} = \left[\frac{2.1\times10^5\times10^4/10^3}{1+\dfrac{.25\times2.1\times10^9}{1.2\times10^7\times10^4\left(\dfrac{2.5}{100}\right)}}\right]^{1/2}$$

$$= \frac{1450}{(1+.175)^{1/2}} = \frac{1450}{1.083} = 1338.87\ \text{m/s}$$

$$= 1339 \text{ m/s}$$

$$p_i = \frac{2\sigma t_p}{D}$$

$$= (2 \times 10^3 \times 10^4) \times 2 \times \frac{2.5}{100}$$

$$= 10 \times 10^5 \text{ N/m}^2$$

Now, $$p_i = \rho c V$$

$\therefore$ $$10 \times 10^3 = 10^3\ (1339)\ V$$

$\therefore$ $$V = \frac{10\times10^5}{10^3\times1339} = 0.74\ \text{m/s}$$

$$\therefore \qquad Q = \frac{\pi}{4} D^2 V = .78\,(.25)^2\,(.74) = \mathbf{3.64\ m^3/s.} \qquad \text{...(Ans.)}$$

■ **Problem 13.11:** *For the pipe given above in problem 13.10, draw a typical pressure variation at one quarter point along the length of the pipe due to sudden closure of valve.*

Solution:

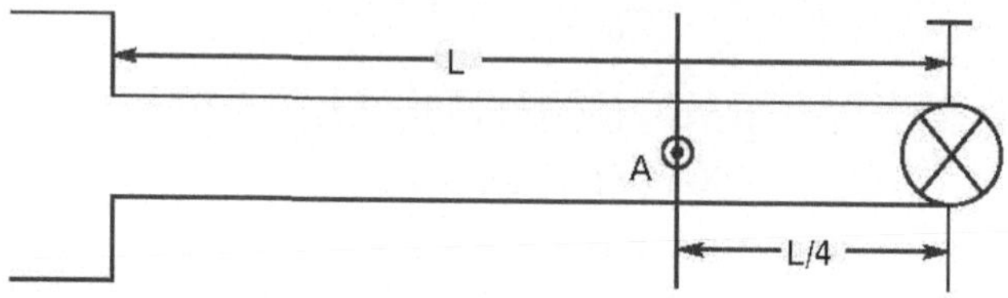

Fig. 13.6

As L is not given, assume = 2 km = 2000 m

$$\text{time to teach quarter point } A = \frac{\frac{1}{4}L}{c} = \frac{200/4}{1339}$$

$$= 0.37 \text{ s}$$

$$\text{time to reach the source} = \frac{\frac{3}{4}L}{c} = \frac{(.75)\,2000}{1339} = 1.12 \text{ s}$$

$$\text{time to reflect back} = 1.12 \text{ s}$$

$$\therefore \qquad .37 + 1.12 + 1.12 = 2.61 \text{ s}$$

i.e., For 2.61 s, p_i + ve will be at A

$$T = \frac{2L}{c} = \frac{2 \times 2000}{1339} = 2.98 \text{ s} \rightarrow 3 \text{ s}$$

i.e., from 3.35 s to **3 × 2 = 6 s** it will be p_i – ve. ...**(Ans.)**

This is shown in Fig. 13.7

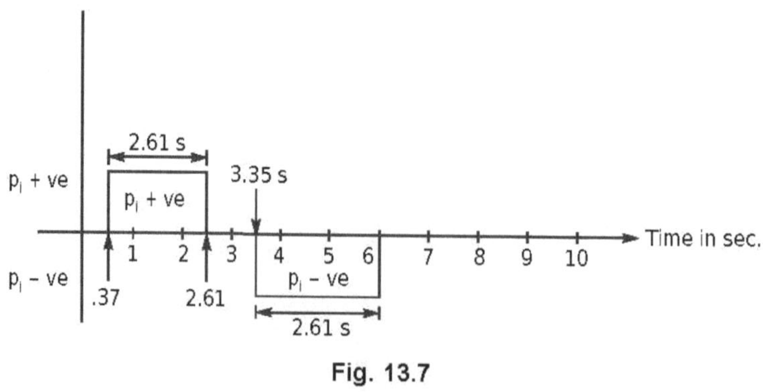

Fig. 13.7

■ **Problem 13.12:** *A pipe of 500 mm diameter and 2.5 km long conveys water at velocity of 1.75 m/s. Find pressure rise due to closure of a valve at the end of the pipe in 1.5 seconds, taking pipe as rigid K = 19.6 × 10⁴ N/cm².*

Show pressure variation at mid length of pipe.

Solution:

For rigid pipe, $c = \sqrt{K/\rho}$

$$= \sqrt{\frac{19.6 \times 10^4 \times 10^4}{1000}}$$

$$= 1400 \text{ m/s}$$

$$\therefore \quad T = \frac{2L}{C} = \frac{2(2.5) \times 1000}{1400} = 3.57 \text{ seconds} > t \text{ which is 1.5 second.}$$

∴ Rapid closure of valve.

$$p_1 = \text{r}cV = 100\ (1400)\ (1.75) = \mathbf{2450} \text{ KPa} \quad \text{or} \quad \mathbf{2.45 \times 10^6} \text{ N.}$$

Time for pressure wave to reach B, mid point of pipe from valve end

$$= \frac{\frac{1}{2}(2.5 \times 1000)}{1400} = 0.892 \text{ second}$$

∴ Time to reach source from B = 0.892 second.

Time to reach B after reflected back = 0.892 second.

Duration of pressure rise (–ve) at B = (.892 +.892) = 1984s

and it is from = .892 second to 3(.892) = 2.676 second.

$$T \text{ for half cycle} = \frac{2L}{C} = \frac{5000}{1400} = 3.57\text{s}$$

∴ $-p_i$ will be at B at t = 3.57 + .892

= 4.462 s

and will last upto t = 4.462 + 2(.892) = 6.246s

T for complete cycle = 3.57 × 2 = **7.14 s**

This is shown in Fig. 13.8

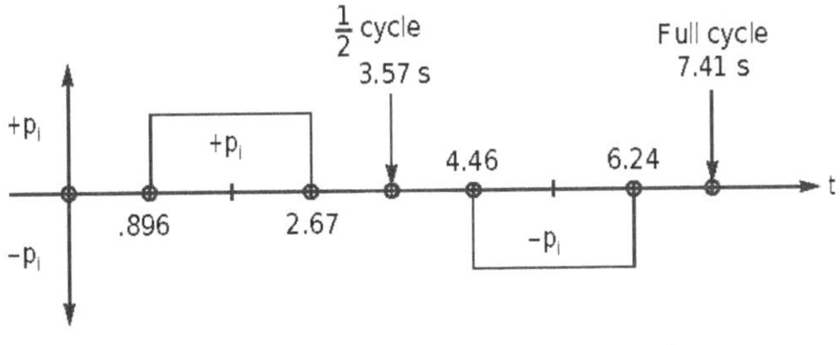

Fig. 13.8 Variation of p at mid point with respect to time

Exercises

1. A pipe of diameter 100 cm and thickness of wall 10 mm, is 2 km long and carries water at 2 m/s. If at its d/s end valve is closed suddenly, find rise in the pressure.
   (*i*) by treating pipe rigid.
   (*ii*) by considering elasticity of pipe wall.
   Take $E = 2.1 \times 10^7$ N/cm², $K = 2.0 \times 10^5$ N/cm².
   (Ans. (*i*) 2828 KPa (*ii*) 2702 KPa**)**

2. (*a*) A 300 mm diameter pipe of MS has 6 mm thickness and carries water at 200 LPS. Find pressure rise for rapid valve closure, given length of pipe 8 km.
   $$E = 2 \times 10^2 \text{ N/cm}^2$$
   $$K = 2 \times 10^5 \text{ N/cm}^2.$$
   (Ans. (*a*) p_i = 3301KPa**)**
   (*b*) Sketch the variation of p_i at the mid point of the pipe.
   For (*b*):

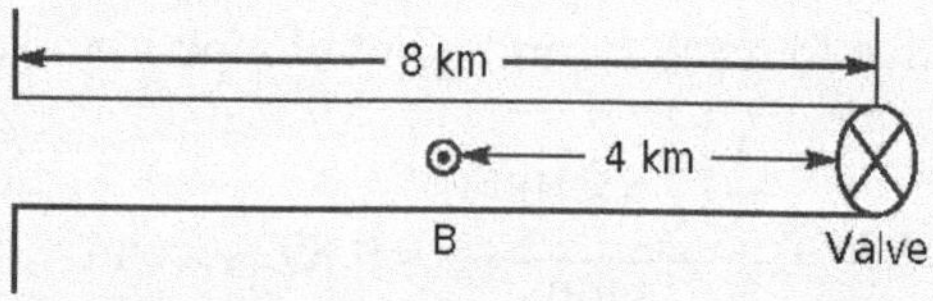

Fig. 13.8

t to reach $\quad B = \dfrac{4000}{c} \quad c = 1159$ m/s as per part (*a*)

$$= \frac{4000}{1159} = 3.45 \text{ s}$$

and then to reach source = 3.45 + 3.45 = 6.9 s and get reflected back at B

6.9 + 3,45 = 10.35 s

Now, $\quad T = \dfrac{2L}{c} = \dfrac{2 \times 8000}{1159} = 13.8 \text{ s}$

∴ between t = 13.8 + 3.45 = 17.25 s

and 17.25 + 6.9 = 24.15 s, p_i will be –ve. **(Ans.** (*b*) is shown in Fig. 13.9**)**

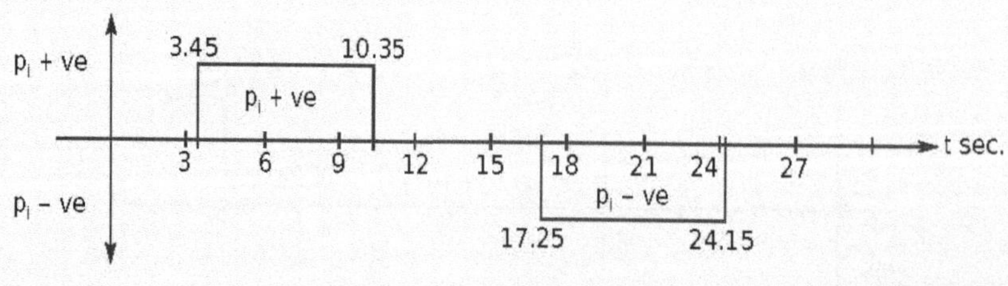

Fig. 13.9

3. A 2000 m long steel pipe of diameter 40 cm supplies water at 200 m head. If pipe thickness is 10 mm and valve is closed such that velocity reduces from 3 m/s to 0.5 m/s in 5 seconds, find pressure rise, and state whether it is a case of slow or rapid closure. Find total pressure. ($K_{water} = 2 \times 10^9$ Pa and $E_{steel} = 2 \times 10^{11}$ Pa).
(**Ans.** $p_i = 1994$ KPa, slow closure; $p_{total} = 1994 + 1962 = 3956$ KPa)
4. A steel pipe 2000 m long and of 20 cm diameter supplies oil at 50 LPS. A valve at its end is closed in 2 s. If pipe thickness is 8 mm, find hoop streets in pipe due to water hammer and type of closure of valve. ($\rho_{oil} = 800$ kg/m^3, $K_{oil} = 1.52 \times 10^9$ Pa, $E_{steel} = 2 \times 10^{11}$ Pa).
(**Ans.** rapid closure, $\rho = 20.2$ N/mm^2)
5. A 50 cm diameter steel pipe 2 km long discharges water at 2000 LPS under a static head of 160 m. If thickness of pipe is 6 mm and working stress in pipe wall 0.1 kN/mm^2, find minimum time of closure so that pipe is safe. ($K = 2 \times 10^9$ Pa, $E = 2 \times 10^{11}$ Pa).
(**Ans.** 4.92 seconds)

14

Boundary Layer and Forces on Submerged Bodies

14.1 BOUNDARY LAYER ALONG A FLAT PLATE

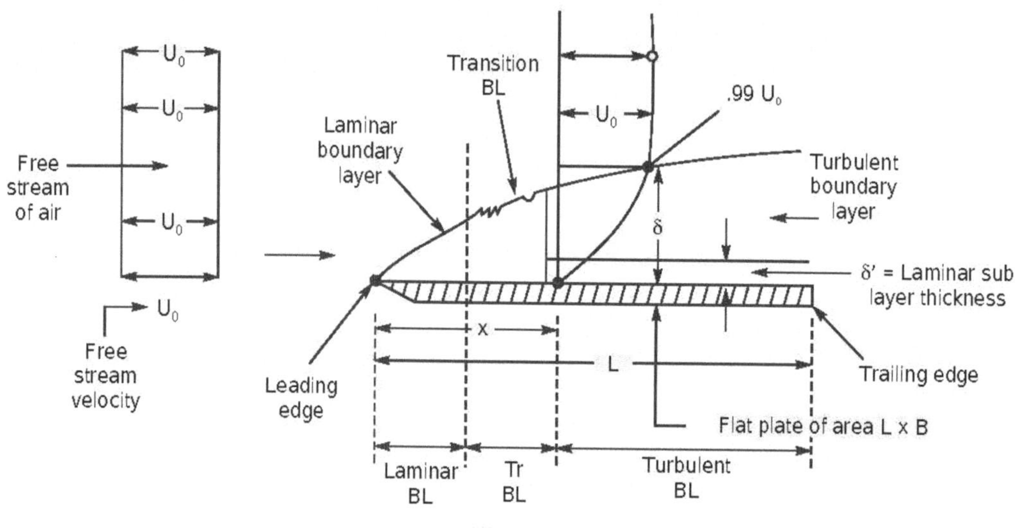

Fig. 14.1

A layer of small thickness adjacent to flat plate at rest, in which velocity is changing from zero at plate to 0.99 U_0 at a normal distance **δ**, is called Boundary Layer and **δ** is nominal boundary layer thickness. Angle of incidence that leading edge of the plate makes with U_0 is zero and also pressure gradient $\frac{dp}{dx}$ is zero. Front edge of the plate is leading edge and end part of the plate is trailing edge. For a small distance x from leading edge, boundary layer (BL) is Laminar and then for some distance it is transition type; after which it is turbulent boundary layer. A layer of small thickness δ' adjacent to plate in turbulent boundary layer zone is known as Laminar sublayer.

For boundary layer to be laminar,

$$\text{Reynolds number} \quad R = \frac{\rho U_0 x}{\mu} < 5 \times 10^5$$

and at $R \geq 5 \times 10^5$, it is turbulent boundary layer. Here x is measured from leading edge of the plate, μ and ρ are dynamic viscosity and mass density of flowing fluid, and U_0 is free stream value of velocity.

$$\delta' = \text{laminary sublayer thickness}$$

$$= \frac{11.6\,v}{u^*}, \text{ here } u^* = \sqrt{\frac{\tau_0}{\rho}} = \text{shear velocity}$$

and $$v = \frac{\mu}{\rho} = \text{kinematic viscosity.}$$

Boundary layer thickness δ varies from zero at leading edge to highest value at trailing edge. As velocity is changing from zero at the plate to 0.99 U_0 at δ in y direction *i.e.* direction normal to the plate, there are momentum changes in this player and hence an additional force, called Drag Force, F_D, acts on the plate. Value of F_D is dependent on δ and hence determination of δ is a first step towards calculation of F_D.

In order to determine value of δ, following additional terms are introduced:

(*a*) δ^* = delta star = displacement thickness,

(*b*) $\delta_m = \delta_\theta$ or θ = momentum thickness,

(*c*) and δ_e = energy thickness,

(*d*) The ratio $\dfrac{\delta^*}{\delta_m}$ is shape factor of boundary layer

and is denoted by H *i.e.* $H = \dfrac{\delta^*}{\theta}$.

(*e*) δ = nominal thickness of boundary layer and is value of y at which $u = 0.99\ U_0$.

Displacement thickness, δ^*:

Let u = velocity at normal distance y from the plate. Consider a strip of thickness dy at y. At y, reduction in velocity = $U_0 - u$, as such there is reduction in flow rate in the boundary layer. If δ^* is considered as a thickness by which if the plate is displaced backward so that loss in the flow rate in the boundary layer is compensated then,

$$U_0 (B \times \delta^*) = \int_0^\delta (U_0 - u)\, B\, dy$$

$$\therefore \quad \delta^* = \int_0^\delta \left(1 - \frac{u}{U_0}\right) dy \qquad \text{...(14.1)}$$

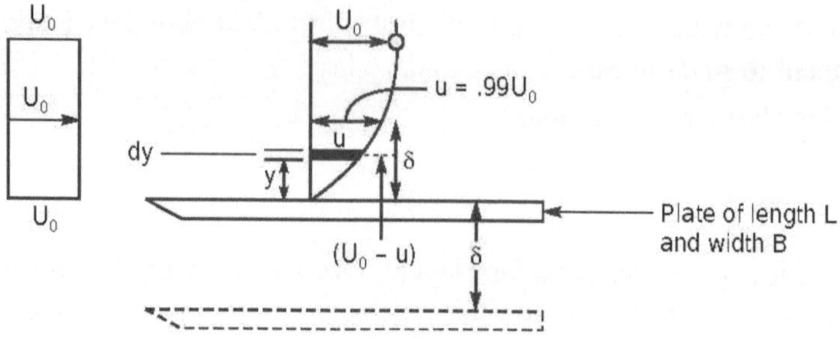

Fig. 14.2

Similarly if δ_m or δ_θ or θ is momentum thickness and is a thickness by which if the plate is shifted backwards to compensate the loss in momentum in boundary layer, then

$$(\rho\, U_0\, B\, \delta_m)\, U_0 = \int_0^\delta (\rho\, u\, B\, dy)\,(U_0 - u)$$

$$\therefore \qquad \delta_m = \theta = \int_0^\delta \frac{u}{U_0}\left(1 - \frac{u}{U_0}\right) dy \qquad \text{...(14.2)}$$

Similarly we can get δ_e also by considering compensation of reduction in KE over thickness δ_e. Here KE $= \dfrac{1}{2}$ mass × (Velocity)^2.

$$\therefore \qquad \frac{1}{2}(\rho U_0\, B\, \delta_e)\, U_0^2 = \int_0^\delta \frac{1}{2}(\rho\, B\, dy\, u)\,(U_0^2 - u^2)$$

$$\therefore \qquad \delta_e = \int_0^\delta \frac{u}{U_0}\left(1 - \frac{u^2}{U_0^2}\right) dy \qquad \text{...(14.3)}$$

To illustrate the above concept of δ^*, δ_m, δ_e and shape factor H etc. following numerical problem is given.

14.1.1 Solved Problem

■ **Problem 14.1:** *For the following velocity distribution in the boundary layer on a flat plate, find* δ^*, δ_θ, δ_e *and* H.

$$\frac{u}{U_0} = \frac{1}{2}\left(\frac{y}{d}\right).$$

Solution: Put $\qquad n = \dfrac{y}{\delta} \quad \therefore \quad dn = \dfrac{dy}{\delta} \quad \therefore \quad dy = \delta\, dn$

and when $\qquad y = 0, \quad n = 0$

$\qquad y = \delta \quad n = 1$

(*a*) $$\delta^* = \int_0^\delta \left(1 - \frac{u}{U_0}\right) dy = \int_0^1 \delta\left(1 - \frac{1}{2}n\right) dn$$

$$= \delta\left[n - \frac{n^2}{4}\right]_0^1$$

$$= \frac{3}{4}\delta$$

(b) $$\theta = \int_0^\delta \frac{u}{U_0}\left(1 - \frac{u}{U_0}\right)dy = \delta \int_0^1 \left(\frac{1}{2}n\right)\left(1 - \frac{1}{2}n\right)dn$$

$$= \delta\left[\frac{n^2}{4} - \left(\frac{1}{2}\right)^2\left(\frac{n^3}{3}\right)\right]_0^1 = \frac{\delta}{6}$$

$\therefore$ $$\theta = \frac{\delta}{6}$$

(c) $$\delta_e = \int_0^\delta \frac{u}{U_0}\left(1 - \frac{u^2}{U_0^2}\right)dy$$

$$= \int_0^1 \delta\left(\frac{1}{2}n\right)\left(1 - \frac{n^2}{4}\right)dn$$

$$= \delta\int_0^1 \left[\frac{n}{2} - \frac{n^3}{8}\right]dn$$

$$= \delta\left[\frac{n^2}{4} - \frac{n^4}{32}\right]_0^1$$

$$= \frac{7}{32}\delta$$

$$H = \frac{\delta^*}{\delta_\theta} = \frac{3\delta/4}{\delta/6} = \frac{3}{4}\times 6 = \frac{9}{2}.$$ ...(Ans.)

14.2 VON KARMAN MOMENTUM INTEGRAL EQUATION

Let D_x = Drag Force at x from leading edge of the plate.

Take a small strip of thickness dy at y from the plate, then mass of fluid flowing through the strip = ($\rho u B\,dy$) and change in velocity flow = ($U_0 - u$).

$\therefore$ $$D_x = \int_0^\delta (\rho u B\,dy)(U_0 - u)\times\frac{U_0^2}{U_0^2}$$ (Multiply and divide by U_0^2)

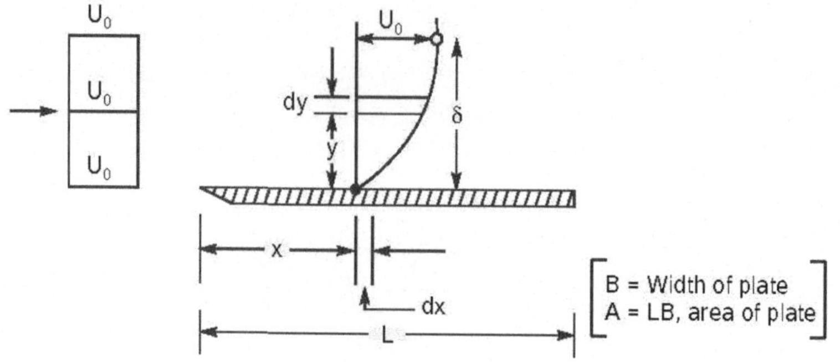

Fig. 14.3

$$= \rho B U_0^2 \int_0^\delta \frac{u}{U_0}\left(1-\frac{u}{U_0}\right) dy$$

$$= (\rho U_0^2 B)\ (\theta), \quad \text{here,} \quad \theta = \text{Momentum thickness} = \int_0^\delta \frac{u}{U_0}\left(1-\frac{u}{U_0}\right) dy$$

$$\therefore \quad dD_x = \rho U_0^2 B\,(d\theta)$$

Also, $dD_x = \tau_0\,(B\, d_x)$, here $\tau_0 = \mu \dfrac{du}{dy}$ at $y = 0$

$$\therefore \quad \rho U_0^2 B\,(d\theta) = \tau_0\, B\,(dx)$$

$$\therefore \quad \frac{\tau_0}{\rho U_0^2} = \frac{d\theta}{dx} \qquad \text{...(14.4)}$$

Eqn. (14.4) is known as VON KARMAN MOMENTUM INTEGRAL EQUATION

Let F_D = Drag force on plate of length $x = L$

$$= \int_0^L d\,D_x = \int_0^L \tau_0\, B\, dx$$

$$C_D = \text{Coefficient of drag} = \frac{\text{Actual drag force } i.e.\ F_D}{\text{Theoretical value of } F_D}$$

$$= \frac{F_D}{\frac{1}{2}\rho A U_0^2} \qquad (\text{here } A = B \times L)$$

$$C_f = \text{Local coefficient of drag} = \frac{\tau_0}{\frac{1}{2}\rho U_0^2}$$

To illustrate above theory, following problems are given:

14.2.1 Solved Problems

■ **Problem 14.2:** *For the velocity profile for laminar boundary layer given by*

$$\frac{u}{U_0} = 2\left(\frac{y}{\delta}\right) - \left(\frac{y}{\delta}\right)^2$$

Find: δ, τ_0, F_D, C_D, C_f.

Solution:

$$\frac{u}{U_0} = 2\left(\frac{y}{\delta}\right) - \left(\frac{y}{\delta}\right)^2$$

Put $\frac{y}{\delta} = n \quad \therefore \quad \delta dn = dy$ and when $y = 0$, $n = 0$ and when $y = \delta$, $n = 1$

$$\therefore \quad \frac{u}{U_0} = 2(n) - (n)^2$$

By Von–Karman Momentum Integral (MI) eq. (4).

$$\tau_0 = \rho U_0^2 \frac{d\theta}{dx}, \quad \text{here } \theta = \int_0^\delta \frac{u}{U_0}\left(1 - \frac{u}{U_0}\right) dy$$

$$\therefore \quad \theta = \delta \int_0^1 (2n - n^2)(1 - 2n + n^2)\, dn$$

$$= \delta \int_0^1 (2n - n^2 - 4n^2 + 2n^3 + 2n^3 - n^4)\, dn$$

$$= \delta \left[\frac{2n^2}{2} - \frac{5n^3}{3} + \frac{4n^4}{4} - \frac{n^5}{5}\right]_0^1$$

$$= \delta\left[1 - \frac{5}{3} + 1 - \frac{1}{5}\right] = \delta\left[2 - \frac{5}{3} - \frac{1}{5}\right] = \frac{2}{15}\delta$$

$$\therefore \quad \tau_0 = \rho U_0^2 \frac{d}{dx}\left(\frac{2}{15}\delta\right)$$

$$= \frac{2}{15}\rho U_0^2 \frac{d\delta}{dx} \qquad \text{...(1)}$$

Also

$$\tau_0 = \mu\left(\frac{du}{dy}\right)_{y=0} = \mu\left(\frac{d\left(\frac{u}{U_0}\right)U_0}{dy}\right). \quad \text{(multiply and divide by } U_0\text{)}$$

$$= \mu U_0 \left[\frac{d\,(2n - n^2)}{\delta\, dn}\right]$$

$$= \frac{\mu U_0}{\delta}(2-2n), \text{ here at } y = 0, n = 0$$

$$\therefore \quad \tau_0 = \frac{\mu U_0 2}{\delta} \qquad ...(2)$$

From (1) and (2), we get

$$\frac{2}{15}\rho U_0^2 \frac{d\delta}{dx} = \frac{\mu U_0 2}{\delta}$$

$$\therefore \quad \delta d\delta = \frac{15\mu}{\rho U_0} dx$$

$$\therefore \quad \frac{\delta^2}{2} = \frac{15\mu}{\rho U_0} x + C$$

Here, C = integrating constant

$= 0$ as when $x = 0$, $\delta = 0$.

$$\therefore \quad \delta^2 = \frac{30\mu x}{\rho U_0}$$

$$\therefore \quad \delta = 5.48\sqrt{\frac{\mu x}{\rho U_0} \times \frac{x}{x}}, \qquad \text{(multiple and divide by } x)$$

$$= 5.48\sqrt{\frac{x^2}{\left(\frac{\rho U_0 x}{\mu}\right)}}$$

$$= 5.48\sqrt{\frac{x^2}{R_x}}, \qquad \text{here } R_x = \frac{\rho U_0 x}{\mu}$$

$$\therefore \quad \delta = \frac{5.48\, x}{\sqrt{R_x}} \qquad ...(14.5)$$

Thus for laminar boundary layer, boundary layer thickness δ is directly proportional to x and inversely proportional to $\sqrt{R_x}$.

Note: If velocity distribution is **not given** in a numerical problem then as per **Blasius Exact Analytical Solution** for Laminar Boundary layer along a flat plate, following value of d, C_D and C_f can be taken:

(i) $$\delta = \frac{5x}{\sqrt{R_x}}$$

(ii) $$C_D = 1.328/\sqrt{R_L}$$

and (*iii*) $C_f = 0.664/\sqrt{R_x}$.

Now, $$\tau_0 = \frac{2U_0\mu}{\delta}$$

∴ $$\tau_0 = \frac{2U_0\mu\sqrt{R_x}}{5.48x} = 0.365\frac{\mu U_0\sqrt{R_x}}{x}$$

$$F_D = \int_0^L \tau_0\, B\, dx = \int_0^L 0.365\frac{\mu U_0}{x}\sqrt{\frac{\rho U_0 x}{\mu}}\,(B)\, dx$$

∴ $$F_D = \int_0^L \left(0.365\,\mu U_0 \frac{\sqrt{\rho U_0}\,.\,B}{\sqrt{\mu}}\right) x^{-1/2}\, dx$$

$$= (0.365U_0\sqrt{\rho U_0\mu}(B))\left[\frac{x^{-1/2+1}}{-\frac{1}{2}+1}\right]_0^L$$

$$= (0.365\,U_0\,\sqrt{\rho U_0\mu}\,(B))\,(2\sqrt{x})_0^L$$

$$= 0.73\sqrt{\rho U_0\mu}\,(U_0B)\sqrt{L}$$

$$C_D = \frac{F_D}{\frac{1}{2}\rho A U_0^2} = \frac{F_D}{\frac{1}{2}\rho\,(LB)\,U_0^2}$$

∴ $$C_D = \frac{0.73\sqrt{\rho U_0\mu}\,(U_0B)\sqrt{L}}{\frac{1}{2}\rho\,(LB)U_0^2}$$

∴ $$C_D = \frac{1.46}{\sqrt{R_L}}, \quad \text{here } R_L = \frac{\rho U_0 L}{\mu}$$

and $$C_f = \frac{\tau_0}{\frac{1}{2}\rho U_0^2} = \frac{0.365\,\mu U_0\sqrt{R_x}}{\frac{1}{2}(x)\,\rho U_0^2} = \frac{0.73\sqrt{R_x}}{\left(\frac{\rho U_0 x}{\mu}\right)}$$

$$= \frac{0.73\sqrt{R_x}}{R_x}$$

$$= \frac{0.73}{\sqrt{R_x}}, \quad \text{here } R_x = \frac{\rho U_0 x}{\mu}.$$

■ **Problem 14.3:** *If laminar boundary layer velocity distribution is* $\frac{u}{U_0} = \sin\left(\frac{\pi}{2}\frac{y}{\delta}\right)$, *find* δ, τ_0, F_D, F_D, C_D *and* C_f.

Solution:

$$\theta = \int_0^\delta \frac{u}{U_0}\left(1-\frac{u}{U_0}\right)dy$$

$$= \int_0^\delta \sin\left(\frac{\pi}{2}\frac{y}{\delta}\right)\left[1-\sin\left(\frac{\pi}{2}\frac{y}{\delta}\right)\right]dy$$

$$= \int_0^\delta \left[\sin\left(\frac{\pi}{2}\frac{y}{\delta}\right)-\sin^2\left(\frac{\pi}{2}\frac{y}{\delta}\right)\right]dy$$

Note:

$$\int \sin^2 x\,dx = \frac{x}{2}-\frac{\sin 2x}{4}$$

$$\therefore \qquad \theta = \left[\frac{-\cos\left(\frac{\pi}{2}\frac{y}{\delta}\right)}{\frac{\pi}{2}\left(\frac{1}{\delta}\right)}\right]_0^\delta - \left[\frac{\frac{\pi y}{2(2\delta)}}{\frac{\pi}{2\delta}} - \frac{\sin 2\left(\frac{\pi}{2}\frac{y}{\delta}\right)}{4\left(\frac{\pi}{2\delta}\right)}\right]_0^\delta$$

Putting limits $y = \delta$ and $y = 0$,

$$\theta = \left[\frac{-\cos\left(\frac{\pi}{2}\right)}{\frac{\pi}{2\delta}} - \frac{-\cos(0)}{\frac{\pi}{2\delta}}\right] - \left[\left(\frac{\delta}{2}-0\right)-(0-0)\right]$$

$$= \left[0+\frac{2\delta}{\pi}\right]-\frac{\delta}{2}$$

$$\therefore \qquad \theta = \delta\left[\frac{2}{\pi}-\frac{1}{2}\right] = 0.136\,(\delta)$$

Then according to Von Karman Momentum Integral eqn.

$$\frac{\tau_0}{\rho U_0^2} = \frac{d\theta}{dx} = 0.136\frac{d\delta}{dx} \qquad \text{...(1)}$$

Also, $$\tau_0 = \mu\left(\frac{du}{dy}\right)_{y=0}$$

$$= \mu U_0 \left. \frac{d\left(\dfrac{u}{U_0}\right)}{dy} \right|_{y=0} = \mu U_0 \frac{d}{dy}\left[\sin\left(\frac{\pi}{2}\frac{y}{\delta}\right)\right]_{y=0}$$

$$= \mu U_0 \left[\cos\left(\frac{\pi}{2}\frac{y}{\delta}\right) \times \frac{\pi}{2\delta}\right]_{y=0}$$

$$= \mu U_0 \left[(1)\frac{\pi}{2\delta}\right]$$

$$= \frac{\mu U_0 \pi}{2\delta} \qquad \text{...(2)}$$

From (1) and (2),

$$\rho U_0^2 \,(0.136) \frac{d\delta}{dx} = \frac{\mu U_0 \pi}{2\delta}$$

$$\rho U_0^2 \,(0.272)\, \delta\, d\delta = (\mu U_0 \pi)\, dx$$

$$\therefore \qquad \delta\, d\delta = \left(\frac{\mu U_0 \pi}{\rho U_0^2\,(0.272)}\right) dx$$

$$\frac{\delta^2}{2} = \left(11.5 \frac{\mu}{\rho U_0}\right) + C$$

$$= \frac{11.5\,\mu x}{\rho U_0} \times \frac{x}{x} \qquad [\because \; C = 0 \text{ at } \delta = 0 \text{ when } x = 0]$$

$$= \frac{11.5\,x^2}{\left(\dfrac{\rho U_0 x}{\mu}\right)}$$

$$\therefore \qquad \delta^2 = \frac{23x^2}{\left(\dfrac{\rho U_0 x}{\mu}\right)}$$

$$\therefore \qquad \delta = \frac{4.79x}{\sqrt{R_x}} = \frac{4.8x}{\sqrt{R_x}}$$

$$\therefore \qquad \tau_0 = \frac{\mu U_0 \pi}{2\delta} = \frac{\mu U_0 \pi \sqrt{R_x}}{2 \times 4.79x}$$

$$= 0.327 \frac{\mu U_0 \sqrt{R_x}}{x}$$

$$\therefore \qquad F_D = \int_0^L \tau_0 \, B \, dx$$

$$= 0.655 \, \mu U_0 \, B \sqrt{R_L}$$

$$\therefore \qquad C_D = \frac{F_D}{\frac{1}{2}\rho A U_0^2} = \frac{0.655 \, \mu U_0 B \sqrt{R_L}}{\frac{1}{2}\rho (BL) U_0^2}$$

$$= \frac{1.31\sqrt{R_L}}{\left(\frac{\rho U_0 L}{\mu}\right)} = \frac{1.31}{\sqrt{R_L}}$$

and similarly
$$C_f = \frac{\tau_0}{\frac{1}{2}\rho U_0^2} = \frac{0.65}{\sqrt{R_x}}$$

Thus for various velocity distribution for laminar boundary layer, value δ, C_D, C_f are given in following table:

Table 14.1

l.b.l. velocity distribution	δ	C_D	C_f
(1) As per Blasius. (**Note:** If in a problem velocity distribution is not given, then use these values).	$\frac{5x}{\sqrt{R_x}}$	$\frac{1.328}{\sqrt{R_L}}$	$\frac{0.664}{\sqrt{R_x}}$
(2) $\frac{u}{U_0} = \frac{y}{\delta}$	$\frac{3.46\,x}{\sqrt{R_x}}$	$\frac{1.154}{\sqrt{R_L}}$	$\frac{0.577}{\sqrt{R_x}}$
(3) $\frac{u}{U_0} = \sin\left(\frac{\pi}{2}\frac{y}{\delta}\right)$	$\frac{4.8\,x}{\sqrt{R_x}}$	$\frac{1.31}{\sqrt{R_L}}$	$\frac{0.65}{\sqrt{R_x}}$
(4) $\frac{u}{U_0} = 2\left(\frac{y}{\delta}\right) - \left(\frac{y}{\delta}\right)^2$	$\frac{5.48\,x}{\sqrt{R_x}}$	$\frac{1.46}{\sqrt{R_L}}$	$\frac{0.73}{\sqrt{R_x}}$
(5) $\frac{u}{U_0} = \frac{3}{2}\left(\frac{y}{\delta}\right) - \frac{1}{2}\left(\frac{y}{\delta}\right)^3$	$\frac{4.64\,x}{\sqrt{R_x}}$	$\frac{1.29}{\sqrt{R_L}}$	$\frac{0.648}{\sqrt{R_x}}$
(6) $\frac{u}{U_0} = 2\left(\frac{y}{\delta}\right) - 2\left(\frac{y}{\delta}\right)^3 + \left(\frac{y}{\delta}\right)^4$	$\frac{5.84\,x}{\sqrt{R_x}}$	$\frac{1.328}{\sqrt{R_L}}$	$\frac{0.664}{\sqrt{R_x}}$

■ **Problem 14.4:** *For a Turbulent Boundary Layer (TBL), on a flat plate, velocity distribution is given by* $\frac{1}{7}$ *th power law,*

$$\frac{u}{U_0} = \left(\frac{y}{\delta}\right)^{1/7}$$

find δ, τ_0, F_D, C_D *and* C_f;

subject to condition *that* $\tau_0 = 0.0225\,\rho U_0^2 \left(\frac{\mu}{\rho U_0 \delta}\right)^{1/4}$.

Solution:

$$\theta = \int_0^\delta \frac{u}{U_0}\left(1 - \frac{u}{U_0}\right) dy$$

Here,

$$\frac{u}{U_0} = \left(\frac{y}{\delta}\right)^{1/7} = n^{1/7},$$

where

$$n = \frac{y}{\delta}$$

and

$$dy = \delta dn$$

and

$$n = 1 \text{ for } y = \delta$$

$$n = 0 \text{ for } y = 0.$$

$\therefore$

$$\theta = \delta \int_0^1 n^{1/7}(1 - n^{1/7})\, dn$$

$$= \delta \int_0^1 (n^{1/7} - n^{2/7})\, dn$$

$$= \delta \left[\frac{7}{8}(n)^{8/7} - \frac{7}{9}(n)^{9/7}\right]_0^1$$

$\therefore$

$$\theta = \delta\left[\frac{7}{8} - \frac{7}{9}\right] = \left(\frac{7}{72}\right)\delta$$

Now, according to Von Karman Momentum Integral eqn.

$$\frac{\tau_0}{\rho U_0^2} = \frac{d\theta}{dx} = \frac{7}{72}\frac{d\delta}{dx}$$

$\therefore$

$$\frac{0.0225\,\rho U_0^2 \left(\frac{\mu}{\rho U_0 \delta}\right)^{1/4}}{\rho U_0^2} = \frac{7}{72}\frac{d\delta}{dx}$$

$\therefore$

$$\int \delta^{1/4}\, d\delta = 0.0225\left(\frac{72}{7}\right)\left(\frac{\mu}{\rho U_0}\right)^{1/4} \int dx$$

$$\therefore \quad \frac{\delta^{1/4+1}}{\frac{1}{4}+1} = 0.2341\left(\frac{\mu}{\rho U_0}\right)^{1/4} x + C \qquad \text{(Here } C = 0 \text{ for } \delta = 0 \text{ at } x = 0\text{)}$$

$$\therefore \quad \delta^{5/4} = 0.2314\left(\frac{5}{4}\right)\left(\frac{\mu}{\rho U_0}\right)^{1/4} x$$

$$\therefore \quad \delta = \left[0.289\left(\frac{\mu}{\rho U_0}\right)^{1/4} . x\right]^{4/5}$$

$$\therefore \quad \delta = 0.37\left(\frac{\mu}{\rho U_0}\right)^{1/5} (x)^{4/5}$$

Multiple and divide RHS by $x^{1/5}$

$$\therefore \quad \delta = \frac{(0.37x)}{\left(\frac{\rho U_0 x}{\mu}\right)^{1/5}}$$

$$= \frac{0.37x}{(R_x)^{1/5}} \qquad \text{here } R_x = \frac{\rho U_0 x}{\mu}$$

Thus for TBL, $$\delta = \frac{0.37x}{(R_x)^{1/5}} \qquad ...(1)$$

Now it is given that $\tau_0 = 0.0225\,\rho U_0^2 \left(\frac{\mu}{\rho U_0 \delta}\right)^{1/4}$

$$\therefore \quad \tau_0 = 0.0225\,\rho U_0^2 \left[\frac{\mu}{\rho U_0 \left(\frac{0.37x}{(R_x)^{1/5}}\right)}\right]^{1/4}$$

$$\tau_0 = \frac{0225}{(.37)^{1/4}}(\rho U_0^2)\left[\frac{\mu}{\frac{\rho U_0 x}{(R_x)^{1/5}}}\right]^{1/4}$$

$$= 0.0577\left(\frac{\rho U_0^2}{2}\right)\left[\frac{1}{R_x} . R_x^{1/5}\right]^{1/4}$$

$\therefore$ $$\tau_0 = 0.0577\left(\frac{\rho U_0^2}{2}\right)\left(\frac{1}{R_x^{1/5}}\right) \qquad ...(2)$$

Now, $$F_D = \int_0^L \tau_0 \, B \, dx$$

$$= 0.072\left(\frac{\rho U_0^2}{2}\right)\left(\frac{1}{R_L^{1/5}}\right)A$$

$\therefore$ $$C_D = \frac{F_D}{\frac{1}{2}\rho A U_0^2} = \frac{0.072}{(R_L)^{1/5}} \qquad ...(3)$$

Also 1, $$C_f = \frac{\tau_0}{\frac{1}{2}\rho U_0^2} = \frac{0.0577}{(R_x)^{1/5}} \qquad ...(4)$$

Note: All above values for Turbulent Boundary Layer are for R between 5×10^5 to 2×10^7. If R is between 2×10^7 to 10^9, Logarithmic form of velocity distribution given by **H. Schlichting** is applicable and in that case,

$$\delta = \frac{(0.22)\,x}{(R_x)^{1/6}}, \; C_D = \frac{0.455}{(\log R_L)^{2.58}}$$

and $$C_f = \frac{0.37}{(\log R_x)^{2.58}} \text{ for } R_x > 2 \times 10^7 \text{ and } \leq 10^9.$$

14.3 SOLVED PROBLEMS ON LAMINAR BOUNDARY LAYER AND TURBULENT BOUNDARY LAYER

■ **Problem 14.5:** *Air of kinematic viscosity 0.15×10^{-4} m²/s and $\rho = 0.1264$ slug/m³ is flowing over a flat plate of size 40 cm × 50 cm, side 50 cm parallel to $U_0 = 5$ m/s. Find δ_L, τ_0 at $x = \frac{1}{2}L$, and F_D on both side of plate; given that*

$$\frac{u}{U_0} = \sin\left(\frac{\pi}{2}\frac{y}{\delta}\right).$$

Solution:

For velocity distribution $$\frac{u}{U_0} = \sin\left(\frac{\pi}{2}\frac{y}{\delta}\right),$$

we have $$\delta = \frac{4.79x}{\sqrt{R_x}} \text{ and } \tau_0 = 0.327\frac{\mu U_0\sqrt{R_x}}{x}:$$

Also, $F_D = 0.655\,\mu\, U_0 B \sqrt{R_L}$, see Table 14.1.

$$R_x = \frac{\rho U_0 x}{\mu} = \frac{U_0 x}{v} = \frac{5 \times 0.5}{0.15 \times 10^{-4}} = 16.66 \times 10^4.$$

$$R_L = 1.66 \times 10^3 < 5 \times 10^5$$

$\therefore$ Boundary Layer in **laminar.**

$$\delta_L\,(L = 50 \text{ cm}) = \frac{4.79 \times 0.5}{\sqrt{1.66 \times 10^5}} = \frac{4.79 \times 0.5}{407} = 5.88 \times 10^{-3} = 0.58 \text{ cm}$$

...(Ans.)

$$R_x\,(x = 25 \text{ cm}) = \frac{U_0(0.25)}{\gamma} = \frac{5 \times 0.25}{0.15 \times 10^{-4}} = 8.33 \times 10^4$$

$$\therefore \quad \tau_0\,(\text{at } x = 25 \text{ cm}) = 0.327\,\frac{\mu U_0 \sqrt{8.33 \times 10^4}}{0.25}$$

$$\mu = v\rho = 0.15 \times 10^{-4} \times 0.1264$$

$$= 0.0189 \times 10^{-4} \text{ kg–s/m}^2$$

$$\therefore \quad \tau_0\,(\text{at } x = 25 \text{ cm}) = 0.327\,\frac{0.0189 \times 10^{-4} \times 5 \times 2.88 \times 10^2}{0.25}$$

$$= 3.56 \times 10^{-2} \text{ N/m}^2$$ **...(Ans.)**

$$F_D\,(\text{on both side}) = 2 \times 0.655\,\mu\, U_0 B \sqrt{R_L}, \qquad \text{here } B = 40 \text{ cm}$$

$$= 2 \times 0.655 \times 0.0189 \times 10^{-4} \times 5 \times 0.4 \times \sqrt{1.66 \times 10^5}$$

$$= 2 \times 10 \times 10^{-4} = 0.002 \; kgf \text{ or } 0.02 \text{ N}$$ **...(Ans.)**

■ **Problem 14.6:** *Find δ_L and F_D on both sides of flat plate of size (B = 2m) × (L = 4m), U_0 = 5 m/s, v_{air} = 0.15 × 10^{-4} m²/s and ρ_{air} = 0.12 slugs/m³.*

Solution:

$$R_L = \frac{U_0 L}{v} = \frac{5 \times 4}{0.15 \times 10^{-4}} = 133 \times 10^4 = 13.3 \times 10^5 > 5 \times 10^5$$

$\therefore$ Boundary layer is turbulent boundary layer.

$$\therefore \quad \delta_L = \frac{0.37\,L}{(R_L)^{1/5}} = \frac{0.37(4)}{(13.3 \times 10^5)^{1/5}} = \frac{0.37 \times 4}{16.7} = 0.088 \text{ m}$$ **...(Ans.)**

$$S_D = \frac{0.072}{(R_L)^{1/5}} = \frac{0.072}{16.7} = 4.31 \times 10^{-3}$$

$$\therefore \quad F_D = 2 \times \frac{1}{2} \rho A U_0^2\, C_D$$

$$= C_D\, \rho A U_0^2$$

$$= (4.31 \times 10^{-3})(0.12)(2 \times 4)(5)^2$$
$$= 103.4 \times 10^{-3}$$
$$= 0.1034 \text{ kgf or } 1.034 \text{ N.} \qquad ...\textbf{(Ans.)}$$

■ **Problem 14.7:** *If velocity distribution in a laminar boundary layer on a flat plate is*

$$f(n) = \frac{u}{U_0} = a + bn + cn^2 + dn^3$$

where $n = \frac{y}{\delta}$, *find coefficients a, b, c, d.*

Solution: For laminar boundary layer boundary conditions are

(1) at $y = 0$, $n = 0$, $u = 0$, $\therefore$ $f(n) = 0$ and $f''(n) = 0$

$$\therefore \quad f(n) = 0 = a + b(0) + c(0)^2 + d(0)^3$$
$$\therefore \quad a = 0$$
$$f'(n) = b + 2cn + 3dn^2$$
$$\therefore \quad f''(n) = 2c + 6dn$$
$$= 0 \text{ at } n = 0$$
$$\therefore \quad c = 0$$

(2) at $y = \delta$, $n = 1$, $u = U_0$, $f(n) = 1$ and $f'(n) = 0$

$$\therefore \quad f(n) = 1 = b + d, \quad \therefore \quad b = 1 - d$$
$$f'(n) = 0 = b + 3d$$
$$= 1 - d + 3d$$
$$= 1 + 2d$$
$$\therefore \quad d = -\frac{1}{2}, \quad \therefore \quad b = \frac{3}{2} \qquad ...\textbf{(Ans.)}$$
$$\therefore \quad f(n) = \frac{u}{U_0} = \frac{3}{2}n - \frac{1}{2}n^3. \qquad ...\textbf{(Ans.)}$$

■ **Problem 14.8:** *For laminar boundary layer,* $\frac{u}{U_0} = f(n) = a + bn + cn^2$, *find coefficients a, b, c and then* δ^*, δ_θ *and H. Here* $n = \frac{y}{\delta}$ *and using boundary conditions for laminar boundary layer.*

Solution:

(1) at $y = 0$, $n = 0$, $u = 0$, $f(n) = 0$ and $f''(n) = 0$.

$$\therefore \quad f(n) = 0 = a + b(0) + c(0)^2$$
$$\therefore \quad a = 0$$

(2) at $y = \delta$, $n = 1$, $u = U_0$, $f(n) = 1$,

$$\therefore \quad f(n) = 1 = a + bn + cn^2$$
$$1 = 0 + b + c$$
$$1 = b + c \qquad ...(i)$$

$\therefore \quad f'(n) = 0 = b + 2cn$

$= b + 2c$

$\therefore \quad b = -2c$, Now put this value of b in (i), $\therefore \quad 1 = (-2c) + c = -c$

$\therefore \quad c = -1$

$\therefore \quad b = +2$

$$\therefore \quad \frac{u}{U_0} = 2n - n^2$$

Now,

$$\delta^* = \int_0^\delta \left(1 - \frac{u}{U_0}\right) dy = \int_0^1 \delta(1 - 2n + n^2)\, dn$$

$$= \delta\left[n - \frac{2n^2}{2} + \frac{n^3}{3}\right]_0^1$$

$$= \delta\left[1 - 1 + \frac{1}{3}\right]$$

$$= \frac{\delta}{3}$$

$$\delta_\theta = \int_0^\delta \frac{u}{U_0}\left(1 - \frac{u}{U_0}\right) dy = \delta \int_0^1 (2n - n^2)(1 - 2n + n^2)\, dn$$

$$= \delta\left[\int_0^1 (2n - n^2 - 4n^2 + 2n^3 + 2n^3 - n^4)\, dn\right]$$

$$= \delta\left[2\frac{n^2}{2} - 5\frac{n^3}{3} + 4\frac{n^4}{4} - \frac{n^5}{5}\right]_0^1$$

$$= \delta\left[1 - \frac{5}{3} + 1 - \frac{1}{5}\right]$$

$$= \delta\left[2 - \frac{5}{3} - \frac{1}{5}\right]$$

$$= \delta\,[2 - 1.67 - 0.2]$$

$$\therefore \quad \delta_\theta = \frac{2}{15}\delta$$

$$H = \frac{\delta^*}{\delta_0}$$

$$= \frac{\delta}{3} \times \frac{15}{2\delta}$$

$$= 2.5.$$

■ **Problem 14.9:** *Find* δ, τ_0, F_D, C_D, C_f *for laminar boundary layer having velocity distribution as*

$$\frac{u}{U_0} = \frac{3}{2}\left(\frac{y}{\delta}\right) - \frac{1}{2}\left(\frac{y}{\delta}\right)^3 \tag{1}$$

Solution:

Put $\frac{y}{\delta} = n$ in above eqn. (1) $\therefore$ $\frac{u}{U_0} = \frac{3}{2}(n) - \frac{1}{2}(n)^3$

and $dy = dn \,.\, \delta,$

and at $y = \delta$, $n = 1$

and at $y = 0$, $n = 0$

$$\theta = \int_0^\delta \frac{u}{U_0}\left(1 - \frac{u}{U_0}\right) dy$$

$$\therefore \quad \theta = \delta \int_0^1 \left(\frac{3}{2}n - \frac{1}{2}n^3\right)\left(1 - \frac{3}{2}n + \frac{1}{2}n^3\right) dn$$

$$= \delta \int_0^1 \left(\frac{3}{2}n - \frac{9}{4}n^2 + \frac{3}{4}n^4 - \frac{1}{2}n^3 + \frac{3}{4}n^4 - \frac{1}{4}n^6\right) dn$$

$$= \delta \int_0^1 \left(\frac{3}{2}n - \frac{9}{4}n^2 + \frac{3}{2}n^4 - \frac{1}{2}n^3 - \frac{1}{4}n^6\right) dn$$

$$= \delta \left[\frac{3}{2}\frac{n^2}{2} - \frac{9}{4}\frac{n^3}{3} + \frac{3}{2}\frac{n^5}{5} - \frac{1}{2}\frac{n^4}{4} - \frac{1}{4}\frac{n^7}{7}\right]_0^1$$

$$= \delta \left[\frac{3}{4} - \frac{9}{12} + \frac{3}{10} - \frac{1}{8} - \frac{1}{28}\right]$$

$$= \delta[0.75 - 0.75 + 0.3 - 0.125 - 0.035]$$

$$= 0.\ 14\ \delta$$

$\therefore$ By Von Karman Momentum Integral eqn., we get

$$\frac{\tau_o}{\rho U_0^2} = \frac{d(\theta)}{dx} = 0.14\ \frac{d\delta}{dx} \quad \text{...(1)}$$

Also $\tau_0 = \mu \frac{du}{dy} \times \frac{U_0}{U_0}$ [Divide and multiply by U_0]

$$= \mu U_0 \frac{d\left(\frac{u}{U_0}\right)}{dy}$$

$$= \mu U_0 \left. \frac{d\left(\frac{3}{2}n - \frac{1}{2}n^3\right)}{\delta\, dn} \right|_{n=0}$$

$$= \frac{\mu U_0}{d}\left[\frac{3}{2} - \frac{1}{2}3n^2\right]_{n=0}$$

$$= \frac{3\mu U_0}{2\delta}$$

Substitute this value of τ_0 in (1),

$$\therefore \quad \frac{3\mu U_0}{2\delta\rho U_0^2} = 0.14\,\frac{d\delta}{dx}$$

$$\therefore \quad \left(\frac{10.7\mu}{\rho U_0}\right) dx = \delta\, d\,\delta$$

$$\therefore \quad \left(\frac{10.7\mu}{\rho U_0}\right) x = \frac{\delta^2}{2} + C \qquad (C = 0 \text{ at } x = 0, \delta = 0)$$

$$\therefore \quad \delta^2 = \frac{21.42\mu}{\rho U_0} x \times \frac{x}{x} \qquad \text{(Divide and multiply by } x\text{)}$$

$$\therefore \quad \delta^2 = \frac{21.42\mu x^2}{\rho U_0 x} = \frac{21.42x^2}{\left(\frac{\rho U_0 x}{\mu}\right)}$$

$$\therefore \quad \delta = \frac{4.63x}{\sqrt{R_x}} \qquad \text{...(Ans.)}$$

Now,
$$\tau_0 = \frac{3\mu U_0}{2\delta} = \frac{3\mu U_0}{2\left(\frac{4.63x}{\sqrt{R_x}}\right)} = 0.324\,\frac{\mu U_0 \sqrt{R_x}}{x}$$

$$F_D = \int_0^L \tau_0 B\, dx = \int_0^L 0.324\,\frac{\mu U_0 \sqrt{\rho U_0 x}}{\sqrt{\mu x}} B\, dx$$

$$= \int_0^L (0.324\sqrt{\mu}\, U_0 \sqrt{\rho U_0} B)\left(\frac{dx}{\sqrt{x}}\right)$$

$$= \left[0.324\, U_0 \sqrt{\rho U_0 \mu}\, B\, \frac{x^{1/2}}{1/2}\right]_0^L$$

$$= (0.648\, U_0 \sqrt{\rho U_0 \mu}\,(B)\sqrt{L} \times \frac{\sqrt{L}}{\sqrt{L}}$$

[Multiply and divide by $\sqrt{L}$]

$$C_D = \frac{F_D}{\frac{1}{2}\rho A U_0^2} = \frac{0.648\, U_0 \sqrt{\rho U_0 \mu}\,(A)}{\frac{1}{2}\rho\, A U_0^2 \sqrt{L}} = \frac{1.3}{\sqrt{\frac{\rho U_0 L}{\mu}}} = \frac{1.3}{\sqrt{R_L}} \quad \text{...(Ans.)}$$

$$C_f = \frac{\tau_0}{\frac{\rho U_0^2}{2}} = \frac{0.324\,\mu\, U_0 \sqrt{R_x}}{x\frac{\rho U_0^2}{2}}$$

$$= \frac{0.648\sqrt{R_x}}{\left(\frac{\rho U_0 x}{\mu}\right)} = \frac{0.648}{\sqrt{R_x}} \quad \text{...(Ans.)}$$

■ **Problem 14.10:** *For a flat plate kept parallel to stream of air having R = 10⁷, find fraction of length of plate from leading edge so that drag force on it is equal to half the drag force on the whole plate.*

Solution:

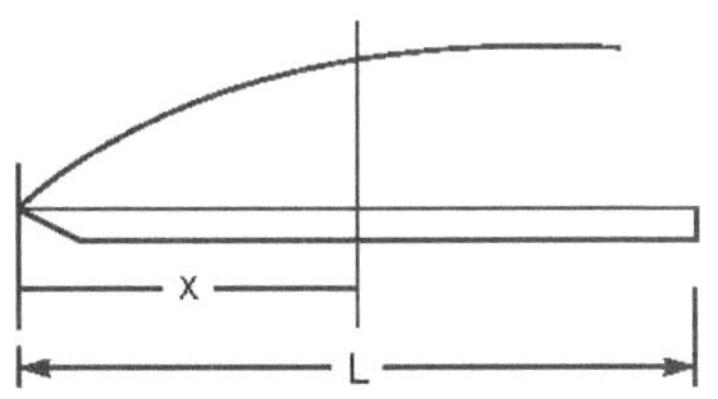

Fig. 14.4

According to given data, here we have to find value of $\frac{x}{L}$ for $\frac{F_{Dx}}{F_{DL}} = \frac{1}{2}$.

$$F_{Dx} = B\int_0^x \tau_0\, dx = \frac{1}{2} C_D (Bx)\rho U_0^2$$

$$R = 10^7, \quad \therefore \quad \text{BL is TBL}, \quad \therefore \quad C_D = \frac{0.074}{(R_x)^{1/5}}$$

$$\therefore \qquad F_{Dx} = \frac{0.074}{(R_L)^{1/5}}(Bx)\left(\frac{\rho U_0^2}{2}\right) \quad \text{...(1)}$$

and

$$F_{DL} = \frac{0.074}{(R_L)^{1/5}}(\text{BL})\left(\frac{\rho U_0^2}{2}\right) \quad \text{...(2)}$$

Divide (1) by (2),

$$\therefore \qquad \frac{F_{Dx}}{F_{DL}} = \frac{(R_L)^{1/5}}{(R_x)^{1/5}}\left(\frac{x}{L}\right)$$

$$= \frac{\left(\frac{\rho U_0 L}{\mu}\right)^{1/5}}{\left(\frac{\rho U_0 x}{\mu}\right)^{1/5}} \times \left(\frac{x}{L}\right)$$

$$= \left(\frac{L}{x}\right)^{1/5}\left(\frac{x}{L}\right) = \left(\frac{x}{L}\right)^{4/5}$$

But $$\frac{F_{Dx}}{F_{DL}} = \frac{1}{2}$$

$$\therefore \qquad \left(\frac{x}{L}\right)^{4/5} = \frac{1}{2} \quad \therefore \quad \frac{x}{L} = 0.42. \qquad \text{...(Ans.)}$$

■ **Problem 14.11:** *A plate 2 m × 10 m is facing flow of water lengthwise at $U_0 = 3$ m/s. Find:*

(1) extent of lbl and its thickness.

(2) b.l. thickness at trailing edge.

(3) shear stress at trailing edge.

Given: $\nu_{water} = 10^{-6}$ *m²/s,* $\rho_{water} = 1000$ *kg/m³.*

Solution:

$$R_L = \frac{U_0 L}{\nu} = \frac{3 \times 10}{10^{-6}} = 3 \times 10^7 > 5 \times 10^5 \quad \therefore \quad \text{TBL}$$

$$R_{\text{critical}} = 5 \times 10^5 = \frac{U_0 x}{\nu}$$

$$\therefore \qquad x = \frac{5 \times 10^5 \times 10^{-6}}{3} = 0.166 \text{ m} \qquad \text{...(Ans.)}$$

$$\delta_x = \frac{5x}{\sqrt{R_x}} \quad \text{(as per Blasius's exact solutions),}$$

$$= \frac{5\,(0.166)}{\sqrt{5 \times 10^5}} = \frac{0.25}{7.07 \times 10^2} = \frac{0.25}{707} = 1.17 \times 10^{-3} \text{ m}$$

$$= 1.17 \text{ mm} \qquad \text{...(Ans.)}$$

We have $R_L = 3 \times 10^7$,

$$\therefore \qquad \delta_L = \frac{0.22}{(R_L)^{1/6}} \text{ as per Schlichting's logarithmic velocity distribution}$$

as $R > 10^7$

$$= \frac{0.22\,(10)}{(3\times10^7)^{1/6}} = \frac{2.2}{17.6} = 0.125 \text{ m} \qquad \text{...(Ans.)}$$

$$\tau_{0_L} = C_{f_L}\frac{\rho U_0^2}{2}$$

$$C_{f_L} = \frac{0.37}{(\log R_L)^{2.58}}$$

$$= \frac{0.37}{187.4}$$

$$= 1.97 \times 10^{-3}$$

$$\therefore \qquad \tau_{0_L} = (1.97\times10^{-3})\frac{1000\times9}{2}$$

$$= 9 \text{ Pa.} \qquad \text{...(Ans.)}$$

14.4 BOUNDARY LAYER SEPARATION

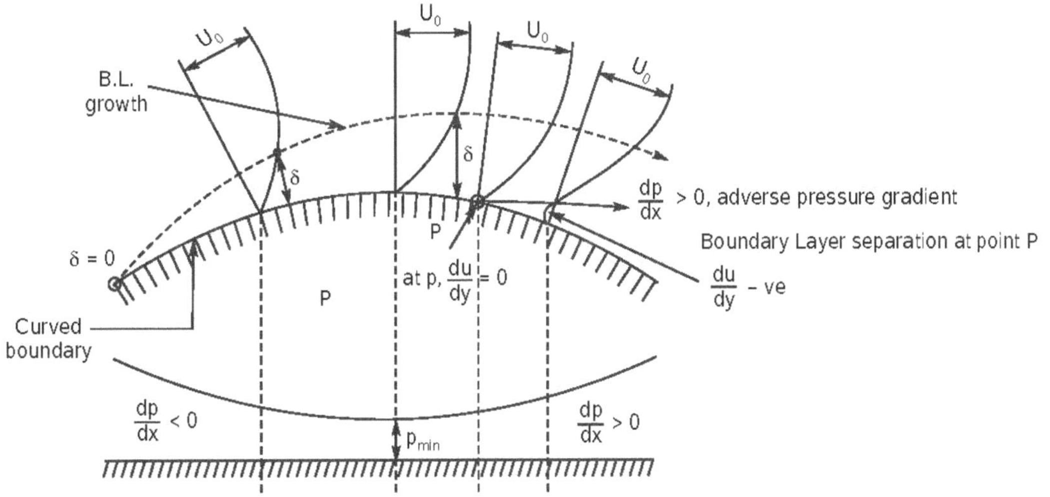

Fig. 14.5 Boundary layer separation or Growth of Boundary layer along a curved surface.

We have already defined that a layer of small thickness adjacent to boundary in which velocity variation in y direction takes place from zero at boundary to $0.99\,U_0$ at $y = \delta$, is called boundary layer. In this layer fluid flow has to overcome friction drag at the expense of kinetic energy. Thus velocity of flow goes on decreasing, this will lead to a stage when b.l. cannot keep contact with the boundary, *i.e.* boundary layer will leave the boundary and on account of averse pressure gradient $\left(\frac{dp}{dx} > 0\right)$, it will be forced to get diverted back towards the boundary, creating a wake zone, as shown in Fig. 14.6. As the curved surface becomes convex, velocity will increase and pressure will decrease and $\frac{dp}{dx}$ will be negative, but as the surface curvature falls after reaching a peak, velocity will decrease and pressure will increase and therefore $\frac{dp}{dx} > 0$ *i.e.* adverse see Fig. 14.5 B.L. gets separated in zone of adverse pressure gradient and at point of separation *p*, $\frac{du}{dy} = 0$ at $y = 0$. Due to b.l. separation wake zone develops in which pressure may be negative; whereas on u/s of stagnation point, pressure will be positive. This will cause vibration of the immersed body and may lead to failure of the structure. The boundary layer after separation is forced back to have curvature towards the surface (see Fig. 14.6) on account of adverse pressure gradient, in the form of vortices distributed on either side of the immerse body leaving a straight path centrally, called Von Karman vortex street. Frequency of Vortex shedding *n*, is dependent on Strouhal Number, *S*, given by

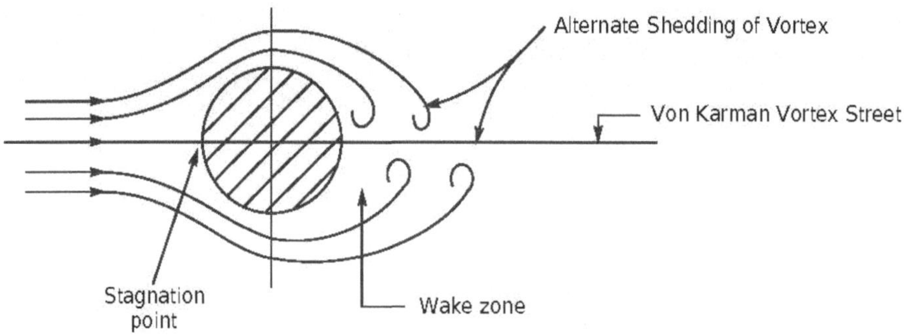

Fig. 14.6

$$S = \frac{nD}{U_0}$$

here n = frequency of vortax shedding in Hertz, *i.e.* cycles per sec.

$$\therefore \quad S = \frac{\left[\frac{1}{T}(L)\right]}{L/T} \quad \text{(dimensionless number.)}$$

Value of S will depend on Reynolds number, and is given by

$$S = 0.21 \text{ for } R > 10^3$$

$$= 0.2\left(1 - \frac{20}{R}\right) \text{ for } R < 10^3.$$

Illustrative problem No. 10 will give more insight into phenomenon of separation and vortex shedding.

14.4.1 Method of Prevention of Separation of Boundary Layer

In the wake zone as shown in Fig. 14.6, back flow and continuous formation of vortices will create loss of KE and vibrations, hence boundary layer separation is not a desirable feature and therefore controlling measures have to be developed. Some of the measures for control of boundary layers are listed below:

(1) Suction of fluid by suction slot.

(2) Supply of additional fluid by a blower.

(3) Rotating the boundary in direction of flow.

(4) Provide a wire ring in laminar region for flow over sphere.

14.4.2 Solved Problem

Problem 14.12: *A cylindrical cable 6 cm in diameter is suspended between two supports: Wind is blowing across it at 100 kmph. Calculate:*

(a) Drag force per unit length of cable.

(b) Frequency of vortex shedding, if

$$S = 0.21 \text{ for } R > 10^3,\ \nu = 1.5 \times 10^{-5}\ m^2/s.$$

For cyl. body, $C_D = 1.2 \text{ for } R \leq 5 \times 10^5,\ \rho_{air} = 1.2\ kg/m^3$

Solution:

$$U_0 = 100 \text{ kmph} = 27 \text{ m/s.}$$

$$R = \frac{U_0 D}{\nu} = \frac{27 \times \frac{6}{100}}{1.5 \times 10^{-5}} = 1.08 \times 10^5 < 5 \times 10^5$$

$\therefore$ $C_D = 1.2$ for cylindrical body

$\therefore$ $$F_D = C_D A \frac{\rho U_0^2}{2}$$

$$= 1.2\,(0.06 \times 1) \times \frac{1.2\,(27)^2}{2}$$

$$= 31.05 \text{ N/m length of cable}$$

$$S = 0.21 = \frac{nD}{U_o} = \frac{n(0.06)}{27}$$

$\therefore$ $$n = \frac{0.21 \times 27}{0.06} = 94.5 \text{ Hertz}$$

= frequency of vortex shedding.

14.5 SINGING OF TELEPHONE WIRES

When high wind is blowing across a cylindrical cable, alternate shedding of vortices on either side of Von Karman Street produces periodic transverse forces on the cable which tend to cause transverse oscillations. If natural frequency of vibration of the cable is close to frequency of vortex shedding, the cable will be subject to severe deflection and it may result in its failure. Singing of telephone wire or transmission line is also due to frequency of vortex shedding tending to be equal to natural frequency of wire.

14.6 TERMINAL VELOCITY OF A BODY

Terminal velocity of a body is defined as maximum constant velocity of a falling body. When a body is allowed to fall freely from rest into the atmosphere, its velocity will increase due to acceleration of gravity. With increase in velocity, drag force opposing the motion will also increase. A stage will come when the upward force due to drag will be equal to weight of the body, then the net external force acting on the body will be zero and body will travel with a constant velocity, known as terminal velocity of the body.

If the body is dropped in a fluid, and when it acquires terminal velocity, its weight W will be equal to drag force F_D and buoyant force F_B acting on it.

i.e. $$W = F_D + F_B$$

For spherical body of diameter D,

$$F_D = 3\pi\mu D U_0$$

$$= C_D(A)\frac{\rho U_0^2}{2}, \text{ here } A = \text{projected area of the sphere} = \frac{\pi}{4}D^2$$

$$= C_D\left(\frac{\pi}{4}D^2\right)\frac{\rho U_0^2}{2}$$

$$\therefore \quad C_D = \frac{3\pi\mu D U_0}{\frac{\pi}{4}D^2\frac{\rho U_0^2}{2}} = \frac{24\mu}{\rho U_0 D} = \frac{24}{R} = 24 \text{ for } R \le 1 \qquad ...(14.6)$$

As per Stoke's Law also,

$$C_D = \frac{24}{R}\left[1 + \left(\frac{3}{16}\right)R\right]^{1/2} \text{ for } R \text{ between 1 to 100} \qquad ...(14.7)$$

$$= 0.5 \text{ for } R = 10^5$$

$$= 0.2 \text{ for } R > 2 \times 10^5.$$

14.7 DRAG AND LIFT FORCES ON SUBMERGED BODIES

Submerged bodies under the influence of relative motion of the fluid and ambient pressure will have drag force and lift force acting on them. Force in direction of delet motion of fluid will be **drag force** and normal to direction of fluid motion will be **Lift force**. This is illustrated in Fig. 14.7.

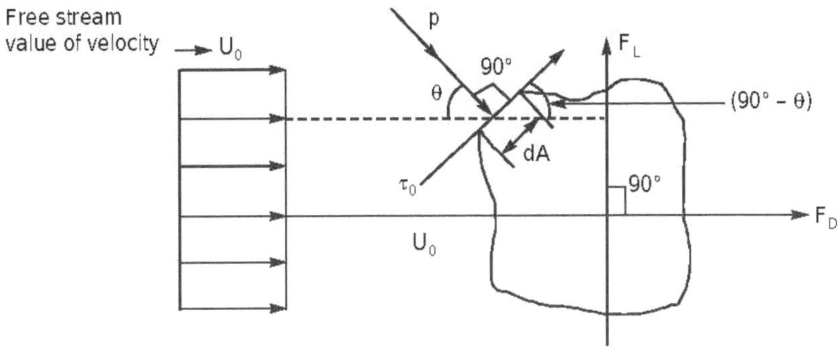

Fig. 14.7

Here, (*a*) $$F_D = \frac{1}{2} C_D A \rho U_0^2 \quad ...(14.8)$$

(*b*) $$F_L = \frac{1}{2} C_L A \rho U_0^2 \quad ...(14.9)$$

(*c*) p = ambient pressure acting on elemental area dA making θ to U_0.

(*d*) τ_0 = shear stress, acting tangentially on elemental area dA.

C_D = coefficient of drag.

C_L = coefficient of lift.

A = projected area on plane normal to U_0.

A = plan form area of the body as seen from top; usually for thin flat surfaces, see Fig. 14.8.

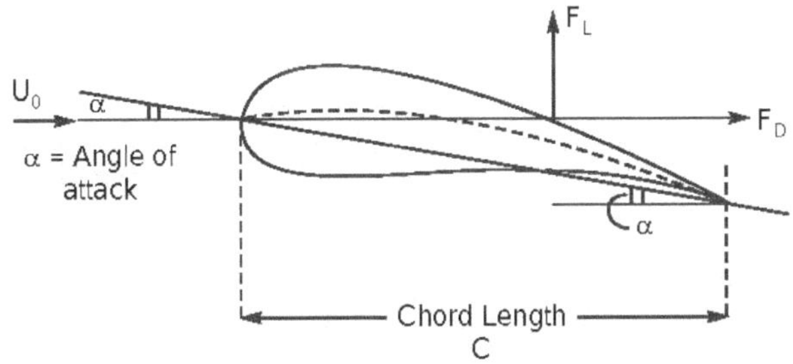

Fig. 14.8 Forces acting on airofoil.

In Fig. 14.8, cross-section of an airofoil subject to free stream velocity U_0 is shown. Here chord length C and span of airofoil normal to its section is L. ∴ Plan form area, $A = CL$.

Airofoil being a lifting body will have large area A with small thickness.

With ref. to Fig. 14.7,

(*a*) dF_D = drag force on elemental area dA in direction of U_0

= force due to pressure + force due to shear stress

$= (pdA) \cos \theta + (\tau_0\, dA) \cos (90 - \theta)$

$$= pdA \cos \theta + \tau_0 \, dA \sin \theta$$

$\therefore$
$$F_D = \int dA \cos \theta + \int \tau_0 dA \sin \theta \quad \text{...(14.10)}$$

pressure drag friction drag
or or
form drag shear drag

(*b*) dF_L = lift force on elemental area dA in direction normal to U_0

$$= -pdA \sin \theta + \tau_0 \, dA \cos \theta$$

$\therefore$
$$F_L = \int \tau_0 \, dA \cos \theta - \int p \, dA \sin \theta \quad \text{...(14.11)}$$

$$F_R = \text{Resultant force} = \sqrt{F_D^2 + F_L^2} \quad \text{...(14.12)}$$

14.7.1 Solved Problems

■ **Problem 14.13:** *In a test section of a wind tunnel a flat plate of 2 m × 1.5 m is kept in a stream of air having velocity equal to 60 kmph. Find lift, drag and resultant force, its angle and power required to hold the plate in position.*

Given: $\rho_{air} = 1.15 \text{ kg/m}^2$, $C_D = 0.15$, $C_L = 0.75$. *Here* $A = 2 \times 1.5 = 3m^2$.

Solution:

$$A = 60 \text{ kmph} = 16.6 = \text{m/s}$$

$$F_L = C_L A \left(\frac{\rho U_0^2}{2}\right) = 0.75\ (3) \left(\frac{1.15 \times (16.6)^2}{2}\right)$$

$$= 356 \text{ N}$$

$$F_D = C_D A \left(\frac{\rho U_0^2}{2}\right) = (0.15)\ (3) \left(\frac{1.15 \times (16.6)^2}{2}\right)$$

$$= 71.3 \text{ N}$$

$$\text{Power} = F_D U_0 = 71.3 \times 16.6 = 1{,}180 \text{ Watts}$$

$$F_R = \sqrt{F_D^2 + F_L^2} = \sqrt{(71)^2 + (356)^2} = 363 \text{ N}$$

$$\theta = \tan^{-1}\left(\frac{F_L}{F_D}\right)$$

$$= 78°$$ **...(Ans.)**

■ **Problem 14.14:** *A string holding a kite of weight 1 Network, develops tension of 10 N when inclined at 45° to vertical, Calculate ratio of Lift to Drag force acting on the kite.*

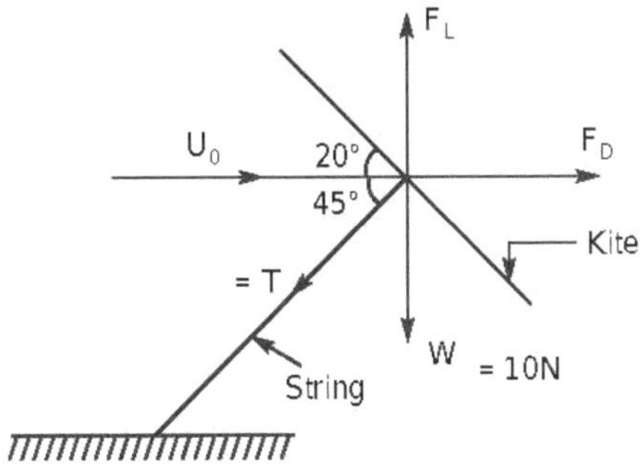

Fig. 14.9

Solution:

$$F_D = T\cos 45 = 10\,(0.707) = 7.07\text{ N}$$

$$F_L = T\sin 45 + 1.0$$

$$= 10\sin 45 + 1$$

$$= 7.07 + 1 = 8.07\text{ N}$$

$$\therefore \quad \frac{F_L}{F_D} = \frac{8.07}{7.07} = 1.14. \qquad \text{...(Ans.)}$$

■ **Problem 14.15:** *A kite having 10 N weight has effective area = 0.6 m² and makes an angle of 20° to horizontal in air. The string attached to the kite makes 45° to horizontal, C_D = 0.6, C_L = 0.8, find speed of air and tension in string ρ_{air} = 1.25 kg/m³.*

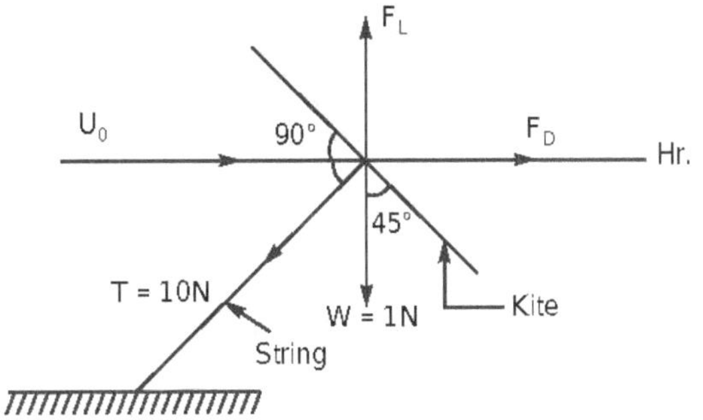

Fig. 14.10

Note: Effective area A = 0.6 m² of kite is to be used in calculating of *FD* and *FL* as effect of its inclination to horizontal is taken care of in values of C_D and C_L

Solution:

$$F_D = T\cos 45 = C_D A\,\frac{\rho U_0^2}{2} = 0.6\,(0.6)\,\frac{1.25\,U_0^2}{2}$$

$$\therefore \quad T\,(0.707) = 0.225\,U_0^2 \qquad \text{...(1)}$$

$$F_L = T\sin 45 + 10 = C_L A\,\frac{\rho U_0^2}{2}$$

$$= 0.8\,(06)\,\frac{1.25\,U_0^2}{2} = 0.3\,U_0^2$$

$\therefore \quad T = (0.707) + 10 = 0.3\ U_0^2$ ...(2)

Subtracting (1) from (2), we get

$$10 = (0.3 - 0.225)U_0^2$$

$$\therefore \quad U_0^2 = \frac{10}{0.075} = 133$$

$\therefore \quad U_0 = 11.5 \text{ m/s} = 41 \text{ kmph}$ ...(Ans.)

and

$$T = \frac{0.225\,(11.5)^2}{0.707}$$

$= 42.08$ N. ...(Ans.)

■ **Problem 14.16:** *A chimney has a diameter of 2 m and is 40 m tall, find bending moment at its base if wind blows across it at 90 kmph.*

Given: $\rho_{air} = 1.2 \text{ kg/m}^3$, $v_{air} = 1.5 \times 10^{-5} \text{ m}^2\text{/s}$

$C_D = 1.2$ if $R \leq 5 \times 10^5$.

Solution: $= 0.33$ if $R > 5 \times 10^5$

$U_0 = 90 \text{ kmph} = 25 \text{ m/s}$

$$R = \frac{U_0 D}{v} = \frac{25\,(2)}{1.5 \times 10^{-5}} = 33.33 \times 10^5, \therefore C_D = 0.33$$

$$\text{Drag Force on Chimney} = F_D = C_D\ (LD)\ \frac{\rho U_0^2}{2}$$

$$= 0.33\ (40 \times 2)\ \frac{1.2\,(25)^2}{2}$$

$= 9.9$ kN

$$\therefore \text{ Bending Moment at its base} = F_D \times \left(\frac{L}{2}\right)$$

$$= 9.9 \times 10^3 \times \frac{40}{2} = 198 \text{ kNm.}$$ ...(Ans.)

■ **Problem 14.17:** *An anemometer consists of two cups of 10 cm diameter each, and mounted in opposite direction as shown in Fig. 14.11. It rotates about a vertical axis at middle of the horizontal rod. Neglecting friction, find RPM of the anemometer in a wind velocity of 80 kmph. $C_D = 1.33$ and 0.34 depending on its frontal shape, $\rho_{air} = 1.2$ kg/m³.*

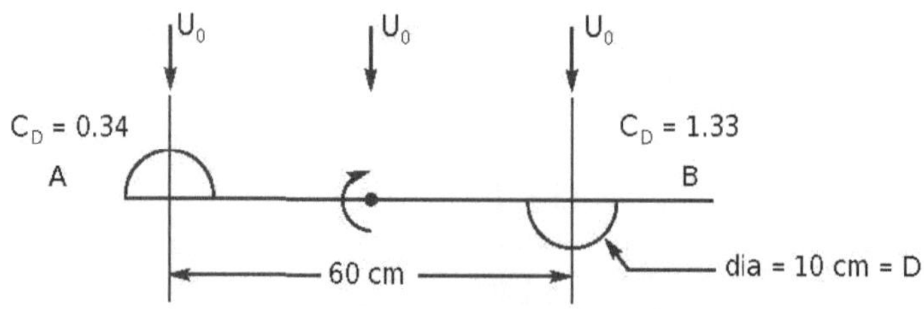

Fig. 14.11

Solution:

$U_0 = 80$ kmph $= 22.2$ m/s.

V = cup velocity = ωr

For cup A, $$F_{DA} = C_D\, A\frac{\rho U_0^2}{2} = 0.34\left(\frac{\pi}{4}D^2\right)\frac{\rho}{2}(U_0 + \omega r)^2$$

For cup B, $$F_{DB} = C_D\, A\frac{\rho U_0^2}{2} = 1.33\left(\frac{\pi}{4}D^2\right)\frac{\rho}{2}(U_0 - \omega r)^2$$

$$\text{Torque} = (F_{DB} - F_{DA})\, r = 0$$

$$\therefore \quad F_{DB} = F_{DA}$$

$$\therefore \quad 1.33\left(\frac{\pi}{4}D^2\right)\frac{\rho}{2}(U_0 - \omega r)^2 = 0.34\left(\frac{\pi}{4}D^2\right)\frac{\rho}{2}(U_0 + \omega r)^2$$

$$\therefore \quad 1.33\,(U_0 - \omega r)^2 = 0.34\,(U_0 + \omega r)^2, \qquad r = \frac{60}{2} = 30 \text{ cm}$$

$$\therefore \quad \left(\frac{1.33}{0.34}\right)^{1/2}(U_0 - 0.30\,\omega) = U_0 + 0.3\,\omega$$

$$\therefore \quad 2\,(U_0 - 0.3\,\omega) = U_0 + 0.3\,\omega$$

$$\therefore \quad U_0 = 0.3\,\omega + 0.6\,\omega$$

$$= 0.9\,\omega$$

$$\therefore \quad \omega = \frac{U_0}{0.9} = \frac{22.2}{0.9}$$

$$= 24.6 = \frac{2\pi N}{60}$$

$$\therefore \quad N = \frac{24.6 \times 60}{2\pi} = 235 \text{ RPM.}$$ **...(Ans.)**

14.8 MAGNUS EFFECT ON ROTATING CYLINDER

If a cylinder is rotating about its axis and is placed in free stream velocity of U_0, then lift force produced on account of its rotation is known as Magnus Effect.

Let V_C = tangential velocity on circumference of the cylinder = $\omega R = \frac{2\pi N}{60}R = \frac{\pi DN}{60}$

Here R = radius of cylinder

D = diameter of cylinder

N = RPM of cylinder

L = Length of cylinder

$$\Gamma = \text{Circulation} = \oint V_C\, ds$$

$$= 2\pi R\, V_C, \quad \therefore \quad V_C = \frac{\Gamma}{2\pi R}$$

Lift force $\qquad F_L = \rho L\, U_0 \Gamma = C_L A\, \dfrac{\rho U_0^2}{2}.$

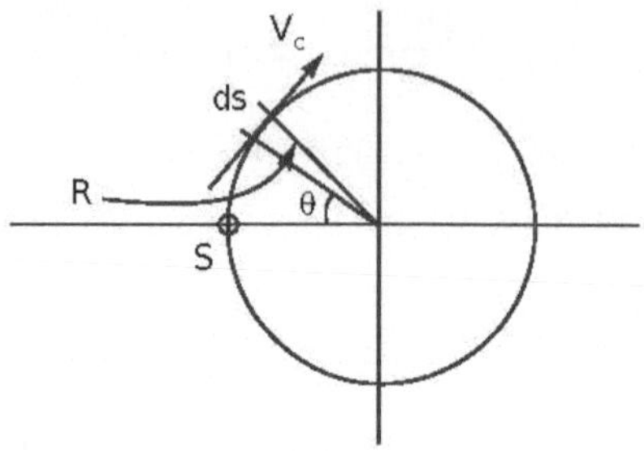

Fig. 14.12 Cylinder with rotating velocity ω case (1).

If a cylinder is placed in a free stream velocity field of U_0, then

$$u_0 = U_0 \left(1 + \frac{R^2}{r^2}\right) \sin\theta \text{ as per ideal fluid flow theory, see Fig. 14.13}$$

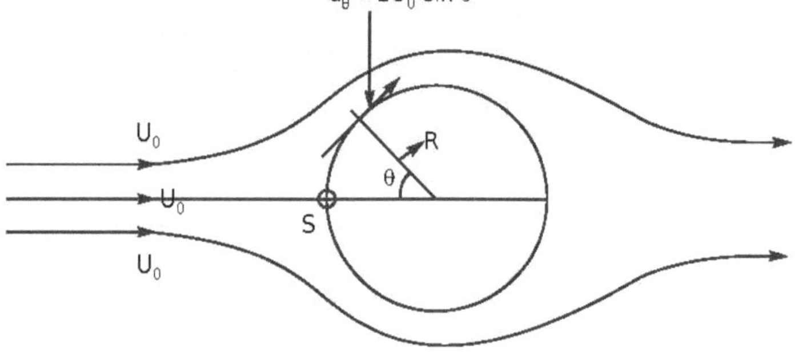

Fig. 14.13 Flow past a non rotating cylinder case (2).

Here $\qquad u_\theta$ = Velocity on circumference of cylinder due to U_0

If $\qquad R = r$ at circumference, then

$$u_\theta = 2U_0 \sin\theta$$

Also $\qquad V_C = \dfrac{\Gamma}{2\pi R}$ due to rotation of cylinder

$\therefore$ Velocity on surface of cylinder = u_s is given by

$$u_s = 2U_0 \sin\theta + \frac{\Gamma}{2\pi R}$$

Thus velocity on surface of cylinder is sum of effect of U_0 on cylinder and V_C.

At stagnation point $u_s = 0$.

$$\therefore \qquad 0 = 2U_0 \sin\theta + \frac{\Gamma}{2\pi R}$$

$$\therefore \qquad 2U_0 \sin\theta = -\frac{\Gamma}{2\pi R} = -V_C$$

$$\therefore \qquad \sin\theta = \left(-\frac{1}{2}\frac{V_C}{U_0}\right) = -1 \text{ for a single stagnation point at } \theta = 270°$$

and $$V_C = 2U_0 \text{ see Fig. 14.14 } (a).$$

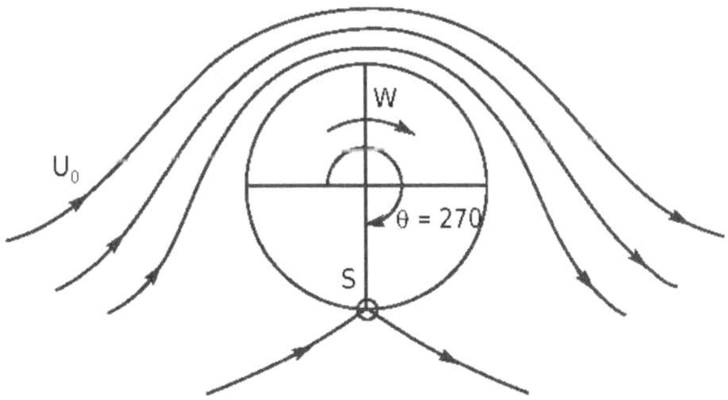

Fig. 14.14 (*a*) Single stagnation point ($V_C = 2U_0$).

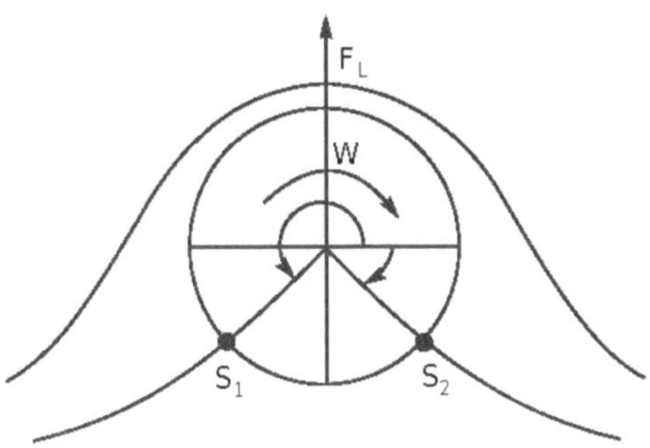

Fig. 14.14 (*b*) Double stagnation points S_1, S_2 $V_C < 2U_0$

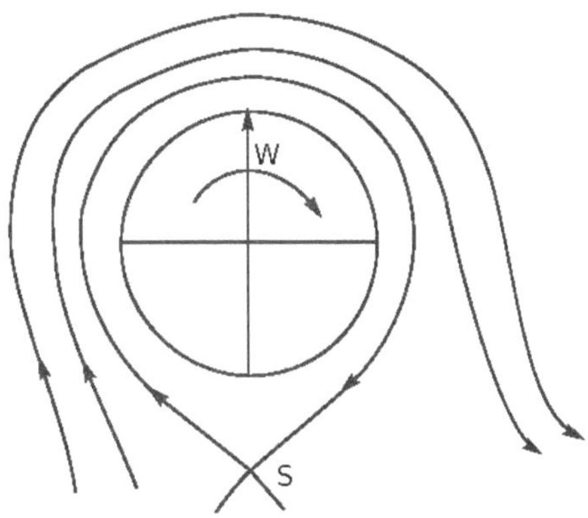

Fig. 14.14 (*c*) Stagnation point away from cylinder $V_C > 2U_0$

Fig. 14.14 (a), (b), (c).

In Fig. 14 (*a*), case of single stagnation point is shown,

and we have $$2\,U_0 \sin\theta = -\frac{\Gamma}{2\pi R}$$

$$\therefore \qquad \sin\theta = -\frac{\Gamma}{4\pi R U_0}$$

and at $\theta = 270, \sin\theta = -1$

$$\therefore \quad -\frac{\Gamma}{4\pi RU_0} = 1, \quad \therefore \quad \Gamma = 4\pi RU_0 \text{ and } V_C = 2U_0 \text{ for } \theta = 270.$$

In Fig. 14.14 (*b*), $V_C < 2\,U_0$, $\therefore$ $\sin\theta > -1$, giving two stagnation points S_1, S_2.

In Fig. 14.14 (*c*), $V_C > 2U_0$, $\therefore$ $\sin\theta > -1$, giving single stagnation point S away form the cylinder.

14.8.1 Solved Problems

■ **Problem 14.18:** *A cylinder of 1.0 m diameter is rotated about its axis in air having velocity of 120 kmph. A lift of 6 kN per m length of cylinder is developed. Assume ideal fluid flow theory and find RPM of cylinder and location of stagnation point,* $\rho_{air} = 1.25\ kg/m^3$.

Solution:

$$U_0 = 120 \text{ kmph} = 33 \text{ m/s}$$

$$F_L = \rho L\,U_0\,\Gamma$$

$$\therefore \quad \frac{F_L}{L} = \rho U_0\,\Gamma = 6000$$

$$\therefore \quad \Gamma = \frac{6000}{1.25\times 33} = 145 \text{ m}^2\text{/s}$$

$$\omega_R = V_C = \frac{\Gamma}{2\pi R} = \frac{145}{2\pi(0.5)} = 46.3 = \left(\frac{2\pi N}{60}\right)R, \quad \text{here } R = 0.5 \text{ m}$$

$$\therefore \quad N = \frac{46.3\times 60}{2\pi(0.5)} = 885 \text{ RPM}$$

$$u_s = 2U_0\sin\theta + \frac{\Gamma}{2\pi R} = 0 \text{ for stagnation points}$$

$$\therefore \quad \sin\theta = -\frac{\Gamma}{4\pi RU_0} = -\frac{145}{4\pi(0.5)\,33}$$

$$= -0.699 < -1, \quad \therefore \quad 2 \text{ stagnation points.}$$

$\therefore$ $\theta = -44.4°$ and $(180 + 44.4)$ *i.e.* $224.4°$ giving S_1 and S_2 see Fig. 14.15.

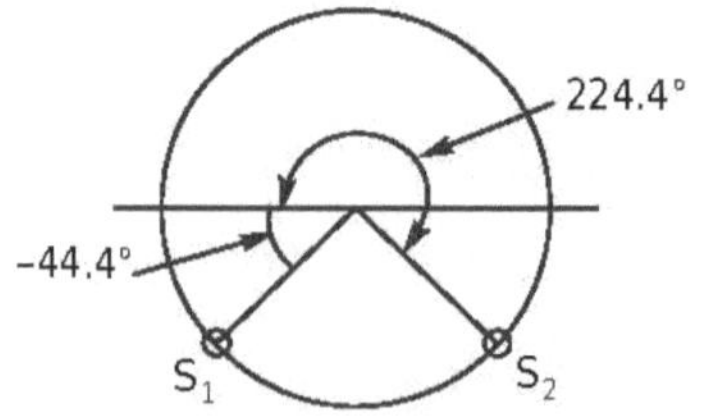

Fig. 14.15

■ Problem 14.19: *A cylinder of 1.2 m dia and length = 10 m, is rotated at 200 RPM with its axis normal to air stream of U_0 = 10 m/s. Find circulation around cylinder, lift force, coefficient of lift and stagnation points. ρ_{air} = 1.2 kg/m³.*

Solution:

$$V_C = \frac{\pi DN}{60} = \frac{\pi(1.2)(200)}{60} = 12.56 \text{ m/s}$$

$$U_0 = 10 \text{ m/s}$$

$$\therefore \quad \frac{V_C}{U_0} = \frac{12.56}{10} = 1.256$$

$$\Gamma = \text{circulation} = 2\pi R\, V_C = 2\pi\left(\frac{1.2}{2}\right)(12.56)$$

$$= 47.32 \text{ m}^2/\text{s} \qquad \text{...(Ans.)}$$

$$F_L = \text{lift force} = \rho L\, U_0\, \Gamma = \frac{1}{2} C_L\, A \rho U_0^2 = \frac{1}{2} C_L (LD) \rho U_0^2$$

$$= 1.2\,(10)\,(10)\,(47.32)$$

$$= 5678.4 \text{ N}$$

$$= 5.67 \text{ kN}$$

$$\therefore \quad C_L = \frac{2\Gamma}{DU_0}$$

But $$\Gamma = \pi DU_0$$

$$\therefore \quad C_L = \frac{2\pi DV_C}{DU_0}$$

$$= 2\pi\frac{V_C}{U_0}$$

$$C_L = 2\pi\frac{V_C}{U_0}$$

$$= 2\pi\,(1.256) = 7.88$$

For stagnation points,

$$\theta = \sin^{-1}\left(-\frac{1}{2}\frac{V_C}{U_0}\right)$$

$$= \sin^{-1}\left[-\frac{1}{2}(1.256)\right]$$

$$= \sin^{-1}(-0.628)$$

$$\theta = 38.9^\circ = S_1 \text{ and } (180 + 38.9) = 218.9 = 218.9^\circ$$

$$= S_2 \text{ giving } S_1 \text{ and } S_2. \qquad \text{...(Ans.)}$$

■ **Problem 14.20:** *For the following velocity profiles check whether the boundary layer separation will take place or not.*

(*a*) $$\frac{u}{U_0} = \left(\frac{y}{\delta}\right) - \frac{1}{2}\left(\frac{y}{\delta}\right)^3$$

(*b*) $$\frac{u}{U_0} = \left(\frac{y}{\delta}\right)^2 - \left(\frac{y}{\delta}\right)^3$$

In case of (*a*) $$\frac{u}{U_0} = \left(\frac{y}{\delta}\right) - \frac{1}{2}\left(\frac{y}{\delta}\right)^3, \quad \therefore \; u = U_0\left(\frac{y}{\delta}\right) - \frac{U_0}{2}\left(\frac{y}{\delta}\right)^3$$

$$\therefore \quad \frac{du}{dy} = \frac{U_0}{\delta} - \frac{3U_0 y^2}{2\delta}$$

Put $y = 0$,

$$\therefore \quad \frac{du}{dy} = \frac{U_0}{\delta} > 0 \text{ at } y = 0$$

∴ Boundary layer will not separate. ...(**Ans.**)

In case (*b*), $$u = U_0\left(\frac{y}{\delta}\right)^2 - U_0\left(\frac{y}{\delta}\right)^3$$

$$\therefore \quad \frac{\partial u}{\partial y} = \frac{2U_0 y}{\delta} - \frac{3U_0 y^2}{\delta}, \text{ put } y = 0$$

$$\therefore \quad \frac{\partial u}{\partial y} = 0 \text{ at } y = 0.$$

∴ Boundary layer will separate. ...(**Ans.**)

Exercises

1. Calculate δ^* and δ_θ in terms of nominal b.l. thickness δ, for following velocity distribution:

(*a*) $\frac{u}{U_0} = \frac{3}{2}\left(\frac{y}{\delta}\right)$ (*b*) $\frac{u}{U_0} = \left(\frac{y}{\delta}\right)^{1/7}$.

$$\left(\textbf{Ans. } (a)\ \delta^* = \frac{1}{4}\delta \text{ and } \delta_\theta = 0 \quad (b)\ \delta^* = \frac{1}{8}\delta, \delta_\theta = \frac{7}{72}\delta\right)$$

2. Calculate δ^*, δ_θ and H in terms of δ for velocity distribution,

$$\frac{u}{U_0} = a + b\left(\frac{y}{\delta}\right) + C\left(\frac{y}{\delta}\right)^2. \qquad (BU\ 1999)$$

$$\left(\textbf{Ans. } a = 0,\ b = 2,\ c = -1,\ \delta^* = \frac{\delta}{3},\ \delta_\theta = \frac{2}{15}\delta,\ H = \frac{\delta^*}{\delta_\theta} = 2.5\right)$$

3. A plate 0.5 m × 0.4 m is facing stream of oil lengthwise, having velocity equal to 6 m/s. Find δ and τ_0 at mid point of the plate.
$\rho_{oil} = 900$ kg/m³, $v = 1 \times 10^{-4}$ m²/s. Also find drag force acting on both sides of plate.
(**Ans.** $\delta = 1.0$ cm, $\tau_0 = 88$ N/m² at mid point. F_D on 2 sides = 49 N)
(**Hint**: Whenever velocity distribution for l.b.l. not given, follow Blasius exact solution.)

4. For the velocity distribution in b.l. along a flat plate given by power low, $\frac{u}{U_0} = \left(\frac{y}{\delta}\right)^{0.22}$,
prove that $\delta^* = 0.18\,\delta$, $\delta_\theta = 0.125\,\delta$, $\delta_e = 0.1278$ where δ = nominal b.l. thickness.
(AMIE 1982)

5. Oil with a velocity of 2 m/s flows over a thin flat plate of size 2 m × 2 m. Calculate b.l. thickness and shear stress at trailing edge and F_D acting on 2 sides of the plate.
[Take $\rho_{oil} = 860$ kg/m³, $v_{oil} = 1 \times 10^{-5}$ m²/s] *(AMIE 1982)*
(**Ans.** $\delta = 1.55$ cm, $\tau_0 = 18.4$ kN/m², $F_D = 29.4$ N)

6. What would be the frequency (f) of oscillations of 2 mm diameter wire held normal to air stream of $U_0 = 72$ kmph? $v_{air} = 0.16$ stokes.

$$\left(\textbf{Hint. } \text{frequency } f = \frac{0.2\,U_0}{D}\left(1 - \frac{20}{R}\right) \text{here } R = \text{Reynolds number.}\right)$$

(**Ans.** f = 1960 cycles/sec)

7. A 1 cm diameter wire is stretched over two electrical transmission towers which are stationed 100 m apart. If wind blows at 100 kmph, find F_D on wire.
Given $v_{air} = 15 \times 10^{-6}$ m²/s, $\rho_{air} = 1.2$ kg/m³, $C_D = 1.1$ for $R > 15000$.
(**Ans.** F_D = 517 N)

8. A 3 mm diameter steel sphere falls in glycerine at terminal velocity of 0.035 m/s. Find viscosity of glycerine, F_D and C_D.
$\gamma_{steel} = 75$ kN/m², $\gamma_{glycerine} = 12.5$ kN/m³.

$$\left[\textbf{Hint. } \text{Terminal velocity } U_0 = \frac{D^2}{18\,\mu}(\gamma_s - \gamma_g) \text{ and } F_D = 3\pi\mu D U_0,\ D = \text{dia. of sphere}\right]$$

$$\left(\textbf{Ans. } \mu = 0.89 \text{ N–s/m}^2;\ F_D = 8.8 \times 10^{-4} \text{ N};\ C_D = \frac{24}{R} = 16.3\right)$$

9. A 2 m diameter and 10 m long cylinder placed normal to air stream of 20 m/s, rotates at 300 RPM.

   Find: (*a*) Circulation Γ (*b*) Lift force, F_L/m length, (*c*) position of stagnation points. Assume $C_L = 3.4$, $\rho_{air} = 1.24$ kg/m^3. (*d*) Also find speed of rotation of cylinder which gives only a single stagnation point.

   (**Ans.** (*a*) $\Gamma = 197$ m^2/s, (*b*) 1719 kgf, (*c*) Stagnation point S_1 and S_2 make $\theta = 231°$, 308°, (*d*) N = 382 RPM for single stagnation point)

15

Flow Through Open Channel

15.1 GENERAL

Flow through irrigation canals, rivers, sewers are some of the examples of channel flow. The characteristic feature of the channel flow is that it is a flow with free surface and all along the surface pressure is atmospheric. The flow is taking place due to bed-gradient. It has to overcome resistance offered by shear stress at the boundary. The boundary may be lined one or unlined one. Canals, rivers are having unlined boundary whereas sewers have lined or rigid boundary because it consists of circular pipe. Recent approach prefers lined canals. All canals constructed earlier *i.e.*, prior to 1980 are mostly unlined. After 1980, some of irrigation projects aided by world bank finance, have to go for lined canals.

15.2 DIFFERENCE BETWEEN PIPE FLOW AND CHANNEL FLOW

It is the pressure gradient that causes flow in the pipe and is a pressure flow with no free surface. It is governed by Reynolds number and loss of head is given by Darcy-Weisbach equation *i.e.*

$$h_f = \frac{fLV^2}{D(2g)} \quad ...(15.1)$$

and Reynolds number is given by

$$R = \frac{\rho VD}{\mu} \quad ...(15.2)$$

here f = friction factor

L = length of pipe line

V = average velocity of flow $= \dfrac{Q}{A}$

D = diameter of the pipe of cross sectioned area $A = \frac{\pi}{4} D^2$

ρ = mass density of flowing fluid

μ = viscosity of fluid.

Channel flow is a free surface flow and is taking place due to bed gradient. It is governed by Froude number, given by

$$F = \frac{V}{\sqrt{gy}} \quad ...(15.3)$$

Here y = depth of flow in channel. Velocity of flow is given by Chezy's formula,

$$V = C\sqrt{RS_o} \quad ...(15.4)$$

Here, C = Chezy's constant

R = hydraulic radius $= \frac{A}{P}$

P = wetted perimeter

S_o = bed gradient.

15.3 DERIVATION OF CHEZY'S AND MANNING'S FORMULA

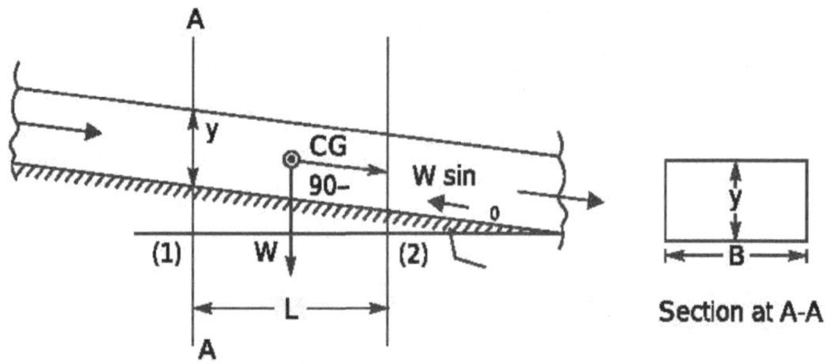

Fig. 15.1

Let W = weight of fluid between section (1) and (2).

θ = angle made by bed with horizontal.

$\therefore$ Component of weight through CG in direction of flow = $W \sin \theta$, and it is opposed by friction at boundary, given by

$\tau_o PL$, P is wetted perimeter and

L is length of channel between 1, 2.

$\therefore \quad \tau_o PL = W \sin \theta.$

$= (\rho g) AL \sin \theta$, as $W = \rho g AL$.

$$\therefore \quad \tau_o = \rho g \left(\frac{A}{P}\right) \sin\theta$$

By putting $\rho g = \gamma$, we get $\tau_o = \gamma R S_o$ ...(15.5)

Here γ is weight density.

But according to Reynolds' experiment for turbulent flow through pipes,

$$\tau_o = \left(\frac{\rho f}{8}\right)V^2 \quad ...(15.6)$$

$$\therefore \quad \left(\frac{\rho f}{8}\right)V^2 = \rho g\left(\frac{A}{P}\right)\sin\theta$$

But $\frac{A}{P} = R$ and $\sin\theta = S_o$ = Bed gradient.

$$\therefore \quad \frac{\rho f}{8}V^2 = \rho g R S_o$$

$$\therefore \quad V^2 = \frac{8g}{f} R S_o$$

$$\therefore \quad V = \sqrt{\frac{8g}{f}}\sqrt{R S_o}$$

$$\therefore \quad V = C\sqrt{R S_o} \quad ...(15.7)$$

Here, C = Chezy's constant = $\sqrt{\frac{8g}{f}}$

and has dimension $\frac{\sqrt{L}}{T}$ *i.e.*, C has dimension of $\frac{\text{m}^{1/2}}{\text{sec}}$ and has values between 40 to 80 depending on type of boundary and value of f.

According to Manning, $C = \frac{1}{n}R^{1/6}$ ...(15.8)

Here, n = Manning's constant, generally varying between 0.01 to 0.02 depending on type of boundary.

$\therefore$ Velocity by Manning's formula is given by,

$$V = \frac{1}{n}R^{2/3}S_o^{1/2} \quad ...(15.9)$$

Value of C can also be worked out by Kutter's formula,

$$C = \frac{23 + \frac{0.00155}{S_o} + \frac{1}{N}}{1 + \left(23 + \frac{0.00155}{S_o}\right)\frac{N}{\sqrt{R}}} \quad ...(15.10)$$

Here, N = 0.025, and is Kutter's constant.

Note: Calculation of velocity in open channel flow problem is always by either Chezy or Manning's, formula and in design of unlined canals for irrigation engineering. Kutter's formula has been recommended by Kennedy.

15.4 TYPES OF FLOW IN CHANNEL

(*a*) **Uniform flow:** When depth of flow does not change over a length of channel, flow is uniform flow. In this type of flow, bed line, water surface line and total energy line all three are parallel, see Fig. 15.2 (*a*). When flow is uniform, depth of flow y is known as normal depth, *i.e.*, y_n and in case of uniform flow only $y_n = y$ = actual depth of flow. Calculation of y_n is by Chezy or Manning's formula,

i.e., $$V = C\sqrt{RS} = C\sqrt{RS_o} \quad \text{here} \quad S = S_0$$

and $$R = \frac{A}{P}, \text{ and is a function of } y_n.$$

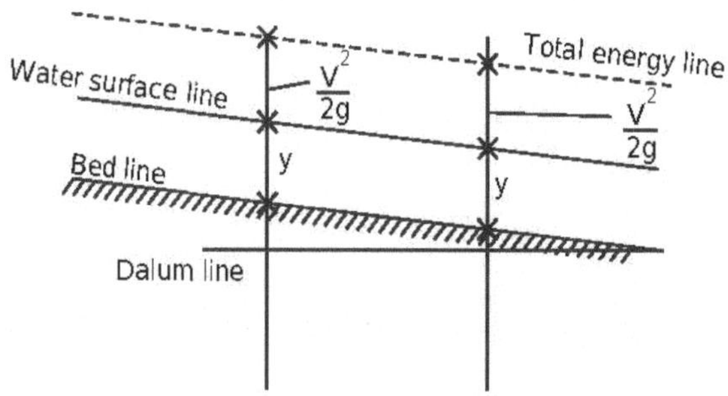

Fig. 15.2 (*a*)

(*b*) **Non uniform flow:** When depth of flow changes over given length of channel, type of flow is non-uniform. Here, total energy line, water surface line and bed line are not parallel to each other, see Fig. 15.2 (*b*).

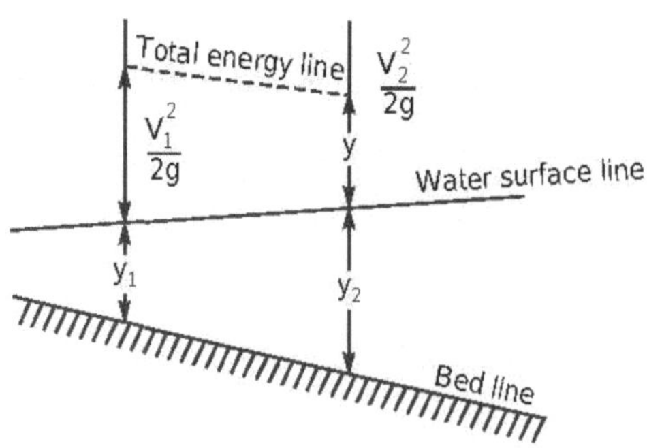

Fig. 15.2 (*b*)

When flow parameters *i.e.*, velocity and depth of flow, do not change with respect to time, flow is said to be **steady type** and if flow parameters change w.r.t. time then it is defined as **unsteady**.

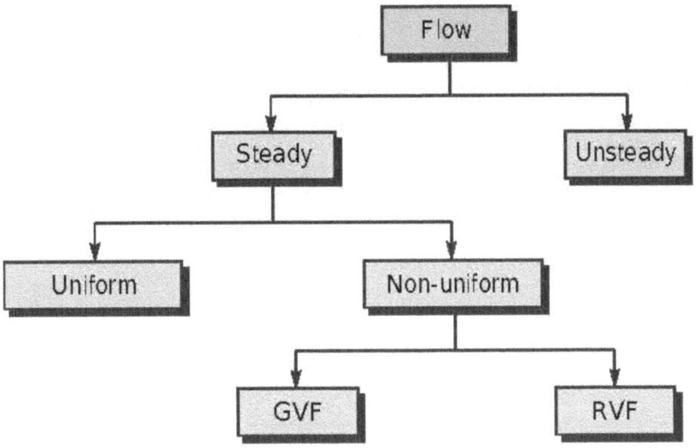

Further, non-uniform flow is classified as:

1. Gradually varied flow, GVF, if depth of flow y changes gradually over given length of channel, and
2. Rapidly varied flow, RVF, if depth of flow y changes suddenly to large values over small interval of channel length. For example, change of water surface level u/s of a dam is case of GVF and is known as Back water curve whereas change of depth of flow at toe of spillway from y_1 to y_2 over a small length is a case of RVF and is known as hydraulic jump, see Fig. 15.3. (*a*) and (*b*).

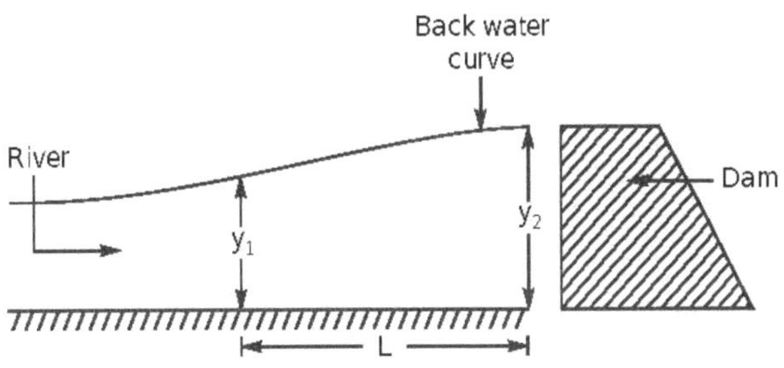

Fig. 15.3 (*a*) Case of GVF.

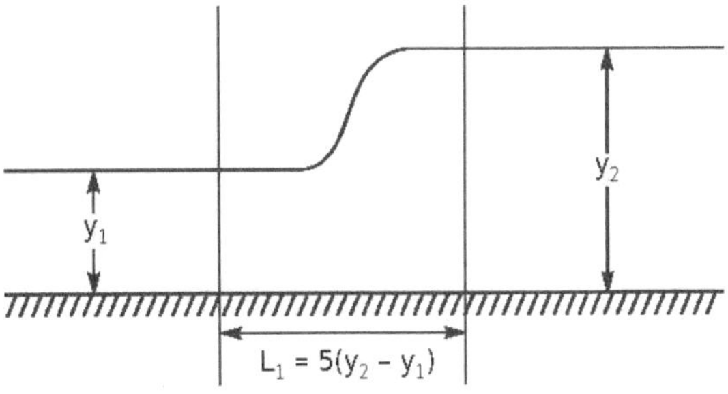

Fig. 15.3 (*b*) Case of RVF.

In case of GVF, $V = C\sqrt{RS_f}$

Here, $S = S_f$ = energy line gradient and R is a function of actual depth y.

when $S = S_o$ = bed gradient, depth of flow is normal depth, y_n and it may not be equal to actual depth y.

15.5 MOST ECONOMICAL HYDRAULIC SECTION OF A CHANNEL

Most economical hydraulic section or hydraulically most efficient section is that which has least perimeter because with P_{min}, V will be maximum and hence for same area discharge will be maximum. Also least perimeter means expense for excavation and lining will be minimum.

There are various type of channel sections:

1. Rectangular
2. Trapezoidal
3. Triangular
4. Circular.

All these types of section can be considered for most economical section and necessary conditions for same can be developed as under:

15.5.1 Most Economical Rectangular Section

Here we will treat given area as constant and P is variable as y is varying. Hence we will find $\frac{dP}{dy}$ and equate it to zero

$$A = By.$$

$$\therefore \quad B = \frac{A}{y}$$

$$P = B + 2y$$

$$\therefore \quad P = \frac{A}{y} + 2y$$

$$\therefore \quad \frac{dP}{dy} = -\frac{A}{y^2} + 2 = 0$$

$$\therefore \quad \frac{A}{y^2} = 2$$

$$\therefore \quad A = 2y^2$$

$$\therefore \quad By = 2y^2$$

$$\therefore \quad B = 2y$$

$$\therefore \quad y = \frac{B}{2} \qquad ...(15.11)$$

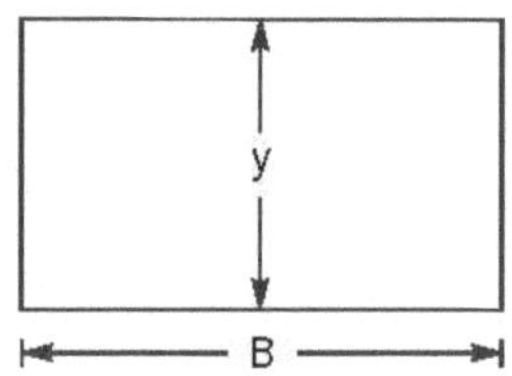

Fig. 15.4

Hence for rectangle section to be most efficient hydraulically, we must have

$$y = \frac{B}{2},$$

Now,

$$R = \frac{A}{P} = \frac{By}{B + 2y}$$

Put $$B = 2y, \quad \therefore \quad R = \frac{(2y)y}{(2y)+2y} = \frac{2y^2}{4y} = \frac{y}{2}.$$

$\therefore$ Hydraulic radius for most efficient rectangular section = $\frac{y}{2}$ and a semicircle can be inscribed in the section with radius equal to y.

Thus, for most economical rectangle section, we have three conditions to be satisfied, *i.e.*

(*i*) $y = B/2$

(*ii*) $R = y/2$

and (*iii*) A semicircle with radius = y can be inscribed.

15.5.2 Most Economical Trapezoidal Section

Both sides having same slope *i.e.*, 1 V to mH.

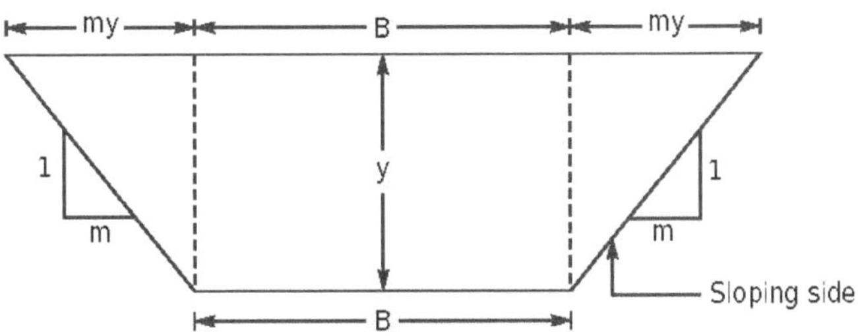

Fig. 15.5

$$\text{sloping side} = \sqrt{(y)^2 + (my)^2}$$

$$= y\sqrt{m^2+1}$$

Here m is constant and y is variable

$$\text{Top width} = T = B + 2my$$

$$\text{Area } A = \frac{1}{2}(T+B)y$$

$$= \frac{1}{2}(B+2my+B)y$$

$$\therefore \quad A = (B+my)y \qquad \text{...(15.12)}$$

$$P = B + 2y\sqrt{m^2+1} \qquad \text{...(15.13)}$$

$\therefore$ From (15.13), $$B = \frac{A}{y} - my$$

$$\therefore \quad P = \frac{A}{y} - my + 2y\sqrt{m^2+1}$$

$$\therefore \quad \frac{dP}{dy} = -\frac{A}{y^2} - m + 2\sqrt{m^2+1} = 0$$

Now we put $A = (B + my)y$ in above equation.

$$\therefore \quad \frac{(B+my)y}{y^2} + m = 2\sqrt{m^2+1}$$

$$\therefore \quad (B+my) + my = 2y\sqrt{m^2+1}$$

$$\therefore \quad B + 2my = 2y\sqrt{m^2+1} \qquad \text{...(15.14)}$$

$\therefore$ Top width = Twice sloping side

or, sloping side = $\frac{1}{2}$(top width)

Now $$R = \frac{A}{P} = \frac{(B+my)y}{B+2\left(y\sqrt{m^2+1}\right)}$$

Replacing $\left(y\sqrt{m^2+1}\right)$ by half of top width, we get

$$R = \frac{(B+my)y}{B+2\left[\frac{1}{2}(B+2my)\right]}$$

$$= \frac{(B+my)y}{(B+2my)} = \frac{y}{2}$$

$$\therefore \quad R = \frac{y}{2} \qquad \text{...(15.15)}$$

Now we prove that a semicircle can be inscribed see Fig. 15.6,

$OE = y$

AD = sloping side = OA (half top width)

$$\therefore \quad OA = y\sqrt{m^2+1}$$

In Fig. 15.6, $AB = OE = y$ and $AD = y\sqrt{m^2+1}$

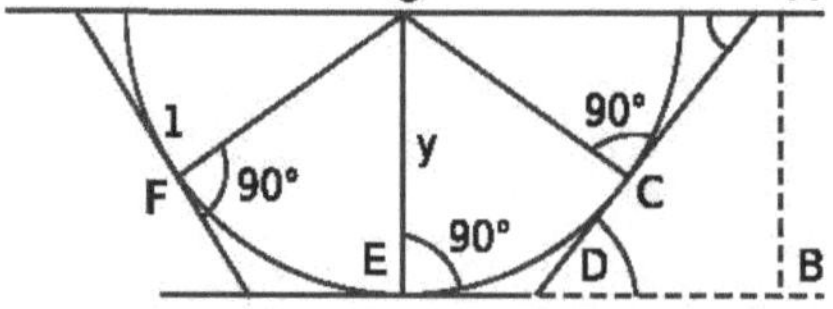

Fig. 15.6

In, Δ ABD, $$\sin\theta = \frac{AB}{AD} = \frac{y}{y\sqrt{m^2+1}}$$

And in $\Delta\, OAC$, $\sin\theta = \dfrac{OC}{OA}$

$$\therefore \quad OC = (OA)\sin\theta$$

$$= \left(y\sqrt{m^2+1}\right)\frac{y}{y\sqrt{m^2+1}}$$

$$= y$$

$$= OE$$

Similarly, $OC = OF = y$.

Thus, a semicircle with radius as y can be inscribed, Fig. 15.6.

We can also prove that most economical trapezoidal section is semi-hexagon as under:

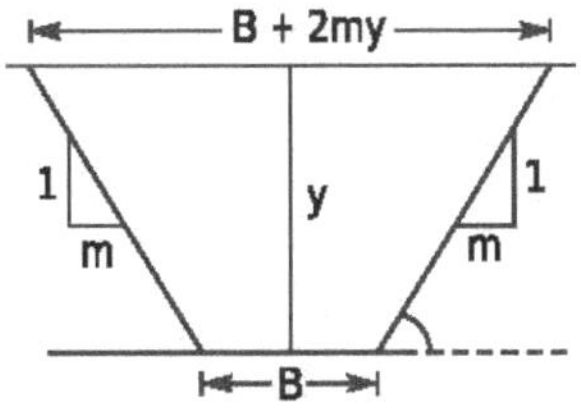

Fig. 15.7

In this case, m is varying and A, y are constant,

$$A = (B + my)y$$

$$\therefore \quad B = \frac{A}{y} - my$$

Now, $P = B + 2y\sqrt{1+m^2}$

$$\therefore \quad P = \frac{A}{y} - my + 2y\sqrt{1+m^2}$$

As P is varying w.r.t. m,

$$\therefore \quad \frac{dP}{dm} = 0 - y + 2y\frac{1}{2}(1+m^2)^{-1/2}\,(2m)$$

$$= 0$$

$$\therefore \quad y = y\frac{2m}{\sqrt{1+m^2}}$$

$$\therefore \quad \sqrt{1+m^2} = 2m$$

$$\therefore \quad 1 + m^2 = 4m^2$$

$$1 = 3m^2$$

$$\therefore \quad m = \frac{1}{\sqrt{3}}$$

$\therefore \qquad \theta = 60°$

Also, $\quad \frac{1}{2}$ top width = sloping side

$$\therefore \quad \frac{1}{2}(B+2my) = y\sqrt{1+m^2} \text{ and } m = \frac{1}{\sqrt{3}},$$

$$\therefore \quad B+2my = 2y\sqrt{1+\frac{1}{3}} = 2y\frac{2}{\sqrt{3}}$$

$$\therefore \quad B+\frac{2}{\sqrt{3}}y = 2y\frac{2}{\sqrt{3}},$$

$$\therefore \quad B = y\frac{2}{\sqrt{3}}$$

and $\qquad$ sloping side $= y\sqrt{m^2+1} = y\frac{2}{\sqrt{3}}.$

$\therefore$ Bed width and both sloping sides are equal and external $\angle A = 69°$.

$\therefore$ Most economical trapezoidal section is "**semi hexagon.**"

15.5.3 Most Economical Triangular Section

It can be proved that triangular channel section is most efficient if apex angle is 90° or a right angled triangle sections is the most economical section.

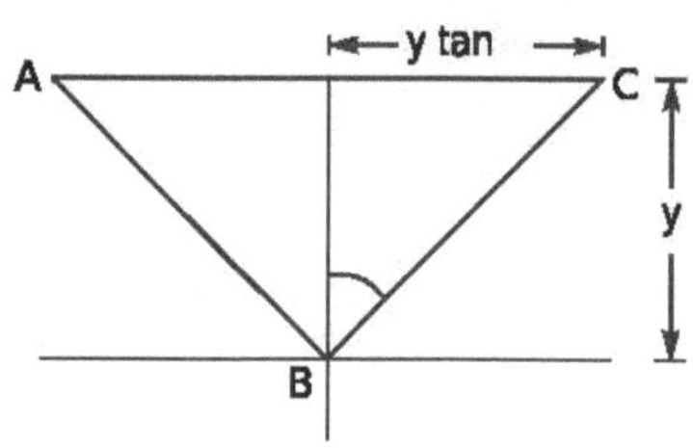

Fig. 15.8

Sloping side $\qquad BC = \sqrt{y^2 + y^2 \tan^2\theta}$

$$= y\sqrt{1+\tan^2\theta}$$

$$= y \sec\theta.$$

Flow area, $\qquad A = 2\left[\frac{1}{2}(y\tan\theta)y\right]$

$$= y^2 \tan\theta$$

$$\therefore \quad y = \sqrt{\frac{A}{\tan\theta}}$$

$$P = 2y \sec \theta = 2\left[\frac{A}{\tan\theta}\right]^{1/2} \sec\theta = 2\sqrt{A}\left[\frac{\sec\theta}{\sqrt{\tan\theta}}\right]$$

$$\therefore \quad \frac{dP}{d\theta} = 2\sqrt{A}\frac{\left[\sqrt{\tan\theta}\,(\sec\theta\tan\theta) - \sec\theta\frac{1}{2}\tan^{1/2}\theta\sec^2\theta\right]}{\tan\theta}$$

$$\therefore \quad \sqrt{\tan\theta}\,(\sec\theta\tan\theta) = \sec\theta\frac{1}{2}\frac{\sec^2\theta}{\sqrt{\tan\theta}}$$

$$\therefore \quad \tan^2\theta = \frac{1}{2}\sec^2\theta$$

$$\therefore \quad \frac{\sin^2\theta}{\cos^2\theta} = \frac{1}{2}\frac{1}{\cos^2\theta}$$

$$\therefore \quad \sin^2\theta = \frac{1}{2}$$

$$\therefore \quad \sin\theta = \frac{1}{\sqrt{2}}$$

$$\therefore \quad \theta = 45°$$

$$\therefore \quad \text{Apex} \angle = 2\theta = 90°$$

∴ Right angled triangular section is the most economical one.

15.5.4 Conditions for Most Economical Circular Section

For circular section, both, area of flow A and perimeter P, are functions of subtended $\angle\theta$ and therefore conditions for V_{max} and Q_{max} will be different and can be derived as under:

(A) For maximum velocity:

See Fig. 15.9, $\quad V = C\sqrt{RS} = C\sqrt{\frac{A}{P}}\sqrt{S}$

∴ V will be V_{max}

when $\sqrt{\frac{A}{P}}$ is maximum.

$$\therefore \quad \frac{d(A/P)}{d\theta} = 0$$

$$\therefore \quad P\frac{dA}{d\theta} - A\frac{dP}{d\theta} = 0$$

$$\therefore \quad P\frac{dA}{d\theta} = A\frac{dP}{d\theta} \qquad \text{...(15.16)}$$

In Fig. 15.9, $OC = r$ = radius of the circle

$$OD = r\cos\left(\frac{\theta}{2}\right)$$

$$DC = r\sin\left(\frac{\theta}{2}\right)$$

$$DB = \text{depth of flow} = y = r - r\cos\left(\frac{\theta}{2}\right)$$

$$y = r(1 - \cos\theta/2) \quad ...(15.17)$$

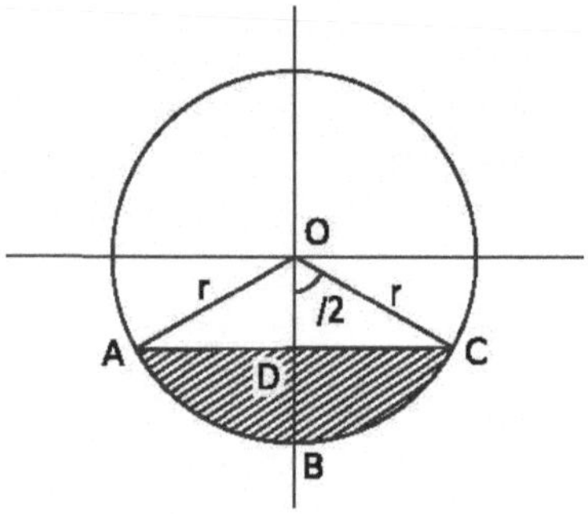

Fig. 15.9

A = Area of flow

= sector $OABC - \Delta\, OAC$

$$\therefore \quad A = \frac{1}{2}r^2\theta - 2\left(\frac{1}{2}r\sin\frac{\theta}{2}\,r\cos\frac{\theta}{2}\right)$$

$$= \frac{1}{2}r^2\theta - r^2\frac{\sin\theta}{2}$$

$$\therefore \quad A = \frac{1}{2}r^2(\theta - \sin\theta) \quad ...(15.18)$$

$$\frac{dA}{d\theta} = \frac{1}{2}r^2(1 - \cos\theta) \quad ...[15.18\ (a)]$$

$$P = r\theta \quad ...(15.19)$$

$$\therefore \quad \frac{dP}{d\theta} = r \quad ...[15.19\ (a)]$$

Now for V_{max}, $P\dfrac{dA}{d\theta} = A\dfrac{dP}{d\theta}$, from eq. (15.16).

$$\therefore \quad (r\theta)\frac{1}{2}r^2(1 - \cos\theta) = \frac{1}{2}r^2(\theta - \sin\theta)\,(r)$$

$$\therefore \quad \theta(1 - \cos\theta) = (\theta - \sin\theta)$$

$$\therefore \quad \theta = \tan\theta$$

$$\therefore \quad \theta = 257^\circ$$

Now, depth of flow, $y = r\left(1 - \cos\frac{\theta}{2}\right)$

$$\therefore \quad y = r\left(1 - \cos\frac{257}{2}\right)$$

Hence depth of flow, $y = 0.81\, D$ for V_{max}

where D = Diameter.

(B) For maximum discharge

$$Q = AV$$

$$= AC\sqrt{RS}$$

$$= AC\sqrt{\frac{A}{P}S}$$

$$= C\sqrt{\frac{A^3}{P}S}$$

$$= [C\sqrt{S}]\left(\sqrt{\frac{A^3}{P}}\right)$$

$\therefore$ Q will be maximum when $\sqrt{\dfrac{A^3}{P}}$ is maximum.

$$\therefore \quad \frac{d\left(\dfrac{A^3}{P}\right)}{d\theta} = \frac{P3A^2\dfrac{dA}{d\theta} - A^3\dfrac{dp}{d\theta}}{P^2} = 0$$

$$\therefore \quad 3P\frac{dA}{d\theta} = A\frac{dP}{d\theta} \qquad \text{...(15.20)}$$

Now substitute values for P, $\dfrac{dA}{d\theta}$, A and $\dfrac{dP}{d\theta}$ from eqn. (15.19), (15.18*a*), (15.18) and (15.19*a*).

$$\therefore \quad 3(r\theta)\frac{r^2}{2}(1 - \cos\theta) = \frac{1}{2}r^2(\theta - \sin\theta)r$$

$$\therefore \quad 3\theta - 3\theta\cos\theta = \theta - \sin\theta$$

$$\therefore \quad \theta = 308^\circ$$

$$\therefore \quad \frac{\theta}{2} = 154^\circ$$

$$y = \text{depth of flow}$$

$$= r - r\cos\frac{\theta}{2}$$

$$= r(1 - \cos 154)$$

$$= r(1 + \cos 26)$$

$$= r(1.89)$$

$$\therefore \quad y = \frac{D}{2}(1.89)$$

$y = 0.95D$ for Q_{max} (by Chezy's formula for velocity).

For circular sections following geometric formulae should be remembered:

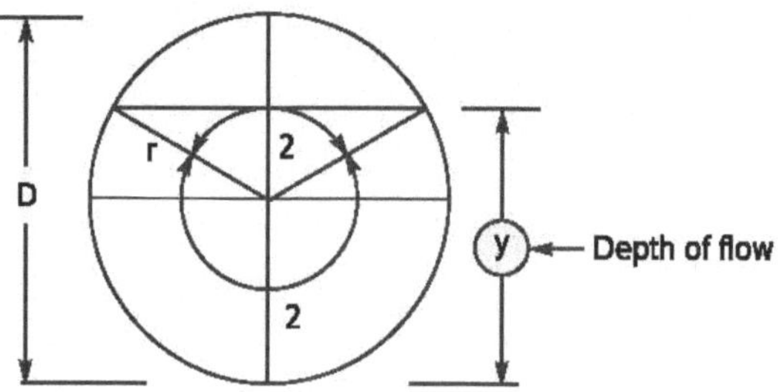

Fig. 15.10

1. A = area of flow

$$= \frac{D^2}{8}[2\theta - \sin 2\theta]$$

2. P = wetted perimeter for depth of flow = y

$$= D\theta$$

3. R = hydraulic radius = $\dfrac{A}{P}$

$$= \frac{D}{8}\left[2 - \frac{\sin 2\theta}{\theta}\right]$$

4. Area of sector with subtended $\angle 2\phi$

$$= \frac{1}{2}r^2[2\phi - \sin 2\phi]$$

5. T = top width of free surface

$$= D\sin\theta$$

6. $\cos\theta = 1 - \left(2\dfrac{y}{D}\right)$

In place of Chezy's formula, if Manning's formula is used, then for V_{max}, there is no change and same condition

$$y = 0.81\,D \text{ can be used}$$

but for Q_{max}, there is a change, given below:

$$Q = AV = A\frac{1}{n}R^{2/3}S_0^{1/2}$$

$$= \frac{S_0^{1/2}}{n}\left(\frac{A^{5/3}}{P^{2/3}}\right)$$

$$= \frac{S_0^{1/2}}{n}\left(\frac{A^5}{P^2}\right)^{1/3}$$

$\therefore$ Q is a maximum when $\left(\dfrac{A^5}{P^2}\right)$ is maximum.

$$\therefore \qquad \frac{d\left(\dfrac{A^5}{P^2}\right)}{d\theta} = 0$$

$$\therefore \qquad P^2 5A^4\frac{dA}{d\theta} - A^5\,2P\frac{dP}{d\theta} = 0$$

$$\therefore \qquad 5P\frac{dA}{d\theta} = 2A\frac{dP}{d\theta} \qquad \text{...(15.21)}$$

This gives θ =302° by substituting values of P, $\dfrac{dA}{d\theta}$, A, $\dfrac{dP}{d\theta}$ derived earlier.

$\therefore$ $\quad$ y = **0.938** $\boldsymbol{D}$ if Manning's formula is used or value of n is given.

15.6 SOLVED PROBLEMS

■ **Problem 15.1:** *A trapezoidal channel of side slope 2 :1 has bottom width of 2 m and depth of flow 1 m, S_o is 1 in 625, and manning's n = 0.013. Find boundary shear, flow rate and value of friction factor.*

Solution:

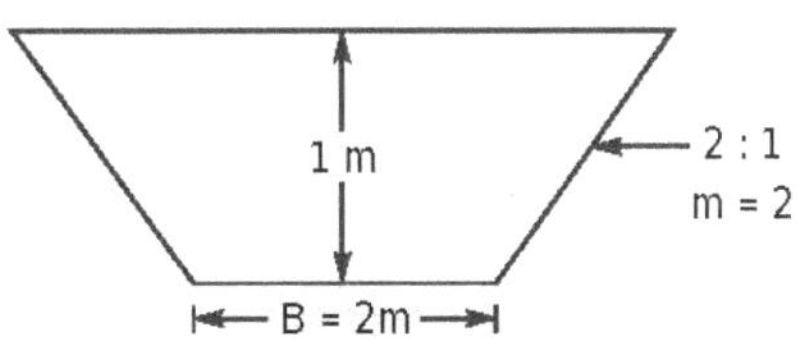

Fig. 15.11

Boundary shear $= \tau_o = \gamma R S_o$

$$R = \frac{A}{P} = \frac{(B+my)y}{B+2y\sqrt{m^2+1}}$$

$$\therefore \quad R = \frac{(2+2\times 1)1}{2+2(1)\sqrt{4+1}} = \frac{4}{6.47} = \mathbf{0.618\,m}$$

$$\therefore \quad \tau_o = \gamma R S_o = 1000(0.618)\frac{1}{625}$$

$$= 0.98 \text{ kgf/m}^2$$ ...(Ans.)

$$Q = AV = AC\sqrt{RS_o}$$

$$= A\frac{1}{n}R^{2/3}S_o^{1/2}$$

$$= (B+my)y\left(\frac{1}{n}R^{2/3}\right)(S_o)^{1/2}$$

$$= \frac{4}{0.013}(0.618)^{2/3}\left(\frac{1}{625}\right)^{1/2}$$

$$= \frac{4}{0.013}(0.724)(0.04)$$

$$= 8.91 \text{ m}^3/\text{s}.$$ ...(Ans.)

We have, $$C = \frac{1}{n}R^{1/6}$$

$$= \frac{1}{0.013}(0.618)^{1/6}$$

$$= 70.9$$

Also, $$C = \sqrt{\frac{8g}{f}}$$

$$\therefore \quad 70.9 = \sqrt{\frac{8(9.81)}{f}}$$

$$\therefore \quad f = \frac{8\times 9.81}{(70.9)^2} = 0.0156$$

$\therefore$ friction factor = 0.0156. ...(Ans.)

■ **Problem 15.2:** *A circular sewer is to carry sewage from a colony of 15000 population, supply of water is 200 lit/head/day; 75% of which appears as sewage. Taking peak factor as 2.5 times average, sewer gradient 1 in 125. Manning's n = 0.014, and assuming sewer runs three fourth full, find the diameter of sewer.*

Solution: $$Q = \frac{1500 \times 200 \times 0.75 \times 2.5}{1000 \times 24 \times 3600} = 0.065 \text{ m}^3/\text{s}$$

Sewer is circular section and is running $\frac{3}{4}$th Full, see Fig. 15.12.

$$\therefore \quad y = \frac{3}{4}\text{ Dia} = \frac{3}{4}D.$$

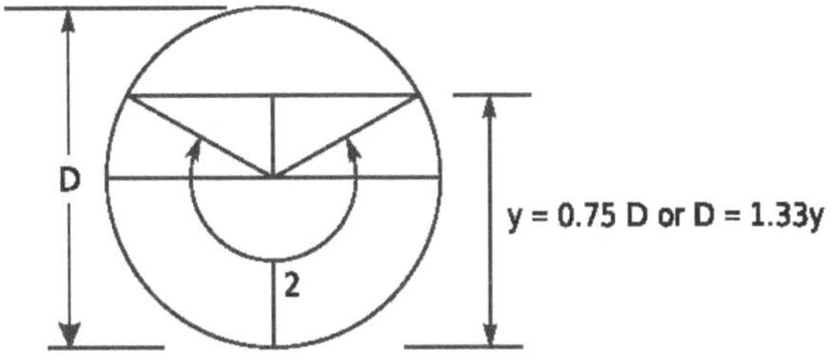

Fig. 15.12

$$\cos\theta = 1 - 2\left(\frac{y}{D}\right) = 1 - 2\left(\frac{0.75D}{D}\right) = 0.5$$

$$\therefore \quad \theta = 120°$$

$$2\theta = 240°$$

Area of flow $$A = \frac{D^2}{8}(2\theta - \sin 2\theta)$$

$$= \frac{(1.33y)^2}{8}\left(\frac{240}{180}\pi + 0.86\right)$$

$$= \frac{(1.33y)^2}{8}(2.1 + 0.86) = \mathbf{1.118y^2}$$

$$P = D\theta = D\frac{120}{180}\pi = \mathbf{2.786y}$$

$$R = \frac{A}{P} = \frac{1.118\,y^2}{2.786y} = 0.40y$$

By Manning's formula,

$$Q = \frac{A}{n}R^{2/3}S_o^{1/2}$$

$$\therefore \quad 0.065 = \frac{1.118\,y^2}{0.014} \times (0.40y)^{2/3}\left(\frac{1}{125}\right)^{1/2}$$

$$\therefore \quad y^{8/3} = 0.01676 \quad \therefore \quad y = \mathbf{0.216\ m}$$

$$\therefore \quad D = 1.33y = 0.2870 \text{ m}$$ **...(Ans.)**

■ **Problem 15.3:** *A circular channel of diameter 0.6 m is having bed gradient of 1 in 3200. Making use of Manning's n = 0.016. Calculate the maximum discharge the channel can carry.*

Solution:

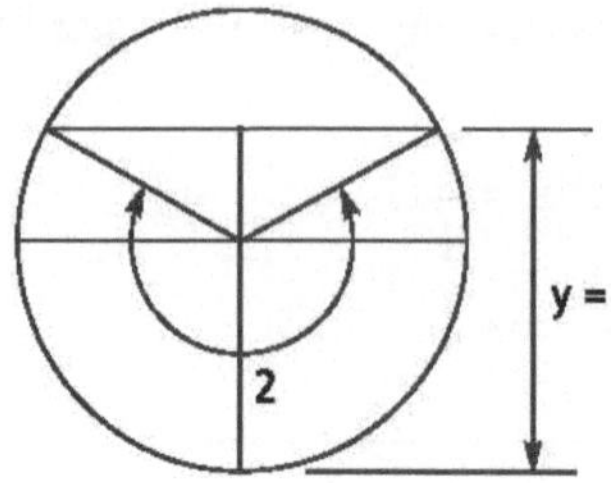

Fig. 15.13

$$\text{For max } Q, y = 0.938\,D$$

$$= 0.94\,D$$

$$y = 0.94\,D \text{ by Manning's formula}$$

$$\cos\theta = 1 - 2\left(\frac{y}{D}\right) = 1 - 2(0.94) = -0.88$$

$$\therefore \quad \theta = 152°$$

$$\therefore \quad 2\theta = 304°,$$

$$A = \frac{D^2}{8}(2\theta - \sin 2\theta)$$

$$= \frac{(0.6)^2}{8}\left[\frac{304}{180}\pi - (-0.82)\right]$$

$$= \mathbf{0.275\ m^2}$$

$$R = \frac{D}{8}\left[2 - \frac{\sin 2\theta}{\theta}\right] = \frac{0.6}{8}\left[2 - \frac{-0.86}{\left(\frac{152}{180}\pi\right)}\right]$$

$$= \mathbf{0.174}$$

$$Q_{max} = \frac{A}{n}(R)^{2/3}(S_o)^{1/2}$$

$$= \frac{0.275}{0.016}(0.174)^{2/3}\left(\frac{1}{3200}\right)^{1/2}$$

$$= \frac{0.275 \times 0.3}{0.016 \times 56.56} = \mathbf{0.091\ m^3/s.}$$ **...(Ans.)**

■ **Problem 15.4:** *A rect. channel 5.4 m wide and 1.2 m deep has a bed slope of 1 in 1000. It is desired to increase the discharge by changing the dimension of channel but maintaining, same amount of lining. Find new dimension and increase in discharge. Take C = 60.*

Solution: For same amount of lining, $P = 5.4 + 2(1.2)$

$$= 7.8 \text{ m.}$$

$$\text{area of lining} = P \times 1 = 7.8 \times 1 = 7.8 \text{ m}^2.$$

Area of lining same but Q to increase, means condition of P_{min} for V_{max}.

$$P = B + 2y, A = By, \quad \therefore \quad B = \frac{A}{y}$$

$$= \frac{A}{y} + 2y$$

$$\therefore \quad \frac{dP}{dy} = -\frac{A}{y^2} + 2 = 0$$

$$\therefore \quad A = 2y^2$$

and $$R = \frac{A}{P} = \frac{y}{2}$$

and $$y = \frac{B}{2}$$

$$\therefore \quad P_{given} = 7.8 = B + 2\left(\frac{B}{2}\right) = 2B$$

$$\therefore \quad B = \frac{7.8}{2} = 3.9 \text{ m}$$

and $$y = \frac{3.9}{2} = 1.95 \text{ m}$$

and $$R = \frac{y}{2}\frac{1.95}{2}$$

$$C = 60.$$

$$Q_{new} = AV$$

$$= 2(1.95)^2 C\sqrt{RS_o}$$

$$= 2(1.95)^2 60\sqrt{\left(\frac{1.95}{2}\right)\frac{1}{1000}}$$

$$= 2(1.95)^2 (60) (0.0312)$$

$$= 14.23 \text{ m}^3/\text{s}.$$

$$Q_{old} = AV = (5.4 \times 1.2)\, 60 \sqrt{\frac{5.4 \times 1.2 \times 1}{(5.4 + 2.4) \times 1000}}$$

$$= 11.2 \text{ m}^3/\text{s}.$$

$\therefore$ Increase in $Q = 14.23 - 11.2$

$$= 3.03 \text{ m}^3/\text{s}.$$

and dimension $B = 3.9$ m, $y = 1.95$ m. ...(Ans.)

■ **Problem 15.5:** *A 20 cm diameter stoneware pipe carries water with depth of flow 15 cm. So 1 in 150 and n = 0.014. Find discharge.*

Solution:

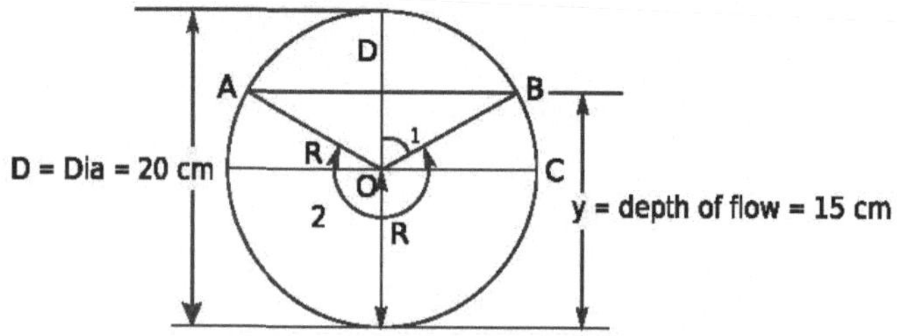

Fig. 15.14

$$y = R + R\cos\theta_1$$

$$= R(1 + \cos\theta_1), \quad R = \frac{D}{2} = 10 \text{ cm}$$

$\therefore$ $15 = 10(1 + \cos\theta_1)$

$\therefore$ $\cos\theta_1 = 0.5$

$\therefore$ $\theta_1 = 60° \quad \therefore \quad \theta = 120°$

$\therefore$ $2\theta = 240$

$$A = \frac{D^2}{8}[2\theta - \sin 2\theta]$$

$$= \frac{(0.2)^2}{8}\left[\frac{240}{180}\pi + 0.86\right]$$

$$= 0.025 \text{ m}^2$$

$\therefore$ $$R = \frac{D}{8}\left[2 - \frac{\sin 2\theta}{\theta}\right]$$

$$= \frac{0.2}{8}[2 + 0.43]$$

$$= 0.03966 \text{ m}$$

$$Q = \frac{A}{n}(R)^{2/3}(S_o)^{1/2}$$

$$= \frac{0.025}{0.014}(0.3966)^{2/3}\left(\frac{1}{150}\right)^{1/2}$$

$$= 0.0173 \text{ m}^3/\text{s}$$

$$= 17.3 \; LPS. \qquad \text{...(Ans.)}$$

■ **Problem 15.6:** *A trapezoidal channel has most economical section with $Q = 15$ cumecs. Side slopes at 45°. S_o 1 in 950*

$C_{lined} = 80$, $C_{unlined} = 55$.

Cost per cu.m. of excavation ₹ 50/-.

Cost per sq. m of lining ₹ 110/-.

Compare the costs between lined and unlined sections.

Solution:

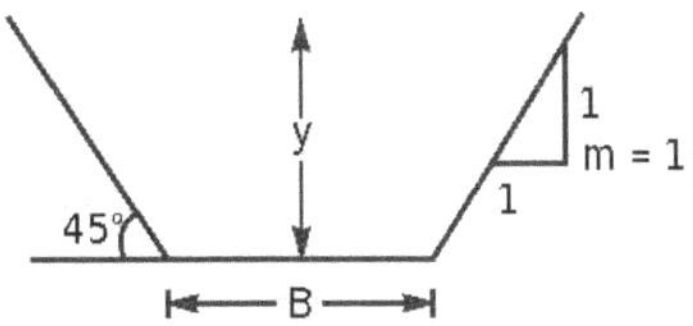

Fig. 15.15

For most economical trapezoidal section,

$$R = \frac{y}{2} \text{ and}$$

$$\text{Top width} = 2(\text{sloping side})$$

$$\therefore \quad B + 2y = 2y\sqrt{1+m^2}, m = 1$$

$$= 2y\sqrt{2}$$

$$\therefore \quad B = 0.82y.$$

For lined section:

$$V = C\sqrt{RS_o}$$

$$= 80\sqrt{\frac{y}{2}\frac{1}{950}} = \frac{80}{43.58}\sqrt{y} = 1.83\sqrt{y} \qquad \text{...(1)}$$

$$= \frac{Q}{A} = \frac{15}{(B+my)y} = \frac{15}{(0.82y+y)y} \qquad \text{...(2)}$$

From (1) and (2), we get

$$1.83\sqrt{y} = \frac{15}{(0.82y+y)y} = \frac{15}{1.82y^2}$$

$$y^{2.5} = 4.5$$

$\therefore$ $y = (4.5)^{\frac{1}{2.5}}$ and $B = 0.82(1.82)$

$\therefore$ $y = \mathbf{1.82\ m}$, $\quad B = \mathbf{1.5\ m}$

$$A = (B + my)y$$

$$= (1.5 + 1.82)1.82 = 3.82 \times 2.1 = 6.04\ \text{m}^2$$

$\therefore$ Volume of excavation $= A \times L = A \times 1 = 6$ m^3/sec/m length of channel.

$\therefore$ excavation cost $= 6 \times 50 =$ **300 ₹**

lining cost $= P \times L \times 110$ (Here $L = 1$m)

$$= (1.50 + 2y\sqrt{2})\,110$$

$= (1.5 + 5.13)\ 110 =$ **730 ₹** per m length of channel.

$\therefore$ Total cost for lined canal $= 300 + 730$

$= 1030$ ₹ per m length.

For unlined canal

$$V = C\sqrt{RS_o}$$

$$= 55\left(\frac{y}{2} \times \frac{1}{950}\right)^{1/2}$$

$$= \frac{55}{43.58}\sqrt{y} = 1.262\sqrt{y} \quad \text{...(3)}$$

$$= \frac{Q}{A} = \frac{15}{(0.82y + y)y} \quad \text{...(4)}$$

From (3) and (4), we get

$$1.26\sqrt{y} = \frac{15}{(0.82y + y)y} = \frac{15}{1.82y^2}$$

$$\therefore \quad y^{2.5} = \frac{15}{1.26 \times 1.82} = 6.54$$

$$\therefore \quad y = (6.54)^{\frac{1}{2.5}} = 2.11\ \text{m}$$

and $B = 0.82y = 0.82(2.11) =$ **1.73 m**

$\therefore$ $A = (B + my)y$

$$= (1.73 + 2.11)\ 2.11 = 8.11\ \text{m}^2$$

Volume of excavation $= A \times 1 = 8.11$ m^3

Cost of excavation $= 8.11 \times 50 =$ **406**

$\therefore$ Cost of unlined canal ₹ 406 $<$ lined canal cost ₹ 1030. **...(Ans.)**

■ **Problem 15.7:** *Determine the most efficient section of a trapezoidal channel with side slope 2H : 1V, carrying a discharge of 11.25 m³/s with a velocity of 0.75 m/s. What should be the bed slope for this channel? Taken = 0.025.*

Solution:

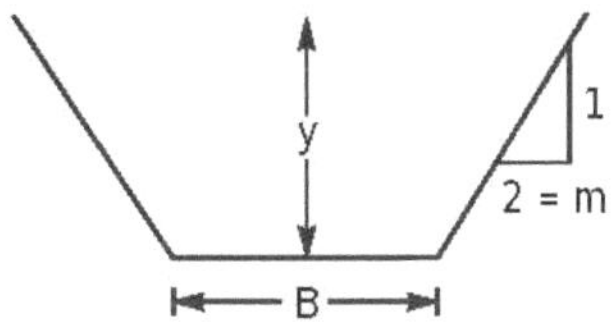

Fig. 15.16

$$Q = 11.25 = AV$$

$$\therefore \quad A = \frac{11.25}{0.75}$$

$$= 15 \text{ m}^2$$

$$A = (B + my)y$$

For most economical section, Top width = 2(slopes side)

$$\therefore \quad B + 2my = 2(y\sqrt{m^2+1})$$

$$m = 2, \quad \therefore \quad B + 4y = 2y\,(2.23)$$

$$\therefore \quad B + 4y = 4.46y$$

$$\therefore \quad B = 0.46y$$

$$\therefore \quad A = (0.46y + 2y)y = 15$$

$$2.46y^2 = 15$$

$$\therefore \quad y = \mathbf{2.46} \qquad \text{...(Ans.)}$$

$$\therefore \quad B = 0.46(2.46)$$

$$= \mathbf{1.135} \qquad \text{...(Ans.)}$$

$$V = \frac{1}{n}(R^{2/3})\left(S_o^{1/2}\right)$$

For most efficient section, $R = \dfrac{y}{2}$

$$\therefore \quad 0.75 = \frac{1}{0.025}\left(\frac{2.46}{2}\right)^{2/3}(S_o)^{1/2}$$

$$\therefore \quad S_o^{1/2} = \frac{0.75 \times 0.025}{1.148} = 0.0163$$

$$\therefore \quad S_o = 2.66 \times 10^{-4} \quad \text{or} \quad 1 \text{ in } 3759. \qquad \text{...(Ans.)}$$

■ **Problem 15.8:** *A trapezoidal channel with one side vertical and other sloping at 2H to 1V has n = 0.014 and delivers 8 m³/ s when bed slope is 0.0001. Find dimension of this channel for minimum lining cost. Find corresponding velocity.*

Solution:

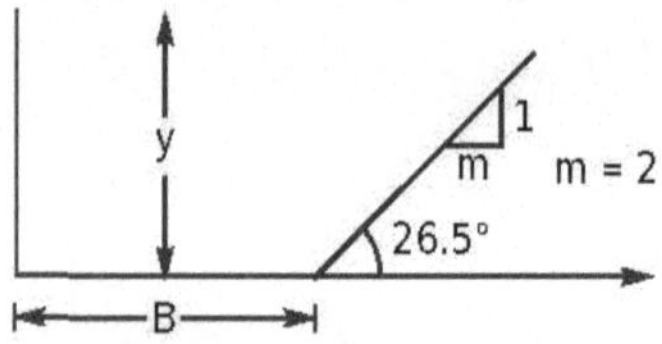

Fig. 15.17

$$Q = 8 \text{ m}^3/\text{s}$$

$$S_o = 0.0001$$

$$A = \frac{1}{2}(B + B + my)y, \; m = 2.$$

$$= \frac{1}{2}(2B + 2y)y = (B + y)y \text{ for } m = 2.$$

$$\therefore \quad B = \frac{A}{y} - y$$

$$P = y + B + y\sqrt{m^2 + 1} = B + y + y\sqrt{4+1}$$

$$\therefore \quad P = B + 3.23y$$

$$P = \frac{A}{y} - y + 3.23y$$

$$= \frac{A}{y} - 2.23y$$

$$\therefore \quad \frac{dP}{dy} = -\frac{A}{y^2} + 2.23 = 0$$

$$\therefore \quad A = 2.23y^2$$

For most economical trapezoidal section, $R = \dfrac{y}{2}$

$$V = \frac{1}{n}\left(\frac{y}{2}\right)^{2/3} S_o^{\,1/2} = \frac{1}{0.014}\left(\frac{y}{2}\right)^{2/3} S_o^{\,1/2}$$

$$= \frac{Q}{A} = \frac{8}{2.23y^2}$$

$$\therefore \quad \frac{8}{2.23y^2} = \frac{1}{0.014}\left(\frac{y}{2}\right)^{2/3}\left(\frac{1}{100}\right)$$

$$y^{8/3} = \frac{8 \times 0.014 \times 100 \times 1.59}{2.23} = 7.98$$

$\therefore \quad y = (7.98)^{3/8}$

$= \mathbf{2.17\ m}$ ...(Ans.)

$\therefore \quad A = 2.23y^2 = 2.23(2.17)^2 = 10.59$

$\therefore \quad B = \frac{A}{y} - y = \frac{10.59}{2.17} - 2.17$

$= 4.88 - 2.17$

$= \mathbf{2.71\ m}$ ...(Ans.)

$V = \frac{8}{2.23\,(2.17)^2} = \frac{3.58}{(2.17)^2} = \mathbf{0.76\ m/s}.$ ...(Ans.)

■ **Problem 15.9:** *Show for an efficient triangular section*, $R = \frac{y}{2\sqrt{2}}$.

Solution:

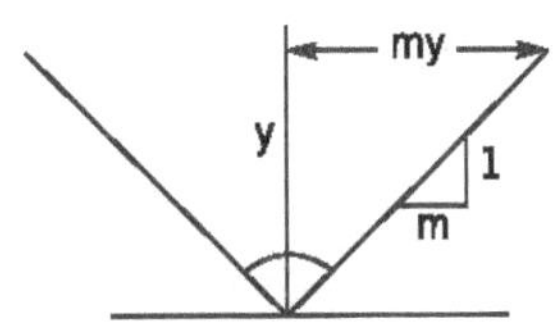

Fig. 15.18

$$A = \frac{1}{2}(2my)y = my^2$$

$$\therefore \quad m = \frac{A}{y^2}$$

$$P = 2y\sqrt{m^2 + 1} = 2y\sqrt{\frac{A^2}{y^4} + 1}$$

$$\therefore \quad = 2\left(\frac{A^2}{y^2} + y^2\right)^{1/2}$$

$$\therefore \quad \frac{d\left(\frac{A^2}{y^2} + y^2\right)}{dy} = -2\frac{A^2}{y^3} + 2y = 0$$

$$\therefore \quad \frac{A^2}{y^3} = y$$

$$\therefore \quad A^2 = y^4$$

$$\therefore \quad A = y^2$$

or $$y = \sqrt{A}$$

$\therefore$ $$m = \frac{A}{y^2} = \frac{A}{A} = 1$$

$$= 1 \quad i.e. \quad = 90°$$

$\therefore$ $$P = 2y\sqrt{1+1}$$

$$= 2y\sqrt{2}$$

$\therefore$ $$R = \frac{A}{P} = \frac{y^2}{2y\sqrt{2}} = \frac{y}{2\sqrt{2}}.$$ **Proved**

■ **Problem 15.10**: *A triangular duct resting on its base carries water with a free surface. Obtain condition for Q_{max} when side slope is $\frac{1}{2}:1$.*

Solution:

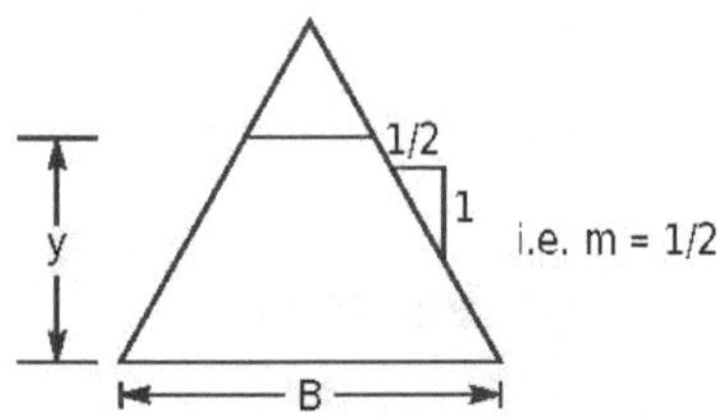

Fig. 15.19

$$Q = \frac{1}{n} A R^{2/3} S_o^{1/2} = \frac{S_0^{1/2}}{n}\left(\frac{A^5}{P^2}\right)^{1/3}$$

$\therefore$ $$\frac{dQ}{dy} = \frac{d}{dy}\left(\frac{A^5}{P^2}\right) = 0$$

$\therefore$ $$P^2 5A^4 \frac{dA}{dy} - A^5 2P\frac{dP}{dy} = 0$$

$\therefore$ $$5P\frac{dA}{dy} = 2A\frac{dP}{dy}$$ is condition for $Q_{max.}$

Now $$A = \frac{1}{2}(B + B - 2my)y = (B - my)y$$

$$A = By - my^2$$

$\therefore$ $$\frac{dA}{dy} = B - 2my = B - y \text{ as } m = \frac{1}{2}$$

$$P = B + 2y\sqrt{m^2+1} \quad \therefore \quad \frac{dP}{dy} = 2\sqrt{m^2+1} = \sqrt{5} = 2.23$$

$$\therefore \quad 5(B + 2.23y)(B - y) = 2\left(By - \frac{1}{2}y^2\right)2.23$$

$$= 4.46\left(B - \frac{y}{2}\right)y$$

$$\therefore \quad (B + 2.23y)(B - y) = 0.89y\left(B - \frac{y}{2}\right)$$

$$\therefore B^2 + 2.23\,By - By - 2.23y^2 = 0.89\,By - \frac{0.89}{2}y^2$$

$$\therefore B^2 + 0.34\,By - 1.78y^2 = 0$$

$$\therefore \quad B = \frac{-0.34y \pm \sqrt{0.11y^2 + 7.12y^2}}{2} = \frac{-0.34y + 2.68y}{2} = 1.17y$$

$$\therefore \quad y = \frac{1}{1.17}B = 0.85B. \qquad \text{...(Ans.)}$$

■ **Problem 15.11:** *A square duct of side (a) is placed with its diagonal vertical and carries water with a free surface.*

Show that Q is maximum when depth of flow is equal to ***1.28a.***

Solution:

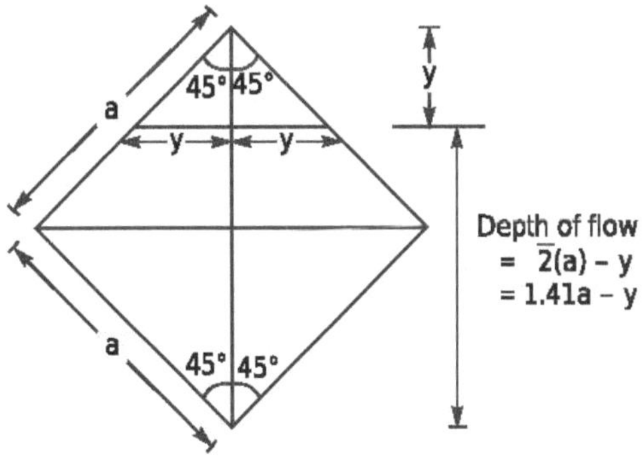

Fig. 15.20

$$\text{Area of flow} = A = a^2 - 2\left(\frac{1}{2}y \cdot y\right)$$

$$\therefore \quad A = a^2 - y^2$$

$$\therefore \quad \frac{dA}{dy} = -2y$$

P = Wetted perimeter = $4a - 2\sqrt{2y}$

$\therefore \qquad P = 4a - 2.82y$

$\therefore \qquad \frac{dP}{dy} = -2.82$

$$Q = AV = AC\sqrt{RS_o}$$

$$= C\sqrt{S_o}\left(\frac{A^3}{P}\right)^{1/2}$$

$\therefore$ For Q_{max}, $\frac{d\left(\frac{A^3}{P}\right)}{dy} = 0$

$\therefore \qquad 3P\frac{dA}{dy} = A\frac{dP}{dy}$

$\therefore \quad 3(4a - 2.82y)(-2y) = (a^2 - y^2)(-2.82)$

$\therefore \quad 2.12y(4a - 2.82y) = a^2 - y^2$

$\quad 8.51ay - 5.97y^2 = a^2 - y^2$

$\therefore \quad y^2 - 1.71\,ay + 0.2a^2 = 0$

$$\therefore \qquad y = \frac{1.71a \pm \sqrt{(1.71a)^2 - 4(1)(0.2a^2)}}{2}$$

$$= \frac{1.71a^2 - 1.45a}{2}$$

$$= \frac{0.26a}{2} = 0.13a$$

$\therefore \qquad$ depth of flow $= 1.41a - 0.13a$

$= 1.28a.$ ...(Ans.)

15.7 CONCEPT OF SPECIFIC ENERGY

Total energy of flow, T consists of depth of flow y, datum head Z and velocity head $\frac{v^2}{2g}$,

$$\therefore \qquad T = Z + y + \frac{v^2}{2g} \qquad ...(15.22)$$

It was in 1912, Bakhmeteff introduced the concept of specific energy, by suggesting that datum head Z can be eliminated if channel bed itself is considered as datum line, thus

$$E = y + \frac{v^2}{2g} \quad ...(15.23)$$

Here E = specific energy

$$V = \frac{Q}{A}$$

$$\therefore \quad E = y + \frac{Q^2}{2g\,A^2}$$

For rectangular channel of bed width B and depth of flow y,

$$A = By$$

$$\therefore \quad E = y + \frac{Q^2}{2g\,B^2 y^2}$$

Now putting $q = \frac{Q}{B}$ = discharge pre unit width of rectangular channel,

$$E = y + \frac{q^2}{2gy^2} \quad ...(15.24)$$

Here, $E \to \infty$ if $y \to \infty$

and $E \to \infty$ if $y \to 0$

that is, if depth of flow varies from zero to infinity specific energy E tends to increase to infinity. Hence if a curve of depth of flow y versus E is drawn, it will be asymptotic to x axis when y tends to zero and will be also asymptotic to a 45° line representing only potential energy, when y tends to increase to infinity. This is shown in Fig. 15.21.

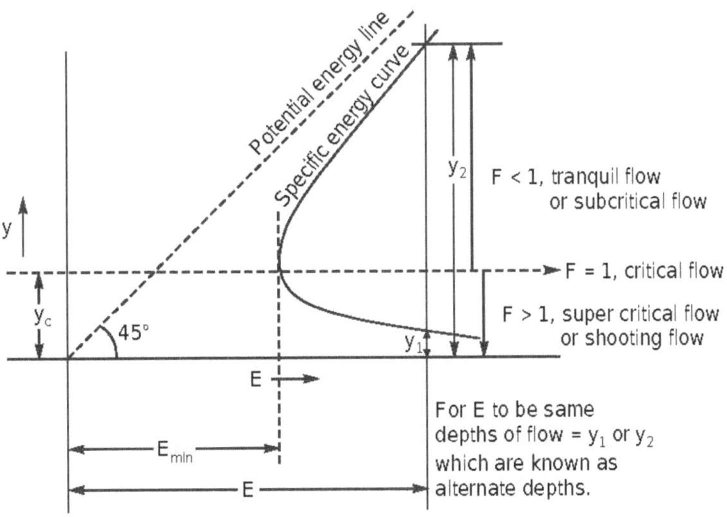

Fig. 15.21 Specific energy diagram.

As can be seen from specific energy curve, at one particular value of depth of flow, E is minimum. This depth of flow is therefore defined as **critical depth,** y_c and its value can be derived mathematically, as under:

We have from eq. (15.21), $E = y + \dfrac{q^2}{2gy^2}$ for rectangular channel.

$$\therefore \quad \frac{dE}{dy} = 1 - \frac{q^2}{gy^3} = 0 \quad \text{for } E_{min}$$

$\therefore \dfrac{q^2}{gy^3} = 1$, here y is y_c as flow is critical.

$$\therefore \quad y_c = \left(\frac{q^2}{g}\right)^{1/3} \qquad \text{...(15.25)}$$

At depth y_c, $\quad F = \dfrac{v}{\sqrt{gy_c}}$

$$\therefore \quad F^2 = \frac{v^2}{gy_c} = \frac{q^2}{gy_c^3} \quad \text{as } q = vy$$

But $\quad \dfrac{q^2}{g} = y_c^3 \quad$ from eq. (15.25)

$$\therefore \quad F^2 = \left(\frac{y_c^3}{y_c^3}\right) = 1$$

$\therefore \quad F = 1$ at critical depth

Thus at critical depth, E is min and F is unity. For any other value of E, we notice from the curve that two depths y_1 and y_2 represent flow and are defined as **alternate depth.** When y_1 is less than y_c zone of flow is defined as shooting or supercritical flow. Whereas, for $y_2 > y_c$, flow is tranquil or subcritical. When actual depth of flow $y = y_c$, flow is defined as critical flow. Thus at critical flow, (*i*) E is min, (*ii*) $F = 1$ and (*iii*) $y_c = \left(\dfrac{q^2}{g}\right)^{1/3}$.

If we substitute $y_c^3 = \dfrac{q^2}{g}$ in eq. (15.24), we get $E = y_c + \dfrac{y_c}{2} = 1.5y_c$ or $y_c = \dfrac{2}{3}E_{min}$.

When flow is supercritical, $y_1 < y_c$ and $F > 1$, but when flow is subcritical, $y_2 > y_c$ and $F < 1$.

15.7.1 Specific Discharge Diagram

Referring to eq. (15.24), we have

$$E = y + \frac{q^2}{2gy^2} \quad \text{for rectangular channel.}$$

$$\therefore \quad q^2 = 2gy^2 (E - y) \quad \text{...(15.26)}$$

If we keep E constant, and study variation of q against that of y, we see that

$q \to 0$ when $y \to E$

and $q \to 0$ when $y \to 0$.

Hence q is maximum at value in between zero and E.

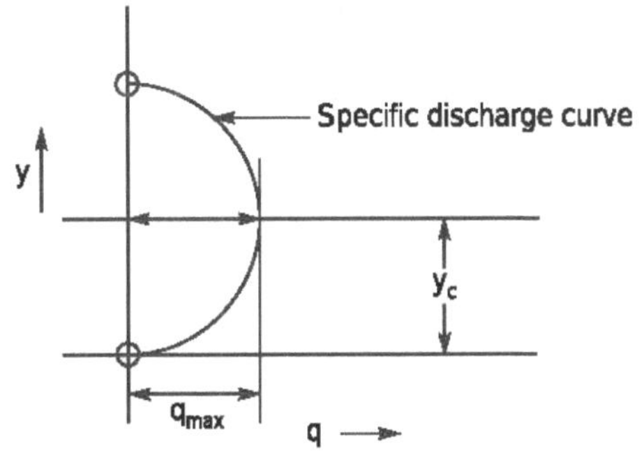

Fig. 15.22

Differentiating eq. (15.26) w.r.t. y, we get

$$2q\frac{dq}{dy} = 2g\,[2Ey - 3y^2] = 0$$

$$\therefore \quad 2Ey = 3y^2$$

$$\therefore \quad y = \frac{2}{3}E = y_c$$

$\therefore$ At $q_{max,}$ depth of flow is critical.

15.7.2 Specific Force Diagram

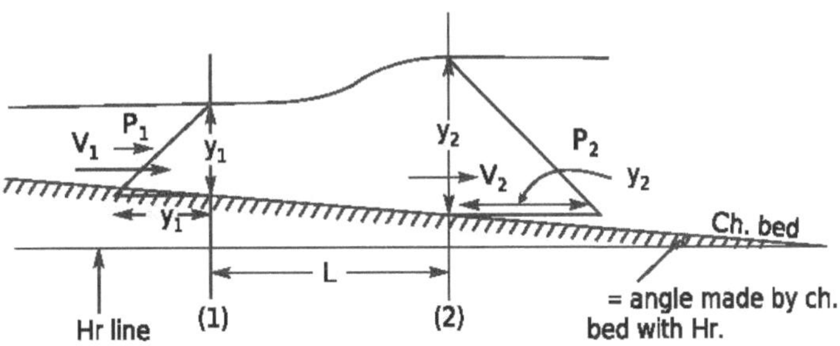

Fig. 15.23

Consider two sections (1) and (2), L distance apart in non-rectangular channel having non-uniform flow as shown in Fig. 15.23. Considering flow in channel equal to Q and weight density of water as γ, we have rate of change of momentum between section (1) and (2) = Forces acting on the volume of water contained between section (1) and (2).

$$\therefore \quad \frac{\gamma Q}{g}(V_2 - V_1) = P_1 - P_2 + W \sin \theta - \text{Friction between (1) and (2)}$$

Neglecting $W \sin \theta$ and Friction, as their values will be very small, we get

$$\frac{\gamma Q}{g}(V_2 - V_1) = P_1 - P_2.$$

$$\therefore \quad \frac{\gamma Q}{g}\left(\frac{Q}{A_2} - \frac{Q}{A_1}\right) = \gamma A_1 \bar{x}_1 - \gamma A_2 \bar{x}_2$$

Here, $\bar{x}_1$ and $\bar{x}_2$ equal to distance of centre of gravity of cross-sectional areas A_1 and A_2 from channel bed.

$$\therefore \quad \gamma A_1 \bar{x}_1 \frac{\gamma Q^2}{gA_1} = \gamma A_2 \bar{x}_2 \frac{\gamma Q^2}{gA_2} \qquad \text{...(15.27)}$$

i.e. (Pressure + Momentum) at section (1) = (Pressure + Momentum) at section (2), etc.

i.e. (P + M) is constant, and is defined as specific force, F.

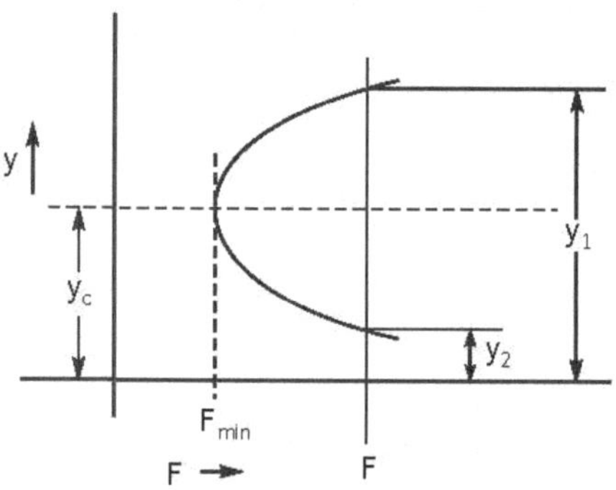

Fig. 15.24

$$\therefore \quad F = (P + M) \text{ at a given section}$$

$$= \frac{1}{2}\gamma y^2 + \frac{\gamma q}{g} v \text{ for rectangular channel}$$

$$= \frac{1}{2}\gamma y^2 + \frac{\gamma q^2}{gy} \text{ as } v = \frac{q}{y} \text{ for rectangular channel}$$

$$\therefore \quad F = \frac{1}{2}\gamma\left(y^2 + \frac{2q^2}{gy}\right) \qquad \text{...(15.28)}$$

In this case also, as $y \to 0, F \to \infty$ and as $y \to \infty, F \to \infty$.

$\therefore$ F if minimum for some value of y.

$$\therefore \quad \frac{dF}{dy} = 2y - \frac{2q^2}{gy^2} = 0$$

$$\therefore \quad 2y\left(1 - \frac{q^2}{gy^3}\right) = 0$$

$$\therefore \quad 1 = \frac{q^2}{gy^3}$$

$$\therefore \quad y^3 = \frac{q^2}{g}$$

$$\therefore \quad y = \left(\frac{q^2}{g}\right)^{1/3} = y_c$$

Thus at F to be minimum, depth of flow is y_c. Thus it can be seen that at critical conditions,

(*i*) Specific energy is minimum.

(*ii*) Discharge is maximum.

(*iii*) Specific force is minimum.

(*iv*) Froude number is unity.

(*v*) $y_c = \left(\frac{q^2}{g}\right)^{1/3} = \frac{2}{3}E_{min}$.

For given value of F, there are two depths possible y_1 and y_2, see Fig. 15.24. They are defined as **conjugate depths.**

15.7.3 Calculation of y_c for non-rectangular Section

From eq. (15.27), we have, specific force, F as

$$F = \gamma\left(\frac{Q^2}{gA} + A\bar{x}\right), \text{ for non-rectangular channel section} \quad \text{...(15.29)}$$

Here, A is a $f(y)$, as can be seen in Fig. 15.25.

In Fig. 15.25 consider top width as T and a small strip of area dA and thickness dy at top of the area A so that new area = $(A + dA)$, and $dA = Tdy$. Taking moment of area A and (Tdy) about free surface.

$$\left[A(\bar{x} + dy) + T(dy)\left(\frac{dy}{2}\right)\right] - (A\bar{x}) = \text{change in value of } (A\bar{x}),$$

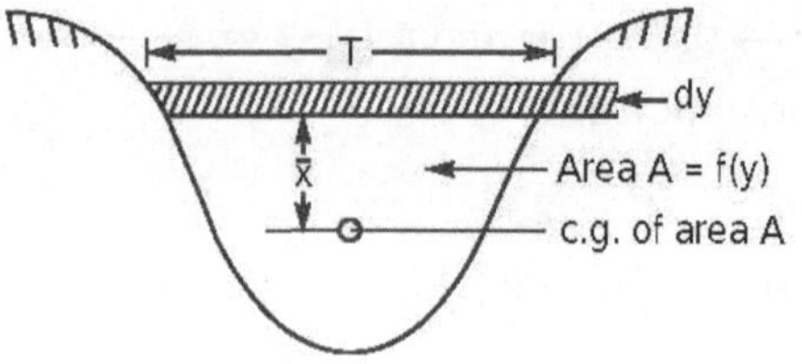

Fig. 15.25

i.e., change in moment of original area about free surface.

$$= d(A\bar{x})$$

Thus, $$d(A\bar{x}) = A\bar{x} + A\,dy + \frac{T}{2}(dy)^2 - A\bar{x}$$

The term containing $(dy)^2$ can be neglected being very small.

$\therefore$ $$d(A\bar{x}) = A\,dy$$

$\therefore$ $$\frac{d}{dy}(A\bar{x}) = A$$

$\therefore$ Differentiating eq. (15.29) w.r.t. to y, we get

$$\frac{dF}{dy} = \frac{d}{dy}\left(\frac{Q^2}{gA}\right) + \frac{d}{dy}(A\bar{x})$$

Now we have got that $\frac{d}{dy}(A\bar{x}) = A$

We can also get value of $\frac{d}{dy}\left(\frac{Q^2}{gA}\right)$ *i.e.*, $\frac{Q^2}{g}\frac{d}{dy}\left(\frac{1}{A}\right)$ as under:

As A is a $f(y)$, $\frac{d}{dy}\left(\frac{1}{A}\right) = -\frac{1}{A^2}\frac{dA}{dy}$ and $\frac{dA}{dy} = T$ from $dA = T\,dy$.

$\therefore$ $$\frac{d}{dy}\left(\frac{Q^2}{gA}\right) = -\frac{Q^2}{g}\frac{\left(\frac{dA}{dy}\right)}{A^2} = -\frac{Q^2T}{gA^2}$$

$\therefore$ $$\frac{dF}{dy} = -\frac{Q^2T}{gA} + A = 0$$

$\therefore$ $$A\left(1 - \frac{Q^2T}{gA^3}\right) = 0$$

$\therefore$ $$1 - \frac{Q^2T}{gA^3} = 0$$

$$\therefore \qquad \frac{Q^2T}{gA^3} = 1 \qquad \text{...(15.30)}$$

Hence for non-rectangular channel section y_c can be calculated from eq. (15.30).

15.8 SOLVED PROBLEMS

■ **Problem 15.12:** *For a constant specific energy of 3 kg-m per kg, calculate maximum discharge that may occur in a rectangular channel 6 m wide. What is Froude number and depth of flow in channel?*

Solution: For E = constant, q is maximum when flow is critical.

$$\therefore \qquad y = y_c = \frac{2}{3}E = \frac{2}{3}(3) = 2\text{m}$$

Also, $$y_c = \left(\frac{q^2}{g}\right)^{1/3}$$

$$\therefore \qquad 2 = \left(\frac{q^2}{9.81}\right)^{1/3}$$

$$\therefore \qquad q^2 = (2)^3\,(9.81) = 78.48$$

$$\therefore \qquad q_{max} = 8.85 \text{ m}^3\text{/s/m} \quad \therefore \quad Q = 6 \times 8.85 = 53.1 \text{ m}^3\text{/s} \qquad \text{...(Ans.)}$$

depth of flow $$= y_c = 2\text{ m},\ F = \frac{q}{\sqrt{gy^3}} = \frac{8.85}{\sqrt{9.81 \times 8}} = \frac{8.85}{8.85} = 1$$

$\therefore$ $F = 1$ as flow is critical at y_c.

■ **Problem 15.13:** *A trapezoidal channel has bottom width of 4 m and side slope 1 : 1, depth of flow y = 2 m, and discharge = 24 m³/s. Find specific energy, critical depth and type flow.*

Solution:

$$E = y + \frac{Q^2}{2gA^2}$$

$$\therefore \qquad E = 2 + \frac{(24)^2}{2g(2)} = 4.44 \text{ m} \qquad \text{...(Ans.)}$$

$$A = (B + my)y = (4 + 2)2 = 12 \text{ m}^2$$

For critical depth calculation in trapezoidal channel, $\dfrac{Q^2T}{gA^3} = 1$

$$\therefore \qquad \frac{Q^2}{g} = \frac{A^3}{T}$$

$$A = (B + y_c)y_c \text{ as } m = 1$$

$$T = B + 2y_c \text{ as } m = 1.$$

$$\therefore \quad \frac{Q^2}{g} = \frac{(24)^2}{9.81} = 58.7 = \frac{[(B+y_c)\,y_c]^3}{(B+2y_c)}$$

$$\therefore \quad \frac{(4+y_c)^3\,y_c^3}{(4+2y_c)} = 58.7$$

By trial and error, y_c 1.35 m

∴ Flow is tranquil as $y_c < 2$ m, given depth of flow.

■ **Problem 15.14:** *A triangular channel section has apex = 120°. Find y_c for $Q = 2\ m^3/s$.*

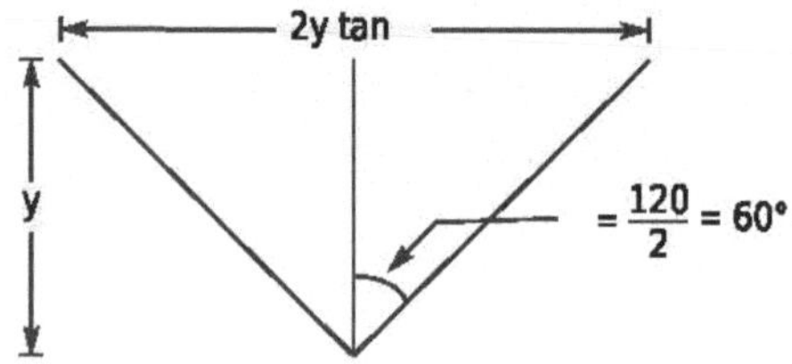

Fig. 15.26

Solution:

$$\text{Top width } T = 2y \tan\theta$$

$$A = 2\left(\frac{1}{2} y \tan\theta \cdot y\right)$$

$$= y^2 \tan\theta$$

For non-rectangular channel section, y_c can be calculated by

$$\frac{Q^2 T}{gA^3} = 1$$

$$\therefore \quad \frac{Q^2}{g} = \frac{A^3}{T} = \frac{(y_c^2 \tan\theta)^3}{2y_c \tan\theta} = \frac{y_c^6 \tan^3\theta}{2y_c \tan\theta}$$

$$\therefore \quad \frac{4}{9.81} = \frac{y_c^5 \tan^2\theta}{2}$$

$$\therefore \quad y_c^{\,5} = \frac{8}{9.81\,(1.73)^2} = \frac{8}{9.81 \times 3} = 0.27$$

$$\therefore \quad y_c = \mathbf{0.77\ m.}$$ ...(**Ans.**)

■ **Problem 15.15:** *On what slope a 3 m wide rect. channel be constructed so that critical flow occurs at normal depth of flow of 1.0 m? Take n = 0.014.*

$$y_n = y_c = 1\ m$$

$$A_c = 3 \times 1 = 3\ m^2.$$

Solution:

$$\text{Top width} = T = 3 \text{ m}$$

$$\frac{Q^2}{g} = \frac{A^3}{T}$$

$$\therefore \quad Q^2 = 9.81\frac{(3)^3}{3} = 88.29$$

$$\therefore \quad Q = 9.39 \text{ m}^3/\text{s}$$

$$\therefore \quad 5.42 = \frac{1}{n} A R^{2/3} S_o^{1/2}$$

$$R = \frac{A}{P} = \frac{3.}{3+2(1)} = \frac{3}{5} = 0.6$$

$$\therefore \quad 5.42 = \frac{1}{0.014}(3)\,(0.6)^{2/3} S_o^{1/2}$$

$$\therefore \quad S_o^{1/2} = \frac{5.42 \times 0.014}{3 \times 0.71} = 0.0356$$

$$\therefore \quad S_o = 1.26 \times 10^{-3}.$$ ...**(Ans.)**

■ **Problem 15.16:** *A circular pipe of 1m diameter is flowing half full at critical condition. Find Q and critical slope. Take n = 0.015.*

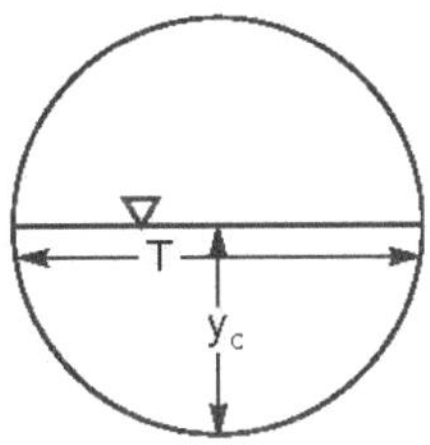

Fig. 15.27

Solution:

For critical condition, we have $\frac{Q^2 T}{g A^3} = 1$.

$$\therefore \quad \frac{Q^2}{g} = \frac{A^3}{T} = \frac{\left(\frac{1}{2}\frac{\pi}{4}(1)^2\right)^3}{1.0} = 0.06$$

$$\therefore \quad Q^2 = 0.06 \times 9.81 \quad \therefore \quad Q = \mathbf{0.7672 \text{ m}^3/\text{s}}$$

$$Q = \frac{1}{n} A R^{2/3} S_o^{1/2}$$

$$R = \frac{A}{P} = \frac{\left(\frac{\pi}{4}D^2\right)\frac{1}{2}}{\frac{1}{2}\pi D} = \frac{D}{4} = \frac{1}{4}$$

$$\therefore \quad 0.7672 = \frac{2}{0.015}(0.39)\left(\frac{1}{4}\right)^{2/3} S_o^{1/2}$$

$$\therefore \quad S_o^{1/2} = \frac{0.7672 \times 0.015}{0.39 \times 2.53} = 0.011$$

$$\therefore \quad S_o = 1.36 \times 10^{-4}. \qquad \text{...(Ans.)}$$

15.9 HYDRAULIC JUMP

When water flowing with high value of kinetic energy ($F_1 > 1$) happens to meet the flow with very low value of KE ($F_2 < 1$), then there is a sudden rise in the depth of flow, known as **hydraulic jump.** This rise is due to corresponding increase in potential energy. This happens at the toe of spillway, where water from crest of spillway is rushing to toe with very high KE and has to flow on almost horizontal apron and therefore there is sudden loss of KE resulting in formation of hydraulic jump. It is coupled with loss in energy which reduces load on foundation work at toe to spillway. Thus formation of hydraulic jump is beneficial in the design of energy dissipating works at toe of spillway. Flow before jump is supercritical type with $F_1 > 1$ and flow after jump is subcritical type with $F_2 < 1$.

Hydraulic jump in rectangular horizontal channel:

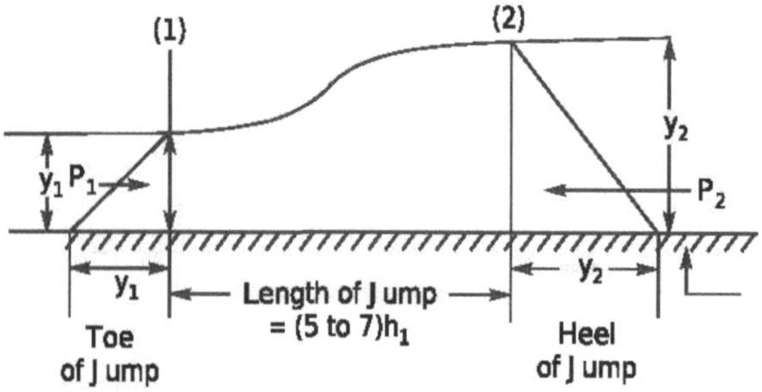

Fig. 15.28

Note:

(*i*) height of jump $= y_2 - y_1 = h_j$

(*ii*) y_2, y_1 are conjugate or sequent depths.

(*iii*) length of jump = (5 to 7) h_j.

Consider sections (1) and (2) in Fig. 15.28 and apply momentum principles which we have consider earlier while defining specific force.

$\therefore \quad (P_1 + M_1)$ at section (1) = $(P_2 + M_2)$ at section (2).

Here $$P_1 = \frac{1}{2}\gamma y_1^2 \quad \text{and} \quad P_2 = \frac{1}{2}\gamma y_2^2$$

$$\therefore \quad \frac{1}{2}\gamma y_1^2 + \frac{\gamma q}{g}(v_1) = \frac{1}{2}\gamma y_2^2 + \frac{\gamma q}{g}(v_2)$$

$$\therefore \quad \frac{1}{2}\gamma (y_2^2 - y_1^2) = \frac{\gamma q}{g}(v_1 - v_2) = \frac{\gamma q}{g}\left(\frac{q}{y_1} - \frac{q}{y_2}\right)$$

Here γ is common on both sides.

$$\therefore \quad \frac{1}{2}(y_2 + y_1)(y_2 - y_1) = \frac{q^2}{g}\left(\frac{1}{y_1} - \frac{1}{y_2}\right)$$

$$= \frac{q^2}{g}\left(\frac{y_2 - y_1}{y_1 y_2}\right)$$

$$\therefore \quad \frac{q^2}{g} = \frac{1}{2} y_1 y_2 (y_1 + y_2) \qquad \text{...(15.31)}$$

This is the basic equation governing formation of hydraulic jump. If y_1 and y_2, which are depths before and after formation of jump are measured accurately, one can calculate q. Thus hydraulic jump can be used as discharge measuring device. Equation (15.31) can be expressed as quadratic equation,

$$\frac{2q^2}{g y_1} = y_1 y_2 + y_2^2$$

$$\therefore \quad y_2^2 + y_1 y_2 - \frac{2q^2}{g y_1} = 0$$

$$\therefore \quad y_2 = \frac{-y_1 \pm \sqrt{y_1^2 - 4\left(-\frac{2q^2}{g y_1}\right)}}{2}$$

$$= \frac{1}{2}\left[-y_1 + \sqrt{y_1^2\left(1 + \frac{8q^2}{g y_1^3}\right)}\right]$$

$$= \frac{1}{2} y_1 \left[-1 + \sqrt{1 + 8F_1^2}\right], \text{ as } \frac{q^2}{g y_1^3} = F_1^2 \qquad \text{...(15.32)}$$

Thus, depth after jump can be worked out if Froude number $F_1 = \frac{v_1}{\sqrt{g y_1}} = \frac{q}{\sqrt{g y_1^3}}$ is known and y_1 depth before jump is known. Equation (15.32) can also be written in the form,

$$y_1 = \frac{1}{2} y_2 \left[-1 + \sqrt{1 + 8F_2^2} \right], \text{ here } F_2^2 = \frac{q^2}{g y_2^3}$$

Note that if y_1 is required, then on RHS we have y_2 and F_2 and if y_2 is required, then on RHS we have y_1 and F_1. F_1 and F_2 are values of Froude number before and after the jump, and are given by

$$F_1^2 = \frac{q^2}{g y_1^3} \text{ and } F_2^2 = \frac{q^2}{g y_2^3}$$

here, y_1 and y_2 are known as conjugate or sequent depths,

Height of jump = $h_j = y_2 - y_1$ and

Length of jump L_j = 5 to 7 $(y_2 - y_1)$ *i.e.*, (5 to 7) h_j.

In Fig. 15.28, portion on LHS is Toe of jump and portion on RHS of jump is known as heel of jump.

E_j = Loss of energy in formation of hydraulic jump and can be worked out as under:

Let E_1 = specific energy before jump and E_2 = specific energy after jump.

$$\therefore \quad E_j = E_1 - E_2$$

$$= \left(y_1 + \frac{v_1^2}{2g} \right) - \left(y_2 + \frac{v_2^2}{2g} \right)$$

$$= \left(y_1 + \frac{q^2}{2g y_1^2} \right) - \left(y_2 + \frac{q^2}{2g y_2^2} \right)$$

$$= (y_1 - y_2) + \frac{q^2}{2g} \left(\frac{1}{y_1^2} - \frac{1}{y_2^2} \right)$$

$$= (y_1 - y_2) + \frac{1}{2} \left[\frac{1}{2} y_1 y_2 (y_1 + y_2) \right] \left(\frac{y_2^2 - y_1^2}{y_1^2 y_2^2} \right)$$

as $\frac{q^2}{g} = \frac{1}{2}(y_1 y_2)(y_1 + y_2)$ as per eq. (15.31)

$$\therefore \quad E_1 = -(y_2 + y_1) + \frac{(y_1 + y_2)(y_2 - y_1)(y_2 + y_1)}{4 y_1 y_2}$$

$$= (y_2 - y_1) \left[-1 + \frac{(y_2 + y_1)^2}{4 y_1 y_2} \right]$$

$$= (y_2 - y_1) \frac{(y_2 - y_1)^2}{4 y_1 y_2}$$

$$\therefore \quad E_1 = \frac{(y_2 - y_1)^3}{4 y_1 y_2} \text{ m per kg per m width of channel} \qquad \text{...(15.33)}$$

$\therefore$ Power dissipated = P = $\gamma Q E_j$ watts = $\rho g Q E_j$ watts. ...(15.34)

Depending on value of Froude number $F_1 = 4$ to 17 value of energy dissipation will be between 45% to 85% of E_1. Note that for formation of hydraulic jump $F_1 > 1$ and $F_2 < 1$. Hydraulic jump is a practical example of RVF (rapidly varied flow) in rectangular channel.

15.9.1 Solved Problems

■ **Problem 15.17:** *A rectangular channel 4 m wide carries a discharge of 32 m³/s. Find if hydraulic jump will occur for initial depth of 0.5 m and if so, find sequent depth and power dissipated. Show by sketch salient feature of the jump.*

Solution:

$$Q = 32, B = 4, \quad \therefore \quad q = \frac{Q}{B} = 8 = v_1 y_1 = v_2 y_2$$

$$\therefore \qquad v_1 = \frac{q}{y_1} = \frac{8}{0.5} = 16 \text{ m/s}.$$

$$F_1 = \frac{v_1}{\sqrt{g y_1}} = \frac{16}{2.21} = 7.2 > 1$$

$\therefore$ Jump will occur

$$y_2 = \frac{1}{2} y_1 \left[-1 + \sqrt{1 + 8F_1^2} \right] = 4.85 \text{ m}$$

$$E_j = \frac{(y_2 - y_1)^3}{4 y_1 y_2} = 9 \text{ m per kg per m width of channel}$$

Salient feature of the jump.

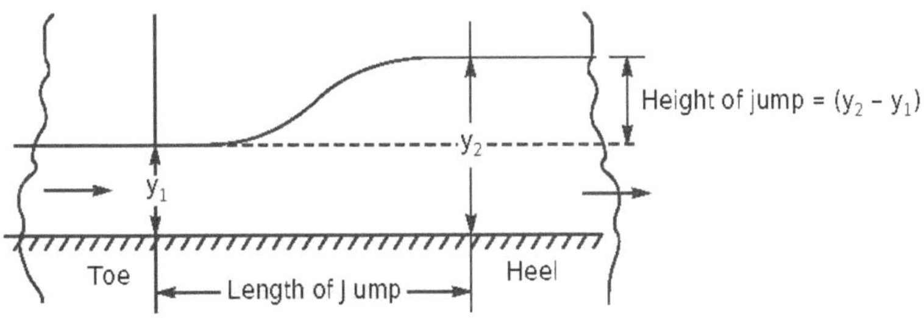

Fig. 15.29

Length of jump, $L_j = 5$ to $7(y_2 - y_1) = 5(4.85 - 0.5)$

$= 5 \times 4.35 =$ **21.75 m**

Height of jump, $h_j = y_2 - y_1 = 4.35$ m

Power dissipated in jump $= \gamma Q E_j$, here γ is wt. density of water

$= \rho g = 1000 \times 9.81 = 9810$ N/m³

$= 9810\ (32)\ (9)$

$=$ **2825 kW**

Check, $$F_2 = \frac{q}{\sqrt{gy_2^3}} = \frac{8}{\sqrt{9.81(4.85)^3}} = \frac{8}{33.45}$$

$$= 0.239 < 1, \textbf{ OK.}$$

■ **Problem 15.18:** *A rectangular channel carries a discharge of 2 m³/s per m width of the channel. If $h_f = 2.75$ m, find conjugate depths.*

Solution: $$h_f = E_j = \frac{(y_2 - y_1)^3}{4y_1y_2} = \frac{y_1^3\left(\frac{y_2}{y_1} - 1\right)^3}{4y_1y_2}$$

∴ $$\frac{E_j}{y_1} = \frac{\left(\frac{y_2}{y_1} - 1\right)^3}{4\left(\frac{y_2}{y_1}\right)}$$

Put $$\frac{y_2}{y_1} = x$$

∴ $$\frac{E_j}{y_1} = \frac{(x-1)^3}{4x} = \frac{2.75}{y_1} \qquad \text{...(1)}$$

Also, $$\frac{y_2}{y_1} = \frac{1}{2}\left[-1 + \sqrt{1 + 8F_1^2}\right]$$

$$= \frac{1}{2}\left[-1 + \sqrt{1 + \frac{8q^2}{gy_1^3}}\right], \quad \text{here } q = 2 \text{ m}^3\text{/s}$$

∴ $$x = \frac{1}{2}\left[-1 + \sqrt{1 + \frac{8(2)^2}{9.81\, y_1^3}}\right]$$

∴ $$2x = \left[-1 + \sqrt{1 + \frac{3.26}{y_1^3}}\right]$$

$$(2x + 1)^2 = 1 + \frac{3.26}{y_1^3} \qquad \text{...(2)}$$

Also from (1), $$(x - 1)^3 = \frac{11x}{y_1} \qquad \text{...(3)}$$

∴ $$y_1 = \frac{11x}{(x-1)^3}$$, putting this value in eqn. (2),

$$(2x + 1)^2 = 1 + \frac{3.26(x-1)^9}{(11x)^3}$$

$$\therefore \quad (2x + 1)^2 - 1 = (2.4\times10^{-3})\frac{(x-1)^9}{x^3}$$

By trial and error, for $x = 8.6$,

LHS = 330 and RHS = 319, which is nearly equal.

$$\therefore \quad x = \mathbf{8.6}$$

$$\therefore \quad y_1 = \frac{11x}{(x-1)^3} = \frac{11(8.6)}{(7.6)^3} = \mathbf{0.215\ m}$$

$$\therefore \quad F_1 = \frac{q}{\sqrt{gy_1^3}} = \frac{2}{\sqrt{9.81\times(0.215)^3}} = 6.40 > 1 \text{ OK}$$

$$\therefore \quad y_2 = \frac{1}{2}y_1\left[-1+\sqrt{1+8F_1^2}\right] = 1.84$$

$\therefore$ Sequent depths are $y_1 = 0.215$ m

and $\quad y_2 = 1.84$ m

Check:

$$F_2 = \frac{q}{\sqrt{gy_2^3}} = \frac{2}{\sqrt{9.81\times(1.84)^3}} = \frac{2}{7.836}$$

$$= 0.255 < 1 \textbf{ OK}$$

$\therefore \quad y_1 = 0.215$ m ...(Ans.)

and $\quad y_2 = 1.84$ m. ...(Ans.)

■ **Problem 15.19**: *Show that for hydraulic jump in a rectangular channel,*

$$F_2^2 = \frac{8F_1^2}{(-1+\sqrt{1+8F_1^2})^3}.$$

Solution: We have

$$F_1^2 = \frac{v_1^2}{gy_1} = \frac{q^2}{gy_1^3} \qquad \text{as } q = v_1y_1 = v_2y_2$$

and

$$F_2^2 = \frac{q^2}{gy_2^3}$$

$$\therefore \quad \frac{F_2^2}{F_1^2} = \frac{q^2}{gy_2^3}\times\frac{gy_1^3}{q^2} = \left(\frac{y_1}{y_2}\right)^3 \qquad ...(1)$$

For hydraulic jump,

$$\frac{y_2}{y_1} = \frac{1}{2}\left[-1+\sqrt{1+8F_1^2}\right]$$

$$\therefore \qquad \left[\frac{y_2}{y_1}\right]^3 = \frac{1}{8}\left[-1+\sqrt{1+8F_1^2}\right]^3$$

$$= \frac{F_1^2}{F_2^2}, \text{ from eq. (1)}$$

$$\therefore \qquad F_2^2 = \frac{8F_1^2}{\left(-1+\sqrt{1+8F_1^2}\right)^3}. \qquad \text{...(Ans.)}$$

■ **Problem 15.20:** *If value of Froude number after jump in a rectangular channel is 0.4, find Froude number of approaching critical flow.*

Solution:

$$\left(\frac{y_1}{y_2}\right) = \frac{1}{2}\left[-1+\sqrt{1+8F_2^2}\right]$$

$$\therefore \qquad \left(\frac{y_1}{y_2}\right)^3 = \frac{1}{8}\left[-1+\sqrt{1+8F_2^2}\right] = \frac{F_2^2}{F_1^2}$$

$$\therefore \qquad F_1^2 = \frac{8F_2^2}{(-1+\sqrt{1+8F_2^2})^3} = \frac{8(0.4)^2}{(-1+\sqrt{1+8(0.16)})^3}$$

$$\therefore \qquad = \frac{1.28}{0.132} = 9.69$$

$$\therefore \qquad F_1^2 = 3.11. \qquad \text{...(Ans.)}$$

■ **Problem 15.21:** *At what value of Froude number of incoming flow, would the loss due to hydraulic jump be fifty per cent of initial specific energy? Also find value of Froude number after the jump.*

Solution:

$$E_1 = y_1 + \frac{v_1^2}{2g} = y_1 + \frac{q^2}{2gy_1^2} \text{ as } v_1 = \frac{q}{y_1}$$

$$\therefore \qquad E_1 = y_1\left(1+\frac{q^2}{2gy_1^3}\right)$$

Now,

$$F_1^2 = \frac{v_1^2}{gy_1} = \frac{q^2}{gy_1^3}$$

$$\therefore \qquad E_1 = y_1\left(1+\frac{F_1^2}{2}\right) \qquad \text{...(1)}$$

Now,

$$E_j = \frac{(y_2-y_1)^3}{4y_1y_2} = \frac{y_1^3\left(\frac{y_2}{y_1}-1\right)^3}{4y_1y_2}$$

$$\therefore \qquad \frac{E_j}{y_1} = \frac{\left(\frac{y_2}{y_1} - 1\right)^3}{4\left(\frac{y_2}{y_1}\right)} \qquad ...(2)$$

But $\qquad E_j = \frac{1}{2}E_1$, given

$$\therefore \qquad E_j = \frac{1}{2}y_1\left(1 + \frac{F_1^2}{2}\right) \text{ from (1)}$$

$$\therefore \qquad \frac{E_j}{y_1} = \frac{1}{2}\left(1 + \frac{F_1^2}{2}\right) \qquad ...(3)$$

From (2) and (3), we get

$$\frac{1}{2}\left(1 + \frac{F_1^2}{2}\right) = \frac{\left(\frac{y_2}{y_1} - 1\right)^3}{4\left(\frac{y_2}{y_1}\right)}$$

But $\qquad \frac{y_2}{y_1} = \frac{1}{2}\left[-1 + \sqrt{8F_1^2 + 1}\right]$

$$\therefore \qquad \frac{1}{2}\left(1 + \frac{F_1^2}{2}\right) = \frac{\left[\frac{1}{2}(-1 + \sqrt{8F_1^2 + 1}) - 1\right]^3}{4\left[\frac{1}{2}(-1 + \sqrt{8F_1^2 + 1})\right]}$$

$$= \frac{\frac{1}{8}(\sqrt{8F_1^2 + 1} - 3)^3}{2(\sqrt{8F_1^2 + 1} - 1)}$$

$$\therefore \qquad 8\left(1 + \frac{F_1^2}{2}\right) = \frac{(\sqrt{8F_1^2 + 1} - 3)^3}{(\sqrt{8F_1^2 + 1} - 1)}$$

$$\therefore \qquad 8\left(1 + \frac{F_1^2}{2}\right)(\sqrt{8F_1^2 + 1} - 1) = (\sqrt{8F_1^2 + 1} - 3)^3 \qquad ...(4)$$

Put $\qquad x = \sqrt{8F_1^2 + 1}$

$$\therefore \qquad x^2 = 8F_1^2 + 1$$

$$\therefore \qquad F_1^2 = \frac{x^2 - 1}{8}$$

Putting these values in eq. (4), we get

$$8\left(1+\frac{x^2-1}{16}\right)(x-1) = (x-3)^3$$

$$(x^2+15)(x-1) = 2(x-3)^3$$

$$\therefore \quad x^3 + 39x = 17x^2 + 39$$

By trial and error, $x = 14.5$ gives

$$\text{LHS} = \text{RHS} = 3613$$

$$\therefore \quad x = 14.5 = \sqrt{8F_1^2+1}$$

$$\therefore \quad F_1 = \mathbf{5.11}$$ ...(Ans.)

$$F_2^2 = \frac{8F_1^2}{(-1+\sqrt{8F_1^2+1})^3} = \frac{8(26.11)}{(-1+14.5)^3}$$

$$= \frac{8\times 26.11}{2460} = 0.085$$

$$\therefore \quad F_2 = \mathbf{0.29.}$$ ...(Ans.)

■ **Problem 15.22:** *If in a rectangular channel, $F_1 = 10$ and $E_j = 3.2$ m, find*

1. *sequent depths*
2. *q*
3. *F_2 and*
4. *% of initial energy lost in HJ.*

Solution:

$$\frac{y_2}{y_1} = \frac{1}{2}(-1+\sqrt{8F_1^2+1})$$

$$= \frac{1}{2}[-1+\sqrt{8(10)^2+1}] = \frac{27.30}{2} = \mathbf{13.65}$$

$$E_j = \frac{(y_2-y_1)^3}{4y_1y_2}$$

$$\therefore \quad \frac{E_j}{y_1} = \frac{\left(\frac{y_2}{y_1}-1\right)^3}{4\left(\frac{y_2}{y_1}\right)}$$

$$\therefore \quad \frac{3.2}{y_1} = \frac{(13.65-1)^3}{4(13.65)} = 37$$

$$\therefore \quad y_1 = \frac{3.7}{37} = \mathbf{0.086\ m}$$

$$\therefore \quad y_2 = 13.65(0.086) = \mathbf{1.18\ m}$$ ...(Ans. 1)

$$F_1 = \frac{v_1}{\sqrt{gy_1}} = 10 \quad \therefore \quad v_1 = 10\sqrt{g(0.086)} = \mathbf{9.2\ m/s}$$

$\therefore$
$$q = v_1 y_1 = 9.2(0.086)$$
$$= \mathbf{0.79\ m^3/s/m}$$ **...(Ans. 2)**

$$F_2 = \frac{v_2}{\sqrt{gy_2}} = \frac{q}{y_2\sqrt{gy^2}} = \frac{0.79}{1.18\sqrt{9.81 \times 1.18}}$$
$$= 0.196 < 1 \ \textbf{OK}$$ **...(Ans. 3)**

$$E_1 = y_1 + \frac{v_1^2}{2g}$$
$$= 0.086 + \frac{(9.2)^2}{2g}$$
$$= 4.39$$

$\therefore$
$$\frac{E_j}{E_1} = \frac{3.2}{4.39} = 0:727$$

i.e., 72.7% of initial energy lost in H.J. **...(Ans. 4)**

■ **Problem 15.23:** *Given $v_2 = 0.8$ m/s, $y_2 = 1.75$ m, find depth before jump, E_j and power dissipated.*

Solution:

$$F_2 = \frac{v_2}{\sqrt{gy_2}} = \frac{0.8}{\sqrt{g(1.75)}} = 0.193$$

$$\frac{y_1}{y_2} = \frac{1}{2}(-1 + \sqrt{8F_2^2 + 1}) = 0.07$$

$\therefore$
$$y_1 = 0.07 \times 1.75 = \mathbf{0.122\ m}$$

$$E_j = \frac{(y_2 - y_1)^3}{4y_1y_2} = 5 \text{ m}$$

$$q = v_2 y_2$$
$$= 0.8 \times 1.75$$
$$= 1.4$$

$$P = \gamma q E_j$$
$$= 9810\,(1.4)5 = \mathbf{68.67\ kW/m.}$$

■ **Problem 15.24:** *An overflow spillway has its crest level at 136 m and its apron at elevation of 102 m. Estimate tail water elevation required to form hydraulic jump when energy line just u/s of spillway crest is at elevation of 138 m. Take $c_d = 0.735$.*

Solution:
$$H = 138 - 136 = 2 \text{ m}$$

$$q = \frac{2}{3} c_d \sqrt{2g}\, H^{3/2} = \frac{2}{3}(0.735)\sqrt{2g}\,(2)^{2/3}$$
$$= 6.139 \text{ m}^3\text{/s/m.}$$

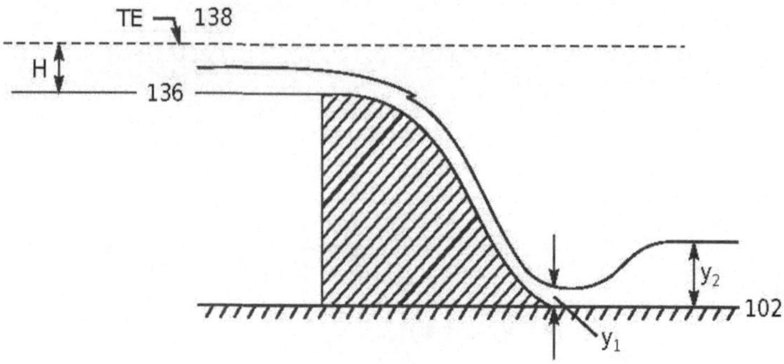

Fig. 15.30

$$E_1 = 138 - 102 = 36$$

$$= y_1 + \frac{v_1^2}{2g} = y_1 + \frac{q^2}{2gy_1^2}$$

$$\therefore \quad y_1 + \frac{(6.139)^2}{2g(y_1)^2} = 36$$

$$\therefore \quad y_1 = 0.2317 \text{ m.} \quad \therefore \quad v_1 = \frac{q}{y_1}$$

$$= 26.49$$

$$F_1 = \frac{v_1}{\sqrt{gy_1}}$$

$$= 17.57$$

$$y_2 = \frac{1}{2}(0.2317)[-1 + \sqrt{8F_1^2 + 1}]$$

$$= 5.644 \text{ m.}$$

∴ Tail water elevation = 102 + 5.644 = **107.644 m.** ...**(Ans.)**

■ **Problem 15.25:** *If y_1 and y_2 are alternate depths in rectangular channel, show that*

$$y_c^3 = \frac{2y_1^2 y_2^2}{y_1 + y_2}$$

and

$$E = \frac{y_1^2 + y_1 y_2 + y_2^2}{(y_1 + y_2)}.$$

Solution:

We have

$$q = y_1 v_1 = y_2 v_2$$

$$E = y_1 + \frac{v_1^2}{2g} = y_2 + \frac{v_2^2}{2g}$$

$$\therefore \quad y_1 + \frac{q^2}{2gy_1^2} = y_2 + \frac{q^2}{2gy_2^2}$$

$$\therefore \qquad y_1 - y_2 = \frac{q^2}{2g}\left[\frac{1}{y_2^2} - \frac{1}{y_1^2}\right]$$

$$= \frac{y_c^3}{2}\left[\frac{y_1^2 - y_2^2}{y_1^2 y_2^2}\right] \text{ as } \frac{q^2}{g} = y_c^3$$

$$\therefore \qquad y_c^3 = \frac{2\, y_1^2 y_2^2}{(y_1 + y_2)} \qquad \text{...(Ans. 1)}$$

$$E = y_1 + \frac{q^2}{2gy_1^2} \text{ ...... here } \frac{q^2}{g} = y_c^3 = \frac{2y_1^2 y_2^2}{y_1 + y_2}$$

$$= y_1 + \frac{1}{2y_1^2}\left(\frac{2y_1^2 y_2^2}{y_1 + y_2}\right)$$

$$= y_1 + \frac{y_2^2}{y_1 + y_2}$$

$$= \frac{y_1^2 + y_1 y_2 + y_2^2}{y_1 + y_2}. \qquad \text{...(Ans. 2)}$$

15.10 GRADUALLY VARIED FLOW IN PRISMATIC AND NON-PRISMATIC CHANNELS

When some obstruction in the path of flow in rivers or channels is introduced, such as dam or weir constructed across a river, then just up stream of this obstruction we find that flow undergoes gradual variation in depth and this type of flow is known as GVF in channels.

Channels having geometric cross-section are defined as prismatic channels and these with irregular cross-section are defined as non-prismatic channels.

We will first try to develop dynamic equation governing GVF in prismatic and non-prismatic channel.

15.10.1 Dynamic Equation Governing GVF

Consider a non-prismatic channel section as shown in Fig. 15.31 (*a*) and (*b*).

Consider sections (1) and (2) in Fig. 15.13*x* distance apart and let depths at flow at these sections be y_1 and y_2 and their corresponding datum be Z_1 and Z_2. Let c/s area at section *A*-*A* be any irregular area as shown in Fig. 15.31 (*b*). Let *T* be top width and area of strip of thickness *dy* at top be *dA*, given by

$$dA = Tdy$$

Let c/s area be a function of *y*.

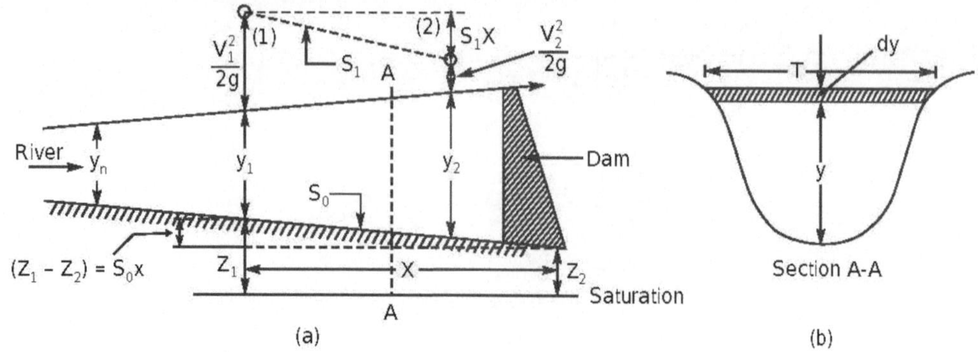

Fig. 15.31

Now taking total energy (TE) at sections (1) and (2), we get

$$Z_1 + y_1 + \frac{V_1^2}{2g} = Z_2 + y_2 + \frac{V_2^2}{2g} + S_f\,(dx)$$

Here S_f = gradient of total energy line

and $S_f(dx)$ = loss due to friction between (1) and (2).

$$\therefore \quad (Z_1 - Z_2) - S_f\,(dx) = (y_2 - y_1) + \left(\frac{V_2^2}{2g} - \frac{V_1^2}{2g}\right)$$

But $Z_1 - Z_2 = S_o\,(dx)$, where S_o = bed slope.

$$\therefore \quad S_o(dx) - S_f\,(dx) = dy + d\left(\frac{V^2}{2g}\right)$$

$$\therefore \quad S_o - S_f = \frac{dy}{dx} + \frac{d}{dx}\left(\frac{V^2}{2g}\right)$$

$$= \frac{dy}{dx} + \frac{d}{dx}\left(\frac{V^2}{2g}\right)\frac{dy}{dx}$$

$$= \frac{dy}{dx}\left[1 + \frac{d}{dy}\left(\frac{Q^2}{2gA^2}\right)\right]$$

Here $V = \frac{Q}{A}$ and Q is constant, whereas A is a function of y.

$$\therefore \quad S_o - S_f = \frac{dy}{dx}\left[1 + 2\frac{Q^2}{2g}\left(-\frac{1}{A^3}\right)\frac{dA}{dy}\right]$$

$$= \frac{dy}{dx}\left[1 - \frac{Q^2T}{gA^3}\right] \quad \text{as} \quad \frac{dA}{dy} = T.$$

$$\therefore \qquad \frac{dy}{dx} = \frac{S_o - S_f}{1 - \frac{Q^2T}{gA^3}}$$

is the dynamic equations for GVF in **non-prismatic channel.** ...(15.35)

Note: It is assumed that depth of flow *y* decreasing in direction of flow is negative and that increasing in direction of flow is positive.

15.10.2 Dynamic Equation for GVF in Wide Rectangle Channel

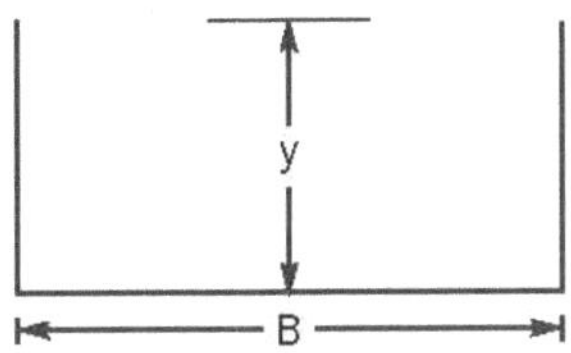

Fig. 15.32

If $B >> y$, then rectangular channel is defined a **wide rectangle channel** and will have.

$$R = \frac{A}{P} = \frac{By}{B + 2y} \approx \frac{By}{B} \quad \text{as} \quad y << B, B + 2y \simeq B.$$

$$= y$$

Thus for **wide rectangular channel,** $R = y$, *i.e.*, hydraulic radius = depth of flow.

Now from eq. (15.35), we get

$$\frac{dy}{dx} = S_o \frac{\left(1 - \frac{S_t}{S_o}\right)}{1 - \frac{Q^2T}{gA^3}}$$

If flow is uniform, depth of flow is y_n and if flow is critical, depth of flow is y_c. Actual depth of flow is always expressed as *y*. Now we have by Chezy's formula,

$$V = C\sqrt{RS} = C\sqrt{y_n S_o}, \qquad S = S_o \text{ for uniform flow.}$$

and

$$q = \frac{Q}{B} = \frac{AV}{B} = \frac{By_n C\sqrt{y_n S_o}}{B}$$

$$= Cy_n\sqrt{y_n S_o} \qquad ...(1)$$

Also if flow is non-uniform, $S = S_f$, and depth of flow is actual depth,

$$\therefore \quad q = \frac{Q}{B} = \frac{AV}{B} = \frac{ByC\sqrt{yS_f}}{B}$$

$$= yC\sqrt{yS_f} \qquad ...(2)$$

$\therefore$ From (1) and (2), we get

$$Cy_n\sqrt{y_nS_o} = yC\sqrt{yS_f}$$

$$\therefore \quad \frac{S_f}{S_o} = \left(\frac{y_n}{y}\right)^3 \qquad ...(3)$$

Also $\frac{Q^2T}{gA^3}$ for wide rectangular section will be

$$= \frac{q^2B^2B}{gy^3B^3} = \frac{q^2}{gy^3} = \frac{y_c^3}{y^3} \quad \text{as } \frac{q^2}{g} = y_c^3$$

$$= \left(\frac{y_c}{y}\right)^3 \qquad ...(4)$$

$$\therefore \quad \frac{dy}{dx} = S_o\left[\frac{1-\left(\frac{y_n}{y}\right)^3}{1-\left(\frac{y_c}{y}\right)^3}\right]$$

is differential equation for GVF in **wide rectangular channel** ...(15.36)

Now, $F = \frac{V}{\sqrt{gy}} \quad \therefore \quad F^2 = \frac{V^2}{gy} = \frac{Q^2}{gyA^2}$

For rectangular channel, $T = B$,

and $A = By$

$$\therefore \quad F^2 = \frac{Q^2}{gyA^2} \times \frac{B}{B} = \frac{Q^2T}{gA^3}, \text{by putting } T = B, \text{ and } By = A$$

$\therefore$ Eq. (15.35) can be used for rectangular channel by putting $F^2 = \frac{Q^2T}{gA^3}$ and hence we get

$$\frac{dy}{dx} = \frac{S_o - S_f}{1 - F^2} \text{ for } \textbf{rectangular channel.}$$

$$= S_o \left[\frac{1-\left(\frac{y_n}{y}\right)^3}{1-\left(\frac{y_c}{y}\right)^3} \right] \quad \textbf{for wide rect. channel.}$$

$$= \frac{S_o - S_f}{1-\frac{Q^2T}{gA^3}} \quad \textbf{for non-prismatic } \textbf{\textit{i.e.}}\textbf{, irregular channel.}$$

Now let us introduce **conveyance factor,** which is defined as, $K = AC\sqrt{R}$ so that Q is given by, $Q = AV = CA\sqrt{RS} = K\sqrt{S}$

If flow is uniform, $S = S_o$ and $K = K_n$ and hence $Q = K_n\sqrt{S_o}$. If flow is non-uniform, $S = S_f$ and therefore $Q = K\sqrt{S_f}$.

$$\therefore \quad K\sqrt{S_f} = K_n\sqrt{S_o}$$

$$\therefore \quad \frac{S_f}{S_o} = \left(\frac{K_n}{K}\right)^2$$

Also section factor, $Z = \sqrt{\frac{A^3}{T}}$ by definition

and we get $\qquad \frac{Q^2T}{gA^3} = \frac{Z_c^2}{Z^2}$

as $\qquad \frac{Q^2}{g} = \frac{A_c^3}{T} = Z_c^2$ for critical condition

and $\qquad \frac{A^3}{T} = Z^2$ by definition for non-critical condition.

$\therefore$ (Eq. 15.35) can also be written in the form,

$$\frac{dy}{dx} = S_o \frac{1-\left(\frac{K_n}{K}\right)^2}{1-\left(\frac{Z_c}{Z}\right)}$$

and can be used with more ease of calculation ...(15.37)
for trapezoidal, triangular and circular sections.

15.10.3 Surface Profiles in Wide Rectangular Channel

For wide rectangular channel we have

$$\frac{dy}{dx} = S_o \frac{1-\left(\frac{y_n}{y}\right)^3}{1-\left(\frac{y_c}{y}\right)^3} \text{ by using Chezy's formula}$$

But if Manning's formula is used, we have

$$\frac{dy}{dx} = S_o \frac{1-\left(\frac{y_n}{y}\right)^{\frac{10}{3}}}{1-\left(\frac{y_c}{y}\right)^3} \quad ...(15.38)$$

Defining **critical slope** represented as C, as that tied gradient which gives $y_n = y_c$ in wide rect. channel, then we can further define mild and steep slopes as under:

(*i*) Mild slope represented as M when $S_0 < S_c$ and $y_n > y_c$

(*ii*) Similarly, steep slope, represented as S, when $S_o > S_c$ and $y_n < y_c$. Thus we have following types of bed gradient defined in case of wide rect. channel as under:

(*i*) Critical slope, C, $S_o = S_c, y_n = y_c$.

(*ii*) Mild slope, M, $S_o < S_c, y_n > y_c$.

(*iii*) Steep slope, S, $S_o > S_c$, $y_n < y_c$.

(*iv*) Horizontal slope, H, $S_o = 0$, $y_n \rightarrow \infty$

(*v*) Adverse slope, A, S_o – ve y_n does not exist.

Thus, we have C, M, S, H, and A types of slopes and in each type we can introduce zone of flow such as

Zone one, two and three as shown in Fig. 15.33 (*i*), (*ii*) and (*iii*).

In case of critical slope zone (2) is absent as $y_n = y_c$ similarly for Horizontal and Adverse slope zone (1) is absent as in case of Horizontal slope $y_n \rightarrow \infty$ and in case of Adverse, y_n does not exist.

Now we consider how to get shape of particular type of profile for a given slope. For example, if given slope is mild, M, then profile in zone (1) is M_1, in zone (2) is M_2 and in zone (3) is M_3 and their shapes can be decided as under:

For M_1 profile, actual depth y is in zone (1) and therefore $y > y_n > y_c$. Now write down differential equation for GVF for wide rect. channel,

$$\frac{dy}{dx} = S_o \frac{1-\left(\frac{y_n}{y}\right)^3}{1-\left(\frac{y_c}{y}\right)^3} = S_o\left(\frac{\text{Numerator, } N}{\text{Denominator, } D}\right)$$

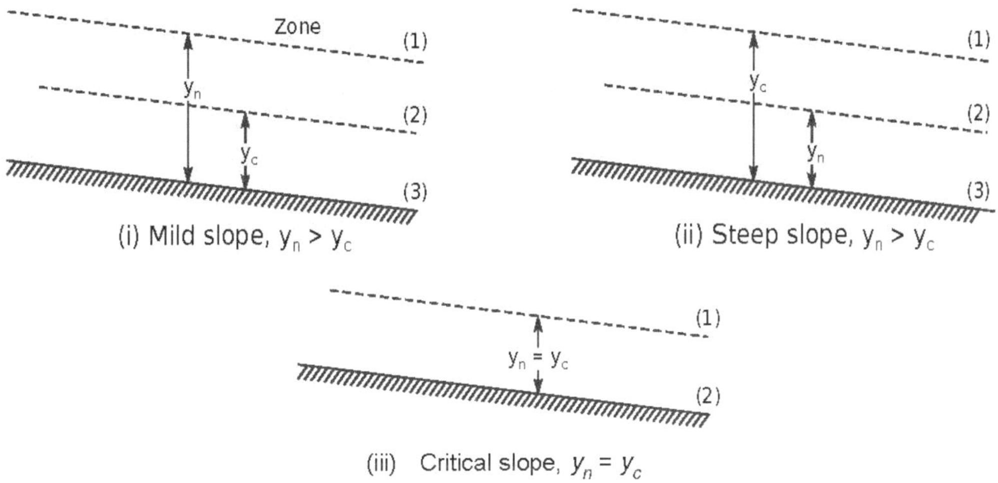

Fig. 15.33

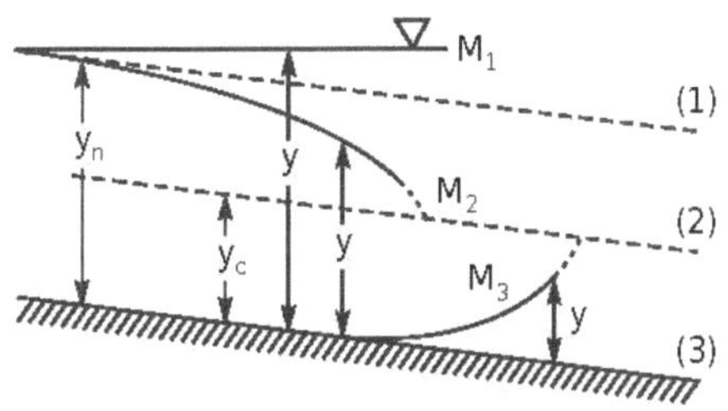

Fig.15.34 Profiles M_1, M_2 and M_3.

As(*i*) $y > y_n$, N (= numerator) is +*ve*

(*ii*) $y > y_c$, D (= denominator) is +*ve*.

$\therefore \quad \dfrac{dy}{dx}$ is **+ve** *i.e.*, water surface will **rise** in direction of flow.

Now apply end conditions, *i.e.*

(*i*) At upper end, $y \to y_n \quad \therefore \quad \dfrac{dy}{dx} \to 0$, *i.e.*, profile starts tangentially to y_n.

(*ii*) At lower end $y \to \infty \quad \therefore \quad \dfrac{dy}{dx} \to S_o$, *i.e.*, profile tends to be horizontal as it approaches obstacles, see M_1 in Fig. 15.34.

For M_2 profile, we have actual depth $y < y_n$ but $y > y_c$ *i.e.*, y is in zone number two. Substituting these conditions in dynamic eq., we have.

(*i*) $y < y_n$, gives N –ve

(*ii*) $y > y_c$, gives D +ve

$\therefore \quad \dfrac{dy}{dx}$ is –ve, *i.e.*, **falling** in direction of flow.

Now apply end condition, *i.e.*, when

(*i*) $y \to y_n \quad \therefore \quad \dfrac{dy}{dx} \to 0$, *i.e.*, profile starts tangentially to y_n.

(*ii*) $y \to y_c \quad \therefore \quad \dfrac{dy}{dx} \to -\infty$, *i.e.*, profile meets y_c line vertically upward see M_2 in Fig. 15.34.

For M_3 profile, we have actual depth, $y < y_c$, *i.e.*, y is in zone number 3. Substituting these condition in dynamic equation, we have

(*i*) $y < y_c$, D is –ve

(*iii*) $y < y_n$, N is –ve

$\therefore \quad \dfrac{dy}{dx}$ +ve, *i.e.*, profile is **rising** in direction of flow.

Now apply end condition:

(*i*) $y \to 0 \quad \therefore \quad \dfrac{dy}{dx} = S_o$ *i.e.*, profile starts tangentially to the bed.

(*ii*) $y \to y_c \quad \therefore \quad \dfrac{dy}{dx} = +\infty$ *i.e.*, profile meets y_c line vertically upward, see M_3 in Fig. 15.34.

Similarly shapes of profiles for *S*, *C*, *H* and *A* types of slope can be developed using above method of analysis and they are given in Fig. 15.35:

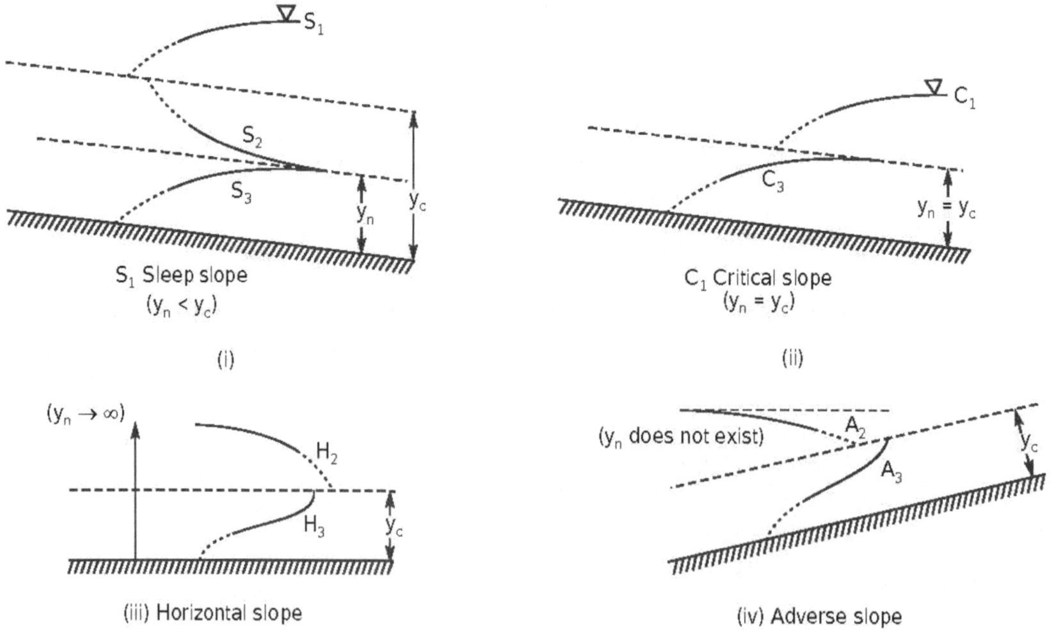

Fig. 15.35 (*i*), (*ii*), (*iii*) and (*iv*).

It may be noted that profiles in zone (1) and zone (3) for all types of slope increase in direction of flow *i.e.*, $\frac{dy}{dx}$ is +ve in zone (1) and (3) whereas $\frac{dy}{dx}$ is –ve in zone (2) *i.e.*, profiles fall in direction of flow in all types of slopes. In all there are twelve profiles, 3 for M, 3 for S, 2 for C, H and A each. C_2, H and A_1 profiles are absent.

M_1 profile represents back water curve on u/s of obstruction whereas M_2 represents drop down curve. H and A profiles are for flow coming out of sluice gate with either horizontal or adverse type of floors.

15.10.4 Single Step Method to get Length of Profile

Eq. (15.36) can be, rewritten as under:

$$\frac{dy}{dx} = S_o \frac{1-\left(\frac{y_n}{y}\right)^3}{1-\left(\frac{y_c}{y}\right)^3} \quad \text{for wide rect. channel}$$

It can be integrated by Bresse, Bakhmeteff or Chow's methods but is out of scope of this text and so not given here, but a simplified approach to solve it by single step method to get length of profile is given as under:

Referring to Fig. 15.31, we have

$$Z_1 + y_1 + \frac{v_1^2}{2g} = Z_2 + y_2 + \frac{v_2^2}{2g} + S_f x$$

$$\therefore \quad (Z_1 - Z_2) - S_f x = \left(y_2 + \frac{v_2^2}{2g}\right) - \left(y_1 + \frac{v_1^2}{2g}\right)$$

$$\therefore \quad S_o x - S_f x = E_2 - E_1$$

$$\therefore \quad (S_o - S_f)x = E_2 - E_1$$

$$\therefore \quad x = \frac{E_2 - E_1}{S_o - \overline{S}_f} \qquad \text{...(15.39)}$$

Here $$S_f = \overline{S}_f \text{ and } \overline{S}_f = \frac{S_{f1} + S_{f2}}{2} \qquad \text{..(15.40)}$$

15.11 SOLVED PROBLEMS

■ **Problem 15.26:** *A wide rect. channel is to carry $q = 2.5\ m^3/s/m$ at a Froude number of 0.5. Take Mannings $n = 0.015$, find (i) y_n (ii) S_o (iii) τ_o.*

Solution: $$q = \frac{Q}{B} = \frac{AV}{B} = \frac{By_nV}{B} = Vy$$

Given channel is wise rect., $\therefore$ $R = y$,

$$F = \frac{V}{\sqrt{gy}} = \frac{\left(\frac{q}{y}\right)}{\sqrt{gy}}$$

$$F^2 = \frac{q^2}{gy^3} = (0.5)^2$$

$$\therefore \quad y^3 = \frac{(2.5)^2}{g(0.5)^2}$$

$$\therefore \quad y = 1.36 \text{ m}$$

$$\therefore \quad V = \frac{q}{y} = \frac{1}{n} y^{2/3} S_o^{1/2}$$

$$\therefore \quad \frac{q^2}{y^2} = \frac{1}{n^2} y^{4/3} S_o$$

$$\therefore \quad \frac{q^2 n^2}{y^{10/3}} = S_o = \frac{(2.5)^2 (0.015)^2}{(1.36)^{10/3}} = \frac{1.4 \times 10^{-3}}{2.78}$$

$$\therefore \quad S_o = 0.503 \times 10^{-3}$$ ...(Ans.)

$$\tau_o = \gamma R S_o = (9810)(1.36)(0.503 \times 10^{-3})$$

$$= \mathbf{6.71 \text{ Pa}}$$ ...(Ans.)

■ **Problem 15.27:** *For a wide rect. horizontal channel, show that length of GVE profile is given by*

$$x = \frac{C^2 y}{g}\left[1 - \frac{1}{4}\left(\frac{y}{y_c}\right)^3\right] + \textit{constant},$$

here, C = *Chezy's constant.*

Solution: Writing differential, equation for GVF in wide rect. channel,

$$\frac{dy}{dx} = \frac{S_o - S_f}{1 - \frac{Q^2 T}{gA^3}}$$

Here, $S_o = 0$ as given channel is horizontal, and considering unit width, $T = B = 1$, $\frac{Q}{B} = q = Vy$, $R = y$ and by Chezy's formula,

$$V = C\sqrt{RS} - C\sqrt{yS_f}$$

$$\therefore \quad S_f = \frac{V^2}{C^2 y} = \frac{q^2}{C^2 y^3}$$

$$\therefore \quad \frac{dy}{dx} = \frac{-S_f}{1 - \frac{Q^2 T}{gA^3}} = \frac{-\frac{q^2}{C^2 y^3}}{1 - \frac{q^2}{gy^3}}$$

$$= \frac{-\frac{q^2}{C^2 y^3} \times \frac{g}{g}}{1 - \left(\frac{yc}{y}\right)^3} \quad \text{as } \frac{q^2}{g} = yc^3$$

$$= \frac{-\frac{g}{C^2}\left(\frac{yc}{y}\right)^3}{1 - \left(\frac{yc}{y}\right)^3}$$

$$\therefore \qquad \frac{dx}{dy} = \frac{1 - \left(\frac{yc}{y}\right)^3}{-\frac{g}{C^2}\left(\frac{yc}{y}\right)^3}$$

$$\therefore \qquad dx = \left[-\left(\frac{C^2}{gy_c^3}\right)y^3 + \frac{C^2}{g}\right]dy$$

$$\therefore \qquad x = \left[-\frac{C^2}{gy_c^3}\left(\frac{y^4}{4}\right) + \frac{C^2}{g}y\right] + \text{constant}$$

$$\therefore \qquad x = \frac{C^2 y}{g}\left[1 - \frac{1}{4}\left(\frac{y}{yc}\right)^3\right] + \text{constant} \qquad \text{...(Ans.)}$$

■ **Problem 15.28:** *A sluice gate discharge 2 m^3/s/m into a wide rect. horizontal channel. The depth at vena contracta is 0.16 m, k tail water depth is 2 m and n = 0.015, find how far away from sluice the jump will occur.*

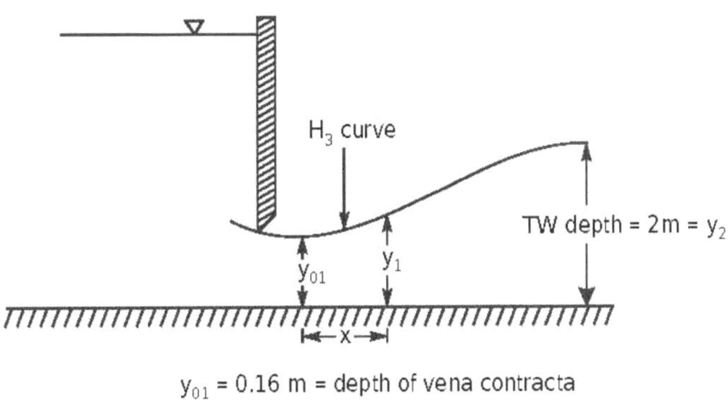

Fig. 15.36

Solution:

At vena contracta, $V_{01} = \dfrac{q}{y_{01}} = \dfrac{2}{0.16} = 12.5$ m/s

$$F_{01} = \frac{V_{01}}{\sqrt{gy_{01}}} = \frac{12.5}{\sqrt{g(0.16)}} = \frac{12.5}{1.25}$$

$$= 10$$

If a jump is to occur at vena contracta,

$$\frac{y_{02}}{y_{01}} = \frac{1}{2}[-1+\sqrt{8F_{01}^2+1}] = 13.65$$

∴ $y_{02} = 13.65\,(y_{01}) = 13.65 \times 0.16 = 2.18$ m

As the actual tail water depth = 2 m is less than 2.18 m, jump will be repelled *i.e.*, it will take place at x distance d/s of vena contracta where depth y_1 should be equal to depth sequent to tail water depth *i.e.*, $2\,m = y_2$.

Now, $$\frac{y_1}{y_2} = \frac{1}{2}[-1+\sqrt{8F_2^2+1}]$$

$$F_2 = \frac{V_2}{\sqrt{gy_2}} + \frac{q}{\sqrt{gy_2^3}} = \frac{2}{\sqrt{9.81(2)^3}}$$

$$= 0.225$$

∴ $$\frac{y_1}{y_2} = \frac{1}{2}[-1+\sqrt{8(0.225)^2+1}]$$

$$= 0.092$$

∴ $y_1 = 0.092\,(2) = 0.185$ m = depth a toe of jump.

At vena contracta $F_{01} = 10 > 1$

∴ flow is supercritical and $y < y_c$, channel is horizontal.

∴ surface profile between vena contracta and toe of jump will be H_3 curve. Distance x between $y_{01} = 0.16$ m to $y_1 = 0.185$ m is calculated by single step method:

$$x = \frac{E_2 - E_1}{S_o - \bar{S}_f} = \frac{E_2 - E_1}{0 - \left(\dfrac{sf_1 + sf_2}{2}\right)}$$

as $S_o = 0$, as channel is horizontal.

$$= \frac{2(E_1 - E_2)}{sf_1 + sf_2}$$

$$E_2 = y_{01} + \frac{v_{01}^2}{2g} = 0.16 + \frac{(12.5)^2}{2g}$$

$$= 0.16 + 7.96 = \mathbf{8.12\ m}$$

$$E_1 = y_1 + \frac{v_1^2}{2g} = 0.185 + \frac{\left(\frac{2}{0.185}\right)^2}{2g} = 0.185 + 5.95 = \mathbf{6.14\ m}$$

$$S_{f1} = \frac{n^2 v_{01}^2}{(y_{01})^{4/3}} = \frac{n^2 q^2}{(y_{01})^{10/3}} = \frac{(0.015)^2\ (2)^2}{(0.16)^{10/3}} = \frac{9\times10^{-4}}{2.23\times10^{-3}} = 0.403$$

$$S_{f2} = \frac{n^2 v_1^2}{(y_1)^{4/3}} = \frac{n^2 q^2}{(y_1)^{10/3}} = \frac{(0.015)^2\ (2)^2}{(0.72)^{10/3}} = \mathbf{0.00268}$$

$\therefore$
$$x = \frac{2(8.12 - 6.14)}{0.403 + 0.00268}$$

$$= 9.77\ \text{m}$$

$\therefore$ Jump will be formed at a distance of $x = 6.15$ m from vena contracta. ...**(Ans.)**

■ **Problem 15.29**: *A triangular channel of side slope 1:1, carries water at the rate of 0.25 m³/s and its bed slope is 0.0012. Find whether the channel has mild, steep or critical slope. Take n = 0.015. For what range of depths will the flow be of type 1, 2 or 3 curve?*

Solution:

Let depth of flow $= y$

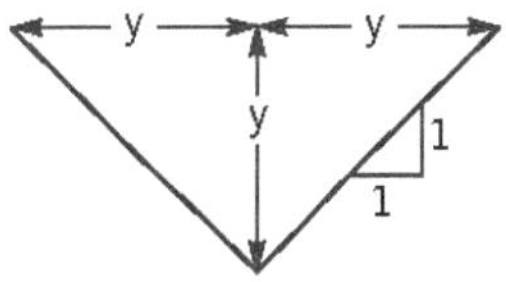

Fig. 15.37

$\therefore$
$$A = 2\left(\frac{1}{2} y \cdot y\right) = y^2$$

$$T = 2y$$

$$R = \frac{A}{P} = \frac{y^2}{2y\sqrt{2}} = \frac{y}{2\sqrt{2}}$$

For **critical depth,**
$$\frac{Q^2}{g} = \frac{A_c^3}{T} = \frac{(y_c^2)^3}{2y_c}$$

$$= \frac{y_c^5}{2}$$

$\therefore$
$$y_c = \left(\frac{2Q^2}{g}\right)^{1/5} = \left[\frac{2\times(0.25)^2}{9.81}\right]^{1/3}$$

$$= \mathbf{0.417\ m}$$

For normal depth y_n:

$$Q = \frac{1}{n} AR^{2/3} (S_o)^{1/2}$$

$$= \frac{1}{0.015}(y_n)^2\left(\frac{y_n}{2\sqrt{2}}\right)^{2/3} (0.0012)^{1/2}$$

$\therefore$ $$0.25 = 1.15\, y_n^{8/3}$$

$\therefore$ $$y_n = \left(\frac{0.25}{1.15}\right)^{3/8} = \mathbf{0.564\ m}$$

$\therefore$ $y_n > y_c$ $\therefore$ given slope of channel is **Mild.**

For M_1 curve $y > 0.564$ m

M_2 $0.564 > y > 0.417$ ...**(Ans.)**

M_3 $y < 0.417$.

■ **Problem 15. 30:** *A 10 m wide rectangular channel with $S_o = 0.00016$ and $n = 0.014$, carries flow at uniform depth of 2.0 m, If depth of flow is changed to 12 m, by constructing a dam, find how far u/s will the depth be 2.5 m? Use step method, state type of profile.*

Solution:

$$Q = AV = (10\times 2)\frac{1}{0.014}\left(\frac{10\times 2}{10+4}\right)^{2/3} (0.00016)^{1/2}$$

$$= \frac{20\times 0.0126\times 1.27}{0.014} = \mathbf{22.8\,m^3/s}$$

$$q = \frac{Q}{B} = \frac{22.8}{10} = 2.28\ \text{m}^3/\text{s/m}$$

$$y_c = \left(\frac{q^2}{g}\right)^{1/3} = \left(\frac{2.28^2}{9.81}\right)^{1/3} = \mathbf{0.81\ m}$$

$$y_n = 2\ \text{m}$$

$\therefore$ $y_n > y_c$, mild slope

actual depth $y_1 = 2.5\ \text{m} > y_n$

$\therefore$ M_1profile.

Consider sections (1) and (2) at x distance apart as shown in above Fig.

$\therefore$ $$R_1 = \frac{A_1}{P_1} = \frac{10\times 2.5}{10+2(2.5)} = 1.66\ \text{m}$$

$$R_2 = \frac{A_2}{P_2} = \frac{10\times 12}{10+24} = 3.52\ \text{m}$$

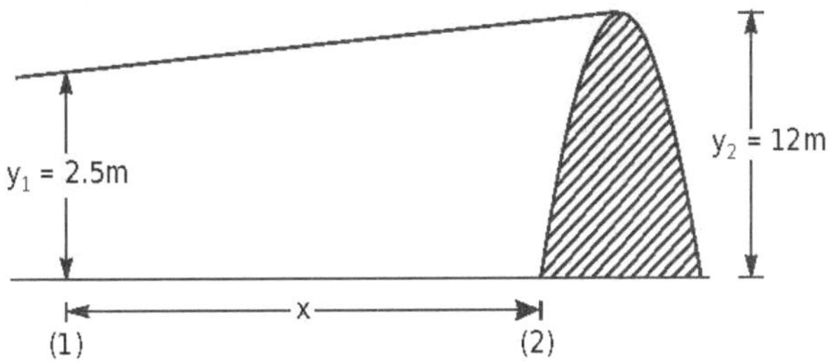

Fig. 15.38

$$V_1 = \frac{Q}{10 \times 2.5} = \frac{2.28}{2.5} = 0.912 \text{ m/s}$$

$$V_2 = \frac{2.28}{12} = 0.19 \text{ m/s}$$

$$\therefore \quad E_1 = y_1 + \frac{V_1^2}{2g} = 2.5 + \left(\frac{0.912^2}{2g}\right) = 2.542$$

$$= 2.5 + 0.042$$

$$E_2 = y_2 + \frac{V_2^2}{2g} = 12 + \left(\frac{0.19^2}{2g}\right)$$

$$= 12 + 0.0018$$
$$= 12.0018$$

$$S_{f1} = \frac{V_1^2 n^2}{(R_1)^{4/3}} = \frac{0.831 \times 1.96 \times 10^{-4}}{(1.66)^{4/3}} = 0.831 \times 10^{-4}$$

$$S_{f2} = \frac{V_2^2 n^2}{(R_2)^{4/3}} = \frac{(0.19)^2 (0.014)^2}{(3.52)^{4/3}} = \frac{0.036 \times 1.96 \times 10^{-4}}{5.332}$$

$$= 0.0132 \times 10^{-4}$$

$$\therefore \quad \bar{S}_f = \frac{S_{f1} + S_{f2}}{2} = \frac{0.831 \times 10^{-4} + 0.0132 \times 10^{-4}}{5.332}$$

$$= 0.4221 \times 10^{-4}$$

$$S_o = 0.00016 = 1.6 \times 10^{-4}$$

$$\therefore \quad x = \frac{E_2 - E_1}{S_o - \bar{S}_f} = \frac{12.0018 - 2.542}{1.6 \times 10^{-4} - 0.422 \times 10^{-4}}$$

$$= \frac{9.4598}{1.178 \times 10^{-4}} = 8.03 \times 10^4 = 80.3 \text{ km} \quad \text{Profile } M_1$$ ...(**Ans.**)

15.12 DISCHARGE MEASUREMENT BY FLUMES

For measurement of discharge through channels (*i*) Venturi Flume, and (*ii*) Standing Wave Flume are used.

15.12.1 Venturi Flume

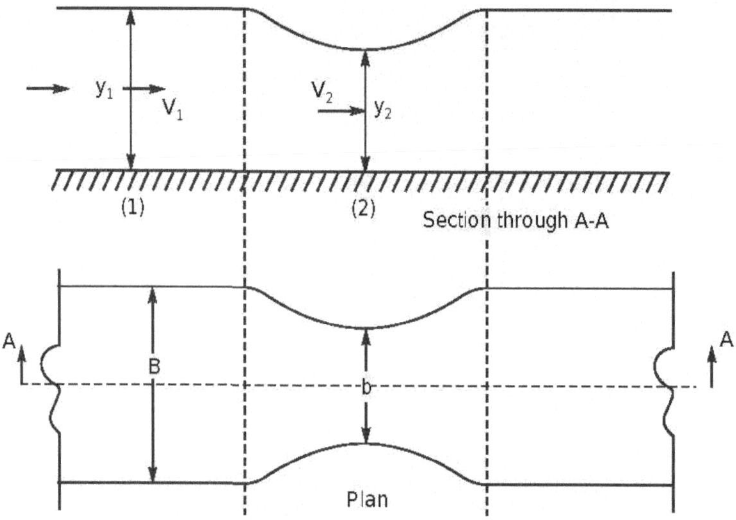

Fig. 15.39 Venturi flume.

Venturi flume is similar to Venturi-meter used for discharge measurement in pipe line at sections (1) and (2) as shown in Fig. 15.39

$$Q = A_1 \ V_1 = A_2 V_2$$

Also specific energy E_1 at section (1) = E_2 at section (2)

$$\therefore \quad y_1 + \frac{Q^2}{2gA_1^2} = y_2 + \frac{Q^2}{2gA_2^2}$$

$$\therefore \quad \frac{Q^2}{2gA_1^2} - \frac{Q^2}{2gA_2^2} = y_2 - y_1$$

$$\therefore \quad \frac{Q^2}{2g}\left[\frac{A_2^2 - A_1^2}{A_1^2 \ A_2^2}\right] = y_2 - y_1$$

$$\therefore \quad Q^2 = \frac{2g\,(y_2 - y_1)\,A_1^2\,A_2^2}{A_2^2 - A_1^2}$$

$$\therefore \quad Q = c_d \frac{A_1 \ A_2}{\sqrt{A_1^2 - A_2^2}} \sqrt{2g\,(y_1 - y_2)} \qquad \text{...(15.40)}$$

Here $\quad A_1 = By_1$ and $A_2 = by_2$

15.12.2 Standing Wave Flume or Critical Depth Flume or Broad Crested Weir

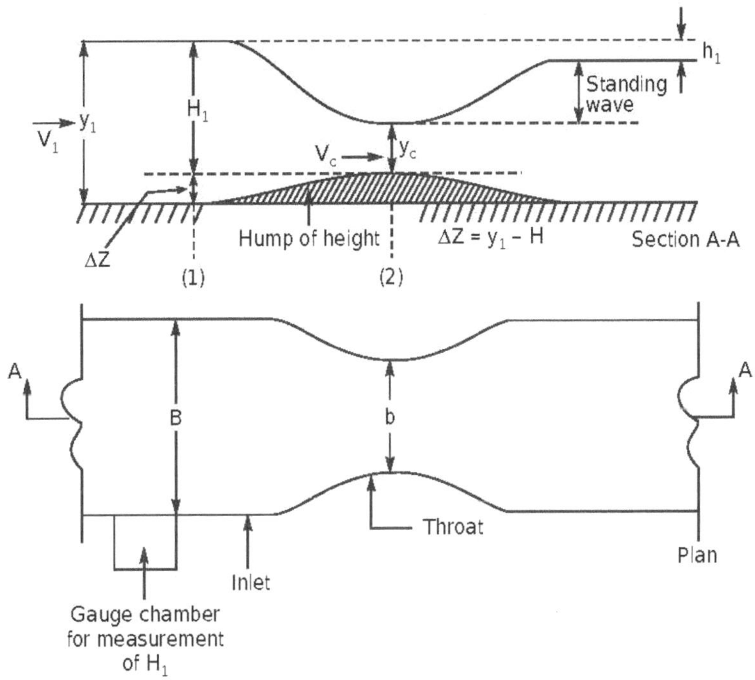

Fig. 15.40

A standing wave flume has at its throat a hump of height ΔZ provided for the purpose of developing critical flow conditions in the throat portion so that discharge measurement by taking only one reading in gauge chamber is made possible. In venturi flume, measurement of y_1 and y_2 both are required to calculate discharge, whereas in case of standing wave flume only one depth measurement is required. In this case, velocity of flow at throat is greater than critical velocity and hence a standing wave or a weak hydraulic jump is formed towards the edge of the hump. Also because velocity of flow at throat is greater than critical velocity, depth of flow at a section u/s of inlet remains independent of changes in *d*/s depth until *d*/*s* depth is less than 0.7 H_1 and discharge is then a function of H_1 only. Hence only one reading H_1 is required to calculate Q.

Taking section (1) u/s of hump and (2) near the edge of hump,

$$y_1 + \frac{V_1^2}{2g} = \Delta Z + \frac{V_C^{\ 2}}{2g} \text{ (neglecting hf)}$$

Put
$$H_1 = \left(y_1 + \frac{v_1^{\ 2}}{2g} \right) - \Delta Z$$

$\therefore$
$$H_1 = y_c + \frac{v_c^2}{2g}$$

$$\therefore \quad v_c = \sqrt{2g\,(H_1 - y_c)}$$

$$q = v_c y_c = y_c\sqrt{2g\,(H_1 - y_c)}$$

Here, $y_c = \frac{2}{3}H_1$ as per definition of critical depth, *i.e.* $E_{min} = \frac{3}{2}y_c = H_1$

$$\therefore \quad q = c_d\left(\frac{2}{3}H_1\right)\sqrt{2g\left(H_1 - \frac{2}{3}H_1\right)}$$

$$= c_d\frac{2}{3}H_1^{3/2}\sqrt{2g\left(\frac{1}{3}\right)} = c_d\,1.705\,\mathrm{H}_1^{3/2}$$

$$Q = bq = c_d 1.705\; bH1^{3/2} \qquad \text{...(15.41)}$$

here $H_1 = E_1 - \Delta Z$

and b = width of throat ...(15.42)

and **minimum** height of hump, $\Delta S = E_1 - \frac{3}{2}y_c$.

■ **Problem 15.31:** *A rect. channel carries discharge of 7640 LPs per meter width at a uniform depth of 2 m. Find height of hump, for a standing wave flume to be provided in this channel. Neglect carries.*

Solution:

$$q = 7640 \text{ LPS/m width}$$

$$\therefore \quad y_c = \left(\frac{q^2}{g}\right)^{1/3} = \left(\frac{7.64^2}{9.81}\right)^{1/3}$$

$$= 1.8 \text{ m}$$

$$E_1 = y_1 + \frac{v_1^2}{2g}$$

$$= 2 + \frac{\left(\frac{7.64}{2}\right)^2}{2(9.81)}$$

$$= 2 + 0.743 = 2.742 \qquad H_1 = \frac{3}{2}(y_c)$$

$$\Delta Z = E_1 - H_1 \qquad = 2.7 \text{ m}$$

$$= 2.743 - 2.7 = 0.043 \text{ m}$$

$$= \mathbf{4.3\ cm.}$$ **...(Ans.)**

■ **Problem 15.32:** *A 4 m wide rect. channel carries water at depth of 1.6. m. In order to measure discharge, width is reduced to 2.7 m and depth by 0.25 m. Calculate discharge if water surface in contracted section drops by 0.15 m. Assume no loss.*

Solution:

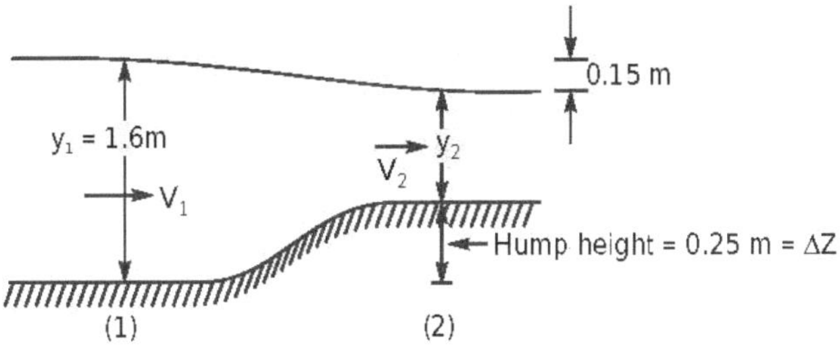

Fig. 15.41

Writing specific energy at section (1) and (2), we get

$$y_1 + \frac{v_1^2}{2g} = \Delta Z + y_2 + \frac{v_2^2}{2g}$$

Here, $y_1 - y_2 - \Delta Z = 0.15$, see Fig. 15.41

$\therefore$ $$\frac{v_2^2}{2g} - \frac{v_1^2}{2g} = 0.15$$

Also as $y_1 - y_2 = \Delta Z = 0.15$, we get

$$y_2 = y_1 = \Delta Z - 0.15 = 1.6 - 0.25 - 0.15$$
$$= 1.2\text{m}$$

$$v_2 = \frac{Q}{A_2} = \frac{Q}{b_2\, y_2} = \frac{Q}{2.7 \times 1.2}$$

$$v_1 = \frac{Q}{A_1} = \frac{Q}{b_1 \times y_1} = \frac{Q}{4 \times 1.6}$$

$\therefore$ From eq. (1), we get

$$\frac{Q^2}{2g\,(2.7 \times 1.2)^2} - \frac{Q^2}{2g\,(4 \times 1.6)^2} = 0.15$$

$$\frac{Q^2}{2g}[0.095 - 0.024] = 0.15$$

$\therefore$ $$Q^2 = \frac{0.15 \times 2g}{0.071} = 41.4$$

$\therefore$ $Q = 6.43 \text{ m}^3/\text{s}$. ...(Ans.)

■ **Problem 15.33**: *A weir is 2.0 m long and has a head of 1.5 m over its crest. Neglect velocity of approach, find Q if*

(*i*) *weir is broad crested weir with well rounded entrance.*

(*ii*) *weir is broad crested weir with square entrance.*

Solution:

$Q = 1.705\, C_d L H^{3/2}$

Case (*i*) $Q = 1.705\,(0.98)\,(2)\,(1.5)^{3/2}$, here $C_d = 0.98$

$= 6.13$ m^3/s ...(Ans.)

Case (*ii*) $Q = 1.705\,(0.85)\,(2)\,(1.5)^{3/2}$, here $C_d = 0.85$ ...(Ans.)

$= 5.32$ m^3/s.

Exercises

(A) UNIFORM FLOW

1. In a wide rectangular channel having depth of flow = y = 1.2 m, velocity at 0.2 (y) is 2.5 m/s and at 0.8 (y) from water surface is 1.0 m/s.Find discharge per meter width and shear stress at bed if S_o = 0.0004. (Note for wide rect. channel $R = y$)

   (**Ans.** $q = 2.1$ m^3/s/m^2, $\tau_o = rRS_o = 4.8$ N/m^2)

2. In a trapezoidal channel of side slope 1 : 1 and bottom width 2*m*, depth of flow is 1.0 m. If channel has Manning's n = 0.014, find Chezy's coefficient and Darcy-Weisbach friction factor. (**Ans.** $C = 66, f = 0.018$)

3. Find rate of flow of water through a circular channel of diameter 1.2 m, running $\frac{3}{4}$th full. Take $C = 60$, $S_o = 0.001$.

   (**Ans.** $Q = 1.03$ m^3/s) $\left(\textbf{Hint: } \text{Running } \frac{3}{4}\text{th full means depth of flow} = \frac{3}{4}D\right)$

(B) MOST EFFICIENT HYDRAULIC CHANNEL SECTIONS

1. Calculate maximum velocity and maximum discharge a circular channel of diameter 1.0 m can develop when laid at a slope of 1 in 4000. $n = 0.015$.

   (**Ans.** $V_{max} = 0.47$ m/s, $Q_{max} = 0.35$ m^3/s)

   (**Hint:** For V_{max}, $y = 0.81D$. For Q_{max} $y = 0.95\,D$ by Chezy and $y = 0.94\,D$ by Manning.)

2. Find dimensions of a trapezoidal channel having most efficient hydraulic section to carry a discharge of 12 m^3/s. Take $S_o = 0.006$ and $n = 0.015$.

   (**Ans.** It is a semi hexagon of side **1.53 m** and depth of flow = **1.33 m** and external $\angle\theta = 60°$ or $m = 0.577$)

3. A 6 m wide and 2 m deep rect. channel has a bed slope of 0.001 and lined with cement mortar giving $n = 0.015$. It is desired to increase the discharge to a maximum by changing the dimension of the channel but keeping same quantity of lining. Find new dimension and percentage increase in the discharge. Assume no change in value of n and bed gradient. (**Ans.** Dim: $B = 5$ m, $y = 2.5$ m, % increase in $Q = 7.1\%$)

4. A triangular duct resting on its base B carries water with a free surface. Obtain condition for maximum velocity for side slope of 1:1. (**Ans.** $y = 0.338\ B$)
5. Prove that a semi hexagon is the most economical trapezoidal channel section.
6. Calculate flow rate through a trapezoidal channel of base width 1.3 m, side slopes at 60° with horizontal and depth of flow at its optimum value. S_o is 1 in 1300 and $n = 0.011$ (**Ans.** $Q = 3.774\ m^3/s$)

   (**Hint:** "Optimum depth" means condition for most economical section.)

(C) SPECIFIC ENERGY AND CRITICAL DEPTH

1. A rect. channel 3 m wide carries a discharge of 9 m³/s. Find y_c and specific energy at this depth. (**Ans.** $y_c = 0.97$ m, $E_c = 1.458$ m)
2. What is the maximum discharge a 3 m rect. channel can carry if specify energy of flow is 3 m? (**Ans.** $Q_{max} = 26.57\ m^3/s$)

   (**Hint:** Q will be maximum at y_c.)
3. A channel of triangular section has apex angle of 90°. It carries a discharge of 2 m³/s, find y_c. It is laid at a slope of 0.01, find y_n. State type of flow. (**Ans.** $y_c = 0.89$ m, $y_n = 0.478$ m, supercritical)
4. If in a rect. channel F_1 and F_2 are Froude numbers at alternate depths, y_1 and y_2 respectively, prove that

$$\frac{y_1}{y_2} = \left[\frac{F_2}{F_1}\right]^{2/3} = \frac{2+F_2^2}{2+F_1^2}.$$

5. On what slope a 4 m wide rect. channel should be constructed so that critical flow will occur at normal depth of 1.0 m? Take $C = 60$. (**Ans.** $S_o = 4 \times 10^{-3}$)
6. If a trapezoidal channel of bed width $B = 2$ m and carrying a discharge of 8 m³/s, has side slope 1:1, find critical depth. If bed slope is 0.0001 and $n = 0.015$, find normal depth and type of flow. (**Ans.** $y_c = 1$ m, $y_n = 2.4$ m, subcritical flow)

(D) HYDRAULIC JUMP

1. If in a horizontal rect. channel; hydraulic jump occurs with sequent depth 0.8 m and 4 m, find discharge intensity, energy lost and F_1. (**Ans.** $q = 8.67\ m^3/s/m$, $E_j = 2.56$ m, $F_1 = 3.86$)
2. If it is desired to have a loss of energy of 6 *m* in an energy dissipator provided at top of spillway when incoming flow has $F_1 = 9$, find sequent depths, length of energy dissipator and percentage of initial energy lost.

$$\left(\textbf{Ans. } y_1 = 0.2\text{ m},\ y_2 = 2.44\text{ m},\ L = 11.2\text{ m to }15.68\text{ m as }L = 5\text{ to }7\,(y_2 - y_1),\ \frac{E_j}{E_1} = 72.2\%\right)$$

3. At the toe of spillway of length 30 m, velocity of flow is 30 m/s and depth of flow 1.0 m. Determine if hydraulic jump will occur or not. If yes, find height and length of jump and power dissipated.
(**Ans.** ∴ Yes, $F = 9.5 > 1$ ∴ Jump occurs, Height of jump = 12 m, L_{jump} = 5 to 7 (12) m, P = 298.8 MW)
4. At the toe of a hydraulic jump, the Froude number and depth of flow are 10 and 0.5 m, find specific energy head at the heel of the jump. (**Ans.** E_2 = 7.0 m)

(E) GRADUALLY VARIED FLOW AND FLUME

1. A wide rect. channel having $q = 4\text{m}^3/\text{s/m}$ and $S_0 = 0.0001$, $n = 0.015$, has depth of flow = 1.4 m at a certain section. How far u/s or *d/s* or will the depth of flow be 2.0 m? Sketch the profile. (**Ans.** Δx = 588 m, u/s of y_1 = 1.4 m, M_2 profile)
2. A wide rect. channel having $q = 5\ \text{m}^3/\text{s/m}$ and $S_o = 0.0009$, $n = 0.015$, has depth of flow = 1.4 m at a certain section. How far u/s or d/s will the depth of flow be 1.6 m? Sketch the profile. (**Ans.** Δx = 95 m, u/s of y_1 = 1.4 m, S_2 profile)
3. A wide rect. channel $n = 0.015$ has $q = 3\ \text{m}^3/\text{s/m}$ and $S_o = 0.006$, find whether the channel slope is M, S or C? (**Ans.** Steep, y_n = 0.72 m, y_c = 0.97 m)
4. A wide rect. channel has $q = 5\ \text{m}^3/\text{s/m}$, $S_o = 0.0004$, and $n = 0.016$. Calculate GVF profile produced if the channel bed has a sudden drop.
(**Ans.** M_2 profile from y_n = 2.29 m to y_c = 1.36 m)
(**Note:** If a channel bed drops suddenly, depth just u/s of the drop is y_c.)
5. In a rect. channel 3.5 m wide having bed slope of 0.0036 and $n = 0.015$, uniform flow occurs at depth of 2 m.
(*i*) Find how high can a hump be raised on the channel bed without causing a change in u/s depth. (**Ans.** ΔZ = 0.026 m)
(*ii*) If u/s depth be increased to 2.4 m, what should be height of hump? (**Ans.** 19.9 cm
6. A sluice gate discharges into a wide rect. channel at a depth of 0.3 m at vena contracta. If a hydraulic jump takes place *d/s* of the gate to the normal depth of 2.0 m in the channel, find distance between toe of the jump and vena contracta. Take $n = 0.015$ and $S_o = 0.001$. (**Ans.** 82 m from vena contracta)
7. (*i*) A 3 m × 1.5 m venturi flume has depth at entrance = 0.75 m and at throat 0.65 m. Find discharge through the flume. (**Ans.** $Q = 1.4\ \text{m}^3/\text{s}$)
(*ii*) If a 0.2 m high stream lined hump is provided in the throat, work out up stream depth for the same discharge. (**Ans.** y_1 = 0.89 m)

16

Dimensional Analysis and Model Testing

16.1 GENERAL

Any physical phenomenon can be expressed in terms of number of variables involved in the phenomenon, for example, flow of fluid in a pipe line is given by

$$Q = \left[\frac{12D^5 h_f}{fL}\right]^{1/2}$$

Here value of Q is dependent on pipe diameter D, loss of head h_f, friction factor f and pipe length L *i.e.*

$$Q = f_n\,(D, h_f, f, L)$$

Also in value of h_f, pressure drop over length, mass density of fluid ρ and acceleration due to gravity g are involved, thus Q is a function of about six independent variables. To study the effect of relationship of these six variables on the phenomenon, permutation and combination of the variables will require 720 experimental trials and hence not manageable. But if we try to form non-dimensional groups of these variables, the number can be reduced to two or three and it will be possible to find out relationship existing between phenomenon and non-dimensional groups of variables. This process is known as dimensional Analysis, and the relationship can be determined by performing experiments on suitable models which is known as model testing.

16.2 DIMENSIONAL HOMOGENEITY

Mathematical equation governing relationship between variables in a physical phenomenon is homogeneous if its left hand side (LHS) and right hand side (RHS) balance dimensionally, for example, discharge from an orifice is given by

$$Q = C_d A\sqrt{2gH}$$

Here $Q = L^3/T$

and $C_D A \sqrt{2gH}$ will have dimension $L^2 \left(\frac{L}{T^2} L\right)^{1/2}$ i.e. $\frac{L^3}{T}$

and hence it is a dimensionally homogeneous equation, but in case of Lacy's formula for wetted perimeter $P = 2.67 \sqrt{Q}$, we find that LHS is P and its dimension is L, whereas on RHS we find

$\sqrt{Q}$ has dimension of $\left(\frac{L^3}{T}\right)^{1/2}$ which does not balance with LHS and so the equine $P = 2.67$

$\sqrt{Q}$ is dimensionally not homogeneous.

16.3 METHOD OF DIMENSIONAL ANALYSIS

There are two methods for Dimensional Analysis, (*i*) Raleigh's method and (*ii*) Buckingham's P_i Theorem method.

16.3.1 Raleigh's Method

If A is a dependent variable and X, Y, Z are independent variables occurring in a phenomenon, then A can be expressed as

$$A = f_n(X, Y, Z)$$
$$= K X^a Y^b Z^c$$

where, K is a constant of proportionality. The fundamental dimensions of each of X, Y, Z and A are written and sum of exponents of each of fundamental dimension on both sides are equated *i.e.* if X has dimension $L^{a1} M^{b1} T^{c1}$, Y had dimension $L^{a2} M^{b2} T^{c2}$, Z has dimension $L^{a3} M^{b3} T^{c3}$, and A has dimension $L^2 M^0 T^0$, then

$$2 = a + b + c \quad ...(1)$$
$$0 = a + b + c \quad ...(2)$$
$$0 = a + b + c \quad ...(3)$$

Thus we have three unknown and three equation and so values of a, b, c can be determined. This method is suitable only if number of variables are three or four, but if they are more than four, it is not advisable to use this method. In that case Buckingham's P_i Theorem method is applicable.

16.3.2 Buckingham's P_i Theorem

Statement of the theorem:

The P_i theorem states that if there are 'm' number of fundamental dimensions (*i.e.* L, M, T) involved in a phenomenon controlled by 'n' number of variables, then the phenomenon can be described by $(n - m)$ independent dimensionless groups known as π terms, (P_i Terms).

In the application of this method, m number of repeating variables are chosen. Then these repeating variables along with one of the remaining variable will form one π term and similarly other π terms are formed. Repeating variables will be two if m is two or three if m is three. This method is also known as repeating variable method. Following rules should be followed in selecting repeating variables.

(*i*) They must have amongst themselves all basic dimensions involved in the phenomenon.

(*ii*) Dependent variables must not be chosen as repeating variable.

(*iii*) Repeating variables must consist of:

(*a*) Length parameter representing geometry of the phenomenon.

(*b*) Flow parameter, *i.e.* velocity.

(*c*) Fluid property parameter *i.e.* density, viscosity, etc.

Both of the above methods will be more clear with the help of numerical problems given in section 16.4. However, before attempting numerical problem, following table giving fundamental dimension of various quantities should be prepared thoroughly.

Table showing common variables in fluid flow phenomenon

Quantity	*Notation*	*Dimension (M, L, T system)*
Length	L	L
Area	A	L^2
Volume	$\forall$	L^3
Mass	M	M
Force	F	MLT^{-2}
Velocity	V	LT^{-1}
Acceleration	a	LT^{-2}
Angle	θ	$M^0 L^0 T^0$
Angular velocity	ϖ	T^{-1}
Frequency	f	T^{-1}
Discharge	Q	$L^3 T^{-1}$
Mass Density	ρ	ML^{-3}
Dynamic viscosity	μ	$ML^{-1} T^{-1}$
Kinematic viscosity	υ	$L^2 T^{-1}$
Surface tension	σ	MT^{-2}
Specific weight	γ	$ML^{-2}T^{-2}$
Specific gravity or relative density	G (or) RD	$M^0 L^0 T^0$
Volume modulus of elasticity	K	$ML^{-1} T^{-2}$
Moment	M	$ML^2 T^{-2}$
Torque	T	$ML^2 T^{-2}$
Momentum	M	$ML T^{-1}$
Work or Energy	W, E	$ML^2 T^{-2}$
Power	P	$ML^2 T^{-3}$
Rotation	N, RPM	$M^0 L^0 T^0$
Strain	–	$M^0 L^0 T^0$
Stress, pressure	p	$ML^{-1} T^{-2}$
Temperature	T	θ

16.3.3 Non-Dimensional Numbers

In fluid mechanics, there are number of non-dimensional numbers such as Reynolds, Fraud, Mach, Weber, Euler, etc. Each one is a ratio of Inertia Force to the force that is dominant in a given phenomenon.

(*i*) Reynolds number, $R = \dfrac{\text{Inertia Force, IF}}{\text{Viscous Force, VF}}$

In a pipe line since viscous force is dominant, Reynolds number is prominent in pipe flow problem.

Now,

$$\begin{aligned}
\text{IF} &= \text{Inertia Force} \\
&= \text{Mass} \times \text{Acceleration} \\
&= M \frac{L}{T^2} \\
&= \rho L^3 \frac{L}{T^2} \\
&= \rho L^2 \frac{L^2}{T^2} = \rho L^2 V^2 \\
\text{VF} &= \text{Viscous Force} = \text{Shear stress} \times \text{Area} \\
&= \tau L^2 \\
&= \mu \frac{du}{dy} L^2 \\
&= \mu \frac{L/T}{L} L^2 = \mu \frac{L^2}{T} \\
&= \mu L^2 T^{-1}
\end{aligned}$$

$$\therefore \quad R = \frac{\text{IF}}{\text{VF}} = \frac{\rho L^2 V^2}{\mu L^2 T^{-1}} = \frac{\rho L^2 V^2}{\mu\left(\dfrac{L}{T}\right)L}$$

$$= \frac{\rho L^2 V^2}{\mu V L} = \frac{\rho L V}{\mu}$$

$$\therefore \quad R = \frac{\rho L V}{\mu}$$

(*ii*) Froude number, $F = \dfrac{(\text{IF})^{1/2}}{(\text{Gravitational Force, GF})^{1/2}}$

$$= \left(\frac{\text{IF}}{\text{GF}}\right)^{1/2}$$

Now $\text{IF} = \rho L^2V^2$

and $\text{GF} = \text{Mass} \times \text{gravity}, g$

$$= \rho L^3 g$$

$$\therefore \quad F = \left(\frac{\rho L^2 V^2}{\rho L^3 g}\right)^{1/2} = \left(\frac{V^2}{Lg}\right)^{1/2}.$$

$$= \frac{V}{\sqrt{Lg}} = \frac{V}{\sqrt{gy}}$$

where, y = depth of flow in channel.

In channel flow, gravity force is prominent and therefore Froude number is a ruling number in channel flow problem.

(*iii*) Mach number, $M = \dfrac{(\text{IF})^{1/2}}{(\text{Compressibility Force})^{1/2}}$

$$= \frac{(\rho L^2 V^2)^{1/2}}{(KL^2)^{1/2}}, \text{ here } K = \text{bulk of vol. modulus of elasticity.}$$

$$= \frac{V}{\sqrt{\dfrac{K}{\rho}}} = \frac{V}{C}$$

$$= \frac{\text{Velocity of flow, } V}{\text{Velocity of sound, } C}, \text{ here } c = \sqrt{\frac{K}{\rho}}$$

In compressible fluids, compressibility of fluid is a very important feature of flow and so Mach number is a ruling number.

(*iv*) Weber number, $W = \dfrac{\text{IF}}{\text{Surface Tension Force}}$

$$= \frac{\rho L^2 V^2}{\sigma L} = \frac{\rho L V^2}{\sigma}$$

This number is important for spillway problem.

(*v*) Euler number, $E = \left(\dfrac{\text{IF}}{\text{Pressure Force}}\right)^{1/2}$

$$= \left(\frac{\rho L^2 V^2}{\Delta p L^2}\right)^{1/2}$$

$$= \frac{V}{\sqrt{\Delta p / \rho}}$$

This number is useful for aeronautical field.

16.4 SOLVED PROBLEMS

■ **Problem 16.1:** *Discharge Q over rectangular weir depends on head over weir H, acceleration due to gravity g, length of weir L, height of weir crest above channel bottom Z, mass density* **ρ**, *and dynamic visocity* **μ** *of liquid. By dimensional analysis, find Q in terms of dimensionless parameters, making use of Buckingham's* **π** *Theorem.*

Solution: As per given data,

$$Q = f_n (H, g, L, Z, \rho, \mu)$$

i.e. $(Q, H, g, L, Z, \rho, \mu) = 0$

Here number of variables $n = 7$ in which fundamental dimensions (L, M, T) involved are three, ∴ $m = 3$ ∴ π terms $= (n - m) = 4$.

$$= \pi_1, \pi_2, \pi_3, \pi_4$$

Here, (H, g, ρ) are chosen as repeating variables, and one from remaining variables is taken to form a π form.

$$\pi_1 = (H)^a (g)^b (\rho)^c Q$$

$$\pi_2 = (H)^a (g)^b (\rho)^c L$$

$$\pi_3 = (H)^a (g)^b (\rho)^c Z$$

$$\pi_4 = (H)^a (g)^b (\rho)^c \mu$$

∴ for π_1, $L^0 M^0 T^0 = (L)^a (LT^{-2})^b (ML^{-3})^c (L^3T^{-1})$

Equating power for L, $0 = a + b - 3c = 3$

for M, $0 = c$

for T, $0 = -2b - 1$

$$\therefore \quad 2b = -1 \quad \therefore \quad b = -\frac{1}{2}$$

$$\therefore \quad 0 = a + \left(-\frac{1}{2}\right) - 0 + 3$$

$$\therefore \quad a = \frac{-5}{2}$$

$$\therefore \quad \pi_1 = (H)^{\frac{-5}{2}} (g)^{\frac{-1}{2}} (\rho)^0 Q = \frac{Q}{H^2\sqrt{gH}}$$

For π_2, $L^0 M^0 T^0 = (L)^a (LT^{-2})^b (ML^{-3})^c L$

Equating power for L, $0 = a + b - 3c + 1$

for M, $0 = c$

for T, $0 = -2b$, ∴ $b = 0$

$\therefore \quad a = -1$

$\therefore \quad \pi_2 = (H)^{-1} (g)^0 (\rho)^0 L$

$$= \frac{L}{H}$$

For π_3, $\quad L^0 M^0 L^0 = (L)^a (LT^{-2})^b (ML^{-3})^c L$

$\therefore \quad \pi_3 = \frac{Z}{H}$, it is similar to π_2.

For π_4, $\quad L^0 M^0 T^0 = (L)^a (LT^{-2})^b (ML^{-3})^c \frac{\mu}{LT}$

$\therefore \quad 0 = a + -3c - 1$, by equating power for L

$0 = c + 1 \quad$ for M

$0 = -2b - 1$ for T

$\therefore \quad c = -1,\ b = \frac{-1}{2},\ a = \frac{-3}{2}$

$\therefore \quad \pi_4 = (H)^{\frac{-3}{2}} (g)^{\frac{-1}{2}} (\rho)^{-1} \mu$

$$= \frac{\mu}{\rho g^{\frac{1}{2}} H^{\frac{3}{2}}}$$

$$= \frac{\mu}{H\rho\sqrt{gH}}.$$

Note: As a check, put fundamental dimension for each variable in π term and see that it is dimensionless. If not, there is a mistake which should be found out and corrected. Thus there is no chance in getting a wrong answer in this type of problem.

■ **Problem 16.2:** *The power P required to drive a propeller depends on diameter D and angular velocity ω of the propeller, density ρ, viscosity μ and modulus K of fluid and free stream velocity V. Prove that,*

$$P = (\rho V^3 D^2)\, f_n\left[\frac{\omega D}{V}, \frac{\mu}{\rho VD}, \frac{K}{\rho V^2}\right].$$

Solution: Variables are: P, ρ V, D, ω, μ, K.

$\therefore \quad n = 7,\ m = 3.$

$\therefore \quad \pi$ terms $= (n - m) = 4.$

Chose D, V, ρ as repeating variables

$\pi_1 = (D)^a (V)^b (\rho)^c P$

$\pi_2 = (D)^a (V)^b (\rho)^c \omega$

$\pi_3 = (D)^a (V)^b (\rho)^c \mu$

$\pi_3 = (D)^a (V)^b (\rho)^c K$

$\therefore$ For π_1, $L^0 M^0 T^0 = (L)^a \left(\frac{L}{T}\right)^b \left(\frac{M}{L^3}\right)^c \left(\frac{ML^2}{T^3}\right)$

Equating power for L, $0 = a + b - 3c + 2$ $\therefore$ $a = -2$, as $c = -1$, $b = -3$ from below

M, $0 = c + 1$ $\therefore$ $c = -1$

T, $0 = -b - 3$ $\therefore$ $b = -3$

$$\therefore \quad \pi_1 = (D)^{-2} (V)^{-3} (\rho)^{-1} P = \frac{P}{\rho D^2 V^3}$$

for π_2, $L^0 M^0 T^0 = (L)^a \left(\frac{L}{T}\right)^b \left(\frac{M}{L^3}\right)^c \left(\frac{1}{T}\right)$

Equating power for L, $0 = a + b - 3c$ $\therefore$ $a = 1$ as $c = 0$, $b = -1$ from below

M, $0 = c$

T, $0 = -b - 1$ $\therefore$ $b = -1$

$$\therefore \quad \pi_2 = (D)^1 (V)^{-1} (\rho)^0 \omega = \frac{\omega D}{V}$$

Equating power for π_3, $L^0 M^0 T^0 = (L)^a \left(\frac{L}{T}\right)^b \left(\frac{M}{L^3}\right)^c \left(\frac{M}{LT}\right)$

for L, $0 = a + b - 3c - 1$ $\therefore a = -1$ as c -1, $b = -1$ from below

M, $0 = c + 1$ $\therefore c = -1$

T, $0 = -b - 1$ $\therefore b = -1$

$$\therefore \quad \pi_3 = (D)^{-1} (V)^{-1} (\rho)^{-1} \mu = \frac{\mu}{\rho VD}$$

for π_4, $L^0 M^0 T^0 = (L)^a \left(\frac{L}{T}\right)^b \left(\frac{M}{L^3}\right)^c \left(\frac{M}{LT^2}\right)$

$\therefore$ for L, $0 = a + b - 3c - 1$, $a = 0$

M, $0 = c + 1$, $c = -1$

T, $0 = -b - 2$ $\therefore$ $b = -2$

$$\therefore \quad \pi_2 = (D)^0 (V)^{-2} (\rho)^{-1} K = \frac{K}{\rho V^2}$$

$$\therefore \quad \frac{P}{\rho D^2 V^3} = f_n \left[\frac{\omega D}{V}, \frac{\mu}{\rho VD}, \frac{K}{\rho V^2}\right]. \qquad \text{...(Ans.)}$$

■ **Problem 16.3:** *The capillary rise h of a fluid of density* ρ *and surface tension* σ *in a tube of diameter D depends on contact* $\angle\theta$ *and gravity g. Prove by* ***Raleigh's method,***

$$\frac{h}{D} = f_n\left[\frac{s}{\rho g D^2}\theta\right].$$

Solution: Variables are $h, \rho, \sigma, D, \theta, g$.

Here $h = f_n[\rho, \sigma, D, \theta, g]$

$= f_n[\rho, \sigma, D, \theta, g]$ as θ itself is non-dimension term.

$\therefore$ $h = f_n(\rho)^a(\sigma)^b(D)^c(g)^d$

$$\therefore \quad L^0M^0T^0 = f_n\left(\frac{M}{L^3}\right)^a (MT^{-2})^b (L)^c \left(\frac{L}{T^2}\right)^d$$

Equating powers of $L, 1 = -3a + c + d$ ...(1)

Equating powers of $M, 0 = a + b$

Equating powers of $T, 0 = -2b - 2d$

$\therefore$ $\mathbf{b = -a}$, $2d = -2(-a) = 2a$

$\therefore$ $\mathbf{d = a}$, putting values of b and d in (1), we get

$\therefore$ $\mathbf{c = 1 + 2a}$

$\therefore$ $h = f_n[(\rho^a)(\sigma)^{-a}(D)^{1+2a}(g)^a]$

$$= f_n\left[\left(\frac{\sigma g D^2}{\sigma}\right)^a (D)\right],$$

$$\left(\text{transfer } D \text{ to LHS giving } \frac{h}{D}\right)$$

$$\therefore \quad \frac{h}{D} = f_n\left[\frac{\sigma}{\rho g D^2}, \theta\right],$$

(θ itself is non-dimensional term and so added as π term).

■ **Problem 16.4:** *Flow velocity u near a rotating disk depends on the angular velocity* ω *of the disk, radial distance r, vertical distance Z, kinematic viscosity* υ*, prove that*

$$\frac{u}{\omega r} = f_n\left[\frac{Z}{r}, \frac{\omega r^2}{\upsilon}\right].$$

Solution: Here variables are

$u, \omega, r, Z, \upsilon$

i.e. $n = 5$.

Now in these variables, all L, M, T are not found *i.e.*

$$u \rightarrow \frac{L}{T}$$

$$\omega \rightarrow \frac{1}{T}$$

$$r \rightarrow L$$

$$Z \rightarrow L$$

$$\upsilon \rightarrow \frac{L^2}{T}$$

i.e. M is absent.

$\therefore$ $m = 2$, as only L and T occur in the given variables.

$\therefore$ $n - m = 5 - 2 = 3$ π terms will be formed.

Note that in this repeating variables will be only <u>2 as $m = 2$</u>, and they are

(*i*) r (geometric property)

(*ii*) ω (angular velocity)

Then from the remaining variable u, z, υ one by one will be put with the repeating variables to form 3π terms as under:

$$\pi_1 = (r)^a \; (\omega)^b \; u$$

$$\pi_2 = (r)^a \; (\omega)^b \; Z$$

$$\pi_3 = (r)^a \; (\omega)^b \; \upsilon$$

$\therefore$ form π_1, $L^0 M^0 T^0 = (L)^a \left(\frac{1}{T}\right)^b \left(\frac{L}{T}\right)$

$\therefore$ for L, $\quad 0 = a + 1 \quad \therefore \quad a = -1$

for T, $\quad 0 = -b - 1 \quad \therefore \quad b = -1$

$$\therefore \quad \pi_1 = (r)^{-1} \; (\omega)^{-1} \; u = \frac{u}{\omega r}$$

for π_2, $\quad L^0 M^0 T^0 = (L)^a \left(\frac{1}{T}\right)^b (L)$

$\therefore$ for L, $\quad 0 = a + 1 \quad \therefore \quad a = -1$

for T, $\quad 0 = -b \quad \therefore \quad b = 0$

$$\therefore \quad \pi_2 = (r)^{-1} \; (\omega)^0 \; Z = \frac{Z}{r}$$

for π_3, $\quad L^0 M^0 T^0 = (L)^a \left(\frac{1}{T}\right)^b \left(\frac{L^2}{T}\right)$

$\therefore$ for L, $\quad 0 = a + 2 \quad \therefore a = -2$

for T, $\quad 0 = -b - 1 \quad \therefore b = -1$

$$\therefore \quad \pi_3 = (r)^{-2} (\omega)^{-1} \upsilon$$

$$= \frac{\upsilon}{\omega r^2} \text{ or } \pi_3 = \frac{\omega r^2}{v}, \text{ as it is non-dimensional it is OK.}$$

$$\therefore \quad \frac{\upsilon}{\omega r} = f_n \left[\frac{Z}{r'} \frac{\omega r^2}{\upsilon} \right].$$

16.5 MODEL TESTING

Safety of civil engineering structures like dams, spillways, bridges, culverts etc. is of prime importance in engineering profession and so design of such structures are always checked by performing experiments with their models. These models have to be hydraulically similar and must possess proper dynamic similarity besides geometric similarity. Hence models of prototype are constructed by following (*i*) geometric (*ii*) kinematic and (*iii*) dynamic similarities between model and prototype.

16.5.1 Hydraulic Similitude

When geometric, kinematic and dynamic similarities exist between prototypes and their models, model testing results will give reliable predictions about behaviour of prototype. This is known as hydraulic similitude.

(A) Geometric similarity

This is dependent on

(*i*) Length scale ratio, $L_r = \dfrac{\text{Length of model}}{\text{Length of prototype}}$

$$= \frac{L_m}{L_p}$$

(*ii*) Area ratio, $\left(\dfrac{L_m}{L_p} \right)^2 = L_r^2$

(*iii*) Volume ratio, $\left(\dfrac{L_m}{L_p} \right)^3 = L_r^3$

(B) Kinematic similarity

This is dependent on

(*i*) Velocity ratio, $V_r = \dfrac{L_r}{T_r}$

where T_r = time scale ratio, and is dependent on Reynolds or Froude's model laws as the case may be.

(*ii*) Acceleration ratio, $a_r = \dfrac{L_r}{T_r^2}$

(*iii*) Discharge ratio, $Q_r = \dfrac{L_r^3}{T_r}$

(C) Dynamic similarity

Two systems are dynamically similar if geometric and kinematic similarities exist between them and also ratios of corresponding forces in the two systems are same.

(D) Reynolds Model Law:

As per this Law, Reynolds number in model and Reynold number in prototype must be same.

$$\therefore \quad \left(\frac{\rho LV}{\mu}\right)_{\text{model}} = \left(\frac{\rho LV}{\mu}\right)_{\text{prototype}}$$

If fluids in model and prototype are possessing same value of ρ and μ, then

$$V_m L_m = V_p L_p$$

$$\therefore \quad \frac{V_m}{V_p} = \frac{L_p}{L_m}, \text{ but } \frac{V_m}{V_p} = V_r$$

$$\therefore \quad V_r = \frac{L_r}{T_r} = \frac{1}{L_r}$$

$$\therefore \quad Tr = L_r^2 \text{ as per Reynolds model law.}$$

(E) Froude Model Law

As per this law, Froude number in model and Froude number in prototype must be same.

$$\therefore \quad \left(\frac{V}{\sqrt{gL}}\right)_m = \left(\frac{V}{\sqrt{gL}}\right)_p$$

$$\therefore \quad \frac{V_m}{V_p} = \left(\frac{L_m}{L_p}\right)^{1/2}$$

$$\therefore \quad V_r = \sqrt{L_r}$$

But $\quad V_r = \dfrac{L_r}{T_r}$

$$\therefore \qquad \frac{L_r}{T_r} = \sqrt{L_r}$$

$$\therefore \qquad T_r = \sqrt{L_r} \text{ as per Froude model law.}$$

16.5.2 Distorted Models and Scale Effect

If prototype is of large magnitude then is model cannot be constructed with perfect geometric similarity, for example, a river model if constructed as per geometric similarity, it will be too long to be accommodated in a laboratory and so in such cases horizontal and vertical scales are kept different. These types of models are known as distorted models. Models for rivers, docks, harbours, etc. fall in this category. The discrepancy between the results of distorted models and prototype is known as scale effect.

Perfect geometric similarity cannot be attained, for example, similarity of roughness of surfaces of pipes and moving bed material of rivers and canals cannot be attained hundred per cent. So even if model and prototype may have perfect geometric similarity, yet surface roughness, type of moving bed material, depth of water or fluid may not have geometric similarity and this can also produce scale effect. Also a distorted model of a river or lake may suffer of not having perfect dynamic similarity, for example, surface tension effects which are negligible in prototype may be found pronounced in the distorted models. Thus model testing of distorted models have to be carried out giving due consideration for scale effect and departure from dynamic similarity.

16.6 SOLVED PROBLEMS

■ **Problem 16.5:** *Estimate for a 1 : 25 model of spillway*

(*i*) Q_p *for* Q_m *of* $0.12\ m^3/s$

(*ii*) V_m *for* V_p *of* $3.5\ m/s$

(*iii*) Q_p *per m length when* Q_m *is* $0.15\ m^3/s$ *and* L_m *of spillway model is 40 cm.*

Solution:

(*i*)

$$\frac{Q_m}{Q_p} = \frac{L_m^3}{T_m} \times \frac{T_p}{L_p^3}$$

$$= \left(\frac{L_m}{L_p}\right)^3 \left(\frac{T_p}{L_m}\right)$$

$$= L_r^3 \times \frac{1}{T_r}$$

As per Froude model law, $T_r = \sqrt{L_r}$

$$\therefore \quad \frac{Q_m}{Q_p} = L_r^3 \times \frac{1}{\sqrt{L_r}} L_r^{5/2}$$

$$\therefore \quad Q_r = \text{discharge ratio} = L_r^{5/2}$$

Now $\quad Q_m = 0.12 \text{ m}^3\text{/s}$

$$\therefore \quad \frac{0.12}{Q_p} = (L_r)^{5/2} = \left(\frac{1}{25}\right)^{5/2}$$

$$\therefore \quad Q_p = (0.12)\,(25)^{5/2} = 0.12 \times 3125$$

$$= 375 \text{ m}^3\text{/s} \quad \textbf{Ans. } (i)$$

(*ii*) Now $\quad \frac{V_m}{V_p} = V_r = \frac{L_r}{T_r} = \frac{L_r}{\sqrt{L_r}} = \sqrt{L_r}$ as per Froudel law,

$$\therefore \quad V_m = V_p \sqrt{L_r} = 3.5 \times \sqrt{\frac{1}{25}}$$

$$= \frac{3.5}{5} = 0.7 \text{ m/s} \quad \textbf{Ans. } (ii)$$

(*iii*) $\quad Q_p = 0.15 \times 3125$

$= 468 \text{ m}^3\text{/s}$ per *m* length **Ans.** (*iii*).

■ **Problem 16.6:** *A model of an open channel is built to a scale of 1 in 100. If the channel has Manning's n = 0.028, what should be the value of n for model?*

Solution: As per Froude model laws:

$$\frac{V_m}{\sqrt{gL_m}} = \frac{V_p}{\sqrt{gL_p}}$$

$$\therefore \quad \frac{V_m}{V_p} = \sqrt{\frac{L_m}{L_p}} = \sqrt{L_r}$$

$$\therefore \quad V_r = \sqrt{L_r}$$

As per Manning's, $\quad V = \frac{1}{n} R^{2/3} S_0^{1/2}$

dimension of $\quad R = L$

and dimension of $\quad S = M^0 L^0 T^0$

Now $\quad n = \frac{R^{2/3}}{V} S_0^{1/2}$

$$\therefore \quad \frac{n_m}{n_p} = n_r = \frac{L_r^{2/3}}{V_r} = \frac{L_r^{2/3}}{\sqrt{L_r}} = L_r^{1/6}$$

$$\therefore \quad n_m = n_p\,(L_r)^{1/6}$$

$$= 0.028 \left(\frac{1}{100}\right)^{1/6}$$

$$= \frac{0.028}{2.15} = 0.013. \qquad \text{...(Ans.)}$$

■ **Problem 16.7:** *Calculate for a model of* $\frac{1}{20}$ *of a spillway.*

(*i*) *prototype velocity corresponding to model velocity of 2 m/s.*

(*ii*) *prototype discharge per m width corresponding to* Q_m *of 0.25* m^3 */s/m*

(*iii*) *pressure head in prototype corresponding to* p_m *of 6 cm of mercury.*

(*iv*) *power dissipated in prototype corresponding to* P_m *= .028 Watts.*

Solution: Froude Model Law is applicable in this case as the flow is over the spillway.

(*i*)
$$V_r = \sqrt{L_r} \text{ and } L_r = \frac{L_m}{L_p} = \frac{1}{20}$$

$$\therefore \quad \frac{V_m}{V_p} = \left(\frac{1}{20}\right)^{1/2}$$

$$\therefore \quad V_p = V_m\,(20)^{1/2} = 2(20)^{1/2} = 8.94 \text{ m/s}, \qquad \text{...(Ans.)}$$

(*ii*) Ratio of discharge per unit width

$$q_r = \frac{(Q/L)_m}{(Q/L)_p} = \frac{Q_r}{L_r} = \frac{L_r^{5/2}}{L_r}$$

$$= L_r^{3/2} = \frac{q_m}{q_p}$$

$$\therefore \quad q_p = \frac{0.25}{\left(\frac{1}{20}\right)^{3/2}} = 0.25\,(20)^{3/2}$$

$$= 22.36 \text{ m}^3\text{/s/m width.} \qquad \text{...(Ans.)}$$

(*iii*) Pressure ratio
$$p_r = \left(\frac{\text{Force}}{\text{Area}}\right)_r$$

$$= \left(\frac{\rho L^2 V^2}{L^2}\right)_r$$

$$= \rho_r V_r^2$$

$$= V_r^2, \text{ since } \rho_r = \frac{\rho_m}{\rho_p} = 1.0$$

But $V_r = \sqrt{L_r}$

$\therefore$ $p_r = L_r$

$\therefore$ $\dfrac{p_m}{p_p} = L_r = \dfrac{1}{20}$

$\therefore$ $p_p = p_m \times 20 = 6 \times 20 = 120$ cm of Hg, ...(Ans.)

(*iv*) Power ratio $P_r = (\text{Force} \times \text{Velocity})_r$

$= (\rho L^2V^2 \times V)_r$

$= \rho_r L_r^2 V_r^3$

$= \rho_r L_r^2 (\sqrt{L_r})^3 = \rho_r (L_r)^{7/2} (\sqrt{L_r})^{7/2}$ as $\rho_r = 1$

$\therefore$ $P_r = (L_r)^{7/2} = \dfrac{P_m}{P_p}$

$\therefore$ $P_p = \dfrac{P_m}{(L_r)^{7/2}} = \dfrac{1028}{\left(\dfrac{1}{20}\right)^{7/3}} = 1000$ Watts $= 1.0$ KW. ...(Ans.)

■ **Problem 16.8:** *A 1 : 10 model of a car is tested in a wind tunnel. The car velocity is 70 kmph. If the drag is 300 N, what is the drag and power required to overcome the drag in the prototype. Assume υ_{air} for model and prototype to be same.*

Solution: Here Reynolds law is applicable.

$$\left(\frac{\rho VL}{\mu}\right)_m = \left(\frac{\rho VL}{\mu}\right)_p, \text{ assume } \rho_m = \rho_p$$

$\therefore$ $\dfrac{V_m}{V_p} = \dfrac{L_p}{L_m} = \dfrac{1}{L_r} = V_r$

$\therefore$ $V_m = \dfrac{V_p}{L_r} = \dfrac{70}{\left(\dfrac{1}{10}\right)} = 700$ kmph

$= \rho_r L_r^{\,2}$

Force $= \rho L^2V^2$

$\therefore$ $\dfrac{F_m}{F_p} = F_r = \dfrac{\rho_m L_m^2 V_m^2}{\rho_p L_p^2 V_p^2} = \rho_r L_r^2 V_r^2 = \rho_r L_r^2 \dfrac{1}{L_r^{2'}}$ *here* $\rho_r = 1$

$\therefore$ $F_m = F_p$

Now $F_m = 300$ N

$\therefore$ $F_p = 300$N ...(Ans.)

Power to overcome drag in prototype

$$P_p = F_p \quad V_p = 300\left(\frac{70\times10^3}{3600}\right)$$

$$= 300 \times 19.4$$

$$= 5.833 \text{ KW.}$$ ...(Ans.)

■ **Problem 16.9:** *A pipe of 2m diameter is transporting oil of kinematic viscosity, υ = 0.03 stoke, at a rate of 4000 LPS. If a 10 cm diameter pipe with water having υ = 0.01 stoke is used for model testing, find velocity and rate of flow in the model.*

Solution: Here Reynolds model law is applicable as it is a pipe flow problem.

$$\therefore \quad \left(\frac{\rho VD}{\mu}\right)_m = \left(\frac{\rho VD}{\mu}\right)_p$$

$$\therefore \quad \left(\frac{VD}{\upsilon}\right)_m = \left(\frac{VD}{\upsilon}\right)_p$$

$$\therefore \quad V_m = \frac{\upsilon_m}{\upsilon_p}\times\frac{D_p}{D_m}V_p$$

Now,
$$V_p = \frac{Q}{\frac{\pi}{4}D^2} = \frac{4}{\frac{\pi}{4}(2)^2} = \frac{4}{\pi} = 1.27 \text{ m/s}$$

$$\therefore \quad V_m = \frac{0.01}{0.03}\times\frac{2}{0.1}\times 1.27$$

$$= 8.49 \text{ m/s,}$$ ...(Ans.)

$$Q_m = \frac{\pi}{4}(0.1)^2\,(8.49) = 0.066 \text{ m}^3\text{/s}.$$ ...(Ans.)

Exercises

1. The critical depth y_c in a rectangular channel depends on discharge Q, bottom width B and the gravity γ. Prove by Raleigh's method

$$\frac{y_c}{B} = f_n\left(\frac{Q}{B^2\sqrt{gB}}\right).$$

2. The stagnation pressure p_s on the nose of an airfoil depends upon ambient pressure P_0, free stream velocity V_0, and density ρ of air. Prove by Raleigh's method.

$$\frac{P_s}{p_0} = f_n\left(\frac{p_0}{\rho V^2}\right).$$

3. The motion of a floating body through water depends on drag force F, speed V, length L, gravity g, density ρ and viscosity μ of water. Apply Buckingham's π theorem to obtain.

$$F = \rho L^2 V^2 f_n\left(\frac{\sqrt{gL}}{V'} \frac{\mu}{\rho LV}\right).$$

4. The discharge Q from a centrifugal group is a function of N (rpm), impeller diameter D, head H, gravity g and fluid properties ρ and μ. Prove that

$$Q = (D^4\, g^{1/2})\, f_n\left(\frac{N\sqrt{D}}{\sqrt{g}}, \frac{H}{D}, \frac{\mu D^2}{\rho Q}\right).$$

5. A channel has Manning's $n = 0.018$. Using model scale of 1.30, find value on n for model. (**Ans.** $n_m = 0.01$)
6. A hydraulic jump occurs at toe of a spillway. A 1 : 30 model is used to study the jump characteristics. If prototype values of incoming velocity, entrance Froude number and power dissipated are 10 m/s, 9, 2, kW/m width, respectively, find corresponding values for the model testing. (**Ans.** $V_m = 1.82$ m/s, (Froude No.)$_m$ = 9 (This should be same in model and prototype as it is a non-dimensional no.), $P_m = 0.4$ W per m width)
7. If gravity, viscosity are surface tension are equally important in a model, show that for dynamic similarity,

$$\frac{\mu_r\, L_r^{1/2}}{\sigma_r} = 1.$$

8. A venturimeter fixed in a 50 cm pipe discharging water is modelled to a scale of 1 : 5 model using air. If $\rho_{air} = 1.2$ kg/m^3, $\rho_{watet} = 1000$ kg/m^3, $\mu_{air} = 2 \times 10^{-5} \frac{\text{N-S}}{\text{m}^2}$ and $\mu_{water} = 0.001 \frac{\text{N-S}}{\text{m}^2}$, find prototype discharge corresponding to model discharge of 6 m^3/s. (**Ans.** $Q_p = 1.49$ m^3/s)

17

Compressible Fluid Flow

17.1 GENERAL

Civil Engineers have to deal with water which is for all practical purposes regarded as incompressible. Only in case of transient flow through penstocks, compressibility of water has to be considered, however, basic knowledge of compressible fluid flow is essential for all branches of engineering. Value of Mach number M is a deciding factor in finding out whether given flow is compressible or incompressible.

Just as Reynold number R is a ruling parameter for pressure flow in pipe line and Froude number F in case of channel flow, similarly Mach number M is a very important nontraditional number in case of compressible flow. It is defined as ratio of velocity of flow V to velocity of sound (c) in the same fluid

$$\therefore \qquad M = \frac{V}{c}$$

Fundamentally,
$$M = \sqrt{\frac{\text{Inertial Force}}{\text{Elastic Force}}} = \left(\frac{\rho L^2 V^2}{K L^2}\right)^{1/2}$$

here K = bulk modulus of given fluid

$$\therefore \qquad M = \left(\frac{V^2}{K/\rho}\right)^{1/2} = \frac{V}{\sqrt{K/\rho}} = \frac{V}{c} \text{ as } \sqrt{K/\rho} = c,$$

which will be proved in next section.

If $M > 1$, supersonic flow,
$M < 1$, subsonic flow,
$M = 1$, sonic flow,

$M > 3$ hypersonic flow

For $M = 0.8$ to 1.2, transonic conditions prevail.

Thus value of M is a ruling factor in deciding whether given flow is supersonic or sonic or subsonic.

17.2 TO PROVE THAT $c = \sqrt{K/\rho}$

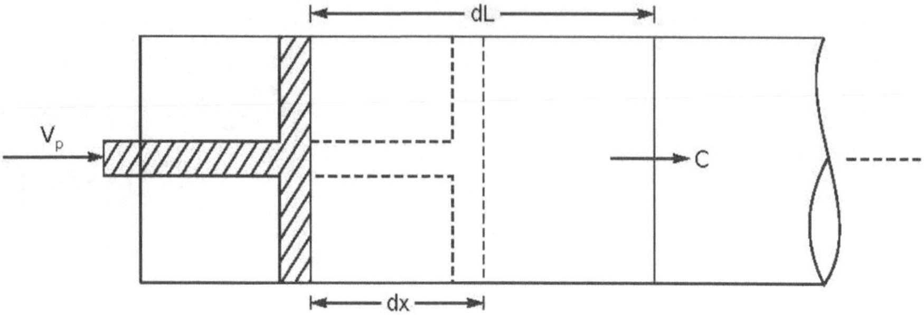

Fig. 17.1

Assume air flow in the pipe shown in Fig. 17.1.

Consider that a piston moves in the pipe with velocity V_p so that in interval of time dt, it will travel $dx = V_p\,dt$.

Pressure wave in the pipe in the same interval of time dt will travel a distance

$$dL = cdt.$$

As per law of continuity,

$$\rho\,(dL.A) = (\rho + d\rho)\,(dL - dx)\,A,\ A = \text{c/s area of the pipe}$$

$\therefore$ $$\rho dL = (\rho + d\rho)\,(dL - dx)$$

But $$dL = cdt \text{ and } dx = V_p\,dt$$

$\therefore$ $$\rho(cdt) = (\rho + d\rho)\,(cdt - V_p\,dt)$$

$\therefore$ $$\rho c = (\rho + d\rho)\,(c - V_p)$$

$\therefore$ $$\rho c = \rho c + cd\rho - V_p\rho - d\rho\,V_p$$

$\therefore$ $$c(d\rho) = \rho V_p \text{ as } V_p << c,\ (d\rho\,V_p) \text{ can be neglected}$$

$\therefore$ $$c = \frac{\rho V_p}{d\rho} \qquad \text{...(17.1)}$$

From momentum considerations,

$$\Sigma Fx = (\text{mass})\,(\text{rate of change of velocity})$$

$\therefore$ $$dp.A = (\rho dLA)\left(\frac{V_p - 0}{dt}\right)$$

$\therefore$ $$dp = \rho\frac{dL}{dt}V_p$$

$$= \rho c\,V_p$$

$$\therefore \qquad c = \frac{dp}{\rho V_p} \qquad ...(17.2)$$

Multiplying (17.1) and (17.2),

$$c^2 = \frac{dp}{d\rho} \quad \therefore \quad c = \sqrt{\frac{dp}{d\rho}} \qquad ...(17.3)$$

Let $\quad K$ = bulk modulus of given fluid

$$\therefore \qquad K = -\frac{dp}{\left(\frac{d\forall}{\forall}\right)} \text{ by definition of } K,$$

Here $\quad \forall$ = volume of fluid

$d\forall$ = change in volume of fluid

dp = change in pressure intensity.

As $\forall$ is proportional to $1/\rho$,

$$\rho\forall = \text{constant}$$

$$\therefore \qquad \forall d\rho + \rho d\forall = 0$$

$$\therefore \qquad \frac{d\forall}{\forall} = -\frac{d\rho}{\rho}$$

$$\therefore \qquad K = -\frac{dp}{\left(-\frac{d\rho}{\rho}\right)} = \frac{(\rho)dp}{d\rho} = \rho c^2 \qquad \text{as from (17.3), } \frac{dp}{d\rho} = c^2$$

$$\therefore \qquad c = \sqrt{K/\rho} \qquad ...(17.4)$$

Here $\quad c$ = value of velocity of pressure wave that will travel through fluid of mass density ρ and bulk modulus K.

= celerity of pressure wave

(*i*) c for isentropic flow of gases is given by

$$c = \sqrt{kRT}, \text{ as } \frac{p}{\rho} = RT$$

and

$$k = \frac{c_p}{c_v} = 1.4 \qquad ...(17.4a)$$

(*ii*) c has dimension of L/T as can be seen from

$$c = \sqrt{\frac{K}{\rho}} = \sqrt{\frac{F/A}{M/L^3}}$$

$$= \sqrt{\frac{\left(M\frac{L}{T^2}\right)\Big/L^2}{M/L^3}} = \sqrt{\frac{L^2}{T^2}}$$

$$= \frac{L}{T}.$$

17.3 AREA-VELOCITY RELATIONSHIP FOR COMPRESSIBLE FLOW

$\left(\text{or to prove that} \frac{dA}{A} = \frac{dV}{V}(M^2 - 1)\right)$

For compressible flow, continuity equality is

$$\rho AV = \text{constant}$$

By differentiation we get

$$\rho A dV + AV d\rho + \rho V dA = 0$$

and by dividing by ρAV, we get

$$\frac{dV}{V} + \frac{d\rho}{\rho} + \frac{dA}{A} = 0$$

$$\therefore \quad \frac{dA}{A} = -\left(\frac{dV}{V} + \frac{d\rho}{\rho}\right) \quad ...(17.5)$$

For frictionless adiabatic conditions *i.e.* for isentropic flow, Bernoulli Theorem can be written as

$$\frac{p}{\rho} + \frac{V^2}{2} + Z = \text{constant}$$

Neglecting datum,

$$\frac{p}{\rho} + \frac{V^2}{2} = \text{constant}$$

$$\therefore \quad \frac{dp}{\rho} + \frac{2VdV}{2} = 0$$

$$\therefore \quad \frac{dp}{\rho} = -VdV \quad ...(17.6)$$

Multiply and divide the term $\frac{dp}{\rho}$ by $d\rho$

$$\therefore \quad \frac{dp}{\rho}\left(\frac{d\rho}{d\rho}\right) = -VdV$$

$$\therefore \quad \frac{dp}{d\rho}\left(\frac{d\rho}{\rho}\right) = -VdV$$

But $\frac{dp}{d\rho} = c^2$ from eq. (17.3)

$$\therefore \quad c^2 \frac{d\rho}{\rho} = -VdV$$

$$\therefore \quad \frac{d\rho}{\rho} = -\frac{VdV}{c^2} \quad \text{...(17.7)}$$

Put this value of $\frac{d\rho}{\rho}$ in eq. (17.5),

$$\therefore \quad \frac{dA}{A} = -\left(\frac{dV}{V} - \frac{VdV}{c^2}\right)$$

$$= \frac{dV}{V}\left(-1 + \frac{V^2}{c^2}\right)$$

$$\therefore \quad \frac{dA}{A} = \frac{dV}{V}(M^2 - 1) \text{ as } M = \frac{V}{c} \quad \text{...(17.8)}$$

Interpretations of eq. (17.8) as per values of M:

(*i*) If $M < 1$, subsonic flow, $\frac{dV}{V} < 0$ and $\frac{dA}{A} > 0$.

i.e. with increase in area, velocity will decrease.

(*ii*) If $M > 1$, $\frac{dV}{V} > 0$ and $\frac{dA}{A} > 0$. (*i.e.* for supersonic flow)

i.e. with increase in area, velocity will also increase.

(*iii*) If $M = 1$, $\frac{dA}{A} = 0$, $\therefore$ A is constant. (*i.e.* for sonic condition)

Thus, the effect of area variation on subsonic flow ($M < 1$), is same as that for incompressible flow, but the effect of area variation on supersonic flow ($M > 1$), is exactly opposite to that for subsonic flow. In order to accelerate the flow of compressible fluid at $M > 1$, the flow passages must diverge. The divergence of flow-passage is necessary because in supersonic flow ($M > 1$) of compressible fluids, the decrease in the density of the fluid is greater than increase in flow velocity but mass flow rate (ρVA) must remain constant and therefore area of flow A must increase.

When $M = 1$, $V = c$, and $dA = 0$,

i.e. if velocity of flow equals velocity of sound, it must do so where the cross-section area is minimum.

Thus it is necessary to have convergent passage followed by divergent in order to convert initially subsonic flow into supersonic flow in a nozzle.

17.4 STAGNATION PROPERTIES

When a fluid flows past an immersed body, at a point 2 on the body, velocity will be zero and the point is called stagnation point. Values of pressure, temperature and density at this point of stagnation s, are called stagnation properties, denoted by p_s, T_s and ρ_s respectively.

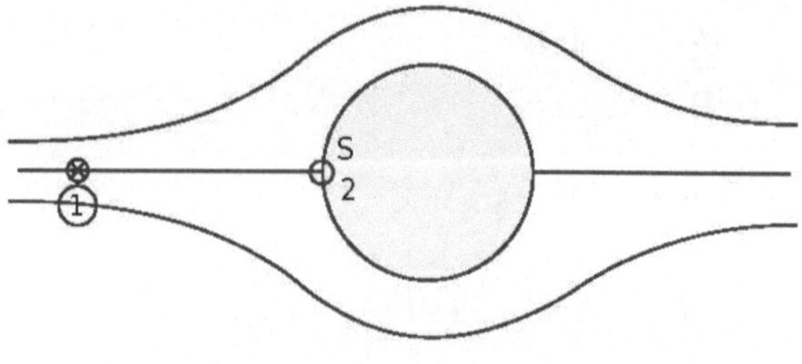

Fig. 17.2

It can be proved that

$$p_s = p_1\left[1+\frac{k-1}{2}M_1^2\right]^{\frac{k}{k-1}}$$

Here p_s = stagnation pressure at point 2

p_1 = ambient pressure at point 1

M_1 = Mach number at point 1 = $\frac{V_1}{c_1}$

$k = \frac{c_p}{c_v}$ = specific heat ratio.

Referring to Fig. 17.2, apply B – Theorem for adiabatic flow with friction at points 1, 2.

$$\left(\frac{k}{k-1}\right)\frac{p_1}{\rho_1}+\frac{V_1^2}{2}=\left(\frac{k}{k-1}\right)\frac{p_2}{\rho_2}+\frac{V_2^2}{2} \text{ taking } Z_1 = Z_2 \textit{ i.e. same datum}$$

At point 2, $V_2 = 0$ $p_2 = p_s$ and $\rho_2 = \rho_s$

$$\therefore \quad \left(\frac{k}{k-1}\right)\frac{p_1}{\rho_1}+\frac{V_1^2}{2} = \left(\frac{k}{k-1}\right)\frac{p_s}{\rho_s}$$

$$\therefore \quad \left(\frac{k}{k-1}\right)\left[\frac{p_1}{\rho_1}-\frac{p_s}{\rho_s}\right] = -\frac{V_1^2}{2} \qquad \text{...(17.9)}$$

$\therefore$ For adiabatic process, $\frac{p}{\rho^k}$ = constant

$$\therefore \quad \frac{p_1}{\rho_1^k}=\frac{p_s}{\rho_s^k}$$

$$\therefore \quad \frac{p_1}{p_s} = \left(\frac{\rho_1}{\rho_s}\right)^k \text{ and } \frac{\rho_1}{\rho_s}=\left(\frac{p_1}{p_s}\right)^{\frac{1}{k}}=\left(\frac{p_s}{p_1}\right)^{-\frac{1}{k}}$$

Putting these values in eq. (17.9),

$$\left(\frac{k}{k-1}\right)\left(\frac{p_1}{\rho_1}\right)\left[1-\left(\frac{p_s}{p_1}\right)\left(\frac{\rho_1}{\rho_s}\right)\right] = -\frac{V_1^2}{2}$$

$$\left(\frac{k}{k-1}\right)\left(\frac{p_1}{\rho_1}\right)\left[1-\left(\frac{p_s}{p_1}\right)^{1-\frac{1}{k}}\right] = -\frac{V_1^2}{2}$$

$$\left[1-\left(\frac{p_s}{p_1}\right)^{\frac{k-1}{k}}\right] = -\frac{V_1^2}{2}\left(\frac{k-1}{k}\right)\left(\frac{\rho_1}{p_1}\right)$$

$$\therefore \quad 1+\frac{V_1^2}{2}\left(\frac{k-1}{k}\right)\left(\frac{\rho_1}{p_1}\right) = \left(\frac{p_s}{p_1}\right)^{\frac{k-1}{k}} \qquad \text{...(17.10)}$$

For adiabatic process,

$$c = \sqrt{kRT} \quad \text{and} \quad \frac{p}{\rho} = RT$$

here, R = gas constant = 287 J/(kg-Kelvin)

J = Joule

$$k = c_p / c_v = \frac{\text{specific heat at constant pressure}}{\text{specific heat at constant volume}}$$

= 1.4 for air.

R is also equal to $c_p - c_v$

Now as $c = \sqrt{kRT}$ and $RT = p/\rho$

$$\therefore \quad c = \sqrt{k\left(\frac{p}{\rho}\right)}$$

$$\therefore \quad c_1^2 = k\left(\frac{p_1}{\rho_1}\right)$$

$$\therefore \quad \frac{\rho_1}{p_1} = \frac{k}{c_1^2}$$

Putting this value in eq. (17.10),

$$1+\frac{V_1^2}{2}\left(\frac{k-1}{k}\right)\left(\frac{k}{c_1^2}\right) = \left(\frac{p_s}{p_1}\right)^{\frac{k-1}{k}}$$

$$\therefore \quad 1+\frac{1}{2}\left(\frac{V_1^2}{c_1^2}\right)(k-1) = \left(\frac{p_s}{p_1}\right)^{\frac{k-1}{k}}$$

$$\therefore \quad \left[1+\frac{k-1}{2}(M_1^2)\right]^{\frac{k-1}{k}} = \frac{p_s}{p_1}$$

$$\therefore \quad p_s = p_1\left[1+\left(\frac{k-1}{2}\right)M_1^2\right]^{\frac{k}{k-1}} \qquad ...(17.11)$$

Similarly,

$$\rho_s = \rho_1\left[1+\left(\frac{k-1}{2}\right)M_1^2\right]^{\frac{1}{k-1}} \qquad ...(17.12)$$

and

$$T_s = T_1\left[1+\frac{k-1}{2}M_1^2\right] \qquad ...(17.13)$$

To get eq. (17.12), put value of $\frac{p_s}{p_1} = \left(\frac{\rho_s}{\rho_1}\right)^k$ in eq. (17.11)

i.e.

$$\left(\frac{\rho_s}{\rho_1}\right)^k = \left[1+\left(\frac{k-1}{2}\right)M_1^2\right]^{\frac{k}{k-1}}$$

$$\therefore \quad \rho_s = \rho_1\left[1+\left(\frac{k-1}{2}\right)M_1^2\right]^{\frac{1}{k-1}}$$

Also

$$\rho_s = \frac{p_s}{R_s T_s} \text{ from } p = \rho RT \qquad ...(1713A)$$

Similarly fro eq. (13),
we have

$$p = \rho RT$$

$$\therefore \quad T_s = \left(\frac{p_s}{\rho_s}\right)\left(\frac{1}{R_s}\right)$$

But

$$\frac{p_s}{\rho_s} = \frac{p_1\left[1+\left(\frac{k-1}{2}\right)M_1^2\right]^{\frac{k}{k-1}}}{\rho_1\left[1+\left(\frac{k-1}{2}\right)M_1^2\right]^{\frac{1}{k-1}}}$$

$$= \frac{p_1}{\rho_1}\left[1+\left(\frac{k-1}{2}\right)M_1^2\right], \text{ as } \left(\frac{k}{k-1}-\frac{1}{k-1}=\frac{k-1}{k-1}=1\right)$$

$$\therefore \qquad T_s = \frac{p_1}{\rho_1}\left[1+\left(\frac{k-1}{2}\right)M_1^2\right]\frac{1}{R_s}$$

Now $\quad R_s = R_1$ since it is a gas constant

$$= \frac{p_1}{\rho_1}\left(\frac{1}{T_1}\right) \text{ from } p = \rho RT$$

$$\therefore \qquad T_s = \frac{p_1}{\rho_1}\left[1+\left(\frac{k-1}{2}\right)M_1^2\right]\frac{\rho_1}{p_1}T_1$$

$$= T_1\left[1+\left(\frac{k-1}{2}\right)M_1^2\right] \qquad \text{...(17.13B)}$$

17.5 PROPAGATION OF PRESSURE WAVE IN COMPRESSIBLE FLOW

Case (*i*): $M < 1$

For subsonic flow, $\frac{V}{c} < 1$

$\therefore \qquad V < c$

$\therefore$ Pressure wave which travels with velocity c will be always ahead of disturbance source which travels with velocity V.

Case (*ii*): $M = 1$

$\therefore \qquad V = c$

In the case of sonic flow, as velocity of wave and disturbance source is same, pressure wave will coincide with the disturbance source.

Case (*iii*): $M > 1$

$\therefore \qquad V > c$

$AB = c$

$AP = V$

$$\sin\alpha = \frac{AB}{AP} = \frac{c}{V} = \frac{1}{M}$$

In case of supersonic flow, source of disturbance will be always ahead of pressure wave as $V > c$. It creates a cone of disturbance which is a conical space created by joining tangent points B, C, D etc. Half the angle of cone is Mach angle and

$$\sin\alpha = \frac{1}{M} = \frac{c}{V}$$

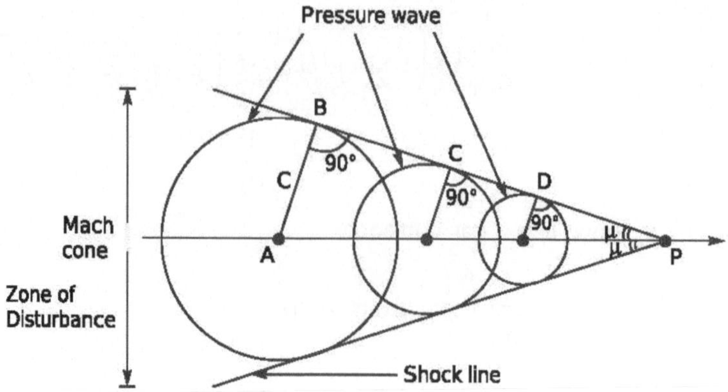

Fig. 17.3

Effect of disturbance is felt only inside mach cone. Outside the cone no disturbance will be felt.

17.6 NORMAL SHOCK WAVE

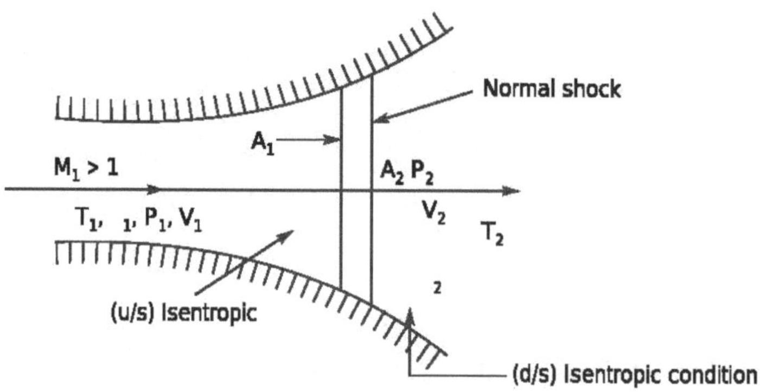

Fig. 17.4

In case of supersonic flow through a convergent-divergent nozzle as shown in Fig. 17.4, a shock wave normal to the flow direction may occur and flow may change to subsonic condition after the shock. It has a very little thickness and is similar to hydraulic jump in open channel. Consider section 1 on u/s and 2 on d/s of the shock wave. As the thickness is little, c/s area

$$A_1 = A_2 = A$$

Change in entropy(s) across the shock is given by

$$s_2 - s_1 = C_v \ln\left[\left(\frac{p_2}{p_1}\right)\left(\frac{\rho_1}{\rho_2}\right)^k\right] \qquad ...(17.14)$$

Relationships between fluid and flow parameter on either side are given below:

(1) Mach Number:

$$M_2^2 = \frac{2+(k-1)M_1^2}{2kM_1^2-(k-1)} \quad ...(17.15)$$

$$M_1^2 = \frac{2+(k-1)M_2^2}{2k\,M_2^2-(k-1)} \quad ...(17.16)$$

(2) Pressure Ratio:

$$\frac{p_2}{p_1} = \frac{1+kM_1^2}{1+kM_2^2} \quad ...(17.17)$$

(3) Density Ratio:

$$\frac{\rho_2}{\rho_1} = \frac{M_1^2\,(k+1)}{2+M_1^2\,(k-1)} \quad ...(17.18)$$

(4) Velocity Ratio:

$$\frac{V_2}{V_1} = \frac{\rho_1}{\rho_2} = \frac{2+M_1^2\,(k-1)}{M_1^2\,(k+1)} \quad ...(17.19)$$

(5) Temperature Ratio:

Stagnation temperature is constant across the shock

$$\therefore \quad T_1 = T_2$$

(6) Entropy(s) is defined as capacity to do mechanical work.

Characteristics of the normal shock:

(1) u/s flow supersonic and d/s subsonic.

(2) Stagnation temperature remains same across the shock.

(3) Entropy increases across the shock with consequent decrease in stagnation pressure and stagnation density across the shock.

17.7 SOLVED PROBLEMS

■ **Problem 17.1:** *A jet fighter is designed to travel at 1200 kmph at temperature of – 10° C through still air at pressure of 91 kN/m². Determine Mach number and stagnation pressure at nose of plane.*

Given: R = 290 J/kg - K, k = 1.4.

Solution:

$$V = 1200 \text{ kmph} = 333 \text{ m/s}$$

$$c = \sqrt{kRT} = \sqrt{1.4\times 290\times 263}, \text{ (here } T = -10+273 = 263 \text{ K)}$$

$$= 326 \text{ m/s}$$

$$M = \frac{V}{c} = \frac{333}{326} = 1.02 \qquad \text{...(Ans.)}$$

$$p_s = p_1\left[1 + \frac{k-1}{2}M_1^2\right]^{\frac{k}{k-1}}$$

$$= 91 \times 10^3\left[1 + \frac{1.4-1}{2}(1.02)^2\right]^{\frac{1.4}{1.4-1}}$$

$$= 91 \times 10^3 \times (1.208)^{3.5}$$

$$= 176.3 \text{ kN/m}^2. \qquad \text{...(Ans.)}$$

■ **Problem 17.2:** *A bullet is fired into atmosphere having temperature = 15°C. Find the velocity of the bullet of Mach angle is 30°. Given R = 30 m/°K, k = 1.4.*

Solution:

Here $R = 30 \text{ m/}^\circ K = 30 \times 9.81 = 294.3 \text{ J/kg-K}$

$k = 1.4, T = 15 + 273 = 288 \text{ K}$

$$c = \sqrt{kRT} = \sqrt{1.4 \times 294.3 \times 288} = 344 \text{ m/s}$$

$$\sin \alpha = \frac{c}{V}$$

$$\therefore \quad \sin 30 = \frac{344}{V} \quad \therefore V = \mathbf{688 \text{ m/s}} \qquad \text{...(Ans.)}$$

■ **Problem 17.3:** *Calculate Mach number and state type of flow if an aircraft flies at 1200 kmph at sea level where temperature is 20° C. Take k = 1.4, R = 287 J/kg-K.*

Solution: $V = 1200 \text{ kmph} = 333 \text{ m/s.}$

$T = 20 + 273 = 293 \text{ Kelvin (K)}$

$$c = \sqrt{kRT} = \sqrt{1.4 \times 287 \times 293} = 343 \text{ m/s}$$

$$\therefore \quad M = \frac{V}{c} = \frac{333}{343} = \mathbf{0.97 < 1, \text{ subsonic flow}} \qquad \text{...(Ans.)}$$

■ **Problem 17.4:** *Calculate stagnation properties on nose of a plane flying at 1000 kmph through still air having ambient pressure of 0.8 kg f/cm² and temperature – 10°C. Take R = 287 J/kg - K and k = 1.4.*

Solution: $V = 1000 \text{ kmph} = 278 \text{ m/s}$

$p_1 = 0.8 \times 10^4 \times 9.81 = 7.85 \times 10^4 \text{ N/m}^2$

$= 78.5 \text{ kN/m}^2$

$T_1 = -10 + 273 = 263 \text{ K}$

$R = 287 \text{ J/kg-K}$ and $k = 1.4$. $\therefore$ $c = \sqrt{kRT} = 325 \text{ m/s}$

$$p_s = p_1\left[1+\frac{k-1}{2}M_1^2\right]^{\frac{k}{k-1}}$$

$$= 78.5\left[1+\frac{1.4-1}{2}(.855)^2\right]^{\frac{1.4}{0.4}} \text{ here } M_1 = \frac{V}{c} = \frac{278}{325} = 0.855$$

$$= 78.5\,[1 + 0.2 \times (0.73)]^{3.5}$$

$$= 78.5\,(1.146)^{3.5}$$

$$= 78.5 \times 1.612 = \mathbf{126.5\ kN/m^2} \quad \text{...(Ans.)}$$

$$T_s = T_1\left[1+\frac{k-1}{2}M_1^2\right]$$

$$= 263\,[1 + 0.2 \times (0.73)] = 263\,(1.146) = \mathbf{301.4\ K}$$

$\therefore$ temp. = 301.4 – 273 = **28.4°C** ...(Ans.)

$$\rho_s = \frac{p_s}{RT_s} \text{ from eq. (13}a\text{)}$$

$$= \frac{126.5\times10^3}{287\times301.4} = 1.462\ \text{kg/m}^3. \quad \text{...(Ans.)}$$

■ **Problem 17.5:** *A plane flies at altitude of 2500 m where temperature is – 10°C. An observer on ground hears the sonic boom after 6 s the plane has past over his head. Find plane velocity and Mach number. R = 287 J/ kg - K and k = 1.4.*

Solution:

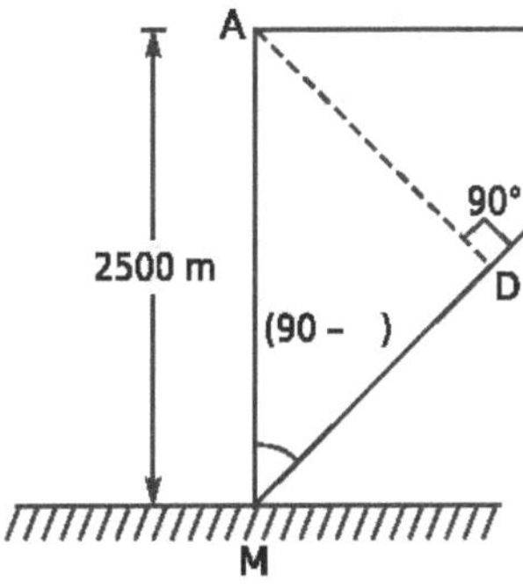

Fig. 17.5

$$T = -10 + 273 = 263$$

$$c = \sqrt{kRT}$$

$$= \sqrt{1.4\,(287)\,(263)}$$

$$= 325 \text{ m/s}$$

Let B be the location of plane when boom is heard by observer at M, on the ground, see Fig. 17.5

$$\angle ABM = \alpha = \text{half cone angle}$$

Let a ⊥ r AD be drawn on MB

$$\therefore \quad AD = ct$$

and $$AB = Vt$$

$$\frac{AD}{AM} = \frac{ct}{AM} = \frac{325\,(6)}{2500} = 0.78$$

But $$\frac{AD}{AM} = \sin(90 - \alpha) = \cos\alpha$$

$$= (1 - \sin^2\alpha)^{1/2}$$

$$= \left(1 - \frac{1}{M^2}\right)^{1/2}$$

$$\therefore \quad .78 = \left(1 - \frac{1}{M^2}\right)^{1/2}$$

$$\therefore \quad 1 - \frac{1}{M^2} = 0.6$$

$$\therefore \quad \frac{1}{M^2} = 0.4$$

$$\therefore \quad M^2 = \frac{1}{0.4} = 2.5$$

$$\therefore \quad M = 1.58 = \frac{V}{c}$$

$$\therefore \quad V = 1.58\,(325) = 513 \text{ m/s.}$$

Exercises

1. Find celerity of pressure wave in gas of $\rho = 1.12$ kg/m^3 and pressure 80 KPa abs. Given $k = 1.4$, **(Ans.** $c = 326$ m/s**)**
2. Find sonic velocity through mercury if its $K = 2.65 \times 10^{10}$ Pa. **(Ans.** 1390 m/s**)**
3. Find sonic velocity in oxygen at 20°C, given $R = 280$ J/kg-K, $k = 1.4$. **(Ans.** 339 m/s**)**

4. A plane is flying at $M = 3$, at elevation of 1000 m, and temperature 20°C, find time that will elapse after sonic boom reaches an observer. What will be the distance of the plane from the observer? Given $R = 280$ J/kg-K, $k = 1.4$.

(**Ans.** $t = 2.82$ s, distance 2828 m)

5. Find stagnation properties at the nose of a plane flying at 653 m/s in atmosphere where the pressure is 12 KPa abs, density is 0.19 kg/m³. Given = $R = 287$ J/kg-K, $k = 1.4$.

(**Hint:** $$T_1 = \frac{p_1}{\rho_1 R} = \frac{12\times10^3}{0.19\,(287)} = 200\text{ K}$$

Then find $$c = \sqrt{kRT}$$
$$= 297\text{ m/s and then}$$

$$M_1 \frac{V}{c} = \frac{653}{297} = 2.2)$$

(**Ans.** $p_s = 128$ KPa (abs); $\rho_s = 1.05$ kg/ m³; $T_s = 160$°C)

18

Impact of Jet on Plates and Jet Propulsion

18.1 INTRODUCTION

For power transmission through pipes, nozzles are fitted on the pipes so that water issues out as jet. If a plate is placed in the path of the jet, a force is exerted by the jet on the plate. The plate may be straight or curved and moving or stationary. The jet may strike the plate in a normal direction or it may strike it with an angle of inclination. The plates may be fitted on a wheel and in that case it becomes a problem of jet striking series if plates. The plate can be stationary but hinged at top and so it may rotate under the influence of jet. Thus we have varieties of problems under this topic. Moreover this topic is a prerequisite for turbomachines and centrifugal pumps.

18.2 CLASSIFICATION OF PROBLEMS

The classification of problems is given as:

(*a*) Jet striking a stationary flat plate,

(*i*) when plate makes a 90° angle with the jet.

(*ii*) when plate makes an angle other than 90° with the jet.

(*iii*) when plate is hinged at top and free to rotate and jet may strike at any angle.

(*b*) Jet striking a stationary curved plate.

(*c*) Jet striking a moving plate.

(*i*) plate may be flat.

(*ii*) plate may be curved.

(*d*) Jet striking a series of flat or curved plates.

18.2.1 Jet Striking a Stationary Flat Plate

(*a*) Let the jet make an angle of 90° with the plate.

Let the jet strike the plate at 90° with velocity V and cross-sectional area of jet as 'a' and its diameter 'd'.

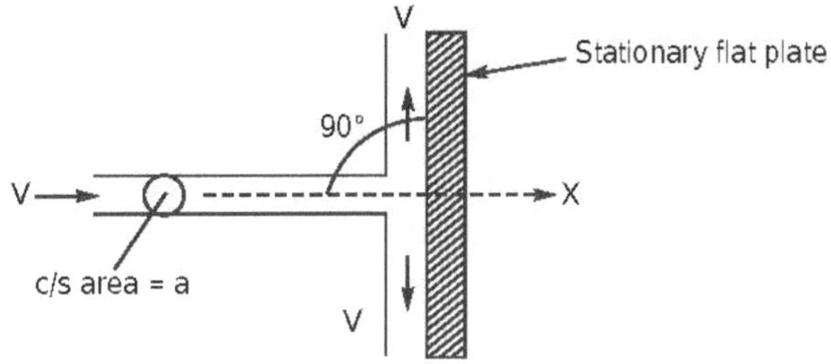

Fig. 18.1

∴ Force exerted by the jet on the plate

$$= F_x = \text{(Mass/sec) (Change is velocity)}$$

$$= (\rho aV)(V - 0)$$

∴ $$F_x = \rho aV^2 \qquad ...(18.1)$$

(*b*) Stationary flat plate making $\angle\theta$ with horizontal or the jet strikes the plate at $\angle\theta$.

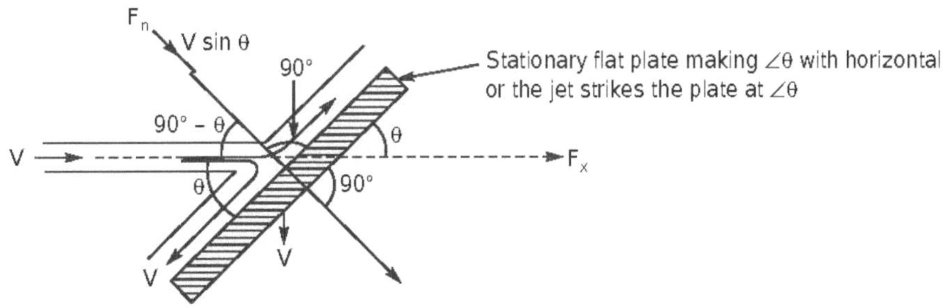

Fig. 18.2

∴ Component of velocity in direction normal to the plate is $V \cos (90 - \theta) = V \sin \theta$

∴ $$F_n = (\rho aV)(V \sin \theta - 0)$$

$$= \rho aV^2 \sin \theta \qquad ...(18.2)$$

Now, $$F_x = F_n \cos (90 - \theta)$$

∴ $$F_x = F_n \sin \theta$$

$$= \rho aV^2 \sin^2 \theta \qquad ...(18.3)$$

and $$F_y = \rho aV^2 \sin \theta \cos \theta \qquad ...(18.4)$$

18.2.2 Force Exerted by Jet on Hinged Plate

Let a plate of dimension ($L \times B$) be suspended from a hinge at O and let its centre of gravity G be at y distance from O. When a horizontal jet strikes the plate with velocity V, the plate gets deflected through $\angle\theta$ and its equilibrium in that position is due to the horizontal force F_x of the jet. In its inclined position, G will be at a horizontal distance of ($y \sin \theta$) from original position of G of the plate. Taking moment at hinge,

$$F_x(y) = W(y \sin \theta)$$

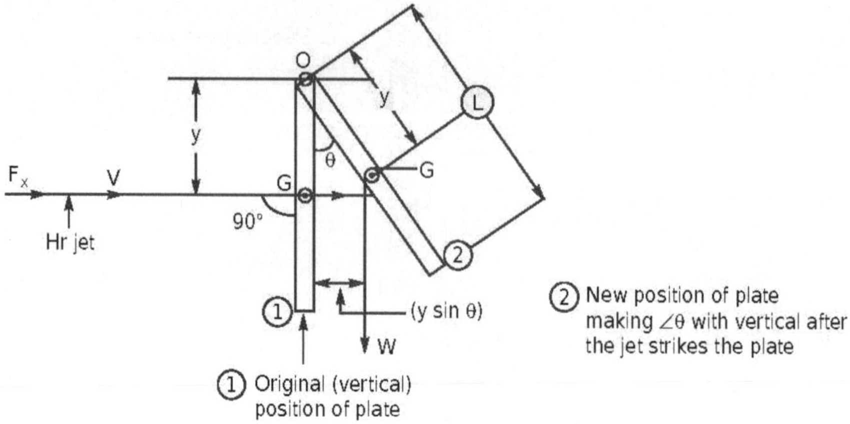

Fig. 18.3

But $$F_x = \rho a V^2$$

$\therefore$ $$\rho a V^2 (y) = W(y \sin \theta)$$

$\therefore$ $$\rho a V^2 = W \sin \theta$$

$\therefore$ $$W = \frac{\rho a V^2}{\sin \theta} \quad ...(18.5)$$

Now, $$W = (LB)(t)(\rho g),$$

where, t = thickness of plate

ρ = mass density of plate material.

This arrangement is useful in finding out experimentally value of C_v as V of jet is given by $V = C_v \sqrt{2gH}$, and the heat H is known.

18.2.3 Jet Striking a Stationary Symmetrical Curved Plate at its Centre

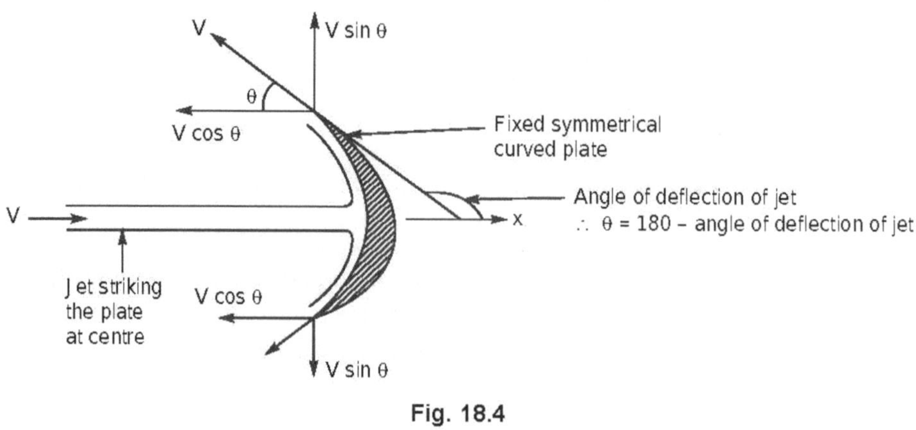

Fig. 18.4

Let a jet strike fixed symmetrical and smooth plate centrally, then velocity of water at outlet is also same *i.e.* V. As water mass is divided into two at the outlet, for calculation of force only one of the outlets is considered.

$$\therefore \quad F_x = \text{(mass per sec) (change in velocity)}$$
$$= \rho a V[V - (-V\cos\theta)]$$
$$= \rho a V^2 (1 + \cos\theta) \quad \text{...(18.6)}$$
$$F_y = \rho a V(0 - V\sin\theta)$$
$$= -\rho a V^2 \sin\theta \quad \text{...(18.7)}$$

18.2.4 Jet Striking a Stationary Curved Plate at One End Tangentially (Plate unsymmetrical)

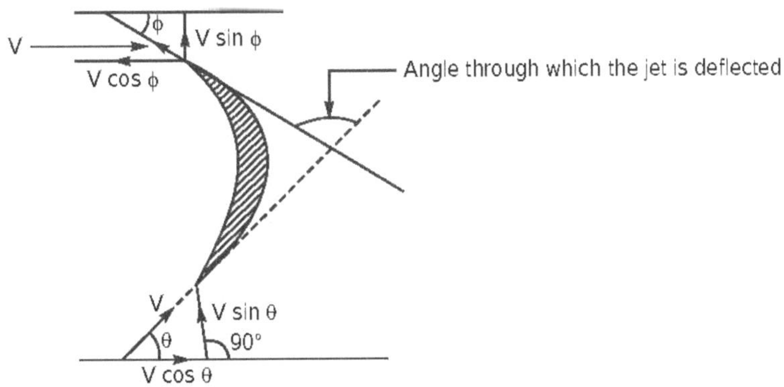

Fig. 18.5

Let the plate be unsymmetrical then θ = angle made by jet at inlet and ϕ = angle made by jet at outlet. (If plate is symmetrical, $\theta = \phi$).

$$F_x = \rho a V[V\cos\theta - (-V\cos\phi)] \quad \text{...(18.8)}$$
$$= \rho a V^2 (\cos\theta + \cos\phi) \text{ for unsymmetrical}$$
$$= \rho a V^2 (2\cos\theta) \text{ for symmetrical}$$

and
$$F_y = \rho a V^2 (\sin\theta - \sin\phi).$$

18.3 JET STRIKING A MOVING FLAT PLATE

Case (1) Vertical Flat Plate:

Let a jet of velocity V strike a plate which is moving at a velocity u in the direction of jet, then mass of water striking the plate is reduced by u

$$F_x = \text{mass striking per sec. (Change in velocity)}$$
$$= \rho a(V-u)\,[(V-u) - 0]$$
$$= \rho a(V-u)^2 \quad \text{...(18.9)}$$

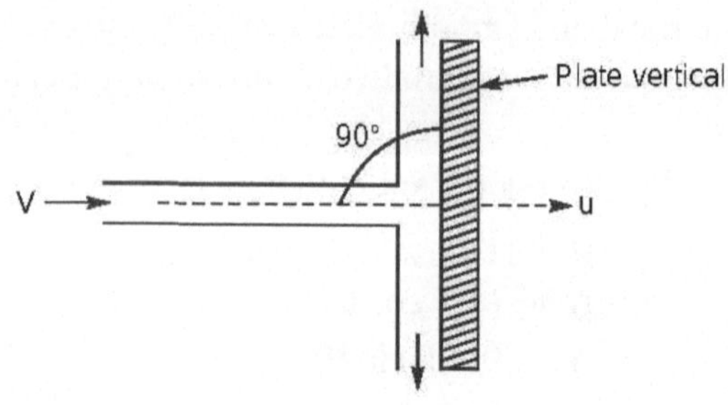

Fig. 18.6

Case (2) Inclined Flat Plate:

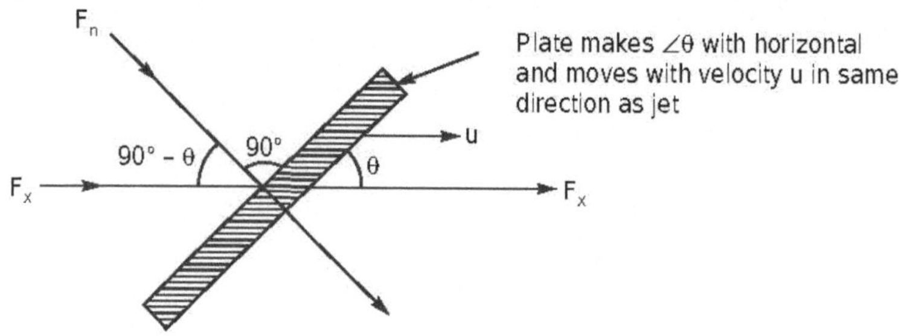

Fig. 18.7

$$F_n = \text{Force normal to plate}$$

$$\therefore \quad = \rho a(V - u)\,[(V - u)\sin\theta - 0]$$

$$= \rho a(V - u)^2 \sin\theta$$

$$\therefore \quad F_x = F_n \cos(90 - \theta)$$

$$= F_n \sin\theta$$

$$= \rho a(V - u)^2 \sin^2\theta \qquad \text{...(18.10)}$$

18.3.1 Jet Striking a Symmetrical Curved Plate Moving in Direction of Jet

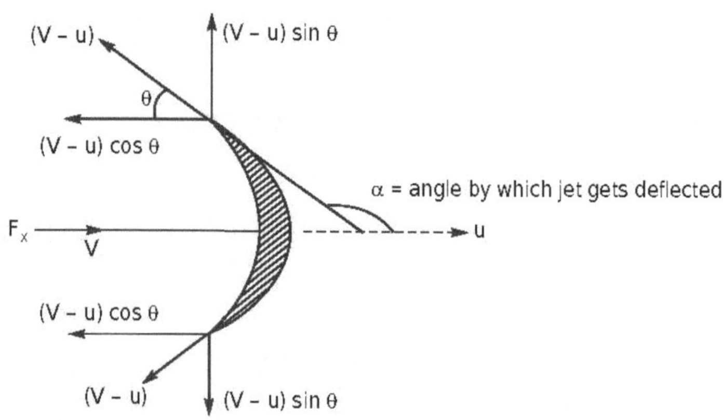

Fig. 18.8

$$\therefore \quad \theta = 180 - \alpha$$

$$= \text{angle jet makes with plate at outlet}$$

$$F_x = \text{Mass striking per sec (Change in velocity)}$$

$$= \rho a(V - u)\,[(V - u) - (-(V - u)\cos\theta)]$$

$$= \rho a(V - u)^2 (1 + \cos\theta) \qquad ...(18.11)$$

$$F_y = \rho a(V - u)\,[0 - (V - u)\sin\theta]$$

$$= -\rho a\,(V - u)^2 \sin\theta \qquad ...(18.12)$$

18.3.2 Jet Striking Unsymmetrical Curved Plate Moving in Direction Different From Jet

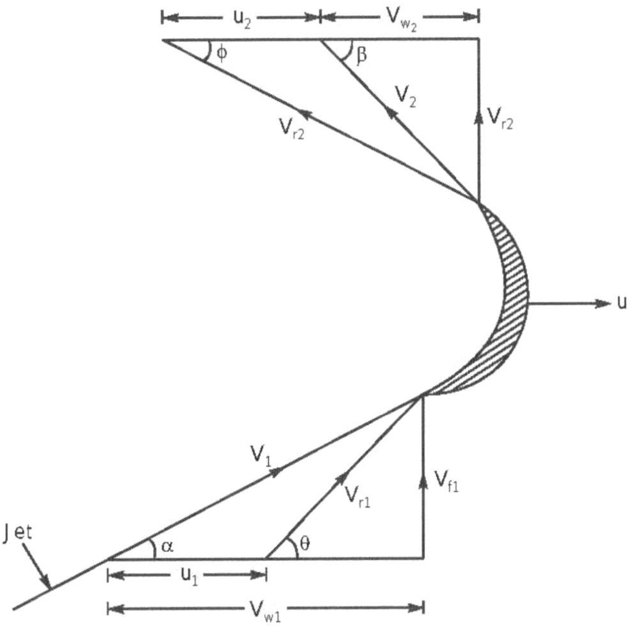

Fig. 18.9

Let the jet strike the plate at one end and make $\angle\alpha$ with the horizontal. Plate is moving with velocity u which is in different direction than that of jet. Relative velocity at inlet (V_{r1}) will be equal to vector difference of V and u. This gives a velocity Δ at inlet and also at outlet. For both velocity Δ^s, notations to be followed are as under:

(*a*) Velocity Δ at inlet:

V_1 = absolute velocity of jet at inlet

u_1 = velocity of plate

V_{r1} = relative velocity of jet and plate

α = angle between V_1 and u_1

θ = angle between V_{r1} and u_1 or plate angle at inlet

V_{w1} = velocity of whirl
V_{f1} = velocity of flow

(*b*) Velocity Δ at outlet:

V_2 = absolute velocity of jet leaving the plate
u_2 = velocity of plate
V_{r2} = relative velocity
ϕ = angle between V_{r2} and u_2 or plate angle at outlet
β = angle between V_2 and u_2
V_{w2} = velocity of whirl
V_{f2} = velocity of flow

θ and ϕ are blade ∠s at inlet and outlet.

α and β are ∠s made by jet at inlet and outlet.

Note that $u = u_1 = u_2$ and $V_{r1} = V_{r2}$ if there is no friction over the plate, assuming plate to be smooth.

Let F_x = force exerted by jet in direction of motion of the plate.

$$= \text{mass of water striking per sec} \times \left[\begin{array}{c}\text{(Initial velocity – Final velocity) of} \\ \text{the jet in direction of motion of plate}\end{array}\right]$$

Now mass/sec $= \rho a V_{r1}$

Initial velocity of jet in direction of motion of the plate

$$= V_{r1} \cos \theta$$
$$= V_{w1} - u_1, \text{ sec inlet } \Delta \text{ of velocity}$$

Final velocity of jet in direction of motion of the plate

$$= -V_{r2} \cos \phi$$
$$= -(u_2 + V_{w2}), \text{ the outlet } \Delta \text{ of velocity.}$$

$$\therefore \quad F_x = \rho a V_{r1} [(V_{w1} - u_1) - (-u_2 + V_{w2})]$$
$$= \rho a V_{r1} [(V_{w1} + V_{w2}] \qquad \text{as } u_1 = u_2 = u \qquad (\text{for } \beta < 90°)$$

and
$$F_y = \rho a V_{r1} [V_{f1} - V_{f2}]$$

Here,
$$V_{w1} = V_1 \cos \alpha$$

and
$$V_{w2} = V_{r2} \cos \phi - u_2$$
$$V_{f1} = V_1 \sin \alpha$$
$$= V_{r1} \sin \theta$$
$$V_{f2} = V_{r2} \sin \phi$$
$$= V_2 \sin \beta$$

$$\text{Resultant Force} = \sqrt{F_x^2 + F_y^2} \text{ at } \theta = \tan^{-1}\left(\frac{F_y}{F_x}\right)$$

If β is acute *i.e.* < 90°, $F_x = \rho a V_{r1} (V_{w1} + V_{w2})$ ...(18.13)

as shown above, but if β is > 90°, *i.e.* obtuse, then

$$F_x = \rho a V_{r1} (V_{w1} - V_{w2}) \quad ...(18.14)$$

If $\beta = 90°, F_x = \rho a V_{r1} (V_{w1})$ as $V_{w2} = 0$.

Work-done per second per unit weight of striking fluid

$$= \frac{\rho a V_{r1} (V_{w1} \pm V_{w2}) u}{(\rho a V_{r1}) g}$$

$$= \frac{1}{g} (V_{w1} \pm V_{w2}) u \quad ...(18.15)$$

18.4 JET STRIKING SERIES OF VANES

Case (*i*) Flat plates mounted on a wheel:

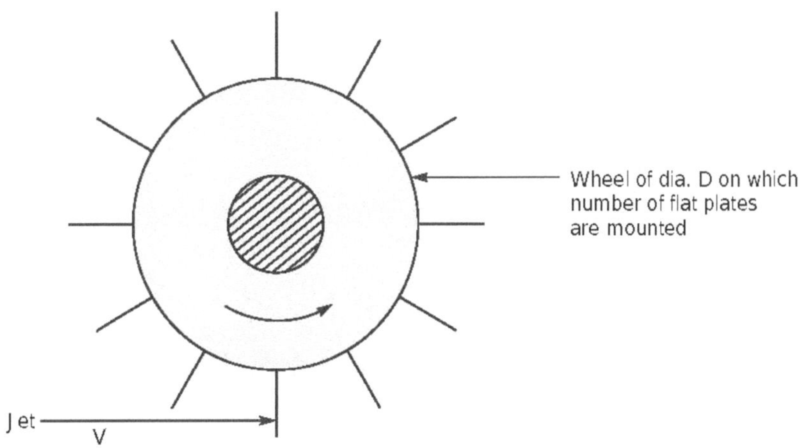

Fig. 18.10

Let the wheel move with (N) RPM

$$\therefore \quad u = \frac{\pi D N}{60} = \text{tangential velo of wheel}$$

In this case mass per sec. striking the vane

$$= \rho a V$$

$$\therefore \quad F_x = \rho a V [(V - u) - 0]$$

$$= \rho a V (V - u)$$

$$\text{Work done} = F_x(u) = \rho a V (V - u) u$$

$$\text{eff., } \eta = \frac{\rho a V (V - u) u}{\frac{1}{2} \rho a V (V^2)}$$

$$= \frac{2u (V - u)}{V^2}$$

$$\therefore \qquad \frac{d\eta}{du} = 2V - 4u = 0$$

$$\therefore \qquad u = \frac{V}{2} \text{ for max. efficiency}$$

$$\therefore \qquad \eta_{max} = \frac{2u\,(2u-u)}{(2u)^2} = \frac{1}{2} = 50\%$$

Case (*ii*) Curved vanes mounted on the wheel:

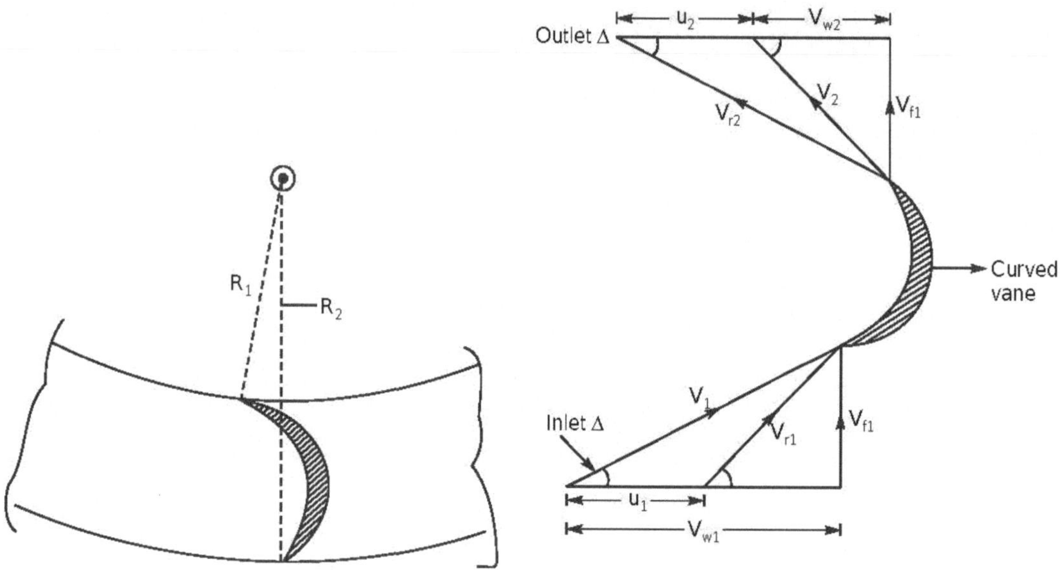

Fig. 18.11

$$u_1 = \varpi R_1 = \frac{2\pi N}{60} R_1 = \frac{\pi D_1 N}{60}$$

$$u_2 = \varpi R_2 = \frac{2\pi N}{60} R_2 = \frac{\pi D_2 N}{60}$$

Moment of water striking the curved vane at inlet

$= \text{(mass) (tangential component of } V_1 \text{ at inlet)}$

$= (\rho a V_1)\,(V_1 \cos \alpha)$

$= \rho a V_1\,(V_{w1}) \qquad \text{as } V_{w1} = V_1 \cos \alpha$

Moment of water leaving the vane at outlet

$= (\rho a V_1) \text{ (component of } V_2 \text{ in tangential direction)}$

$= \rho a V_1\,(-\,V_2 \cos \beta)$

$= -\,\rho a V_1\,(V_{w2}) \qquad \text{as } V_{w2} = V_2 \cos \beta$

Non-angular momentum at inlet

$= \text{moment at inlet} \times \text{radius at inlet}$

$$= \rho a V_1 (V_{w1}) (R_1)$$

and angular momentum at outlet

$$= -\rho a V_1 (V_{w2}) (R_2)$$

$\therefore$ Torque exerted by water on the wheel

$$= T = \rho a V_1 (V_{w1} R_1) - (-\rho a V_1 V_{w2} R_2)$$

$$\therefore \quad T = \rho a V_1 (V_{w1} R_1 + V_{w1} R_2) \qquad \text{(assuming } \beta \text{ as acute)}$$

Work done per sec. $= \text{Torque} \times \text{angular velocity}$

$$= T\varpi$$

$$= \rho a V_1 [V_{w1}(R_1 \omega) + V_{w2}(R_2 \omega)]$$

But $u_1 = \omega R_1$ and $u_2 = \omega R_2$

$\therefore$ Work done per sec. $= \rho a V_1 (V_{w1} u_1 + V_{w2} u_2)$

If β is obtuse,

Work done per sec. $= \rho a V_1 (V_{w1} u_1 - V_{w2} u_2)$

If $\beta = 90°, V_{w2} = 0$

$\therefore$ Work done/sec $= \rho a V_1 (V_{w1} u_1)$

η = efficiency of curved vane

$$= \frac{\text{Work done per sec}}{\text{KE of jet}}$$

$$= \frac{\rho a V_1 (V_{w1} u_1 \pm V_{w2} u_2)}{\frac{1}{2} \rho a V_1 (V_1^2)}.$$

18.5 SOLVED PROBLEMS

■ **Problem 18.1:** *A rectangular plate 1 m × 1 m × 5 mm size is suspended vertically by a hinge on its top edge. Specific gravity of plate material is 7.66. A horizontal jet of water 40 mm diameter strikes the plate 100 mm below the centre of gravity of the plate. Find velocity of the jet if the plate is deflected through 30°.*

Solution:

$$\theta = 30°$$

$$W = \text{wt. of plate}$$

$$= 1 \times 1 \times 0.005 \times 7.66 \times 1000 \times 9.81$$

$$= 375 \text{ N}$$

Taking moment at hinge

$$F_x (0.5 + 0.1) = W (0.5 \sin \theta)$$

$$\rho a V^2 (0.6) = 375 (0.5 \sin 30)$$

$$1000 \left[\frac{\pi}{4} \left(\frac{40}{1000} \right)^2 \right] V^2 (0.6) = 375 \times 0.5 \times 0.5$$

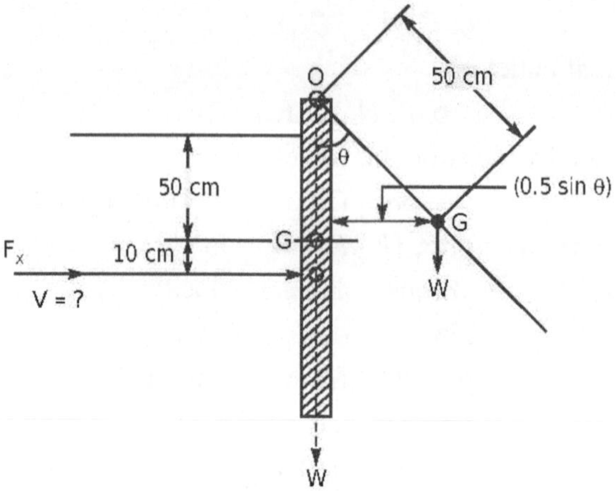

Fig. 18.12

$$\therefore \qquad V^2 = \frac{375 \times 0.25}{1000 \times 0.78 \times 1.6 \times 10^{-3}}$$

$$= 75.12$$

$$\therefore \qquad V = 8.66 \text{ m/s.} \qquad \text{...(Ans.)}$$

■ **Problem 18.2:** *A jet of water having a velocity of 19 m/s and diameter of 15 cm strikes a curved blade. The inlet and outlet angles of the blade are 0°, and 45° respectively. When the blade is stationary find the resultant force and find change in force when blade moves at 6 m/s in direction of jet.*

Solution:

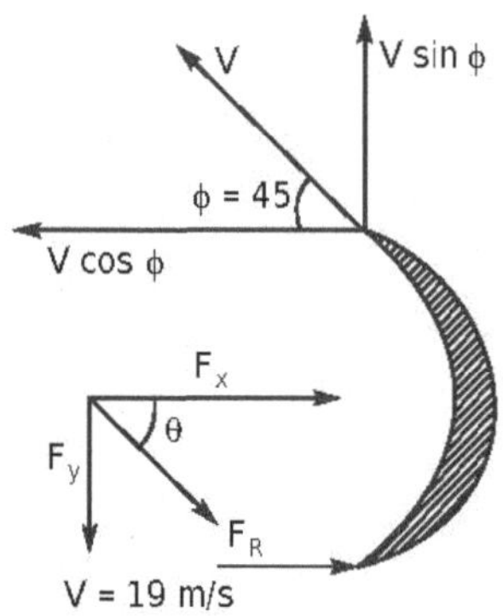

Fig. 18.13

$$\phi = 45°$$

$$\angle \text{ at inlet} = 0$$

$$V = 19 \text{ m/s}$$

$$a = \frac{\pi}{4}d^2 = 0.78(0.15)^2 = 0.0175 \text{ m}^2$$

$$d = 15 \text{ cm.}$$

(*i*) Plate stationary:

$$F_x = (\text{Mass/sec})\ [V - (-V\cos\phi)]$$
$$= \rho a V^2 (1 + \cos\phi)$$
$$= 1000(0.78 \times 0.15^2 \times 19^2)(1 + \cos 45)$$
$$= 1000(0.78 \times 0.0225 \times 361)(1.707)$$
$$= 10.81 \text{ kN}$$
$$F_x = \rho a V^2 (-\sin 45)\ [-\text{ve means } F_y \text{ acts in downward direction}]$$
$$= -1000(0.78 \times 0.0225 \times 361)(-0.707)$$
$$= -4.47 \text{ kN}$$

$$\therefore \quad F_R = \sqrt{F_x^2 + F_y^2} = \sqrt{116.8 + 19.9} = \mathbf{11.69\ kN} \quad \text{...(Ans.)}$$

$$\tan\theta = \frac{F_y}{F_x} = \frac{4.47}{10.81} = 0.41$$

$$\therefore \quad \theta = 22.4°. \quad \text{...(Ans.)}$$

(*ii*) Plate moves with a velocity of 6 m/s:

$$F_x = \rho a (V - u)^2 (1 + \cos\phi)$$
$$= 1000(0.0175)(19 - 6)^2 (1.707)$$
$$= \mathbf{5.0\ kN}$$
$$F_y = \rho a (V - u)^2 (-\sin 45)$$
$$= 1000(0.175)(13)^2 (-0.707)$$
$$= \mathbf{-2\ kN}$$

$$\therefore \quad F_R = \sqrt{(5)^2 + (-2)^2} = \mathbf{5.38\ kN}$$

$$\tan\theta = \frac{-2}{5} = -0.4,\ \theta = (180 - 21.8) = \mathbf{158.2°}. \quad \text{...(Ans.)}$$

■ **Problem 18.3:** *A jet of water, 40 mm diameter, strikes a hinged vertical plate of 800 N weight, normally at its centre at 15 m/s. Find*

(i) angle of deflection

(ii) force F that must be applied at lower edge to keep the plate vertical.

Solution:

$$W = 800 \text{ N},$$

$$\text{Area of jet} = a$$

$$\therefore \quad a = \frac{\pi}{r} d^2$$

$$= 0.78\left(\frac{40}{1000}\right)^2 = 1.24 \times 10^3 \text{ m}^2$$

Case 1:

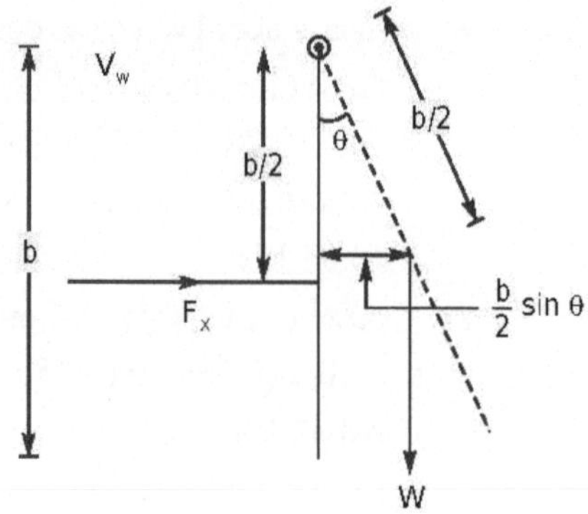

Fig. 18.14

Take moment at hinge,

$$\therefore \quad F_x\left(\frac{b}{2}\right) = W\left(\frac{b}{2}\sin\theta\right)$$

But $\quad F_x = \rho a V^2$

$$\therefore \quad \rho a V^2 = W \sin\theta$$

$$\therefore \quad \sin\theta = \frac{\rho a V^2}{W}$$

$$\therefore \quad \sin\theta = \frac{1000\,(1.24\times10^{-3})\,(15)^2}{800}$$

$$= 0.348$$

$$\therefore \quad \boldsymbol{\theta = 20.4^\circ}.$$ ...(Ans.)

Case 2:

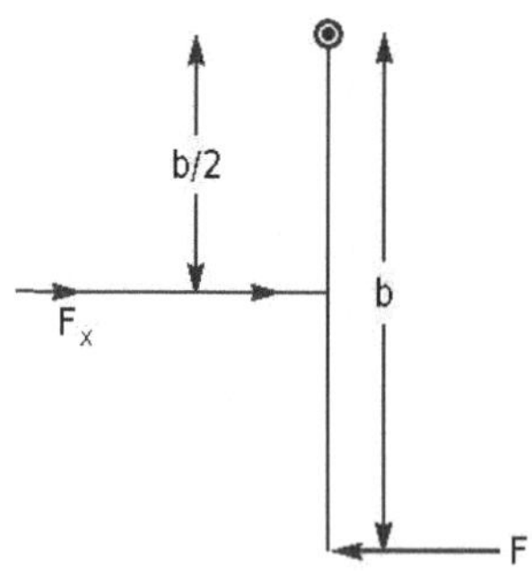

Fig. 18.15

$$F_x \times \frac{b}{2} = F(b)$$

$$\therefore \quad F = \frac{1}{2}F_x = \frac{1}{2}\rho a V^2$$

$$= \frac{1}{2} F_x = \frac{1}{2} \rho a V^2$$

$$= \frac{1}{2} 1000\,(1.24 \times 10^{-3})\,(15)^2$$

$= \mathbf{139.5\ N.}$ ...**(Ans.)**

■ **Problem 18.4:** *A jet of water 10 cm diameter strikes a curved vane at a velocity of 25 m/s. The inlet angle of vane is zero and outlet ∠30°. Find resultant force on vane when it is stationary and when it is moving with a velocity of 10 m/s in direction of jet.*

Solution:

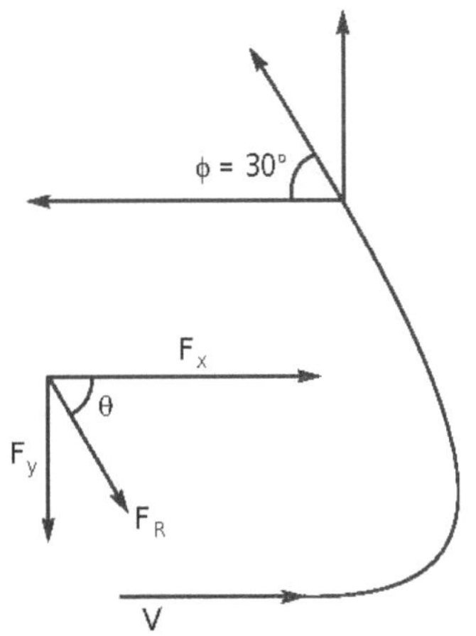

Fig. 18.16

$\phi = 30°$, ∠ at inlet $= 0$

$$a = \frac{\pi}{4}(0.1)^2 = 0.78 \times 10^{-2}\ \text{m}^2$$

$V = 25$ m/s

(*i*) Plate stationary:

$$F_x = \rho a V^2 (1 + \cos \phi)$$
$$= 1000\,(0.78 \times 10^{-2})\,(25)^2\,(1 + \cos 30)$$
$$= \mathbf{9.1\ kN}$$

$$F_y = -\rho a V^2 \sin 30$$
$$= -1000\,(0.78 \times 10^{-2})\,(25)^2 \sin 30$$

$= \mathbf{-2.43\ kN}$ (– ve, means downward)

∴ $F_R = \sqrt{F_x^2 + F_y^2} = \sqrt{(9.1)^2 + (2.43)^2}$

$= \mathbf{9.42\ kN}$ at $\tan \theta = \dfrac{F_y}{F_x} = \dfrac{2.43}{9.1} = 0.26$

∴ $\boldsymbol{\theta = 15°}$. ...**(Ans.)**

(*ii*) Plate moves with $u = 10$ m/s

$$\therefore \quad F_x = \rho a (V - u) [V - (-V \cos \phi + u)]$$
$$= 1000 (0.78 \times 10^{-2}) (25 - 10) (25 + 15 \cos 30 - 10)$$
$$= 1000 (0.78 \times 10^{-2}) (15) (25 + 13 - 10)$$
$$= 1000 (0.78 \times 10^{-2}) (15) (28)$$
$$= \mathbf{3.27\ kN}$$
$$F_y = \rho a (V - u) [-(V - u) \sin 30]$$
$$= 1000 (0.78 \times 10^{-2}) (15) \left(-\frac{15}{2}\right)$$
$$= -\mathbf{0.87\ kN}$$
$$\therefore \quad F_R = \sqrt{F_x^2 + F_y^2}$$
$$= \sqrt{(3.27)^2 + (0.87)^2}$$
$$= 3.36 \text{ kN} \qquad \textbf{...(Ans.)}$$

and
$$\theta = \tan^{-1}\left(\frac{0.87}{3.27}\right) = 14.81. \qquad \textbf{...(Ans.)}$$

■ **Problem 18.5:** *A jet of water diameter 12 cm and having a velocity of 6 m/s, strikes tangentially at inlet of a curved vane moving with 6 m/s in the same direction as the jet. If the jet gets deflected through 130°, and vane is smooth, find (1) Force (2) Power (3) efficiency of vane. Assume* β *acute.*

Solution:

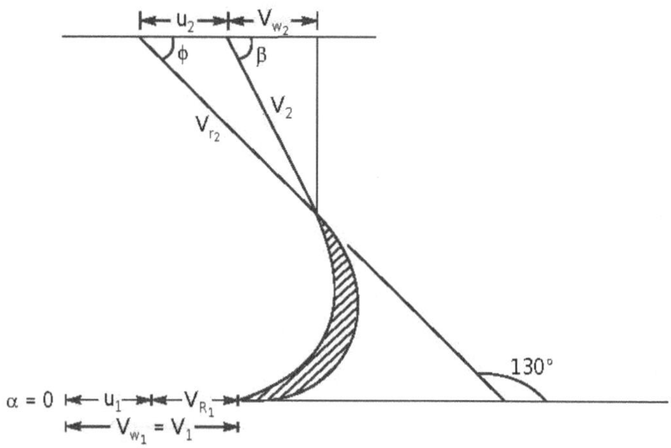

Fig. 18.17

Jet strikes at inlet tangentially

$$\therefore \quad \alpha = 0$$

and
$$V_1 = V_{w1}$$
$$\phi = 180 - 130$$
$$= 50°$$

Plate is smooth, $\therefore$ $V_{r1} = V_{r2}$

$$u_1 = u_2 = 6 \text{ m/s}$$

$$V_1 = 16 \text{ m/s} = V_{w1} = u_1 + V_{r1}$$

$$\therefore \quad V_{r1} = 16 - u_1 = 16 - 6 = 10 = V_{r2}$$

$$V_{r2} \cos\phi = u_2 + V_{w2}$$

$$\therefore \quad V_{w2} = 10 \cos 50 - 6 = 10\,(0.642) - 6 = 0.42 \text{ m/s}$$

1. $$F_x = \rho a V_{r1}(V_{r1} + V_{w2}) \qquad (\beta \text{ is acute})$$

$$= (1000)\frac{\pi}{4}(0.12)^2(10)(16 + 0.42)$$

$$= 1000\,(0.011)\,(16.42)\,(10)$$

$$= \mathbf{1.84\ kN}$$ ...(Ans.)

2. Power $= F_x u = 1.84\,(6) = \mathbf{11.04\ kW}$ ...(Ans.)

3. $$\text{efficiency} = \frac{\text{Work done by jet}}{\text{KE of jet}}$$

$$= \frac{F_x(u)}{\frac{1}{2}(\rho a V_1) V_1^2}$$

$$= \frac{1.84 \times 1000 \times 6}{\frac{1}{2}(1000 \times 0.011 \times 16)(16)^2}$$

$$= 48.8\%.$$ ...(Ans.)

■ **Problem 18.6**: *A jet of water having velocity of 40 m/s strikes series of curved vanes moving at 12 m/s. If angle of jet at inlet* $\alpha = 20°$, $V_{r1} = V_{r2}$ *and velocity of outlet is normal to the wheel, find vane angles at inlet and outlet, and efficiency.*

Solution:

$$u_1 = u_2 = 12 \text{ m/s}$$

$$V_1 = 40 \text{ m/s}$$

$$\alpha = 20°$$

$$\theta, \phi = ?$$

At inlet Δ, apply cosine rule,

$$\therefore \quad V_{r1}^2 = (V_1)^2 - (u_1)^2 + 2u_1 V_1 \cos\alpha$$

$$= (40)^2 + (12)^2 + 2(12)(40) \cos 20$$

$$= 1600 + 144 + 902$$

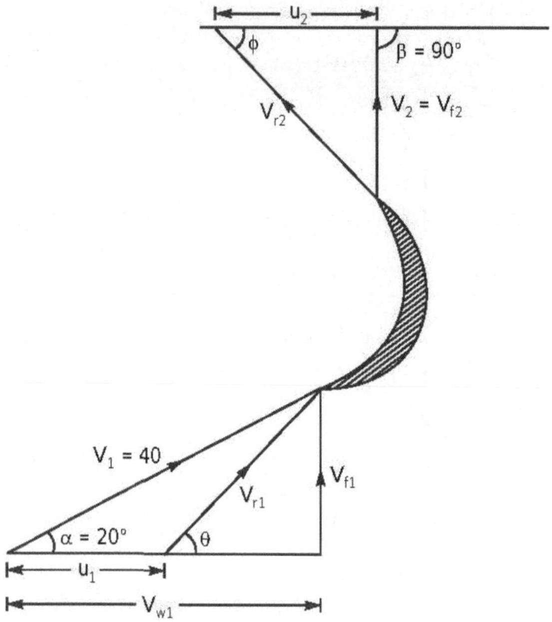

Fig. 18.18

$V_{r1} = 51.43$

$= V_{r2}$

$V_{w1} = V_1 \cos \alpha = 40 \cos 20$

$= 37.5$

$V_{f1} = V_1 \sin \alpha$

$= 40 (\sin 20) = 13.6$

$$\therefore \quad \tan \theta = \frac{V_{f1}}{V_{w1} - u_1} = \frac{13.6}{37.5 - 12} = \frac{13.6}{25.5}$$

$= 0.533$

$\therefore$ $\boldsymbol{\theta = 28°}$ ...(Ans.)

$\cos \phi = \dfrac{u_2}{V_{r2}} = \dfrac{12}{51.43}$ $\therefore$ $\boldsymbol{\phi = 76.5°}$ ...(Ans.)

Work done/sec/kg $= \dfrac{1}{g}(V_{w1} u_1)$, (here $V_{w2} = 0$ and $\beta = 90°$)

$$= \frac{1}{9.81}(37.5 \times 12)$$

$= 45.8$ N m/sec/N.

$$\text{Efficiency} = \frac{\text{Work done}}{\left(\dfrac{V_1^2}{2g}\right)} = \frac{45.8}{\left(\dfrac{40\times40}{2\times9.81}\right)} = \frac{45.8}{81.5}$$

$= \mathbf{56\%}$. **...(Ans.)**

■ **Problem 18.7:** *A jet of water having velocity of 60 m/s, strikes series of curved vanes tangentially. The jet is deflected through 120°. If $V_{r2} = 0.9\ V_{r1}$ and windage loss is $0.5\left(\dfrac{u^2}{2g}\right)$ per kg of water, find condition for maximum efficiency, efficiency and work done per sec kg of water. Assume β obtuse and vane velocity as u m/sec.*

Solution:

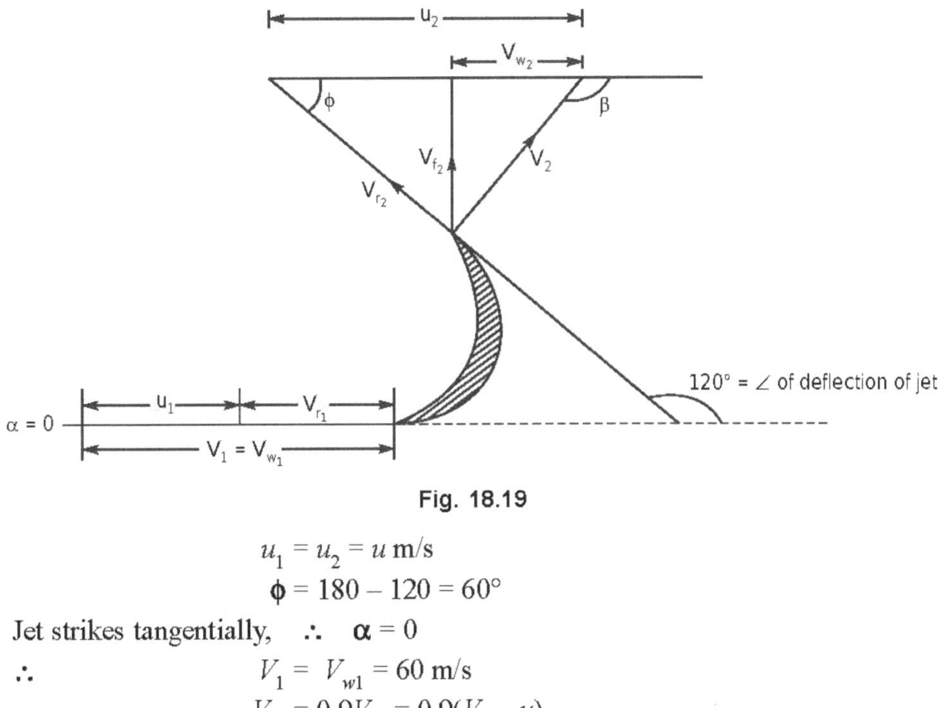

Fig. 18.19

$$u_1 = u_2 = u \text{ m/s}$$
$$\phi = 180 - 120 = 60°$$

Jet strikes tangentially, ∴ $\alpha = 0$

∴
$$V_1 = V_{w1} = 60 \text{ m/s}$$
$$V_{r2} = 0.9V_{r1} = 0.9(V_1 - u)$$
$$V_{w2} = u_2 - V_{r2}\cos\phi$$
$$= u - 0.9\,(V_1 - u)\cos 60$$
$$= u - 0.45\,(V_1 - u)$$

Work done per sec per kg

$$= \frac{1}{g}\,[V_{w1}u_1 - V_{w2}u_2], \qquad \text{(–ve as } \beta \text{ is obtuse)}$$

and
$$\text{KE of jet} = \frac{1}{2}\left(\frac{V_1^2}{g}\right) \text{ per kg of water}$$

$$\therefore \quad \eta = \text{efficiency} = \frac{\frac{1}{g}[V_{w1}u_1 - V_{w2}u_2] - 0.5\frac{u^2}{2g}}{\left(\frac{V_1^2}{2g}\right)} \quad (\text{here } u_1 = u_2 = u)$$

$$= \frac{2[V_1 u - (u - 0.45\,(V_1 - u))\,u] - 0.5u^2}{V_1^2}$$

$$\therefore \quad \frac{d\eta}{du} = 2[V_1 - 2u + 0.45V_1 \;- 0.9u] - u = 0$$

$$\therefore \quad 2.9\,V_1 - 6.8u = 0$$

$$\therefore \quad u = \frac{2.9}{6.8} = 0.426V_1$$

$\therefore \quad u = 0.426\ V_1$ **is condition for max η**

$= 0.426\ (60)$ ...(Ans.)

$= 25.6$ m/s ...(Ans.)

$$\eta = \frac{2[60(25.6) - (25.6 - 0.45\,(60 - 25.6))\,25.6] - \frac{1}{2}(25.6)^2}{(60)^2}$$

$$= \frac{2[1536 - 258] - 327}{3600}$$

$$= \frac{2556 - 327}{3600} = \frac{2229}{3600} = \mathbf{62\%}$$ ...(Ans.)

Work done per sec per kg

$$= \frac{1}{g}\,[V_{w1}u_1 - V_{w2}u_2]$$

$$= \frac{1}{9.81}\,[V_1 u - (u - 0.45\,(V_1 - u))\,u]$$

$$= \frac{1}{9.81}\,[60 \times 25.6 - (10.1 \times 25.6)]$$

$$= \frac{1280}{9.81} = 130.5 \text{ kgf – m/sec/kg of water.}$$ ...(Ans.)

■ **Problem 18.8:** *A jet of water having velocity of 10 m/s strikes a symmetrical vane which deflects the jet through 120°. If vane is moving at 6 m/s, find angle of jet so that there is no shock at entry. What is absolute velocity of jet at exit?*

Solution:

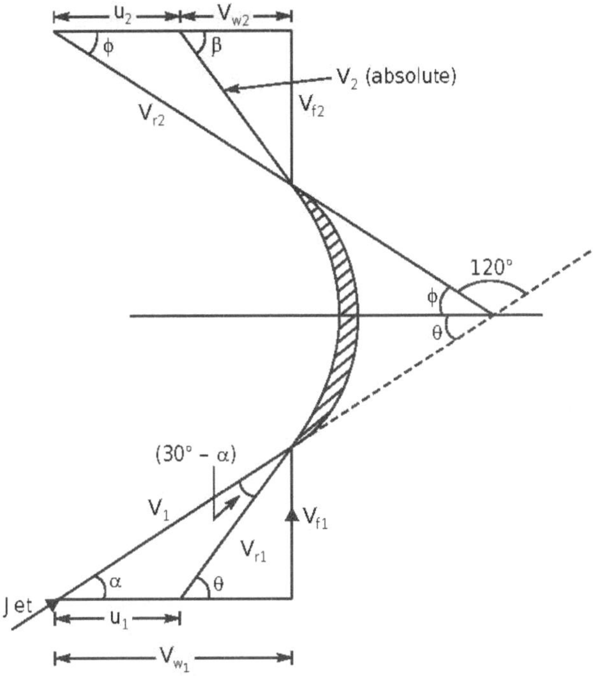

Fig. 18.20

$$\theta + \phi = 180 - 120 = 60$$

Vane symmetrical, $\therefore$ $\theta = \phi = 30°$

$$u = u_1 = u_2 = 6 \text{ m/s}$$

$$V_1 = 10 \text{ m/s}$$

From Inlet Δ, $$\frac{V_1}{\sin(180 - \theta)} = \frac{u_1}{\sin(30 - \alpha)}$$

$\therefore$ $10 \sin(30 - \alpha) = 6 \sin 30 = 3$

$\therefore$ $30 - \alpha = 17.45°$ $\therefore$ $\alpha =$ **12.54°** ...(Ans.)

$= \text{jet} \angle \text{ at entry}$

From inlet Δ, $$V_{r1} = \frac{V_1 \sin \alpha}{\sin 30} = \frac{10 \sin (12.54)}{\sin 30}$$

$$= \frac{10(0.217)}{0.5} = 4.34 = V_{r2},$$ as no shock

at outlet Δ, $$V_{r2} \cos \phi = u_2 + V_{w2}$$

$\therefore$ $4.34 \cos 30 = 6 + V_{w2}$

$\therefore$ $V_{w2} = 2.24 \text{ m/s}$

$$V_{f2} = V_{r2} \sin \phi = 4.34 \sin 30 = 2.17$$

$$\therefore \quad V_2 = \sqrt{(2.24)^2 + (2.17)^2}$$

$$= 3.11 \text{ m/s} = \text{absolute velocity at exit.} \quad \text{...(Ans.)}$$

$$\tan \beta = \frac{V_{f2}}{V_{w2}} = \frac{2.17}{2.24}$$

$$\therefore \quad \beta = 44° = \text{angle } V_2 \text{ makes at exit.} \quad \text{...(Ans.)}$$

■ **Problem 18.9:** *A jet of water having velocity 20 m/s strikes a symmetrically curved vane moving with a velocity of 6 m/s. The jet gets deflected through 140°. Find angle of jet at inlet such that there is no shock. Also find absolute velocity of water at outlet and work done per sec per kg of water. Assume vane to be smooth.*

Solution:

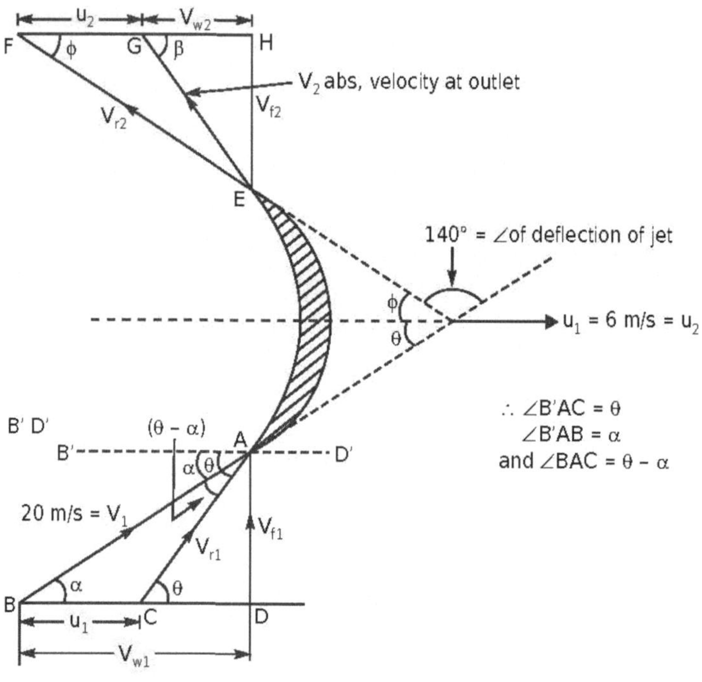

Fig. 18.21

As vane is symmetrical, $\theta = \phi$

and $140 = 180 - (\theta + \phi)$

$\therefore \quad \theta = \phi = 20°$

Let jet make $\angle\alpha$ a inlet

$\therefore$ In ΔABC, $\quad \angle BAC = (\theta - \alpha)$ opposite to side BC.

Vane is smooth, $\therefore \quad V_{r1} = V_{r2}$

Apply sine rule to Δ ABC,

$$\therefore \quad \frac{AB}{\sin(180-\theta)} = \frac{BC}{\sin(\theta-\alpha)} = \frac{AC}{\sin\alpha}$$

$$\therefore \quad \frac{V_1}{\sin(180-\theta)} = \frac{u_1}{\sin(\theta-\alpha)}$$

$$\therefore \quad \frac{20}{\sin(180-\theta)} = \frac{6}{\sin(\theta-\alpha)}$$

$$\therefore \quad \frac{20}{\sin\theta} = \frac{6}{\sin(\theta-\alpha)}$$

But $\theta = 20$, $\therefore \quad \dfrac{20}{\sin 20} = \dfrac{6}{\sin(20-\alpha)}$

$$\therefore \quad \sin(20-\alpha) = \frac{6}{58.47}$$

$$\therefore \quad 20-\alpha = 5.88^\circ$$

$$\therefore \quad \alpha = 14.12^\circ$$

$$\therefore \quad \frac{V_1}{\sin\theta} = \frac{V_{r1}}{\sin(14.12^\circ)}$$

$$\therefore \quad V_{r1} = 20\,\frac{\sin(14.12)}{\sin(20)} = 20\,\frac{0.243}{0.342}$$

$$= 14.2 \text{ m/s}$$

$$\therefore \quad V_{r1} = V_{r2} = 14.2 \text{ m/s}$$

At outlet, from ΔHEF,

$$V_{r2}\cos\phi = u_2 + V_{w2}$$

$$\therefore \quad 14.2\cos 20 = 6 + V_{w2}$$

$$\therefore \quad V_{w2} = 13.34 - 6 = \mathbf{7.34 \text{ m/s}}$$

Also, $\quad V_{r2}\sin\phi = V_{f2} = (14.2)\sin 20 = 4.85$ m/s

$$\therefore \quad V_2 = \sqrt{V_{f2}^{\,2} + V_{w2}^{\,2}}$$

$$= \sqrt{(4.85)^2 + (7.34)^2}$$

$$= 8.79 \text{ m/s} \qquad \text{...(Ans.)}$$

and $\quad \tan\beta = \dfrac{V_{f2}}{V_{w2}} = \dfrac{4.85}{7.34} = 0.66$

$$\therefore \quad \beta = 33.4^\circ$$

$$\text{Work done per sec per kg} = \frac{1}{g}[V_{w1}u_1 + V_{w2}u_2]$$

$$= \frac{1}{9.81}[(20\cos 20)\,6 + 7.34(6)]$$

$$= \frac{112.76 + 44.04}{9.81}$$

$$= 16 \text{ kgf-m/sec/kg.} \qquad \text{...(Ans.)}$$

■ **Problem 18.10**: *A square plate of 30 cm side and weight 150 N is suspended from a hinge and a jet of water 2 cm in diameter strikes it horizontally at its centre with a velocity of 15 m/s. Find force required to be applied at its lower edge to keep it vertical. It allowed to swing freely, find the angle it makes with vertical.*

Solution:

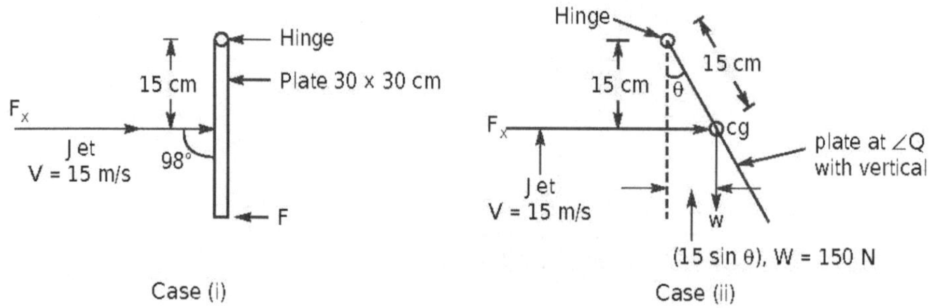

Fig. 18.22 case (*i*) and case (*ii*)

Case (*i*)

$$F_X = \rho a V^2 = 1000\left[\frac{\pi}{4}\left(\frac{2}{100}\right)^2\right](15)^2$$

$$= 70 \text{ N}$$

Taking moment at hinge,

$$F_x(15) = F(30)$$

$$\therefore \quad F = 70\left(\frac{15}{30}\right) = \mathbf{35\ N} \qquad \text{...(Ans. (i))}$$

Case (*ii*)

Taking moment at hinge,

$$F_x(15) = W(15\sin\theta)$$

$$\therefore \quad 70(15) = 150(15\sin\theta)$$

$$\therefore \quad \sin\theta = \frac{70}{150} = 0.466$$

$$\therefore \quad \theta = 27.8° \text{ with vertical.} \qquad \text{...(Ans. (ii))}$$

■ **Problem 18.11:** *A jet of water of velocity 30 m/s strikes a series of curved vanes moving at 20 m/s and makes an angle of 30° to the direction of vane velocity at inlet, and at outlet it makes an angle of 130°. Draw velocity triangles at inlet and outlet and find out*

(*i*) *vane angles* θ *and* ϕ *for* $V_{r1} = V_{r2}$

(*ii*) *work done per kg of water entering the vane*

(*iii*) *efficiency.*

Solution:

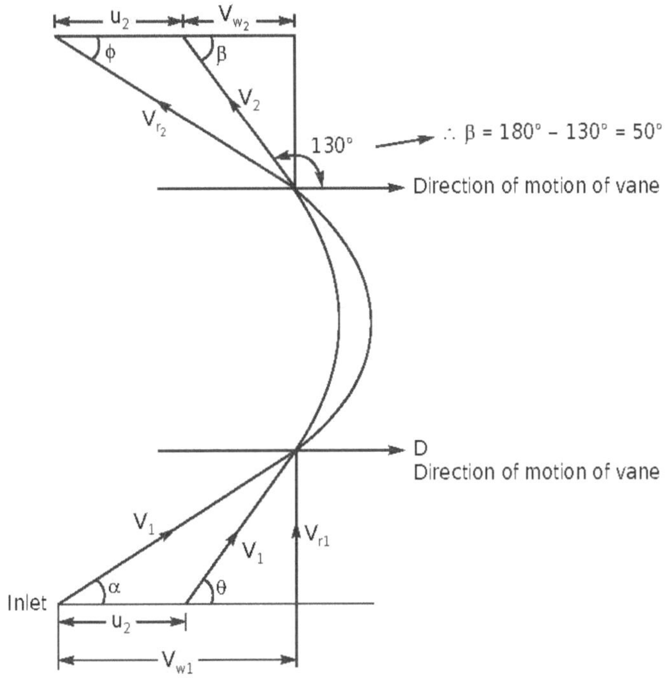

Fig. 18.23

$$\alpha = 30°$$

$$\theta \text{ and } \phi?$$

$$u_1 = u_2 = u = 20 \text{ m/s}$$

$$V_{f1} = V_1 \sin \alpha$$

$$= 30 \cos 30 = 26 \text{ m/s}$$

$$\therefore \quad \tan \theta = \frac{V_{f1}}{V_{w1} - u_1} = \frac{15}{26 - 20} = 2.5$$

$$\therefore \quad \theta = 68° = \text{Vane} \angle \text{ at inlet} \qquad \text{...(Ans.)}$$

Apply sine rule to inlet Δ $\dfrac{V_{r1}}{\sin \alpha} = \dfrac{V_1}{\sin(180 - \theta)} = \dfrac{V_1}{\sin \theta}$

$$\therefore \quad V_{r1} = \frac{30}{\sin 68} \sin 30 = 16.17 \text{ m/s}$$

$$= V_{r2} \quad \text{as no shock at entry and exit.}$$

Apply sine rule to **outlet Δ**, see **Fig. 18.24**

$$\therefore \quad \frac{V_{r2}}{\sin 130} = \frac{u_2}{\sin(50-\phi)}$$

$$\frac{16.17}{0.766} = \frac{20}{\sin(50-\phi)}$$

$$\therefore \quad \sin(50-\phi) = \frac{20 \times 0.766}{16.17} = 0.947$$

$$\therefore \quad 50 - \phi = 71.34°$$

$$\therefore \quad \phi = \mathbf{21.34°} = \text{angle of vane at outlet} \qquad \text{...(Ans.)}$$

$$V_{w2} = V_{r2} \cos\phi - u_2$$

$$= 16.17 \cos(21.34) - 20$$

$$= 15 - 20 = -5 \quad \textit{i.e.} \quad V_{w2} u_2 \text{ will be –ve.}$$

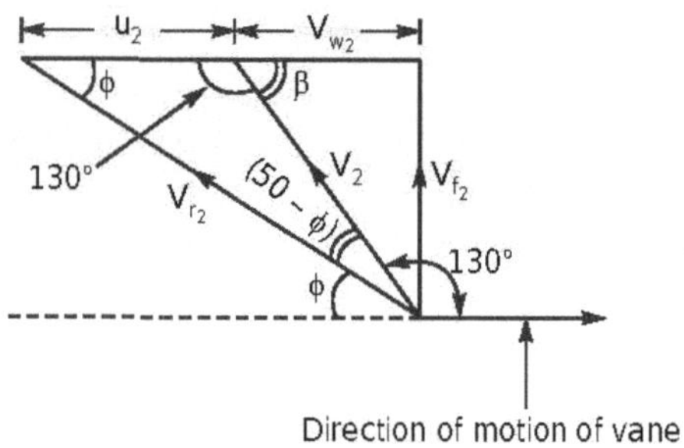

Fig. 18.24

$$\text{Work done per kg} = \frac{1}{g}[V_{w1}u_1 - V_{w2}u_2]$$

$$= \frac{1}{9.81}[26(20) - (5)\,20]$$

$$= \frac{20}{9.81}[26 - 5] = \frac{20 \times 21}{9.81} = 42.8 \text{ kgf-m/sec per kg}$$

$$\eta = \text{efficiency} = \frac{\text{Work done per kg}}{\text{KE of jet per kg}}$$

$$= \frac{42.8}{\left(\frac{V_1^2}{2g}\right)} = \frac{42.8}{\left(\frac{30^2}{2 \times 9.81}\right)} = \frac{42.8}{45.92} = 0.93 = \mathbf{93\%}. \qquad \text{...(Ans.)}$$

■ **Problem 18.12:** *A jet of water having velocity of 40 m/s impinges a series of curved vanes mounted on a wheel rotating at 240 RPM. The jet makes an angle of 30 at inlet and 120° at outlet. The wheel has inner radius of 0.5 m and outer radius of 0.8 m. If $V_{r1} = V_{r2}$, find*

(*i*) *angle of vanes at inlet and outlet.*

(*ii*) *work done per kg of water*

(*iii*) *efficiency.*

Solution:

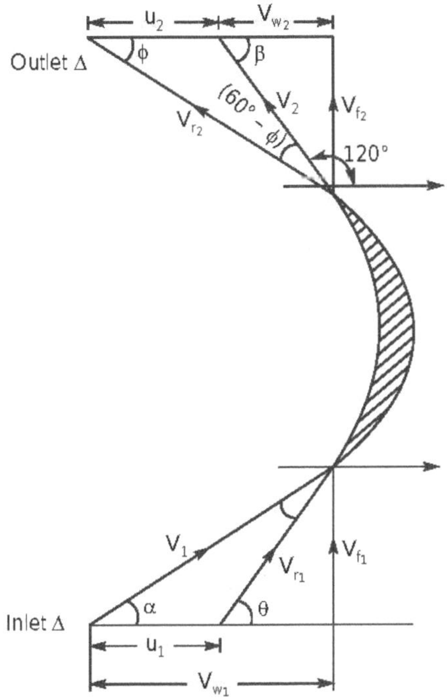

Fig. 18.25

$V_1 = 40$ m/s; $\alpha = 30°$

$N = 240$ rpm

$\beta = 180 - 120 = 60°$

$R_1 = 0.8$ m (outer radius)

$R_2 = 0.5$ m (inner radius)

$$\varpi = \frac{2\pi N}{60} = \frac{2\pi(240)}{60}$$

$= 25.12$ radius/sec.

$u_1 = \varpi R_1 = 25.12\ (0.8)$

$= 20$ m/s

$u_2 = \varpi R_2 = 25.12\ (0.5)$

$= 12.56$ m/s

From inlet Δ, $V_{w1} = V_1 \cos \alpha = 40 \cos 30 = 34.6$ m/s

$$V_{f1} = V_1 \sin \alpha = 40 \sin 30 = 20 \text{ m/s}$$

$$\therefore \quad \tan \theta = \frac{V_{f1}}{V_{w1} - u_1} = \frac{20}{34.6 - 25.2}$$

$$= \frac{20}{9.52} = 2.10$$

$$\therefore \quad \theta = \mathbf{64.5°} \qquad \text{...(Ans.)}$$

$$\therefore \quad \sin \theta = \frac{V_{f1}}{V_{r1}} \quad \therefore \quad V_{r1} = \frac{V_{f1}}{\sin \theta} = \frac{20}{\sin (64.5)}$$

$$= 22.2 \text{ m/s}$$

$$= V_{r2} \text{ (given that } V_{r1} = V_{r2})$$

From outlet Δ,

$$\frac{V_{r2}}{\sin 120} = \frac{u_2}{\sin (60 - \phi)}$$

$$\therefore \quad \sin (60 - \phi) = \frac{12.56}{22.2} \sin 120 = 0.489$$

$$\therefore \quad 60 - \phi = 29.33, \quad \therefore \phi = \mathbf{30.66°} \qquad \text{...(Ans.)}$$

$$V_{w2} = V_{r2} \cos\phi - u_2 = 22.2 \cos (30.6) - 12.56 = 6.53 \text{ m/s}$$

$$\therefore \text{ Work done per } kg = \frac{1}{g} [V_{w1}u_1 + V_{w2}u_2]$$

$$= \frac{1}{9.81} [34.6(20) + 6.53(12.56)]$$

$$= \frac{[692 + 82.1]}{9.81}$$

$$= 78.89 \text{ kgf – m/sec/kg} \qquad \text{...(Ans.)}$$

$$\eta = \text{efficiency} = \frac{\text{Work done/kg}}{\text{KE/kg}}$$

$$= \frac{78.98}{\left(\frac{V_1^2}{wg}\right)} = \frac{78.89}{\left(\frac{(40)^2}{19.6}\right)} = \frac{78.89}{81.63}$$

$$= 96.64\% \qquad \text{...(Ans.)}$$

18.6 JET PROPULSION

We have seen that jet striking a plate exerts a force on the plate. Now if the jet is issuing out from an orifice situated on one side of a tank, it will produce a reaction on the tank while leaving the tank. As per Newton's Law that action and reaction are equal and opposite, this reaction will also be equal to the force of the jet and opposite to force in direction. If tank is free to move and if there is no friction at its supporting wheels, then it will move in direction opposite to that of jet velocity. This is jet propulsion. Ships, aeroplanes, submarines etc. use this principle of jet propulsion.

18.6.1 Effect of Jet Propulsion on a Tank

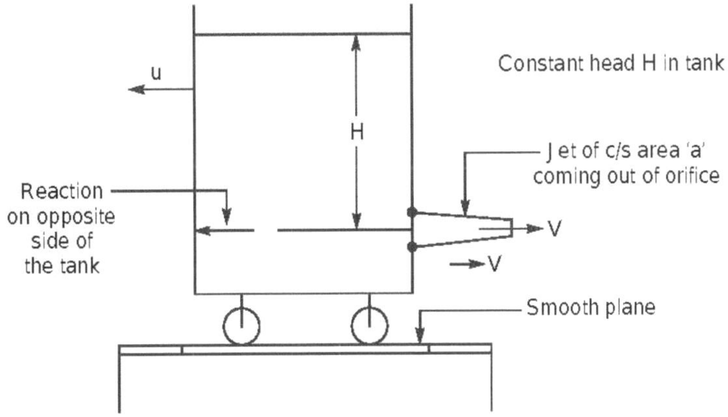

Fig. 18.26

Here absolute velocity of jet $= V = C_v\sqrt{2gH}$

and Force of jet $= \rho a V^2$

This force will produce a reaction on the tank and it will start moving in opposite direction with a velocity u.

$\therefore$ Relative velocity of jet $= V - (-u) = V + u$

$\therefore$ Mass of water per sec $= \rho a\,(V + u)$

$\therefore$ Force exerted on the tank

$$= \text{(mass per sec) (Change of velocity)}$$
$$= \rho a\,(V + u)\,[(V + u) - u]$$
$$= \rho a\,(V + u)\,V$$

$\therefore$ Work done = Force × tank velocity $= \rho a\,(V + u)\,Vu$

$$\eta = \text{efficiency of propulsion}$$
$$= \frac{\text{Work done}}{\text{KE of jet}}$$
$$= \frac{\rho a\,(V + u)\,Vu}{\frac{1}{2}[\rho a\,(V + u)]\,(V + u)^2}$$
$$= \frac{2Vu}{(V + u)^2}$$

∴ For maximum efficiency,

$$\frac{d\eta}{du} = \frac{(V+u)^2\,(2V)-(2Vu)[2(V+u)]}{(V+u)^4} = 0$$

∴ $(V + u) - 2u = 0$

∴ $V - u = 0$

∴ $V = u$

∴ $$\eta_{max} = \frac{2(u)u}{(u+u)^2} = \frac{1}{2} = 50\%.$$

18.6.2 Jet Propulsion of Ships

Ships develops its motion by making use of principle of jet propulsion. Ship carries a centrifugal pump in it and water from surrounding sea is drawn inside the ship. This water is discharged through orifice provided at its back, known as stern. Reaction of the jet coming out at back of ship propels the ship in forward direction. Sea water is taken into the ship either through

1. inlet orifice provided at right angle direction of ship motion, *i.e.* on its side or
2. inlet orifice facing the direction of motion of ship, *i.e.* on its front.

Case (*i*): Jet propulsion of ship when orifice is at its side. See Fig. 18.27.

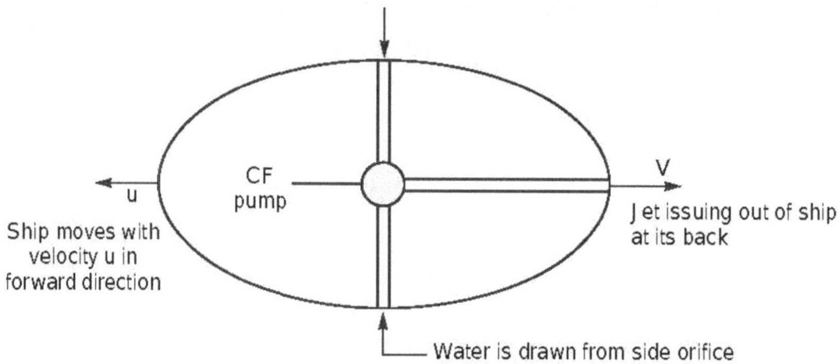

Fig. 18.27 Ship in Plan.

Mass of water issuing at back of ship

$= \rho a\,(V + u)$

Propulsive force on ship = F.

∴ $F = \rho a\,(V + u)\,V$

Work done per sec = $\rho a\,(V + u)\,Vu$

efficiency = $\dfrac{2Vu}{(V+u)^2}$ and its

maximum value = 50%

Case (*ii*): Jet propulsion of ship when orifice is at its front.

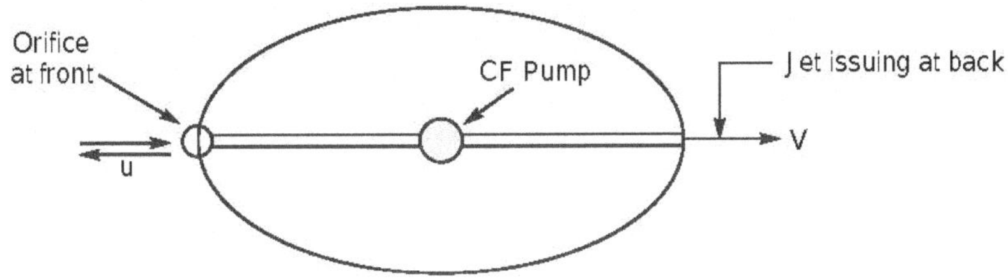

Fig. 18.28 Ship in Plan.

In this case expression for propulsive force and work done is same as in case (*i*), but KE of jet will be different, because water enters the ship with velocity equal to that of ship.

$$\therefore \qquad \text{KE of jet} = \frac{1}{2}\,[\rho a\,(V+u)]\,[(V+u)^2 - u^2]$$

$$\eta,\ \text{efficiency} = \frac{\text{Work done}}{\text{KE of jet}} = \frac{\rho a\,(V+u)\,Vu}{\frac{1}{2}\rho a\,(V+u)\,[(V+u)^2 - u^2]}$$

$$\therefore \qquad \eta = \frac{2Vu}{(V+u)^2 - u^2}$$

$$= \frac{2u}{V+2u}.$$

18.7 SOLVED PROBLEMS

■ **Problem 18.13:** *A jet of water comes out of a tank from a 10 cm diameter orifice. Head in the tank is constant at 2 m above centre of orifice. If force on tank is kept 290 N, find C_v of orifice.*

Solution:

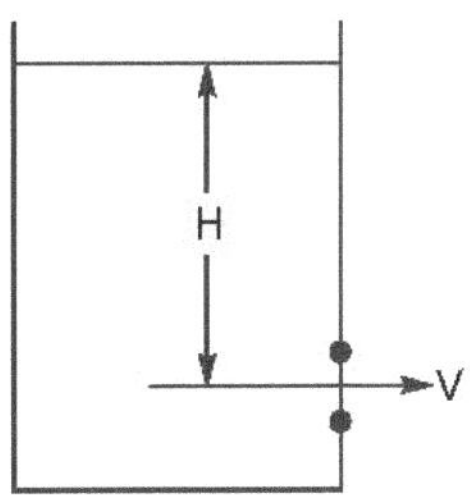

Fig. 18.29

$$H = 2\text{ m}$$

$$a = \frac{\pi}{4}(d)^2 = \frac{\pi}{4}\,(0.1)^2$$

$$= 0.0078\text{ m}^2$$

$$F = \rho a V^2$$

$$290 = 1000(0.0078)\ C_v[C_v\sqrt{2gH}\,]^2$$

$$290 = 1000(0.078)\ C_v^2\ 2g(2)$$

$$\therefore \qquad C_v^2 = \frac{290}{7.8 \times 19.6 \times 2} = 0.948$$

$$\therefore \qquad C_v = 0.973.$$ ...(Ans.)

■ **Problem 18.14:** *A jet of water comes out from a tank through 15 cm diameter orifice having a head of water of 6 m above its centre. If tank velocity is 4 m/s due to reaction of jet, find*

(*a*) *propelling force on tank*

(*b*) *work done per sec and*

(*c*) *efficiency of propulsion, if* $C_v = 0.97$.

Solution:

(*a*) $$\text{Force} = \rho a\,(V + u)V$$

$$= 1000\,\frac{\pi}{4}\,(0.15)^2\,(V + 4)\,V$$

$$V = C_v\,\sqrt{2gH} = 0.97\,\sqrt{2g6} = 10.5 \text{ m/s}$$

$$\therefore \qquad \text{Force} = 1000(0.78)\,(0.0225)\,(10.5 + 4)\,10.5$$

$$= 2.67 \text{ kN}$$ ...(Ans.)

(*b*) $$\text{Work done/sec} = \rho a(V + u)Vu$$

$$= 2.67 \times 4$$

$$= 10.68 \text{ kN-m/sec.}$$ ...(Ans.)

(*c*) $$\text{Efficiency} = \frac{2Vu}{(V + u)^2}$$

$$= \frac{2(10.5)4}{(14.5)^2} = 0.399$$

$$= 39.9\%.$$ ...(Ans.)

■ **Problem 18.15:** *A jet propelled ship draws water from its sides and discharging at its back with an absolute velocity of 30 m/s. If the jet diameter is 22.5 cm, and ship velocity is 30 kmph, find*

(*a*) *propelling force*

(*b*) *power developed*

(*c*) *efficiency of propulsion.*

Solution:

$$u = 30 \text{ kmph}$$

$$= 8.33 \text{ m/s}$$

(*a*) Force $= \rho a (V + u)V$

$= 1000[0.78(0.225)^2] (30 + 8.33) 30$

$= 46$ kN ...(Ans.)

(*b*) Work done/sec = power

$=$ Force $\times u$

$= 46 \times 8.33 =$ **383.14 kW** ...(Ans.)

(*c*)
$$\text{Efficiency} = \frac{2Vu}{(V+u)^2}$$

$$= \frac{2(30)\,8.33}{(38.33)^2}$$

$= 0.34$

$= 34\%$. ...(Ans.)

■ **Problem 18.16:** *A jet propelled ship draws water from orifices provided at its front, and is moving at 40 kmph. The absolute velocity of jet a its back is 40 m/s and jet diameter is 22.5 cm. Find propelling force and propulsion efficiency.*

$V = 40$ m/s

$u = 40$ kmph

$= 11$ m/s

$F = \rho a(V + u) V$

$= 1000(0.04) (40 + 11) 40$

$=$ **81.6 kN** ...(Ans.)

$$\eta = \frac{2u}{V+2u} = \frac{2\times 11}{40+22} = \frac{22}{62} = 0.35 = 35\%. \qquad \text{...(Ans.)}$$

Exercises

1. A 15 cm diameter jet of water strikes a flat plate at an angle of 30° to the normal. If jet velocity is 16 m/s, find the force exerted on the plate. **(Ans:** 3897 N)
2. A 20 cm diameter jet of water strikes a flat plate normally. The plate is moving with a velocity of 3 m/s in direction of jet. Calculate absolute velocity of jet if the force exerted on the plate is 3370 N. **(Ans:** $V = 12$ m/s)
3. A stationary curved plate deflects a 10 cm diameter jet through 120° in the horizontal plane. Calculate the force required to hold this plate in position if velocity of jet is 10 m/s. **(Ans:** Rusultant Force = 1345 N makes $\angle\theta = 30°$ with x-axis)
4. A 20 cm diameter jet of velocity 20 m/s strikes a vane having velocity 10 m/s at 30° to direction of motion. Vane angle at outlet is 30°. Find vane angle at inlet and force in direction of motion. **(Ans:** $\theta = 53.79°$, $F_x = 7066$ N)

5.

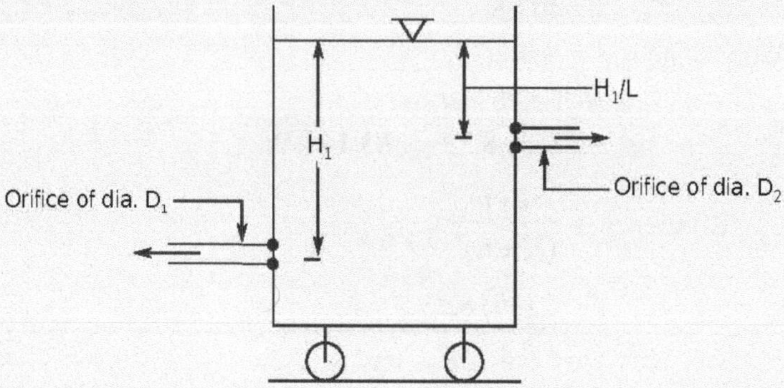

Fig. 18.30

A tank shown in above figure is mounted on a wheel and has an orifice of diameter 2 cm at a depth of H_1 m. On the opposite side of the tank, another orifice of diameter D_2 is provided below $H_1/2$ from free surface. Find diameter D_2 so that net horizontal force on the tank is zero. (**Ans:** $D_2 = 2.82$ cm)

6. (*a*) A stationary vane having inlet angle of zero degree and outlet angle of 25° receives water at 50 m/s. Find resultant force acting on vane per kg of water.

   (*b*) If above vane is moving with a velocity of 20 m/s in direction of jet find resultant force acting on vane per kg of water.

   (**Ans:** (*a*) $F_x = 9.7$ kgf, $F_y = -2.15$ kgf and $R = 9.95$ kgf at $\theta = 12.5°$ with *x*-axis (*b*) $F_x = 5.8$ kgf, $F_y = -1.3$ kgf, $R = 5.9$ kgf at $\theta = 12.5°$ with *x*-axis)

7. A jet of water of 15 cm diameter strikes a curved vane with a velocity of 20 m/s. The inlet and outlet angles of blade are zero and 45° respectively. Find resultant force on the blade when the blade moves against the direction of water of 5 m/s. Neglect friction.

   (**Ans:** $R = 20.3$ kN at $\theta = 22.5°$ ($F_x = 18.6$ kN and $F_y = 7.6$ kN))

8. A jet of water having velocity of 50 m/s strikes without shock a series of curved vanes moving at 20 m/s. The jet makes an angle of 20° to the direction of vane velocity. If $V_{r2} = 0.9\ V_{r1}$, and absolute velocity at exit makes a 90° angle with vane velocity, find vane angles at inlet and outlet, work done per kg and efficiency of jet.

   (**Ans:** (*a*) Inlet $\angle\theta = 32°$, outlet $\angle\phi = 23°$, (*b*) Work done/kg = 95.8 kg – m/kg (*c*) efficiency = 75%)

9. A jet propelled ship draws water from side orifices and discharges at its back with absolute velocity of 50 m/s. If jet diameter is 25 cm, and ship velocity is 40 kmph, find (*a*) propelling force (*c*) efficiency of propulsion.

   (**Ans:** (*a*) Force = 148.9 kN (*b*) 1654 kW (*c*) $\eta = 30\%$)

❑❑❑

19

Hydraulic Turbines

19.1 INTRODUCTION

In civil engineering profession, use of centrifugal pumps is required often and most of multipurpose reservoirs make use of water for irrigation as well as for hydro-power production. Thus knowledge of hydraulic machines such as pumps, turbines, lift, brake etc. is of great value in civil engineering profession. Hydraulic energy is converted into mechanical energy through turbines and mechanical energy is converted into electric power through generators. Electrical power is utilized to run pumps and pumps are essential for water supply and minor irrigation schemes. Impact of water jet on curved vanes mounted on a wheel produces rotational motion and is utilized for power production. This is how Pelton wheel was developed in 1880 and then after Francis, Kaplan and other varieties of turbines got developed. If vanes are forced to rotate through water mass, the result is production of higher kinetic energy at exit and centrifugal pumps came into existence. Thus hydraulic machines are responsible for industrial revolution and help its growth.

19.2 CLASSIFICATION OF TURBINES

The turbines are classified as impulse, reaction type and axial flow type. Pelton is impulse type, Francis is reaction type and Kaplan is axial flow type. Pelton wheel works under higher water heads of the order of 150 m to 1500 m, Francis turbine works with medium heads varying from 20 to 200 m and Kaplan is suitable for low heads varying from 2 to 3 m to 30 or 40 m. Thus, turbines are classified as per heads, *i.e.* high head, low head and medium head turbines. They are also classified as per direction of flow with respect to rotor axis, *i.e.* if flow is parallel to rotor axis, turbine is known as axial flow machine, if flow is in radial direction, turbine is radial. Flow may be partly radial and partly axial and in that case turbine is mixed flow machine. Classification is also based on specific speed, which will be given later.

19.3 IMPULSE TURBINE OR PELTON WHEEL

A. K. Pelton was an American engineer (1829 – 1908) who developed Pelton turbine in 1880.

Fig 19.1 shows schematic diagram of a hydro electric plant using Pelton turbine. Penstock is a steel pipe, receiving water with high pressure from reservoir and supplies to nozzle which converts pressure head into kinetic energy head and jet issuing from nozzle strikes the curved buckets attached to Pelton wheel which produces rotational motion and hence electric power. Pressure at exit of nozzle is atmospheric and therefore the Pelton wheel can be operated freely in air, however a casing is always provided.

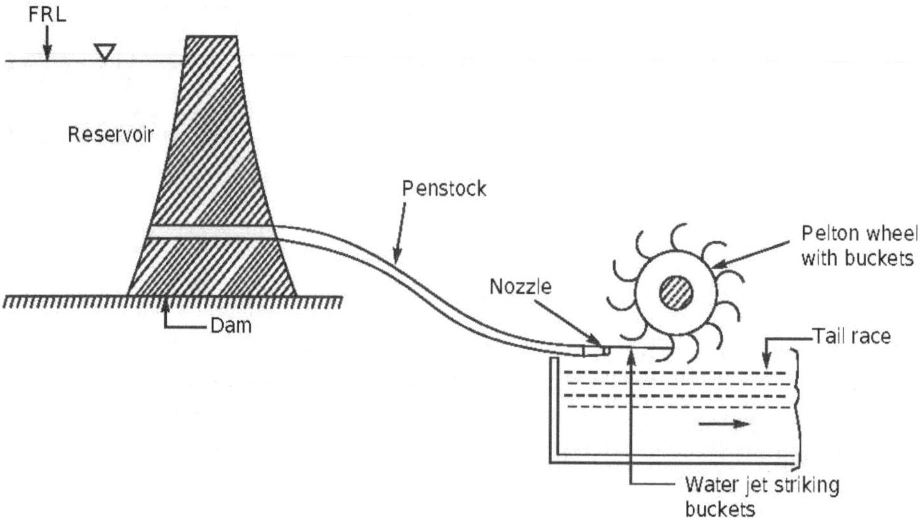

Fig. 19.1 Schematic diagram of a Hydro power plant.

Components parts of an impulse turbine or Pelton wheel are:

1. Penstock fitted with nozzle and spear valve
2. Wheel and buckets
3. Casing.

They are shown in Fig. 19.2.

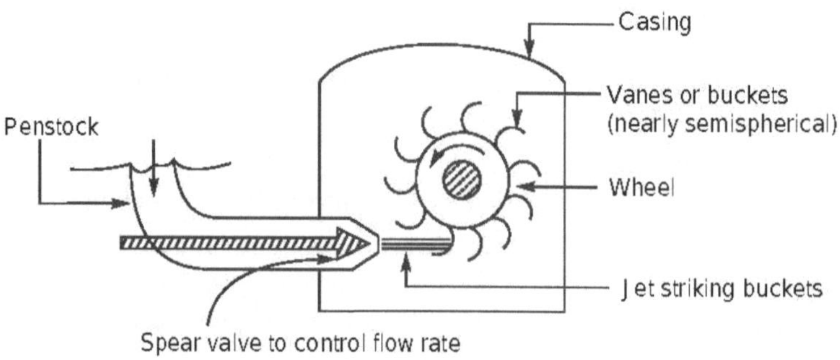

Fig. 19.2 Pelton turbine.

1. Nozzle and spear valve: Water in form of jet strikes the bucket. Jet comes out of nozzle fitted to Penstock. Control of water flow through nozzle is by means of spear valve. The spear is a conical needle which when pushed forward reduces the flow and vice versa.

2. Wheel or runner with buckets: On the periphery of runner number of buckets are spaced at uniform interval. The buckets are hemispherical twin cups and between two cups there is a dividing part which is known as splitter. The buckets are shaped such that they deflect the jet through 160 to 165°. Buckets are made up of stainless steel or bronze.

3. Casing is provided to prevent splashing of water and to guide water to tail race. It consists of steel plates fabricated to required shape. Pressure in casing atmospheric.

19.4 VELOCITY TRIANGLES, WORK DONE AND RELATED INFORMATION ABOUT PELTON WHEEL

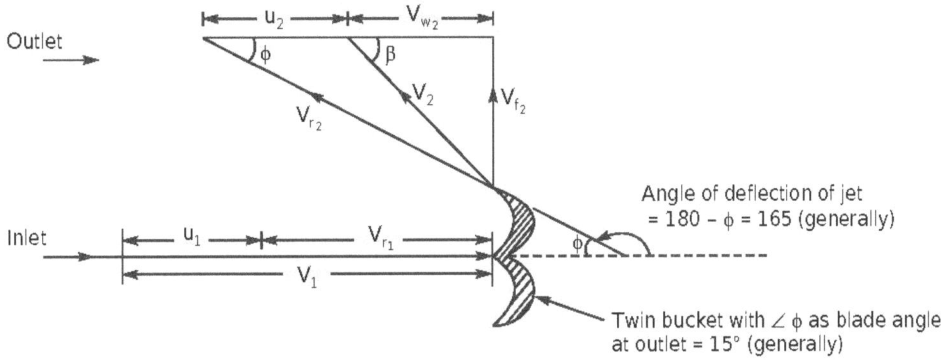

Fig. 19.3

H = Head acting on turbine

$= H_g - h_f$

H_g = gross head

h_f = friction in Penstock pipe $= \dfrac{fLV^2}{2gD_1}$

L = Length of Penstock of diameter D_1

V = Velocity in Penstock

f = friction factor of Penstock, generally 0.02

β = Angle of jet at exit

V_1 = Velocity of jet at inlet $= C_V\sqrt{2gH}$

N = rpm of wheel

D = diameter of wheel, d_j = diameter of jet

$$u = u_1 = u_2 = \frac{\pi DN}{60} = \text{tangential velocity of wheel}$$

$V_{r1} = V_1 - u_1$ = relative velocity at inlet

V_{w1} = Velocity of whirl at inlet = V_1 in this case only as

$\alpha = 0$ = jet angle at inlet, and

$\theta = 0$ = bucket angle at inlet, ϕ = bucket angle at out let

At out let: $V_{r2} = V_{r1}$; if no friction loss in vanes or $V_{r2} = kV_{r1}$

and

$$V_{w2} = V_{r2} \cos\phi - u_2$$

$$= k\, V_{r1} \cos\phi - u \quad (k = \text{coefficient due to friction})$$

$$= k\,(V_1 - u) \cos\phi - u$$

F_x = Force exerted by jet on wheel

$= \rho a\, V_1\, [V_{w1} \pm V_{w2}]$ (+ve sign if β is acute, –ve if β is obtuse)

As series of vanes/buckets are mounted on wheel, mass of water striking the bucket $= \rho a V_1$

where a = c/s area of jet $= \dfrac{\pi}{4} d_j^2$

d_j = jet diameter

Work done by jet on wheel

$$= F_x(u)$$

$$= \rho a\, V_1\, [V_{w1} + V_{w2}]\, u$$

$$= \rho a\, V_1\, [V_1 + k\,(V_1 - u)] \cos\phi - u]\, u$$

$$= \rho a\, V_1\, [(V_1 - u)\,(1 + k \cos\phi)]\, u$$

Work done per unit weight of water striking the bucket

$$= \frac{\rho a\, V_1\, [V_{w1} + V_{w2}]\, u}{\rho a\, V_1\, (g)}$$

$$= \frac{1}{g}[V_{w1} + V_{w2}]\, u \text{ kg – m per kg of water}$$

$$= \frac{1}{g}\, [(V_1 - u)\,(1 + k \cos\phi)]\, u$$

η_h = hydraulic efficiency

$$= \frac{\text{work done per sec.}}{\text{KE of jet per sec.}} \text{ or } = \frac{\text{Runner power}}{\text{Water power}} = \frac{\text{RP}}{\text{WP}}$$

$$= \frac{\rho a\, V_1\, [V_{w1} + V_{w2}]}{\frac{1}{2}(\rho a\, V_1)\, V_1^2}$$

$$\therefore \quad \eta_h = \frac{2\,(V_{w1} + V_{w2})\, u}{V_1^2} = \eta_b = \text{blading efficiency}$$

Here, $V_{w1} = V_1$

$$V_{w_2} = V_{r2} \cos \phi - u_2$$
$$= (V_1 - u) \cos \phi - u$$

as $V_{r2} = k (V_{r1}) = k (V_1 - u_1) = k (V_1 - u)$ as $u_1 = u_2 = u$

$$\therefore \quad \eta_h = \frac{2[V_1 + k (V_1 - u) \cos \phi - u] u}{V_1^2}$$

$$= \frac{2 (V_1 - u)(1 + k \cos \phi) u}{V_1^2} \qquad ...(19.1)$$

For max. eff. $\dfrac{d(\eta_h)}{du} = 0$

$$\therefore \quad \frac{(1 + k \cos \phi)}{V_1^2} \frac{d}{du} (2uV_1 - 2u^2) = 0$$

$$\therefore \quad 2V_1 - 4u = 0$$

$$\therefore \quad u = \frac{V_1}{2}$$

$$\therefore \quad \eta_{h(\max)} = \frac{2\left(V_1 - \dfrac{V_1}{2}\right)(1 + k \cos \phi) \times \dfrac{V_1}{2}}{V_1^2} = \frac{(1 + k \cos \phi)}{2} \qquad ...(19.2)$$

or $\eta_{b(\max)} = \dfrac{(1 + k \cos \phi)}{2}$, here ϕ is bucket angle at outlet and $k = \dfrac{V_{r2}}{V_{r1}}$

$$\text{Speed ratio} = k_u = \frac{\text{bucket speed}}{\text{jet speed}}$$

$$= \frac{u}{\sqrt{2gH}} = 0.43 \text{ to } 0.48, \text{ say } 0.45$$

$$m = \text{jet ratio} = \frac{\text{pitch diameter or diameter of wheel, } D}{\text{diameter of jet, } d_j}.$$

$$= \frac{D}{d_j} = 10 \text{ to } 12$$

Note: Hydraulic efficiency η_h and blading efficiency η_b are one and same

Z = number of buckets on runner or wheel

$$= 15 + \frac{D}{d_j} \qquad ...(19.3)$$

$$= (15 + 0.5 \text{ m}), \text{ varies from 18 to 24}$$

$$\text{Number of jets} = \frac{Q}{\left(\frac{\pi}{4} d_j^2\right)} = \frac{\text{Flow rate (total)}}{\text{Flow rate of single jet of diameter } d_j}$$

$$V_1 = C_v \sqrt{2gH}$$

$$C_v = 0.98 \text{ and } H = \text{net head on wheel}$$

Mechanical efficiency,

$$\eta_m = \frac{\text{Shaft power}}{\text{Power developed by Runner}} = \frac{\text{SP}}{\text{RP}} \quad \text{...(19.4)}$$

$$\eta_0 = \text{Overall efficiency}$$

$$= \frac{\text{Shaft Power}}{\text{Water Power supplied to turbine}} = \frac{\text{SP}}{\text{WP}} = \frac{\text{SP}}{\left(\frac{\gamma QH}{1000}\right)} \quad \text{...(19.5)}$$

$$= \frac{\text{SP}}{\text{WP}} \times \frac{\text{RP}}{\text{RP}} \text{ (Multiply and divide by RP)}$$

$$= \frac{\text{SP}}{\text{WP}} \times \frac{\text{RP}}{\text{RP}} = \frac{\text{SP}}{\text{RP}} \times \frac{\text{RP}}{\text{WP}}$$

$$= \eta_m \times \eta_h = \text{(mech eff.} \times \text{hyd. eff.)} \quad \text{...(19.6)}$$

$$\eta_0 = \frac{\text{Shaft power in kW, P}}{\left(\frac{\rho g\, QH}{1000}\right)} = \frac{P}{\left(\frac{\rho g\, QH}{1000}\right)} \quad \text{...(19.7)}$$

$$\eta_v = \text{Volumetric efficiency}$$

$$= \frac{\text{Actual volume of water striking the runner}}{\text{Volume of water supplied to the turbine}}$$

$$= \frac{\text{(Vol. of water supplied to turbine)} - \text{(Losses)}}{\text{Vol. of water supplied to turbine}} = \frac{Q - \Delta Q}{Q} \quad \text{...(19.8)}$$

Additional points to be remembered:

If d_j = diameter of jet

1. Width of bucket = $5 \times d_j$
2. Depth of bucket = $1.2\, d_j$
3. If $h_f = \frac{1}{3} H$ then d = dia. of nozzle = $\left(\frac{D_1^5}{8 fL}\right)^{1/4}$ for maximum power transmitted

through Penstock pipe.

Here, D_1 = pipe diameter (Penstock),
L = pipe length, (Penstock)
f = friction factor of pipe.

19.5 STEPS INVOLVED IN DESIGN OF PELTON WHEEL

(*a*) Find Q from overall efficiency $\eta_0 = \dfrac{P}{\left(\dfrac{\rho g Q H}{1000}\right)}$. Here P = Power in kW.

(*b*) Calculate velocity V_1 of jet from $V_1 = C_v\sqrt{2gH}$

(*c*) Calculate total area of jet $a = \dfrac{Q}{V_1}$

(*d*) Calculate diameter D of wheel from $u = \dfrac{\pi D N}{60}$

(*e*) Calculate diameter d_j of jet from $\dfrac{D}{d_j} = m$ = jet ratio. If not given, take $m = 12$.

(*f*) Number of jets $= \dfrac{a}{\left(\dfrac{\pi}{4}d_j^2\right)}$

(*g*) Number of buckets $= 15 + \dfrac{D}{2d_j}$

(*h*) Calculate nozzle diameter d from $\left(\dfrac{\pi}{4}d^2\right)V_1 = Q$.

19.6 SOLVED PROBLEMS

■ **Problem 19.1:** *A penstock supplies water from a reservoir to the Pelton wheel with a gross head of 600 m; and one third of it is lost in friction. Rate of flow from nozzle fitted to penstock is 2 m³/s. Jet gets deflected through 165°. Find HP of runner and hydraulic efficiency.*

Given: $k_u = 0.45$, $C_v = 1.0$.

Solution:

Here, $H_g = 600$ m

$$h_f = \frac{1}{3}H_g = \frac{600}{3} = 200 \text{ m}$$

∴ $H = 600 - 200 = 400$ m

$Q = 2\ \text{m}^3/\text{s}$

Bucket $\angle\phi = 180 - 165 = 15°$

Speed ratio $k_u = 0.45 = \dfrac{u}{\sqrt{2gH}}$

$\therefore$ $u = 0.45\sqrt{2g\,(400)} = 40 \text{ m/s} = u_1 = u_2$

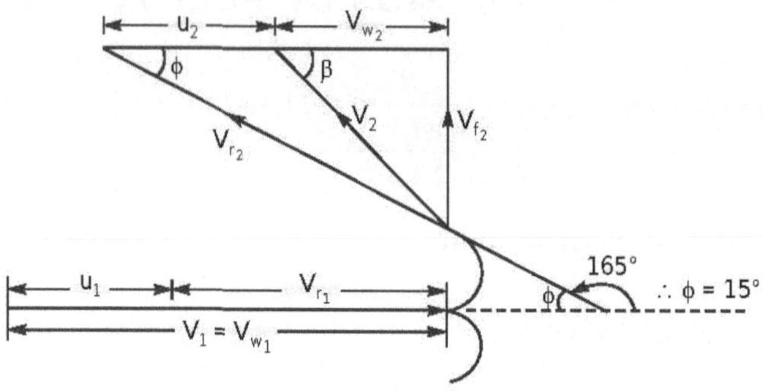

Fig. 19.4

$$V_1 = C_v\sqrt{2gH} = (1)\sqrt{2g\,(400)} = 88.5 \text{ m/s} \quad (C_v = 1)$$

$$V_{r1} = V_1 - u_1 = 88.5 - 40 = 48.5 \text{ m/s}$$

$$V_{w1} = V_1 = 88.5 \text{ m/s}$$

$$V_{r2} = V_{r1} = 48.5 \text{ m/s} \quad (k = 1)$$

$$V_{r2}\cos\phi = u_2 + V_{w2}$$

$\therefore$ $V_{w2} = 48.5\cos(15) - 40$

$$= 46.8 - 40 = 6.8 \text{ m/s}$$

Work done per sec. $= \rho a V_1 [V_{w1} + V_{w2}]\,u$

$$aV_1 = Q = 2 \text{ m}^3/\text{s}$$

$\therefore$ Work done per sec. $= 1000\,(2)\,[88.5 + 6.8]\,40$

$$= 7624 \text{ kW.}$$

Note: 1 metric HP = 735 watts

$$\text{HP} = \frac{\text{Power in Watts}}{735} = \frac{7624 \times 1000}{735} = 10372 \text{ HP}$$

$$\eta_h = \frac{2(V_{w1} + V_{w2})\,u}{V_1^2} = \frac{2\,(88.5 + 6.8)\,40}{(88.5)^2} = 97.3\%. \qquad \text{...(Ans.)}$$

■ **Problem 19.2:** *A Pelton wheel is working under a head of 220 m and its nozzle diameter is 20 cm with $C_v = 0.98$. Speed of wheel is 250 RPM and develops a power of 3.75 MW. Assuming blade to jet speed ratio as 0.46, find wheel diameter at the pitch circle of the blades. If blade outlet ∠16°, calculate blading efficiency and turbine efficiency. Neglet frictional effect.*

Solution:

$$V_1 = C_V\sqrt{2gH} = 0.98\sqrt{2g(220)}$$

$$= 64.35 \text{ m/s}$$

a = nozzle area

$$= \frac{\pi}{4}(d^2) = \frac{\pi}{4}(0.2)^2 = 0.0312 \text{ m}^2$$

$$k_u = \text{Blade to jet speed ratio} = \frac{u}{V_1} = 0.46$$

$$\therefore \quad u = 0.46\ (64.35) = 29.6 \text{ m/s} = \frac{\pi DN}{60}$$

$$\therefore \quad D = \frac{60 \times 29.6}{\pi(250)} = 2.26 \text{ m} \qquad \text{...(Ans.)}$$

Blading efficiency by assuming $k = 1$,

$$\eta_b = 2\frac{u}{V_1}\left(1 - \frac{u}{V_1}\right)(1 + k\cos\phi) \qquad \text{...(1)}$$

This is same as hyd. eff.; $\eta_h = \dfrac{2u\,(V_1 - u)\,(1 + \cos\phi)}{V_1^2}$ ...(2)

Putting $\dfrac{u}{V_1} = 0.46$ in (1),

We get $\eta_b = 2\ (0.46)\ (1 - 0.46)\ (1 + \cos 16)$

$= 97.37\%$ ...(Ans.)

$$\eta_t = \text{turbine efficiency} = \frac{\text{Turbine output (given in data)}}{\text{Turbine input}}$$

$$= \frac{3.75 \times 10^6}{(\text{mass flow rate})\ gH}$$

$$= \frac{3.75 \times 10^6}{(a V_1 \rho)\ gH}$$

$$= \frac{3.75 \times 10^6}{(0.0312 \times 64.35 \times 1000)\ 9.81 \times 220}$$

$$= \frac{3.75 \times 10^6}{4.33 \times 10^6} = 86.6\%. \qquad \text{...(Ans.)}$$

■ **Problem 19.3:** *A Pelton turbine delivers a maximum power of 15000 kW when working under a head of 500 m and running at 800 RPM. Find diameter of orifice at nozzle tip, least diameter of jet and mean diameter of the wheel. Specify number of buckets for the wheel. Take* $\eta_0 = 0.9$, $\eta_h = 0.8$, $C_v = 0.98$ *and* $k_u = 0.45$. *Is jet ratio within limit?*

Solution:

$$\eta_0 = \frac{P}{\left(\frac{\rho g\, QH}{1000}\right)} = 0.9$$

$$\therefore \quad \frac{15000}{\left(\frac{1000\,(9.81)\,Q\,(500)}{1000}\right)} = 0.9$$

$$\therefore \quad Q = \frac{15000}{9.81 \times 500 \times 0.9} = 3.39 \text{ m}^3/\text{s}$$

$$\eta_n = \frac{2\,(V_{w1} + V_{w2})\,u}{V_1^2}, \qquad V_1 = C_v\,\sqrt{2gH}$$

$$0.8 = \frac{2\,(V_1 + V_{w2})\,u}{V_1^2} \qquad = 0.98\,\sqrt{2g\,(500)}$$

$$= 97 \text{ m/s} = V_{w1}$$

$$k_u = 0.45 = \frac{u}{C_v\,\sqrt{2gH}} = \frac{u}{0.98\sqrt{2g\,500}}$$

$$\therefore \quad u = 0.45 \times 0.98\,\sqrt{2g\,(500)} = 0.44 \times 99 = 43.6 \text{ m/s}$$

$$\therefore \quad 0.8 = \frac{2\,(97 + V_{w2})\,43.6}{(97)^2}$$

$$(97 + V_{w2}) = \frac{0.8 \times (97)^2}{2 \times 43.6} = 86.32$$

$$\therefore \quad V_{w2} = 97 - 86.32 = 10.67 \text{ m/s}$$

$$u = \frac{\pi DN}{60}, \quad \therefore \quad 43.6 = \frac{\pi D\,(800)}{60}$$

$$\therefore \quad D = \frac{43.6 \times 60}{800\,\pi} = 1.04 \text{ m} = \text{wheel dia.}$$ ...**(Ans.)**

$$Q = \left(\frac{\pi}{4} d^2\right) V_1$$

$$3.39 = \frac{\pi}{4}\, d^2\,(97)$$

$$d^2 = \frac{3.39}{0.78 \times 97}$$

$$\therefore \quad d = 0.21 \text{ m}$$

$$= 21 \text{ cm}$$

$$\therefore \qquad D_1 = \frac{3.39}{0.78(97)} = 0.044$$

$\therefore$ $d = 0.21$ m = 21 cm (nozzle diameter) ...(Ans.)

Z = Number of buckets on wheel

$$= 15 + \frac{D}{2d}, \text{ here } \frac{D}{d} = \text{jet ratio} = \frac{1.04}{0.21} = 5 < 12$$

$\therefore$ not adequate. ...(Ans.)

$$= 15 + \frac{1.04}{2(0.21)}$$

$$= 15 + 2.52$$

$$= 17.52$$

= 18, Number of buckets be provided. ...(Ans.)

For least diameter of jet, take jet ratio $\frac{D}{d} = 12$

$$\therefore \qquad \frac{1.04}{d} = 12$$

$$\therefore \qquad d = \frac{1.04}{12} = 0.08 \text{ m} = 8.8 \text{ cm.}$$

■ **Problem 19.4:** *At a hydroelectric plant, the difference in water levels in the intake and tail race is 180 m. When the flow is 2.25 cumec, friction loss in Penstock is 18 m and head utilized by turbine is 138 m. The mechanical friction in turbine is 75 kW and leakage loss is 85 LPS, find*

(*a*) *hydraulic, volumetric, mechanical and overall efficiencies.*

(*b*) *power delivered to shaft.*

(*c*) *power delivered to runner.*

Solution: $H_{total} = 180$ m

$Q = 2.25$ m^3/s,

leakage = 85 LPS

$h_f = 18$ m, H on turbine = 138 m

Friction loss due to mechanical aspect = 75 kW

$$\eta_{vol.} = \frac{\text{Water available to runner}}{\text{Water supplied to turbine}}$$

$$= \frac{2.25 - \frac{85}{1000}}{2.25} = \frac{2.25 - 0.085}{2.25} = \frac{2.165}{2.25}$$

$= 0.962 = 96.2\%$ ...(Ans.)

$$\text{Runner Power} = \frac{\rho g Q\,(\text{H}_{\text{utilized by turbine}})}{1000} = \frac{1000\,(9.81)\,2.25 \times 138}{1000}$$

$$= 3046 \text{ kW}$$

$$\text{Water power (supplied to turbine)} = \frac{\rho g QH}{1000} = \frac{1000\,(9.81)\,(2.25)\,(180-18)}{1000}$$

$$= 3575 \text{ kW}$$

$$\eta_h = \frac{\text{Runner Power}}{\text{Power supplied}}$$

$$= \frac{3046}{3575} = 0.852 = 85.2\% \qquad \text{...(Ans.)}$$

$$\eta_m = \frac{\text{Shaft Power}}{\text{Runner Power}}$$

$$= \frac{\text{Runner power} - \text{Mechanical Losses}}{\text{Runner Power}}$$

$$= \frac{3046-75}{3046}$$

$$= \frac{2971}{3046} = 0.975 = 97.5\% \qquad \text{...(Ans.)}$$

$$\eta_0 = \eta_m \times \eta_h = 0.975 \times 0.852$$

$$= 0.83$$

$$= 83\%$$

$$= \frac{\text{Shaft Power}}{\text{Power Supplied}} = \frac{2971}{3575} = 83\%, \text{ checked, OK}$$

Power delivered to shaft = 2971 kW ...(**Ans.**)

Power delivered to runner = 3046 kW. ...(**Ans.**)

■ **Problem 19.5:** *A Pelton wheel works under a head of 525 m, and produces 11,170 kW, while running at 300 RPM. If $\eta_0 = 84\%$, $C_v = 0.98$, find diameters of jet and nozzle, mean diameter of wheel and number of buckets.*

Solution:

$$\eta_0 = \frac{P}{\left(\dfrac{\rho g QH}{1000}\right)}$$

$$\therefore \qquad 0.84 = \frac{11170}{\dfrac{1000\,(9.81)\,Q\,(525)}{1000}}$$

$$\therefore \qquad Q = \frac{11170}{9.81 \times 525 \times 0.84}$$

$$= 2.58 \text{ m}^3\text{/s}$$

$$= \frac{\pi}{4}\, d^2\, V_1,$$

here d = dia. of nozzle

But $V_1 = C_v\sqrt{2gH} = 0.98\sqrt{2g\,(525)}$

$= 99.4$ m/s

$\therefore \quad 2.58 = 0.78\, d^2\, (99.4)$

$\therefore \quad d^2 = \dfrac{2.58}{99.4 \times 0.78} = 0.0332$

$\therefore \quad d = 0.182 = 18.2$ cm = dia. of jet and nozzle (same as per data given)

Assume sped ratio $= 0.45 = \dfrac{u}{\sqrt{2gH}}$

$u = 0.45\sqrt{2g\,(525)}$

$= 45.6 \text{ m/s} = \dfrac{\pi DN}{60}$, ($N$ = 300 RPM)

$\therefore \quad D$ = Wheel dia. $= \dfrac{45.6 \times 60}{\pi\,(300)}$

$= 2.9$ m

Jet ratio $= \dfrac{D}{d} = \dfrac{2.9}{0.182} = 15.9$

Z = Number of buckets

$= 15 + \dfrac{D}{2d} = 15 + \dfrac{15.9}{2} = 23.$ ...(**Ans.**)

■ **Problem 19.6:** *A Pelton wheel is to be designed for following data:*

$$P = 6000 \text{ kW}, H_{net} = 300 \text{ m}, N = 600 \text{ RPM}$$

$$\text{Jet ratio} = 10, \eta_0 = 85\%$$

$$C_v = 0.98, k_u = 0.46.$$

Find number of jets, jet diameter, diameter of wheel, quality of water required.

Solution: $V_1 = C_v\sqrt{2gH} = 0.98\sqrt{2g300} = 75$ m/s

$u = k_u\sqrt{2gH} = 0.46\sqrt{2g300} = 35.2$ m/s

Now, $u = \dfrac{\pi DN}{60}$, $\therefore \quad 35.2 = \dfrac{\pi D\,(600)}{60}$

$\therefore \quad D = 1.12$ m

= wheel dia. ...(**Ans.**)

$$\eta_0 = 0.85 = \frac{P}{\left(\dfrac{\rho g\,QH}{1000}\right)}$$

$$\therefore \qquad 0.85 = \frac{6000}{\left(\frac{1000 \times 9.81 \times Q \times 300}{1000}\right)}$$

$$\therefore \qquad Q = \frac{6000}{0.85 \times 9.81 \times 300} = 2.4 \text{ m}^3/\text{s}$$

= quantity of water required ...(Ans.)

$$\text{Jet ratio} = 10 = \frac{D}{d_j} = \frac{1.12}{d_j}$$

$$\therefore \qquad d_j = \frac{D}{10} = \frac{1.12}{10} = 0.112 \text{ m}$$

∴ Jet diameter = 0.112 m ...(Ans.)

$$\text{Number of jets} = \frac{Q/V_1}{\frac{\pi}{4}(d_j)^2} = \frac{2.4/75}{0.78\,(0.112)^2}$$

= 3.27

∴ Provide 4 number of jets. ...(Ans.)

■ **Problem 19.7**: *A Pelton wheel nozzle for which C_v = 0.98 is 425 m below water surface of reservoir. The jet diameter is 85 mm and is deflected through 165° by buckets. Bucket speed is 0.45 times jet speed and bucket friction reduces outlet relative velocity by 15%. Mechanical efficiency = 80%. Considering maximum efficiency of transmission of power through Penstock pipes, determine the flow rate and shaft power developed by the turbine.*

Solution: H_g = 425m, ϕ = 180 – 165 = 15°

For max power,

$$h_f = \frac{1}{3}(425)$$

= 141.6 m

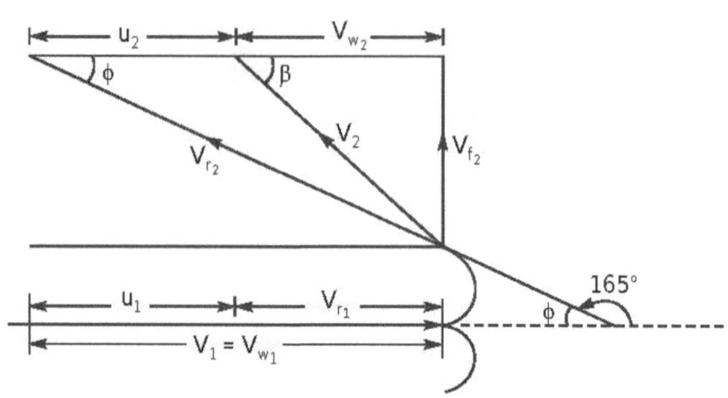

Fig. 19.5

$$\therefore \quad H \text{ on turbine} = 425 - 141.6$$

$$= 283.9 \text{ m}$$

$$C_V = 0.98, \quad \therefore \quad V_1 = C_v\sqrt{2gH} = 0.98\sqrt{2g\,(283.4)}$$

$$= 73 \text{ m/s}$$

$$u = u_1 = u_2 = 0.45\,(73) = 32.87$$

$$V_{r1} = V_1 - u_1$$

$$= 73 - 32.87$$

$$= 40.13 \text{ m/s}$$

$$V_{r2} = 0.85\, V_{r1}$$

$$= 0.85\,(40.13)$$

$$= 34.11 \text{ m/s}$$

$$V_{r2} \cos \phi = u_2 + V_{w2}$$

$$34.11\,(\cos 15) = 32.86 + V_{w2}$$

$$\therefore \quad V_{w2} = 32.94 - 32.86 = 0.087 \text{ m/s (negligible)}$$

$$\text{Flow rate} = Q = \frac{\pi}{4}\,(d^2)\, V_1$$

$$= 0.78\left(\frac{85}{1000}\right)^2 (73) = 0.411 \text{ m}^3\text{/s} = aV_1 \qquad \text{...(Ans.)}$$

$$P = \frac{\text{Work done/sec.}}{1000} = \frac{\rho a V_1\,(V_{w1} + V_{w2})\,u}{1000}$$

$$= \frac{1000\,(0.411)\,(73.087)\,32.86}{1000}$$

$$= 988 \text{ kW}$$

$$\therefore \quad \text{Shaft Power} = n_m\,(988) = 0.8\,(988) = 790 \text{ kW.} \qquad \text{...(Ans.)}$$

■ **Problem 19.8:** *A Pelton wheel has bucket speed of 12 m/s and is supplied with water at 700 LPS under a head of 30 m. If the buckets deflect the jet through 160°, find HP and over all efficiency of turbine. Take $C_v = 0.99$ and $k = 1$.*

Solution: $V_1 = C_v\sqrt{2gH} = 0.99\sqrt{2 \times g \times 30} = 24$ m/s and $u = 12$ m/s, $k = 1$

$$\phi = 180 - 160 = 20.$$

$$P = \frac{\rho Q\,[(V_1 - u)\,(1 + k\cos\phi)]\,u}{1000} \text{ kW}$$

$$= \frac{1000\left(\frac{700}{1000}\right)[(24.0 - 12)\,(1 + \cos 20)]\,12}{1000}$$

$$= \frac{700\,(12)\,(1.94)\,12}{1000}$$

$$= 195.5 \text{ kW}$$

$$\therefore \qquad \text{HP} = \frac{195.5 \times 1000}{735} = 266 \qquad \text{...(Ans.)}$$

$$\eta_0 = \frac{P}{\left(\frac{\rho g Q H}{1000}\right)} = \frac{195.5}{\left(\frac{1000\,(9.81)\,(0.7)\,(30)}{1000}\right)}$$

$$= \frac{195.5}{206} = 94.9\%. \qquad \text{...(Ans.)}$$

■ **Problem 19.9:** *A pipe line 1200 m long supplies water at 600 LPS to a Pelton wheel. Head above nozzle is 360 m, C_v = 0.98, friction factor 0.02, η_0 = 85%, N = 560 RPM, h_f = 12 m.*

Find: *1. Power developed (HP)*
2. Nozzle diameter
3. Pipe diameter.

Solution:

$$H_{\text{net}} = 360 - 12 = 348 \text{ m}$$

$$\eta_0 = \frac{\rho}{\frac{\rho g Q H}{1000}} = \frac{P}{\left(\frac{1000\,(9.81)\left(\frac{600}{1000}\right)(348)}{1000}\right)}$$

$$0.85 = \frac{P}{2048}$$

$$\therefore \qquad P = 0.85\,(2048) = 1741 \text{ kW}$$

$$\therefore \qquad \text{HP} = \frac{1741 \times 1000}{735} = 2368 \qquad \text{...(Ans.)}$$

$$h_f = \frac{flQ^2}{12D^5} = \frac{0.2\,(1200)\,(0.6)^2}{12\,(D)^5}$$

It is given that h_f $= 12$ m

$$\therefore \qquad 12 = \frac{0.02\,(1200)\,(0.6)^2}{12\,D^5}$$

$$\therefore \qquad D1 = 0.06$$

$$\therefore \qquad D^5 = 0.569 \text{ m} = \text{pipe diameter} \qquad \text{...(Ans.)}$$

$$V_1 = C_v\,\sqrt{2gH} = 0.98\,\sqrt{2g \times 348} = 81 \text{ m/s}$$

$$Q = \frac{\pi}{4} d^2\, V_1,$$

here d = dia. of nozzle

$$d^2 = \frac{Q}{0.78(81)} = \frac{0.6}{0.78(81)} = 9.5 \times 10^{-3}$$

$\therefore$ $d = 0.097$ m

$= 9.7$ cm $=$ nozzle diameter. ...(Ans.)

■ **Problem 19.10:** *A Pelton wheel which is required to developed 7350 HP has a specific speed of 23.5 and is supplied with water at a head of 300 m above nozzle, find out:*

(*a*) *rotational speed of wheel*

(*b*) *mean dia. of bucket circle*

(*c*) *diameter of jet and their number*

(*d*) *number of buckets.*

Assume $C_v = 0.97$, $k_u = 0.46$, jet ratio = 12, $\eta_0 = 85\%$.

Solution:

$$N_s = \frac{N\sqrt{P}}{H^{5/4}}, \text{ Here } P \text{ in kW} \qquad \text{(take 0.735 kW = 1 HP)}$$

$$23.5 = \frac{N\sqrt{7350 \times 0.735}}{(300)^{5/4}}$$

$\therefore$ $N = 400$ RPM ...(Ans.)

$$\eta_0 = \frac{P}{\left(\dfrac{\rho QgH}{1000}\right)} = \frac{7350 \times 0.735}{\left(\dfrac{1000\, Q\, 9.81 \times 300}{1000}\right)}$$

$= 0.85$

$$\therefore \quad Q = \frac{7350 \times 0.735}{0.85 \times 9.81 \times 300}$$

$= 2.15$ m^3/s

$$V = C_v \sqrt{2gH} = 0.97\sqrt{2g \times 300}$$

$= 74.3$ m/s

$$u = k_u \sqrt{2gH}$$

$$= 0.46\sqrt{2gH} = 35.27 \text{ m/s}$$

$$= \frac{\pi DN}{60} = \frac{\pi D(400)}{60}$$

$\therefore$ $D = 1.68$ m ...(Ans.)

$Q = aV$; (where, a = total area of jet)

$$a = \frac{Q}{V} = \frac{2.15}{74.3} = 0.029 \text{ m}^2$$

$$\text{Jet ratio} = 12 = \frac{D}{d_j}$$

$$\therefore \qquad d_j = \frac{D}{12} = \frac{1.68}{12} = 0.14 \text{ m}$$

$$\therefore \qquad \text{Area of one jet} = \frac{\pi}{4}(0.14)^2$$

$$= 0.015 \text{ m}^2$$

$$\therefore \qquad \text{Number of jets} = \frac{a}{0.015}$$

$$= \frac{0.029}{0.015} = 1.933$$

Provide 2 number of jets each of 14 cm dia. ...(Ans.)

$$Z = \text{bucket number}$$

$$= 15 + \frac{D}{2d_j}$$

$$= 15 + \frac{12}{2} = 21 \text{ number.} \qquad \text{...(Ans.)}$$

■ **Problem 19.11:** *A double jet Pelton wheel is required to generate 7500 kW under a head of 400 m. The jet is deflected through 165° and relative velocity of jet is reduced by 15% in passing over the buckets. Find*

(*a*) *dia. of each jet*

(*b*) *total flow rate*

(*c*) *force exerted by jet on bucket in tangential direction and*

(*d*) η_h *if* $k = 0.9$.

Assume $\eta_0 = 80\%$, *generator efficiency* = 95%, $C_v = 0.97$ *and* $k_u = 0.46$

Solution: As generator efficiency of 95% given,

$$\therefore \qquad P = \frac{7500}{0.95} = 7895 \text{ kW}$$

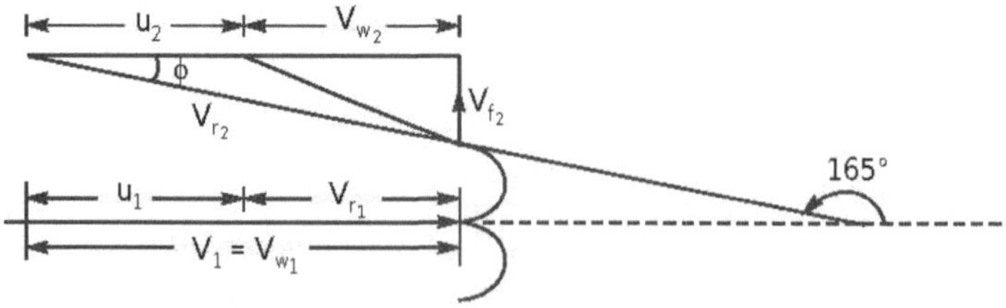

Fig. 19.6

$$\therefore \qquad \eta_0 = \frac{P}{\left(\dfrac{\rho QgH}{1000}\right)} = \frac{7895}{\left(\dfrac{1000\, Q\, 9.81 \times 400}{1000}\right)} = 0.8$$

$$\therefore \qquad Q = \frac{7895}{0.8 \times 9.81 \times 400}$$

$$= 2.51 \text{ m}^3/\text{s} \qquad \text{...(Ans.)}$$

$$V_1 = C_v \sqrt{2gH}$$

$$= 0.97 \sqrt{19.6\,(400)} = 86.5 \text{ m/s}$$

$$u_1 = k_u \sqrt{2gH} = 0.46 \sqrt{1.96 \times 400}$$

$$= 40.7 \text{ m/s} = u_2$$

$$\therefore \qquad \phi = 180 - 165 = 15°$$

$$V_{r2} = 0.85\, V_{r1}$$

$$= 0.85\,(V_1 - u_1)$$

$$= 0.85\,(86.5 - 40.7)$$

$$= 39.1 \text{ m/s}$$

$$V_{r2} \cos\phi = 39.1 \cos 15 = 37.76 = u + V_{w2}$$

$$\therefore \qquad V_{w2} = 37.76 - u = -3 \text{ m/s}$$

Force exerted by each jet on bucket

$$= \frac{\rho Q\,[V_{w1} \pm V_{w2}]}{2}$$

$$= \frac{\rho Q\,(V_1 - 3)}{2} \quad (\text{–ve as } V_{w2} \text{ is – ve})$$

$$= \frac{1000\,(2.51)\,(86.5 - 3)}{2}$$

$$= 104792 \text{ N or } 10682 \text{ kg} \qquad \text{...(Ans.)}$$

$$Q = aV_1$$

$$\therefore \qquad a = \frac{Q}{V_1} = \frac{2.51}{86.5} = 0.029 \text{ m}^2$$

$$= 2 \times \frac{\pi}{4} d_j^2 \qquad \text{(2 no. of jets)}$$

$$\therefore \qquad d_j = 0.136 \text{ m}$$

$$= 13.6 \text{ cm} \qquad \text{...(Ans.)}$$

$$\eta_h = \frac{2u_1\,(V_1 - u_1)\,(1 + k\cos\phi)}{V_1^2}$$

$$= \frac{2\,(40.7)\,(86.5 - 40.7)\,(1.8693)}{(86.5)^2}$$

$$= 0.931$$

$$= 93.1\%. \qquad \text{...(Ans.)}$$

■ **Problem 19.12:** *A twin jet pelton wheel runs at 330 RPM under a head of 550 m. The jet diameter is 10 cm and gets deflected through 165°. If $V_{r2} = 0.85\ V_{r1}$, $C_v = 0.98$, $k_u = 0.46$, calculate (1) Wheel diameter, (2) Power developed and (3) η_0 (4) η_h (5) η_m.*

Solution:

$$V_1 = C_v \times \sqrt{2gH} = 0.98\sqrt{2g\,(550)} = 101.75 \text{ m/s}$$

$$u = k_u \times \sqrt{2gH} = 0.46\sqrt{2g\,(550)} = 47.7 \text{ m/s}$$

$$u = \frac{\pi DN}{60} \quad \therefore \quad D = \frac{47.7 \times 60}{\pi\,(330)} = 2.76 \text{ m}$$ ...**(Ans.)**

Here as $V_{r2} = 0.85\ V_{r1}$, as $k = 0.85$,

$$a = \frac{\pi}{4}\,(d_j)^2 \times 2 = 0.78\,(0.1)^2 \times 2 = 0.0156$$

$$P = \text{Power developed} = \frac{\rho a V_1\,[(V_1 - u)(1 + k\cos\phi)]\,u}{1000}$$

$$\therefore \quad P = \frac{1000\,(0.0156)\,(101.75)}{1000}\,[(101.75 - 47.7)\,(1 + 0.85\cos 15)]\,47.7$$

$$= 1.587\,[54 \times 1.82]\,47.7$$

$$= 7444 \text{ kW}$$ ...**(Ans.)**

$$\eta_0 = \frac{P}{\left(\dfrac{\rho QhH}{1000}\right)} = \frac{7444}{0.0156\,(101.75)\,9.81 \times 550}$$

$$= 0.869 = 86.9\%$$ ...**(Ans.)**

Hydraulic efficiency η_h is calculated below:

$$(\eta)_h = \frac{2\,(V_1 - u)\,(1 + k\cos\phi)\,u}{V_1^2}$$

$$= \frac{2\,(101.75 - 47.7)\,(1 + 0.85\cos 15)\,74.7}{(101.75)^2}$$

$$= 0.90 = 90\%$$ ...**(Ans.)**

$$\eta_m = \text{mech. efficiency} = \frac{\eta_0}{\eta_h}$$

$$= \frac{86.9}{90} = 96.5\%.$$ ...**(Ans.)**

19.7 REACTION TURBINES

The man distinguishing feature of reaction turbine is that the rotor develops rotational motion on account of conversion of pressure energy into kinetic energy. When water enters the inlet of reaction turbine, it is possessing pressure as well as kinetic energy and when it flows through the blades, its pressure energy gets converted into kinetic energy and the turbine develops rotational speed. Water flowing through runner is under pressure and hence reaction turbine has to be completely enclosed by air tight casings and it must run full of water. There are two types of reaction turbines: (1) Francis and (2) Kaplan, but Francis is radial flow type whereas Kaplan is axial flow type. We shall consider Francis turbine first and Kaplan turbine later.

19.8 FRANCIS TURBINE

An eminent American engineer, J.B. Francis (1815-1892) developed Francs Turbine in 1849 as inward radial flow type reaction turbine. Later on modifications took place and at present it is a mixed flow type in which water enters the runner radially and leaves axially at its central portion around the shaft, known as eye.

The main parts of a radial flow reaction turbine are:

(*a*) Casing

(*b*) Guide blades

(*c*) Runner consisting of unsymmetrical curved blades

(*d*) Draft tube

(*e*) Tail race.

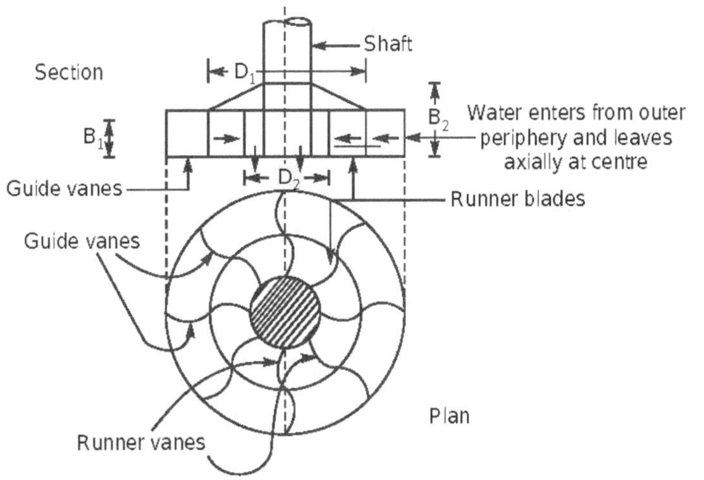

Fig. 19.7 Inward flow reaction turbine.

Fig. 19.7 shows plan and section of inward flow reaction turbine in which it is shown that water enters from outer periphery, flows over guide vanes and from guide vanes, enters runner blades from where it leaves the turbine axially at its centre, *i.e.* through the opening around the shaft *i.e.* eye. Draft tube and tail race will be considered later on.

19.9 VELOCITY TRIANGLES

Nomenclature used are given below w.r.t. Figs. 19.7 and 19.8:

1. θ, ϕ, blade $\angle$s at inlet and outlet.

2. α, β jet $\angle$s at inlet and outlet.
3. $\angle\alpha$ is also known as guide blade angle.
4. $\angle\beta$ may be acute, 90° or > 90°.
5. V_1, V_2 absolute velocity of jet at inlet and outlet.
6. V_{r1}, V_{r2} relative velocity of jet at inlet and outlet.
7. V_{w1}, V_{w2} velocity of whirl at inlet and outlet.
8. V_{f1}, V_{f2} velocity of flow at inlet and outlet.

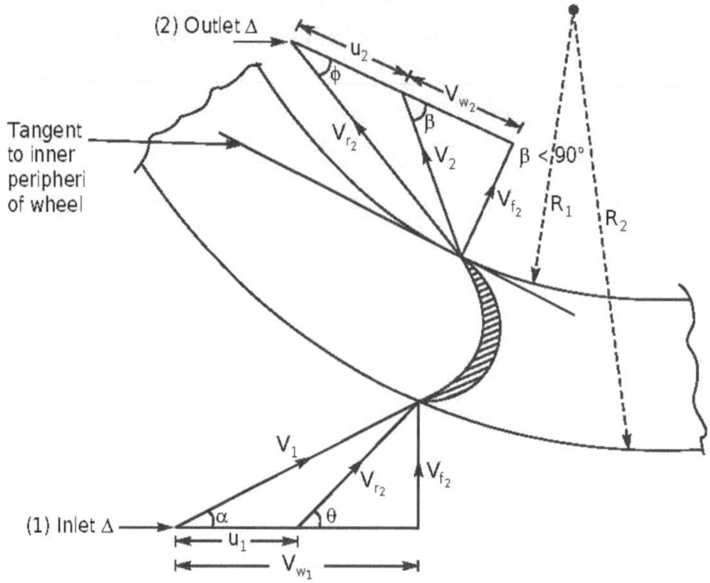

Fig. 19.8

9. u_1, u_2 tangential velocity of wheel at inlet and outlet.

From velocity triangles for inlet and outlet shown in Figs. 19.7 and 19.8, we can write expression for work done by runner of inward flow reaction turbine as under:

$$\text{Output} = \text{Work done} = \rho Q\,[V_{w1}\,u_1 \pm V_w\,u_2]\ \text{kg-m/sec.} \qquad ...(19.9)$$

(+ sign if $\beta < 90°$, –ve if $\beta > 90$)

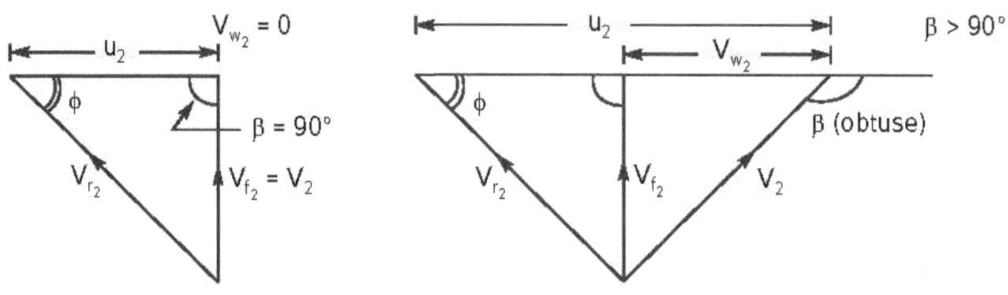

Fig 19.9 Outlet Δ^s for $\beta = 90°$ and $\beta > 90°$.

(This is already derived in chapter 18)

where Q = discharge through turbine

$$= \pi D_1 B_1 V_{f1}$$
$$= \pi D_2 B_2 V_{f2}$$

where B_1, B_2 = width of turbine at inlet, and outlet

$$u_1 = \frac{\pi D_1 N}{60} \text{ and } u_2 = \frac{\pi D_2 N}{60}$$

where N = speed of turbine in RPM

If thickness of blade = t and number of blades are n, then

$$Q = (\pi D_1 - nt) B_1 V_{f1}$$

Head H on turbine is given by

$$H = \frac{p_1}{(\rho g)} + \frac{V_1^2}{2g}$$

If discharge at exit is radial, $\beta = 90°$ and $V_{w2} = 0$.

If there is no loss due to friction when water flows through runner, then

$$H - \frac{V_2^2}{2g} = \frac{\rho Q}{g} [V_{w1} u_1 \pm V_{w2} u_2] \qquad ...(19.10)$$

$$\text{Hydraulic efficiency, } \eta_h = \frac{V_{w1} u_1 \pm V_{w2} u_2}{gH} \qquad ...(19.11)$$

$$\text{If } V_{w2} = 0 \text{ when } \beta = 90°, \eta_h = \frac{V_{w1} u_1}{gH} \qquad ...(19.12)$$

$$\psi = \text{Flow ratio} = \frac{V_{f1}}{\sqrt{2gH}} = 0.15 \text{ to } 0.3$$

$$k_u = \text{Speed ratio} = \frac{u_1}{\sqrt{2gH}} = 0.6 \text{ to } 0.9$$

$$\text{HP developed by machine} = \frac{\text{Work done/sec.}}{735}$$
$$= \frac{\rho Q (V_{w1} u_1 \pm V_{w2} u_2)}{735}$$

$$\text{Power } P \text{ in kW} = \frac{\rho Q (V_{w1} u_1 \pm V_{w2} u_2)}{1000}$$

$$\text{Width or Breadth ratio} = \frac{\text{Width or Breadth of wheel at inlet}}{\text{Dia. of wheel at inlet}}$$
$$= \frac{B_1}{D_1} = 0.1 \text{ to } 0.4$$

$$\text{Work done/sec./unit wt. of water } (\beta = 90°) = \frac{\rho Q (V_{w1} u_1)}{(\rho Q g)} = \frac{1}{g} (V_{w1} u_1) \qquad ...(19.13)$$

$$= \frac{1}{g}\,[V_{w1}u_1 \pm V_{w2}u_2]\ (+ \text{ if } \beta < 90°, - \text{ if } \beta > 90°)$$

η_0 = overall efficiency

$$= \frac{P \text{ in kW}}{\left(\dfrac{\rho g Q H}{1000}\right)} \quad ...(19.14)$$

$$= \frac{P \text{ in HP} \times 0.735}{\left(\dfrac{\rho g Q H}{1000}\right)} \quad ...(19.15)$$

19.10 SOLVED PROBLEMS

■ **Problem 19.13:** *An inward flow reaction turbine works at 450 RPM under head of 120 m. Its diameter at inlet is 1.2 m and flow area 0.4 m². The angles made by absolute and relative velocities at inlet area 20°, and 60° with the tangential velocity of the wheel.*

Find: (*a*) *Volume flow rate*

(*b*) *HP developed*

(*c*) *Efficiency.*

Assume whirl at outlet to be zero.

Solution: Given values:

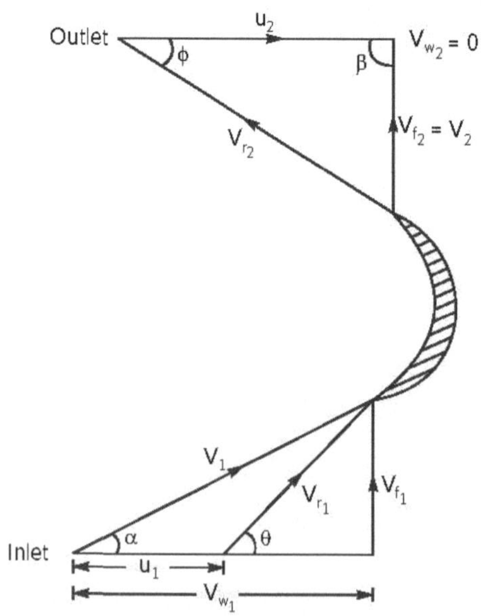

Fig. 19.10

$$\beta = 90°,\ V_{w2} = 0,\ \pi D_1 B_1 = 0.4 \text{ m}^2$$
$$\alpha = 20,\ \theta = 60°,\ N = 450 \text{ RPM}$$

$$D_1 = 1.2 \text{ m} \quad \text{and} \quad H = 120 \text{ m}$$

$$u_1 = \frac{\pi D_1 N}{60} = \frac{\pi (1.2)\, 450}{60}$$

$$= 28.26 \text{ m/s}$$

From inlet Δ

$$\tan \alpha = \frac{V_{f1}}{V_{w1}}$$

$\therefore$ $$V_{f1} = V_{w1} \tan 20 = 0.363\ V_{w1}$$

Also, $$\tan \theta = \frac{V_{f1}}{V_{w1} - u_1} = \frac{0.363\, V_{w1}}{V_{w1} - 28.26}$$

$\therefore$ $$\tan 60 = 1.73 = \frac{0.363\, V_{w1}}{V_{w1} - 28.26}$$

$\therefore$ $$0.363\ V_{w1} = 1.73\ (V_{w1} - 28.26)$$

$\therefore$ $$0.2\ V_{w1} = V_{w1} - 28.26$$

$\therefore$ $$0.8\ V_{w1} = 28.26$$

$\therefore$ $$V_{w1} = 35.3 \text{ m/s}$$

$\therefore$ $$V_{f1} = 0.363\ (35.3)$$

$$= 12.8 \text{ m/s}$$

$\therefore$ $$Q = \pi D_1 B_1 V_{f1}$$

But $\pi D_1 B_1 = 0.4\ m^2$, given.

$\therefore$ $$Q = 0.4\ (12.,8) = 512 \text{ m}^3/\text{s}$$ ...(Ans.)

$$\text{HP developed} = \frac{\text{Work done /sec}}{735} = \frac{\rho Q V_{w1} u_1}{735}$$

$$= \frac{1000\,(5.12)\,35.3\,(28.26)}{735} = 6950$$ ...(Ans.)

$$\text{eff.} = \eta_h = \frac{V_{w_1} u_1}{gH} = \frac{35.3 \times 28.26}{9.81 \times 120} = 0.847 = 84.7\%.$$ ...(Ans.)

■ **Problem 19.14:** *An inward flow reaction turbine has $D_1 = 1.2$ m and $D_2 = 0.6$ m, $\eta_h = 92\%$ and $H = 40$ m. Discharge at exit is radial and $V_{f2} = 2.5$ m/s. If width of wheel is 10 cm and at outlet vane $\angle 15°$, find*

(*a*) *guide blade angle,* α

(*b*) *speed of turbine, N*

(*c*) *vane $\angle$ at inlet,* θ

(*d*) *power developed by engine , P in kW.*

Solution:

Discharge radial at exit,

$$\therefore \quad \beta = 90°, V_{w2} = 0.\ \phi = 15°$$

$$\alpha = ?, N = ?, \phi = ?, P = ?$$

$$\eta_h = 0.92 = \frac{V_{W_1} u_1}{gH}$$

$$V_{w1}u_1 = 0.92(9.81)\ 40 = 361$$

$$V_{f2} = 2.5 \text{ m/s (given)}$$

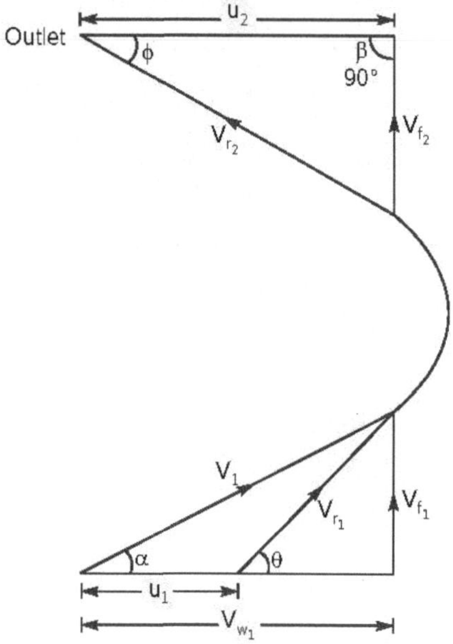

Fig. 19.11

$$\tan \phi = \frac{V_{f2}}{u_2} = \tan 15$$

$$\therefore \quad u_2 = \frac{2.5}{0.267} = 9.36 \text{ m/s}$$

$$Q = \pi D_2 B_2 V_{f2}$$

$$= \pi\,(0.6)\,(0.10)\,(2.5) = 0.47 \text{ m}^3\text{/s}$$

$$= \pi\, D_1\, B_1\, V_{f1}$$

$$= 3.14\,(1.2)\,(0.1)\, V_{f1}$$

$$\therefore \quad V_{f1} = 1.25 \text{ m/s}$$

$$u_2 = \frac{\pi D_2 N}{60}$$

$$\therefore \quad 9.36 = \frac{\pi(0.6)\,N}{60}, \therefore N = \frac{9.36 \times 60}{\pi\,(0.6)} = 298 \text{ RPM}$$

$$u_1 = \frac{\pi D_1 N}{60} = \frac{3.14(1.2)\,298}{60} \qquad \text{...(Ans.)}$$
$$= 18.72 \text{ m/s}$$

Now $\quad V_{w1}u_1 = 361, \quad \therefore \quad V_{w1} = \frac{361}{18.72} = 19.3 \text{ m/s}$

$\therefore \quad \tan\alpha = \frac{V_{f_1}}{V_{w_1}} = \frac{1.25}{19.3}; \quad \therefore \quad \alpha\, 3.7° \qquad$ ...(Ans.)

$$\tan\theta = \frac{V_{f1}}{V_{wl1} - u_1} = \frac{1.25}{19.3 - 18.72} = \frac{1.25}{0.58} = 2.15$$

$\therefore \quad \theta = 65° \qquad$ ...(Ans.)

$$P = \frac{\rho Q(V_{w_1} u_1)}{1000}$$
$$= \frac{1000\,(0.47)\,(19.3 \times 18.72)}{1000}$$
$$= 169.8 \text{ kW.} \qquad \text{...(Ans.)}$$

■ **Problem 19.15:** *Design a Francis turbine runner with following data:*

Net head $H = 70$ *m*

Speed $N = 750$ *RPM*

Power $P = 325$ *kW*

hyd. eff. $\eta_h = 94\ \%$

$\eta_o = 85\ \%$

flow ratio $\psi = 0.15$

Breath ratio $= 0.1 = \frac{B_1}{D_1}$

Outer to inner diameter ratio $= 2 = \frac{D_1}{D_2}$

Circumferential area of vane thickness = 6%

Flow is radial.

Velocity of flow is constant.

Solution: From given data as above, we have to design the turbine, *i.e.* find α, θ, ϕ, D_1, D_2 and B_1.

Flow is radial.

$\therefore \quad \beta = 90°$

$\therefore \quad V_{w2} = 0.$

Velocity of flow constant

$\therefore \quad V_{f1} = V_{f2}$

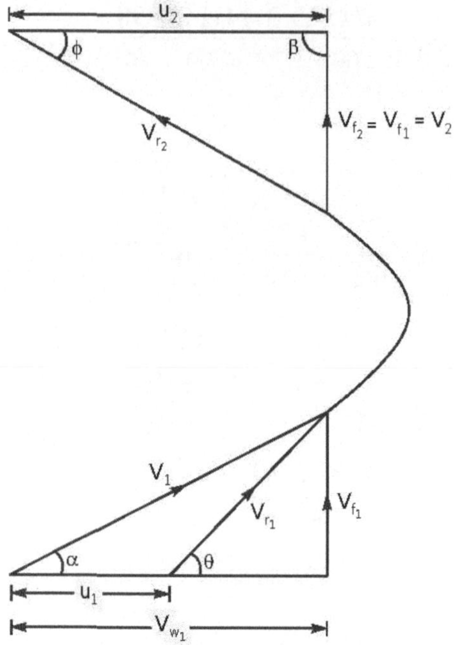

Fig. 19.12

$$D_1 = 2D_2,\ H = 70 \text{ m}$$

$$\text{Flow ratio } \psi = \frac{V_{f_1}}{\sqrt{2gH}} = 0.15$$

$$\therefore \quad V_{f1} = 0.15\sqrt{2g \times 70}$$

$$= 5.55 \text{ m/s} = v_{f2} = V_2$$

$$\eta_0 = 0.85 = \frac{\text{P(in Kw)}}{\left(\frac{\rho gQH}{1000}\right)}$$

$$= \frac{325}{\left(\frac{1000\,(9.81)\,Q\,(70)}{1000}\right)}$$

$$Q = \frac{325}{0.85 \times 9.81 \times 70} = 0.556 \text{ m}^3/\text{s}$$

$$\text{Actual area of flow} = [(100 - 6)\%]\,(\pi D_1 B_1) = 0.94\,\pi\, D_1\, B_1$$

$$\therefore \quad Q = 0.94\,(\pi D_1 B_1)\, V_{f1} = 0.94\,(\pi D_1\ 0.1\, D_1)\, V_{f1}$$

$$\therefore \quad 0.556 = 0.94\,(\pi D_1^2 \times 0.1)\, 5.55$$

$$\therefore \quad D_1^2 = \frac{0.556}{0.94\,(\pi \times 0.1)\, 5.55}$$

$$= 0.338$$

$\therefore \quad D_1 = 0.582 \text{ m} \quad i.e. \quad 58.2 \text{ cm}$ ...(Ans.)

Now, $\dfrac{B_1}{D_1} = 0.1$

$\therefore \quad B_1 = 0.1\,(D_1) = 0.1\,(0.582) = 0.0582 \text{ m} = 5.82 \text{ cm}$ ...(Ans.)

$$u_1 = \frac{\pi D_1 N}{60} = \frac{\pi(0.58)\,750}{60}$$

$$= 22.86 \text{ m/s}$$

$$D_1 = 2D_2$$

$\therefore \quad D_2 = \dfrac{0.58}{2} = 0.29 \text{ m} = 29 \text{ cm}$ ....(Ans.)

$$u_2 = \frac{\pi D_2 N}{60} = \frac{3.14\,(0.29)\,750}{60}$$

$$= 11.43 \text{ m/s}$$

$$\tan\phi = \frac{V_{f_2}}{u_2} = \frac{5.53}{11.43} = 0.485 \qquad \therefore \quad \phi = 26°$$

$\therefore \quad n_h = 0.94 = \dfrac{V_{w_1} u_1}{gH} = \dfrac{V_{w1}\,(22.87)}{9.81\,(70)}$

$\therefore \quad V_{w1} = \dfrac{0.94\,(9.81)\,(70)}{22.87} = 28.22 \text{ m/s}$

$\therefore \quad \tan\alpha = \dfrac{V_{f_1}}{V_{w_1}} = \dfrac{5.55}{28.22} = 0.196, \quad \therefore \quad \alpha = 11°$

$\therefore \quad \alpha = 11° =$ guide blade angle at inlet. ...(Ans.)

$$\tan\theta = \frac{V_{f_1}}{V_{w_1} - u_1} = \frac{5.55}{28.23 - 22.84} = \frac{5.55}{5.38} = 1.03$$

$\therefore \quad \theta = 46° =$ Vane angle at inlet. ...(Ans.)

■ **Problem 19.16:** *The degree of reaction for an inward flow reaction turbine is 0.6. The rotor diameter at exit is half that at entry. The peripheral velocity of blades at entry is 10 m/s. The velocity of flow is constant at 2.4 m. Neglecting frictional losses and assuming no whirl, find blade angles at entrance and exit.*

Solution: $D_1 =$ diameter at inlet

$$\text{Dia. at outlet} = D_2 = \frac{1}{2} D_1$$

$$u_1 = \frac{\pi D_1 N}{60} \quad \text{and} \quad u_2 = \frac{\pi D_2 N}{60}$$

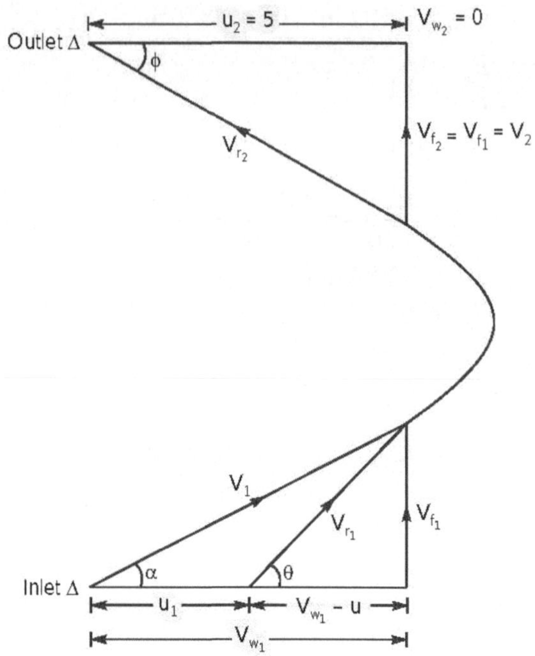

Fig. 19.13

$$\therefore \qquad \frac{u_1}{u_2} = \frac{D_1}{D_2} = \frac{D_1}{\frac{1}{2}D_1} = 2$$

$$\therefore \qquad u_2 = \frac{10}{2} = 5 \text{ m/s}$$

$$u_1 = 10 \text{ m/s (given)}$$

$$V_{w2} = 0 \text{ (given)}. \; V_{f1} = V_{f2} = 2.4 \text{ m/s}$$

∴ From outlet **Δ**,

$$\tan \phi = \frac{V_{f_2}}{u_2} = \frac{2.4}{5} = 0.48$$

$$\therefore \qquad \phi = 25.6°$$

$$= \text{outlet angle}$$ ...(**Ans.**)

$$\text{Degree of reaction } R = \frac{\left(\dfrac{u_1^2 - u_2^2}{2g}\right) + \left(\dfrac{Vr_2^2 - Vr_1^2}{2g}\right)}{\text{Work done per kg}}$$

$$\text{Now work done per kg} = \frac{(V_{w1}\, u_1 \pm V_{w2}\, u_2)}{g}$$

But, $V_{w2} = 0$ (given)

$\therefore$ Work done per kg $= \dfrac{V_{w_1} u_1}{g}$

$$\therefore \qquad R = \frac{(u_1^2 - u_2^2) + (Vr_2^2 - Vr_1^2)}{2 V_{w1}\, u_1}$$

Now referring to velocity Δ^s given in Fig. 19.13,

$$Vr_2^2 = u_2^2 + V_{f_2}^2 \quad \text{and} \quad Vr_1^2 = V_{f_1}^2 + (V_{W_1} - u_1)^2$$

$$= V_{f_2}^2 + (V_{W_1} - u_1)^2 \text{as } V_{f_1} = V_{f_2} \text{ (given)}$$

$$\therefore \qquad R = \frac{u_1^2 - (Vr_2^2 - V_{f_2}^2) + [Vr_2^2 - V_{f_1}^2 - (V_{w_1} - u_1)^2]}{2 V_{w_1}\, u_1}$$

$$= \frac{u_1^2 - (V_{w_1} - u_1)^2}{2 V_{w_1}\, u_1}$$

$$= \frac{(u_1 + V_{w_1} - u_1)(u_1 - V_{w_1} + u_1)}{2 V_{w_1}\, u_1}$$

$$= \frac{V_{w_1}(2u_1 - V_{w_1})}{2V_{w_1}\, u_1} = \frac{2u_1 - V_{w_1}}{2u_1}$$

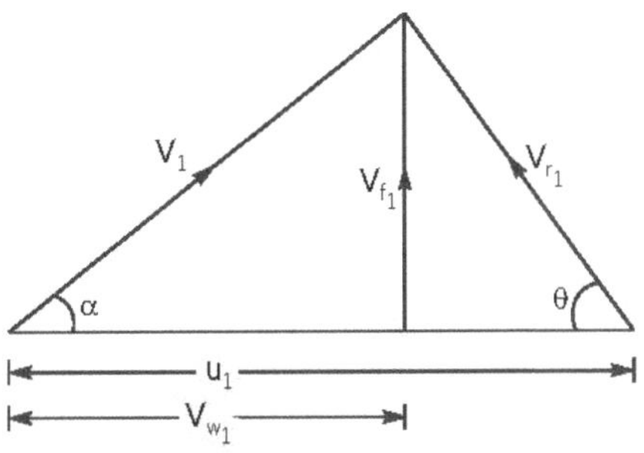

Fig. 19.14 Revised inlet Δ.

$$\therefore \qquad R = 1 - \frac{Vw_1}{2u_1} \quad \text{for given data}$$

Now $\qquad R = 0.6 \quad \therefore \quad 0.6 = 1 - \dfrac{Vw_1}{2u_1}$

$$\therefore \qquad 0.4 = \frac{V_{w1}}{2u_1}$$

$\therefore$ $V_{w1} = 0.8u_1 = 0.8\,(10) = 8$ m/s

Now $u_1 = 10$ m/s and $V_{w1} = 8$ m/s

$\therefore$ $u_1 > V_{w1}$ and $\therefore$ inlet Δ is to be redrawn and is given in Fig. 19.14.

$\therefore$ From inlet Δ given in Fig. 19.14,

$$\tan\theta = \frac{V_{f_1}}{u_1 - V_{w_1}} = \frac{2.4}{10-8} = \frac{2.4}{2}$$

$$= 1.2$$

$\therefore$ $\boldsymbol{\theta = 50.19°}$

$\therefore$ Inlet angle = 50.19°. ...**(Ans.)**

■ **Problem 19.17**: *An outward flow reaction turbine has internal and external diameters of the runner as 0.5 m and 1.0 m. respectively. The guide blade angle is 15° and velocity of flow is 3.0 m/s and is constant. If its speed is 250 rpm, head 10 m and discharge at outlet is radial, find*

(*a*) *runner vane Ls at inlet and outlet.*

(*b*) *work done/sec./kg of water*

(*c*) *hydraulic efficiency.*

Solution: Outward flow:

$\therefore$
$$D_1 = 0.5$$
$$D_2 = 1.0$$
$$\alpha = 15°$$
$$N = 250 \text{ RPM}$$

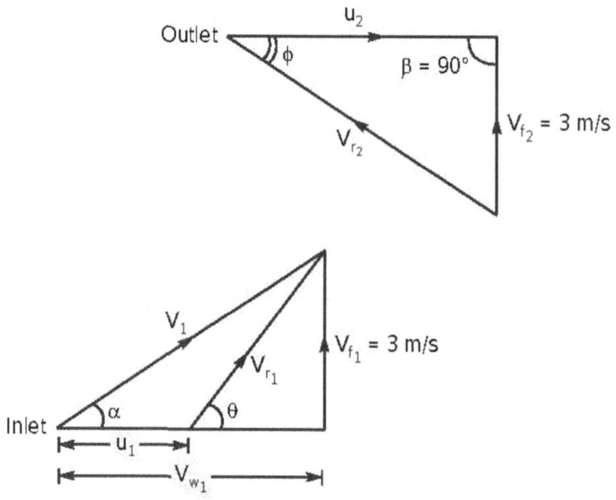

Fig. 19.15

$$u_2 = \frac{\pi D_2 N}{60} = \frac{3.14\,(1)\,250}{60} = 13 \text{ m/s}$$

$$u_1 = \frac{\pi D_1 N}{60} = \frac{3.14\,(0.5)\,250}{60} = 6.5 \text{ m/s}$$

From outlet **Δ**, $\tan\phi = \frac{V_{f_2}}{u_2} = \frac{3}{13} = 0.23$

$\phi = 13° = \text{Blade angle at outlet}$ ...**(Ans.)**

From inlet **Δ**,

$$\tan\alpha = \frac{V_{f_1}}{V_{w_1}}$$

$$\therefore \quad V_{w1} = \frac{3}{\tan\alpha} = \frac{3}{\tan 15} = \frac{3}{0.267} = 11.23 \text{ m/s}$$

$$\therefore \quad \tan\theta = \frac{V_{f_1}}{V_{w_1} - u_1} = \frac{3}{11.23 - 6.5} = \frac{3}{4.73} = 0.634$$

$$\therefore \quad \theta = 32.3° = \text{blade angle at inlet}$$ ...**(Ans.)**

$$\text{Work done/sec/kg} = \frac{1}{g}(V_{w_1} u_1) \text{ as } V_{w2} = 0 \text{ (as discharge is radial)}$$

$$= \frac{11.23(6.5)}{9.81} = 7.44 \text{ kgf-m per sec.}$$

$$\eta_h = \frac{V_{w1} u_1}{gH} = \frac{11.23(6.5)}{9.81(10)} = 0.744 = 74.4\%.$$ ...**(Ans.)**

■ **Problem 19.18:** *For no loss of energy in the runner of a Francis turbine and its discharge at outlet radial, prove that hydraulic efficiency η_h is given by*

$$\eta_h = \frac{1}{1 + \dfrac{\tan^2\alpha}{2\left(1 - \dfrac{\tan\alpha}{\tan\theta}\right)}}$$

and further if vane angle at inlet is 90°,

$$\eta_h = \frac{2}{2 + \tan^2\alpha}$$

Assume that velocity of flow is constant.

Solution: Given that:

(1) $\beta = 90°,\ V_{w2} = 0$

(2) $V_{f1} = V_{f2} = V_2$

(3) $H - \frac{V_2^2}{2g} = \frac{V_{w1} u_1}{gH}$ for no loss in runner.

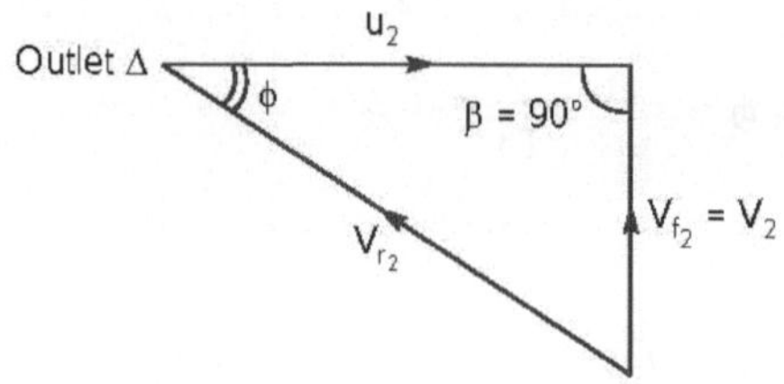

Fig. 19.16

From inlet velocity **Δ**,

$$\tan\alpha = \frac{V_{f_1}}{V_{w_1}}$$

$$\therefore \quad V_{f1} = V_{w1} \times \tan\alpha \qquad ...(1)$$

Also,
$$\tan\theta = \frac{V_{f_1}}{V_{w_1} - u_1}$$

$$\therefore \quad V_{f1} = (V_{w1} - u_1)\tan\theta$$

$$\therefore \quad V_{w1}\tan\alpha = (V_{w1} - u_1)\tan\theta$$

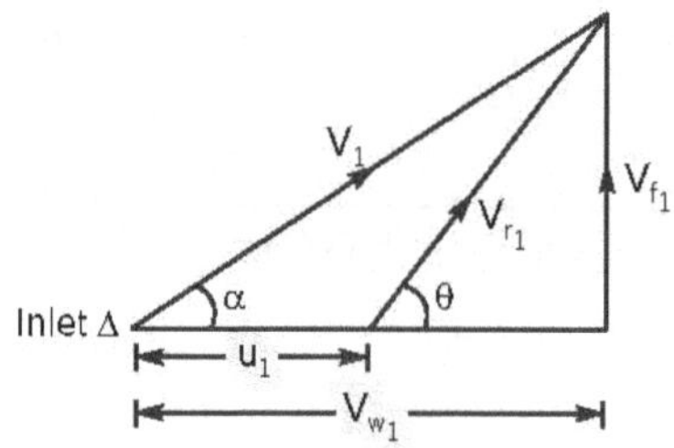

Fig. 19.17

$$\therefore \quad u_1 = V_{w1} - V_{w1}\frac{\tan\alpha}{\tan\theta}$$

$$= V_{w1}\left(1 - \frac{\tan\alpha}{\tan\theta}\right) \qquad ...(2)$$

For no loss of energy in runner and discharge radial, we have

$$H - \frac{V_2^2}{2g} = \frac{V_{w1}\, u_1}{g}$$

$$\therefore \quad H - \frac{V_{f1}^{\,2}}{2g} = \frac{V_{w_1}\, u_1}{g}$$

$$\therefore \quad H = \frac{V_{f1}^{\,2}}{2g} + \frac{V_{w_1}\, u_1}{g} = \frac{V_{w1}^{\,2}\tan^2\alpha}{2g} + \frac{V_{w1}^{\,2}\left(1 - \frac{\tan\alpha}{\tan\theta}\right)}{g}, \text{ from (1) and (2).}$$

$$\therefore \qquad H = \frac{V_{w1}^2}{g}\left[\frac{1}{2}\tan^2\alpha + 1 - \frac{\tan\alpha}{\tan\theta}\right] \qquad \text{...(3)}$$

Now hyd eff.

$$\eta_h = \frac{V_{w_1} u_1}{g_h}$$

$$\eta_h = \frac{V_{w_1} u_1}{g\left(\frac{V_{w1}^2}{g}\right)\left[1 - \frac{\tan\alpha}{\tan\theta} + \frac{1}{2}\tan^2\alpha\right]} \qquad \text{...From (3)}$$

$$\therefore \qquad \eta_h = \frac{u_1}{V_{w_1}\left[1 - \frac{\tan\alpha}{\tan\theta} + \frac{\tan^2\alpha}{2}\right]} \qquad \text{...(4)}$$

Now we have $u_1 = V_{w1}\left(1 - \frac{\tan\alpha}{\tan\theta}\right)$ from eqn. (2)

Putting this value in (4), we get

$$\therefore \qquad \eta_h = \frac{V_{w_1}\left(1 - \frac{\tan\alpha}{\tan\theta}\right)}{V_{w_1}\left[1 - \frac{\tan\alpha}{\tan\theta} + \frac{\tan^2\alpha}{2}\right]}$$

$$= \frac{\left(1 - \frac{\tan\alpha}{\tan\theta}\right)}{\left(1 - \frac{\tan\alpha}{\tan\theta} + \frac{\tan^2\alpha}{2}\right)}$$

Dividing by $\left(1 - \frac{\tan\alpha}{\tan\theta}\right)$, we get

$$\eta_h = \frac{1}{\left[1 + \frac{\tan^2\alpha}{2\left(1 - \frac{\tan\alpha}{\tan\theta}\right)}\right]} \qquad \text{...(Ans. (i))}$$

If $\theta = 90°, \tan\theta = \infty$

$$\therefore \qquad \eta_h = \frac{2}{2 + \tan^2\alpha} \qquad \text{...(Ans. (ii))}$$

■ **Problem 19.19:** *A Francis turbine has $H = 30m$, $D_1 = 1.2$ m at inlet and $D_2 = 0.6$ m at outlet. Guide blade angle is 15° and vane angle at inlet 90°. Water at exit leaves the vanes without any* *tangential velocity and velocity of flow is constant. Assume no frictional losses, find speed of wheel and vane angle at exit.*

Solution: From given data:

$$H = 30$$
$$D_1 = 1.2 \text{ m}$$

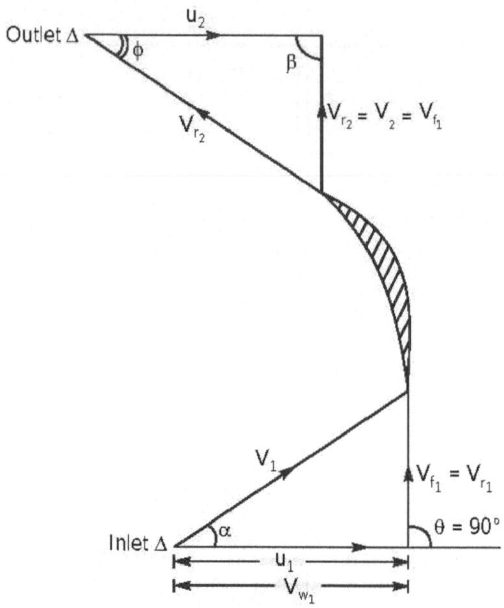

Fig. 19.18

$$D_2 = 0.6 \text{ m}$$
$$\theta = 90° \quad \alpha = 15°$$

No tangential velocity of vane at exit means

$$V_{w2} = 0$$

$$\therefore \quad \beta = 90°$$
$$V_2 = V_{f1} = V_{f2}$$

For no loss in runner, we have

$$H - \frac{V_2^2}{2g} = \frac{1}{g}[V_{w_1} u_1] \qquad \text{as } V_{w2} = 0$$

Now from Fig. 19.18 $V_{w1} = u_1$ as $\theta = 90°$

$$\therefore \quad H - \frac{V_2^2}{2g} = \frac{u_1^2}{g} \qquad ...(1)$$

$$\tan \alpha = \frac{V_{f_1}}{u_1}$$

$$\therefore \quad V_{f1} = u_1 \tan \alpha = u_1 \tan (15) = 0.267\,(u_1) = V_{f2} = V_2$$

Putting this value in (1) above,

$$H - \frac{(0.267\,u_1)^2}{2g} = \frac{1}{g}\left[u_1^2\right]$$

Now $H = 30$ m

$\therefore$ $30\,(g) - 0.035\,u_1^2 = u_1^2$

$\therefore$ $30 \times 9.81 = 1.035\,u_1^2$

$\therefore$ $u_1^2 = \dfrac{30 \times 9.81}{1.035} = 284.3$

$\therefore$ $u_1 = 16.80 \text{ m/s} = \dfrac{\pi D_1 N}{60}$

$\therefore$ $N = \dfrac{16.8 \times 60}{\pi (1.2)} = 268$ RPM ...(Ans.)

From outlet $\Delta \tan \phi = \dfrac{V_{f_2}}{u_2} = \dfrac{0.267\,u_1}{u_2}$

$$u_2 = \frac{\pi D_2 N}{60} = \frac{\pi (0.6)(268)}{60} = 8.43 \text{ m/s}$$

$\therefore$ $\tan \phi = \dfrac{0.267\,(16.8)}{8.43} = 0.532$, $\therefore$ $\phi = 28°$. ...(Ans.)

■ **Problem 19.20:** *A Francis turbine receives 2.4 cumecs of water under a head of 90 m, the constant velocity of flow through the runner is 15 m/s. Width of runner at inlet is 0.15 times inlet diameter and outlet diameter is 0.6 times inlet diameter. The runner blade angle at inlet is 90°. The speed of rotation is 460 RPM; 10% blockage to flow due to blade thickness. Find inlet angle of guide vane, runner blade angle at outlet and wheel diameter. If hydraulic efficiency is 60%, find absolute velocity of water at exit.*

Solution:

$Q = 2.4$ cumecs

$H = 90$ m

$B_1 = 0.15\,D_1$

$D_2 = 0.6\,D_1$

$N = 460$ RPM

10% blockage to flow area

$\therefore$ $Q = 0.9\,\pi\,D_1\,B_1\,V_{f1}$

$2.4 = 0.9\,\pi\,D_1(0.15 D_1)\,15$

$\therefore$ $D_1^2 = \dfrac{2.4}{0.9\,\pi \times 0.15 \times 15} = 0.377$

$\therefore$ $D_1 = 0.61$ m ...(Ans.)

$\therefore$ $D_2 = 0.6\,D_1 = 0.6\,(0.61) = 0.368$ m ...(Ans.)

$$u_1 = \frac{\pi D_1 N}{60}$$

$$= \frac{3.14\,(0.61)\,460}{60} = 14.68 \text{ m/s}$$

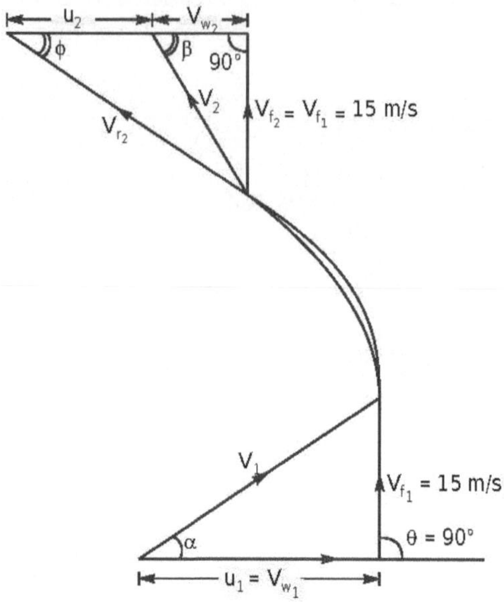

Fig. 19.19

$$u_2 = \frac{\pi D_2 N}{60} = \frac{3.14\,(0.368)\,460}{60} = 8.85 \text{ m/s}$$

From Inlet Δ, $\tan\alpha = \frac{V_{f_1}}{u_1} = \frac{15}{14.68} = 1.02$

∴ $\alpha = 45.6° =$ guide blade ∠ at inlet

$$\eta_h = 0.6 = \frac{V_{w_1}u_1 + v_{W_2}u_2}{gH}$$

$$= \frac{u_1^2 + V_{w_2}(8.85)}{9.81 \times 90}$$

∴ $0.6\,(883) = (14.68)^2 + V_{w2}(8.85)$

∴ $V_{w2} = \frac{308}{8.85} = 35$ m/s

∴ $V_2^2 = V_{w2}^{\ 2} + V_{f2}^{\ 2} = 1225 + 225 = 1450$

∴ $V_2 = 38$ m/s = abs. velocity at exit. ...(Ans.)

$$\tan\phi = \frac{V_{f_2}}{u_2 + V_{w_2}} = \frac{15}{8.85 + 35} = \frac{15}{43.85} = 0.34$$

∴ $\phi = 18.8° =$ runner blade ∠ at outlet ...(Ans.)

$$\tan\beta = \frac{15}{35}$$

$$\therefore \qquad \beta = 23° = \text{angle of } V_2 \text{ at exit.}$$

19.11 DRAFT TUBE OF REACTION TURBINE

As exit pressure of reaction turbine is generally negative, water cannot be discharged directly into tail race. A conical type tube is therefore provided at exit, connecting its inlet diameter to outlet of turbine runner and larger diameter of the tube is kept immersed in tail race water, this reduces the exit velocity and tries to build up pressure in the tube. This conical type tube is known as draft tube and is suitable for Francis turbine. For Kaplan turbine an elbow type draft tube with a small circular inlet and large rectangular outlet is suitable. Both these types of draft tubes are shown in Fig. 19.20 (*a*) and (*b*).

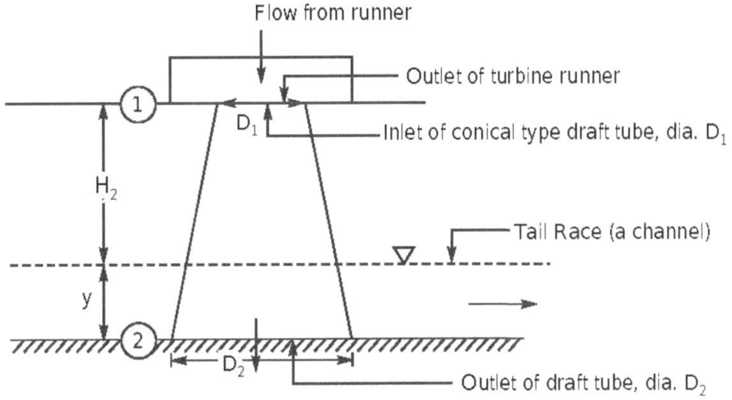

Fig. 19.20 (*a*) Conical draft tube.

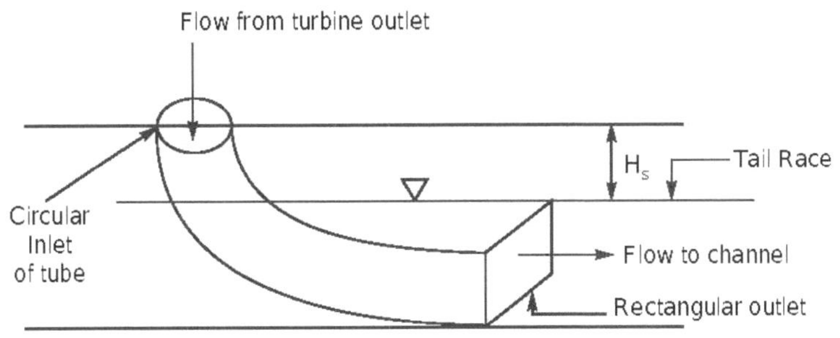

Fig. 19.20 (*b*) Draft tube for Kaplan turbine.

19.12 DRAFT TUBE EFFICIENCY

Consider conical type of draft tube shown in Fig. 19.20 (*a*).

H_s = height of inlet from tail race level

y = depth of immersion of outlet in tail race

Apply Bernoulli's theorem at sections (1) and (2),

$$\frac{p_1}{\rho g} = \frac{V_1^2}{2g} + (H_s + y) = \frac{p_a}{\rho g} + y + \frac{V_2^2}{2g} + h_{f_{1-2}}$$

Here, $$\frac{P_a}{\rho g} = \text{atmospheric pressure head} = 10.3 \text{ m}$$

$$\therefore \quad \frac{P_1}{\rho g} = \frac{P_a}{\rho g} - H_s - \left(\frac{V_1^2}{2g} - \frac{V_2^2}{2g} - h_{f_{1-2}}\right) \qquad ...(19.16)$$

$$= \text{pressure in runner at its outlet}$$

$$\eta_d = \text{efficiency of draft tube}$$

$$= \frac{\text{Conversion of KE into pressure head}}{\text{KE at inlet}}$$

$$= \frac{\left(\frac{V_1^2}{2g} - \frac{V_2^2}{2g}\right) - h_f}{\left(\frac{V_1^2}{2g}\right)} \qquad ...(19.17)$$

19.12.1 Sloved Problems

■ **Problem 19.21:** *Inlet and outlet diameters of a conical draft tube are 1.2 m and 1.8 m and velocity at its outlet is 2.8 m/s. The tube is 5 m above tail race level and its remaining 2 m length is below tail race level. Taking atmospheric pressure head as 10.3 m, and h_f in tube equal to 20% of velocity head at outlet of tube, find efficiency to tube and pressure at outlet of turbine.*

Solution: Refer to Fig. 19.20 (*a*).

Here, we have $D_1 = 1.2$ m, $D_2 = 1.8$ m

$$V_2 = 2.8 \text{ m / s}$$

$$H_s = 5 \text{ m}$$

$$y = 2 \text{ m}$$

$$\frac{p_a}{\rho g} = 10.3 \text{ m}$$

$$h_f = 0.2\left(\frac{V^2}{2g}\right)$$

$$= 0.2\left(\frac{2.8^2}{2g}\right) = 0.08 \text{ m}$$

$$Q = A_2 V_2$$
$$= \frac{\pi}{4}(1.8)^2\ (2.8) = 7\ \text{m}^3/\text{s}$$
$$\therefore \quad V_1 = \frac{Q}{A_1} = \frac{7}{0.78\,(1.2)^2} = 6.3\ \text{m/s}$$

Pressure at outlet of turbine = pressure at inlet of tube = $\frac{p_1}{\rho g}$

$$\therefore \quad \frac{p_1}{\rho g} = \frac{p_a}{\rho g} - H_s - \left(\frac{V_1^2}{2g} - \frac{V_2^2}{2g} - h_f\right)$$
$$= 10.3 - 5 - \left(\frac{6.3^2}{2g} - \frac{2.8^2}{2g} - 0.08\right)$$
$$= 10.3 - 5 - (2.02 - 0.4 - 0.08)$$
$$= 10.3 - 5 - 1.54$$
$$= 3.76\ \text{m (abs)} = \text{pressure at outlet of runner} \quad \text{...(Ans.)}$$

$$\text{Efficiency of tube} = \eta_d = \frac{\left(\frac{V_1^2}{2g} - \frac{V_2^2}{2g} - h_f\right)}{\left(\frac{V_1^2}{2g}\right)}$$
$$= \frac{1.54}{2.02}$$
$$= 0.762 = 76.2\%. \quad \text{...(Ans.)}$$

■ **Problem 19.22:** *A turbine runner discharges water into a draft tube at a velocity of 5 m / s and velocity at draft tube exit is 1 m /s. The tail water is 4 m below entrance of draft tube and losses in tube are 0.1 m. Determine pressure head at draft tube entrance.* (M.U. 2001)

Solution: Apply Bernoulli's theorem at entrance and exit of the tube *i.e.* at point (1) and (2) as shown in the Fig. 19.21.

$$\therefore \quad \frac{p_1}{\rho g} + \frac{V_1^2}{2g} + H_s = \frac{p_2}{\rho g} + h_f + \frac{V_2^2}{2g}$$
$$\therefore \quad \frac{p_1}{\rho g} + \frac{(5)^2}{2g} + u = 0 + 0.1 + \frac{(1)^2}{2g}$$

Here $\quad \frac{p_2}{\rho g}$ = atmospheric pressure at tail race level

$$\therefore \quad \frac{p_1}{\rho g} = (0.1 + 0.05) - \frac{25}{19.6} - 4$$

$= 0.15 - 1.27 - 4$

$= -5.12$ m ...(**Ans.**)

= Pressure head at entrance of draft tube and at exit of turbine.

(It is negative, *i.e.* suction.)

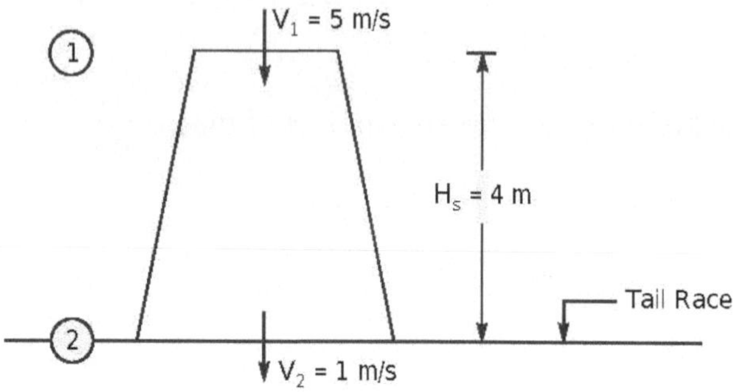

Fig. 19.21

19.13 SPECIFIC SPEED, N_S

It is defined as speed of a model turbine of such size that will develop unit metric HP when working under unit head and is denoted by N_s. Concept of specific speed is useful in comparing the different types of turbines. We can derive N_s as under:

Overall efficiency, $\eta_0 = \dfrac{P}{\left(\dfrac{\rho g Q H}{1000}\right)}$ (P in kW)

$\therefore$ $P \propto QH$ ...(1)

If D = dia. of given turbine

N = speed of given turbine

u = peripheral velocity of turbine

V = absolute velocity of water at inlet and

H = head available to turbine, then

We have, $u = k_u \sqrt{2gH} = \dfrac{\pi D N}{60}$

$\therefore$ $u \propto \sqrt{H}$ and also $\propto (DN)$

$\therefore$ $\sqrt{H} \propto (DN)$

$Q = (\pi D B)\, V_f$ = area $\times$ velocity of flow

$B = nD$ and $V_f = \Psi \sqrt{2gH}$

$\therefore$ $Q \propto (D^2 \sqrt{H})$

$$\propto \left(\frac{\sqrt{H}}{N}\right)^2 \sqrt{H}$$

$$\propto \frac{H^{3/2}}{N^2} \qquad \text{...(2)}$$

$$\therefore \qquad P \propto \left(\frac{H^{3/2}}{N^2}\right) H \text{ by substituting above value of } Q \text{ in (1)}$$

$$\therefore \qquad P \propto \frac{H^{5/2}}{N^2}$$

$$\therefore \qquad P = K\frac{H^{5/2}}{N^2}$$

Now by definition, if $P = 1$ kW, $H = 1$ m, $N = N_s$

$$\therefore \qquad N_s^2 = K$$

$$\therefore \qquad P = N_s^2\frac{H^{5/2}}{N^2} \quad \therefore \quad N_s = \frac{N\sqrt{P}}{H^{5/4}}, \text{ here } P \text{ in kW}, H \text{ in m. (SI units)}$$

If P is metric HP and H in m, then

$$N_s = \frac{N\sqrt{P}}{H^{5/4}} \text{ is in MKS units}$$

But if P is in KW, H in m then

$$N_s = \frac{N\sqrt{P}}{H^{5/4}} \text{ is in SI units}$$

and dimension of $N_s = [F^{1/2} L^{-3/4} T^{-3/2}]$

but as a convection, units are not written. A dimensionless form of specific speed is shape number, S_p and is given by

$$S_p = \frac{N\sqrt{P}}{\rho^{1/2}(gH)^{5/4}}, \text{ (Non-dimensional } N_s)$$

Specific speed N_s is useful in selecting type of turbine. For each type of turbine values of N, N_s and Head are given in the following table:

Type of Turbine	*N rpm*	*N_s SI units*	*Head m*
Pelton (single jet)	75–1000	10–35	100–1800
Pelton (multiple jet)	do	35–60	do
Francis	70–1000	40–420	30–450
Kaplan and Propeller	70–600	380–950	1.5–75

19.14 SIMILARITY LAWS AND UNIT QUANTITIES

In conducting model studies of turbine, geometric similarity is of prime importance. Following non-dimensional relationships between model and prototype are helpful in analysis of model studies of turbine:

Using m subscript for model and p subscript for prototype,

(1) $$\left(\frac{ND}{\sqrt{H}}\right)_m = \left(\frac{ND}{\sqrt{H}}\right)_p$$

(2) $$\left(\frac{Q}{ND^3}\right)_m = \left(\frac{Q}{ND^3}\right)_p$$

(3) $$\left(\frac{P}{N^3D^5}\right)_m = \left(\frac{P}{N^3D^5}\right)_p$$

(4) $$(N_s)_m = (N_s)_p$$

Unit Quantities:

For a given diameter ratio, following proportionalities exist:

(1) $N \propto \sqrt{H}$

(2) $Q \propto \sqrt{H}$

(3) $P \propto H^{3/2}$

Based on above proportionality, unit quantities are defined as under:

(1) $$N_u = \frac{N}{\sqrt{H}} = \text{unit speed}$$

(2) $$Q_u = \frac{Q}{\sqrt{H}} = \text{unit discharge}$$

(3) $$P_u = \frac{P}{H^{3/2}} = \text{unit power}$$

Above relationship helps in studying performance characteristics of a turbine.

19.14.1 Sloved Problems

■ **Problem 19.23:** *Prove that hydraulic efficiency for Francis Turbine having radial discharge at exit and constant velocity of flow is given by*

$$\eta_h = \left[1 - \frac{1}{1 - 2\cot\alpha(\cot\alpha + \cot\beta)}\right]$$

Given: (α = guide blade angle at inlet, β = vane angle at inlet).

Solution:

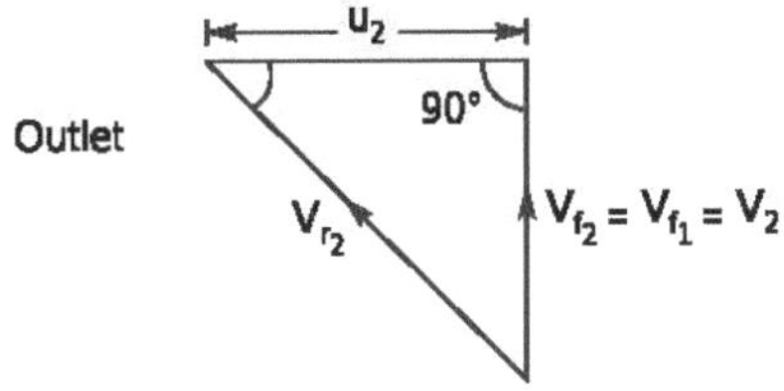

Fig. 19.22 (*a*)

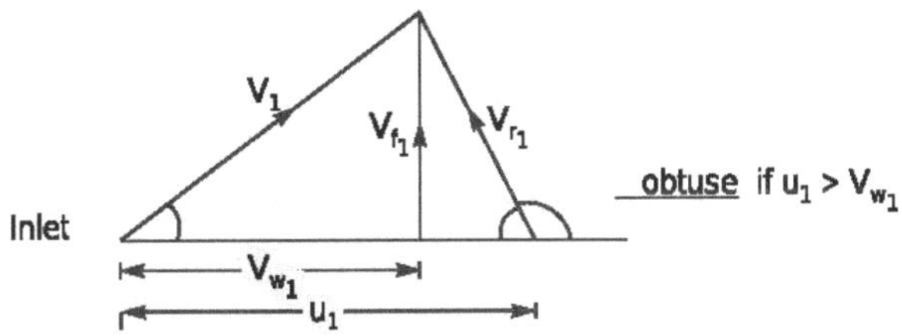

Fig. 19.22 (*b*)

From inlet Δ, $\tan\alpha = \dfrac{V_{f_1}}{V_{w_1}}, \quad \therefore \; V_{w_1} = V_{f_1}\cot\alpha$

and $\tan\beta = \dfrac{V_{f_1}}{u_1 - V_{w_1}} \quad \therefore \; u_1 - V_{w_1} = V_{f_1}\cot\beta$

$$\therefore \quad u_1 = V_{w_1} + V_{f_1}\cot\beta$$

$$= V_{f_1}\cot\alpha + V_{f_1}\cot\beta$$

$$= V_{f_1}(\cot\alpha + \cot\beta)$$

$$\therefore \quad V_{w_1}u_1 = V_{f_1}^2\cot\alpha\,(\cot\alpha + \cot\beta) \qquad \text{...(1)}$$

$$H - \frac{V_2^2}{2g} = \frac{V_{w_1}u_1}{g} \text{ as discharge is radial at exit.}$$

$$= H - \frac{V_{f_1}^2}{2g} \text{ as } V_{f_2} = V_{f_1} = V_2 \text{ for } \beta = 90^\circ$$

$$\therefore \quad H = \frac{V_{w_1}u_1}{g} + \frac{V_{f_1}^2}{2g}$$

$$\therefore \quad gH = V_{w_1}u_1 + \frac{1}{2}V_{f_1}^2 = \frac{1}{2}[2V_{w_1}u_1 + V_{f_1}^2]$$

$$= \frac{1}{2}\left[2V_{f_1}^2 \cot\alpha(\cot\alpha + \cot\beta) + V_{f_1}^2\right] \quad \text{...From (1)}$$

$$= \frac{1}{2} V_{f_1}^2 [2\cot\alpha(\cot\alpha + \cot\beta) + 1]$$

$$\eta_h = \frac{V_{w_1} u_1}{g} = \frac{V_{f_1}^2 \cot\alpha(\cot\alpha + \cot\beta)}{\frac{1}{2}V_{f_1}^2 [2\cot\alpha(\cot\alpha + \cot\beta) + 1]}$$

$$\therefore \quad \eta_h = \frac{2\cot\alpha(\cot\alpha + \cot\beta)}{1 + 2\cot\alpha(\cot\alpha + \cot\beta)}$$

$$= 1 - \left(\frac{1}{1 + 2\cot\alpha(\cot\alpha + \cot\beta)}\right).$$

■ **Problem 19.24:** *A Francis turbine of 3 m diameter and running at 300 RPM develops 6750 kW power under a head of 45 m. A geometrically similar model of ratio 1 : 10 is to be tested at a head of 10 m. Estimate size, speed, discharge and power develop by the model. What will be specific speed of model?*

Assume overall efficiency as 0.80 for prototype and model.

Solution:

$$P = \eta_0 \rho g Q H$$

$$\therefore \quad 6750 \times 1000 = 0.8\,(1000)\,(9.81)\,Q \times 45$$

$$\therefore \quad Q_p = 19.1 \text{ m}^3/\text{s}$$

Now scale ratio given is 1 : 10,

$$\therefore \quad \frac{D_m}{D_p} = \frac{1}{10}, D_p = 3 \text{ m}$$

$$\therefore \quad D_m = \frac{3}{10} = 0.3 \text{ m} = \text{dia. of model.} \quad \text{...(Ans.)}$$

$$\frac{H_m}{H_p} = \frac{10}{45} = \frac{2}{9}$$

Using similarity relationship between model and prototype,

(1) For speed : $\left(\frac{ND}{\sqrt{H}}\right)_m = \left(\frac{ND}{\sqrt{H}}\right)_p$

$$\therefore \quad N_m = N_p\left(\frac{D_p}{D_m}\right)\left(\sqrt{\frac{H_m}{H_p}}\right)$$

$$= 300\,(10)\sqrt{\frac{2}{9}}$$

$$= 1414 \text{ RPM} = \text{model speed} \quad \text{...(Ans.)}$$

(2) For discharge:

$$\left(\frac{Q}{ND^3}\right)_m = \left(\frac{Q}{ND^3}\right)_p$$

$\therefore$ Q_m = Model discharge

$$= Q_p \frac{(ND^3)_m}{(ND^3)_p}$$

$$= 19.1\left[\frac{1414}{300}\left(\frac{1}{10}\right)^3\right]$$

$$= \frac{90}{1000} = 0.09\ \text{m}^3/\text{s} = \text{discharge for model.} \qquad \text{...(Ans.)}$$

(3) For power:

$$\left(\frac{P}{N^3D^5}\right)_m = \left(\frac{P}{N^3D^5}\right)_p$$

$$\therefore \quad P_m = P_p \frac{(N^3D^5)_m}{(N^3D^5)_p}$$

$$= 6750\left(\frac{1414}{300}\right)^3\left(\frac{1}{10}\right)^5$$

$$= 7.06\ \text{kW} = \text{power for model.} \qquad \text{...(Ans.)}$$

(4) $$(N_s)_m = \left(\frac{N\sqrt{P}}{H^{5/4}}\right)_m = \frac{1414\sqrt{7.06}}{(10)^{5/4}} = \frac{1414 \times 2.657}{17.78}$$

$$= 211.3$$

$$(N_s)_p = \left(\frac{N\sqrt{P}}{H^{5/4}}\right)_p = \frac{300\sqrt{6750}}{(45)^{5/4}} = \frac{300 \times 82.15}{116.5} = 211.5. \qquad \text{...(Ans.)}$$

It may be noted N_s for model and prototype is same, it is a check on calculation.

■ **Problem 19.25:** *A turbine develops 8000 kW at 100 RPM. If its head is reduced from 30 m to 10 m, find speed and power of turbine.*

Solution: For geometrically similar turbine,

Unit speed $$N_u = \frac{N}{\sqrt{H}}$$

$$\therefore \quad \frac{N_1}{\sqrt{H_1}} = \frac{N_2}{\sqrt{H_2}}$$

$$\therefore \quad N_2 = N_1 \sqrt{\frac{H_2}{H_1}}$$

$$= 100\sqrt{\frac{10}{30}}$$

$$= 57.7 \text{ RPM} \qquad \text{...(Ans.)}$$

and Unit power $P_u = \dfrac{P}{H^{3/2}}$

$$\therefore \quad \frac{P_1}{H_1^{3/2}} = \frac{P_2}{H_2^{3/2}}$$

$$\therefore \quad P_2 = P_1 = \left(\frac{H_2}{H_1}\right)^{3/2}$$

$$= 8000\left(\frac{10}{30}\right)^{3/2}$$

$$= 1539.6 \text{ kW}$$

■ **Problem 19.26:** *A turbine develops 7000 kW at 400 RPM under a head of 50 m with η_0 = 85%. What would be RPM, Q and P if the head is 60 m under homologous condition?*

Solution: $P = \eta_0 (\rho g) QH$

$$\therefore \quad (7000 \times 1000) = 0.85\ (1000 \times 9.81)\ Q\ (50)$$

$$\therefore \quad Q = 16 \text{ m}^3\text{/s}$$

Using unit relationship, $N_u = \dfrac{N}{\sqrt{H}} \quad \therefore \quad \dfrac{N_1}{\sqrt{H_1}} = \dfrac{N_2}{\sqrt{H_2}}$

$$\therefore \quad N_2 = N_1\sqrt{\frac{H_2}{H_1}} = 400\left(\frac{60}{50}\right)^{1/2}$$

$$= 438 \qquad \text{...(Ans.)}$$

Similarly, $Q_2 = Q_1\sqrt{\dfrac{H_2}{H_1}} = 16\left(\dfrac{60}{50}\right)^{1/2} = 17.5 \text{ m}^3\text{/s}$ ...(Ans.)

$$P_2 = P_1\left(\frac{H_2}{H_1}\right)^{3/2} = 7000\left(\frac{60}{50}\right)^{3/2}$$

$$= 9201.7 \text{ kW.} \qquad \text{...(Ans.)}$$

19.15 KAPLAN OR PROPELLER TURBINE

Kaplan Victor (1876–1934) was an Austrian engineer who developed this turbine for low heads with large volume of flow. Kaplan turbine is axial flow reaction turbine like Francis which has radial entry of water but exit is axial.

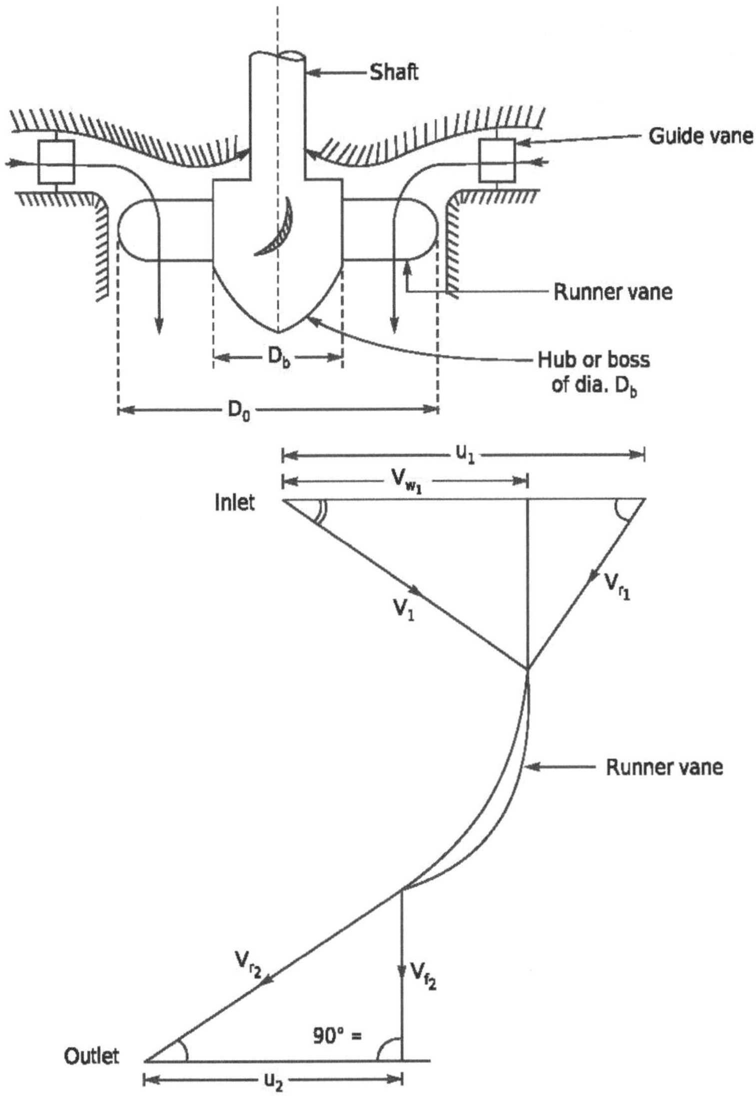

Fig. 19.23 Kaplan Turbine.

In Kaplan, entry of water is axial as well as it leaves axially. In Francis number of runner blades are 16 to 24 where as in Kaplan they are 3 to 8 only.

Kaplan is low head turbine whereas Francis is medium head turbine.

$$Q \text{ through Kaplan} = \frac{\pi}{4}(D_0^2 - D_b^2)\,V_f$$

Velocity Δ_s for Kaplan are shown in Fig. 19.23 and are similar to that of Francis turbine but with following changes:

(1) $u_1 = u_2 = \dfrac{\pi D_0 N}{60}$ = Peripheral velocity at inlet as well as outlet.

(2) $V_{f_1} = V_{f_2}$ = Velocity of flow constant.

(3) Flow area = $\frac{\pi}{4}(D_0^2 - D_b^2)$, same at inlet and outlet

(4) Flow leaves runner at 900, $\therefore$ $\beta = 90°$, $V_{w_2} = 0$

(5) Specific speed = $N_s = \frac{N\sqrt{P}}{H^{5/4}}$ = 380 to 950.

(6) K_u = speed ratio = $\frac{u}{\sqrt{2gH}}$ = 2 to 1.4

(7) Flow ratio = $\psi = \frac{V_f}{\sqrt{2gH}} = 0.6$

(8) Hub or boss diameter $D_b = 0.35\ D_0$

(9) $\eta_h = \frac{V_{w_1} u_1}{gH}$ as $V_{w_2} = 0$

(10) $\eta_0 = \frac{P}{\left(\frac{\rho g Q H}{1000}\right)}$, (here P in kW)

19.15.1 Solved Problems

■ **Problem 19.27:** *A Kaplan turbine develops 16000 kW at 40 m head. Diameter of boss is 0.35 times diameter of runner. Speed ratio = 2.0, flow ratio = 0.65, η_0 = 90%, find runner diameter speed and specific speed.*

Solution:

Speed ratio, $K_u = 2 = \frac{u_1}{\sqrt{2gH}}$

$$\therefore \quad u_1 = 2\sqrt{19.6 \times 40}$$
$$= 56 \text{ m/s}$$

$$\text{Flow ratio} = \psi = 0.65 = \frac{V_f}{\sqrt{2gH}}$$

$$\therefore \quad V_f = 0.65\sqrt{19.6 \times 40}$$
$$= 18.2 \text{ m/s}$$

$$\eta_0 = \frac{P}{\left(\frac{\rho g Q H}{1000}\right)}$$

$$\therefore \quad \frac{16000}{\frac{1000(9.81)Q(40)}{1000}} = 0.9$$

$$\therefore \quad Q = 45.3 \text{ m}^3/\text{s}$$

$$= \frac{\pi}{4}(D_0^2 - D_b^2)V_f$$

$$\therefore \quad 45.3 = 0.78\ (D_0^2)\ [1-(0.35)^2]\ 18.2$$

$$\therefore \quad D_0^2 = \frac{45.3}{12.45} = 3.638$$

$$\therefore \quad D_0 = 1.9 \text{ m} \qquad \text{...(Ans.)}$$

$$D_b = 0.35\ (1.9) = 0.66 \text{ m}$$

$$u_1 = \frac{\pi D_0 N}{60}$$

$$56 = \frac{\pi(1.9)N}{60}$$

$$\therefore \quad N = \frac{56 \times 60}{\pi(1.9)}$$

$$= 563 \text{ RPM}$$

$$N_s = \frac{N\sqrt{P}}{H^{5/4}} = \frac{563\sqrt{16000}}{(40)^{5/4}} \qquad \text{...(Ans.)}$$

$$= \frac{563 \times 126.49}{100.59} = 708.$$

■ **Problem 19.28:** *A Kaplan turbine develops P = 3000 kW under a head of 6 m. A draft tube with inlet dia. of 3 m is fitted to outlet of the turbine and is 1.6 m above tail race level. A vacuum gauge connected to draft tube inlet gives reading of 5 m of water. If efficiency of draft tube is 80%, find efficiency to turbine.*

Solution: $\frac{p}{\rho g}$ = pressure at inlet of draft tube = –5 m (given)

$$-5 = -\left[H_s + \frac{V_2^2 - V_3^2}{2g}\right]$$

$$\therefore \quad 5 = \left[1.6 + \frac{V_2^2 - V_3^2}{2g}\right]$$

$$\therefore \quad \frac{V_2^2 - V_3^2}{2g} = 3.4$$

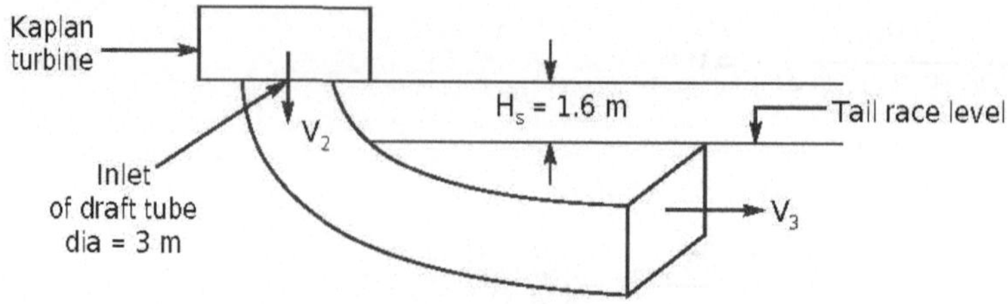

Fig. 19.24

$$\eta_{\text{draft tube}} = \frac{\frac{(V_2^2 - V_3^2)}{2g}}{\left(\frac{V_2^2}{2g}\right)} \quad \text{(neglecting } h_f)$$

$$\therefore \quad \frac{V_2^2}{2g} = \frac{3.4}{0.8} = 4.25$$

$$\therefore \quad V_2 = \sqrt{4.25 \times 19.6} = 9.12 \text{ m/s}$$

$$Q = \frac{\pi}{4} (3)^2 (9.12) = 64 \text{ m}^3/\text{s}$$

$$\therefore \quad \eta_0 = \frac{P}{\rho g Q H} = \frac{3000 \times 10^3}{1000 \times 9.81 \times 64 \times 6}$$

$$= 0.796$$

$$= 79.6\%.$$ ...(Ans.)

■ **Problem 19.29**: *A Kaplan turbine develops 2100 kW under a net head of 7.2 m with η_0 = 85%. It is to be fitted with an elbow type draft tube of efficiency 88%, and having inlet dia. = 1.8 m. Determine setting height of draft tube so that at its inlet vacuum pressure does not exceed 460 mm of mercury.*

Solution: $\frac{p}{\rho g}$ = pressure at inlet of draft tube

$$= -\frac{460}{1000}(13.6) = -6.25 \text{ m}$$

$$\eta_0 = 0.85 = \frac{P \times 10^3}{\rho g Q H} = \frac{2100 \times 10^3}{10^3 (9.81) Q \times 7.2}$$

$$\therefore \quad Q = \frac{2100}{9.81 \times 0.85 \times 7.2} = 35 \text{ m}^3/\text{s}$$

$$= \frac{\pi}{4} D^2 V_f$$

But, $D = 1.8$ m (given)

$\therefore$ $$V_f = \frac{35}{0.78\,(1.8)^2} = 13.8 \text{ m/s}$$

= Velocity at inlet of tube

$= V_2$

$$\eta_d = \frac{\left(\frac{V_2^2}{2g} - \frac{V_3^2}{2g}\right)}{\left(\frac{V_2^2}{2g}\right)}$$

$\therefore$ $$0.88 = \frac{\left(\frac{V_2^2}{2g} - \frac{V_3^2}{2g}\right)}{\left[\frac{(13.8)^2}{2g}\right]}$$

$\therefore$ $$\left(\frac{V_2^2}{2g} - \frac{V_3^2}{2g}\right) = 0.88\,(9.7) = 8.55 \text{ m}$$

$$\frac{p}{\rho g} = -\left[H_s + \frac{V_2^2 - V_2^3}{2g}\right]$$

$\therefore$ $-6.25 = -[H_s + 8.55]$

$\therefore$ $H_s = 6.25 - 8.55 = -2.29$ m.

i.e. 2.29 m above tail race level, the inlet of draft tube should be.

■ **Problem 19.30:** *A Kaplan turbine under a head of 7.5 m develops 1835 kW with an overall efficiency of 87%. The turbine is set 2.5 m above the tail water level and vacuum gauge inserted at turbine outlet records a suction head of 3.15 m. Calculate efficiency of the draft tube if it has an inlet diameter of 3 m and loss of head due to friction in the draft tube equals 25% of kinetic head of outlet.*

Solution: $$\eta_0 = \frac{P \times 10^3}{\rho g\, QH}$$

$\therefore$ $$0.87 = \frac{1835 \times 10^3}{10^3\,(9.81)\,Q\,(7.5)}$$

$\therefore$ $$Q = \frac{1835}{9.81 \times 0.87 \times 7.5} = 28.66 \text{ m}^3\text{/s}$$

Also $$Q = \frac{\pi}{4}(3)^2\, V_1$$

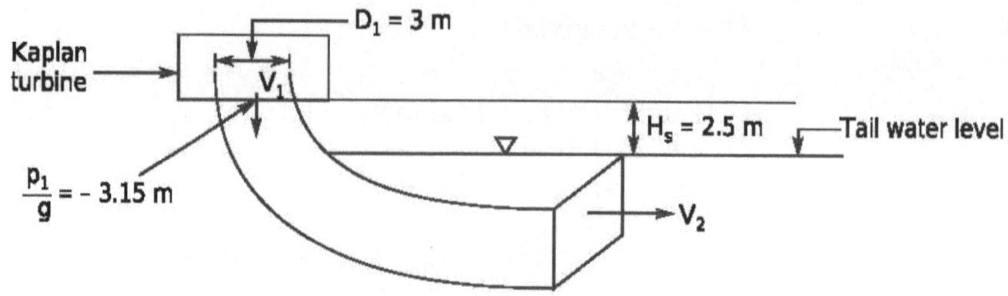

Fig. 19.25

$$\therefore \qquad V_1 = \frac{28.66}{0.78 \times 9} = 4 \text{ m/s}$$

For draft tube, $$\frac{p_1}{\rho g} = -H_s - \left(\frac{V_1^2}{2g} - \frac{V_2^2}{2g} - h_f\right)$$

$$-3.15 = -2.15 - \left(\frac{V_1^2}{2g} - \frac{V_2^2}{2g} - 0.25\frac{V_2^2}{2g}\right)$$

$$0.65 = \frac{V_1^2}{2g} - \frac{V_2^2}{2g} - 0.25\frac{V_2^2}{2g}$$

$$= \frac{(4)^2}{2g} - \frac{V_2^2}{2g}(1 + 0.25)$$

$$\therefore \qquad 0.65 - 0.816 = -\frac{V_2^2}{2g}(1.25)$$

$$\therefore \qquad \frac{V_2^2}{2g} = \frac{0.166}{1.25} = 0.133 \text{ m}$$

Draft tube efficiency

$$\eta_d = \frac{\left(\frac{V_1^2}{2g} - \frac{V_2^2}{2g} - h_f\right)}{\frac{V_1^2}{2g}} = \frac{[0.816 - 0.133 - 0.25\,(0.133)]}{0.816}$$

$$= \frac{0.65}{0.816} = 0.796 = 79.6\%.$$ **...(Ans.)**

■ **Problem 19.31:** *A conical draft tube having inlet and outlet diameters as 0.2 m and 0.3 m discharges water at outlet with a velocity of 3 m/s. The total length of draft tube is 1.5 m and 0.3 m of its length is immersed in water. In h_f of tube = 0.25 times velocity head at outlet of tube, find*

(1) pressure head at inlet (2) efficiency of draft tube.

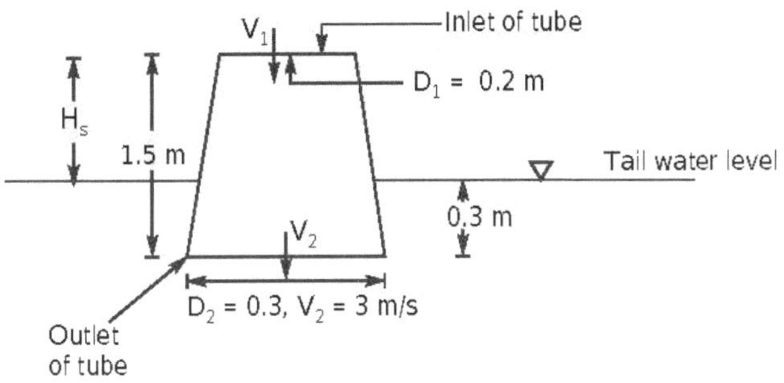

Fig. 19.26

Solution:

$$D_2 = 0.3 \text{ m}; \; V_2 = 3 \text{ m/s}$$

$$H_s = 1.5 - 0.3 = 1.2 \text{ m/s}$$

$$\frac{\pi}{4} D_1^2 V_1 = \frac{\pi}{4} D_2^2 V_2$$

$$\therefore \quad V_1 = \left(\frac{D_2}{D_1}\right)^2 V_2 = \left(\frac{0.3}{0.2}\right)^2 (3) = 6.75 \text{ m/s}$$

$$\frac{p_1}{\rho g} = -H_s - \left[\frac{V_1^2}{2g} - \frac{V_2^2}{2g} - h_f\right]$$

$$= -1.2 - \left[\frac{(6.75)^2}{2g} - \frac{(3)^2}{2g} - 0.25\frac{(3)^2}{2g}\right]$$

$= -2.95$ m (vacuum) = pressure head at inlet of tube

$= -2.95 + 10.3$

$= +\,7.35$ m (absolute) ...(**Ans.**)

$$\eta_d = \frac{\left[\frac{V_1^2}{2g} - \frac{V_2^2}{2g}\right] - h_f}{\left(\frac{V_1^2}{2g}\right)} = \frac{(2.32 - 0.46) - 0.11}{2.32}$$

$$= \frac{1.75}{2.32} = 0.754 = 75.4\%.$$ ...(**Ans.**)

■ **Problem 19.32:** *A hydraulic turbine is to develop 1000 kW when running at 150 RPM under a head of 10 m. Find maximum flow rate and specific speed of the turbine if η_0 at best operating point is 90%. In order to predict its performance a 1 : 10 scale model is tested a head of 6 m. What would be speed, power output and water consumption of the model if it runs under condition similar to prototype.*

Solution:

$$N_s = \frac{N\sqrt{P}}{H^{5/4}} = \frac{150\sqrt{1000}}{(10)^{5/4}} = 266 \; (SI \text{ units})$$ ...(**Ans.**)

$$\eta_0 = 90\% = \frac{P \times 10^3}{\rho g\, QH}$$

$\therefore$ $$Q = \frac{1000 \times 10^3}{10^3 \times 9.81 \times 0.9 \times 10} = 11.3 \text{ m}^3/\text{s}$$ ...(Ans.)

1 : 10 model

$$H_1 = 10 \text{ m}, P_1 = 1000 \text{ kW}, N_1 = 150, Q_1 = 11.3, H_2 = 6 \text{ m}$$

From unit speed definition, $\frac{N_1}{\sqrt{H_1}} = \frac{N_2}{\sqrt{H_2}}$

$\therefore$ $$N_2 = N_1 \sqrt{\frac{H_2}{H_1}} = 150 \sqrt{\frac{6}{10}} = 116 \text{ RPM}$$ ...(Ans.)

Similarly $$P_2 = P_1 \left(\frac{H_2}{H_1}\right)^{3/2}$$

$$= 1000\,(0.6)^{3/2} = 460 \text{ kW}$$ ...(Ans.)

and $$Q_2 = \left(\frac{H_2}{H_1}\right)^{1/2} \times Q_1$$

$$= 0.17 \times 11.3 = 8.75 \text{ m}^3/\text{s}.$$ ...(Ans.)

■ **Problem 19.33:** *Outer diameter of Kaplan turbine is 4 m and hub diameter is 2 m and works under a head of 16 m and gives 10,000 kW. Guide vane angle is 35°, η_h = 90% and η_0 = 0.85, velocity of whirl at outlet is nil. Find runner blade angles at inlet and outlet and speed of turbine and specific speed.*

Given:

$$D_0 = 4 \text{ m}$$
$$D_b = 2 \text{ m}$$
$$H = 16 \text{ m}$$
$$\alpha = 35^o$$
$$P = 10{,}000 \text{ kW}$$
$$\eta_h = 0.9 \;\; \eta_0 = 0.85.$$

Solution: To find θ, ϕ and N

$$\eta_0 = \frac{P \times 10^3}{\rho g\, QH}$$

$\therefore$ $$0.85 = \frac{10000 \times 10^3}{10^3\,(9.81)\,Q\,(16)}$$ $\therefore$ $Q = 75 \text{ m}^3/\text{s}$

$$Q = \frac{\pi}{4}(D_0^2 - D_b^2) V_f$$

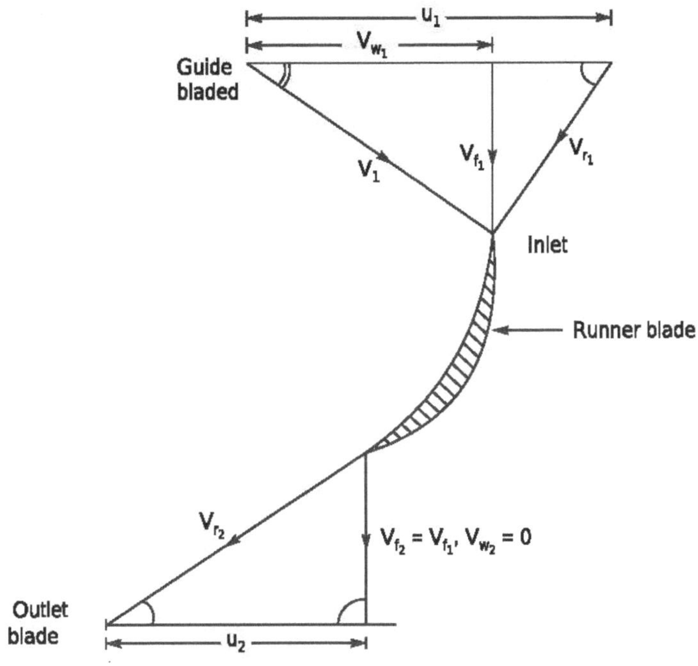

Fig. 19.27

$$\therefore \quad V_f = \frac{75}{0.78(16-4)} = 8 \text{ m/s} = V_{f_1} = V_{f_2}$$

$$\therefore \quad V_{f_1} = \frac{V_{w_1} u_1}{gH}$$

$$\therefore \quad V_{w_1}(u_1) = 0.9\,(9.81)\,(16) = 141$$

From inlet Δ, $\tan\alpha = \dfrac{V_{f_1}}{V_{w_1}}$

$$\therefore \quad V_{w_1} = \frac{8}{\tan 35} = \frac{8}{0.7} = 11.42 \text{ m/s}$$

$$\therefore \quad u_1 = \frac{141}{11.42} = 12.3 = \frac{\pi D_1 N}{60}$$

$\therefore \quad N = 59$ RPM ...(Ans.)

For Kaplan turbine $u_1 = u_2$

From outlet Δ, $\tan\phi = \dfrac{V_{f_2}}{u_2} = \dfrac{8}{12.3} \quad \therefore \quad \phi = 33°$ ...(Ans.)

$$u_1 - V_{w_1} = 12.3 - 11.4 = 0.9$$

$$\therefore \qquad \tan\theta = \frac{V_{f_1}}{u_1 - V_{w_1}} = \frac{8}{0.9} \quad \therefore \quad \theta = 83.5^\circ \qquad \text{...(Ans.)}$$

$$\text{Specific} = N_s = \frac{N\sqrt{P}}{H^{5/4}} = \frac{59\sqrt{10,000}}{(16)^{5/4}} = 184.3. \qquad \text{...(Ans.)}$$

■ **Problem 19.34**: *Determine overall efficiency of a Kaplan turbine developing 3000 kW under a head of 6 m. It is provided with a draft tube of inlet diameter 3 m and set at 1.6 m above tail race level. A vacuum gauge connected to the draft tube inlet gives a reading of 5 m of water. Draft tube efficiency is 78%.*

Solution: For a draft tube we have

$$\frac{p_1}{\rho g} = -\left[H_s + \frac{V_1^2 - V_2^2}{2g}\right]$$

$$\therefore \qquad -5 = -\left[1.6 + \frac{V_1^2 - V_2^2}{2g}\right]$$

$$\therefore \qquad \frac{V_1^2 - V_2^2}{2g} = 3.4$$

$$\eta_d = \frac{\left(\frac{V_1^2}{2g} - \frac{V_2^2}{2g}\right)}{\left(\frac{V_1^2}{2g}\right)}$$

$$\therefore \qquad 0.78 = \frac{3.4}{\left(\frac{V_1^2}{2g}\right)}$$

$$\therefore \qquad \frac{V_1^2}{2g} = \frac{3.4}{0.78} = 4.35$$

$$\therefore \qquad V_1^2 = 4.35 \times 19.6 = 85.43$$

$$\therefore \qquad V_1 = 9.24 \text{ m/s} = \text{Velocity at outlet of turbine}$$

$$\therefore \qquad Q = \frac{\pi}{4}(D^2)V_1$$

$$= \frac{\pi}{4}(3)^2(9.24) = 65 \text{ m}^3\text{/s}$$

$$\therefore \qquad \eta_0 = \frac{P \times 10^3}{\rho g QH} = \frac{3000 \times 10^3}{10^3 (9.81)(65)(6)}$$

$$= 0784 = 78.4\%. \qquad \text{...(Ans.)}$$

■ **Problem 19.35:** *An inward flow reaction turbine with a radial discharge and $\eta_0 = 80\%$ is developing 150 kW of power. If head is 9 m, speed ratio 0.96, flow ratio 0.36, speed of wheel 150 RPM, and hydraulic losses in turbine are 20% of available energy; find*

(*a*) *guide blade angle*

(*b*) *runner vane angle at inlet*

(*c*) *diameter of wheel*

(*d*) *width of wheel at inlet.*

Solution: $\eta_0 = 80\%, H = 9$ m, $P = 150$ kW, $N = 150$ RPM, speed ratio = 0.96, $u_1 = 0.96\sqrt{2gH}$

$= 0.96\sqrt{2g\,(9)} = 12.75$ m/s. Flow ratio = 0.36, $\therefore$ $V_{f_1} = 0.36\sqrt{2g\,(9)} = 4.78$ m/s.

Hydraulic losses in turbine = 20%

$$\therefore \quad \eta_h = \text{hyd. efficiency} = 100 - 20$$

$$\therefore \quad 0.8 = \frac{V_{w_1} u_1}{gH} \quad (V_{w_2} = 0 \text{ as discharge is radial})$$

$$\therefore \quad V_{w_1} = \frac{0.8\,(9.81)\,(9)}{12.75}$$

$$= 5.53 \text{ m/s.}$$

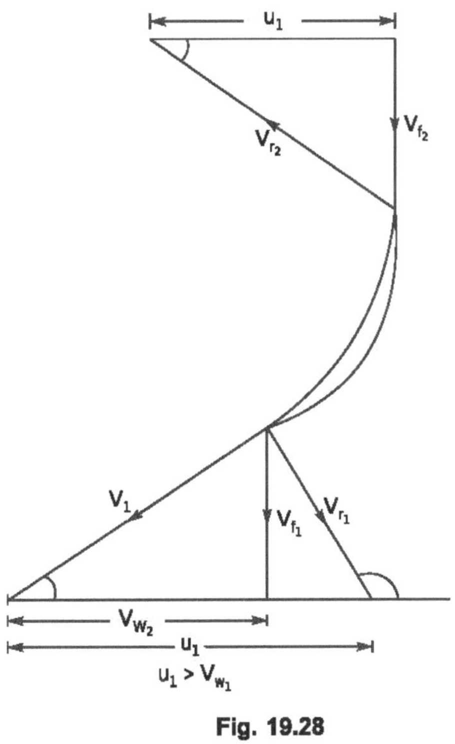

Fig. 19.28

From inlet Δ, $\tan \alpha = \dfrac{V_{f_1}}{V_{w_1}} = \dfrac{4.78}{5.53}$

$\therefore \quad \alpha = 40^\circ$ ...(**Ans.**) (1)

As $u_1 > V_{w_1}$, θ is obtuse in inlet Δ

$$\therefore \quad \tan(180 - \theta) = \frac{V_{f_1}}{u_1 - V_{w_1}} = \frac{4.78}{12.75 - 5.53}$$

$$\therefore \quad \tan(180 - \theta) = \frac{4.78}{7.22} = 0.662$$

$$\therefore \quad 180 - \theta = 33.5$$

$\therefore \quad \theta = 146.5^\circ$ ...(**Ans.**) (2)

$$u_1 = \frac{\pi D_1 N}{60}$$

$$\therefore \quad 12.75 = \frac{\pi D_1 (150)}{60}$$

$\therefore \quad D_1 = 1.62 \text{ m}$ ...(**Ans.**) (3)

We have $$\eta_0 = \frac{P \times 10^3}{\rho g Q H}$$

$$\therefore \quad \eta_0 = \frac{150 \times 10^3}{10^3 (9.81) Q (9)} = 0.8$$

$$\therefore \quad Q = \frac{150}{0.8 (9.81)(9)}$$

$$= 2.12 \text{ m}^3/\text{s}$$

$$= \pi D_1 B_1 V_{f_1}$$

$$\therefore \quad B_1 = \frac{2.12}{\pi (1.62)(4.78)}$$

$$= 0.087 \text{ m}$$

$= 8.7$ cm. ...(**Ans.**) (4)

■ **Problem 19.36:** *An inward flow reaction turbine has radial discharge and constant velocity of flow, show that degree of reaction R can be expressed as:*

$$R = 1 - \frac{1}{2}\left[\frac{1}{1 - \tan \alpha \cot \theta}\right]$$

where α and θ are guide and runner blade angles is at inlet.

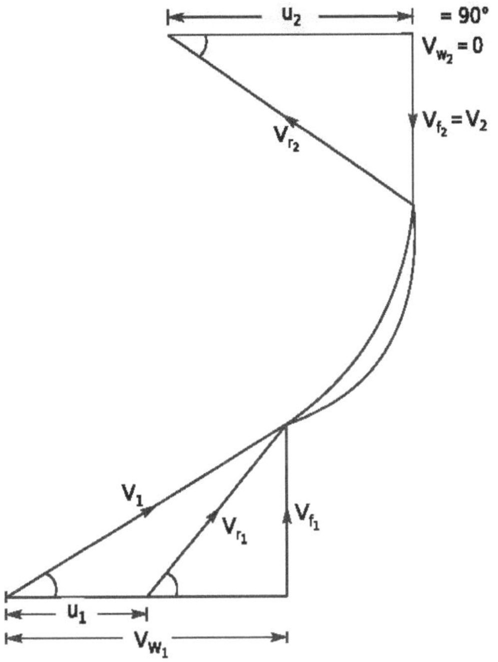

Fig. 19.29

Solution: Apply *B–Th* between inlet and outlet of runner of an inward flow reaction turbine with radial discharge, we get.

$$\frac{p_1}{\rho g}+\frac{V_1^2}{2g}=\frac{p_2}{\rho g}+\frac{V_2^2}{2g}+\frac{V_{w_1}u_1}{g}$$

$$\therefore \qquad \frac{p_1-p_2}{\rho g}=\frac{V_2^2-V_1^2}{2g}+\frac{V_{w_1}u_1}{g}$$

Now degree of reaction $R=\dfrac{\left(\dfrac{p_1-p_2}{\rho g}\right)}{\left(\dfrac{V_{w_1}u_1}{g}\right)}$

$$\therefore \qquad R=\frac{\dfrac{V_2^2-V_1^2}{2g}+\dfrac{V_{w_1}u_1}{g}}{\dfrac{V_{w_1}u_1}{g}}$$

$$=1+\frac{1}{2}\left[\frac{V_2^2-V_1^2}{V_{w_1}u_1}\right]=1+\frac{1}{2}\left[\frac{V_{f1}^2-V_1^2}{V_{w_1}u_1}\right] \qquad \ldots(1)$$

From inlet Δ

$$\tan \theta = \frac{V_{f_1}}{(V_{w_1} - u_1)}$$

$$\sin \alpha = \frac{V_{f_1}}{V_1}$$

$$\text{con } \alpha = \frac{V_{w_1}}{V_1} \qquad \text{...(2A)}$$

$$\therefore \qquad u_1 = V_{w_1} - \cot \theta \, V_{f_1}$$

$$= V_1 \cos \alpha - V_{f_1} \cot \theta$$

$$= V_1 \cos \alpha - V_1 \sin \alpha \cot \theta$$

$$= V_1 (\cos \alpha - \sin \alpha \cot \theta) \qquad \text{...(2)}$$

Now from inlet Δ, $V_{f1}^2 = V_1^2 - V_{w1}^2$

$$\therefore \qquad V_{f1}^2 - V_1^2 = -V_{w1}^2 \qquad \text{...(3)}$$

Substituting (3) in (1), we get

$$R = 1 - \frac{1}{2}\left[\frac{V_{w1}^2}{V_{w_1} u_1}\right]$$

$$= 1 - \frac{1}{2}\left[\frac{V_{w_1}}{u_1}\right]$$

Putting value of V_{w_1} and u_1 as derived in (2*A*) and (2),

$$R = 1 - \frac{1}{2}\left[\frac{V_1 \cos \alpha}{V_1 (\cos \alpha - \sin \alpha \cot \theta)}\right]$$

$$= 1 - \frac{1}{2}\left[\frac{\cos \alpha}{\cos \alpha - \sin \alpha \cot \theta)}\right],$$

Multiply Numerator and Denominator for the terms in the braket by $\left(\frac{1}{\cos \alpha}\right)$

$$\therefore \qquad R = 1 - \frac{1}{2}\left[\frac{1}{1 - \tan \alpha \cot \theta}\right]$$

19.16 DEGREE OF REACTION

$$W = \text{Workdone in case of a turbine}$$

$$= \frac{1}{g}[V_{w_1} u_1 \pm V_{w_2} u_2] \text{ per unit weight of water}$$

If there is no loss of energy in runner vanes,

$$\text{Work done (per kg)} = \frac{1}{2g}[V_1^2 - V_2^2]$$

$$\therefore \quad \frac{[V_{w_1} u_1 \pm V_{w_2} u_2]}{g} = \frac{V_1^2 - V_2^2}{2g} \quad ...(1)$$

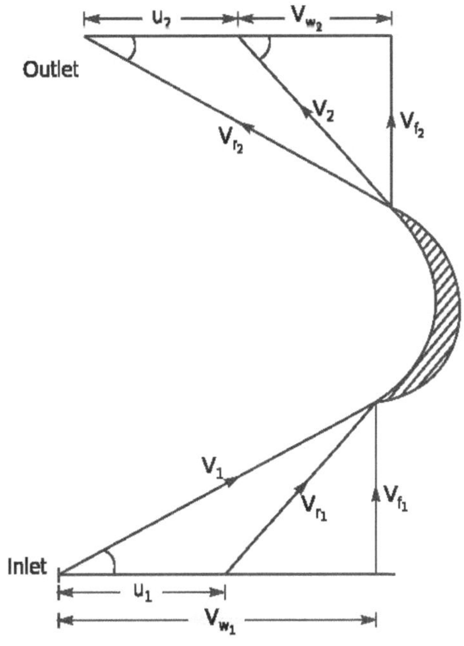

Fig. 19.30

From velocity Δs at inlet and outlet, of a radial flow reaction turbine

$$V_1^2 = V_{w1}^2 + V_{f1}^2 \quad ...(2)$$

$$V_2^2 = V_{w2}^2 + V_{f2}^2 \quad ...(3)$$

$$\therefore \quad V_1^2 - V_2^2 = (V_{w1}^2 - V_{w2}^2) + (V_{f1}^2 - V_{f2}^2) \quad ...(4)$$

Also from inlet Δ,

$$V_{r1}^2 = V_{f1}^2 + (V_{w_1} - u_1)^2$$

$$\therefore \quad V_{r1}^2 = (V_{f1})^2 + V_{w1}^2 - 2V_{w_1} u_1 + u_1^2 \quad ...(5)$$

Similarly from outlet Δ,

$$V_{r2}^2 = V_{f2}^2 + (V_{w_2} + u_2)^2$$

$$= V_{f2}^2 + V_{w2}^2 + 2V_{w_2} u_2 + u_2^2 \quad ...(6)$$

Equations (5) – (6) give us,

$$V_{r1}^2 - V_{r2}^2 = (V_{f1}^2 - V_{f2}^2) + (u_1^2 - u_2^2) + (V_{w1}^2 - V_{w2}^2) - 2(V_{w_1} u_1 - V_{w_2} u_2)$$

$$\therefore \quad 2(V_{w_1} u_1 - V_{w_2} u_2) = (V_{f1}^2 - V_{f2}^2) + (u_1^2 - u_2^2) + (V_{w1}^2 - V_{w2}^2) - (V_{r1}^2 - V_{r2}^2) \quad ...(7)$$

Now from eqn. (4), $V_{w1}^2 - V_{w2}^2 = (V_1^2 - V_2^2) - (V_{f1}^2 - V_{f2}^2)$

Substituting this in (7), we get

$$2(V_{w_1} u_1 - V_{w_2} u_2) = (V_1^2 - V_2^2) + (u_1^2 - u_2^2) + (V_{r2}^2 - V_{r1}^2)$$

$$\therefore \quad \frac{1}{g}(V_{w_1} u_1 - V_{w_2} u_2) = \frac{V_1^2 - V_2^2}{2g} + \frac{u_1^2 - u_2^2}{2g} + \frac{V_{r2}^2 - V_{r1}^2}{2g}$$

Thus work done = Change in (KE head + static pressure head (as in case of forced vertex motion) + relative velocity head)

Thus, head developed in rotating bladed impeller/runner is a combination of three distinct changes *i.e.*, changes in KE head, Pressure head and relative velocity head. This we can write in the form

$$\Delta p_t = \Delta p_d + \Delta p_s$$

where

$$\Delta p_d = \rho\left(\frac{V_1^2 - V_2^2}{2}\right)$$

$$\Delta p_s = \rho\left[\frac{u_1^2 - u_2^2}{2} + \frac{V_{r2}^2 - V_{r1}^2}{2}\right]$$

Thus effect of work interaction in the rotor is a combination in the changes of static and dynamic pressure. Degree of reaction R is then defined as a measure of the relative importance of the static components,

$$R = \frac{\Delta p_s}{\Delta p_t}$$

$$= \frac{(u_1^2 - u_2^2) + (V_{r2}^1 - V_{r1}^2)}{(V_1^2 - V_2^2) + (u_1^2 - u_2^2) + (V_{r2}^2 - V_{r1}^2)}$$

A rotor for which $R = 0$ is a called **impulse** type and can be operated open to atmosphere just as Peloton wheel. In this case fluid static pressure does not vary due to blade action.

In case of rotor of a reaction type turbine, fluid static pressure continuously changes and as such these machines are operated with pressure sealings. In reaction type machine, degree of reaction $R < 1$.

Degree of reaction *R* can also be defined as the ratio of pressure drop to the hydraulic work done in runner if losses in the runner are negligible as per this definition,

$$R = \frac{\left(\dfrac{p_1 - p_2}{\rho g}\right)}{\left(\dfrac{V_{w_1} u_1}{g}\right)} \qquad \text{(assuming } V_{w_2} = 0\text{) (See problem 19.16)}$$

19.17 CHARACTERISTIC CURVES OF TURBINES

To know performance of turbines under different working conditions, characteristic curves are plotted from the results of tests performed to study relationship of following variables governing working of turbines:

(*a*) Speed *N*, head *H*, discharge *Q* which are independent variables and

(*b*) Power *P*, overall efficiency η_0 and gate opening which are dependent variables.

Following characteristic curves are of prime importance in studying performance of turbines:

(1) Constant Head Curve.

(2) Constant Speed Curve.

(3) Constant Efficiency Curve

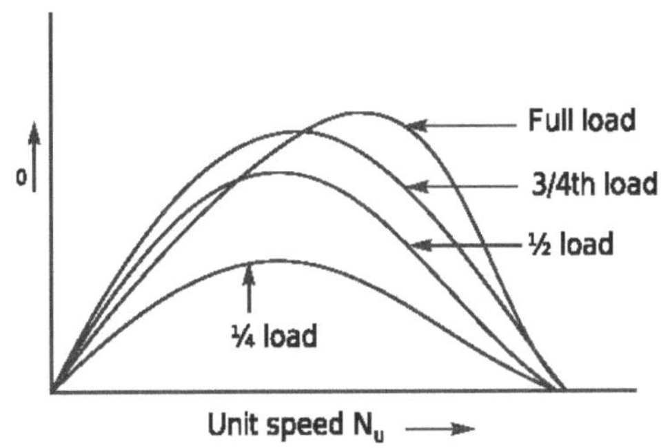

Fig. 19.31

Constant head curves for Pelton wheel are shown in Fig. 19.31

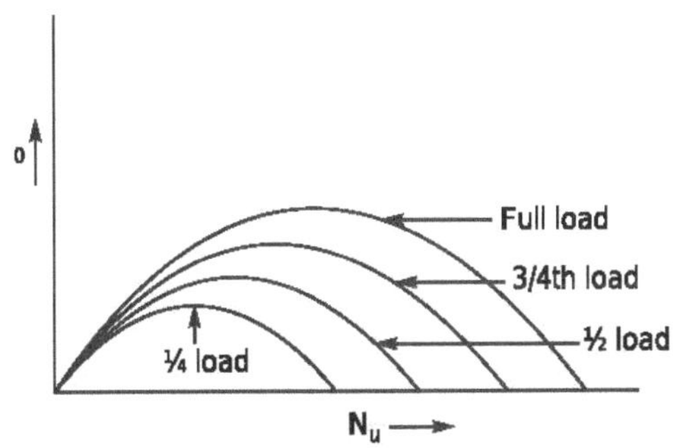

Fig. 19.32

Constant head curves for Francis Turbine are shown in Fig. 19.32

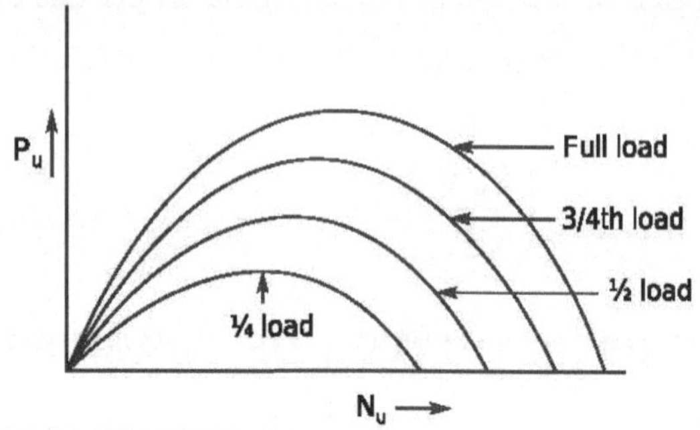

Fig. 19.33

Constant head curves for Kaplan turbine are shown in Fig 19.33

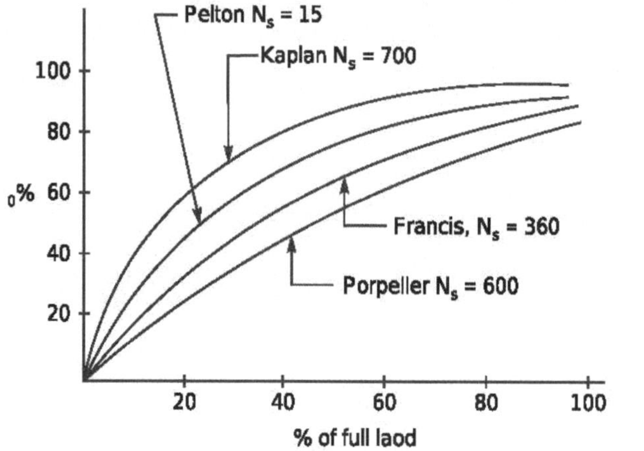

Fig. 19.34

Constant speed (N_s) curves are shown in Fig. 19.34

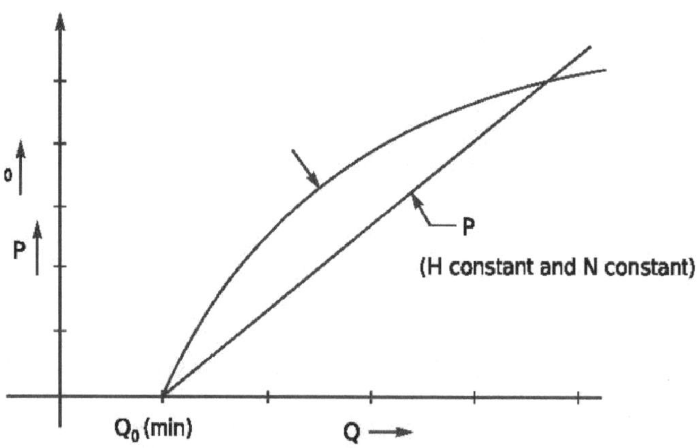

Fig. 19.35

Curves for $P\ V_s\ Q$ and $n\ V_s\ Q$ are shown in Fig. 19.35. These curves are plotted from a certain minimum discharge Q_0 which is required to initiate motion of runner from its state of rest. Power is directly proportional to discharge if head is constant, whereas efficiency η_0 increases with discharge and remains constant beyond a particular value of discharge.

19.18 CAVITATION IN TURBINES

Towards the edge of rotor of reaction turbine we find very low pressure which may be negative *i.e.,* below atmospheric. This is because pressure head is utilised in doing work on the blades. In region of high velocity such as exit of blades or inlet of draft tube, pressure could be negative, and if it is lower than permissible value of vapour pressure (2.4 m abs) vapour bubbles will be formed. Apart from vapour bubbles causing discontinuity of flow, their collapse can cause severe structural damage to turbine runner and blades. The phenomenon of formation and collapse of bubbles is called caviation.

Assessment of occurrence of Cavitation is made through Thoma's Cavitation number, σ as given below:

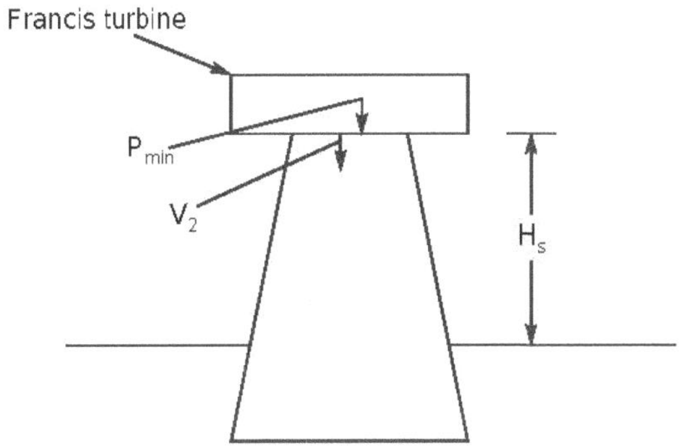

Fig. 19.36

For a draft tube connected at outlet of Francis Turbine we have

$$\frac{p_{min}}{\rho g} + \frac{V_2^2}{2g} + H_s = \frac{p_{atm}}{\rho g}$$

If H is head on turbine, we divide above terms by H to make them non-dimensional,

$$\therefore \qquad \frac{V_2^2}{2gH} = \frac{p_{atm}}{\rho gH} - \frac{p_{min}}{\rho gH} - \frac{H_s}{H} = \sigma = \text{Thoma number}$$

and $\dfrac{p_{atm} - p_v}{\rho gH} - \dfrac{H_s}{H} = \sigma_c$ = Thoma number at critical condition. (Here $P_v = P_{min}$ = vapour pressure)

For safety, $p_{min} > p_v$ and therefore $\sigma > \sigma_c$ is the condition for safety against Cavitation. Usual empirical value prescribed for $\sigma_c = 0.1$.

19.18.1 Solved Problems

■ **Problem 19.37:** *A turbine $\sigma_c = 0.1$ is to be installed where barometric pressure is 1 bar (10.2 m). Net head available to turbine is 50 m and p_v = vapour pressure = 2.4 m. Calculate maximum permissible height of turbine rotor above tail water level.*

Solution:

$$\sigma_c H = \frac{p_{atm} - p_v}{\rho g} - H_{s_{max}}$$

$$\therefore \quad H_{smax} = \frac{p_{atm} - p_v}{\rho g} - \sigma_c H$$

$$= (10.3 - 2.4) - 0.1\,(50)$$

$$= 7.9 - 5$$

$$= 2.9 \text{ m} \qquad \text{...(Ans)}$$

It may be noted that runner of a reaction turbine may also sometimes be placed below the tail water level to prevent cavitation. The draft tube of a reaction turbine is a diffusing passage to recover exit KE and provide structural support for installation of turbine.

Exercises

(A) PELTON WHEEL

1. Design a Pelton wheel for following data:

   Power P = 12000 kW

   Head H = 400 m

   Speed N = 700 RPM

   $\eta_0 = 85\%$

   Jet ratio = 6, Speed ratio = 0.45, $C_v = 0.98$

   Find wheel diameter, number of jets, diameter of each jet.

   (**Ans.** D = 1.1m, no. of jets = 4, d_j = 12 cm)

2. A Pelton wheel works under a head of 400 m. it is supplied with water by Penstock of dia. 1 m, and length 5 km, and its friction factor 0.032. Jet of 15 cm dia. strikes the buckets and gets deflected through 165°. If $V_{r_2} = 0.85\ V_{r_1}$,= speed ratio 0.45 and $\eta_m = 0.85$, find:

   (1) Power developed by runner

   (2) Shaft power

   (3) η_h and η_0. (**Ans.** (1) 5028 kW, (2) 4274 kW, (3) $\eta_h = 0.9$, $\eta_0 = 0.76$)

3. Shaft power developed by a Pelton wheel is 15400 kW. Three jets each of 16 cm dia. strike the buckets under a head of 400 m and get deflected through 160°. If $C_v = 0.99$, $K_u = 0.45$, find overall efficiency, hydraulic efficiency and mechanical efficiency.

   (**Ans.** η_0.=, $\eta_h = 0.96$, $\eta_m = 0.77$)

4. A Pelton wheel has a nozzle diameter of 16 cm and head available at nozzle is 400 m. If C_v= 0.98 , wheel diameter 1.75 m, jet gets deflected through 150°, and wheel to jet speed ratio 0.46, find power developed by turbine, its speed and hydraulic efficiency.

(**Ans.** 6065 kW, 436 RPM, 89 %)

(B) FRANCIS TURBINE

1. An inward flow reaction turbine has peripheral velocity of 24 m/s at inlet. The axial and whirl velocity components at inlet are 2 m/s and 18 m/s. The passage width and flow area at inlet are 150 mm an 0.4 m², discharge is radial, η_h= 80%. Find wheel diameter at inlet and outlet, power developed, impressed head, rotational speed and blade angle at inlet and outlet. Assume $D_2 = 0.5\ D_1$ and velocity of flow constant.

(**Ans.** $D_1 = 0.85$ m, $\pi = 345$ kW, $D_2 = 0.425$ m, $H = 55$ m, $N = 540$ RPM, $\theta = 18.43°$, $\phi = 9.46°$)

2. An inward flow reaction turbine has $\eta_0 = 80\%$ and develops 136 kW. Head is 16 m and K_u= 0.75, flow ratio 0.25, N = 120 rpm and hydraulic losses are 15% of a available energy. Find.

(*a*) Wheel diameter (*b*) discharge through turbine

(*c*) guide blade angle (*d*) runner blade angle θ.

(**Ans.** (*a*) $D = 2.1$ m (*b*) $Q = 1.08$ m³/s (*c*) $\alpha = 23.5°$ (*d*) $\theta = 55°$ or (180 – 55 = 125°))

3. An inward flow Francis turbine develops 735 kW at 750 RPM under a head of 100 m. The guide vane angle at inlet is 15°, breadth ratio = 0.1, $D_2 = \frac{D_1}{2}$, velocity of flow is constant and discharge is radial. The runner blade thickness blocks 5% of flow area at inlet, if $\eta_0 = 84$ % find wheel diameter, wheel width at inlet, runner blade angle at inlet and at outlet. (**Ans.** $D_1 = 0.574$ m, $B_1 = 5.74$ cm, $\theta = 38.78°$, $\phi = 24°$)

4. An inward flow Francis turbine has outer and inner diameters as 60 cm and 40 cm with a 5 cm width at inlet. The wheel blade angels are 95° and 14°. Velocity of flow is constant and 8 % blockage of flow area due to blade thickness. If $H = 54$ m, $\eta_h = 88\%$, $\eta_0 = 81\%$, and discharge at exit radial, find

(*a*) RPM of wheel (*b*) Power developed by runner. (**Ans.** $N = 692$ rpm, $P = 128$ kW)

5. A Kaplan turbine develops 20,000 kW at a head of 35 m and 420 rpm outer diameter = 2.5 m and inner diameter = 0.85 m. If $\eta_h = 90\%$ and $\eta_0 = 85\%$, find discharge, guide vane angle, runner blade angle at inlet and specific speed.

(**Ans.** $Q = 68.6$ m³/s, $\alpha = 70.5°$, $\theta = 17.7°$ $N_s = 698$ (SI units))

6. A turbine develops 8000 kW at 1000 RPM and under a head of 30 m. If head is reduced to 18 m, find speed and power developed by the turbine

(**Ans.** 77.5 rpm, 3710 kW)

❑❑❑

20

Centrifugal Pumps

20.1 INTRODUCTION

A centrifugal pump is just reverse of inward flow reaction turbine *i.e.,* it is a rotodynamic pump in which electrical energy is converted into mechanical and dynamic pressure developed in the machine enables the lifting of liquids from lower level to higher level. The basic principle on which centrifugal pump works is that the rotational motion of impeller of the pump develops a centrifugal head at its peripheral and a suction at its eye so that liquid rushes to the central part and gets lifted up at its peripheral part on account of centrifugal action. A reciprocating pump is a positive displacement type of pump and can handle relatively small quantites of pure liquids whereas centrifugal pump can handle large quantities of pure and as well as impure and viscous liquids. Oils, muddy and sewage water, paper pulp, ready mix concrete, cement slurry, etc., can be transported through pipe lines with the help of centrifugal pump. This pump can be operated at high speed without danger of separation and cavitation and can be coupled directly to electric motors. As against this, reciprocating pumps suffer of low speed and higher maintenance and is belt driven. However, reciprocating pump can build up very high pressure, and as such they are useful in lifting oil from very deep wells. An axial flow pump is just reverse of Kaplan turbine and mixed flow pump is reverse of mixed flow type Francis turbine. However, all these three types are generally known as centrifugal pumps.

20.2 PRIMING AND WORKING OF CENTRIFUGAL PUMP

Before a centrifugal pump is set to work, its suction pipe and the pump itself should be filled with the liquid which is required to be lifted up; this is known as priming of centrifugal pump. Its impeller is then set to run by electrical motor shunted to the pump. The rotational motion of impeller causes a forced vertex action on the liquid which results in (*a*) increase of velocity and pressure with increase in radius and (*b*) a partial vacuum near impeller centre, called "eye". Liquid from sump then gets sucked into the pump through suction pipe connected to pump at its inlet and is discharged with higher velocity and pressure at periphery of impeller. A valve at the end of suction pipe known as foot value is provided so that liquid poured for priming action is retained in the pipe and pump casing. Foot value will also not permit impurities in liquid to enter suction pipe.

A centrifugal pump may have a double inlet impeller for handling large volume of liquid and it balances the axial thrust. When several impellers are arranged in series on a common shaft, the pump is known as multistaged pump. Discharge from one one impeller is connected to suction of the following impeller causing higher rise in pressure.

The blades of centrifugal pump are usually curved backward. Straight radial blades are used when liquid to be handled is non-newtonian type *i.e.,* containing loose floating particles such as in cement slurry, sewage etc.

20.3 COMPONENT PARTS OF CENTRIFUGAL PUMP

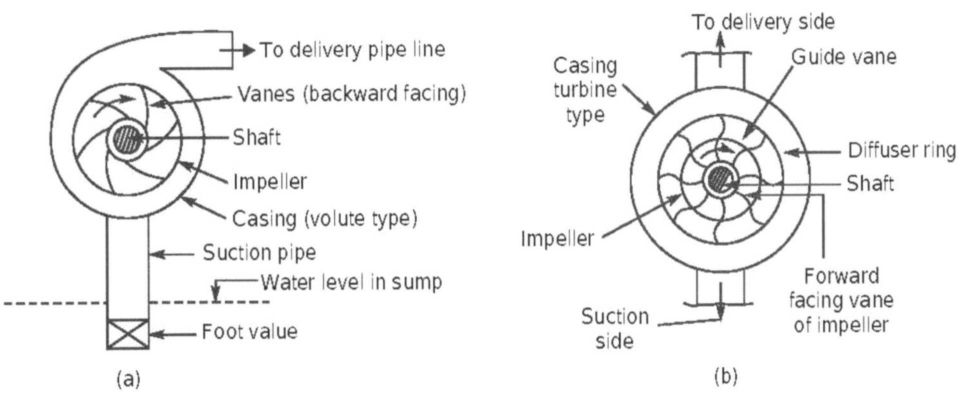

Fig. 20.1 Component of centrifugal pump (*a*) Volute type (*b*) Turbine type.

A centrifugal pump consists of a rotating element, called an impeller, which has an eye at its centre and curved vanes spanning centre to periphery of the impeller. The vanes may be curved backward with respect to rotational direction or they can have a forward curvature or they may be radial.

According to type of casing, centrifugal pump is known as (*a*) volute pump or (*b*) diffuser or turbine pump. In a volute type, the impeller is put in a spiral casing as shown in Fig. 20.1 (*a*), whereas in diffuser type (Fig. 201 (*b*)) impeller is surrounded by series of guide vanes mounted on a ring called diffuser ring. Compared to volute type, turbine type converts 75% of KE into pressure energy. Volute type is provided with vortex chamber so that it can also convert high percentage of KE into pressure energy. A centrifugal pump developing head less than 15 m is low head type whereas if head is between 15 to 40 m it is medium type and higher than 40 m, it is high head centrifugal pump. Generally high heads pumps are multistage pumps.

20.4 WORK DONE AND EFFICIENCY OF PUMP

Inlet velocity Δ, entry of water radial (see Fig. 20.2). $\therefore$ $\alpha = 90°$ and velocity of whirl $V_{w1} = 0$

Vane $\angle$ at inlet = θ = angle between V_{r1} and u_1.

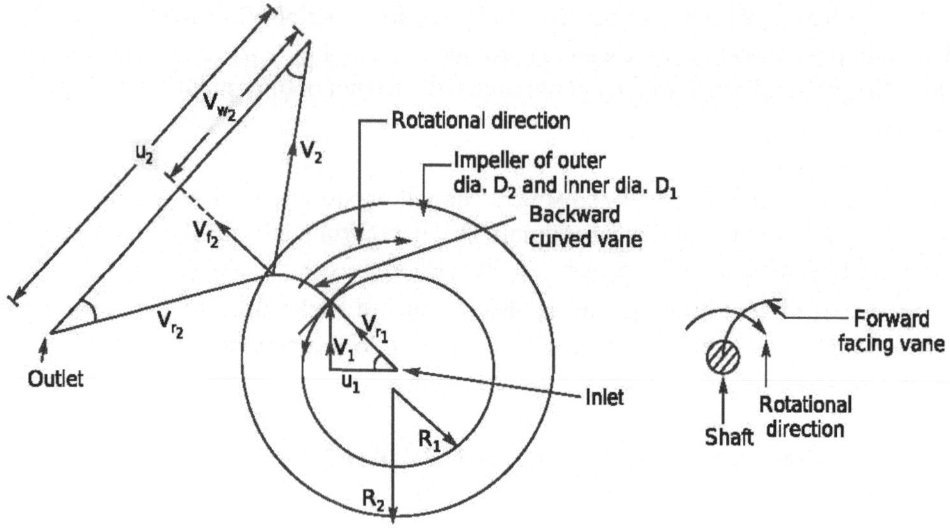

Fig. 20.2

u_1 = tangential velocity of inlet = $\dfrac{\pi D_1 N}{60}$

N = RPM of pump;

V_1 = absolute velocity of water at inlet

Outlet velocity Δ,

$\phi = \angle$ between V_{r2} and u_2

= vane angle at outlet

V_2 = absolute velocity of water at outlet making $\angle \beta$ with tangent to the impeller

u_2 = peripheral velocity at outlet = $\left(\dfrac{\pi D_2 N}{60}\right)$

$\phi > 90°$ backward facing vane

$= 90°$ for radial vane,

$> 90°$ for forward facing vane

V_{w2} = velocity of whirl

V_{f2} = velocity of flow at outlet

β = direction of absolute velocity at exit

$Q = \pi D_2\, b_2 = V_{f2} = \pi D_1\, b1\ V_{f1}$

b_1 = width of impeller at inlet

b_2 = width of impeller at outlet

$u_2 = k_u = \left(\sqrt{2gH_m}\right)$ and $V_{f2} = \psi\left(\sqrt{2gH_m}\right)$

where, k_u = speed ratio and ψ = flow ratio.

Work done is similar to inward flow reaction turbine but with a = 90° and $V_{w1} = 0$.

$$\therefore \quad \text{Work done} = \frac{W}{g}[V_{w1}u_1 \pm V_{w2}u_2]$$

$$= \frac{W}{g}[V_{w2}u_2] \quad \text{as } V_{w1} = 0$$

W = wt. water = $(\rho g)\,Q$

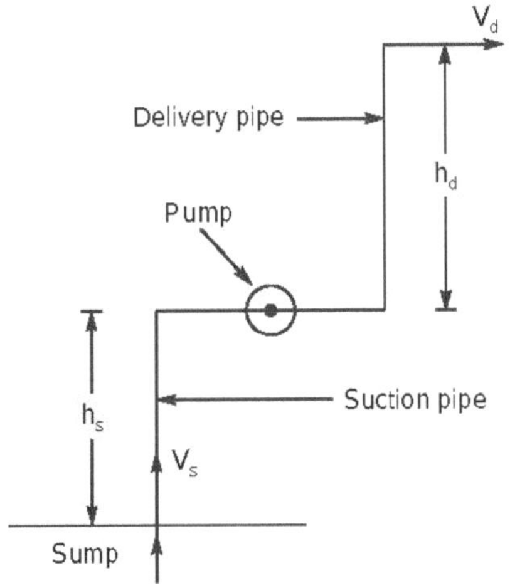

Fig. 20.3

Let H_m = manometric head

$$= h_s + h_d + h_{fs} + h_{fd} + \frac{V_d^2}{g} = \text{pump output}$$

$$= \frac{V_{w2}u_2}{g} - k\frac{V_2^2}{2g}, \text{ here } k \text{ is friction coefficient.}$$

h_s = suction head, L_s = length of suction pipe

h_d = delivery head, L_d = length of delivery pipe

$h_s + h_d$ = static head

h_{fs} = friction loss in suction pipe = $\dfrac{fL_s V_s^2}{2D_s g}$

h_{fd} = friction loss in delivery pipe

$$= \frac{fL_d V_d^2}{D_d 2g}, f = \text{friction factor} = \text{usually } 0.02$$

V_s = velocity in suction pipe

V_d = velocity in delivery pipe

Pump input = $\dfrac{V_{w2}u_2}{g}$, Pump output = H_m

$$\therefore \quad \eta_{manometric} = \eta_{mano} = \eta_m = \frac{gH_m}{Vw_2u_2}$$

$$= \frac{H_m}{H_m + \text{losses in pump}}$$

$$\eta_{vol} = \text{Volumetric efficiency}$$

$$= \frac{Q}{Q+\Delta Q}, \qquad \Delta Q = \text{leakage from impeller}$$

$$\eta_0 = \text{overall efficiency} = \frac{(\rho g)QH_m}{P = \text{power given to shaft}}$$

$$\eta_{mech} = \frac{\rho g\,(Q+\Delta Q)\dfrac{V_{w2}u_2}{g}}{p \text{ to shaft}}$$

$$= \frac{\rho\,(Q+\Delta Q)\,V_{w2}\,u_2}{P \text{ given to shaft or SHP of motor}}$$

$$\eta_0 = \eta_{mano} \times \eta_{vol} \times \eta_{mech.}$$

$$\tan\phi = \frac{Vf_2}{u_2 - V_{w2}}, \text{ for finding vane angle at outlet}$$

20.5 CAVITATION IN CENTRIFUGAL PUMP

Centrifugal pump and reaction turbine are likely to suffer of cavitation problem and their vanes and casing may get damaged. According to Prof. Thoma, cavitation in pump or turbine will occur if

$$\sigma \le \sigma_c$$

Here, σ = Thoma's cavitation factor = $\dfrac{\text{NPSH}}{H_m}$

$$= \frac{H_b - H_s - h_{fs}}{H_m}$$

$$= \frac{\left(\dfrac{p_a}{\gamma} - \dfrac{p_V}{\gamma}\right) - \dfrac{p_s}{\gamma} - h_{f_s}}{H}$$

Here, H_b = barometric head in m of water

$$= \left(\frac{p_a}{\gamma} - \frac{p_v}{\gamma}\right),$$

= atmospheric pressure head-vapour pressure head

H_m = net head on turbine or pump

$H_s = \frac{p_s}{\gamma}$ = suction pressure head, $\gamma = \rho g$

h_{fs} = friction head of suction pipe

NPSH = net positive suction head = $H_b - H_s - h_{fs}$

σ_c = critical cavitation factor

$= \sigma_{min}$ for no cavitation to occur in pump

$$= 0.103 \left(\frac{N_s}{1000}\right)^{4/3}$$

N_s = specific speed = $\frac{N\sqrt{Q}}{(H)^{5/4}}$ for pump

$= \frac{N\sqrt{p}}{(H)^{5/4}}$ for turbine, in this formula, by putting $P \propto QH$, above expression of N_s for pump is obtained.

N_s	Type of Pump
< 10	Low speed radial flow
10 – 20	Medium speed radial flow
20 – 80	High speed radial flow
> 80	Axial flow

20.6 MINIMUM SPEED FOR STARTING A CENTRIFUGAL PUMP

Centrifugal head developed by impeller = $\frac{u_2^2 - u_1^2}{2g}$

Flow is possible if $\frac{(u_2^2 - u_1^2)}{2g} \geq H_m$

$\therefore$ For min. speed, $\frac{u_2^2 - u_1^2}{2g} = H_m$ ...(1)

Now, $\eta_m = \frac{gH_m}{V_{w2}u_2}$

$\therefore$ $H_m = \eta_m \left(\frac{V_{w2}u_2}{g}\right)$

and $u_1 = \frac{\pi D_1 N}{60}$ and

$$u_2 = \frac{\pi D_2 N}{60}$$

Putting these values eqn. (1), we get,

$$\therefore \frac{1}{2g}\left[\left(\frac{\pi D_2 N}{60}\right)^2 - \left(\frac{\pi D_1 N}{60}\right)^2\right] = \eta_m \frac{V_{w_2}}{g}\left(\frac{\pi D_2 N}{60}\right)$$

$$\left(\frac{\pi N}{60g}\right) \text{ will cancel on both sides}$$

$$\therefore \quad \frac{\pi N}{120g}(D_2^2 - D_1^2) = \eta m\,(V_{w2} D_2)$$

$$\therefore \quad N_{\min} = \frac{120\,\eta_m V_{w2} D_2}{\pi(D_2^2 - D_1^2)}$$

20.7 RELATIONSHIP OF MANOMETRIC EFFICIENCY WITH ϕ

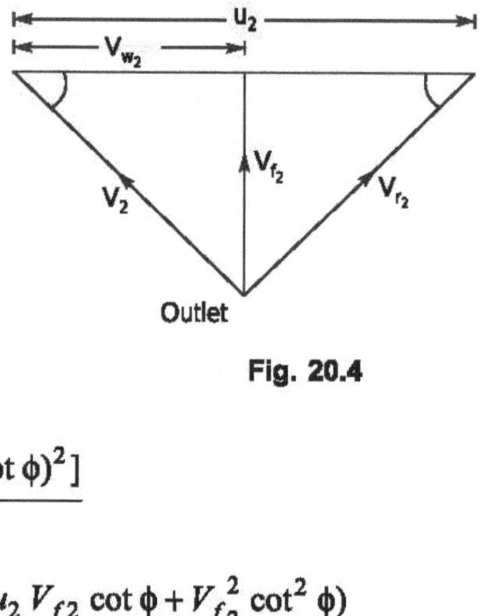

Fig. 20.4

$$H_m = \frac{v_{W_2} u_2}{g} - \frac{V_2^2}{2g}$$

ϕ = vane angle at outlet

$$V_2^2 = V_{f_2}^2 + Vw_2^2$$

$$V_{w_2} = u_2 - V_{f2} = \cot\phi$$

$$\therefore \quad H_m = \frac{(u_2 - V_{f2}\cot\phi)u_2}{g} - \frac{(V_f + W_{w2}^2)_2^2}{2g}$$

$$= \frac{2(u_2^2 - u_2 V_{f2}\cot\phi)[V_{f_2}^2 + u_2 - v_{f_2}\cot\phi)^2]}{2g}$$

$$H_m = \frac{2u_2^2 - 2u_2 V_{f2}\cot\phi - (V_{f_2}^2 + U_2^2 - 2u_2 V_{f2}\cot\phi + V_{f_2}^2\cot^2\phi)}{2g}$$

$$= \frac{u_2^2 - V_{f_2}^2(1 + \cot^2\phi)}{2g}$$

$$= \frac{u_2^2 - V_{f2}\,\mathrm{cosec}^2\,\phi}{2g}$$

Now, $\eta_{\text{mano}} = \eta_m = \dfrac{gH_m}{V_{w_2} u_2}$

$$\therefore \qquad \eta_m = \frac{g\,(u_2^2 - V_{f_2}^2 \operatorname{cosec}^2 \phi)}{2g\,(u_2 - V_{f2} \cot \phi)\, u_2}$$

$$= \frac{u_2^2 - V_{f_2}^2 \operatorname{cosec}^2 \phi}{2u_2\,(u_2 - V_{f2} \cot \phi)}$$

Here, $V_{f2} = \psi\sqrt{2g\,H_m}$

and $u_2 = k_u\sqrt{2g\,H_m}$

$\therefore$ η_m is dependent on ϕ for given value of H_m.

20.8 SIMILARITY LAWS OF CENTRIFUGAL PUMP

In the model testing of pumps, we have to find relationship between rotational speed N, diameter of impeller D, shaft power P, between model and prototype. Hence similarity laws are developed on the lines adopted for turbines and we have the following relationship:

(1) $$\left(\frac{H}{N^2 D^2}\right)_m = \left(\frac{H}{N^2 D^2}\right)_p$$

(suffix m for model and p for prototype)

(2) $$\left(\frac{H}{ND^3}\right)_m = \left(\frac{Q}{ND^3}\right)_p$$

(3) $$\left(\frac{P}{(\rho g)\,D^5 N^3}\right)_m = \left(\frac{P}{(\rho g)\,D^5 N^3}\right)_p$$

For two homologous pumps, N_s will be same

(4) $$\left(\frac{N\sqrt{Q}}{H_m^{\;3/4}}\right)_m = \left(\frac{N\sqrt{Q}}{H_m^{\;3/4}}\right)_p$$

where, H_m = manometric head

20.9 PUMPS IN PARALLEL

If two pumps are connected in parallel then combined distance Q is given by

$$Q = Q_1 + Q_2$$

However, H_m head remains same *i.e.*

$$H_m = H_{m1} = H_{m2}$$

This is a case similar to two pipes running in parallel. Pumps in parallel help in having higher Q for same monometric head.

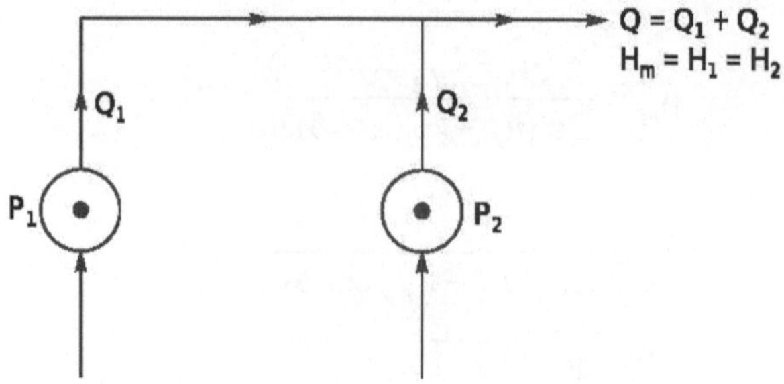

Fig. 20.5

20.10 PUMPS IN SERIES OF MULTISTAGE PUMP

If more head is required for same value of Q, "pumps in series" connection is used or a mutistaged centrifugal pump is used.

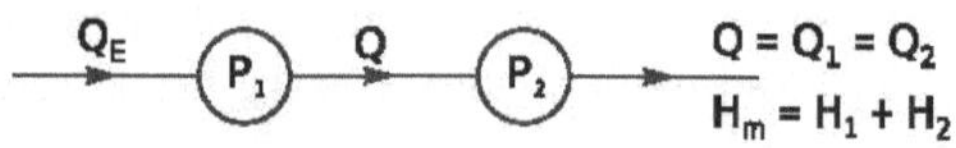

This is similar to pipes in series.

20.11 SOLVED PROBLEMS

■ **Problem 20.1:** *A centrifugal pump is to discharge 100 lps at a speed of 1450 rpm against a head of 15 m. The impeller has an outer diameter of 25 cm with a width of 6 cm. The manometric efficiency is 80%. Find blade angle at outlet*

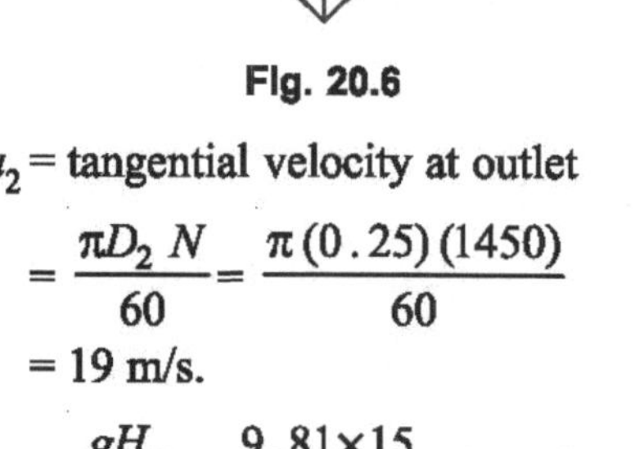

Fig. 20.6

Solution:

$$u_2 = \text{tangential velocity at outlet}$$

$$= \frac{\pi D_2 N}{60} = \frac{\pi (0.25)(1450)}{60}$$

$$= 19 \text{ m/s.}$$

$$\eta_{mano} = \frac{gH_m}{V_{w2}u_2} = \frac{9.81 \times 15}{V_{w_2}(19)} = 0.8 \text{ (Note } \eta_{mano} \text{ and } \eta_m \text{ is same)}$$

$\therefore$ $$Q = \pi \Delta_2 b_2 Vf_2$$

$\therefore$ $$\frac{100}{1000} = \pi (0.25)\left(\frac{6}{100}\right) V_{f_2}$$

$\therefore \quad V_{f2} = 2.12$ m/s

$$\therefore \quad \tan\phi = \frac{V_{f2}}{u_2 - V_{w2}} = \frac{2.12}{19 - 9.7} = 0.22$$

$\phi = 12.84°$ ...(Ans.)

■ **Problem 20.2:** *Show that pressure rise in the impeller of a centrifugal pump when frictional and other losses are neglected is given by*

$$\frac{p_2 - p_1}{\rho g} = \frac{1}{2g}\left[V_{f_2}^2 + u_2^2 - Vf_2^2 \operatorname{cosec}^2\phi\right].$$

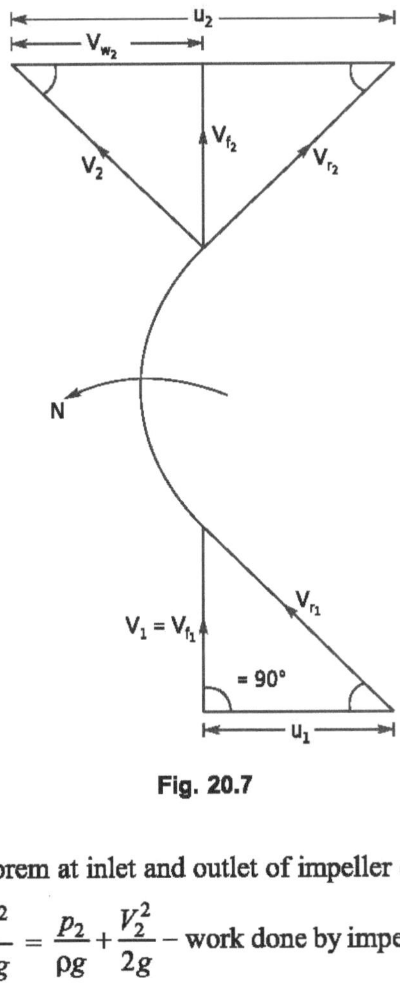

Fig. 20.7

Solution:

Apply Bernoulli's theorem at inlet and outlet of impeller of centrifugal pump.

$$\frac{p_1}{\rho g} + \frac{V_1^2}{2g} = \frac{p_2}{\rho g} + \frac{V_2^2}{2g} - \text{work done by impeller}$$

$$\therefore \quad \frac{p_2 - p_1}{\rho g} = \frac{V_1^2 - v_2^2}{2g} + \frac{V_{w_2}(u_2)}{g}$$

$V_1 = V_{f1}$ as $\alpha = 90°$ (see inlet Δ in Fig. 20.7)

$V_2^2 = V_{f_2}^2 + V_{w2}^2$ (outlet Δ)

Also $$V_{w2} = u_2 - \frac{V_{f2}}{\tan\phi} = u_2 - V_{f2} = \cot\phi$$

$$\therefore \quad V_2^2 = V_{f_2}^2 + (u_2 - V_{f_2} \cot\phi)^2$$

$$= V_{f_2}^2 + u_2^2 - 2u_2 V_{f_2} \cot\phi - V_{f_2}^2 \cot^2\phi$$

$$= V_{f_2}^2 (1 + \cot^2\phi) + u_2^2 - 2u_2 V_{f_2} \cot\phi$$

$$\therefore \quad \frac{p_2 - p_1}{\rho g} = \frac{Vf_1^2 - [V_{f_2}^2 (1 + \cot^2\phi) + u_2^2 - 2u_2 V_{f_2} \cot\phi]}{2g} + \frac{2u_2 (u_2 - V_{f_2} \cot\phi)}{2g}$$

$$= \frac{1}{2g}[V_{f_1}^2 + u_2^2 - V_{f_2}^2 \operatorname{cosec}^2\phi] \qquad \text{...(proved)}$$

■ **Problem 20.3:** *Show that $H_m = AN^2 = BNQ + CQ^2$ where, A, B, C are constant, N = RPM and Q = discharge from a centrifugal pump and H_m = menometric head.*

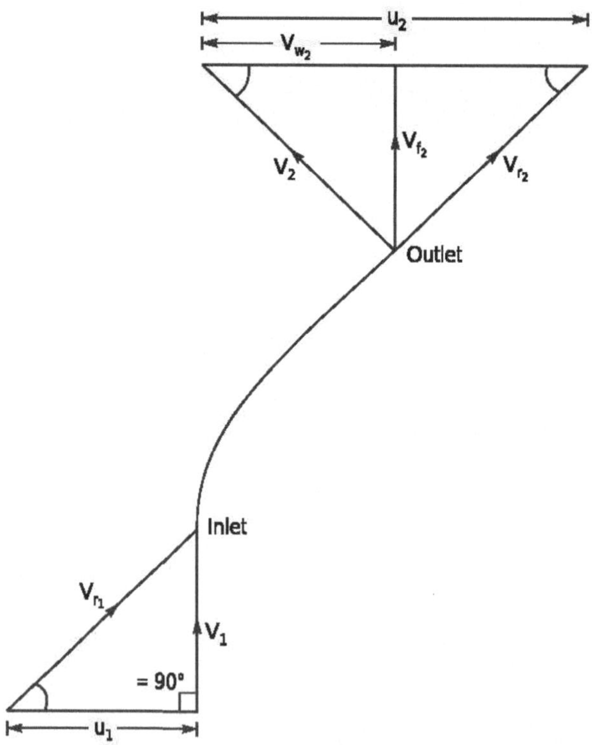

Fig. 20.8

Solution:

We have in centrifugal pump

$$H_m = \frac{V_{w2}u_2}{g} - K\frac{V_2^2}{2g}$$

$$u_2 = \frac{\pi D_2 N}{60} = k_1 = N$$

$$Q = \pi D_2 b_2 V_{f2}$$

$$\therefore \quad V_{f2} = \frac{Q}{\pi D_2 b_2} = k_2 Q \qquad \text{where } k_1 = k_2 = \text{constant.}$$

$$\tan\phi = \frac{V_{f2}}{u_2 - V_{w2}}$$

$$\therefore \quad u_2 - V_{w2} = \frac{V_{f2}}{\tan\phi} = V_{f2}\cot\phi$$

$$\therefore \quad V_{w2} = u_2 - V_{f2}\cot\phi$$

$$= u_2 - k_3 Q, \qquad ...(k_3 = k_2\cot\phi)$$

$$= k_1 N - k_3 Q$$

From outlet Δ,

$$V_2^2 = V_{f2}^2 + V_{w2}^2$$

$$= (k_2 Q)^2 + (k_1 N - k_3 Q)^2$$

Now, $H_{\text{mano}} = \dfrac{V_{w2}u_2}{g} - \dfrac{kV_2^2}{2g}$

$$= \frac{(k_1 N - k_3 Q)(k_1 N)}{g} - \frac{k[k_2 Q)^2 + (k_1 N - k_3 Q)^2]}{2g}$$

$$= \frac{1}{2g}[2(k_1 N)^2 - 2k_1 k_3 NQ - k k_2^2 Q^2 - k(k_1 N)^2 + 2k_1 N k_3 Q k + k kj_3^2 Q^2]$$

$$= \frac{1}{2g}[N^2(2k_1^2 - kk_1^2) NQ(2k k_1 k_3 - 2k_1 k_3) + Q^2(-kk_2^2 - kk_3^2)]$$

$$= \frac{1}{2g}[AN^2 + BNQ + CQ^2], \text{ here } A = (2k_1^2 - kk_1^2); (2kk_1 k_3 - 2k_1 k_3) \text{ and } C = -kk_2^2 - kk_3^2$$

■ **Problem 20.4**: *A centrifugal having Q = 1200 l pm, head = 30 m, N = 1450 rpm,* $\eta_{mano} = 0.75$, *loss of head =* $0.7\dfrac{V_2^2}{2g}$ *has an impeller of diameter 400 mm.*

Find velocity of flow and blade angle at outlet.

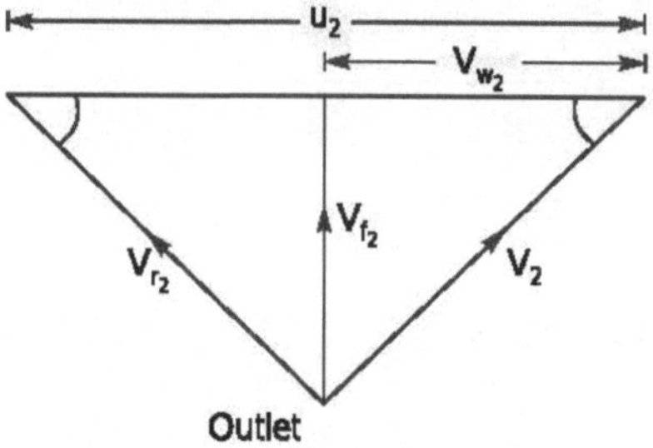

Fig.20.9

Solution:

$$\tan\phi = \frac{V_{f2}}{u_2 - V_{w2}}$$

$$u_2 = \frac{\pi D_2 N}{60} = \frac{\pi(0.4)1450}{60}$$

$$= 30.3 \text{ m/s}$$

$$\eta_{mano} = 0.75 = \frac{gH_m}{V_{w2}\,u_2}$$

$$V_{w2} = \frac{9.81(30)}{0.75(30.3)} = 13 \text{ m/s}$$

$$V_{f_2}^2 = V_2^2 - V_{w2}^2$$

$$H_m = \frac{V_{w2}\,u_2}{g} - k\frac{V_2^2}{2g}$$

$\therefore$ $$k\frac{V_2^2}{2g} = \frac{V_{w2}\,u_2}{g} - H_m$$

$$= \frac{13(30.3)}{9.81} - 30$$

$$= 40.15 - 30 = 10.115$$

$$k = 0.7, \quad \therefore \quad \frac{V_2^2}{2g} = \frac{10.15}{0.7} = 14.5$$

$\therefore$ $$V_2^2 = 14.5 \times 19.6 = 284.2$$

$\therefore$ $$V_{f_2}^2 = 284.2 - (13)^2 = 115.2$$

$\therefore$ $$V_{f2} = 10.73$$

$\therefore$ $$\tan\phi = \frac{V_{f2}}{u_2 - V_{w2}} = \frac{10.73}{30.3 - 13} = \frac{10.73}{17.3} = 0.62$$

$\therefore$ $$\phi = 31.8°$$ ...(Ans.)

■ **Problem 20.5**: *The suction lift and delivery head of a centrifugal pump are 3.3 and 30 m, The suction and delivery pipe diameter are 7.5 cm and 5 cm. and head loss in suction and delivery pipe are 2 m and 10 m. Impeller = 30 cm and its width 3 cm. Rotational speed = 1400 rpm,, blade angle at exit 35°, and* η_{mano} *= 80% m* η_0 *= 70%, find power required to run pump and discharge from pump.*

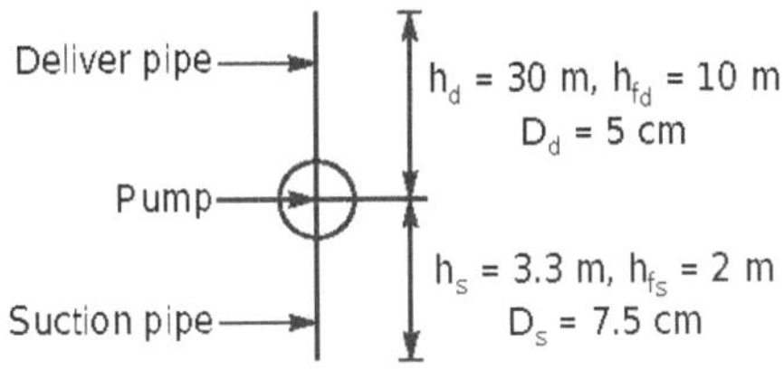

Fig. 20.10

Solution:

$$\phi = 35°$$

$$D_2 \text{ of impeller} = 30 \text{ cm}$$

$$b_2 = 3$$

$$N = 1400 \text{ rpm}$$

$$H_m = h_s + h_d + h_{fs} + h_{fd} + \frac{V_p^2}{2g}$$

$$= 3.3 + 30 + 2 + 10, \quad (\text{neglecting } V_p)$$

$$= 45.3$$

$$u_2 = \frac{\pi D_2 N}{60} = \frac{\pi(0.3)\,1400}{60-} = 22 \text{m/s}$$

$$\eta_{\text{mano}} = 0.8 = \frac{gH_m}{V_{w2}\,u_2}$$

$$\therefore \quad V_{w2} = \frac{9.81 \times 45.3}{0.8\,(22)}$$

$$= 25.2 \text{ m/s} > u_2$$

$$\tan\phi = \frac{V_{f2}}{u_2 - V_{w2}}$$

$$\therefore \quad V_{f2} = \tan 35\,(22 - 25.2)$$

as $V_{w2} > u_2$ = (see Fig. 20.11) take $\tan(180 - 35) = -0.7$

$$\therefore \quad V_{f2} = -0.7\,(-3.2) = 2.24 \text{ m/s}$$

$$Q = \pi D_1 b_2 V_{f2} = \pi\,(0.3)\,(0.03)\,(2.24)$$

$$= 0.063 \text{ m}^3/\text{s}$$ **...(Ans.)**

$$\eta_0 = \frac{(\rho g)\,QH_m}{\text{Power of shaft}}$$

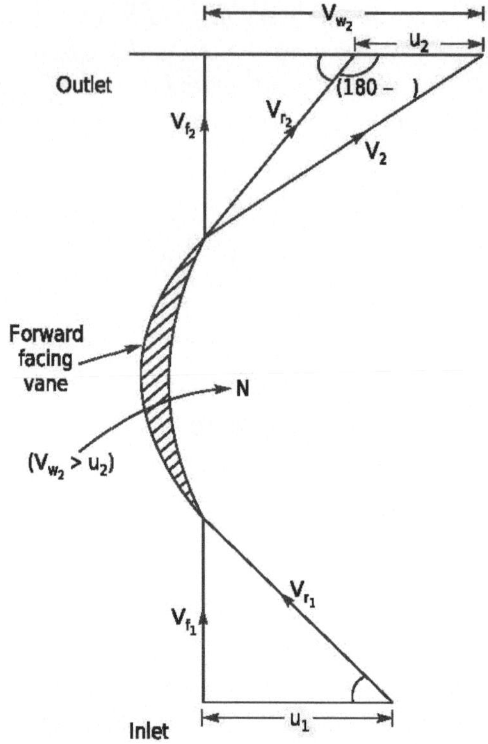

Fig. 20.11

$$\text{Power} = \frac{1000\,(9.81)\,(0.063)\,45.3}{0.7} = 39.9 \text{ kW} \qquad \text{...(Ans.)}$$

■ **Problem 20.6:** *A centrifugal pump lifts water against a static head of 32 m of which is suction lift. The suction and delivery pipes both have 12.7 cm diameter. The loss of head in suction pipe is 1 m and delivery pipe 6 m. The impeller diameter is 30.5 cm and width 2.5 cm. and width 2.5 cm. Its rotational speed is 1450 rpm and blade angle at exit 35°.* η_{mano} *= 80% and* η_0 *= 68%.*

Find:

(a) discharge of pump

(b) power required to drive the pump

(c) pressure in suction and delivery pipe.

Solution:

$$\eta_{mano} = \text{manometric efficiency} = \frac{gH_m}{V_{w2}\,u_2} = 80\%$$

and

$$\eta_0 = \frac{(\rho g)\,QH_m}{\text{Power required to drive pump}} = 68\%$$

$$u_2 = \frac{pD_2N}{60} = 23.1 \text{ m/s}$$

Neglecting velocity head in delivery pipe, $H_m = (h_s + h_d) + h_{fs} + h_{fd} = 32 + 1 + 6 = 39$ m

$$V_{w2} = \frac{9.81(39)}{0.8 \times 23.1}$$ [**Note:** here $(h_s + h_d)$ = static head = 32 m]

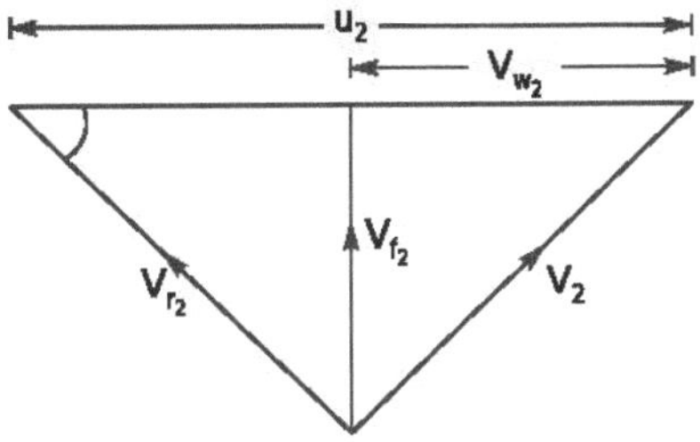

Fig. 201.2

$$\tan\phi = \frac{V_{f2}}{u_2 - V_{w2}} = \frac{V_{f2}}{23 - 20.7} = \frac{V_{f2}}{2.4}$$

∴ $V_{f2} = 2.4 \tan 35 = 1.68$

$$Q = \pi D_2 b_2 V_{f2} = 3.14\ (0.305) \left(\frac{25}{100}\right) 1.68$$

$= 0.04\ m^3/s$ ...**(Ans. 1)**

$$\text{Power to drive pump} = \frac{(\rho g) Q\, H_m}{0.68} = \frac{1000\,(9.81)\,(0.04)\,39}{0.68}$$

$= 22.63$ kW ...**(Ans. 2)**

$$\text{Pressure in suction pipe} = \frac{p_s}{\rho g} = -h_s - h_{fs} - h_{fs} - \frac{V_s^2}{2g}$$

$$V_s = V_d = \frac{Q}{A} = \frac{0.04}{\frac{\pi}{4}\left(\frac{12.7}{100}\right)^2} = 3.17 \text{ m/s}$$

∴ $$\frac{p_s}{\rho g} = -3 - 1 - \frac{(3.17)^2}{19.6}$$

$= -4 - 0.512 = -4.512$ m ...**(Ans.)**

$$= \text{pressure in delivery pipe} = h_d + h_{fd} + \frac{V_d^2}{2g}$$

$= (32 - 3) + 6 + 0.512 = 35.512$ m. ...**(Ans.)**

■ **Problem 20.7:** *A centrifugal pump running at a speed of 600 RPM discharges 280 LPS against a manometric head of 60 m. Flow is radial at inlet at 9 m/s and losses due to friction and leakage may be assumed to be each 2%. If velocity of whirl at outlet is one half that of peripheral speed at exit, find exit dimension of the impeller and power required to drive the pump. Determine inlet and outlet blade angle. Assume impeller consisting of 8 vanes of 12.5 mm thickness and* $\eta_0 = 75\%$.

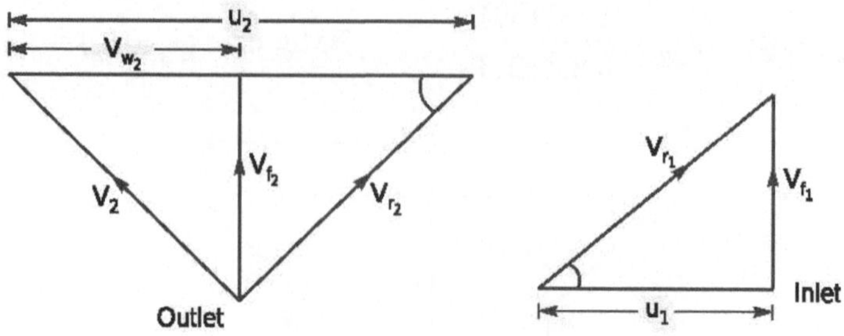

Fig. 20.13

Solution: Given $H_m = 60$ m, $Q = 280$ *LPS* $= 0.28$ m³/s

$$V_{w_2} = \frac{1}{2} u_2, \eta_0 = 75\%, N = 600 \; RPM$$

$$H_m = \frac{V_{w_2} u_2}{g} - \text{losses which are 4\%}$$

$$\therefore \quad \frac{V_{w_2} u_2}{g} = 1.04 \, H_m = 1.04\,(60)$$

$$\therefore \quad 2V_{w2}^2 = 9.81\,(1.04)\,(60)$$

$$\therefore \quad V_{w_2} = 17.5 \text{ m/s}$$

$$\therefore \quad u_2 = 35 \text{ m/s} = \frac{\pi D_2 N}{60} = \frac{\pi D_2\,(600)}{60}$$

$$\therefore \quad D_2 = 1.11 \text{ m}$$ ...(Ans.)

$$Q = (\pi D_2 - t)\, V_{f_2}\, b_2, \qquad b_2 = b_1 = 5 \text{ cm} \quad \text{(assumed)}$$

$$\therefore \quad V_{f_2} = \frac{Q}{[\pi D_2 - 8\,(0.0125)]\,(0.05)} = \frac{0.28}{(\pi(1.11) - 0.1)\,(0.05)}$$

$$= \frac{0.28}{0.169} = 1.65 \text{ m/s}$$

$$\therefore \quad \text{from outlet } \Delta, \tan\phi = \frac{V_{f_2}}{(u_2 - V_{w_2})} = \frac{1.65}{17.5} = 0.094$$

$$\therefore \quad \phi = 5.4°$$ ...(Ans.)

$$\text{from inlet } \Delta, \tan\theta = \frac{V_{f_1}}{u_1}$$

$$Q = [\pi D_1 - 8\,A(0.0125)]\; b_1\, V_{f_1}$$

$$\therefore \quad \pi D_1 - 0.1 = \frac{Q}{b_1 V_{f_1}} = \frac{0.28}{(0.05)\,(9)}$$

$$= 0.62$$

$$\therefore \quad \pi D_1 = 0.72$$

$$\therefore \quad D_1 = \frac{0.72}{\pi} = 0.23 \text{ m} \qquad \text{...(Ans.)}$$

$$\therefore \quad u_1 = \frac{\pi D_1 N}{60} = \frac{\pi (0.23) 600}{60}$$

$$= 7.2 \text{ m/s}$$

$$\therefore \quad \tan\theta = \frac{V_{f_1}}{u_1} = \frac{9}{7.2}$$

$\therefore \theta = 51.3° =$ inlet blade angle ...(**Ans.**)

$$\eta_0 = \frac{(\rho g) Q H_m}{P}$$

$$\therefore \quad P = \frac{(\rho g)(0.28) 60}{0.75}$$

$$= \frac{1000 \times 9.81 \times 0.28 \times 60}{0.75}$$

$$= 219 \text{ kW.} \qquad \text{...(Ans.)}$$

■ **Problem 20.8:** *A centrifugal pump while running at 1000 rpm discharges 80 LPS against a net head of 16 m. The manometric efficiency of the pump is 0.85. If vane angle at outlet is 35° and velocity of flow 1.5 m/s; estimate outer diameter of impeller and its width.*

Solution: Given data: $H_m = 16$ m, $N = 1000$, $Q = \frac{80}{1000} = 0.08$ m^3/s

$$\eta_{mano} = 0.85, \quad \phi = 35°, \; V_{f_2} = 1.5 \text{ m/s}, D_2 = ?, b_2 = ?$$

$$0.85 = \frac{gH_m}{V_{w_2} u_2} \qquad \therefore \; V_{w_2} u_2 = \frac{9.81(16)}{0.85} = 184.6 \qquad \text{...(1)}$$

$$\tan\phi = \frac{V_{f_2}}{u_2 - V_{w_2}} \qquad \therefore \; u_2 - V_{w_2} = \frac{1.5}{\tan(35)} = 2.14$$

$$\therefore \quad u_2 - \frac{184.6}{u_2} = 2.14$$

$$\therefore \quad u_2^2 - 2.14\, u_2 - 184.6 = 0$$

$$\therefore \quad u_2 = \frac{2.14 \pm \sqrt{(2.14)^2 + 4(184.6)}}{2}$$

$$= \frac{2.14 + 27.2}{2}$$

$$= 14.67 \text{ m/s} = \frac{\pi D_2 N}{60}$$

$$\therefore \quad D_2 = \frac{14.67 \times 60}{\pi (1000)} = 0.28 \text{ m} \quad \text{...(Ans.)}$$

$$Q = \pi D_2 b_2 V_{f_2}$$

$$\therefore \quad 0.08 = \pi (0.28)\, b_2 (1.5)$$

$$\therefore \quad b_2 = \frac{0.8}{\pi (0.28)(1.5)} = 0.06 \text{ m}$$

$$= 6 \text{ cm.} \quad \text{...(Ans.)}$$

■ **Problem 20.9:** *A pump can deliver a discharge of 0.1 m³/s to a head of 30 m. The critical cavitation number σ_c for the pump is 0.12. The pump is to be installed at a location where barometric pressure is 96 kPa (abs) and vapour pressure is 3.0 kPa (abs). Assuming intake pipe friction as 0.3 m, find minimum vale of NPSH. What will be the maximum allowable elevation above sump water level at which pumb can be located?*

Solution:

$$\sigma_c = 0.12 = \frac{H_{atm} - H_V - H_s - h_{f_s}}{H_m} = \frac{(NPSH)_{min}}{H_m}$$

Here, atm. pr. = 96 kPa

$$= 96 \times 10^3 \text{ N/m}^2$$

$$\therefore \quad H_{atm} \text{ (head)} = \frac{96 \times 10^3}{\rho g} = \frac{96 \times 10^3}{(10^3)(9.81)} = 9.78 \text{ m}$$

Similarly

$$H_V = \frac{3 \times 10^3}{(10^3)(9.81)} = 0.3 \text{ m}$$

$$h_{f_s} = 0.3 \text{ m} \quad \text{and} \quad H_m = 30 \text{ m}$$

$$\therefore \quad (\text{NPSH})_{min} = 0.12\,(H_m) = 0.12\,(30) = 3.6 \text{ m} \quad \text{...(Ans.)}$$

$$\sigma_c = 0.12 = \frac{9.78 - 0.3 - H_s - 0.3}{30}$$

$$\therefore \quad (0.12 \times 30) - 9.18 = -H_s$$

$$\therefore \quad H_s = 9.18 - 3.6 = 5.58 \text{ m} = \text{elevation for pump's location.} \quad \text{...(Ans.)}$$

■ **Problem 20.10:** *A centrifugal pump running at 440 RPM delivers 150 LPS. The diameter of impeller at inlet and outlet are 25 cm and 55 cm. The widths at inlet and at outlet are 10 cm and 6 cm. The impeller vanes are curved back to give a discharge angle of 30°. Neglecting losses, find head developed by pump. If diameters of suction and delivery pipes are 10 cm and their lengths 2 m and 15 m, and friction factor = 0.02, η_0 = 80%, find power required to run the pump.*

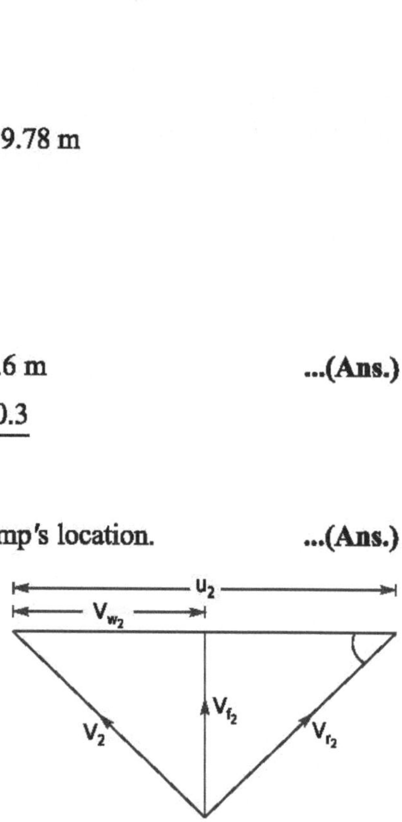

Fig. 20.14

Solution:

$$H_m = \text{pump head}$$

$$= \frac{V_{w_2} u_2}{g}$$

$$u_2 = \frac{\pi D_2 N}{60} = \frac{\pi (0.55)\, 440}{60}$$

$$= 12.66 \text{ m/s}$$

$$Q = 0.15 = \pi D_2 b_2 V_{f_2}$$

$$\therefore \quad V_{f_2} = \frac{0.15}{\pi (0.55)(0.06)} = 1.44 \text{ m/s}$$

$$\therefore \quad \tan \phi = \frac{V_{f_2}}{u_2 - V_{w_2}}$$

$$\therefore \quad \tan 30 = \frac{1.44}{12.66 - V_{w_2}}$$

$$\therefore \quad 12.66 - V_{w_2} = \frac{1.44}{0.577} = 2.49$$

$$\therefore \quad V_{w_2} = 12.66 - 2.49 = 10.17 \text{ m/s}$$

$$\therefore \quad H_m = \frac{V_{w_2} u_2}{g} = \frac{10.17\,(12.66)}{9.81} = 13.12 \text{ m}$$

$$V = \frac{Q}{\frac{\pi}{4}(0.1)^2} = \frac{0.15}{0.78\,(0.1)^2}$$

$$\therefore \quad V = 19.2 \text{ m/s}$$

$$(h_{f_s} + h_{f_d}) = \frac{fLV^2}{D(2g)} = \frac{0.02\,(2+15)\,(19.2)^2}{(0.1)\,(9.81)} = 64 \text{ m},$$

$$\therefore \quad \text{Head (total)} = 13.12 + 64 = 73.12 \text{ m} = H$$

$$P = \frac{(\rho g) QH}{\eta_0} = \frac{1000\,(9.81)\,(0.15)\,(73.12)}{0.8}$$

$$= 134.5 \text{ kW}$$ ...(Ans.)

■ **Problem 20.11**: *Calculate power required for centrifugal pump to deliver 24 LPS, under a static head of 24 m. Diameter of suction and delivery pipes are 15 cm and their total length 46 m.*

Solution:

$$\eta_0 = 5\%; \; f = 0.022.$$

$$H_m = \text{static head} + \text{friction head}$$

$$= 24 + \frac{fL V_p^2}{D2g}; \quad V_p = \text{velocity in suction and delivery pipe}$$

$$V_p = \frac{Q}{\frac{\pi}{4}(D^2)} = \frac{24/1000}{0.78\,(0.15)^2} = 1.36 \text{ m/s}$$

$$\therefore \quad H_m = 24 + \frac{0.022\,(46)\,(1.36)^2}{(0.15)\,19.6}$$

$$= 24 + 0.636 = 24.636 \text{ m}$$

$$\eta_0 = \frac{(\rho g)\,Q\,H_m}{P}$$

$$\therefore \quad P = \frac{(\rho g)\,Q\,H_m}{\eta_0} = \frac{1000\,(9.81)\,(0.024)\,(24.636)}{0.75}$$

$$= 7.73 \text{ kW.}$$ ...(Ans.)

■ **Problem 20.12:** *A centrifugal pump with impeller dia. of 15 cm discharges 2250 lpm when running at 1440 rpm under a head of 4 m. Calculate speed and head for geometrically similar pump having an impeller of 40 cm dia. and delivering 46 cum/min.*

Solution: For geometrically similar pumps, we have

$$\left(\frac{Q}{ND^3}\right)_m = \left(\frac{Q}{ND^3}\right)_p$$

$$\therefore \quad \left(\frac{22.50}{1440\,(0.15)^3}\right)_m = \left(\frac{46}{N\,(0.40)^3}\right)_p$$

$$\therefore \quad N_p = \frac{46}{(0.4)^3} \times \frac{1440\,(0.15)^3}{2.250}$$

$$= \frac{46}{0.064} \times \frac{1440\,(3.375 \times 10^{-3})}{2.250}$$

$$= 1552 \text{ RPM}$$ ...(Ans.)

Also,

$$\left(\frac{H}{N^2 D^2}\right)_m = \left(\frac{H}{N^2 D^2}\right)_p$$

$$\therefore \quad \left(\frac{4}{(1440)^2\,(0.15)^2}\right) = \frac{H_p}{(1552)^2\,(0.4)^2}$$

$$\therefore \quad H_p = \left(\frac{1552}{1440}\right)^2 \left(\frac{0.4}{0.15}\right)^2 (4) \quad \text{...(4)}$$

$$= (1.16)\,(7.11)\,(4)$$

$$= 32.99$$

$$= 33 \text{ m.}$$ ...(Ans.)

■ **Problem 20.13:** *A single stage centrifugal pump with an impeller diameter of 25 cm delivers 2000 lpm when run at 2000 rpm to a height of 35 m. Find the number of stages and diameter of each impeller of a multistage pump to lift 4000 LPM at 1000 RPM to a height of 150 m. Take efficiency = 80%.* (M.U. 1996)

Solution: For single stage pump:

$$D_1 = 25 \text{ cm}$$
$$N_1 = 2000 \text{ RPM}$$
$$Q_1 = 2000 \text{ LPM}$$
$$H_{m_1} = 35 \text{ m}$$

For muti stage pump:

Let head per stage = H_{m_2}, total head = 150 m

$$D_2 = ?$$
$$Q_2 = 4000 \text{ LPM}$$
$$N_2 = 1000 \text{ RPM}$$

N_s for both cases must be same

$$\therefore \quad \left(\frac{N\sqrt{Q}}{H_m^{3/4}}\right)_1 = \left(\frac{N\sqrt{Q}}{H_m^{3/4}}\right)_2$$

$$\therefore \quad H_{m_2}^{3/4} = \frac{N_2}{N_1}\left(\frac{Q_2}{Q_1}\right)^{1/2} (H_{m_1})^{3/4}$$

$$= \frac{1000}{2000}\left(\frac{4000}{2000}\right)^{1/2} (35)^{3/4}$$

$$= (0.5)\,(1.41)\,(14.38)$$

$$= 10.14$$

$$\therefore \quad H_{m2} = (10.14)^{4/3} = 21.9 \text{ m}$$

$$\therefore \quad \text{No. of stages} = \frac{150}{21.9} = 6.84, \text{ i.e. } 7 \text{ No.}$$ ...(Ans.)

For dia. D_2 of each impeller of multi stage pumps.

$$\left(\frac{H}{N^2D^2}\right)_1 = \left(\frac{H}{N^2D^2}\right)_2$$

$$\therefore \quad \frac{35}{(2000)^2\,(0.25)^2} = \frac{21.9}{(1000)^2\,(D_2)^2}$$

$$\therefore \qquad (D_2)^2 = \frac{21.9}{35}\left(\frac{2000}{1000}\right)^2 (0.25)^2$$

$$= (0.625)\,(4)\,(0.0625)$$

$$= 0.156$$

$$\therefore \qquad D_2 = 0.395 \text{ m, rounded to} = 0.4 \text{ m} = 40 \text{ cm.} \qquad \text{...(Ans.)}$$

■ **Problem 20.14:** *A 1 : 5 scale model of a pump was tested at 1000 RPM. The head developed and the power input at best efficiency point were found to be 8 m and 30 kW. If prototype pump has to work against a head of 25 m, determine its working speed, power required to drive it, and ratio of flow rates handled by two pumps.*

Solution: We have for geometrical similar pumps:

1. For N:

$$\left(\frac{H}{D^2N^2}\right)_m = \left(\frac{H}{D^2N^2}\right)_p$$

$$\therefore \qquad N_p^2 = \left(\frac{25}{8}\right)\left(\frac{D_m}{D_p}\right)^2 N_m^2$$

$$= \frac{25}{8}\left(\frac{1}{5}\right)^2 (1000)^2,$$

$$\left(\text{As per given scale, } \frac{D_m}{D_p} = \frac{1}{5}\right)$$

$$\therefore \qquad N_p = 1.76\left(\frac{1}{5}\right)(1000)$$

$$= 353 \text{ RPM} \qquad \text{...(Ans.)}$$

2. For power:

$$\left(\frac{P}{N^3D^5}\right)_m = \left(\frac{P}{N^3D^5}\right)_p$$

$$\therefore \text{ Power for prototype} = \left(\frac{N_p}{N_m}\right)^3\left(\frac{D_p}{N_m}\right)^5 P_m$$

$$= \left(\frac{353}{1000}\right)^3 (5)^5\,(30)$$

$$= 0.0439 \times 3125 \times 30$$

$$= 4115 \text{ kW} \qquad \text{...(Ans.)}$$

3. For flow ratio:

$$\left(\frac{Q}{ND^3}\right)_m = \left(\frac{Q}{ND^3}\right)_p$$

$$\therefore \quad \frac{Q_m}{Q_p} = \frac{(ND^3)_m}{(ND^3)_p} = \frac{1000}{353}\left(\frac{1}{5}\right)^3 = 0.0226$$

$$\therefore \quad \frac{Q_p}{Q_m} = 44.12. \qquad \text{...(Ans.)}$$

20.12 SUCTION LIMITS

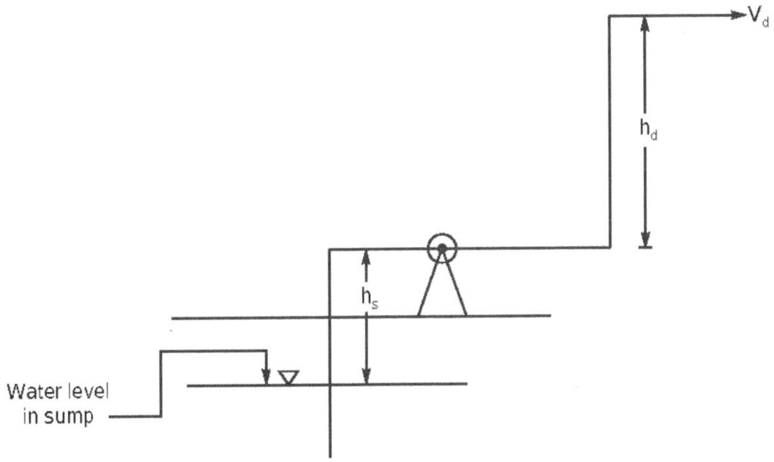

Fig. 20.15

A pump is an energy conversion device and lifts Q m³/s of a liquid through a static head H, which is given by $H = h_s + h_d + \frac{V_d^2}{2g}$ and the power required is P given by

$$P = \rho g\, QH \text{ watts}$$

The liquid rises through suction pipe to impeller eye due to pressure difference between atmospheric pressure on sump water surface and pressure at pump inlet p_s, *i.e.*,

$$\left(\frac{p_{atm}}{\rho g} - \frac{p_s}{\rho g}\right) = h_s + \frac{V_s^2}{2g} + h_{f_s}$$

where h_s = suction lift,

V_s = velocity in suction pipe

h_{f_s} = friction loss in suction pipe

Minimum value of $\frac{p_s}{\rho g} = \frac{p_v}{\rho g}$ where p_v is vapour pressure.

If h_s and V_s are increased, p_s may become equal p_v and cavitation conditions may develop at inlet. Therefore, suction pipe length is kept short and its diameter is kept larger or at least equal to that of delivery pipe. The pump manufacturer prescribes a net positive suction head, NPSH as a measure of permissible value of inlet pressure p_s. Thus,

$$\text{NPSH} = \frac{p_s - p_v}{\rho g}$$

NPSH is also prescribed in head of liquid by Thoma's number σ.

$$\text{NPSH} = \sigma H$$

$$\therefore \text{ Maximum suction lift } h_s = \frac{p_{atm} - p_v}{\rho g} - \text{NPSH}$$

This will be more clear from following numerical problem:

■ **Problem 20.15:** *A centrifugal pump has NPSH of 2.3 m at a head of 26 m. Find Thoma's number and maximum suction lift given p_v = 0.97 m of water at 45° C.*

Solution: Thoma's number $= \sigma = \frac{\text{NPSH}}{H} = \frac{2.3}{26} = 0.088$

$$h_s = \text{suction lift} = \frac{p_{atm} - p_v}{\rho g} - \text{NPSH}$$

$$= 10.3 - 0.97 - 2.3$$

$$= 7.03 \text{ m}$$

As a general practice suction lift is restricted to 7 m. If water is required to be lifted up from a greater depths, submersible pumps are used.

20.13 CHARACTERISTIC CURVES OF CENTRIFUGAL PUMP

The characteristic curve of a centrifugal pump are:

(1) Main characteristic curves which are obtained by plotting speed (*N*) *v/s* (*a*) power, *P* (*b*) Head, *H* and (*c*) discharge, *Q* as shown is Fig. 20.16.

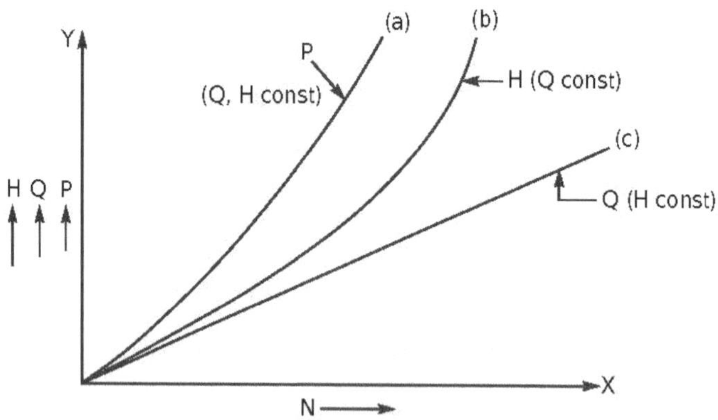

Fig. 20.16

(2) Operating characteristic curve: These are obtained by keeping speed constant and plotting Q on X-axis and η, p, H on Y-axis as shown in Fig. 20.17.

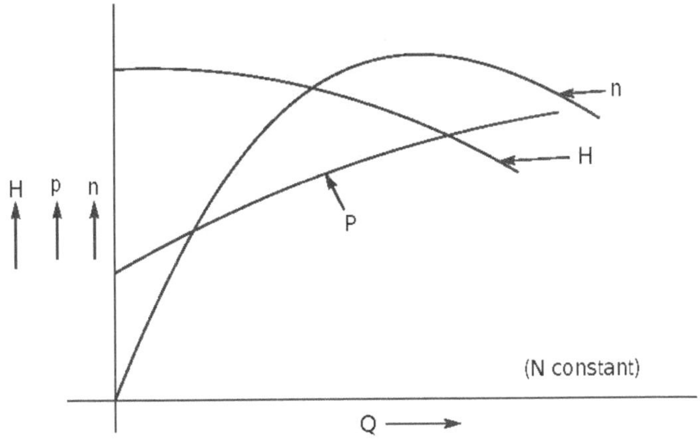

Fig. 20.17

The use of above curves will be more clear from following numerical problem:

■ **Problem 20.16:** *Tests on single stage centrifugal pump at constant speed of 1000 rpm gave following results:*

Q (LPM)	*0*	*225*	*455*	*680*	*910*	*1135*
H (m)	*12.7*	*12.5*	*11.9*	*10.4*	*7.3*	*3.7*
n%	*0*	*48*	*68*	*76*	*70*	*50*

The such pumps in parallel have common suction and delivery pipes with useful lift of 6.4 m. Friction and other losses = 2.02 $Q^2 \times 10^{-6}$ m where Q is in lpm. Find specific speed and also find delivery in LPM and driving power required for pump when

(*i*) *only one pump is connected.*

(*ii*) *two pumps work in parallel.*

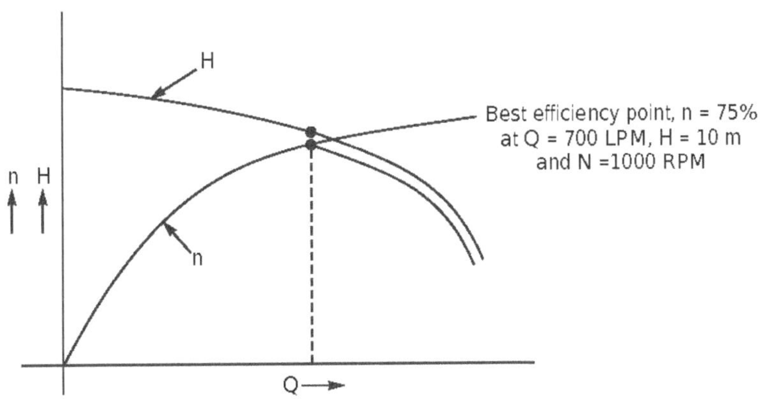

Fig. 20.18

Solution: From given data, plot the curves

1. Q vs η
2. Q vs H and obtain at best efficiency point values of Q and H, as shown in Fig. 20.15.

At best efficiency of 75%, $Q = 700$ LPM and $H = 10$ m.

$$Q = 700 \text{ LPM} = 0.011 \text{ m}^3/\text{s}$$

$$N_s = \frac{N\sqrt{Q}}{H^{3/4}} = \frac{1000\,(0.011)^{1/2}}{(10^{3/4})}$$

$$\therefore \quad N_s = \frac{1000\,(0.1)}{5.62} = 17.8 \text{ (SI units)} \qquad \text{...(Ans.)}$$

For single pump:

For actual $H = 6.4$, $Q = 380$ from graph. ...(Ans.)

$$H_{\text{Theoretical}} = H_{\text{actual}} + \text{losses}$$
$$= 6.4 + (2.02\, Q^2 \times 10^{-6})$$
$$= 6.4 + 0.29 \text{ for } Q = 380 \text{ LPM}$$
$$= 6.69$$

$$P = \rho g\, Q H_{\text{Th}} = \frac{1000\,(9.81)}{735}\left(\frac{380}{1000 \times 60}\right)(6.69)$$

$$= 0.565\ HP$$

For two pumps in parallel:

$$Q = 380 \times 2 = 760 \text{ LPM}$$

$$\therefore \quad P = 0.565 \times 2 = 1.13\ HP.$$

■ **Problem 20.17:** *If impeller diameter of a centrifugal pump at outlet is double that at inlet, and $\eta_{mano} = 0.7$, show that*

$$D_2 = \frac{81.7\sqrt{H_m}}{N} \text{ for starting speed of } N$$

Solution: For min. speed, $\dfrac{u_2^2 - u_1^2}{2g} = H_m = \eta_{\text{mano}}\left(\dfrac{V_{w_2} u_2}{g}\right)$

$$\therefore \quad H_m = \frac{1}{\eta_m}\left(\frac{u_2^2 - u_1^2}{2g}\right), \quad \text{given the } D_2 = 2D_1$$

$$= \frac{1}{\eta_m\,(2g)}\left(\frac{\pi N}{60}\right)^2 (D_2^2 - D_1^2)$$

$$= \frac{1}{\eta_m\,(2g)}\left(\frac{\pi N}{60}\right)^2 \left(D_2^2 - \frac{D_2^2}{4}\right)$$

$$= \frac{0.75}{0.7(2g)}\left(\frac{\pi}{60}\right)^2 N^2 D_2^2$$

$$\therefore \qquad D_2 = 81.7\,\frac{\sqrt{H_m}}{N}.$$

■ **Problem 20.18:** *Impeller diameter of a centrifugal pump at inlet and outlet are 25 cm and 50 cm. If menometric head is 30 m, find minimum starting speed.*

Solution: For min speed we have

$$\frac{u_2^2 - u_1^2}{2g} = H_m \text{ and } u_2 = \frac{\pi D_2 N}{60} \text{ and } u_1 = \frac{\pi D_1 N}{60}$$

$$\therefore \qquad \frac{1}{2g}\left(\frac{\pi N}{60}\right)^2 (D_2^2 - D_1^2) = H_m.$$

$$\therefore \qquad \frac{1}{2g}\left(\frac{\pi N}{60}\right)^2 (N^2)\,((0.5)^2 - (0.25)^2) = 30$$

$$(1.39 \times 10^{-4} N^2 (0.25 - 0.0625) = 30$$

$$\therefore \qquad N^2 = \frac{30}{1.39 \times 10^{-4} \times 0.1825}$$

$$= 115.1 \times 10^4$$

$$N = 1072 \text{ RPM.}$$ ...**(Ans.)**

■ **Problem 20.19:** *A centrifugal pump lifts water under a static head of 36 m of which 4 m is suction head. Dia. of suction and delivery pipes are 15 cm and friction loss in them 1.5 m and 7.0 m respectively. If impeller dia. is 38 cm and its width 2.5 cm, N = 1200 rpm, ϕ = 38°, η_m = 80% find discharge and pressures on suction and delivery sides.*

Solution: $H_m = 36 + 7 + 1.5 = 44.5$ m

$$u_2 = \frac{\pi D_2 N}{60} = 23.8 \text{ m/s}$$

$$\eta_m = 80\% = \frac{gH_m}{V_{w_2} u_2},$$

$$\therefore \qquad V_{w_2} = \frac{9.81(44.5)}{0.8 \times 23.8}$$

$$= 22.8 \text{ m/s}$$

From outlet Δ, $$\tan\phi = \frac{V_{f_2}}{u_2 - V_{w_2}} = \tan 38$$

$$\therefore \qquad V_{f_2} = 0.8 \text{ m/s}$$

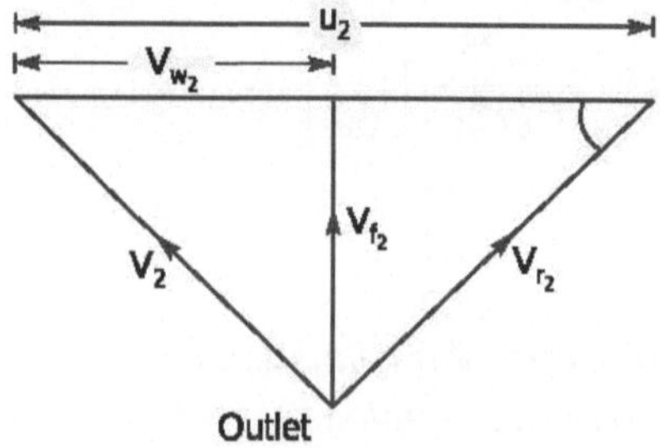

Fig. 20.19

$$Q = \pi D_2 b_2 V_{f_2} = \pi\,(0.38)\,(0.025)\,(0.8) = 0.023 \text{ m}^3/\text{s}$$

$$V_s = V_d = \frac{Q}{\frac{\pi}{4}(0.15)^2} = \frac{0.023}{0.78\,(0.15)^2} = 1.311 \text{ m/s}$$

$$\therefore \quad \frac{V_s^2}{2g} = \frac{V_d^2}{2g} = 0.0876 \text{ m.}$$

Ans. Pressure on suction side $= \frac{p_s}{\rho g} = 4 + 1.5 + 0.0876 = 5.5876$ m vacuum (–ve) = 54.81 kN/m^2

Pressure on deliver side $= \frac{p_d}{\rho g} = (36 - 4) + 7 + 0.0876 = 39.0876$ m = 383.45 kN/m^2 (+ve)

■ **Problem 20.20:** *A centrifugal pump has impeller diameter at outlet 400 mm and width 80 mm. The vanes are curved background at 35° and vane thickness occupies 20% of peripheral area. If velocity of flow is constant and impeller speed is 900 RPM and discharge 150 LPS.*

Find (a) pressure rise in impeller.

(b) percentage of work converted to KE.

Solution: $D_2 = 40$ cm, $b_2 = 8$ cm, $\phi = 35°$, $N = 900$

Vane thickness occupies 20% of $\pi D_2 b_2$,

i.e., area of flow – 0.8 $(\pi D_2 b_2)$

$$\therefore \quad Q = 0.8\,\pi D_2\, b_2\, V_{f_2} = 0.15, \quad \therefore\ V_{f_2} = 1.86 \text{ m/s} = V_{f_1}$$

$$u_2 = \frac{\pi D_2 N}{60} = \frac{\pi\,(0.4)\,900}{60} = 18.84 \text{ m/s}$$

$$\tan\phi = \frac{V_{f_2}}{u_2 - V_{w_2}}$$

$$\therefore \quad \tan 35 = \frac{1.86}{18.84 - V_{w_2}} = 0.7$$

$$\therefore \quad V_{w_2} = 18.84 - \frac{1.86}{0.7} = 18.84 - 2.65$$

$$= 16.19 \text{ m/s}$$

$$\text{Pressure rise} = \frac{1}{2g}[V_{f1}^2 + u_2^2 - V_{f2}^2 \operatorname{cosec}^2 \phi], \text{ (see problem 20.2)}$$

$$= \frac{1}{2g}\left[(1.86)^2 + (18.84)^2 - (1.86)^2 \frac{1}{\sin^2 \phi}\right]$$

$$= \frac{1}{2g}\left[3.45 + 355 \frac{3.45}{0.328}\right]$$

$$= \frac{358.45 - 10.5}{19.6} = 17.75 \text{ m of water}$$ ...(**Ans.**(*i*))

$$\text{Also velocity at outlet} = V_2 = \sqrt{V_{f2}^2 + V_{w2}^2}$$

$$= \sqrt{(1.86)^2 + (16.19)^2}$$

$$= 16.29 \text{ m/s}$$

$$\therefore \quad KE \text{ per kg} = \frac{V_2^2}{2g} = 13.5 \text{ Nm}$$

$$\text{Work done per kg} = \frac{1}{g}[V_{w_2} u_2] = \frac{16.19 \times 18.84}{9.81}$$

$$= 31 \text{Nm}$$

$$\therefore \% \text{ of work converted to } KE = \frac{13.5}{31} = 0.435 = 43.5\%.$$ ...(**Ans.**)

Exercises

1. A centrifugal pump having discharge equal to 140 lps and head 13 m, $N = 600$ rpm, $D_1 = \frac{1}{2} D_2$ and $D_2 = 50$ cm, outlet angle 35° and area of flow 0.07 m^2.

   Find: (*a*) Monometric efficiency. (*b*) Vane angle at inlet.

   (**Ans.** (*a*) 64%; (*b*) $\theta = 14.5\%$)

2. Outer diameter of a centrifugal pump is 40 cm and its width 5 cm, $N = 800$ RPM and H_m 15 m. If outlet angle = 40° and $\eta_m = 75\%$, find discharge from the pump and absolute velocity at outlet. (**Ans.** (*a*) $Q = 270$ LPS (*b*) $V_2 = 12.56$ m/s at $\beta = 20°$)

3. A centrifugal pump has $D_2 = 2D_1$ and $D_1 = 20$ cm. Vane angles at outlet and inlet are 35° and 30° respectively. Velocity of flow constant and $N = 1000$ RPM, $\eta_{mono} = 0.8$. Find menometric head developed. **(Ans.** 18.5 m)
4. A centrifugal pump has $D_1 = 25$ cm and $D_2 = 50$ cm. If flow is shut off from delivery pipe, and impeller rotates at 600 rpm, find centrifugal head developed in kN/m^2. **(Ans.** 92.5 kN/m^2)
5. A centrifugal pump has $D_2 = 2D_1$ and $D_1 = 25$ cm and is required to develop a head of 20 m. Find minimum speed to start pumping. **(Ans.** 875 RPM)
6. A centrifugal pump has the following dimensions:
   $D_1 = 25$ cm, $D_2 = 50$ cm, $N = 1200$ RPM, $Q = 150$ LPS, b_1 = width of impeller at inlet = 8 cm at outlet $b_2 = 5$ cm. Vanes are curved backward and has $\phi = 25°$.
   $\eta_{mano} = 0.9$ and $\eta_0 = 0.7$.
   Find net head produced, power required to run pump, and specific speed of pump. **(Ans.** $H_m = 78.5$ m, 150 kW, $N_s = 17.6$)
7. A centrifugal pump has impeller of size 30 × 15 cm and vane angle at inlet and outlet 30° and 35°, and $N = 1000$ RPM. If velocity of flow is constant, and $\eta_{mano} = 0.92$, find net head develops by the pump and its width at outlet if $N_s = 45$. **(Ans.** $H_m = 13.5$ m, $b_2 = 2.3$ cm)
8. A 3 stage centrifugal pump has impeller diameter of 40 cm and width 2 cm. Vane angle at outlet 45°. If pump delivers 60 LPS, $\eta_0 = 70\%$ find:
   (*a*) power required by pump
   (*b*) net head of pump
   (*c*) specific speed. **(Ans.** (*a*) 75.67 kW (*b*) 90 m (30 × 3) (*c*) 19)
9. Two geometrically similar pumps run at 1000 RPM. One of pumps has diameter of 0.4 m and discharge of 30 LPS at a head of 20 m. If other pump has half of this discharge, find its head and diameter. **(Ans.** $H_2 = 12.6$ m, $D_2 = 0.317$ m)
10. A centrifugal pump running at 750 RPM has $Q = 100$ LPS against a head of 10 m. A second pump working at 500 rpm, has $Q = 50$ LPS. What will be design head of 2nd pump and scale ratio between pump 1 and 2? **(Ans.** $H_2 = 3.67$ m, $L_r = 1.32$)

❑❑❑

21

Miscellaneous Hydraulic Machinery

21.1 INTRODUCTION

Power can be transmitted from one place to another with the help of water which is generally referred by a term 'hydraulic power transmission'. The machines which use hydraulic energy for their operation are called as hydraulically operated machines or hydraulic machines.

Some important hydraulic devices are:

(1) Hydraulic accumulator

(2) Hydraulic intensifier

(3) Hydraulic press

(4) Hydraulic crane

(5) Hydraulic ram.

21.2 HYDRAULIC ACCUMULATOR

Hydraulic accumulator stores the energy under pressure and supply it whenever needed by the hydraulic machines connected to it. When the crane or lift moves in downward direction or during their idle period they need less water than average and when the lift or crane moves in upward direction it requires more water. But the water pump discharges water at a constant rate. So when the lift moves in downward direction the excess water is stored in accumulator. The stored water is then supplied to lift along with the discharge from pump when the lift moves in upward direction.

Hydraulic accumulator consists of a fixed cylinder in which a ram is sliding. The ram is loaded on its top. At the bottom of the cylinder inlet and outlet is provided. Pump which discharges water under pressure is connected to the inlet and outlet is connected to the hydraulic machine like lift or crane.

When the water enters the accumulator the sliding ram moves in upward direction. Maximum amount of pressure energy will be stored when the sliding ram will be at topmost position. This stored water with pressure moves towards lift or crane when it needs more energy and ram will move in downward direction.

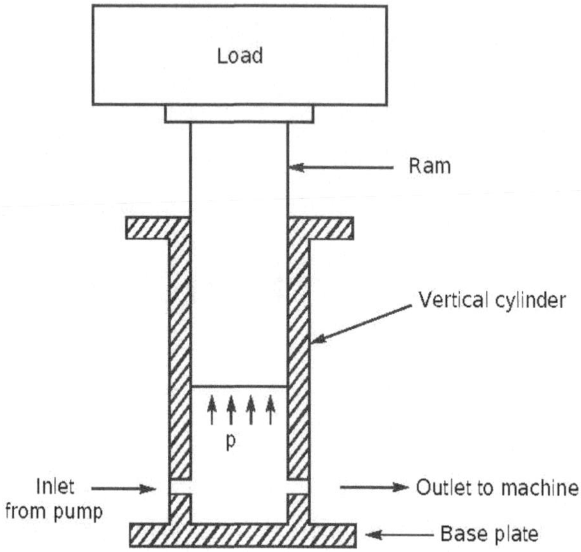

Fig. 21.1 Simple accumulator.

21.2.1 Capacity of Hydraulic Accumulator

Capacity of Hydraulic Accumulator is defined as the maximum amount of pressure energy stored in the accumulator.

Let W = Total load on sliding ram (N)

A = Area of sliding ram (m^2)

h = Strok or height or fall of moving ram (m)

p = Pressure of water supplied by the pump (N/m^2)

Now from Fig. 21.1

Energy stored in the accumulator = work done in lifting the ram

$\therefore$ Work done = Force $\times$ distance moved

$= p \times A \times h$

$= p \times (A \times h)$

$= p \times$ Volume of cylinder

$\therefore$ By definition

Capacity of accumulator = $p \times$ Volume of cylinder ...(21.1)

21.2.2 Differential Accumulator

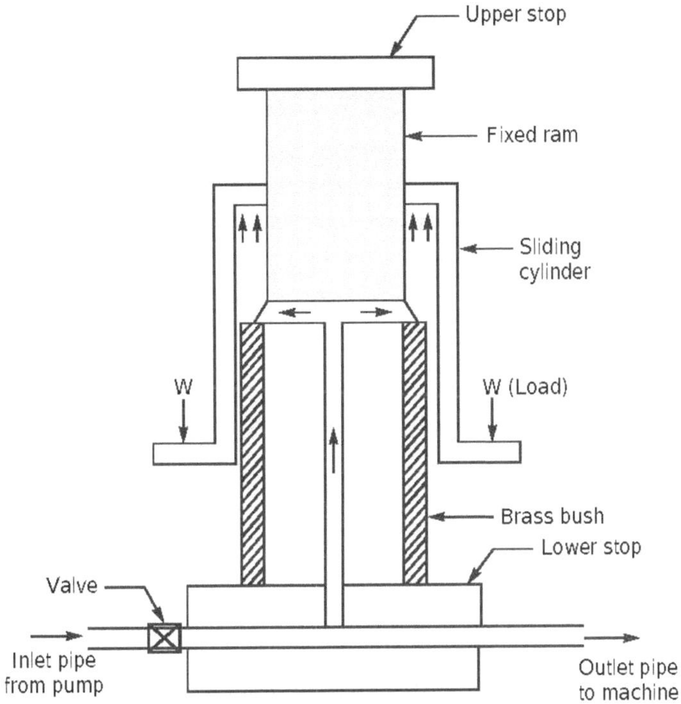

Fig. 21.2 Differential accumulator.

Differential accumulator consists of a fixed ram. On its lower part brass plates are provided. The sliding cylinder which is loaded with cast iron ring weights slides along the fixed ram. The inlet and outlet are provided for water to enter and to leave the cylinder.

Water enters the cylinder through the inlet and passes through the passage provided in the ram to enter the cylinder. Due to the pressure of water the cylinder moves in upward direction till it reaches the end of the stroke.

When the machine connected on downstream side of the accumulator needs extra water under pressure it takes it from the accumulator because of which the cylinder slides down till it touches the lower stop.

For differential accumulator

Total load on cylinder $= W = p \times a$

where p = pressure of water supplied by pump

$$a = \frac{\pi(D^2 - d^2)}{4} = \text{area of brass bush}$$

(D = external diameter of brass bush,
d = diameter of the fixed ram)

and capacity of accumulator $= p \times a \times h$

$$= W \times h \quad ...(21.2)$$

$$\text{power supplied by accumulator} = \frac{W \times h}{t} \quad ...(21.3)$$

■ **Problem 21.1:** *The sliding ram of a accumulation carries a load of W Newtons. The diameter of the ram is 35 cm and the intensity of pressure inside the accumulator is 900 N/cm². If the frictional resistance against the movement of the ram is 6% of the total weight W. Find the weight on the ram and the pressure intensity when the ram is moving up with uniform velocity.*

Given $d = 35 \text{ cm} = 0.35 \text{ m}$

$p = 900 \text{ N/cm}^2 = 900 \times 10^4 \text{ N/m}^2$

Frictional resistance $= 0.06\ W.$

Solution: Load required to overcome frictional resistance = 0.06 W

(*a*) When the ram moves down with a uniform velocity, the frictional resistance acts vertically upwards

∴ The net load on the ram $= W - 0.06\ W$

$= 0.94$ W Newtons

$$\text{Pressure intensity} = \frac{\text{Net load}}{\text{area of ram}}$$

$$900 \times 10^4 = \frac{0.94\ W}{\left(\frac{\pi \times 0.35^2}{4}\right)} = \frac{0.94\ W}{0.0962}$$

∴ $W = 92 \times 10^4 \text{ N} = 920 \text{ kN}.$

(*b*) When the ram moves up with a uniform velocity, the frictional resistance acts vertically downwards.

∴ The net load on the ram $= W + 0.06\ W$

$= 1.06\ W = 1.06 \times 92 \times 10^4 \text{ N}$

$$\therefore \quad \text{Pressure intensity} = \frac{\text{Net load}}{\text{area of ram}}$$

$$= \frac{1.06 \times 92 \times 10^4}{0.0962}$$

$$= 1013 \times 10^4 \text{ N/m}^2$$

$$= 1013 \text{ N/cm}^2.$$

■ **Problem 21.2:** *An accumulator with ram diameter 25 cm and stroke length of 5 m is loaded with 350 kN. The frictional resistance (packing friction) is 5 per cent of load on the accumulator. The ram takes 100 seconds to fall through its full range. Find the total work supplied and power delivered to the hydraulic machine when the pump delivers 7 lit/sec of water during the downward movement of the ram at the stated velocity.*

Given $W = 350\ kN = 350 \times 10^3\ N$

$d = 25\ cm = 0.25\ m$

$t = 100\ sec$

Stroke of ram $= h = 5\ cm$

Frictional resistance $= 0.05\ W$ *Newtons*

$Q = 7\ lit/sec = 0.007\ m^3/sec.$

Solution: Area of ram $= A = \dfrac{\pi d^2}{4} = \dfrac{\pi \times 0.25^2}{4} = 0.049\ m^2$

Then net load on the ram $= W - 0.05\ W$

(When it moves down)

$= 0.95\ W$

$= 0.95 \times 350 \times 10^3\ N$

$= 332.50 \times 10^3\ N$

Distance moved by the ram per sec $= \dfrac{h}{t}$

$= \dfrac{5}{100} = 0.05\ m/sec$

Work supplied by the accumulator = Net load on ram × Distance moved by ram per sec.

$= 332.50 \times 10^3 \times 0.05$

$= 16625\ Nm/sec$

Intensity of pressure of water $= p = \dfrac{\text{Net load}}{\text{Area of ram}}$

$= \dfrac{332.50 \times 10^3}{0.049} = 6785.71 \times 10^3\ N/m^2$

Pressure head of water supplied $= H = \dfrac{p}{w}$

$= \dfrac{6785.71 \times 10^3}{9810}$

$= 691.71$ m of water

Work supplied by the pump $= wQH$

$= 9810 \times 0.007 \times 691.71$

$= 47499.97\ Nm/sec$

Total work supplied to hydraulic machine

$= 16625 + 47499.97 = 64124.97\ Nm/sec$

∴ Power supplied to the hydraulic machine

$= \dfrac{64124.97}{736} = 87.1263$ HP.

21.3 HYDRAULIC INTENSIFIER

Hydraulic intensifier is a device which increases the intensity of pressure of water by utilising the energy of a large quantity of liquid at low pressure. Water is supplied through intensifier to those hydraulic machines which needs water at very high pressure for its operation like press, crane, lift etc.

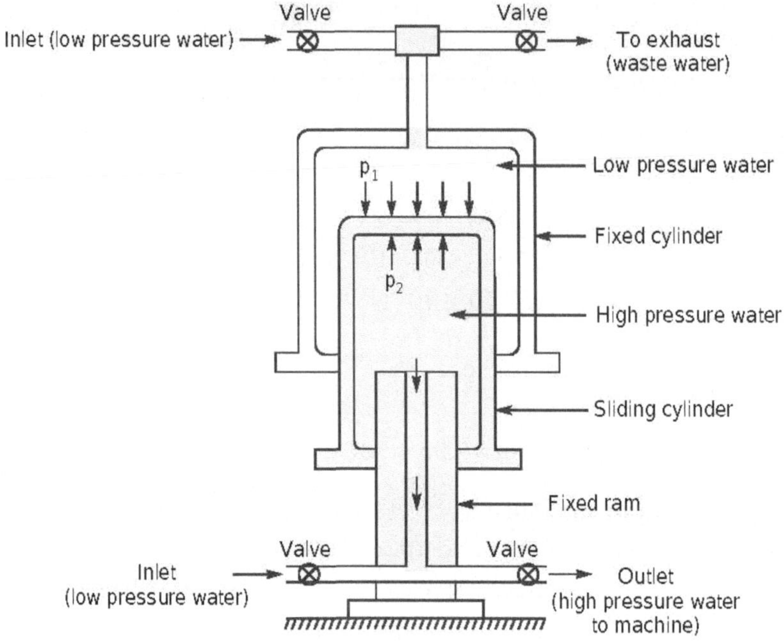

Fig. 21.3 Hydraulic intensifier.

It consists of one fixed cylinder, one movable cylinder and one fixed ram. The lower cylinder slides over the fixed ram. To the fixed cylinder one inlet and one outlet is provided. The inlet admits low pressure water from a pump and through the outlet waste water is discharged. A passage is provided for water through the fixed ram which admits low pressure water from a pump and discharges high pressure water to hydraulic machines. For proper control and regulations values are provided as shown if Fig. 21.3.

Initially let the sliding cylinder be at the bottom of the its stroke. The outlet valve of the fixed cylinder and the inlet valve of the fixed ram are opened while the inlet valve of the fixed cylinder and outlet valve of the fixed ram are kept closed. So the low pressure water enters into the sliding cylinder forcing it to rise up and reaches the end of its upward stroke.

Then the discharge valve of the fixed cylinder and inlet valve of fixed ram are closed. Simultaneously the inlet valve of fixed cylinder and outlet valve of fixed ram are opened. So the low pressure water enters inside the fixed cylinder from the top, which in turn forces the sliding cylinder in downward direction. When the sliding cylinder moves in downward direction forces the high pressure water from sliding water to the hydraulic machines through the passage of water provided in the fixed ram. This is continued till the sliding ram reached to the end of its stroke.

The above process is repeated.

The force exerted by the high pressure water on the sliding cylinder in the upward direction

$$= p_2 \times a \quad ...(21.4)$$

The force exerted by the high pressure water on the sliding cylinder in the downward direction

$$= p_1 \times A \quad ...(21.5)$$

Equating (21.4) and (21.5)

$$p_2 \times a = p_1 \times A$$

$$\therefore \quad p_2 = \frac{A}{a} p_1 \quad ...(21.6)$$

■ **Problem 21.3:** *A hydraulic intensifier has a sliding cylinder diameter of 30 cm. Find the diameter of the fixed ram of the intensifier if the pressure intensity of water supplied to an intensifier is 175 N/cm² and the pressure intensity of water leaving the intensifier is 950 N/cm².*

Given $D = 0.3\ m$

$p_1 = 175\ N/cm^2 = 175 \times 10^4\ N/m^2$

$p_2 = 950\ N/cm^2 = 950 \times 10^4\ N/m^2.$

Solution:

Area of sliding cylinder $= A = \dfrac{\pi D^2}{4}$

$$= \frac{\pi \times 0.3^2}{4} = 0.0707\ \text{m}^2$$

using the equation (21.5)

$$p_1 A = p_2 a$$

$$\therefore \quad 175 \times 10^4 \times 0.0707 = 950 \times 10^4 \times a$$

now $$a = \frac{\pi d^2}{4} = 0.0130$$

$$\therefore \quad d = \sqrt{\frac{0.0130 \times 4}{\pi}} = 0.1287\ \text{m} = 12.87\ \text{cm}$$

The diameter of the fixed ram is 12.87 cm.

21.4 HYDRAULIC PRESS

Hydraulic press is a device used to lift heavier loads by applying a much smaller force. It works on the Pascal's law which states that liquid exerts equal pressure in all directions.

The hydraulic press consists of two cylinder of different diameters. The larger cylinder contains a ram which lifts load and the second smaller cylinder contains a plunger on which a effort is applied. The two cylinders are connected by a pipe to carry liquid from one cylinder to another.

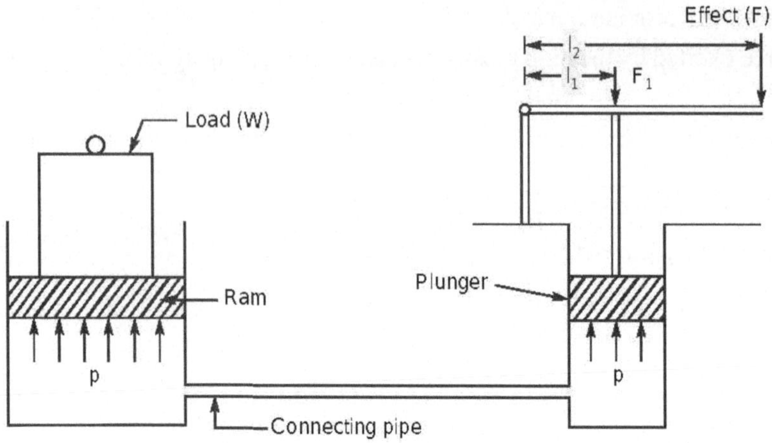

Fig. 21.4 Hydraulic press.

When a effort (F) is applied on the plunger in the small cylinder the pressure intensity in the liquid will be same on the same level which is responsible for lifting the ram placed in the large cylinder with the load on it.

∴ By Pascal's law

Pressure intensity on ram = pressure intensity on plunger

$$\frac{W}{A} = \frac{F_1}{a} \quad \therefore \quad W = \frac{A}{a} F_1 \qquad \text{...(21.7)}$$

where A = Area of ram

and a = Area of plunger

If a lever is used for applying force on the plunger then from Fig. 21.4

$$F \times l_2 = F_1 \times l_1$$

$$\therefore \quad F_1 = \frac{F \times l_2}{l_1}$$

put in equation (21.6)

$$\therefore \quad W = F \times \frac{l_2}{l_1} \times \frac{A}{a} \qquad \text{...(21.8)}$$

■ **Problem 21.4**: *A hydraulic press has a ram and plunger of diameters 250 mm and 35 respectively The frictional resistance of the ram as well as the plunger is 5% of load. The leverage of the handle is 10 to 1. The lift of the load is 1 m and the stroke of the plunger is 250 mm. A load of 150 kN is to be raised in 2 minutes. Determine:*

(1) The force applied at the end of the lever.

(2) H.P. required to drive the plunger

(3) Number of strokes performed by the plunger.

Given $D = 250\ mm = 0.25\ m$

$d = 35\ mm = 0.035\ m$

frictional resistance = *5% of load*

$$\frac{l_2}{l_1} = 10$$

$$Lift = L = 1\ m$$

$$Stroke\ of\ plunger = 250\ mm = 0.25\ m$$

$$W = 150\ kN$$

$$T = 2\ minutes = 120\ sec.$$

Solution: (1) Force applied at the end of lever (F)
using equation (21.7)

$$W = F\left(\frac{l_2}{l_1}\right)\left(\frac{A}{a}\right)$$

Now frictional resistance is given as 5%

∴ The effective force on plunger = $F - 0.05\ F = 0.95\ F$

Similarly effective force responsible for lifting the load = 0.95 (0.95 F)

$$\therefore \qquad F_{(eff)} = 0.95^2\ F$$

equation (21.7) can be written for this problem as

$$W = F_{(eff)}\left(\frac{l_2}{l_1}\right)\left(\frac{A}{a}\right)$$

$$\therefore \qquad 150 \times 10^3 = 0.95^2 F \times (10) \times \left(\frac{\frac{\pi \times 0.25^2}{4}}{\frac{\pi \times 0.035^2}{4}}\right)$$

$$\therefore \qquad F = 325.76\ \text{N}$$

(2) Number of strokes performed by the plunger

$$\frac{A \times L}{a \times l} = \frac{\frac{\pi \times 0.25^2}{4} \times 1}{\frac{\pi \times 0.035^2}{4} \times 0.25}$$

$$= 204 \text{ strokes.}$$

(3) H.P. required to drive the plunger

$$= \frac{\text{Weight lifting} \times \text{distance travelled}}{(0.95)^2 \times \text{time} \times 736}$$

$$= \frac{150 \times 10^3 \times 1}{0.95^2 \times 120 \times 736} = 1.88 \text{ H.P.}$$

21.5 HYDRAULIC LIFT

The hydraulic lift is a device used for carrying passenger or goods from one level to another.

Hydraulic lift consists of a cage which can move vertically upward or downward direction. A jigger consists of a fixed cylinder, a sliding ram and two pulley blocks out of which one is fixed and other is movable. The movable pulley block is connected to the sliding ram. One end of a cable fixed at a point as shown in Fig. 21.5 and it moves over both the pulley block and the other end is connected to the cage.

When the water under pressure enters the fixed cylinder the ram moves in outward direction and the distance between two pulley blocks increases and hence the cable is pulled resulting the upward movement of cage. When the water from the cylinder removed the ram moves inside the cylinder resulting release of cable and hence downward movement of lift.

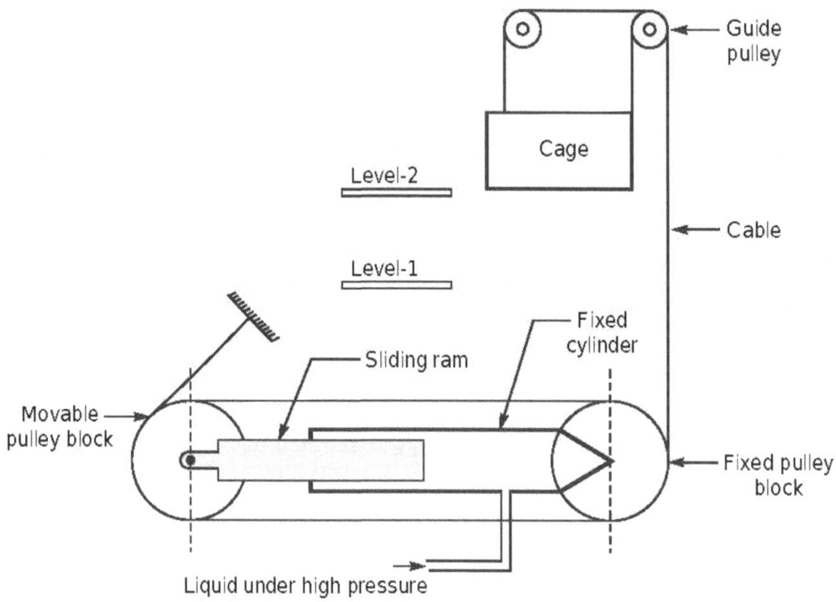

Fig. 21.5 Suspended hydraulic lift.

■ **Problem 21.5:** *A hydraulic lift with a speed of 0.6 m/sec is required to lift a load of 10 kN through a height of 12 m after every 120 second. Find*

(a) HP required to drive the lift.

(b) Working period of lift in seconds.

(c) Idle period of the lift in seconds.

Given $W = 10\ kN = 10 \times 10^3\ N$

$H = 12\ m$

$V = 0.6\ m/sec$

and *time for one operation* $= t = 120$ *seconds.*

Solution:

(*a*) Work done per sec. $= \dfrac{W \times H}{t}$

$= \dfrac{10 \times 10^3 \times 12}{120}$

$= 1000$ Nm/sec

$\therefore$ HP required to drive the lift

$= \dfrac{1000}{736} = 1.36$ HP

(*b*) Working period of lift

$= \dfrac{H}{V} = \dfrac{12}{0.6} = 20$ sec

(*c*) Idle period of the lift

= Total time – Working period

= 120 – 20 = 100 sec.

21.6 HYDRAULIC CRANE

Hydraulic cranes are used to raise and transfer heavy loads.

Its construction is similar to hydraulic lift.

Hydraulic crane consists of a vertical post or mast which is a hollow structure. The jib and tie are connected to the vertical post. The jib can be raised or lowered to increase or decrease the working area of crane. The vertical post along with the jib can rotate to transfer the load anywhere within the crane's action area. One end of tie and jib are connected to the guide pulley over which the cable passes to lift or lower the load. The mechanism of lowering or lifting the load is same as that of lift.

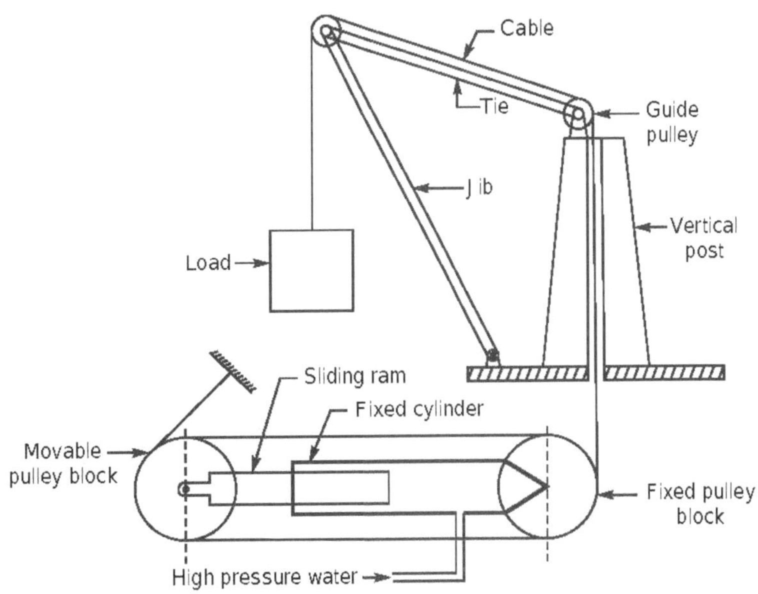

Fig. 21.6 Hydraulic crane.

■ **Problem 21.6:** *For a hydraulic crane the ram diameter is given as 20 cm and the velocity ratio 8. Find the weight lifted by the crane and the volume of water required to lift the weight if the water is supplied under a pressure of 750 N/cm² for lifting a weight through a height of 12 m. Take efficiency of hydraulic crane as 65%.*

Given $D = 0.2\ m$

Velocity ratio $= 8$

$p = 750\ N/cm^2$

$h = 12\ m$

$\eta = 65\% = 0.65.$

Solution: Area of ram $= A = \dfrac{\pi D^2}{4} = \dfrac{\pi \times 0.2^2}{4} = 0.0314\ \text{m}^2$

Force on ram = pressure intensity of water × area of ram

$= 750 \times 10^4 \times 0.0314$

$= 23.55 \times 10^4\ \text{N}$

Efficiency of the hydraulic crane

$$= \eta = \frac{\text{Outlut}}{\text{Input}} = \frac{\text{Weight} \times \text{Distance moved by weight}}{\text{Force} \times \text{Distance moved by force}}$$

$$= \frac{\text{Weight}}{\text{Force}} \times \text{Velocity ratio}$$

$$0.65 = \frac{\text{Weight}}{23.55 \times 10^4} \times 8$$

$$\text{Weight} = 0.65 \times 23.55 \times 10^4 \times 8$$

$= 1224600\ \text{N}$

$= 1224.6\ \text{kN}$

$$\text{Now stroke of the ram} = \frac{\text{Distance moved by weight}}{\text{Velocity ratio}}$$

$$= \frac{h}{\text{Velocity ratio}}$$

$$= \frac{12}{8}$$

$= 1.5\ \text{m}$

∴ Volume of water required to lift the weight

= Area of ram × Stroke of ram

$= 0.0314 \times 1.5$

$= 0.0471\ \text{m}^3.$

21.7 HYDRAULIC RAM

Hydraulic ram lifts small quantifies of water to great heights by utilising a large quantity of water falling through a small height.

A hydraulic ram consists of a supply tank connected to a chamber by a long supply pipe. The chamber has two values on it. One is a waste water valve which opens inside the chamber and second one is a delivery valve which opens outward into the air vessel which is fitted on the top of chamber. A delivery pipe connects the air vessel to the overhead tank or discharge water to the atmosphere.

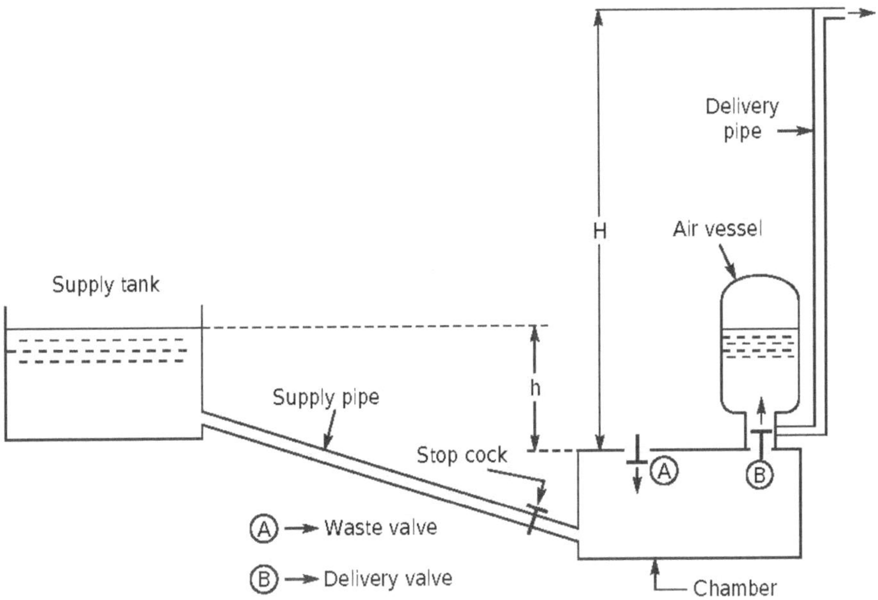

Fig. 21.7 Hydraulic ram.

When stop cock provided on supply pipe opened, water starts flowing from supply tank to chamber. As the water level rise in the chamber the waste water valve 'A' starts moving in upward direction and a stage comes when it suddenly closes. This sudden closure of waste water valve gives rise to a high pressure inside the chamber which opens the delivery valve '**B**'. The water from chamber enters the air vessel. The pressure of air in the air vessel increases and this forces water to flow into the delivery pipe and finally comes out from the delivery end. This reduces the pressures inside the chamber and leads to opening of the waste valve. Water starts flowing from the supply tank to chamber and the whole cycle get repeated.

21.7.1 Efficiencies of Hydraulic Ram

(1) D′ Aubuisson's efficiency:

$$\eta = \frac{\text{Energy delivered by the ram}}{\text{Energy supplied to the ram}}$$

$$= \frac{W_2 \times H}{W_1 \times h} \text{ or } \frac{q \times H}{Q \times h} \quad ...(21.9)$$

where W_2 = Weight of water delivered per second
W_1 = Weight of water supplied per second to chamber
q = Discharge of delivery pipe
Q = Discharge through supply pipe

(2) Rankine's efficiency:

$$\eta = \frac{W_2 \times (H-h)}{(W_1 - W_2) \times h} \text{ or } \frac{q(H-h)}{(Q-q) \times h} \quad ...(21.10)$$

■ **Problem 21.7:** *The water is supplied at the rate of 0.1 m³/sec. From a tank 5 m above the hydraulic ram which raises 0.01 m³/sec of water to a tank 25 m above the ram. Calculate efficiency of the ram.*

Given $Q = 0.1\ m^3/sec$
$h = 5\ m$
$q = 0.01\ m^3/sec$
$H = 25\ m.$

Solution:

(1) Aubuisson's efficiency $= \dfrac{q \times H}{Q \times h}$

$$= \frac{0.01 \times 25}{0.1 \times 5}$$

$= 0.5$ *i.e.* 50%.

(2) Rankine's efficiency $= \dfrac{q(H-h)}{(Q-q) \times h}$

$$= \frac{0.01(25-5)}{(0.1-0.01)\,5}$$

$= 0.4444$ *i.e.* 44.44%. ...(**Ans.**)

■ **Problem 21.8:** *Keeping the same data of problem 21.7.*

If the diameter and length of the delivery pipe is given as 75 mm and 90 m respectively, calculate the efficiency of the ram. Take coefficient of friction f = 0.005.

Given $Q = 0.1\ m^3/sec$
$h = 5\ m$
$q = 0.01\ m^3/sec$
$H = 25\ m$
$d = 75\ mm = 0.075\ m$

$l = 90\ m$

$f = 0.005.$

Solution: Head lost due to friction in delivery pipe is

$$hf = \frac{4flv^2}{2gd}$$

Now $$v = \frac{q}{a} = \frac{0.01}{\left(\frac{\pi \times 0.075^2}{4}\right)} = \frac{0.01}{4.4179 \times 10^{-3}} = 2.26 \text{ m/sec}$$

$\therefore$ $$hf = \frac{4 \times 0.005 \times 90 \times 2.26^2}{2 \times 9.81 \times 0.075}$$

$$= 6.25 \text{ m}$$

$\therefore$ Net head developed by the ram $= H + hf$

$\therefore$ $$H_{net} = 25 + 6.25 = 31.25 \text{ m}.$$

(1) Aubuisson's efficiency $= \dfrac{q \times H_{net}}{Q \times h}$

$$= \frac{0.005 \times 31.25}{0.1 \times 5}$$

$$= 0.625 \ \ i.e.\ \ 62.5\%.$$

(2) Rankine's efficiency $= \dfrac{q\,(H_{net} - h)}{(Q - q) \times h}$

$$= \frac{0.01(31.25 - 5)}{(0.1 - 0.01)\,5}$$

$$= 0.58 \ \ i.e.\ \ 58\%.$$

Exercises

1. The sliding ram of an accumulator carries a load of 920 kN. The diameter of the ram is 25 cm. If the frictional resistance against the movement of the ram is 6% of the total load. Find the pressure inside the accumulator if the ram moves in downward direction. **(Ans.** 900 N/cm^2)
2. A pipe of 100 mm diameter and 1750 m long transmits 35 hp from an accumulator. If the power lost due to friction is 3%, find the diameter of the ram if it carries a load of 1250 kN. Take efficient of friction $f = 0.005$ for the given pipe. Also find the pressure intensity in the accumulator. **(Ans.** $p = 3975796.8$, $D = 0.4$ m)

3. A hydraulic intensifier has a sliding cylinder diameter of 30 cm. If the diameter of the fixed ram of the intensifier is 12.87 cm and pressure intensity of water supplied to an intensifier is 175 N/cm^2. Find the pressure intensity of water leaving the intensifier.

   (**Ans.** 950 N/cm^2)

4. A hydraulic intensifier has a sliding cylinder diameter of 50 cm, pressure at outlet is 2500 N/cm^2 and pressure at inlet is 100 N/cm^2. Take loss due to friction at each of the packings of the intensifier is 3% of total force on each of the packings. Find the diameter of the ram. (**Ans.** 9.7 cm)

5. A hydraulic press has a ram of 15 cm diameter and a plunger of 1.50 cm having a stroke of 25 cm. Calculate the force and power required to raise a load of 25000 N by 50 cm if the load is lifted in 12 minutes. (**Ans.** 250 N, 200 strokes, 17.36 Watts)

6. A hydraulic lift is required to raise a load of 12 tonnes through a height of 10 m once in every 2 minutes, the speed of lifting is 0.75 meter per second. The water is supplied under a pressure of 325 N/cm^2, the efficiency of the lift and pump is 80% and 90% respectively. Find the power required to drive the pump and the minimum capacity of accumulator if the lift works on accumulator which is constantly charged by a pump.

   (**Ans.** 13620.92 Nm/sec, 0.402 m^3)

7. Calculate the efficiency of a hydraulic crane utilising 500 litres of water at a pressure intensity of 450 N/cm^2 to lift the load of 12 tonnes through a height of 10 m.

   (**Ans.** 52.32%)

8. A hydraulic ram is supplied a water under a head of 7 m and the delivers water to a head of 40 m. The ratio of waste water to useful water is 25. Calculate efficiencies of hydraulic ram.

   (**Ans.** D′ Aubuisson's efficiency – 21.98%, Rankine Efficiency = 18.13%)

❑❑❑

22

Introduction to Ideal Fluid Flow

22.1 INTRODUCTION

Ideal Fluid Flow is also called as Potential Flow. In this chapter, a flow of ideal fluid (non-viscous and incompressible) is discussed.

22.2 UNIFORM FLOW

A uniform flow is characterised by straight and parallel streamlines and uniform velocity distribution. Let a uniform flow takes place with a velocity V in x-y plane.

Let u and v are the velocity components V in x and y direction respectively.

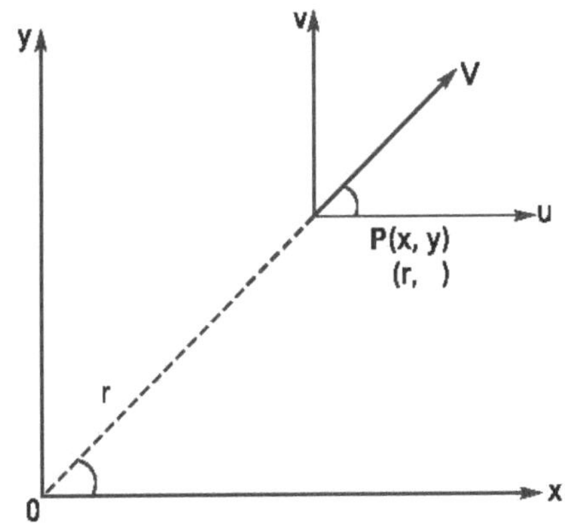

Fig. 22.1 Uniform flow.

At any point 'P' in the flow field having Cartesian co-ordinates (x, y) or polar co-ordinates (r, θ) we have

$$u = V \cos \alpha$$

and $$u = V \sin \alpha$$

where α is the angle made by the velocity vector V with x-axis.

From the definitions of velocity potential function and stream function we have

$$u = \frac{-\partial \phi}{\partial x} = \frac{\partial \psi}{\partial y}$$

and $$v = \frac{-\partial \phi}{\partial y} = \frac{\partial \psi}{\partial x}$$

$$\frac{\partial \phi}{\partial x} = -u$$

$$= -V \cos \alpha$$

Integrating with respect to x

$$\phi = -V \cos \alpha \, . \, x + f(y) \qquad \text{...(22.1)}$$

Differentiating equation (22.1) with respect to y

$$\frac{\partial \phi}{\partial y} = f'(y)$$

$$\therefore \quad f'(y) = -v = -V \sin \alpha$$

$$f(y) = -V \sin \alpha \, . \, y$$

put in equation (22.1)

$$\phi = -V \cos \alpha \, . \, x - V \sin \alpha \, . y \qquad \text{...(22.2)}$$

If $\alpha = 0°$ (*i.e.* streamlines are parallel to x-axis)

$$\therefore \quad \phi = -V \, . \, x$$

$$= -V \, . \, r \cos \theta$$

Similarly, $$\psi = V \cos \alpha \, . \, y - V \sin \alpha \, . \, x \qquad \text{...(22.3)}$$

If $$\alpha = 0°$$

$$\psi = V \, . \, y = V \, . \, r \sin \theta.$$

22.3 SOURCE

Source is a point from which fluid discharges uniformly, radically outward in all directions. For source streamlines are straight radial lines and equipotential lines are concentric circles.

The strength of the source is defined as the volume flow rate per unit depth per unit time and its unit is m²/sec.

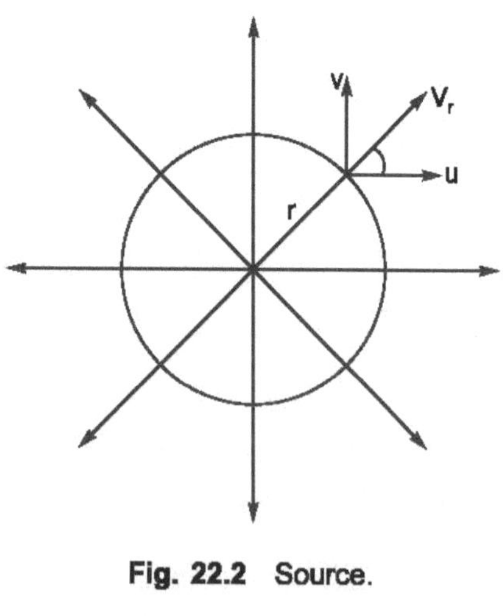

Fig. 22.2 Source.

Let P is a point on the streamline having polar co-ordinates (r, θ) where the velocity is V. Its radial velocity component V_r shall be the same at all the points on a circle of radius r and the tangential velocity component V_θ is zero.

From the definition of strength of source

$$m = \int_0^{2\pi} V_r \,.\, r \,.\, d\theta = V_r \,.\, 2\pi r$$

$$\therefore \qquad V_{r=} \frac{m}{2\pi r} \qquad ...(22.4)$$

$$\text{Now,} \qquad V_r = \frac{m}{2\pi r} = \frac{\partial \phi}{\partial r} = \frac{\partial \psi}{r \partial \theta} \qquad ...(22.5)$$

$$\text{and} \qquad V_0 = 0 = \frac{\partial \phi}{r \partial \theta} = -\frac{\partial \psi}{\partial r} \qquad ...(22.6)$$

From equation (22.5)

$$\frac{\partial d}{\partial r} = \frac{m}{2\pi r}$$

Integrating with respect to r

$$\phi = \frac{m}{2\pi} \log_e r \qquad ...(22.7)$$

$$\text{Similarly,} \qquad \frac{\partial \psi}{r \partial \theta} = \frac{m}{2\pi r}$$

Integrating with respect to θ

$$\psi = \frac{m}{2\pi} \,.\, \theta \qquad ...(22.8)$$

$$\text{Since} \qquad r = \sqrt{x^2 + y^2} \quad \text{and} \quad \tan\theta = \frac{y}{x} \left(i.e.\ \theta = \tan^{-1} \frac{y}{x} \right)$$

equations (22.7) and (22.8) in terms of cartesian co-ordinates

$$\phi = \frac{m}{2\pi} \log_e \sqrt{x^2 + y^2} \qquad ...(22.9)$$

$$\text{and} \qquad \psi = \frac{m}{2\pi} \tan^{-1} \frac{y}{x} \qquad ...(22.10)$$

$$\text{also} \qquad u = V_r \cos\theta = \frac{m}{2\pi r} \cdot \frac{x}{r}$$

$$= \frac{m}{2\pi} \cdot \frac{x}{(x^2 + y^2)} \qquad ...(22.11)$$

$$\text{and} \qquad v = V_r \sin\theta = \frac{m}{2\pi r} \cdot \frac{y}{r}$$

$$= \frac{m}{2\pi} \cdot \frac{y}{(x^2 + y^2)} \qquad ...(22.12)$$

22.4 SINK

Sink is a point to which fluid moves uniformly, radially inward from all directions with radial velocity.

$$V_r = -\frac{m}{2\pi r} \qquad ...(22.13)$$

The stream function and the potential function for a sink are

$$\phi = -\frac{m}{2\pi}\log_e r \qquad ...(22.14)$$

and

$$\psi = -\frac{m}{2\pi}\theta \qquad ...(22.15)$$

22.5 VORTEX FLOW

The flow of a fluid along a curved path or flow of rotating mass of fluid is defined as a vortex flow.

Types of vortex flow:

(1) Forced Vortex Flow.

(2) Free Vortex Flow.

(1) **Forced Vortex:** To rotate the fluid mass external torque need to be applied.

(2) **Free Vortex:** No external torque is required to rotate the fluid mass.

22.5.1 Free Vortex

For a free circular vortex flow the streamlines are curved and hence

$$V_\theta . r = \text{constant} = c \qquad ...(22.16)$$

and the circulation Γ around a streamline of an irrotational vortex is

$$\Gamma = V_\theta . 2\pi r$$
$$= 2\pi . c$$
$$= \text{constant} \qquad ...(22.17)$$

where Γ is called as a strength of the vortex and is taken as positive if the vortex is anticlockwise.

$$\therefore \quad V_\theta = \frac{\Gamma}{2\pi r} \text{ and } V_r = 0 \qquad ...(22.18)$$

Now

$$V_\theta = \frac{\Gamma}{2\pi r} = \frac{\partial\phi}{r\partial\theta} = \frac{-\partial\psi}{\partial r} \qquad ...(22.19)$$

$$V_r = 0 = \frac{\partial\phi}{\partial r} = \frac{\partial\psi}{r\partial\theta} \qquad ...(22.20)$$

From equation (22.19)

$$\frac{\partial \phi}{r\partial \theta} = \frac{\Gamma}{2\pi r}$$

Integrating with respect to θ

$$\phi = \frac{\Gamma}{2\pi}, \theta \qquad ...(22.21)$$

and

$$\frac{-\partial \psi}{\partial r} = \frac{\Gamma}{2\pi r}$$

Integrating with respect to r

$$\psi = \frac{-\Gamma}{2\pi}. \log_e r \qquad ...(22.22)$$

To get the expressions for clockwise vortax replace 'Γ' by '– Γ' in the above expressions.

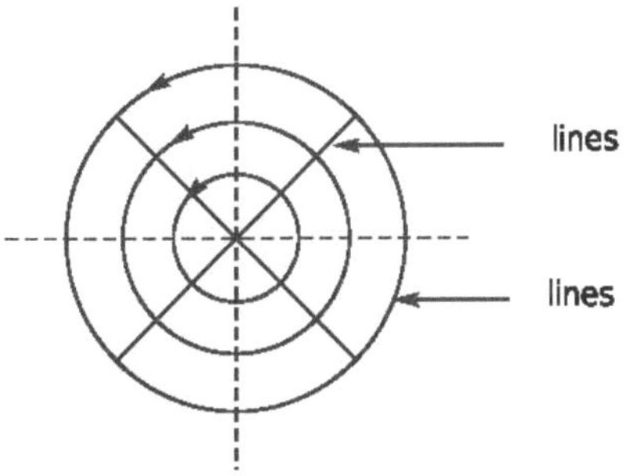

Fig. 22.3 Free vortex flow.

22.6 DOUBLET

A doublet is a pair of source and sink of equal strength 'm' placed '$2a$' distance apart, which approaches each other in a way that the product of their strength and the distance between them remains a finite constant value. It is generally denoted by μ and is called the strength of a doublet.

∴ Strength of doublet = $\mu = 2a$ m

Refer Figure 22.4

The line AB is called a axis of doublet and is + ve in the direction source to sink.

Let A is a source and B is a sink placed '$2a$' distance apart. Let P is a point in the plane. Stream function for a doublet.

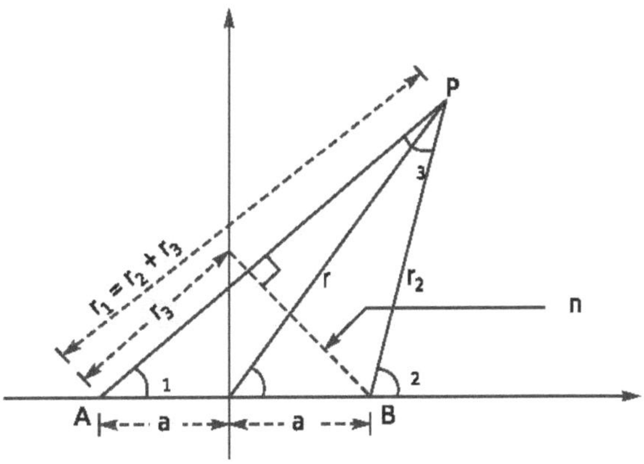

Fig. 22.4 Doublet.

$$\psi = \psi \text{ due to source} + \psi \text{ due to sink}$$

$$\therefore \quad \psi = \frac{m}{2\pi}\theta_1 - \frac{m}{2\pi}\theta_2$$

$$= \frac{m}{2\pi}(\theta_1 - \theta_2)$$

$$= \frac{-m}{2\pi}\Delta\theta$$

$$\approx \frac{-m}{2\pi}\frac{\Delta n}{r_2} \quad \text{...(}\Delta\theta \text{ is small)}$$

$$\approx \frac{-m}{2\pi}\frac{a\sin\theta_1}{r_2} \quad \text{...(}r_1 \approx r_2 + r_3\text{)}$$

By definition of doublet

as $a \to 0$ $ma \to \mu$

For this condition $\theta_1 \to \theta$ and $r_2 \to r$

$$\therefore \quad \psi = \frac{-\mu\sin\theta}{2\pi r} \quad \text{...(22.23)}$$

Similarly velocity potential function for a doublet

$$\phi = \phi \text{ due to source} + \phi \text{ due to sink}$$

$$\therefore \quad \phi = \frac{m}{2\pi}\log_e r_1 - \frac{m}{2\pi}\log_e r_2$$

$$= \frac{m}{2\pi}\log_e\left(\frac{r_1}{r_2}\right)$$

now for small values of a $r_1 \approx r_2 + r_3$

$$\approx \frac{m}{2\pi}\log_e\left(\frac{r_2 + r_3}{r_2}\right)$$

For small values of r_3

$$= \log_e\left(1 + \frac{r_3}{r_2}\right) \approx \frac{r_3}{r_2}$$

$$\therefore \quad \approx \frac{m}{2\pi}\frac{r_3}{r_2}$$

$$= \frac{m}{2\pi}\cdot\frac{a\cos\theta_1}{r_2}$$

∴ By definition of doublet

as $a \to 0$, $ma \to \mu$

$$\therefore \qquad \phi = \frac{\mu \cos\theta}{2\pi r}$$

Also velocity of P is given as

$$V_r = \frac{\partial \phi}{\partial r} = \frac{-\mu \cos\theta}{2\pi r^2}$$

$$V_\theta = \frac{-\partial \psi}{\partial r} = \frac{-\mu \sin\theta}{2\pi r^2}$$

$$\therefore \qquad V = \sqrt{V_r^2 + V_\theta^2} = \frac{\mu}{2\pi r^2}.$$

22.7 SOLVED PROBLEMS

■ **Problem 22.1:** *Find the strength of the doublet to produce a velocity of 5 m/sec at a point (0, 4) in a x-y plane. Also find the streamline value passing through the point P*

Given $\theta = 90°$, $V_r = 0$, $V_\theta = 5$ *m/sec.*

Solution: Now

$$V_\theta = \frac{-\mu \sin\theta}{r^2}$$

$$\therefore \qquad -5 = \frac{-\mu}{4^2}$$

$$\therefore \qquad \mu = 80 \text{ m}^2\text{/sec}$$

Stream function of streamline passing through

$$P = \psi = \frac{-\mu \sin\theta}{4}$$

$$= \frac{-80 \times \sin 90°}{4}$$

$$= -20 \text{ m}^3\text{/sec/m.}$$

■ **Problem 22.2:** *A source of strength 3 m³/s/m is placed at the origin and the other source of strength 4 m³/s/m is placed at (1, 0) find velocity components at point (2, 2).*

Given $m_1 = 3$ *m³/s/m*

$m_2 = 5$ *m³/s/m*

$a = 1, x = 2, y = 2.$

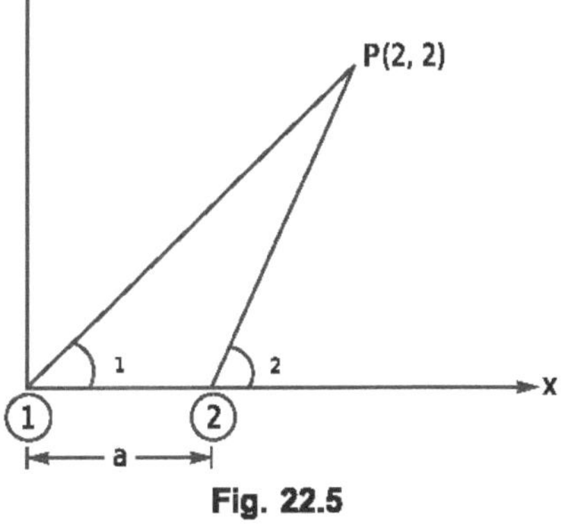

Fig. 22.5

Solution:

Now $$\psi = \frac{m_1}{2\pi}\left[\tan^{-1}\left(\frac{y}{x}\right)\right] + \frac{m_2}{2\pi}\left[\tan^{-1}\left(\frac{y}{x-a}\right)\right]$$

but $$u = \frac{\partial \psi}{\partial y}$$

$$= \frac{m_1}{2\pi}\cdot\frac{x}{x^2+y^2} + \frac{m_2}{2\pi}\frac{(x-a)}{(x-a)^2+y^2}$$

$$= \frac{3}{2\pi}\times\frac{2}{2^2+2^2} + \frac{4}{2\pi}\cdot\frac{(2-1)}{(2-1)^2+2^2}$$

$$= \frac{6}{16\pi} + \frac{4}{8\pi}$$

$$= 0.119 + 0.159 = 0.278 \text{ m/sec}$$

Similarly, $$v = \frac{\partial \psi}{\partial x}$$

$$= -\left[\frac{m_1}{2\pi}\cdot\frac{1}{1+\frac{y^2}{x^2}}\cdot\left(\frac{-y}{2\pi}\right) + \frac{m_2}{2\pi}\frac{1}{1+\frac{y^2}{(x-a)^2}}\left(\frac{-y}{x-a}\right)^2\right]$$

$$= -\left[\frac{3}{2\pi}\cdot\frac{1}{\left(1+\frac{2^2}{2^2}\right)}\cdot\left(\frac{-2}{2^2}\right) + \frac{4}{2\pi}\cdot\frac{1}{1+\frac{2^2}{(2-1)^2}}\left(\frac{-2}{2-1}\right)^2\right]$$

$$= -\left[\frac{-6}{16\pi} - \frac{8}{10\pi}\right]$$

$$= -[-0.119 - 0.255]$$

$$= -0.374 \text{ m/sec.}$$

Appendix

Syllabi

S.E. (CIVIL/CONSTRUCTION) **SEM III**

SUB: FLUID MECHANICS

1. **Properties of Fluids:** Mass density, weight density, specific gravity, specific volume, viscosity, compressibility, bulk modulus, surface tension, capillary action, vapour pressure, types of fluids, basic concepts applicable to fluid mechanics.
2. **Fluid Static:**
   2.1. Pascal's law, pressure variation in fluids at rest, absolute, atmospheric, gauge pressure, measurement of pressures.
   2.2. Hydrostatic force on plane and curved surface
   2.3. Buoyancy and flotation: Metacentre, metacentric, height, equilibrium of floating and submerged bodies.
3. **Liquids in Relative Equilibrium:** Uniform linear acceleration, liquid containers subjected to constant horizontal and vertical acceleration, constant rotation with vertical axis.
4. **Fluid Kinematics:** Types of flow–one, two and three-dimensional flows, steady, unsteady, uniform, non-uniform, laminar, turbulent, compressible, incompressible, rotational, irrotational flows, continuity equation, vorticity.
5. **Fluid Dynamics:** Euler's equation, Bernoulli's equation.
6. **Flow Measuring Devices:**
   6.1. Venturi meter, orifice meter, nozzle meter, pitot tube, rotameter.
   6.2. Orifice: hydraulic coefficient, small and large orifice, time of emptying a tank through orifice.
   6.3. Mouthpieces: External, convergent, Borda's mouthpieces.
   6.4. Notches and weirs: rectangular triangular, Cipolleti weirs, velocity of apprach, end contractions.

7. **Compressible Flow:** (elementary study) basic equations of flow, Mach number, Mach cone, area-velocity relationship, stagnation properties.
8. **Ideal fluid flow:** uniform flow, source and sink, doublet, free vortex.

Practical

List of experiments (At least 6 to be conducted)

1. Determination of metacentric height.
2. Verification of Bernoulli's theorem.
3. Calibration of orifices.
4. Calibration of mouthpieces.
5. Calibration of notches.
6. Calibration of weirs.
7. Calibration of Venturi meter.
8. Calibration of Orifice meter.
9. Calibration of Nozzle meter.

Term work

Each student is to appear for at least one written test during the term.

Report an experiments performed as detailed above and assignments on each topic (at least 5), and the graded answer paper of the class test shall be submitted as term work.

The distribution of term work will be as follows:

Report of the experiments performed	: 10 marks
Assignments	: 05 marks
Written test	: 10 marks

T.E. (CIVIL) SEM V

SUB: APPLIED HYDRAULICS-I

1. **Dynamics of fluid flow:** Momentum principle, applications: force on plates, pipe bends, jet propulsion, moment of momentum equation.
2. **Dimensional analysis:** Dimensional homogeneity, Buckingham's π theorem, Rayleigh's method and other methods, dimensionless groups, similitude, model studies, distorted and undistorted models.
3. **Laminar flow through pipes:** Reynold experiment, critical velocity, steady laminar flow through parallel plates, moving plates, flow through circular pipes and annulus.
4. **Flow through pipes:** Loss of head through pipes, Darcy–Weisbach equation, minor losses, total energy equation, hydraulic gradient line, pipes in series, equivalent pipes in parallel, flow through laterals, flow in dead end pipes, syphon, power transmission through pipes, nozzles.

5. **Impact of jets:** Jet striking stationary, moving inclined and perpendicular flat plates, impact on stationary, moving, curved vane–series of curved vanes.
5. **Turbines:** Classification, details of construction, performance characteristics, model studies, unit quantities of Pelton wheel, Francis and Kaplan turbines, examples illustrating fixing size of different components, calculation of efficiencies, output etc.
7. **Centrifugal pump:** Classification, velocity diagram, series and parallel operation, characteristics curves, efficiencies, model studies, simple examples.
8. **Miscellaneous hydraulic machinery:** Hydraulic ram, press, intensifter, crane and lift, examples.

Practical

List of experiments (At least six to be performed)

1. Reynold's experiment
2. Friction loss through pipes
3. Laminar flow through pipes
4. Minor losses
5. Impact of jet
6. Performance of centrifugal pump
7. Performance of Pelton wheel
8. Performance of Francis turbine
9. Hydraulic ram.

Term work

Each student is to appear for at least one written test during the term.

Report on experiments performed as detailed above and the graded answer paper for the term test shall be submitted as term work.

The distribution of term work marks will be as follows:

Report of the experiments performed : 15 marks

Written test : 10 marks

T.E. (CIVIL) SEM VI

SUB: APPLIED HYDRAULICS-II

1. **Turbulent flow through pipes:** Causes of turbulence, instability, mechanism of turbulience, Reynold stresses, semi-empirical theories of turbulence, Prandtl's mixing length theory, universal velocity distribution equation, resistance equations, applications.
2. **Boundary layer theory:** Development of boundary over flat and curved surfaces, laminar and turbulent boundary layer, boundary layer thickness, Karman's momentum integral equation, boundary layer separation and control, examples.
3. **Flow around submerged bodies:** Drag and lift, streamlined and bluff bodies application, circulation lift and magnums effect, lift characteristics of airfoils.
4. **Analysis of pipe network:** Hardy Cross method, water hammer in pipes and control measures.
5. **Flow through open channel:**
   - **5.1. Steady uniform flow:** Chezy's/Manning's equation, most economical section.
   - **5.2. Gradually varied flow:** governing differential equation, flow profiles with examples, estimation of length of backwater and drawdown curves.
   - **5.3. Rapidly varied flow:** specific energy, specific force, hydraulic jump in rectangular channels, applications.
   - **5.4. Flow measurement:** venturiflume, standing wave flume.

Practical

List of experiments (At least six to be performed)

1. Chezy's roughness factor
2. Study of gradually varied flow
3. Hydraulic jump
4. Venturiflume, standing wave flume
5. Velocity distribution in circular pipe
6. Establishment of flow
7. Boundary layer
8. Studies in wind tunnel.

Term work

Each student is to appear for at least one written test during the term.

Report on experiments performed as detailed above and the graded answer paper for the term test shall be submitted as term work.

The distribution of the term work will be as follows:

Report of the experiments performed	:	15 marks
Written test	:	10 marks

T.E. (MECHANICAL/AUTOMOBILE) SEM V

SUB: FLUID MECHANICS

1. Definition of fluid properties of fluids, Ideal viscous, compressible, incompressible, Newtonian, non Newtonian fluids principle of continuum.
2. **Fluid static's:** Body and surface forces Fundamental equation of fluid statics. Inertial and non inertial frames of reference pressure at a point. Variation of pressure with height inside liquids and gases. Force on plane lamina, centre of pressure, Buoyancy and flotation. Stability Criterion of floating body, metacentre, Accelerated systems; whirling of fluids.
3. **Integral Analysis:** System and control volume, Deformable and non-deformable control volume. Reynolds Transport theorem. Conservation of mass, momentum and energy applied to control volume. Application to problems. [Note: rigorous proof of control volume equations are not required. More emphasis to be placed on application.
4. **Differential Analysis:** Continuity equation for one, two and three dimensional flow in cartesian and cylindrical co-ordinate system. Navier-Stoke equation (without proof) in cartesian and cylindrical coordinates. Euler's momentum equation one and two dimensional; derivation of Bernoulli's equation from Euler equation. Limitation of Bernoulli's equation. Kinetic energy and momentum correction factors. Laminar flow: plane poiseulle flow, Hagen poiseulle flow, Couette flow, flow in annular pipe. Turbulent flow: Origin of turbulence, mean values and fluctuations, intercity and scale of turbulence, normal and shear stress due to turbulence, Prandtl's mixing length theory. Karman similarity hypothesis; universal velocity distribution law. Prandtl's 1/7 th law. Concept of laminar sublayer, buffer layer and turbulent zone, hydraulically smooth and rough surfaces. Upper and lower critical Reynolds numbers.
5. **Pipe Flow:** Head loss due to friction in pipe. Variation of friction factor. Karman Prandtl resistance law for smooth and rough pipes. Colebrook's correlation Moody's diagram.
6. **Dimensional Analysis and dynamic similitude:** Rayleigh and Buckingham Methods. Reynolds number, Froude number, Model studies.
7. **Boundary layer theory:** boundary layer thickness, displacement, momentum and energy thickness. Von Karman momentum integral theorem. Laminar boundary layer analysis using polynomial profiles. Blasius solution from Navier stokes equation analysis of turbulent boundary layer, expression for drag boundary layer on curved surface boundary layer separation methods to control separation.
8. **Potential flow:** potential and stream function, properties Two dimensional source, sink vortex, doublet, uniform flow, flow past a cylinder without and with circulation. Kutta Jouk owsky theorem. Rankine oval and Rankine half body.
9. **Fluid flow measurement:** venturi meter, orifice meter, flow nozzle, dependence of C_d on Reynolds number. Rotometer, elbow meter, Rectangular notch and V notch. Anemomenters, magnetic flow meters.
10. Aerofoil theory, terminology C_L and C_D airfoil of infinite and finite span.

Term work

Term work shall consists of laboratory experiments and assignment based on the syllabus.

Experiments

1. Archimedien principle
2. Metacentric height
3. Venturimeter
4. Orificementer
5. Orifice in a tank
6. Pitot tube
7. Laminar flow through pipe
8. Turbulent flow through pipe
9. Impact of jets
10. Whirling of liquid
11. Application of momentum equation
12. Application of energy equation
13. Determination of friction for a piping system
14. Calibration of pressure gauges and vacuum gauges.

    Assignment: minimum one on each topic, and a class test of TEN marks

---

T.E. (MECHANICAL) **SEM VI**

SUB: FLUID MECHINERY

1. **Turbines:** Definition of head on turbine. Application of momentum equation to stationary and vanes moving with linear velocity. Series of moving vanes. Application of angular momentum principle to turbine rotor. Euler's velocity triangles. Expression for work done. Impulse and Reaction turbines:

   Pelton Turbines: Parts of turbine, salient features, power developed. Hydraulic, Volumetric, Mechanical and Overall efficiencies.

   Reaction Turbines: Inward, Outward flow, radial, mixed and axial flow turbines. Parts of the turbine and their functions.

   Characteristics of turbines: Dimensional analysis of turbines. Affinity relations. Conventional and dimensionless specific speed. Model testing, Scale effect.

   Cavitation: Mechanism of cavitation, types of cavitation. Thoma cavitation parameter.

   Governing of turbines: Methods employed in Pelton, Francis and Kaplan turbines.

   Pumped Storage Plants: Tubular turbines and Deriaz turbines.

2. **Pumps:** Centrifugal, Radial, Mixed and Axial flow pumps. Pressure rise across impeller, pressure conversion devices. Velocity triangles. Manometric head and manometric efficiency.

Effect of finite number of vanes, relative channel circulation, Slip factor, Stodola's correction. Backward and Forward bend blades. Specific speed of pump. Influence of specific speed on shape of impeller, NPSH and cavitation. H-Q characteristics of pumps; System curve.

Determining point of operation. Series and parallel operation of pumps. Blade profiles for single curvature blades.

Design of logarithmic spiral, circular arc blades. Point to point method.

Priming of Pumps, Self priming pump. Use of gland packing or mechanical seal. Axial thrust and methods of balancing axial thrust, balancing chamber, radial-ribs, balancing disc and balancing drum. Radial thrust and methods of balancing.

Reciprocating pump: Single and double acting pumps, inertia head. Calculation of pressure inside cylinder, indicator diagram. Use of air vessels, Negative slip.

Rotor pumps, Gear pump, Vane pump unbalanced and balanced, Radial piston pump, Axial piston pumps.

3. **Compressor:** Centrifugal and Axial flow compressor. Application of one dimensional flow equation. Input work, isentropic work, polytropic work. Representation as area under curve on TS diagram, power input factor.

   Multistage compression. Relation between stage efficiency and compressor efficiency, Intercooling, Stage matching and stage miss match at off design conditions.

Term work

The term work shall consist of laboratory experiments and assignments.

Experiments

Atleast 5 from the following:

1. Impact of jets.
2. Test on Pelton Wheel to determine (*i*) main characteristics, (*ii*) operating characteristics.
3. Test on Francis Turbine.
4. Test on Kaplan Turbine.
5. Similarity Test on any of the three machines mentioned above.
6. Test on Cavitation induced in Venturi.
7. Test on blowers.
8. Performance characteristics and Variable speed characteristics of Centrifugal Pumps.
9. Determine NPSH of Centrifugal Pumps.
10. Performance characteristics of Reciprocating Pumps/other Positive displacement pumps.

Assignment

1. 2 problems on Pelton Wheel.
2. 4 problems of Reaction Turbine.
3. 1 problem on Similarity.
4. 1 problem on Centrifugal Pump (velocity triangles).
5. 1 problem each on Centrifugal Pump system interaction (*a*) Single pump (*b*) Two pumps in Series, (*c*) Two pumps in Parallel.
6. 1 problem on Reciprocating Pump.
7. 2 problem on Blowers and Compressors.

T.E. (CIVIL ENGINEERING) **DIPLOMA**

SUB: HYDRAULICS

UNIT-I: Physical Properties of Fluid

Chapter-1: (A) Introduction

Definition of fluid. Definition of fluid mechanics and hydraulics. Importance of learning hydraulics with special reference to Irrigatin engineering and Environmental engineering. Historical developments of the subject.

(B) Physical Properties of Fluids

Definition and S.I. units: specific weight, volume, mass density, specific gravity, viscosity, surface tension, compressibility. Units of the physical properties. Situations where viscosity surface tension and compressibility comes in picture. Problems on properties of fluid.

UNIT-II: Hydrostatics

Chapter-2: Pressure and its measurements

Definitions: Pressure, free liquid surface, pressure head. Pressure at a point in static liquid. Pascal's law, Variation of pressure in horizontal and vertical direction. Atmospheric pressure, gauge pressure, Absolute pressure relation between them, problems on calculation of gauge pressure/absolute pressure. Measurement of pressure. Different devices for measurement of pressure. Manometers–Simple Manometers, Piezometers, U-tube Manometers, Differential manometers, inverted U-tube manometers, problems on manometers. Mechanical Gauges–Boudron tube pressure gauge.

Chapter-3: Total hydrostatic pressure

Definition of total pressure and centre of pressure. Expression for total pressure and depth of centre off pressure on surface immersed in static liquid, problems. Pressure diagram–Definition and its use. Total pressures on vertical and inclined faces of gravity dam.

UNIT-III: Hydrodynamics

Chapter-4: Fundaments of fluid flow

Types of flow: steady and unsteady, uniform and non-uniform, Lamina and turbulent, compressible and incompressible, various combination of flow with examples pressure head. Discharge and its unit. Continuity equations for liquids. Datum head, velocity head, total head, Bernoulli's theorem, loss of head, modified Bernoulli's theorem, problems on Bernoulli's theorem. Venturimeter–Principal component part, expression for discharge through venturimeter, coefficient of meter. Orifice plate meter expression for discharge, situation where orifice plate meter is used.

Chapter-5: Flow through orifice

Orifice, jet of flow, venna contract, use of orifice. Classification of orifice according to size, shape and discharge condition. Coefficient of contraction, coefficient of velocity, coefficient of discharge. Derivation of relation between them, Determination of C_c, C_v, C_d. Discharge through small circular orifice, problems on calculation of dydraulic, through small circular orifice, problems on calculation of hydraulic, coefficient and discharge through small circular orifice. Discharging free.

Chapter-6: Flow over notches and weirs

Notches: Types of notches, expression for discharge through rectangular and triangular notch. Francis formula, effect of end contraction and velocity of approach on discharge computation, Cippolitte weir. Measurement of head over notches with gauges. Weir–Broad crusted weir, Ogee shaped spillway. Expression for discharge.

Chapter-7: Flow through pipes

Loss of head due to friction, Darcy weight batch equation. Common range of friction factor for different types of pipe material. Reynold's number and its significance, relative roughtness. Determination of coefficient from Moody's diagram. Minor head losses in pipe–loss of head due to sudden contraction, gradual expansion, gradual contraction loss of head at entrance, exit and loss of head in various pipe fittings such as bends, valves, elbows etc. Hydraulic gradient line and Total energy line Problems on flow through pipes and drawing the HGL and EGL. Flow through pipes in series and parallel, compound pipe, equivalent pipe. Water hammer–Causes, effects and remedial measures, surge tank, use of nomograms for design of water distribution system.

Chapter-8: Flow through open channels

Different shapes of artificial channels, wetted perimeter, wetted area, hydraulic mean depth. Chezy's formula and Manning's formula for calculation of discharge through an open channel. Common values of Chezy's constant and Mannings's constant for different types of channel surfaces. Most economical channel section, Expressions for most economical rectangular and trapezoidal channel sections. Hydraulic jump, situations where hydraulic jump occurs, uses of hydraulic jump.

Chapter-9: Flow measurement

Volumetric measurement of discharge by measuring tank. Discharge measuring devices in closed conduits. Watermeters–Principle and use. Discharge measuring devices used in open channel flume venturi flumes, standing wave flume, expression for discharge. Situations where the above devices are used. Velocity measuring devices, Float–Surface float. Pitot tube–principle, types, expression for velocity. Current meter–types. Velocity, area measurement method for channels.

UNIT–IV: Simple Hydraulic Machine

Chapter-10: Simple hydraulic machine

Definition of pump, types of pumps, Centrifugal pumps–principle of working, component parts, priming of pump, calculation of power required for pumps. Reciprocating pumps–component parts and working. Submersible pump and turbine pumps. Selection and choice of type of pump. Turbines–definition and types.

UNIT–V: Applications of principles of hydraulics in Engineering

Chapter-11: Applications of principles of hydraulic in engineering

Applications of principles of hydraulics in various fields of Engineering such as Environmental Engg., Irrigation Engg., Transportation Engg.

Index

E

F

G

H

I

J

K

L

M

N

O

P

R

S

T